FROM THE EDITORS OF BOTTOM LINE

SAY NO TO NURSING HOMES

YOUR ULTIMATE GUIDE TO WORRY-FREE AGING AND INDEPENDENT LIVING

B

BottomLineBooks

BottomLineInc.com

Say No to Nursing Homes

Copyright © 2016 by Bottom Line Inc.

10   9   8   7   6   5   4   3   2   1

ISBN 0-88723-756-8

Bottom Line Books® publishes the advice of expert authorities in many fields. These opinions
may at times conflict as there are often different approaches to solving problems. The use
of a book is not a substitute for legal, accounting, investment, health or any other professional
services. Consult competent professionals for answers to your specific questions.

Offers, prices, rates, addresses, telephone numbers and websites
listed in this book are accurate at the time of publication,
but they are subject to frequent change.

Bottom Line Books® is a registered trademark of Bottom Line Inc.
3 Landmark Square, Suite 201, Stamford, CT 06901

www.BottomLineInc.com

Bottom Line Books® is an imprint of Bottom Line Inc., publisher of print periodicals,
e-letters and books. We are dedicated to bringing you the best information from the most
knowledgeable sources in the world. Our goal is to help you gain greater wealth,
better health, more wisdom, extra time and increased happiness.

Printed in the United States of America

Contents

7 • DRIVE SAFER LONGER...OR LIVE INDEPENDENTLY WITHOUT A CAR

8 • STAY SAFE FROM CRIME AND SCAMS

PART 3: LONG-TERM HEALTH CARE

9 • GET THE BEST MEDICAL CARE

Contents

Contents

15 • HEART HEALTH AND STROKE

Contents

Preface

I t can cost close to $90,000 a year to stay in a nursing home.* Then there's the lack of privacy and freedom…basic dignities that disappear when you end up in institutional living. It's a worthy goal to avoid it at all costs!

This essential volume features actionable and life-saving information you can trust from the best aging, health and money experts in the world—information that will help you completely avoid spending your final years in a "home." In the following chapters you'll find the best scientifically proven health remedies to keep you living a long, happy and active life. You'll also find the answers to your post-salary financial challenges, and more.

Whether it's the latest on nutrition, heart care, cancer recovery, chronic conditions, avoiding falls and accidents, managing money in retirement (including confusing Social Security rules), tax savings or health-care spending, the editors at Bottom Line talk to the

*Cost of Care Survey 2016, Genworth Financial, Inc.

experts—from top doctors to research scientists to leading money people and experts on aging—all who are creating the true innovations to make your life better.

Over the past four decades, we have built a network of literally thousands of leading physicians in both alternative and conventional medicine who are affiliated with the premier medical and research institutions throughout the world. We read the important medical journals and follow the latest research that is reported at universities and beyond. And we regularly talk to our advisors in major teaching hospitals, private practices and government agencies for their insider perspective.

Our expert network also runs deep in the financial and lifestyle arenas, with specialists who provide the smartest strategies that keep your retirement money intact, so that you never outlive your savings and can afford the life you want. You'll discover how to get the support you need. Our experts will guide you through the many options available that keep you living your life to the fullest.

Say No to Nursing Homes: Your Ultimate Guide to Worry-Free Aging and Independent Living is the result of our ongoing research and connection with these experts, and is a compilation of their latest findings and advice. We trust that you will glean new, helpful and affordable information about the health, money and lifestyle topics that concern you most…and find vital topics of interest to family and friends as well.

As a reader of a Bottom Line book, please be assured that you are receiving well-researched information from a trusted resource. But, please use prudence in health and money matters. Always speak to your physician before taking vitamins, supplements or over-the-counter medication…stopping a medication…changing your diet…or beginning an exercise program. Consult a financial advisor or lawyer when exploring specific personal finance or tax options or estate planning. We wish you the greatest success as you enjoy the best years of your life!

Be happy and well,
The Editors, *Bottom Line Inc.*

PART 1

Aging Well

1

Live Longer... and Better

Slow Down the Aging Process—and Add Years to Your Life

The myth about longevity is that we have no control over how long we live. False. We do have some control—even though we all know some people who lived healthfully but died suddenly...and others who didn't take care of themselves and lived on and on. It is easy to fall back on the idea that we can't escape our heredity, but our genes aren't as important as you might think.

While there is no one secret to longevity, we can adopt aspects of healthful aging into our lives and improve our chances of reaching the century mark. I have seen many patients improve their health and add years to their lives. You can do the same by following these recommendations. You'll feel better and have greater vitality right away.

DOES A FAMILY HISTORY OF LONGEVITY HELP?

Having long-lived ancestors and siblings does increase your odds of living to old age, but it doesn't guarantee longevity.

Reason: Your genes, the biological programs that govern the activity of your body's 70 trillion cells, may influence only half of the factors involved in aging, according to the Okinawa Centenarian Study. That means we can have a direct effect on our aging process by focusing on the other factors.

Proof: Americans are living longer than ever, although not as long as people in other countries. The number of centenarians (people who are age 100 years or older) in the US is at an all-time high of over 53,000!

M.J. Friedrich et al., "Biological Secrets of Exceptional Old Age," *The Journal of the American Medical Association*, 2002.

B. Wilcox, et al., "Caloric Restriction, the Traditional Okinawan Diet and Healthy Aging," *Annals of the New York Academy of Sciences*.

Surprise: Centenarians often are in better health than younger seniors. About 20% of centenarians are "escapers," people who have entirely avoided serious diseases, and 40% were escapers until at least age 85, according to a *Journal of the American Medical Association* (*JAMA*) article.

ADD YEARS TO YOUR LIFE BY...

• **Protecting your genes.** A strong nutritional foundation safeguards our genes. Crucial to this protection is vitamin B, which can help repair genes and slow gene damage.

Advice: I recommend that most adults take a high-potency multivitamin each day that contains at least 50 milligrams (mg) each of vitamins B-1 and B-2, 400 micrograms (mcg) of folic acid and 50 mcg to 100 mcg of vitamin B-12. If your multivitamin is low in B vitamins, take an additional B-complex supplement so that you get the amounts listed above. These amounts are safe for everyone except those taking methotrexate for rheumatoid arthritis or as a chemotherapy drug—because high amounts of B supplements can interfere with these treatments

• **Eating healthfully.** Nutrients serve as the building blocks of our biochemistry. Vitamin and mineral deficiencies can impair our normal biochemistry and increase the formation of age-promoting free radical molecules.

A study in *Journal of the American Geriatrics Society* found that centenarians consume, on average, about two-and-a-half times more antioxidant-packed vegetables than seniors ages 70 to 99. Incredibly, the centenarians ate five times more veggies than typical 40-year-olds. All those antioxidants help protect against the types of cell damage involved in aging. Similarly, studies of Seventh Day Adventists in California—who do not smoke or drink but do eat lots of vegetables—have found that they have higher levels of antioxidants and tend to live longer.

Bottom line: Eat your veggies—lots of them.

• **Taking supplements.** It's difficult to study the specific effects of supplements over 80 to 100 years when so many other variables affect longevity. But both animal and human studies demonstrate the health benefits of supplements.

Recommendation: In addition to taking a multivitamin, there's convincing evidence that a combination of the antioxidant alpha-lipoic acid (300 mg to 400 mg daily) and the amino acid acetyl-L-carnitine (800 mg to 1,200 mg daily) has a rejuvenating effect, making people feel more energetic. These two nutrients are involved in the body's production of energy, which powers every cell in the body. They are safe for everyone, although people with diabetes or seizure disorders should take them under a doctor's supervision.

A recent study published in *American Journal of Clinical Nutrition* found that a related supplement, L-carnitine (2 grams daily), which helps transport fatty acids into the mitochondria (cell structures that convert nutrients into energy to power the cells), reduced mental and physical fatigue in centenarians. This supplement is safe for everyone.

Magnesium (400 mg daily) helps maintain the length of telomeres, the protective tips of chromosomes. Resveratrol (100 mg twice daily) activates the SIRT1 gene, which is involved in longevity. And vitamin C (1,000 mg daily) enhances immunity and reduces inflammation, both of which can contribute to longevity. It is safe to take all of these supplements.

• **Eating less.** Animal studies dating back to the 1930s have shown that nutritionally complete, but calorie-restricted, diets (generally with 30% fewer calories than national recommendations) often increase life expectancy by up to 30%. In human terms, that's roughly an extra 22 years, which can bring people very close to the century mark. Studies of people growing up in Okinawa, Japan, during the 1940s and 1950s found that they consumed about 11% fewer calories than their estimated calorie requirements (about 2,000 calories daily for men and 1,600 for women) until middle age, which contributed to greater longevity.

Guaranteed benefit: Eating less will help you maintain a normal weight and lower the odds of developing diabetes and heart disease.

Important: Only 30% of centenarians are overweight.

It takes great willpower to maintain a diet with 30% fewer calories than what feels "normal," but eating less than you do can be an important first step. Assuming that you aren't underweight, I recommend a calorie-reducing compromise—at each meal, eat until you feel 80% full. You may feel hungry initially, but you'll soon adjust to consuming less food.

• **Continuing to learn.** Even more than physical health, mental sharpness (such as memory and the ability to make decisions) is the most likely predictor of independence among people in their 90s and over 100 years of age, according to a *JAMA* article. Researchers say that some deterioration in cognitive function is inevitable as we age but that building a brain "reserve," or extra brain power, can offset part of this decline. Mental activity builds your brain's reserve. Be a lifelong learner by taking challenging classes...reading and discussing difficult material...and exposing yourself to new and provocative ideas. All of these activities increase connections among brain cells.

• **Exercising.** The more exercise you do, the better. A study conducted at King's College London in England found that physically active people have healthier cells than those who don't exercise. Researchers found that exercise lengthened telomeres, the tips of chromosomes, which usually shorten with aging.

Recommendation: If you are not physically active, start by walking for 10 minutes daily. Gradually build up speed, time and distance over a few weeks or months.

• **Getting enough—but not too much—sleep.** Seven hours of sleep nightly is the amount most strongly associated with longevity. Getting less sleep—or more—is associated with shorter life spans. People who sleep less than five hours don't give their bodies enough time for physiological recovery, and that may lead to metabolic dysfunction. Metabolic dysfunction also can result from habitually sleeping for more than eight hours.

• **Maintaining a spiritual foundation.** Having a spiritual foundation is associated with longer life. I find that my own spiritual foundation relieves stress. You can develop your inner life through prayer and/or meditation.

• **Being optimistic.** Centenarians tend to be optimists who feel that they have control over major decisions in their lives.

Helpful reading: Learned Optimism: How to Change Your Mind and Your Life by Martin Seligman.

• **Connecting with others.** Strong ties to family and friends play a big role in longevity. Studies show that married men tend to live longer than bachelors. Research also has shown that having friends is even more important than having family in terms of living longer.

My prescription: Take time to thoroughly enjoy the company of family and friends!

Anti-Aging Secrets From Canyon Ranch's Dr. Mark Liponis

Mark Liponis, MD, corporate medical director of the Canyon Ranch Health Resorts in Tucson, Arizona, and Lenox, Massachusetts. He is the author of *Ultralongevity* and coauthor of *Ultraprevention*.

Scientists still haven't figured out exactly what causes aging. Is it due to oxidation (a natural process that damages the body's cells)? Genetics? Wear and tear from daily living and environmental assaults? Or perhaps the gradual weakening of the immune system?

Recent thinking: An overactive immune system can contribute to premature aging.

Sound far-fetched? This belief stems, in part, from exciting research on biological factors that influence disease and the aging process. Consider these facts...

IMMUNITY AND AGING

A healthy adult's immune system is composed of 30 billion to 50 billion white blood cells that are equipped with powerful molecular weapons to destroy disease-causing bacteria, viruses and fungi. But if that army of white blood cells becomes overactive due to exposure to an excess of those germs, it can cause "collateral" damage that produces aging.

According to this theory, overactive white blood cells chew up neurons in the brain (Alzheimer's disease)…eat through the lining of arteries (heart disease)…and attack cartilage in the joints (arthritis).

An overactive immune system also produces an overabundance of antibodies (proteins in the body that help fight infection). Instead of fighting microbial enemies, these antibodies attack one or more of the body's organs.

A HEALTHY IMMUNE SYSTEM

Dozens of studies have shown that the following steps can help prevent the immune system from becoming overactive…

1. Breathe deeply. Diseases that interfere with normal breathing, such as asthma, bronchitis and sleep apnea (temporary cessation of breathing during sleep), cause an increase in immune activity.

But breathing also is impeded even in people without respiratory disease. It's common to breathe shallowly whenever you're preoccupied—while driving the car, for example, or balancing your checkbook.

Simple step: Become aware of and deepen your breathing.

What to do: Fold your arms across your belly while you're sitting. With each breath in, your arms should rise. That means your abdomen is expanding and you're performing "abdominal breathing"—relaxed, deep breathing that calms your immune system. If your arms don't move up, or they move inward, you need to focus on relaxing and expanding your belly with each breath.

Practice this breathing technique for 15 minutes, once a day. Eventually, you will become more mindful of your breathing during everyday activities.

2. Eat small meals. Eating is stressful for the immune system because it has to filter every substance swallowed to check for potentially harmful bacteria, viruses and other

germs, then gear up to defend against them. The bigger the meal, the greater the stress.

Simple step: Instead of eating three large meals, eat small meals every few hours—breakfast, a mid-morning snack, lunch, a midday snack and dinner. Have a half cup of soup, not a whole cup. Eat half a sandwich. Snack on a handful of nuts. For small meals, high-fiber foods (such as whole grains, beans, fruits, vegetables, nuts and seeds) work best—they're quickly filling and digest slowly, which delays hunger.

3. Get high-quality sleep. Studies of people who have voluntarily stayed awake for up to 80 hours have shown that sleep deprivation can increase CRP levels fivefold. But sleep quality—deep, restful sleep—is as important as the amount of time you spend in bed.

How do you know that you're getting quality sleep? *Ask yourself these questions…*

• **Do I often fall asleep when I'm reading or watching TV?**

• **Do I have to catch up on sleep during weekends?**

• **Do I wake up most mornings feeling tired?**

If you answered "yes" to any of these questions, you may not be getting enough quality sleep.

Simple step: Try a "sleep mantra"—an image, thought or feeling on which to focus—to help clear your mind of disturbing thoughts so that you can peacefully drift off into deep, restful sleep.

Examples: Repeat a phrase, such as "I am so happy to be in bed"…focus on a happy memory from the past…or think about someone you love. Even if you suffer from serious insomnia, this technique can be part of your treatment plan.

4. Try dancing (or other "rhythmic" activities). People who exercise rhythmically—such as by dancing, swimming, rowing or walking to music—have lower levels of immune activation than people who do not exercise this way, such as golfers or tennis players. No one knows why, but perhaps rhythmic exercise synchronizes with the natural rhythms of the body, such as the heartbeat and breathing.

Simple step: For beginners (people who have not been active), try walking at a steady pace while listening to music…swimming… ballroom dancing…or basic aerobics. Intermediates may want to try biking…rowing…jumping rope…or tap, hip-hop or square dancing. For those who are advanced, good choices include rhythmic martial arts (such as karate, tae kwon do, jujitsu and tai chi)…hiking…or strenuous dance forms, such as jitterbug, African dance or polka.

5. Forge strong emotional connections. When you experience deep emotional bonds, such as love for your spouse, children, friends or pets, you are less likely to feel the negative emotions of anxiety, hostility or depression—all of which researchers have linked to an overactive immune system.

Simple step: Keep a daily diary of incidents that reflect your emotional connections.

Examples: Write about an enjoyable phone conversation with a friend…special time spent with your children…or playing Frisbee with your dog in the park. Whenever you feel anxious, angry or sad, open the journal, read it—and remind yourself about the love in your life.

6. Create a soothing environment. Anecdotal evidence suggests that the immune system doesn't like a noisy, chaotic or stressful environment. It prefers an "outside world" that's nurturing and calm.

Simple steps: Play music that relaxes you. Display artwork that you enjoy looking at. Bring wonderful smells, such as fresh flowers or mulled apple cider, into your home.

7. Get your nutrients. Nutritional supplements can help calm an overactive immune system. See a nutritionist for advice on the supplements that are right for you.

Simple step: Take your multivitamin about an hour before your biggest meal of the day. This helps reduce the immune activity that is triggered after you eat.

Having More Aches and Pains? Getting Less Sleep?

John Whyte, MD, MPH, an internist and chief medical expert and vice president, health and medical education, at the Discovery Channel. He is the author of *Is This Normal?: The Essential Guide to Middle Age and Beyond.* DiscoveryChannel.com

With all the physical changes that occur as we grow older, it's tempting to chalk up all our infirmities to the effects of aging.

But that's a mistake. In some cases, physical changes that appear to be a normal part of aging signal the onset of a treatable condition. To protect yourself—and feel as good as possible!—it's crucial to know what's normal and what's not as we grow older. *For example…*

STOOPED POSTURE

The vertebrae in the spine are separated by intervertebral discs, which act like shock absorbers. It's normal for the discs to dehydrate and flatten with age. This is why the average person loses about half an inch in height every decade after about age 40. The same changes can alter the curve of the spine and cause a slight stoop.

What isn't normal: Extreme curvature of the upper spine. In general, aging should cause no more than a 20-degree curvature of the spine. An extreme curvature is typically due to a condition known as "dowager's hump" (kyphosis), which is usually caused by osteoporosis. Weak bones in the spine eventually crumble, changing the alignment of the spine and causing a stooped posture. Osteoporosis that has advanced this far can't be reversed.

That's why prevention is critical. Perform weight-bearing exercises, preferably before the bones have weakened. Walking and even dancing promote the development of new bone and protect your posture later in life. Weight-bearing exercise also can help even after bones are weakened—just be sure not to overdo it since you don't want to cause more damage. Depending on the condition of your bones, you may need to switch to non–weight-bearing exercise, such as swimming.

Important: Make sure you're getting enough vitamin D. Depending on where you live, it's possible to get more than 90% of the vitamin D that you need just from sun exposure—the rest can come from D-fortified foods and/or supplements. Vitamin D enables the movement of calcium from the bloodstream into the bones. Ask a doctor for a blood test to check your vitamin D level. If it's low, he/she can suggest the best ways for you to get more of this crucial vitamin.

PAIN

We all notice more aches and pains as we get older, often due to back problems, arthritis or other common conditions. These aches are normal if they are occasional.

What isn't normal: Pain that's severe or chronic.

Good rule of thumb: See a doctor if you have severe pain and don't know why—or if chronic pain interferes with your ability to live a normal life.

Important: Consider your mental health as well as your physical health. Pain and depression frequently go together—they actually share some of the same biochemical pathways.

That's why drugs called tricyclic antidepressants, such as *imipramine* (Tofranil), are sometimes used to relieve chronic pain—even in patients who aren't depressed. When pain is due to a physical problem, such as arthritis, depression also is common.

Get help right away, either from a doctor or a mental health professional (or both). Otherwise, you could be setting yourself up for a difficult cycle—ongoing pain increases depression, and the more depressed you are, the more pain you'll experience.

Helpful: I strongly advise pain patients to do some kind of exercise, even if it's just gentle stretches. Exercise increases endorphins, the body's natural painkillers.

LESS SLEEP

After about age 50, most people tend to sleep less soundly, and they may sleep fewer total hours than younger people. The reasons for these differences in sleep habits are varied but may include more pain, medication use and nighttime urination in older adults.

What isn't normal: Taking more than 10 to 15 minutes to fall asleep. See your doctor if you have trouble falling asleep more than, say, two nights a week. This delay in sleep onset might be due to stress. Or you could be having side effects from medications. Offenders include decongestants, beta-blockers and some asthma drugs. Don't ignore sleep problems—over time, they can increase one's risk for heart disease, diabetes and other serious conditions.

SLEEPWALKING

We still don't know why people sleepwalk, but it's been shown that sleepwalkers can engage in surprisingly complex activities, such as going to the refrigerator, then preparing—and consuming—a complete meal.

Sleepwalking is more common in children but also occurs in older adults. It's usually not cause for concern unless you are putting yourself in dangerous situations, such as leaving the house or walking outside onto an unprotected balcony.

What isn't normal: A condition known as sun-downing, which can mimic sleepwalking. With sun-downing, older adults sometimes are awake late at night and wander around the house. They're partly conscious but confused and often combative. You can distinguish sun-downing from sleepwalking by the person's degree of engagement. Sun-downers can interact with other people—sleepwalkers usually don't.

If you suspect that you or a loved one may be suffering from sun-downing, see a doctor. It could be a sign of early-stage dementia. Sun-downing can also be a side effect (or wearing off) of medications, such as antidepressants, sleeping pills or antipsychotic drugs. In addition, it can be caused by narcotic painkillers, such as *meperidine* (Demerol). Once a physician changes the person's medications—or adjusts the dosages—the nighttime wandering may stop.

BLURRED VISION

Do you have trouble reading small letters? Welcome to the over-50 club. The lenses of the eyes get less elastic with age, which impairs close vision, such as that required for reading. You can solve it with reading glasses or bifocals.

What isn't normal: Consistently blurry vision. You could be developing "dry" macular degeneration, a leading cause of impaired vision. It occurs when cells in the macula (a structure in the center of the retina) start to deteriorate.

You might notice that words on a page are getting increasingly blurry. You also might have trouble adjusting to dim light. In addition, you'll probably notice a general haziness and perhaps a blurred spot in the center of your vision.

Important: See a doctor immediately if you notice any of the above vision changes. Dry macular degeneration sometimes leads to the "wet" form, a leading cause of blindness. (To read more about macular degeneration, see page 243.)

Interesting: Although color blindness is usually present at birth in those who suffer from the condition, some people lose the ability to see certain colors later in life. For example, many adults age 50 and older have trouble distinguishing greens from blues. The lenses of the eyes, like tooth enamel, yellow with age. The yellow filters out these other colors. This problem is usually minor and requires no treatment.

LOSS OF LIBIDO

It's common for men and women to experience gradual changes in their ability/desire to have sex. In men, there is a decrease in the frequency/strength of erections, often due to reduced blood flow. Women may have reduced lubrication after menopause because of declines in estrogen.

What isn't normal: Significant changes in your desire for sex might be a problem. In general, physical factors, such as pain and/or lower levels of hormones, can cause a loss of libido. But you should consider your history when assessing desire for sex—a 50% or more reduction in frequency is worth discussing with your doctor. It is usually due to excessive stress—from money worries, relationship conflicts, etc.

Helpful: Stress-reducing practices, which can include regular exercise, making time for hobbies and/or practicing relaxation techniques, such as meditation.

---

6 Herbs That Slow Aging

Donald R. Yance, CN, MH, RH (AHG), clinical master herbalist and certified nutritionist. He is author of *Adaptogens in Medical Herbalism*. DonnieYance.com

You can't escape aging. But many Americans are aging prematurely.

Surprising fact: The US ranks 42nd out of 191 countries in life expectancy, according to the Census Bureau and the National Center for Health Statistics.

The leading cause of this rapid, premature aging is chronic stress. Stress is any factor, positive or negative, that requires the body to make a response or change to adapt. It can be psychological stress, including the modern addiction to nonstop stimulation and speed. Or it can be physiological stress—such as eating a highly processed diet...sitting for hours every day...absorbing toxins from food, water and air...and spending time in artificial light.

Chronic stress overwhelms the body's homeostasis, its inborn ability to adapt to stress and stay balanced, strong and healthy. The result?

Your hormonal and immune systems are weakened. Inflammation flares up, damaging cells. Daily energy decreases, fatigue increases and you can't manage life as effectively. You suffer from one or more illnesses, take several medications and find yourself in a downward spiral of worsening health. Even though you might live to be 75 or older, you're surviving, not thriving.

We can reduce stress by making lifestyle changes such as eating better and exercising. You also can help beat stress and slow aging with adaptogens. These powerful herbs balance and strengthen the hormonal and immune systems...give you more energy...and repair cellular damage—thereby boosting your body's ability to adapt to chronic stress.

Important: Adaptogens are generally safe, but always talk with your doctor before taking any supplement.

Here are six of the most powerful adaptogens...

ASHWAGANDHA

This adaptogen from Ayurveda (the ancient system of natural healing from India) can help with a wide range of conditions.

Main actions: It is energizing and improves sleep, and it can help with arthritis, anxiety, depression, dementia and respiratory disorders, such as asthma, bronchitis and emphysema.

Important benefit: It is uniquely useful for cancer—some researchers claim it can help kill cancer cells...reduce the toxicity of chemotherapy (and prevent resistance to chemotherapeutic drugs)...relieve cancer-caused fatigue...and prevent recurrence.

ELEUTHERO

This is the most well-researched adaptogen (with more than 3,000 published studies). It often is called the "king" of adaptogens. (It was introduced in the US as "Siberian ginseng," but it is not a ginseng.)

Main actions: Along with providing energy and vitality, eleuthero protects the body against the ill effects of any kind of stress, such as extremes of heat or cold, excessive exercise and radiation. More than any other adaptogen, it helps normalize any type of physiological abnormality—including high or low blood pressure...and high or low blood sugar.

Important benefit: Eleuthero is a superb "ergogenic" (performance-enhancing) aid that can help anyone involved in sports improve strength and endurance and recover from injury.

GINSENG

Used as a traditional medicine in Asia for more than 5,000 years and the subject of more than 500 scientific papers, ginseng has two primary species—Panax ginseng (Korean or Asian ginseng) and Panax quinquefolius (American ginseng).

Main actions: Ginseng is antifatigue and antiaging. It increases muscle strength and endurance and improves reaction times. It also strengthens the immune system and the heart and helps regulate blood sugar.

Important benefits: American ginseng can be beneficial for recovering from the common cold, pneumonia or bronchitis (particularly with a dry cough)...and chronic stress accompanied by depression or anxiety.

Korean or Asian ginseng is helpful for increasing physical performance, especially endurance and energy. It is effective for restoring adrenal function and neurological health such as learning and memory.

RHAPONTICUM

This herb contains more anabolic (strengthening and muscle-building) compounds than any other plant. It is my number-one favorite herb for increasing stamina and strength.

Main actions: It normalizes the central nervous and cardiovascular systems...improves sleep, appetite and mood...and increases the ability to work and function under stressful conditions.

Important benefit: This herb is wonderful for anyone recovering from injury, trauma or surgery.

RHODIOLA

Rhodiola has gained popularity over the past few years as studies show that it rivals eleuthero and ginseng as an adaptogen. It is widely used by Russian athletes to increase energy.

Main actions: Rhodiola increases blood supply to the muscles and the brain, enhancing physical and mental performance, including memory. It normalizes the cardiovascular system and protects the heart from stress. It also strengthens immunity.

Red flag: Don't use rhodiola alone—it is extremely astringent and drying. It is best used along with other adaptogens in a formula.

SCHISANDRA

This herb has a long history of use as an adaptogen in China, Russia, Japan, Korea and Tibet. The fruit is commonly used, but the seed is more powerful.

Main actions: Schisandra can treat stress-induced fatigue...protect and detoxify the liver...treat insomnia, depression and vision problems...and enhance athletic performance.

Important benefit: This adaptogen may help night vision—one study showed it improved adaptation to darkness by 90%.

COMBINATIONS ARE BEST

Any one herb has limitations in its healing power. But a combination or formula of adaptogenic herbs overcomes those limitations—because the adaptogens act in concert, making them more powerful.

This concept of synergy—multiple herbs acting together are more effective than one herb acting alone—is key to the effectiveness of the herbal formulas of traditional Chinese medicine (TCM) and Ayurveda. Both these ancient forms of medicine often employ a dozen or more herbs in their formulas.

But it's not only the combination of herbs that makes them effective—it's also the quality of the herbs. There are many more poor-quality adaptogens on the market than high-quality (or even mediocre-quality).

My advice: Look for an herbalist or herbal company that knows all about the source and content of the herbs it uses.

Example: Herbalist & Alchemist, a company that grows most of the herbs used in its products.

Or find a product sold to health practitioners, who then sell it to their patients—this type of product is more likely to be high quality.

Example: MediHerb, from Standard Process.

Herbal formulas from my company, Natura Health Products, also meet these criteria for high quality.

You Can Have a Much Younger Body and Mind— A Few Simple Changes Can Turn Back the Clock

Mike Moreno, MD, who practices family medicine in San Diego, where he is on the board of the San Diego Chapter of the American Academy of Family Physicians. He is also the author of *The 17 Day Plan to Stop Aging.* DrMikeDiet.com

What is it that allows some people to remain robust and healthy well into their 80s and 90s while others become frail or virtually incapacitated? It's not just luck. New studies indicate that aging is largely determined by controllable factors.

Case in point: Millions of people have chronic inflammation, which has been linked to practically every "age-related" disease, including arthritis, heart disease and dementia.

Inflammation can usually be controlled with stress management, a healthful diet, weight loss (if needed) and other lifestyle changes, but there are other, even simpler, steps that can strengthen your body and brain so that they perform at the levels of a much younger person.

To turn back your biological clock...

CHALLENGE YOUR LUNGS

You shouldn't be short of breath when you climb a flight of stairs or have sex, but many adults find that they have more trouble breathing as they age—even if they don't have asthma or other lung diseases.

Why: The lungs tend to lose elasticity over time, particularly if you smoke or live in an area with high air pollution. "Stiff" lungs cannot move air efficiently and cause breathing difficulty.

Simple thing you can do: Breathe slowly in and out through a drinking straw for two to three minutes, once or twice daily. Breathe only through your mouth, not your nose. This stretches the lungs, increases lung capacity and improves lung function.

Helpful: Start with an extra-wide straw, and go to a regular straw as you get used to breathing this way.

DRINK THYME TEA

When the lungs do not expand and contract normally (see above), or when the tissues are unusually dry, you're more likely to get colds or other infections, including pneumonia. The herb thyme contains thymol, an antioxidant that may help prevent colds, bronchitis and pneumonia and soothe chronic respiratory problems such as asthma, allergies and emphysema.

Simple thing you can do: Add a cup of thyme tea to your daily routine. If you have a chronic or acute respiratory illness, drink two cups of thyme tea daily—one in the morning and one at night.

To make thyme tea: Steep one tablespoon of dried thyme (or two tablespoons of fresh thyme) in two cups of hot water for five minutes, or use thyme tea bags (available at most health-food stores).

If you take a blood thinner: Talk to your doctor before using thyme—it can increase risk for bleeding. Also, if you're allergic to oregano, you're probably allergic to thyme.

Another simple step: Drink at least six to eight eight-ounce glasses of water every day. This helps loosen lung mucus and flushes out irritants, such as bacteria and viruses.

LOWER YOUR HEART RATE

Heart disease is the leading cause of death in the US. The average American would live at least a decade longer if his/her heart pumped blood more efficiently.

Elite athletes typically have a resting heart rate of about 40 beats a minute, which is about half as fast as the average adult's resting heart rate. This reduced heart rate translates into lower blood pressure, healthier arteries and a much lower rate of heart disease. But you don't have to be an athlete to lower your heart rate—you just have to get a reasonable amount of aerobic exercise.

Simple thing you can do: Aim for a resting heart rate of 50 to 70 beats a minute—a good range for most adults. To do this, get 30 minutes of aerobic exercise, five days a week.

Good aerobic workouts include fast walking, bicycling and swimming. Even if you're not in great shape, regular workouts will lower your resting heart rate.

To check your pulse: Put your index and middle fingers on the carotid artery in your neck, and count the beats for 15 seconds, then multiply by four. Check your pulse before, during and after exercise.

WALK JUST A LITTLE FASTER

A study published in *The Journal of the American Medical Association* found that people who walked faster (at least 2.25 miles per hour) lived longer than those who walked more slowly.

Why: Faster walking not only lowers your heart rate and blood pressure but also improves cholesterol and inhibits blood clots, the cause of most heart attacks.

Simple thing you can do: You don't have to be a speed-walker, but every time you go for a walk, or even when you're walking during the normal course of your day, increase your speed and distance slightly.

Time yourself and measure your distance to monitor your progress, and create new goals every two weeks. Walk as fast as you can but at a speed that still allows you to talk without gasping, or if you're alone, you should be able to whistle. You'll notice improvements in stamina and overall energy within about two to three weeks.

SHAKE UP YOUR MENTAL ROUTINES

In a study of about 3,000 older adults, those who performed mentally challenging tasks, such as memorizing a shopping list or surfing the Internet to research a complex topic, were found to have cognitive skills that were the typical equivalent of someone 10 years younger. You'll get the same benefit from other activities that promote thinking and concentration.

Why: These tasks trigger the development of new neurons in the brain, which boost cognitive function.

Simple thing you can do: Try to change your mental routines daily.

Fun ideas: If you're right-handed, use your left hand to write a note. Study the license number of the car in front of you, and see if you can remember it five minutes later. Listen to a type of music that's new to you. Rearrange your kitchen cabinets so that you have to think about where to find things. Overall, don't let your brain get into the rut of performing the same tasks over and over.

FIGHT BRAIN INFLAMMATION

You've probably heard that good oral hygiene can reduce the risk for heart disease. A new study suggests that it also can promote brain health. Researchers found that men and women over age 60 who had the lowest levels of oral bacteria did better on cognitive tests involving memory and calculations than those who had more bacteria.

Why: Bacteria associated with gum disease also cause inflammation in the brain. This low-level inflammation can damage brain cells and affect cognitive function.

Simple thing you can do: Brush your teeth after every meal—and floss twice a day. I also recommend using an antiseptic mouthwash, which helps eliminate bacteria.

The Extreme Dangers of Belly Fat

Bill Gavin, MD, an interventional cardiologist and medical director of the Heart Program at Providence St. Peter Hospital in Olympia, Washington. He is the author of *No White at Night: The Three-Rule Diet.*

Belly fat—generally associated with an "apple" body shape—presents great risks to our health. Also known as visceral fat, it is stored mostly inside the abdominal cavity, where it wraps around (and sometimes invades) the internal organs, including the heart.

Long known to damage blood vessel linings, belly fat is a metabolically active tissue that secretes harmful inflammatory substances that can contribute to a variety of health problems.

People with an apple body type are far more likely to die of heart attacks than those with a pear shape.

The worst of the worst: Hard belly fat (commonly known as a "beer belly") is even more dangerous than soft belly fat—perhaps because many people with hard belly fat have high levels of C-reactive- protein (CRP), an inflammation marker and risk factor for heart disease. Alcohol has been shown to slow fat metabolism by more than 30%, which is compounded by the fact that beer drinkers tend to eat high-calorie snack foods while drinking and beer itself is high in carbohydrate calories.

Surprising finding: Among those of normal weight who had excess belly fat, dementia risk was 1.89 times higher than for those of normal weight who did not have excess belly fat.

My recommendation: A waist size of 35 inches or less in women and 40 inches or less in men. Even slight increases above these numbers significantly raise your health risks.

Best way to measure your waist: Place a tape measure just below your navel, exhale gently, then record the measurement.

STRATEGIES FOR WAIST LOSS

There are no proven ways to selectively reduce accumulations of visceral fat. *My advice…*

• **Strive for healthy overall weight loss.** People who follow a sensible diet, such as the American Heart Association's No-Fat Diet (*americanheart.org*) or the Weight Watchers plan (*weightwatchers.com*), lose weight proportionally—that is, they lose more weight from areas where they have the most body fat. Someone with a high percentage of visceral fat will show the effects most in the abdomen.

Another advantage of such diets is that they include large amounts of natural, wholesome foods, such as vegetables and whole grains. A plant-based diet supplies large quantities of anti-inflammatory, disease-fighting compounds.

Important: When you're trying to lose weight, avoid or eliminate most dietary sugars—not only from sweet snacks, but also from processed carbohydrates, such as white bread,

13

snacks, beer and fruit juices. These foods have a high-glycemic index—that is, they cause a rapid spike in blood sugar that may increase the accumulation of visceral fat.

• **Drink green tea.** A study in the *Journal of Nutrition* found that obese adults who drank green tea lost about twice as much weight over 12 weeks as a control group even though people in both groups followed similar diets and exercise patterns. It's thought that compounds known as catechins in green tea increase metabolism and accelerate the breakdown of fat.

• **Focus on aerobic exercise.** This is the best way to increase metabolism, burn calories and reduce fat. Aerobic exercise is more effective than resistance workouts (such as lifting weights) because it burns more calories per hour.

There's some evidence that overweight women who engage in sustained aerobic workouts—such as 20 minutes or more of brisk walking daily—can lose up to one inch of belly fat in just four weeks.

• **Turn down the thermostat.** Researchers have recently made exciting discoveries related to so-called "brown" fat, which has been shown to burn energy to generate body heat.

This type of fat was once thought to disappear after infancy, but new studies indicate that it's present in many adults and can be activated by exposure to cool temperatures—roughly 61°F.

People who are overweight or obese may have lower brown fat activity, which could be an under-lying cause of weight gain. Spending a few hours in cool temperatures—say, at night when you sleep—could potentially increase the body's energy expenditure, which, over time, could result in weight loss. More research is needed, but in the meantime, set your thermostat as low as is comfortable year-round.

*To calculate your body mass index, go to the National Heart, Lung and Blood Institute website, *nhlbi. nih.gov*, and search "BMI calculator."

Sarcopenia Is Slowly Stealing Your Muscles, Your Strength—and Maybe Even Your Life

Michael J. Grossman, MD, a specialist in antiaging and regenerative medicine. He is coauthor of *The Vitality Connection: Ten Practical Ways to Optimize Your Health and Reverse the Aging Process.*

You probably know all about osteoporosis, the gradual, age-related loss of bone.

What you may not know: There also is an age-related loss of muscle mass, strength and function—a condition called sarcopenia. And it is a problem for all of us as we age.

Sarcopenia generally starts at age 40. By the time you're 50, you're losing 1% to 2% of your muscle mass every year. And as you lose muscle, you lose strength.

Example: Starting in your 40s, leg strength typically drops by 10% to 15% per decade until you're 70, after which it declines by 25% to 40% per decade.

But you don't have to become physically debilitated to suffer the devastating effects of muscle loss. When you have less muscle, you have more fat—and fat cells produce inflammatory compounds that drive many deadly chronic diseases, such as heart disease and cancer.

The good news: Starting today, there are many actions you can take to slow, stop and even reverse sarcopenia…

WHAT YOU NEED TO KNOW

When sarcopenia is at its worst—what some experts call pathological sarcopenia—you become weak, walk slowly, fall easily, are less likely to recover from an illness and are more likely to die from any cause. That degree of sarcopenia afflicts 14% of people ages 65 to 75 and 45% of those 85 and older.

Sarcopenia is linked to a 77% increased risk for cardiovascular disease. It's also linked to higher death rates in breast cancer survivors and older people with lymphoma.

With less muscle, you burn less glucose (blood sugar), so it becomes harder to prevent, control or reverse type 2 diabetes, a disease of chronically high blood sugar that can plague your life with complications such as vision loss, nerve pain and kidney failure. Diabetes also doubles your risk for heart attack, stroke and Alzheimer's disease.

Studies also link sarcopenia to triple the risk for osteoporosis, a fourfold increase in postoperative infections and severe menopausal symptoms.

NUTRITION

The right diet and supplements can fight muscle loss. (Talk to your doctor before taking any of these supplements, because they could interact with medication or affect a chronic condition, such as kidney disease.)

• **Eat protein-rich food daily.** Increasing the amount of protein in your diet not only can help stop the breakdown of muscle, but it also helps build new muscle.

Scientific evidence: In a three-year study, published in *The American Journal of Clinical Nutrition*, older people who ate the most protein lost 40% less muscle compared with people who ate the least.

My advice: Every day, eat at least four ounces of protein-rich food, such as lean beef, fish, chicken or turkey. A four-ounce serving is about the size of a deck of cards.

Helpful: Whey protein, from milk, is rich in branched-chain amino acids. These three amino acids (leucine, isoleucine and valine) comprise 35% of muscle protein and are uniquely effective in building muscle. Look for a protein powder derived from whey protein, and use at least one scoop daily in a smoothie or shake. You also can get some of these amino acids by eating Greek yogurt, nuts, seeds, cheese and hard-boiled eggs.

• **Take vitamin D.** Vitamin D is widely known to stop bone loss, but it also stops muscle loss.

Scientific evidence: A study published in *Journal of Internal Medicine* linked low blood levels of vitamin D to a fourfold increase in the risk for frailty, a problem of old age that includes pathological sarcopenia.

Vitamin D works to protect muscle by decreasing chronic, low-grade inflammation, which contributes to the breakdown and loss of muscle protein.

Unfortunately, an estimated nine out of 10 Americans have suboptimal blood levels of vitamin D, below 30 nanograms per milliliter (ng/ml). A simple blood test can reveal your vitamin D level. Research shows that people with a blood level of 55 ng/ml or higher of vitamin D have 50% less heart disease and cancer than people with a blood level of 20 ng/ml or below. It also reduces the risk of falling by 19%.

My advice: I recommend the same 55 ng/ml level to control muscle loss. To achieve that level, most people need to take a daily vitamin D supplement that supplies 3,000 international units (IU) to 5,000 IU.

• **Take fish oil.** Like vitamin D, fish oil works to protect muscle by reducing the chronic inflammation that damages muscle cells.

Scientific evidence: In a study in *The American Journal of Clinical Nutrition*, women who participated in strength-training and also took fish oil had much stronger muscles after three months than women who did only strength-training.

My advice: To protect and build muscle, I recommend a supplement containing 1,000 milligrams (mg) of omega-3 fatty acids, with 400 mg of EPA and 300 mg of DHA. Take it twice daily.

• **Consider creatine.** Creatine is an amino acid–like compound found mostly in red meat, pork and fish, such as salmon, tuna and herring. More than 70 clinical studies show that regularly taking a creatine supplement can help build muscle and increase strength.

However: The nutrient works to build muscle only if you are exercising—without that regular challenge to the muscles, supplemental creatine has no effect.

My advice: If you're exercising regularly, take three grams of creatine daily.

EXERCISE

Regular exercise is one of the best ways to stop or reverse muscle loss. You need both aerobic exercise and resistance exercise (which stresses the muscles, causing them to get stronger). *My advice...*

• **For aerobics, use your lower and upper body.** Walking is a good exercise, but it builds only lower-body strength. Also include aerobic exercise that uses the lower and upper body, such as tennis, ballroom dancing or working out on an elliptical machine. Try to participate in 30 to 60 minutes of aerobic exercise five or more days a week.

• **For resistance training, work all your muscles.** I recommend resistance exercise three times a week, concentrating on the different muscle groups at each session—chest and triceps...back and biceps...and legs and shoulders. If you don't like weight-lifting, try another form of resistance exercise, such as resistance bands.

HORMONES

As you age, you lose bone, muscle—and hormones. And many of those hormones, particularly testosterone, are crucial for building muscle in both men and women. (Women manufacture testosterone in the ovaries and adrenal glands.) Estrogen and dehydroepiandrosterone (DHEA) also play a role in creating and maintaining muscle.

My advice: Find a doctor trained in anti-aging medicine and bioidentical hormone replacement therapy (BHRT), which uses compounds that are identical to the hormones that your body manufactures rather than synthetics. Ask the doctor to test your hormone levels and determine if BHRT is right for you.

2

Eat Like This for Longevity

5 Surprising Foods to Help You Live Longer

Whether your blood sugar (glucose) levels are normal and you want to keep them that way…or you have diabetes and glucose control is your mantra…it is smart to eat a well-balanced diet to help keep your glucose readings healthy. In fact, maintaining healthy glucose levels may even help you live longer by avoiding diabetes—one of the leading causes of death in the US.

Most people already know that cinnamon is an excellent choice for blood sugar control. Consuming just one-half teaspoon to three teaspoons a day can reduce glucose levels by up to 24%. Cinnamon is great on cereals, vegetables, cottage cheese and snacks (think fresh apple slices sprinkled with cinnamon).

Other smart food choices…*

*If you take diabetes medication, consult your doctor before making significant changes to your diet—drug dosages may need to be adjusted.

GLUCOSE-CONTROLLING FOOD #1: BLACK BEANS

Beans, in general, are the most underrated food in the supermarket.

Beans are high in protein as well as soluble and insoluble fiber. Soluble fiber helps you feel fuller longer, and insoluble fiber helps prevent constipation. Beans also break down slowly during digestion, which means more stable blood sugar levels.

Black beans, however, are particularly healthful because of their especially high fiber content. For example, one cup of cooked black beans contains 15 g of fiber, while a cup of pink beans has just 9 g.

Bonus: Beans protect the heart by lowering cholesterol and reducing damage from free

Bonnie Taub-Dix, RD, a registered dietitian and owner of BTD Nutrition Consultants located in New York City. A nationally recognized nutrition expert and the author of *Read It Before You Eat It*, she has advised patients on the best ways to control diabetes for more than three decades. BonnieTaubDix.com

17

radicals. For example, one study showed that you can lower your total and LDL ("bad") cholesterol by about 8% simply by eating one-half cup of cooked pinto beans every day.

Helpful: To shorten cooking times, use canned beans instead of dried beans. They are equally nutritious, and you can reduce the sodium in salted canned beans by about 40% by rinsing them.

Another healthful way to use beans: Hummus. In the Middle East, people eat this chickpea (garbanzo bean) spread as often as Americans eat bread. It is much healthier than bread because it contains both protein and olive oil—important for slowing the absorption of carbohydrate sugars and preventing blood sugar "spikes."

Hummus is a good weight-loss dish because it is high in fiber (about 15 g per cup) as well as protein (about 19 g). Ample amounts of protein and fiber allow you to satisfy your appetite with smaller portions of food.

Hummus is made with mashed chickpeas, tahini (a sesame seed paste), lemon juice, garlic, salt and a little olive oil. Stick to the serving size on the label, which is typically two to four tablespoons.

GLUCOSE-CONTROLLING FOOD #2: COCOA

The flavanols in cocoa are potent antioxidants that not only fight heart disease but also help guard against diabetes. In recent studies, cocoa improved insulin sensitivity, the body's ability to transport sugar out of the bloodstream. It's wise for people with diabetes or high blood sugar to choose unsweetened cocoa and add a small amount of sugar or sugar substitute.

Cinnamon hot cocoa combines two glucose-controlling ingredients in one delicious recipe.

To prepare: Mix one-quarter cup of baking cocoa, one tablespoon of sugar (or Truvia to taste) and a pinch of salt. Gradually add one-quarter cup of boiling water and blend well. Add one cup of skim or 1% low-fat milk and a cinnamon stick. While stirring occasionally,

heat on low for 10 minutes. Remove the cinnamon stick and enjoy!

GLUCOSE-CONTROLLING FOOD #3: DATES

These little fruits are sweet enough to qualify as dessert but have more antioxidants per serving than oranges, grapes and even broccoli. The antioxidants can help prevent heart disease as well as neuropathy—nerve damage that frequently occurs in people who have diabetes.

A single serving (for example, seven deglet noor dates) has 4 g of fiber for better blood sugar management.

Be careful: Seven dates also have 140 calories and 32 g of sugar, so this must be added to your total daily carbohydrate intake, especially if you have diabetes. Dates, in general, have a low glycemic index, so they don't spike glucose levels. Medjool dates, however, are not an ideal choice. They have significantly more sugar and calories per serving than deglet noor dates.

GLUCOSE-CONTROLLING FOOD #4: SARDINES

Many people know about the heart-healthy benefits of cold-water fish, such as salmon and mackerel. An analysis of studies involving hundreds of thousands of adults found that just one to two fish servings a week reduced the risk of dying from heart disease by more than one-third.

What's less well known is that the high concentration of omega-3 fatty acids in cold-water fish also helps prevent a too-rapid rise in blood sugar. Besides being low on the glycemic index, fish contains protein, which blunts blood sugar levels.

Best for helping to prevent high blood sugar: In addition to salmon and mackerel, sardines are an excellent choice (when canned with bones, they also are a good source of calcium). Tuna, to a somewhat lesser extent, offers omega-3s (choose canned light—albacore white has higher levels of mercury). Also avoid large fish, such as king mackerel and swordfish, which have more mercury than smaller fish. Aim for a 3.5-ounce serving two or three times a week.

GLUCOSE-CONTROLLING FOOD #5: ALMONDS

High in fiber, protein and beneficial fats, nuts can significantly lower glucose levels. In fact, women who ate a one-ounce serving of nuts at least five times a week were nearly 30% less likely to develop diabetes than women who rarely or never ate nuts, according to one study.

The poly- and monounsaturated fats in nuts improve the body's ability to use insulin. Nuts also help with cholesterol control—important because diabetes increases risk for heart disease.

All nuts are beneficial, but almonds contain more fiber, calcium and protein than most nuts (and are best for blood sugar control). Walnuts are highest in antioxidants and omega-3 fatty acids. Avoid salted nuts—they have too much sodium.

Excellent way to add nuts to your diet: Nut butters. Almost everyone likes peanut butter, and it is healthier than you might think. Like butters made from almonds, cashews or other nuts, the fats it contains are mostly monounsaturated, which are good for the heart. The fiber in nut butters (about 1 g to 2 g per tablespoon, depending on the nut) can help lower blood sugar.

Good choice for blood sugar control: One serving (one to two tablespoons) of almond butter (rich in potassium, vitamin E and calcium) several times a week. Look for nut butters that have a short list of ingredients—they are the most nutritious.

A SIMPLE BLOOD SUGAR BUSTER

Taking two tablespoons of apple-cider vinegar in eight ounces of water with meals or before bedtime can slow the absorption of sugar into the blood—vinegar helps to block the digestive enzymes that change carbs to sugar.

Eat Your Way to Health: DASH Diet

Marla Heller, MS, RD, author of *The DASH Diet Action Plan*, based in Chicago. Her website is DASHDiet.org/Marla.asp.

Maintaining normal blood pressure is vital to staying healthy, but perhaps we've been trained by the mainstream medical community to rely too much on drugs to do it. For many people, there can be a better—and safer—way that requires nothing more than your spoon and fork.

During a five-center study in the 1990s sponsored by the National Institutes of Health, researchers found that participants with high blood pressure (hypertension) who followed a specific dietary plan called DASH (Dietary Approaches to Stop Hypertension) lowered systolic pressure (the higher number in a blood pressure reading) by 11.4 mm/Hg and diastolic pressure by 6 mm/Hg. More recent studies gave the DASH diet added value—at Brigham and Women's Hospital in Boston, an analysis of data from the long-term Nurse's Health Study and Health Professionals Follow-Up Study found that following the DASH diet was associated with lower risk for kidney stones. Other studies find that a DASH diet lowers risk for cardiac disease and stroke...and most recently, at Utah State University in Logan, an 11-year study has demonstrated that elderly adults who followed DASH stayed mentally sharp longer.

HOW TO DO DASH

The diet (more details to follow) basically consists of eating healthy foods with some specific tweaking, plus a salt limitation. Given that the typical diet of Americans today is filled with processed foods high in sugar, salt and fat, DASH is often described as "difficult to follow." But according to Marla Heller, MS, RD, author of *The DASH Diet Action Plan*, it doesn't have to be! She agrees that it usually takes time to overcome a lifetime of bad habits such as living on french fries and soft drinks... but the DASH plan includes a wide variety of delicious, satisfying foods. It is important to follow this dietary plan closely, she said, because in addition to restricting sodium, eating the recommended amounts of foods on DASH provides high amounts of magnesium, potassium and calcium. A diet that is rich in foods with this combination of nutrients is what helps to control blood pressure.

In a nutshell, here's the DASH diet…

•**Whole grains**—six to eight servings a day of products made from 100% whole grains…a serving is one slice of bread, one ounce of dry cereal, or one-half cup of cooked cereal, whole-grain pasta or brown rice.

•**Fruits and vegetables**—eight to 10 servings a day…a serving is defined as one cup of raw, leafy vegetables or one-half cup of cooked veggies, one medium fruit, one-half cup low-sodium vegetable juice, one cup of fresh fruit, or one-half cup of frozen or canned fruit. To reduce calories, Heller suggests limiting starchy vegetables, such as potatoes, corn and the like, but the good news is that you can eat as much as you like of the nonstarchy ones, for example, tomatoes, green beans, leafy greens, peppers and others.

•**Low-fat or nonfat dairy**—two to three servings a day. A serving is one cup of milk or yogurt or one and one-half ounces of cheese. (See update on page 382 "The High-Fat Path to Low Blood Pressure…").

•**Lean meat, fish and poultry**—six or fewer ounces a day. A three-ounce serving is the size of a pack of cards, which is sufficient with a meal.

•**Nuts, seeds and beans**—four to five servings per week…servings include one-half cup of cooked dried beans or peas, one-quarter cup of nuts or two tablespoons of peanut butter. Heller says it is okay to have more beans than this each week, but if so you should balance that by eating less meat, fish and poultry.

•**Fats and oils**—two to three servings a day…with a serving being one teaspoon of margarine or vegetable oil, one tablespoon of mayonnaise or two tablespoons of salad dressing.

•**Sweets**—up to five servings a week…such as one-half cup sorbet, one tablespoon of sugar, jelly or jam, or one cup of lemonade.

•**Sodium**—The National Academy of Science's Institute of Medicine recommends not exceeding 1,500 mg to 2,400 mg of salt per day (1,500 mg is about two-thirds teaspoon of table salt).

Note: Factors such as medications you are on, exercise and diet history should be considered in determining your optimal sodium intake.

Make DASH Delicious…

Here's another reason the DASH diet is tastier and easier to follow than you might think: It follows many of the same principles as the Mediterranean Diet that is so popular today, in particular its focus on a daily bounty of fresh vegetables. It's easy to find restaurants serving these foods (see page 374 for specific restaurant choices).

While many new DASH followers complain about a lack of flavor, what they really are reacting to is the lack of salt. Heller shared some of her favorite cooking tips for flavorful food—and she noted that reducing salt intake is easier if you make the change gradually. She often uses a base of onions, garlic and red wine, which she says makes just about everything tasty. "For sautéing foods, I start with onions and garlic together and at the very end of the dish I add a little bit of red wine and cook it down to evaporate the alcohol," she explains. Herbs add flavor, too—for instance, try a bit of oregano or thyme on vegetables. A sprinkle of reduced-sodium cheese can also be delicious, as is, surprisingly, cinnamon. Another trick of Heller's is to drizzle a bit of olive oil (a tablespoon, she suggests) over foods, which enhances their flavor and adds fat, making them more satisfying and also helping with absorption of nutrients.

To get started on DASH, Heller says, it is vital to clear your kitchen and pantry of all foods that are not on the diet. Then stock up with a wide variety of fresh, tasty and healthy DASH foods. That way, when your stomach rumbles, you will have plenty of satisfying no-cheat choices. For more information on DASH, suggested menus and recipes, go to *dashdiet.org*.

heel…the outside of the heel…the ball of the foot…and just below the pinkie toe.

And here's an exercise that can help you identify a forward-thrusting pelvis and poor weight placement: Stand barefoot and move your hips back until they are over your ankles—when you do this correctly, you should be able to lift all 10 toes off the floor. Do this near a chair or wall in case you need support. Once you learn what this centered position feels like, try to achieve it regularly.

WHAT TO WEAR?

Walk shoeless often, and when footwear is required select heels that are as flat as possible. An elevation of even an inch or so puts too much weight on the ball of the foot—it's like walking downhill. In fact, wear shoes that draw your weight back, onto the heels, such as those made by Earth, Inc. (*earthfootwear.com*). Arch supports may be helpful for people with very high or very low arches, but regular use weakens foot muscles.

Flip-flops are a no-no—they force the wearer to scrunch the toes, which can cause hammer toes and also makes proper weight distribution (those four proper contact points) impossible. Avoid the types of workout shoes that rock the foot and purposely throw off the body's balance to make leg muscles work harder—including "FitFlops" and MBTs. The shape of the sole creates an unnatural gait pattern that can harm the feet, knees, hips and spine.

For dress-up occasions, women should bring heels to put on at the last minute. If you wear them regularly, visit the chiropractor or a naturopathic physician to get some special attention for your feet and sacroiliac joints, which will help to minimize the damage.

EASY STEPS TO FEEL-GOOD FEET

The real path to pain-free feet, however, involves giving them tender, loving care in the form of regular exercises that stretch, balance and strengthen their muscles, tendons and ligaments. Start by simply spreading and lifting your toes as often as possible. *Other easy exercises…*

• **Toe lifts.** While standing, lift your big toe alone, followed in succession by each of the remaining toes…repeat in the opposite direction, big toe last.

• **Toe tucks.** Stand with one foot flat on the floor and the other pointed slightly behind you, toes tucked under so that the tops of your toes are resting on the floor. This stretches your upper foot. (This won't be easy or comfortable at first.)

• **Arch support.** Stand erect, shift your weight to the outside of one of your soles, and lift that foot's ball and toes…slowly lower the ball of the foot without letting your arch collapse, and then relax your toes back to the ground.

• **Toe spacers.** Available at nail-care salons, online and in many stores, they fit between your toes and spread them. They may feel odd at first, but then are soothing. If you use them fairly often, such as while reading or watching TV, your toes will eventually relearn their normal spreading motion.

Yoga Can Change Your Life! An 85-Year-Old Instructor Shares Her Stay-Young Poses

Mary Louise Stefanic, a certified yoga and qigong instructor with a focus on therapeutic yoga. Ms. Stefanic is a staff member at the Loyola Center for Fitness and Loyola University Health System, both in Maywood, Illinois. She has been teaching yoga since 1969.

Not that long ago, yoga was viewed primarily as an activity for "youngish" health nuts who wanted to round out their exercise regimens.

Now: Older adults—meaning people in their 60s, 70s, 80s and beyond—are among the most enthusiastic practitioners of this ancient healing system of exercise and controlled breathing.

YOGA GOES MAINSTREAM

Virtually everyone can benefit from yoga. Unfortunately, many people are reluctant to try it because they assume that it's too unconventional and requires extreme flexibility. Neither belief is true.

What's more, its varied health benefits are largely what's making the practice so popular now with older adults. More than 1,000 scientific studies have shown that yoga can improve conditions ranging from arthritis, asthma, insomnia and depression to heart disease, diabetes and cancer.

You look better, too: Yoga is quite useful in helping to prevent rounding (or hunching) of the back, which occurs so often in older adults.

GETTING STARTED

If you want to see whether you could benefit from yoga, ask your doctor about trying the following poses, which address common physical complaints. These poses are a good first step before taking a yoga class.* Yoga is best performed in loose, comfortable clothing and in your bare feet, so your feet won't slip. *Poses to try…*

•**Knees to chest pose.** For low-back pain and painful, tight hips.

What to do: Lie on your back (on carpet or a yoga mat, available at sports-equipment stores for about $25). With your arms, hug both knees in to your chest. Keep your knees together and your elbows pointing out to each side of your body. Slowly rock from elbow to elbow to massage your back and shoulders. Take deep, abdominal breaths while holding your thighs close to your chest and hold for six complete inhales and exhales.

•**Mecca pose.** This pose also relieves back pain.

*To find a yoga class near you, check your local community center and/or consult the International Association of Yoga Therapists, iayt.org.

What to do: Begin by kneeling on the floor with your knees together. Sit back on your feet, and lean forward from your waist so that your chest and stomach rest atop your thighs. Reach your arms out in front of you, resting your forehead to the floor while stretching your tailbone to your heels. Hold for six complete inhales and exhales.

•**Leg rotation.** For sciatica, a cause of back, pelvic and leg pain.

What to do: Lie on your back with both legs extended. Slowly bring your right knee to your chest and inhale. Rest your right ankle on the front of your left thigh, and exhale as you slowly slide it down along your left knee, shin and ankle to toes. This helps "screw" the top of your right thighbone into the hip socket, easing lower back and leg pain. Repeat on other side. Do three times on each side.

To conclude your session: While in a sitting position, press your palms together. Bring your thumbs into your breastbone. Tuck your elbows in and down, press your breastbone to your thumbs, lifting and opening your chest. Hold for six breaths.

Important: Even when you're not doing yoga, don't forget your breath. Slow, thoughtful, deep breathing is most effective, but don't perform it too quickly. I find the technique to be most effective when you hold the inhalation and exhalation for a certain number of counts.

What to do: Lie on your back, resting your hands on your belly so that your middle fingers touch across your navel. Inhale through your nose for a count of six, pushing your navel out so that your fingertips separate. Pause, then exhale for a count of nine, pulling your navel back in. Perform these steps two more times (more may make you dizzy). Do this in the morning and at night (deep breathing improves mental focus and can be energizing in the morning and calming at night).

4

Grow Younger: Look Good and Feel Good

12 Things That Make You Look Older

As you get older, wardrobe and style choices that worked when you were younger may no longer be serving you well. This goes for both men and women. Without knowing it, you may be looking older than you are. This could cause others to treat you as older and potentially hold you back from employment opportunities and advancements. This also can make you feel like you are not up to your game or comfortable in your skin. When you are not style confident, you are less body confident, which makes you feel less life confident.

Helpful: Seek out style mentors—people who look elegant and modern without chasing youth-oriented trends. Observe them carefully, and adapt elements of their style to your own. TV newscasters make good style mentors because they are required to look contemporary while also projecting dignity and authority.

Give yourself a good, hard look, and ask yourself whether you are looking older than your actual age with any of these common signals…

1. Sneakers for everyday wear. Your feet should be comfortable, but sneakers outside the gym just look sloppy and careless. Young people get away with it—but there are more stylish options when you're older. These include loafers or driving moccasins for men and low-heeled pumps with cushioned soles for women. Wedge-soled shoes are a comfortable alternative to high heels.

2. Baggy pants. Although young men may look trendy in high-waisted, loose-fitting jeans, this style screams old on anyone else. For women, the rear end tends to flatten with age, causing pants to fit loosely in the rear.

Kim Johnson Gross, cocreator of the *Chic Simple* book series and author of *What to Wear for the Rest of Your Life.* KimJohnsonGross.com

And front-pleated pants for women generally are unflattering and unstylish.

Better: Spend the time to find pants that fit well—or figure a tailor into your wardrobe budget. Baggy is dowdy, but overly tight makes you look heavier. Well-fitting clothes make you look slimmer and younger.

3. Boring colors. Skin tone gets duller with age, so the colors you wear should bring light to your face. If you are a woman who has worn black for years, it may be too harsh for you now. Brown makes men fade into the woodwork.

Better: Stand in front of a mirror, and experiment with colors that you never thought you could wear—you may be surprised at what flatters you. Avoid neon brights, which make older skin look sallow, but be open to the rest of the color spectrum. Try contemporary patterns and prints. For neutrals, gray and navy are softer alternatives to black for women, and any shade of blue is a good bet for men.

4. Boring glasses and jewelry. Men and women should have some fun with glasses. It's a great way to update your look and make it more modern. Tell your optician what you're looking for, or bring a stylish friend with you.

As for jewelry for women, wearing a large piece of fab faux jewelry (earrings, necklace, ring) or multiple bracelets adds great style and youth to your look.

5. Turtlenecks. You may think a turtleneck hides a sagging neck and chin, but it is more likely to draw attention to jowls.

Better: A cowl neckline for women, or a loosely draped scarf. A scarf is the single best item to help a woman look thinner, taller, prettier and more chic. You can find several scarf instructional videos online. We like the one at Nordstrom's website: *shop.nordstrom.com/c/ scarf-video.* For a man, an oblong scarf, looped, is a stylish European look that adds a welcome shot of color.

6. Stiff or one-tone hair. An overly styled helmet of hair looks old-fashioned. Hair that's a solid block of color looks unnatural and harsh.

Better: Whether hair is short or shoulder-length, women need layers around the face for softness. As for color, opt for subtle highlights in front and a slightly darker tone toward the back.

Keep in mind that gray hair can be beautiful, modern and sexy. You need a plan to go gray, though, which means a flattering cut and using hair products that enhance the gray. Ask your stylist for recommendations. Also, if your hair is a dull gray, consider getting silver highlights around your face to bring light and "energy" to your hair.

Men who dye their hair should allow a bit of gray at the temples—it looks more natural than monochrome hair. But avoid a comb-over or a toupee. A man who attempts to hide a receding hairline isn't fooling anyone—he just looks insecure.

Better: Treat your thinning hair as a badge of honor. Either keep it neatly trimmed or shave your head.

7. Missing (or bushy) eyebrows. Women's eyebrows tend to disappear with age. Men's are more likely to grow wild.

Better: Women should use eyebrow pencil, powder or both to fill in fading brows. Visit a high-end cosmetics counter, and ask the stylist to show you how. You may need to try several products to find out what works best. Men, make sure that your barber or hair stylist trims your eyebrows regularly.

Also: Women tend not to notice increased facial hair (especially stray hairs) on the chin and upper lip—a result of hormonal change. Pluck!

8. Deeply tanned skin. Baby boomers grew up actively developing suntans using baby oil and sun reflectors. Now pale is the norm. A dark tan not only dates you, it increases your risk for skin cancer and worsens wrinkling.

Better: Wear a hat and sunscreen to shield your skin from sun damage.

9. Less-than-white teeth. Yellowing teeth add decades to your appearance. Everyone's teeth get yellower with age, but with so many teeth-whitening products available, there is no excuse to live with off-color teeth.

Better: Ask your dentist which whitening technique he/she recommends based on the condition of your teeth—over-the-counter whitening strips, bleaching in the dentist's office or a custom bleaching kit you can use at home.

10. Women: Nude or beige hose. Nude stockings on women look hopelessly out-of-date. Bare legs are the norm now for young women, but they are not a good option for older women who have dark veins.

Better: In winter, wear dark stockings or opaque tights. In summer, use spray-on tanner for a light tan…or wear nude fishnet stockings or slacks or capris.

11. Poor-fitting bra. Get a bra that fits. Most women don't know that bra size changes as your body does. Giving your breasts a lift will make you look younger and trimmer.

12. Excess makeup. Thick foundation, heavy eyeliner, bright blusher and red lipstick all add years to your face.

Better: Use a moisturizing (not matte) foundation, and dab it only where needed to even out skin tone. To add color to cheeks, use a small amount of tinted moisturizer, bronzer or cream blush. Use liquid eyeliner in soft shades such as deep blue or brown, and blend it well. For lips, choose soft pinks and mauves, depending on your skin tone.

Bottom line: The idea is to have fun putting yourself together. That inner spark and personal style will show that you are getting better with age.

Sugar Makes You Look Older

People were asked to guess the age of volunteers. The study found that every 0.18-gram increase in the volunteers' blood sugar level was associated with a five-month increase in perceived age.

Possible reason: Glucose can damage skin's collagen and elastin, causing wrinkles and sagging.

Study by researchers from Unilever Discover, Colworth House, Sharnbrook, Bedfordshire, UK, and Leiden University Medical Center, the Netherlands, published in *AGE: Journal of the American Aging Association.*

Skin Care from the Inside Out

Joy Bauer, MS, RD, CDN, a nutritionist/dietitian in private practice in New York City. She is author of several books, including *Joy Bauer's Food Cures: Treat Common Health Concerns, Look Younger & Live Longer.* JoyBauer.com

---

To take care of their skin, most people reach for sunscreen, lotions and creams to protect, smooth and moisturize. These products can help, but beautiful, healthy skin starts with what goes into your body, not what you rub on it. Research shows that good nutrition may reduce the effects of sun damage…minimize redness and wrinkling…and even protect against some skin cancers.

FIRST STEP: HYDRATE

The single most important nutritional factor for keeping skin healthy is water. Staying hydrated keeps cells plump, making skin look firmer and clearer. When cells are dehydrated, they shrivel and can make your skin look wrinkled. Think of it this way—when you dehydrate a juicy grape, you get a raisin. In addition, water transports nutrients into skin cells and helps flush toxins out of the body.

To stay hydrated, drink whenever you feel thirsty.

Helpful sign: If your urine is pale yellow, you are adequately hydrated—but if it is bright or dark yellow, you may need to boost your fluid intake.

Good news: Drinking unsweetened tea helps keep you hydrated, plus you get the benefit of antioxidant nutrients called polyphenols, which may help prevent sun-related skin cancers. Green, white, black and oolong teas provide more polyphenols than herbal teas. It is your choice whether to drink caffeinated or decaffeinated tea. Although caffeine is a mild diuretic (increasing the amount of urine that is passed from the body), the relatively small amount in tea doesn't affect its ability to keep skin hydrated and healthy.

Avoid: Teas sweetened with a lot of sugar —excess sugar can make skin dull and wrinkled.

For extra hydration: Eat "juicy foods" that are at least 75% water by weight—fruits such as apples, berries, cherries, grapes, grapefruit, mangoes, melons, oranges, peaches, plums… and vegetables such as asparagus, beets, carrots, celery, cucumbers and tomatoes.

SKIN-HEALTHY FOODS

Everything we eat is reflected in the health of our skin—for better or for worse. *Among the best nutrients for the skin…*

• **Beta-carotene,** a powerful antioxidant which, once ingested, is converted to vitamin A, a nutrient necessary for skin tissue growth and repair.

Skin-smart: Have at least one serving per day of beta-carotene–rich foods—for instance, orange carrots, sweet potatoes and tomatoes… green arugula, asparagus and spinach…and fruits such as cherries, grapefruit, mangoes and watermelon.

• **Omega-3 fatty acids,** healthful fats that are important building blocks of the membranes that make up cell walls, allowing water and nutrients to enter and keeping out waste and toxins.

Skin-smart: Eat at least three servings of omega-3–rich foods each week—such as wild salmon (farm-raised salmon may have higher levels of potentially dangerous contaminants) …mackerel (not king mackerel, which has too much mercury)…anchovies, herring and sardines. Good fats also are found in smaller amounts in flaxseed, soybeans and walnuts. If you don't eat enough of these omega-3 foods, consider taking daily supplements of fish oil providing 1,000 mg of combined *eicosapentaenoic acid* (EPA) and *docosahexaenoic acid* (DHA), the most biologically active and beneficial components. Look for brands that have been tested for purity, such as Ultimate Omega by Nordic Naturals (*nordicnaturals.com*).

• **Selenium,** a mineral with antioxidant activity thought to help skin elasticity (which means you'll look younger longer) and prevent sun-related skin damage and cancers.

Skin-smart: Eat at least one serving a day of a selenium-rich food—canned light tuna (which has less mercury than canned albacore or white tuna), crab, tilapia…whole-wheat breads and pasta…lean beef…chicken and turkey (breast meat is lowest in fat).

Caution: Taking selenium in supplement form may increase the risk for squamous cell skin cancer in people with a personal or family history of the disease. Selenium in food is safe and healthful.

• **Vitamin C,** an antioxidant that helps build collagen and elastin (proteins that comprise the skin's underlying structure)…and also protects against free radicals (molecules in the body that damage cells) when the skin is exposed to sunlight.

Skin-smart: Eat at least one serving a day of any of these vitamin C-rich foods—cantaloupe, citrus fruits, kiwifruit, papaya, pineapple, strawberries, watermelon…and bell peppers, broccoli, brussels sprouts, cabbage, cauliflower, kale and kidney beans.

• **Zinc,** a mineral that helps maintain collagen. People with zinc deficiencies often develop skin redness and lesions.

Skin-smart: Eat at least one serving of a zinc-rich food daily—chicken or turkey breast, crab, lean beef, pork tenderloin (lower in fat than other cuts)…peanuts and peanut butter…fat-free dairy products (cheese, milk and yogurt).

Wise for everyone: A daily multivitamin that contains 100% of the daily value for vitamins A, C, E and zinc and no more than 70 mcg of selenium.

WHAT TO AVOID

• **Sugar.** Research suggests that sugary foods (such as soda and cookies) may contribute to skin blemishes. These "bad carbs" may promote harmful inflammation throughout the body, which can trigger breakouts. Limit your indulgence in sweet treats to no more than one small serving per day.

•**White flour.** Minimize white-flour foods (such as white bread and pasta) in your diet by choosing whole-grain breads and rolls, cereals, crackers and pasta.

•**Dairy foods.** Milk may contain hormones (especially if cows are pregnant) and iodine from iodine-fortified feed. Although uncommon, both of these components can cause pimples. If you are prone to acne, try going off dairy for a while to see if your skin improves.

•**Cigarette smoke,** including secondhand smoke. It fills your body with toxins, inflammation causing irritants and free radicals that damage every cell they touch...and also limits blood flow, so skin cells don't receive the oxygen and nutrients they need.

A Younger-Looking Neck—Without Surgery

Nelson Lee Novick, MD, clinical professor of dermatology at Mount Sinai School of Medicine and a cosmetic dermatologist in private practice, both in New York City. He is author of *Super Skin* and winner of the American Academy of Dermatology's Leadership Circle Award. DoctorNovick.com

New nonsurgical techniques improve the appearance of "necklace lines" (bands of wrinkles encircling the neck) and "turkey wattle" (saggy chin skin and ropey vertical cords at the front of the neck)—without the pain, risks, recuperation or expense of cosmetic surgery. *Fixes for...*

•**Necklace lines.** Microdroplets of muscle-relaxing Botox* (a purified form of a protein produced by the Clostridium botulinum bacterium) are injected at half-inch intervals along, above and/or below each band (except where covered by hair at the back of the neck). With-

*The FDA now requires Botox and other similar anti-wrinkle drugs to carry warning labels explaining that the material has the potential to spread from the injection site to other parts of the body, with risk of causing serious difficulties.

in 14 days, as the sheetlike platysma muscle relaxes in the treated areas, the muscle in the nontreated areas pulls the skin taut so wrinkles smooth out.

Cost: About $500 to $750 per treatment.

•**Turkey wattle.** Botox injections down the length of each ropey cord make the platysma muscle drape more smoothly...Botox under the jawline allows the muscles above to pull the neck skin upward. Then injections of Radiesse (a synthetic gel of tiny calcium-based spheres) along the jawline and under the chin give added volume where needed to make the neck skin more taut. Radiesse also helps stimulate the body's own production of skin-firming collagen.

Cost: About $1,500 per treatment.

With either procedure: There is minor discomfort as local anesthesia is injected. Only tiny amounts of Botox are given at each site, so swallowing and breathing muscles are not affected. No recovery time or activity restrictions are needed. Minor redness, swelling and bruising disappear within two days. Botox lasts about six months...Radiesse lasts nine to 18 months.

Help for Old-Looking Hands

My hands have started to look very old. Is there anything I can do?

Prominent veins and tendons, thinning skin and brown spots (also known as "liver spots" or "sun spots") are very common as we age. Topical skin lighteners, such as over-the-counter Lumixyl, can be used at home. There are also many in-office treatments for brown spots and crepey skin, including chemical peels, microneedling and laser therapy.

Until recently, little could be done for the veiny hands that often betray our age. But the FDA has now approved Radiesse, a calcium-based volumizing filler that recontours hands and camouflages veins and tendons.

Hyaluronic acid fillers have also been successfully used off-label for hand rejuvenation. The cost of these treatments is not covered by insurance.

Nelson Lee Novick, MD, clinical professor of dermatology, Icahn School of Medicine at Mount Sinai, New York City. DoctorNovick.com

No-Surgery Nose Job— in Just Minutes

Nelson Lee Novick, MD, clinical professor of dermatology at Mount Sinai School of Medicine and a cosmetic dermatologist in private practice, both in New York City. He is author of *Super Skin*. DoctorNovick.com

Using new, safe and practically painless nonsurgical techniques, a dermatologist now can reshape a nose in less than 10 minutes, giving immediate results that last about a year or longer.

Average cost: $750 to $1,500.*

Options…

• **Smooth a bump or straighten a bend.** Radiesse, a synthetic gel of tiny bone-like calcium-based spheres, is injected beneath the skin where desired—for instance, above or below a bump on the bridge or along the side of the nose. Then it is quickly molded like clay to the desired shape and fully retains its shape within about a day. For more precise shaping, the doctor also may inject Juvéderm or Restylane, fillers made of synthetic hyaluronic acid. (In the body, one function of natural hyaluronic acid is to provide volume to the skin.)

• **Lift a long, drooping tip.** Botox** (a purified form of a protein produced by the Clostridium botulinum bacterium) is injected into the crevices on each side and at the base of the nose, weakening the muscles that pull the nose tip downward and permitting mus-

*Prices subject to change.

**The FDA now requires Botox and other similar antiwrinkle drugs to carry warning labels explaining that the material has the potential to spread from the injection site to other parts of the body, with risk of causing serious complications.

cles higher up on the nose to draw the tip upward. Next, Radiesse is injected at the base of the nose to buttress the tip, providing longer-lasting effects than from Botox alone.

With either procedure: Prior to treatment, the area is injected with a local anesthetic plus epinephrine (a blood vessel constrictor).

Recovery: There are no restrictions on activities. You may have minor swelling and bruising for a few days. Risk for infection is very slight. Generally, results last 12 to 18 months with Radiesse…eight to 12 months with Juvéderm and Restylane…and three to six months with Botox. After that, touch-ups may be desirable.

How You Can Stand Taller As You Age

Joel Harper, personal trainer, has designed custom workouts for celebrities and Olympic medalists, and is the creator of the PBS DVD, *Firming Up After 50*. He is based in New York City. JoelHarperFitness.com

Here's a simple antiaging trick that will make you look and feel much younger (and costs nothing at all!)—stand straight and tall. Unfortunately, as you age and your muscles get weaker, this becomes more challenging. Here's a routine that builds strength all over your body, takes just 10 minutes a day and delivers a noticeable improvement in posture in just a few weeks.

Not sure whether you need it? *Here's a test…* With your back against the wall, slide down to sit in an imaginary chair, legs bent, heels directly underneath your knees and thighs parallel to the floor. (If this makes you feel uncomfortable or unsteady, don't try to slide down this far—you've already learned that you could benefit from this routine!) People with reasonably good posture can easily rest the back of their heads and shoulders against the wall in this "chair" position for one full minute…so if you can't, you've got work to do.

Do each of these three pairs in a row every other day for two weeks. These aren't the easiest exercises in the world—but then, re-alistically, the easiest exercises in the world aren't going to fix your posture! Of course, if there's any chance that trying new exercises might not be safe for you, check these with your doctor first.

POSTURE PAIRING #1

"Field Goals" strengthen your shoulders. With your back against a wall, stand with feet together and raise your arms at your sides to make a "T." Then bend your elbows and raise your forearms, forming a 90-degree angle with your palms facing forward and fingers spread. Now lower your hands to make your forearms horizontal—and repeat this last motion, both sides at the same time, 25 times. Resist moving your elbows. Keep your shoulders relaxed, not shrugged. You can add a balance component to this exercise by slightly lifting your heels as you do the arm movements and/or pump it up by adding three-pound hand weights.

"Chicken wing" stretches your shoulders and upper back. Standing up straight with your stomach pulled in, put your left hand on your left hip, fingers behind you. Now reach your right hand in front of your body to grasp your left elbow and gently pull it toward your stom-ach. That'll stretch the left side of your arm, upper back and shoulders. Hold where you feel the stretch and take five deep breaths...then switch sides and repeat. If one side is tighter than the other, repeat on that side, with the goal of eventually making both sides equal.

POSTURE PAIRING #2

"Rickety Table" strengthens the back, arms and glutes. Get down on all fours on a pad-ded surface, with your fingers spread apart, making sure your hands are in line with your shoulders and your knees with your hips. Keep your back flat and parallel to the floor. With your left arm slightly bent (so you work the muscle, not the joint), reach your right arm straight forward and your left foot straight back, stretching them as far away from each other as possible, aiming to keep your right hand one inch higher than your head. Hold for 25 seconds. Work up to that amount of time if you can't do it at first. Or, if this move feels too easy, then simultaneously lower your

right hand and left foot (big toe) to tap them on the floor and then raise them back to hori-zontal position. Repeat this 25 times, then switch sides. An even more advanced version is to tap your elbow to the opposite knee (in-stead of tapping your hand and foot on the ground) and then return to parallel position after each tap.

"Elbow circling" releases tension and stretch-es muscles in your shoulders and neck. You can do this either sitting or standing. Put your right fingertips on top of your right shoulder and your left fingertips on top of your left shoulder and then touch your elbows together in front of you. Keeping your fingers where they are and looking straight ahead, make large circles to-ward the outside of your body with each elbow simultaneously. Inhale on one circle on a count of five and exhale on the next count of five. Do six circles in that direction, and then do six in the opposite direction. This is great to do if you sit at a desk all day.

POSTURE PAIRING #3

"Side-lying kick" strengthens the oblique (side) abdominal and leg muscles. Lie on the ground on your left side, stretching your left arm above your head so that your left ear rests on your arm. Keeping your stomach taut and resisting rocking, bend your left knee to a 45-degree angle with your heel in line with your spine. Lift your right (straight) leg three-feet directly above your left foot...then tap your right knee lightly on the ground in front of your waist. Then lift your leg back up, straighten it and kick three feet in the air above your left foot (or as high as you can). Do this sequence 25 times and then switch sides.

"Airplane stretch" stretches the hips and legs. While seated on a straight-backed chair or stool, put the right side of your right foot onto your left knee. Rest your right elbow on top of your right knee and your right hand on your right ankle. While keeping your back straight, gently lean forward. Look straight ahead. You can increase the stretch by using your left hand to gently turn the sole of your right foot to face up. Hold for 30 seconds, tak-ing deep breaths. Switch sides and repeat. If you find that one side of your body is tighter than the other, then you should repeat on that particular side in order to create balance.

A FINAL TIP

An easy way to keep your posture picture-perfect is to always try to keep your gaze straight ahead. It's almost impossible to have bad posture if you keep your eyes at eye level. It's a simple trick to keep in mind as you go about your busy day, looking younger and feeling great!

Look Younger With the Right Care

Eudene Harry, MD, medical director of Oasis Wellness & Rejuvenation Center in Orlando, Florida. She is the author of *Live Younger in 8 Simple Steps: A Practical Guide to Slowing Down the Aging Process from the Inside Out.* LivingHealthyLookingYounger.com

---

Skin-care products can help smooth wrinkles and provide other benefits, but there are so many on the market that most people are confused about which to use. *Best choices for younger-looking skin...*

•**Topical vitamin C.** About 80% of the dermis (the second layer of skin) consists of that all important protein collagen. Because collagen production declines with age, it's a good idea to promote collagen production any way you can.

That's where vitamin C enters the picture. The body uses vitamin C to produce collagen, but whatever is consumed orally doesn't reach adequate concentrations in the skin to boost collagen. That's why you need to apply it topically.

My advice: Use skin-care products (such as lotions and sunscreens) that have ascorbic acid (vitamin C)—the best form of the vitamin for absorption as well as collagen production and sun protection. Studies show that topical vitamin C can reduce the appearance of fine lines and wrinkles in as little as three months.

To save money: Buy powdered vitamin C at a health-food store, and mix in a small pinch

each time you use a moisturizer/sunscreen that does not contain the vitamin.

•**Retinoic acid.** This is a form of vitamin A that is added to hundreds of over-the-counter (OTC) skin-care products. It is also available by prescription. Retinoic acid increases cellular turnover, the rate at which cells divide. This makes the skin appear brighter, smoother and plumper.

My advice: Use OTC retinol cream once daily. Apply it at night because it temporarily increases the skin's sensitivity to sun. Most products have a concentration of 1% or less. Prescription-strength retinoic acid usually is not necessary.

•**Moisturizer.** Everyone should use this as they age. Adding moisture to skin cells makes them expand, which improves skin volume and texture. Moisturizers protect the skin from environmental factors (heat, dryness and pollution) that undermine skin health.

My advice: Use moisturizer with sunscreen at least twice a day. I advise a vitamin C–enhanced moisturizer that includes green-tea extract. Both ingredients improve the skin's ability to absorb the moisturizer. Compounds in green tea also reduce skin inflammation and sun-related skin damage. Soy moisturizers may provide similar benefits.

Also important: Exfoliation, an effective form of controlled trauma that stimulates the skin to produce more collagen. Every week or two, use a gentle facial scrub with fine grains and a soft facial brush. This practice also removes the dead skin cells that dull your complexion.

Sensitive skin sometimes cannot tolerate even a mild scrub. An ultrasonic brush, such as Clarisonic ($100 to $200 at department stores and online), with a hydrating cleanser is a good alternative.

A chemical peel once or twice a year is another good way to remove dead skin cells. OTC peels contain glycolic acid, lactic acid or salicylic acid, usually in a concentration of about 5% to 10%. Peels should also contain moisturizing ingredients to minimize irritation. If you're new to chemical peels, talk with your dermatologist before using one of these products, since they can irritate skin, especially sensitive skin.

Look 15 Years Younger Just by Going to the Dentist

Marvin A. Fier, DDS, FASDA, a Diplomate of the American Board of Aesthetic Dentistry. He serves as executive vice president of the American Society for Dental Aesthetics. He is an adjunct professor and a guest lecturer at dental schools and major conferences in the US and internationally. He has a private dental practice in Pomona, New York. SmileRockland.com

Teeth show your age just as much as drooping muscles or sagging skin. Even if you get regular dental care and keep your teeth white, you might want to consider other dental enhancements. Age-related changes can dim your smile and even change your facial structure, making you look far older than your age. *Common problems—and the best solutions…*

WORN TEETH

Decades of chewing (or tooth-grinding or clenching) can wear down the upper and lower teeth. As the teeth get shorter, the distance between the chin and nose also shortens.

Result: A shorter face that makes you look older.

Solution: Veneers or crowns that restore natural tooth shapes and dimensions. Veneers are ultrathin pieces of porcelain that, when attached to the surface of existing teeth, become extremely strong. A crown goes over the entire tooth. Crowns are a better choice if your teeth are structurally weak because of fillings, root canals, etc. Sometimes increasing the length of only the upper teeth can create a dramatic improvement.

Crowns and veneers can last at least 10 to 15 years and sometimes longer.

Cost: Between $800 and $2,500 per tooth, depending on the part of the country where you live. Veneers and crowns are roughly the same price. Insurance rarely, if ever, covers any service performed strictly for esthetic reasons. However, if a tooth is structurally compromised, a crown may be covered as a necessary service.

MISSING TEETH

People often don't realize that the shape of the face partly is determined by the teeth. This is particularly true in the cheek areas because the muscles are supported by the side teeth. If you have one or more missing teeth, your cheeks can cave inward and create an older, drawn appearance.

Even one missing tooth can cause a "sunken" appearance if you have a small, narrow face. It will be less apparent if you have a large, broad face.

Solution: A dental implant is ideal as long as the underlying bone is healthy. A dentist will surgically implant a titanium cylinder in the jawbone. After the bone heals, a connector, called an abutment, is attached to the implant. Then a new tooth (a crown) is attached to the abutment.

Dental implants typically last just as long as your regular teeth, and in many cases, even longer.

Warning: Smokers are about two-and-a-half times more likely to have failed implants than nonsmokers.

Cost: Approximately $3,000 to $5,000 per tooth.

Another option: A stationary bridge—often called a permanent, or fixed, bridge (as opposed to a removable one)—that replaces one or more teeth and is connected to the adjacent teeth with supporting crowns. It can cost almost as much as an implant but is more likely to be covered by insurance.

ABNORMAL JAW POSITION

Patients with temporomandibular disorder (TMD) will sometimes experience changes in the jaw joint that cause the chin and lower jaw to move to an abnormal position. This can distort the normal appearance of the face.

Solution: Some patients can correct a TMD problem by wearing a splint—sometimes known as a night guard or a bite guard—when they sleep. This is called occlusal splint therapy. Splints, made from a type of durable plastic, usually slip over all or some of the teeth. They cause changes in the joint that can reposition the lower jaw and both relieve pain and restore a more normal appearance.

Splints are relatively inexpensive, but they can take years to work—and they don't work for every patient. If occlusal splint therapy fails, you might need surgery of the temporomandibular joint to correct the problem.

Important: Don't bother with over-the-counter boil-and-bite splints. They are not effective for a receding jaw. You need a splint that is customized by a dentist to fit your specific teeth and jaw shape.

Cost: Between $400 and $1,000 for occlusal splint therapy, plus the expense of imaging tests, such as an MRI or a CT scan.

DETERIORATED FILLINGS

If you're middle-aged or older, you probably have one or more silver amalgam fillings. These don't last forever. The edges can open up and allow bacteria to get under the fillings. Also, the metal fillings in teeth can darken and appear as gray shadows that are visible through the tooth enamel, imparting an old and unattractive appearance.

Solution: Remove old fillings and replace them with nonmetal, tooth-colored fillings.

Cost: Approximately $150 to $350 per tooth, depending on the size of the original filling and how much work is required for the new one.

DETERIORATED CROWNS

Even if you don't break or "pop" a porcelain crown, it won't maintain its original appearance forever.

Example: The gums often recede with age. This can produce a thin gray or black line between the crown and the gum.

Solution: Replace the crown. A lower-cost option is to use tooth-colored filling material to fill the gap. It isn't as durable or as attractive as a new crown, but it's a good choice for patients with limited funds.

Cost: Filling the gap is about $100.

GUMMY SMILE

You've probably heard the expression, "He/she is long in the tooth." Changes in the shape and health of the gums can make the teeth appear longer. Or they can make the gums disproportionately prominent. Either of these changes can compromise your appearance and make you look older.

Solution: A "gum lift," known technically as a gingivectomy or gingivoplasty. The dentist will use a laser and/or scalpel to give your gums a more even appearance that's in harmony with your face.

Cost: $1,000 to $2,000.

POOR DENTURE FIT

Even if your partial or complete dentures fit perfectly when they were new, they tend to become loose or misaligned as your mouth changes. It's normal for the gums and underlying bone to change over time.

Poorly fitting dentures can sometimes give you jowls and wrinkled skin as your muscles work overtime to keep the dentures in place.

Solution: Ask your dentist to check the fit of your dentures. Most people find that it is worth replacing them every five to 10 years.

Cost: Insurance plans typically cap the expense at about $800 to $900 per upper and lower denture. If you don't have insurance, the cost per denture could range from $1,800 to $5,000 depending on where you live and the design and quality of the denture.

Erase Years from Your Face by Relieving Stress

Sanam Hafeez, PsyD, founder and clinical director of Comprehensive Consultation Psychological Services, with offices in New York City, Forest Hills and Uniondale, New York. ComprehendTheMind.com

Compare the faces of two people in your life. Person One is happy, relaxed and pleased with life. Person Two is overworked, stressed and harried. Guess which face appears younger and more attractive?

Stress can add years to your looks. When you're stressed, your body churns out cortisol, the hormone that primes you for action. Some cortisol is helpful (and motivating), but too much triggers inflammation, which affects every organ in your body, including the skin.

Experts have coined a term for the link between emotions and the skin—psychodermatology. This new field is based on research that shows that chronic stress and other psychological issues can trigger or exacerbate skin changes. But you can reverse those changes using emotional strategies and other lifestyle changes.

Example: Critically ill children who were given relaxing massages showed improvements in itching, redness and other skin conditions, according to researchers at the Touch Research Institute at University of Miami.

You can spend a fortune on anti-aging products and cosmetic procedures, but unless you manage stress at the same time, you'll still look older than you should.

WHAT STRESS DOES TO SKIN

Stress can cause blotches, itching, redness and acne. The cortisol-driven rise in inflammation damages tissues and capillaries that are readily apparent in the mirror. *Stress also causes…*

•**Dryness.** The constant bombardment of cortisol in women with chronic stress can mean a drop in estrogen that's been called mini-menopause. Estrogen is largely responsible for the differences in appearance between young women and older ones. Women who are frequently stressed tend to develop dryness and a loss of skin elasticity.

While women need estrogen more than men and are more impacted on a monthly basis by its regulation, hormonal imbalance also happens in men with the excess secretion of the stress hormone androgen, as well as glucocorticoids. This can cause a loss of estrogen leading to dryness in both men and women and an overproduction of sebum (an oily secretion of the sebaceous glands), which can trigger acne and razor bumps.

•**Wrinkles.** There's a reason that forehead furrows, between-the-eye creases and other wrinkles are known as "frown lines," "worry lines" or even "battle lines." Repeated expressions can etch themselves permanently in your face.

•**Circles under the eyes.** They make you look tired and can age your appearance even more than wrinkles. Some people are genetically prone to under-eye circles. They also can be caused by sun exposure, a lack of sleep or allergic skin conditions, along with stress.

What happens: Stress increases blood flow, and the tiny capillaries under the eyes become engorged. Those dark circles really are blood vessels that are visible through the skin.

•**Under-eye bags.** Like circles under the eyes, these puffy areas are partly due to genetics. But they're also common in people whose stress keeps them up at night. A lack of sleep causes fluids to accumulate under the eyes and makes your face appear puffy and tired.

WHAT TO DO

•**Take "mini-vacations."** Almost everyone can benefit from frequent "mini-vacations" that provide a break from stress. These can be as simple as a lunchtime walk…admiring a piece of art…or listening to a favorite song.

•**Eat an estrogen-enhancing diet** including fresh fruits and vegetables, salmon and whole grains. These antioxidant-rich foods fight inflammation. Fruits and vegetables also are naturally rich in phytoestrogens, plant compounds that mimic the effects of estrogen in the body. Estrogen "plumps" the skin and gives women and men a healthy glow.

•**Avoid excess sugar in all forms,** including refined carbohydrates, alcohol and highly processed foods, such as cake and cookies. These cause the body to produce advanced glycation end-products, toxins that trigger inflammation in the skin. The sugars in carbohydrates attach to certain proteins and can break down skin collagen, causing a loss of elasticity and the plumpness we associate with young skin.

• **Drink more water.** People who stay hydrated tend to have plumper, younger-looking skin. Also, water can flush excess salt from the body, which reduces under-eye puffiness. If you don't care for regular water, try coconut water. It is a natural source of electrolytes that help to keep you hydrated.

• **Relax your face.** You're probably not aware of your facial expressions, but you can learn to relax your face. When you're feeling stressed, remind yourself not to squint or frown. Be mindful of your expressions. Eventually, not frowning will become a habit. If you find yourself frowning, make it a habit to smooth your hand over your forehead and think happy, tranquil thoughts until your face naturally relaxes to a resting state.

• **Get a good night's sleep.** Even if you find that you can't log a full eight hours, at least make sure that the sleep you get is quality sleep. If you can't fall asleep in 15 or 20 minutes, get up and do something relaxing, such as gazing out the window or holding a yoga pose. You want to stay within yourself instead of engaging with electronics or the outside world until you're tired enough to try again. If you find yourself becoming anxious about all the things you have to do, make a list of what needs to be done. You'll feel like you accomplished something and are in control of your tasks. And you won't be worried about forgetting them the next day.

• **Sleep with your head slightly elevated—** a thick pillow will do it. The increased pull of gravity will help fluids drain away from your eyes.

• **Exercise.** Exercise relieves stress. You'll almost instantly see a difference when you attend a yoga class or go for a power walk. Your face will look smoother and younger.

Live in More Than One World…and Other Ways to Get Happy Later in Life

Bruce Rosenstein, MSLS, a lecturer at The Catholic University of America, Washington, DC, and former librarian, researcher and writer for *USA Today*. He is author of *Living in More Than One World: How Peter Drucker's Wisdom Can Inspire and Transform Your Life*. BruceRosenstein.com

Peter Drucker is known as the "father of modern management." His business writings remain widely read and highly influential six years after his death at age 95.

Yet even Drucker's disciples might not realize that the famed guru was an expert in life management as well as business management.

What can we learn about succeeding in life from the man who taught the world so much about succeeding in business? Bruce Rosenstein, author of *Living in More Than One World: How Peter Drucker's Wisdom Can Inspire and Transform Your Life*, identified three of Drucker's core life strategies…

STRATEGY 1:
LIVE IN MORE THAN ONE WORLD

Drucker noted that people who have just one goal or one passion tend to wind up unhappy for several reasons…

• **If you have just one interest,** your circle of friends and allies is likely to be very limited. That's unfortunate, because having lots of friends is highly correlated with happiness…and having lots of allies means more open doors, increasing your odds of success.

• **Having only one goal leaves no fallback position should you be dealt a setback.**

Example: Devote yourself completely to a political cause, and you will feel crushed if the vote goes against you.

• **People with multiple interests tend to spend less time ruminating over mistakes and missed chances.** Obsessing over failures only reduces the odds of future success.

• **A single-minded person tends to feel like a failure unless he/she is 100% suc-**

cessful in his focus area—and total success is rare.

Example: Anything short of reaching a desired spot in a company can feel like failure to someone who has devoted his life entirely to his career.

●**Outside interests provide unique viewpoints,** which can increase the odds of success in one's area of primary interest.

Example: Drucker found that studying Japanese art gave him insight into Japanese culture, which helped him find perspective on—and gain influence in—the Japanese business community.

STRATEGY 2:
CHOOSE A NONFINANCIAL PRIMARY GOAL

Peter Drucker observed that most of the people he knew whose life goal was to make lots of money did, in fact, make lots of money. But Drucker also saw that despite their wealth, most of these people were miserable.

Drucker was not opposed to wealth. He simply believed that there never is a true sense of satisfaction when wealth is the main motivator of achievement. Set out to earn $1 million, and you probably won't feel successful when you do it—you'll decide you need even more money…or wonder why money doesn't make you feel fulfilled.

Drucker thought a better goal was to leave something of value behind when you're gone. *You could leave behind…*

●**A happy, loving family that will continue to be happy thanks to your positive example.**

●**A history of treating everyone you meet with respect,** encouraging them to treat others with respect, too.

●**A profitable company that will continue to provide employment** and products or services after you retire.

If you're not certain what you can leave, spend some time teaching, mentoring or volunteering with a charity. These are among the surest ways to feel you have created a worthwhile legacy.

Added benefits: Teachers and mentors tend to improve their own mastery of the material… while volunteers benefit from a halo effect—others view them more positively because of their public service, increasing the volunteer's odds of success in all aspects of life.

STRATEGY 3:
WORK YOUR STRENGTHS

Drucker advanced an idea more than a quarter century ago called "strengths analysis." This strategy works just as well for individuals as for companies. *Three ways to put strengths analysis to work in your life…*

●**Abandon whatever isn't working.** Regularly question your habits, your hobbies, your relationships, your projects and your time commitments. For each, ask, Would I start this again today knowing what I know now? If the answer is no, end it or at least scale it back—your time is better spent elsewhere.

Drucker disagreed with the saying "If at first you don't succeed, try, try again." He advised, "If at first you don't succeed, try once more, and then try something else."

Example: Drucker published two novels. Neither succeeded, so he never wrote fiction again.

●**Engage in ongoing self-reflection.** Consider what you expected to happen in the past year…what actually happened…and if those two answers differed, why they differed. This analysis could point you toward areas where your abilities are greater than you realize—or away from areas where your abilities are less than you think.

●**Focus forward.** People get too caught up in day-to-day tasks and activities. They don't spend enough time focusing on future opportunities and how to make those opportunities happen.

Our future is more important than the distractions and errands that absorb much of our time in the present. Do not treat the future as a low priority just because it has not yet arrived.

Loneliness Harms Your Health

Gregory T. Eells, PhD, associate director of Gannett Health Services and director of Counseling and Psychological Services at Cornell University in Ithaca, New York. Dr. Eells is also a past president of the Association for University and College Counseling Center Directors.

Oh, those long, lonesome days…and nights! Most of us occasionally feel that way. But what if you are lonely more often than not? Plenty of people are.

Important new finding: Persistent loneliness is being linked to a growing list of health problems, including insomnia, cardiovascular disease and Alzheimer's disease. Even more startling is the fact that loneliness raises the risk for premature death among adults age 50 and older by 14%.

So for the sake of your health—and happiness—here's what you need to know about loneliness…

ARE YOU LONELY?

While it's easy to assume that anyone who is struggling with loneliness would know that he/she is lonely, that's often not the case. For many people, that extreme sense of social disconnection—the feeling that no one really knows you and what your life is like—is so familiar and constant that they don't even realize that they're lonely. And friends and family might not necessarily recognize that a friend or loved one is lonely.

Of course, most of us do need some time by ourselves, and solitude—the opportunity to think and feel quietly without the distraction and demands of other people—is rightly valued. But loneliness is very different.

Here are some red flags that you may be lonely: You spend hours of alone time on the computer (perhaps surfing the Internet or following the activities of "friends" on social media sites)…you have pangs of anger or envy when others around you are happy…and/or you feel a vague sense of dissatisfaction even when you are spending time with other people.

But just as you can be alone without being lonely, you can be lonely without being alone. Someone who looks happy and well connected from the outside—the person who invites 20 of his/her closest friends to a party—may still feel empty and isolated inside. Nor are romantic relationships or marriage a surefire defense against loneliness. Feeling uncomfortably alone and alienated is a frequent complaint of troubled couples.

WHY IT'S BAD FOR YOU

The connection between loneliness and depression has been established for quite some time. People who have depression often withdraw from social situations and have feelings of loneliness. But only recently have researchers discovered that loneliness itself is linked to elevated blood pressure, increased stress hormones and impaired immune function.

A new study has also found that the more lonely that people reported themselves to be, the more fragmented—and less restful—was their average night's sleep.

Loneliness also exacts a huge toll when people turn to unhealthy behaviors to avoid the pain it brings—if we don't try to drink it away, for example, then we might spend far too many hours at work to busy ourselves rather than face painful time alone.

HOW TO OVERCOME LONELINESS

Alleviating loneliness is like falling asleep or growing a garden—you can't force it to happen, but you can create conditions that encourage it to unfold. *Here's how…*

SECRET #1: **Share more about yourself.** Sharing the details of your life with others and showing vulnerability will foster deep connections and minimize loneliness. This may feel risky. After all, you might run up against rejection or disapproval, but such fears are usually groundless. Nothing ventured, nothing gained!

Example: You might ask a friend to have coffee and share with him/her discipline problems you are having with your teenage daughter.

SECRET #2: **Make room for "small" connections.** While quantity doesn't replace quality in relationships, momentary contacts do add to your sense of being part of the social world around you.

Exchange a few extra words with the clerk at your local convenience store, and smile at those you pass on the street. These pleasant interactions will prime you for deeper, more meaningful ones with close friends and family.

SECRET #3: **Be part of something big.** Meaningful activity will bring you in contact with like-minded others. OK, so maybe volunteering in a hospital or soup kitchen isn't your thing. Perhaps you would rather get involved with your local political party…tutor a child who is struggling in school…join a gardening club…or get involved at your house of worship.

Your local newspaper and websites such as *meetup.com* and *groups.yahoo.com* are great resources for finding local groups involved in a wide variety of activities that might interest you.

Show up for whatever new activity you choose for several weeks, and if you're not feeling more connected by the end of that time, then look for something else that might be more to your liking.

SECRET #4: **Don't hole up by yourself when your life changes.** For most people, significant changes such as job loss, the death of a loved one, divorce or retirement provide a good excuse to shut out others—and the perfect setup for loneliness. But don't let the natural tendency to withdraw at such times go on for more than a few months.

Challenge yourself to set up two outings a week with a friend, neighbor or family member to get yourself out of the house.

SECRET #5: **Consider getting a pet.** Pets are more than mere company…dogs, cats, birds and even guinea pigs are, after all, fellow creatures that have their own feelings and are often responsive to ours. These are real connections, too.

If you don't have the time to care for a pet full time, consider sharing a pet. There are several sites (*CityDogShare.org*) that enable you to meet people near you who are interested in doing this. Or volunteer at your local animal shelter.

Both of these activities are great ways to connect with animals and animal lovers.

---

6 Foods Proven to Make You Happy

Tonia Reinhard, MS, RD, a registered dietitian and professor at Wayne State University in Detroit. She is author of *Superfoods: The Healthiest Foods on the Planet* and *Superjuicing: More Than 100 Nutritious Vegetable and Fruit Recipes.*

You can eat your way to a better mood! Certain foods and beverages have been proven to provide the raw materials that you need to feel sharper, more relaxed and just plain happier. *Best choices…*

HAPPY FOOD #1: **Chocolate.** Chocolate can make you feel good—to such an extent that 52% of women would choose chocolate over sex, according to one survey.

Chocolate contains chemical compounds known as polyphenols, which interact with neurotransmitters in the brain and reduce anxiety. An Australian study found that men and women who consumed the most chocolate polyphenols (in the form of a beverage) felt calmer and more content than those who consumed a placebo drink.

Chocolate also boosts serotonin, the same neurotransmitter affected by antidepressant medications. It triggers the release of dopamine and stimulates the "pleasure" parts of the brain.

Then there's the sensual side of chocolate—the intensity of the flavor and the melting sensation as it dissolves in your mouth. The satisfaction that people get from chocolate could be as helpful for happiness as its chemical composition.

Recommended amount: Aim for one ounce of dark chocolate a day. Most studies used dark chocolate with 70% cacao or more.

HAPPY FOOD #2: **Fish.** Fish has been called "brain food" because our brains have a high concentration of omega-3 fatty acids—and so does fish. These fatty acids have

69

been linked to memory and other cognitive functions. In countries where people eat a lot of fish, depression occurs less often than in countries (such as the US) where people eat less.

The omega-3s in fish accumulate in the brain and increase "membrane fluidity," the ability of brain-cell membranes to absorb nutrients and transmit chemical signals.

A study in *Archives of General Psychiatry* looked at patients diagnosed with depression who hadn't responded well to antidepressants. Those who were given 1,000 mg of EPA (a type of omega-3 fatty acid) daily for three months had significant improvements, including less anxiety and better sleep.

Recommended amount: Try to have at least two or three fish meals a week. Cold-water fish—such as sardines, mackerel and salmon—have the highest levels of omega-3s. Or choose a supplement with 1,000 mg of EPA and DHA (another omega-3 fatty acid) in total.

HAPPY FOOD #3: **Dark Green Veggies.** Dark green vegetables such as spinach, asparagus, broccoli and Brussels sprouts are loaded with folate, a B-complex vitamin that plays a key role in regulating mood. A Harvard study found that up to 38% of adults with depression had low or borderline levels of folate. Boosting the folate levels of depressed patients improved their mood.

Dark green vegetables are particularly good, but all vegetables and fruits boost mood. Researchers asked 281 people to note their moods on different days. On the days when the participants consumed the most vegetables and fruits, they reported feeling happier and more energetic. Folate certainly plays a role, but self-satisfaction may have something to do with it as well. People feel good when they eat right and take care of themselves.

Recommended amount: The minimum you should have is five servings of vegetables and fruits a day.

Bonus: Middle-aged men who had 10 servings a day showed reduced blood pressure.

HAPPY FOOD #4: **Beans (including soybeans).** Beans are rich in tryptophan, an essential amino acid that is used by the body to produce serotonin, the neurotransmitter that affects feelings of calmness and relaxation.

Beans also are loaded with folate. Folate, as mentioned in the veggies section, plays a key role in regulating mood.

In addition, beans contain manganese, a trace element that helps prevent mood swings due to low blood sugar.

Recommended amount: For people not used to eating beans, start with one-quarter cup five days a week. Build up to one-half cup daily. This progression will help prevent gastrointestinal symptoms such as flatulence.

HAPPY FOOD #5: **Nuts.** Nuts are high in magnesium, a trace mineral involved in more than 300 processes in the body. People who don't get enough magnesium feel irritable, fatigued and susceptible to stress.

The elderly are more likely than young adults to be low in magnesium—because they don't eat enough magnesium-rich foods and/or because they tend to excrete more magnesium in their urine.

Also, many health problems can accelerate the depletion of magnesium from the body.

Examples: Gastrointestinal disorders (or bariatric surgery), kidney disease and sometimes diabetes.

Recommended amount: Aim for one ounce of nuts a day. Good choices include almonds, walnuts, cashews, hazelnuts and peanuts (the latter is technically a legume). If you don't like nuts, other high-magnesium foods include spinach, pumpkin seeds, fish, beans, whole grains and dairy.

HAPPY FOOD #6: **Coffee.** The caffeine in coffee, tea and other caffeinated beverages is a very beneficial compound. One study found that people with mild cognitive impairment were less likely to develop full-fledged Alzheimer's disease when they had the caffeine equivalent of about three cups of coffee a day.

Caffeine can temporarily improve your memory and performance on tests. It enhances coordination and other parameters of physical performance. When you feel energized, you feel happier. Also, people who feel good from caffeine may be more likely to engage in other happiness-promoting behaviors, such as seeing friends and exercising.

Recommended amount: The challenge is finding the "sweet spot"—just enough caffeine to boost mood but not so much that you get the shakes or start feeling anxious. For those who aren't overly sensitive to caffeine, one to three daily cups of coffee or tea are about right.

WHAT NOT TO EAT

Some people turn to food or drink for comfort when they're feeling down. *Here's what not to eat or drink when you've got the blues...*

• **Alcohol.** Alcohol is a depressant of the central nervous system. When you initially consume alcohol, it produces a euphoric effect and you become more animated and less inhibited. But as you continue drinking and more alcohol crosses the blood-brain barrier, the depressant effect predominates.

• **Baked goods.** When you eat high-sugar, high-fat carbs such as cookies, pastries and donuts, you tend to want more of them. The food gives you a temporary "good feeling," but the excess food intake that typically results causes drowsiness and often self-loathing.

Fight Depression Using Only Your Mind

Zindel Segal, PhD, CPsych, the Cameron Wilson Chair in Depression Studies at the University of Toronto, and head of the Cognitive Behavioural Therapy Unit at the Centre for Addiction and Mental Health, both in Toronto, Canada. He is a coauthor of *The Mindful Way through Depression: Freeing Yourself from Chronic Unhappiness.*

Suffering from depression is very different from being sad. Sadness is a normal part of life. Depression is a constellation of psychological and physical changes that persist, unrelenting, for a minimum of two weeks—and often much longer.

For those affected, depression often becomes an ongoing issue—those who have faced it once have a 40% chance of experiencing an episode in the future and those who already have had multiple episodes face up to an 80% chance of additional recurrences.

Depression is most commonly treated with medication that regulates the brain's chemistry and with professional counseling, which helps people take effective action in the face of the low motivation and pessimism that often define depression.

Exciting tool: In the last decade or so, a new technique has been shown in studies to help sufferers head off depression before it takes hold. The technique is called mindfulness—paying attention to the present moment, without judgment, in order to see things more clearly.

LIFE ON AUTOMATIC PILOT

Mindfulness can prevent depression from taking hold of us because the alternative—our usual state—is that we operate on "automatic pilot." Our minds are elsewhere as we perform mundane activities.

Example: You're taking a shower, but wondering what's waiting in your e-mail.

If we let it, this automatic pilot also will select our moods and our emotional responses to events—and the responses it chooses can be problematic. For instance, if you make a minor misstep in some area of your life, your autopilot might select as your emotional response feelings of anger, failure and/or inadequacy, even though the event might have been completely inconsequential.

Because your mind is not paying full attention to the situation, you might not grasp that the negative feelings are greatly out of proportion to what's really going on. You only know that you feel bad. When these negative feelings persist, they can pull you into the downward spiral of depression.

Example: A friend mentions that one of the stocks in his portfolio has turned a profit. Your investments have not been as successful, and your autopilot selects inadequacy as your primary emotional response. This may sound like an overreaction, but in someone who is prone to depression, these feelings can expand into a full-blown episode.

Mindfulness can be an antidote to automatic pilot. By becoming more aware of the world around us, we experience life directly, not filtered through our minds' relentless ruminations. We learn to see events for what they are rather than what our autopilot might turn them into. That helps us to derail potential episodes of depression before they have a chance to take hold. It typically takes two weeks or longer for depression to fully sink in, so there is often plenty of time to stop the process.

BECOMING MINDFUL

Learning to be mindful involves more than simply paying attention. You must reorient your senses so that you experience a situation with your whole mind and heart and with all of your senses.

Try it out: Pick up a raisin. Hold it, feel it, examine it as if you had never seen anything like it before. Explore the raisin's folds and texture. Watch the way light shines off of its skin. Inhale its aroma. Then gently place it on your tongue. Notice how your hand knows exactly where to put it. Explore the raisin in your mouth before biting. Then chew once or twice. Experience the waves of taste and the sensation of chewing. Notice how the taste and texture change as you chew. Once you swallow, try to feel the raisin moving through your digestive system.

Keep it up: Practice the following three steps every day to make mindfulness a regular part of your life—and episodes of depression less likely…

1. Focus on your breath. Focusing your attention on your breath is perhaps the simplest, most effective way to anchor your mind in the moment. You think only of this breath. You can do this anytime, anywhere.

2. Watch your thoughts drift by like clouds. See them, acknowledge them, but do not attempt to reason them away. Some people attempt to use logic to escape depression. They tell themselves, My life is pretty good—I should be happy. This just leads to troubling questions like If my life is good, why am I so unhappy? What's wrong with me?

It is also tempting to try to push negative thoughts away so that you don't have to deal with them at all. Unfortunately, the thoughts are still there even if you refuse to acknowledge them.

Better: When you feel bad, reflect on what is bothering you. Try to uncover the original thought or event that set off your bad feelings. Then view it as just a thought, something independent from you even though it has popped into your head. Do not dismiss it, though. Even if the thought or the event that caused it was trivial, the feelings it has prompted are real and significant.

Next, notice any physical sensations that you are experiencing. Does your throat feel tight? Is your mouth dry? Are there butterflies in your stomach? Just as you are learning to watch your feelings float by, watch these physical sensations in a detached way. If you can learn to spot the onset of these sensations, you will be able to identify the early signs of depression sooner—and head off the bad feelings before they take root.

3. Take action.

Ask yourself: Does this thought have any merit? Is it connected to negative thoughts that I have had in the past? What can I do to make myself feel better about this issue?

Example: You feel depressed about your work life even though you are doing fine in your job. When you reflect on these negative thoughts, you realize that they began recently, when you learned that your brother received a promotion. You feel left behind because it has been some time since your last promotion.

What actions could you take to allay these negative feelings? Perhaps you could speak with your supervisor about your job performance and your prospects for future promotions…or contact a headhunter to remind yourself that you have other options.

With any problematic thought, identifying it quickly and taking some positive action is often enough to head off depression.

Important: Learning the mindfulness approach can be useful for preventing future bouts of depression—not for combating an episode that is already under way. When people are in the midst of depression, they typically cannot concentrate sufficiently to practice mindfulness. It is better to use the technique between episodes of depression so that it becomes a natural part of your thought process.

WHERE TO FIND
HELP AGAINST DEPRESSION

For information about depression and links to local support, contact...

• **National Institute of Mental Health,** 866-615-6464, *nimh.nih.gov.*

• **National Alliance on Mental Illness,** 800-950-6264, *nami.org.*

Seek Out a Depression Care Manager

Depression in the elderly is best controlled by antidepressants. Over a two-year period, regular use of *paroxetine* (Paxil) was more effective at preventing a recurrence than psychotherapy. Doctors may want to keep depressed patients over age 70 on medication indefinitely—just as they would patients with diabetes or hypertension.

Also important: A depression care manager—a nurse, social worker or psychologist—to make sure the condition is kept under control.

Charles F. Reynolds III, MD, a psychiatrist and professor of psychiatry, neurology and neuroscience at University of Pittsburgh School of Medicine and leader of the study, published in *The New England Journal of Medicine.*

Depressed? Give New Eyeglasses a Try

Eyeglasses ease depression among the elderly.

Recent finding: After two months, seniors who received properly prescribed eyeglasses had higher scores for activities, hobbies and social interaction—and fewer signs of depres-

sion—than seniors with similar visual acuity who were not given new eyeglasses.

Cynthia Owsley, PhD, professor, department of ophthalmology, University of Alabama at Birmingham, and leader of a study of 78 nursing home residents, published in *Archives of Ophthalmology.*

Let Go of Toxic Memories

Thomas H. Crook III, PhD, CEO of Cognitive Research Corporation and a psychologist in private practice in St. Petersburg, Florida. He is author of numerous books, including *The Memory Advantage.* CogRes.com

A toxic memory turned constant companion is a harmful bad habit—and like any bad habit, it can be broken. *Steps...*

1. Select a favorite positive memory. You can choose an event that specifically contradicts your toxic memory (for instance, the day you learned to ski despite being a "hopeless klutz")...or choose a completely unrelated experience, such as your first date with your spouse.

2. Write down as many details as you can recall. Where did you go? What did you wear? Did you dance to a certain song or see a stunning sunset? How did that first kiss feel? Tap into all your senses.

3. Practice conjuring up this happy memory. Let this personal "movie" play inside your head during relaxed moments. Soon you'll be able to recall it vividly at will, even when stressed or depressed.

4. Mentally hit an "eject" button whenever a toxic memory pops into your head, replacing it with thoughts of the happy memory.

FULFILLING EMOTIONAL NEEDS

If the technique above isn't working, your toxic memory may be more than a bad habit—it may be fulfilling some unmet need. Ask yourself, "How am I benefiting by holding onto this painful memory?" This insight will help you explore more productive ways to meet that need, thus diminishing the power of the toxic memory. *Consider...*

• **Does thinking of yourself as unlucky let you avoid taking responsibility for your life?** On a sheet of paper, make two columns, labeled "good luck" and "bad luck," then list examples from your own life of each type of experience. You will see that your whole life hasn't been a series of misfortunes. Next, identify the role played by your own efforts—rather than good luck—in creating each positive experience...and give yourself due credit.

• **Is there a certain pleasure for you in resenting other people for past unpleasantness?** (Be honest with yourself!) Develop a habit of doing small favors that make people respond to you in a positive way. Smile at everyone you pass on the sidewalk, yield to other drivers trying to enter your lane, say a sincere "thank you" to a surly cashier. A conscious and voluntary decision to be of service to others can help you overcome old resentments, relegate toxic memories to the past and find pleasure in the here and now.

If you feel traumatized: After an extremely traumatic experience, it is normal to fixate on the event for a time. However, if you are seriously disturbed by recurrent memories of the trauma months or even years later, you may have post-traumatic stress disorder (PTSD). Symptoms include nightmares or obsessive mental reenactments of the event...frequent fear or anger...trouble concentrating...feelings of guilt, hopelessness or emotional numbness.

Defusing traumatic memories may require the help of a mental-health professional.

Recommended: Cognitive-behavioral therapy (CBT), which focuses on changing harmful thought patterns rather than on lengthy exploration of past experiences.

Referrals: National Association of Cognitive-Behavioral Therapists, *nacbt.org*. With CBT, even seriously toxic memories can become more manageable—and you can move on with your life.

Reconcile with Your Grief... and Live Happily Again

Alan D. Wolfelt, PhD, CT (certified thanatologist, which indicates an expertise in strategies for coping with death), founder and director of the Center for Loss and Life Transition in Fort Collins, Colorado. He is the author of several books, including *Understanding Your Grief and Healing a Spouse's Grieving Heart.* CenterforLoss.com

When someone you love dies, it's natural to feel the pain of your loss—and to grieve. But too many people try hard not to feel the pain. While it's understandable to want to avoid pain, it's a mistake to do so. People who appear to be "doing well" with their grief sometimes develop chronic, low-grade depression, anxiety and/or addiction to alcohol or drugs as they self-treat their emotional pain.

Recent developments: An increasing body of research is now also linking this type of unreconciled grief (meaning an inability to move forward in life without the person who died) to a wide range of physical ailments, including fatigue, headache, high blood pressure and heart disease.

For many people, grief is prolonged and unresolved because there are so many misconceptions surrounding it. *Among the most common—and dangerous—misconceptions about grief...*

MISCONCEPTION #1: **Grief and mourning are the same thing.** People tend to use the words "grieving" and "mourning" interchangeably, but they have different meanings.

Grief is the constellation of internal thoughts and feelings you have when someone you love dies. Mourning is when you take the grief you have on the inside and express it outside yourself.

Examples of mourning: Talking about the person who died. Crying. Expressing your thoughts and feelings through art or music. Celebrating anniversary dates that held meaning for the person who died.

Many people grieve but don't mourn. When you don't honor a loss by acknowledging it—first to yourself, and then to others—your grief will accumulate. The denied losses then come flowing out in other ways, such as depression and physical problems…all of which compound the pain of your loss.

MISCONCEPTION #2: **You should move away from grief, not toward it.** Our society does not give people much time to grieve. They're expected to get "back to normal" in short order.

This attitude leads many people to either grieve in isolation or attempt to run away from their grief through various means, such as overworking or abusing alcohol or drugs. Masking or moving away from your grief creates anxiety, confusion and depression.

What to do: Continually remind yourself that leaning toward—not away—from the pain will help you heal. To lean toward the pain, when you are feeling bad, stop and allow yourself to feel the emotion by talking to someone or writing about it.

MISCONCEPTION #3: **Grief is mainly about the physical loss of the person who died.** The death of a loved one creates many secondary losses—such as connections to yourself and the world around you.

Examples: You can lose the self ("I feel like a part of me died")…identity (such as your role as a spouse or child)…security (for example, a widow may not feel as safe in her home)…and meaning (when dreams for the future are shattered).

Important: Understanding the range and depth of your personal losses can help you be more self-compassionate. This involves showing sensitivity toward yourself for what you're going through.

Physical self-compassion can include eating well, exercising regularly and getting enough sleep.

Mental self-compassion can mean asking yourself two questions on a daily basis that will help you survive the difficult months of grieving and learn to love life again…

1. What do I want? **(now that the person you love is gone).** Ask yourself what's doable and what you'd like to accomplish today.

2. What is wanted of me? **(Who depends on you? What skills and experience can you bring to others?)**

Social self-compassion can include finding a grief "buddy"—a friend who has also had a loss—and/or joining a grief support group. To find a group near you, check with local hospices and funeral homes.

Grief forces us to consider what life is about and what greater purpose there might be for our lives. Spiritual self-compassion can mean starting each day with a meditation or spending time in nature.

MISCONCEPTION #4: **After a loved one dies, the goal should be to "get over" your grief as soon as possible.** Grief is not a problem that you can solve or an illness from which you recover. Rather, you become reconciled to your grief—you integrate the new reality of moving forward in life without the person who died. With reconciliation comes a renewed sense of energy and confidence, an ability to fully acknowledge the reality of the death and a capacity to become re-involved in the activities of living.

MISCONCEPTION #5: **When grief and mourning are fully reconciled,** they never come up again. Grief comes in and out like the tide. Sometimes heightened periods of sadness occur even years after the death.

Example: My dad loved Frank Sinatra's music—and I have bursts of grief almost every time I hear Frank's voice.

You will always, for the rest of your life, feel some grief over a loved one's death. It will no longer dominate your life, but it will always be there, in the background, reminding you of the love you had for the person who died. And you needn't think of that as a bad thing.

If you follow the advice in this article but are still struggling with grief, consider seeing a compassionate grief counselor. To find one, consult the Association for Death Education and Counseling (*ADEC.org*).

PART 2

Stay Self-Reliant and Safe

5

Live at Home Forever

Aging in Place Lets Seniors Stay Comfortably In Their Homes

Back in 1999, Susan McWhinney-Morse faced a dilemma. She loved her Boston town house but was worried that she'd have to struggle to obtain needed support to live there comfortably while she aged.

Her solution: She helped launch a nonprofit group that would provide her—and other retirees in her area who wished to remain in their homes—with help and social activities. Today that nonprofit group, Beacon Hill Village, has nearly 400 members. What's more, it has inspired approximately 150 similar "virtual villages" around the country, with roughly 120 more in the planning stages.

These virtual villages do not typically provide actual day-to-day support to members, just guidance about where and how to obtain support. They vet local service providers— from plumbers to home health aids. (Some of these providers offer discounts to group members.) They connect members in need of assistance with fellow members or local volunteers who are willing to help. And they typically have someone on staff who can advise members about the ins and outs of senior services. Virtual villages also sponsor get-togethers and outings, says McWhinney-Morse, who still is in her town house as she enters her 80s. Membership fees typically are $300 to $500 a year, though a few villages charge as much as $1,000.

The Village to Village Network website (*VTV Network.org*) can help you locate groups in your area. If there is no group nearby, click

Karen Larson, editor of *Bottom Line/Personal.*

Peter Notarstefano, director, Home and Community Based Services (HCBS) at the American Association of Homes and Services for the Aging (AAHSA). He is responsible for developing and implementing AAHSA's HCBS policy agenda and helping providers establish and enhance community service programs.

79

the "Start a Village" link on the site to learn more.

This is a growing trend, with more than 100 aging-in-place communities established and more in the works. Peter Notarstefano, director of Home and Community Based Services at the American Association of Homes and Services for the Aging (AAHSA), said that setting up these organizations can be a lot of work, but those who do so find the rewards well worth the effort.

THE ELEPHANT IN THE ROOM: AFFORDABILITY

Money, for funding an organization as well as paying individual fees, is the biggest barrier to establishing aging-in-place communities, and indeed most of the existing ones are in affluent areas populated by well-educated and well-connected professionals. However, some government and social service agencies are beginning to step up and share funds and expertise. United Jewish Communities, a national nonprofit, has used federal grant money to develop 45 "Naturally Occurring Retirement Communities" (NORCs: *http://www.norcs.org/*) as demonstration projects in neighborhoods or buildings where many older people live, including those who lack the means to join fee-based ones. These programs can take advantage of existing services like Meals on Wheels, and fitness classes and outings sponsored by local organizations such as senior centers and YMCAs. Then they focus on filling in identified gaps, such as providing affordable housing for those who can no longer physically or financially manage a large house but want to remain in their community…funding physical adjustments such as ramps and handrails to support mobility challenges…and providing supportive services, such as case managers.

These are steps in the right direction but the government is not focusing on solving the core problems that would reduce costs in the long-term. Notarstefano calls the government policy on spending for the elderly "short-sighted," pointing out, for example, that Medicare won't pay for fall-preventing safety measures such as inexpensive grab bars in the bathroom, but will readily pay doctor and hospital bills resulting from a fall. Medicaid picks up most of the bills for nursing home care, which costs on average $77,745 a year, according to AAHSA.

Notarstefano's conclusion: Funding and coordinating more services to enable people to stay safely in their own homes is not only kinder and gentler, but in the long run, it's more cost-effective.

WHAT TO DO?

Given that there is no effective oversight of medical practices, billing or program mandates, elders are on their own when it comes to seeking non-medical industry services. *Whether aging in place is a goal you want to pursue on your own—or with like-minded members of your community—there are many resources and organizations to tap into…*

• **AARP** (*www.aarp.org*). This leading nonprofit offers a wealth of resources for aging in place. For example, there's a list of Certified Aging-in-Place Specialists (CAPS), contractors who are specially trained in making home modifications for older people. Click on *http://aarp.org/families/home_design/* to find CAPS in your area.

• **Leading Age** (*leadingage.org*). The 6,000 member organizations of this not-for-profit offer adult day services, home health care, community services, as well as senior housing, assisted living residences, continuing care retirement communities, nursing homes and more.

• **The Eldercare Locator** (*eldercare.gov*). This national service connects older people to resources—such as local agencies and community-based agencies that serve seniors and their caregivers—that help them live independently in their own communities. It is administered in part by the National Association of Area Agencies on Aging.

• The **National Aging In Place Council** (*naipc.org*). NAIPC draws together experts from all areas of expertise—including aging, health care, financial services, legal, design and building sectors—to help make independent living possible. Click on "Practical Advice" for a wide range of practical and helpful tips, from promoting independence to understanding your risks.

High-Tech Ways to Age at Home

Majd Alwan, PhD, senior vice president of technology and executive director of the LeadingAge Center for Aging Services Technologies, a nonprofit for aging advocacy in Washington, DC. LeadingAge.org/CAST

Where do you plan to live during your retirement years—including your latest years? If you're like most people, you want to stay right at home.

But that doesn't work for everyone. People with chronic illnesses and/or physical disabilities may end up moving into assisted-living facilities or nursing homes—and often sooner than they had hoped.

Now: High-tech devices can help you stay in your home much longer than before (even if you live alone) while also giving loved ones the assurance that you are safe.

To stay at home as long as possible, people have traditionally installed ramps, grab bars, brighter lighting and other such products to accommodate their changing needs. But that doesn't scratch the surface of what's available today.

Impressive high-tech devices to help you stay at home as you age…

"CHECKUPS" AT HOME

There's now an easy way to quickly alert your doctor of important changes in your health that may be occurring between office visits.

What's new: Remote patient monitoring. You can use an at-home glucose monitor, weight scale, pulse oximeter (to measure oxygen in the blood) and other devices that store readings, which you can then easily share with your doctor—on a daily, weekly or monthly basis, depending on your condition and how well you're responding to treatments.

Example: A wireless glucose monitor, such as the iHealth Align ($16.95, without test strips), available at iHealthLabs.com. It works with a smartphone to take glucose readings and automatically log/track measurements over time and send them to the doctor.

In development: Systems with wearable sensors that automatically take and transmit important readings. A steering wheel that measures blood glucose? Watch for that too in the next few years!

FALL MONITORS GO HIGH-TECH

We're all familiar with the older fall-monitor systems that require users to press a button on a pendant to initiate communication with a call center. Staffers then contact you (via an intercom-like device) to ask if you need help.

What's new: Devices that don't require the push of a button, so fall victims who are immobilized or unconscious also can be helped.

New-generation fall monitors are equipped with accelerometers that can tell when you've fallen. The units, worn around the neck, on the wrist or clipped to a belt, contact a call center or a designated caregiver. If you don't answer a follow-up call, emergency responders will be sent to your address.

Why the new technology is important: Fall victims who receive help within one hour of a fall are six times more likely to survive than those who wait longer.

Examples: Philips Lifeline HomeSafe with AutoAlert (automatic fall detection with push-button backup, 24-hour call center/emergency response) starts at $44.95/month. GoSafe is a wireless version that starts at $54.95/month, plus a onetime GoSafe mobile button purchase of $149. Both are available at *LifelineSys.com.*

Traditional-style fall monitor: Walgreens Ready Response Vi Alert System (390-foot range, 24-hour call center/emergency response) requires the fall victim to push a button. Available at *WalgreensReadyResponse.com* for $29.99/month.

ACTIVITY MONITORS

By tracking activity—and noting changes in routines—an off-site loved one or caregiver can tell when you've become more or less active or when you're spending more time in certain parts of the house. A sudden increase in bathroom visits, for example, could indicate a urinary tract infection that hasn't yet been diagnosed.

What's new: Sensors that track daily activity—for example, how often refrigerator doors are opened, when the stove is turned on and how often the bathroom is used.

Examples: GrandCare Activity Monitoring Package. A caregiver can log in to the system to view activity reports and/or set up "alert parameters" that will trigger an alert if there is no registered movement at scheduled times. A personalized package is available at *grandcare.com*, starting at $299.99, plus a monthly fee based on system developed.

A less expensive option is Lively Activity Sensors for Living Independently. Small, disk-shaped sensors are attached to household objects such as the refrigerator and a pillbox. The sensors detect and send text/e-mail notifications when there's a movement, such as the opening of a refrigerator door. A package of six is available at *amazon.com* for $43.65, plus $24.95/month.

HOW'S YOUR WALKING

A change in walking speed could indicate that someone has balance problems, muscle weakness or other issues that can interfere with daily living.

What's new: Wearable devices (available from your doctor or physical therapist) that monitor gait, balance and walking speed. The devices store information that can be electronically transmitted to a doctor or physical therapist.

If walking speed has declined, it could mean that an underlying health problem—such as congestive heart failure—isn't well-controlled by medication...or that you need physical therapy to increase muscle strength and stamina. Detecting such changes in gait in high-risk patients can allow treatment adjustments that help prevent falls and improve mobility—critical for staying (and thriving) at home.

Examples: StepWatch from Modus Health straps onto your ankle and has 27 different metrics to measure gait and speed. Available at *modushealth.com*. LEGSys from Biosensics includes portable, wireless sensors that analyze gait and generate easy-to-read reports. It's easy to put on with a Velcro strap. Available at *biosensics.com/products/LEGSys*.

Grab Stuff You Can't Reach

Jim Miller, an advocate for older Americans, writes "Savvy Senior," a weekly information column syndicated in more than 400 newspapers nationwide. Based in Norman, Oklahoma, he also offers a free senior news service at SavvySenior.org.

Do you ever wish you had much longer arms? Then you could reach items on overhead shelves or on the ground without climbing, bending, stooping or straining. You would not have to climb on step ladders or, worse, shaky stools or chairs to reach everyday items.

Well, you may know that there are lightweight, easy-to-use devices called reacher grabbers that extend your arms. But there are so many different types, with various materials, lengths and abilities, that it's not easy to choose the one best for your needs.

Here are some top choices among reacher grabbers that could make your life much easier...

Bargain-priced device for picking up small and lightweight items: Aluminum Reacher with Magnetic Tip by Duro-Med, available in 26- and 32-inch lengths, has a trigger-style handgrip that can be operated with one or two fingers and a serrated jaw that provides a secure grip when lifting objects. It also has a magnet built into the tip for picking up small, lightweight metal objects such as paper clips. And it has a small hook (or horn) that aids in retrieving things such as clothes, shoes or keys. However, because of its lightweight design, it doesn't work well retrieving heavier items such as canned goods from shelves. $12.

All-purpose: Ettore Grip 'n Grab can handle most chores. Available in 16-, 34- and 50-inch lengths, it has a soft, comfortable trigger handgrip and a rubber-lined jaw for a firm grip that's strong enough to lift objects up to five pounds and up to four inches wide, yet sensitive enough to pick up something as small as a dime. The jaw also can swivel 90 degrees to reach things in awkward spaces. $18 to $30.

For people who have trouble gripping: The Medline 31-inch Reacher has a unique handgrip that lets you use all five fingers to close the jaw. $18.

Alternatively, the new HealthSmart GripLoc Sliding Reacher is a 43-inch, two-hand reacher with a "power-slide" handle that makes opening and closing the jaw easier (no hand squeezing required) and a twist-and-click lock that keeps the jaw clenched. $40.

For easy storage: The 32-inch EZ Reacher Collapsible has a slip-joint in the arm that allows it to fold in half. It also has a pistol grip and stainless steel "fingers" with silicone suction-cup tips that do a good job of picking up large and small items. There is a version with a "safety lock" on the handle that lets you lock the jaw onto items without continuously squeezing the handgrip. ($22 to $23, *arcmate.com*)

For adjustable lengths: PikStik TelescoPik has a sliding, lockable shaft that adjusts from 30 to 44 inches. It has a pistol grip and a rubber-lined jaw that can hold up to five pounds and can rotate 90 degrees to reach items in awkward spaces. ($30, *pikstik.com*)

For outdoor use: Unger Nifty Nabber is 36 inches long and can hold up to eight pounds. Its rubber-coated jaw is ideal for outdoor jobs such as picking up trash, broken glass or nails. It also has a built-in magnet and an aluminum handle. $20.

WHERE TO BUY

Reacher grabbers can be purchased at many pharmacies as well as medical-equipment and home-improvement stores, but because they are specialty items, the selection is very limited. Your best option is to buy online through the manufacturer's website (if available) or through *amazon.com*.

30 Handy Aids for Achy Hands

Jim Miller, an advocate for older Americans, writes "Savvy Senior," a weekly information column syndicated in more than 400 newspapers nationwide. Based in Norman, Oklahoma, he also offers a free senior news service at SavvySenior.org.

People typically don't think about how much they use their hands until their hands get stiff and painful.

Arthritis, carpal tunnel syndrome and other conditions can make performing everyday tasks such as turning a doorknob, fastening a button, brushing your teeth, preparing a meal or using a computer mouse difficult and painful. There are various assistive devices and other products to help ease the burden of having achy hands. *Here are some of the best ones…*

KITCHEN AIDS

Dexter DuoGlide knives have soft, textured handles and curved blades that let you chop foods using a rocking motion with less hand strain. Available in six models—paring knife, utility knife, bread slicer, all-purpose knife, cook's knife and chef's knife. From $22.50 to $64.85. *dexter1818.com*

Anolon 14-Inch French Skillet ($59.99) and Circulon 6-Quart Covered Chef Pan ($79.99) both have a large, ergonomically designed handle and a second helper handle on each pan that makes them easier to lift and move around when cooking, cleaning or serving. *potsandpans.com*

West Bend Electric Can Opener is a hands-free can opener that starts and stops automatically once you lock the can in place. A built-in magnet keeps the lid from falling in the food once open. $45.99. *westbend.com*

Zim Jar Opener has a V-shaped grip that holds the lid still as you use both hands to twist open a jar or bottle. Available in wall-mounted ($17.99) and under-counter-mounted ($16.99) versions, these openers require installation. *amazon.com*

Alternative: Hamilton Beach Open Ease Automatic Jar Opener is a small, battery-operated device that opens twist-lids from one to four inches in diameter at the push of a button. $34.95. *amazon.com*

Good Grips Eating Utensils (fork, small spoon, teaspoon, tablespoon, soupspoon and rocker knife) are stainless steel with large, soft 1⅜-inch, nonslip grips that are easy to grasp. The fork and spoons also have a special twist built into the metal shaft that allows them to be bent to any angle for either left- or right-handed use, which helps people with limited hand-to-mouth reach. $10.95 per utensil. *ncmedical.com*

OXO Good Grips makes easy-to-grip cooking and baking utensils with large, soft handles. They range from spatulas and whisks to pizza wheels and ice cream scoops. Large-handled utensils spread your fingers so that they don't close completely around the tool, which reduces hand stress and makes the utensils more comfortable to grasp. Typically from $5 to $13 per item. *oxo.com*

HOUSEHOLD HELPERS

• **Lever faucet handles.** If you have twist-handle kitchen or bathroom faucets, check the brand and then see if lever-styled replacement handles are available through the manufacturer's website or through a home-improvement store. Lever handles provide greater leverage for easier turning.

Example: Danco Decorative Lever Handle, $14.98 each at The Home Depot. If lever-style replacement handles are not available, replace your faucets with lever-handle faucets.

The following items can be found at *maddak.com*…

• **Doorknob extenders** fit over standard doorknobs, converting them into easy-to-turn door levers. $21.20 for a package of two.

• **Key turners attach to a key.** Each turner has two finger holes in the handle to improve grip and leverage. $7.95.

• **Big lamp switch is a large,** three-spoked knob adapter that provides better leverage for turning a lamp switch. $10.35.

PERSONAL CARE

Simplehuman triple wall-mount pump holds liquid soap, shampoo and conditioner and has a T-bar lever at the base of each container that you pull for one-handed dispensing. $70. *simplehuman.com*

Simplehuman sensor pump is a touch-free liquid-hand-soap dispenser that sits by the kitchen or bathroom sink. Place your hand under the spout to dispense the soap automatically. $40. *simplehuman.com*

Touch N Brush: The Hands-Free Toothpaste Dispenser can hold any size tube of toothpaste and attaches to the bathroom mirror or the wall with suction cups. Just touch the pump arm with your toothbrush head to get a strip of toothpaste without squeezing the tube. $9.99. *amazon.com*

Oral-B and Sonicare offer a variety of electric toothbrushes with handles that are easier to hold and are wider than standard manual brushes. Prices for the Oral-B toothbrushes run between $39.99 and $169.99 (*oralb.com*). Sonicare toothbrushes cost between $39.95 and $189.95 (*sonicare.com*).

Cheaper alternative: Foam tubing can be cut down to size and fit onto your toothbrush handle to create a large, soft handgrip. This also can be used on eating utensils, pens and pencils. Available in ¼-inch, ⅜-inch and 1⅛-inch widths, this tubing is slip-resistant and does not absorb water. $14.35. *maddak.com*

Philips Sonicare AirFloss cleans between your teeth by shooting microbursts of air and water droplets, eliminating the need for string floss. $169.95. *sonicare.com*

EASIER DRESSING

Button Hook Zipper Pull is a rubber-grip hand tool with a four-inch-long wire-hook buttoning aid at one end for fastening and unfastening buttons and a brass hook at the other end for pulling zipper tabs. $11.99. *easycomforts.com*

Zipper pulls are three-inch-long polypropylene pulls that attach to zipper tabs, making them easier to grasp. $4.99 for a set of 12 in assorted colors. *easycomforts.com*

Lock Laces are elastic shoelaces that convert lace-ups into slip-ons. To ensure a good fit, they include a spring-activated locking device that can tighten and loosen the shoelaces. Available in a variety of colors for $7.99 or $9.99 per pair. *locklaces.com*

EASIER DRIVING

These are available at *amazon.com*…

• **Car key turner** (around $6) is a curved, five-inch-long plastic handle that attaches to the key to provide leverage.

• **Kinsman gas cap removal tool** ($23) works like a wrench and fits most gas caps.

• **Steering Wheel Cover** ($10 to $15) fits over the steering wheel to make the wheel larger in size and easier to grip. There are numerous options, including heated versions.

READING, WRITING AND COMPUTING

For book readers, electronic e-readers are ideal because they're lightweight and easier to hold than regular books and don't require traditional page turning. But if you like paper publications, there are bookholders such as Levō Book Holder Floor Stand ($169) and Corner Table Clamp Book Holder ($99) that hold hardcovers, paperbacks, magazines and cookbooks in any position. Levō also offers holders for e-readers and tablet computers that cost between $99.99 and $229.99. *bookholder.com*

The Pencil Grip is a small rubber grip that fits on pencils and pens to make holding easier and reduce hand fatigue. $1.79. *thepencilgrip.com*

Pen Again is a Y-shaped pen that cradles your index finger to relieve hand stress when writing. $4.99. *penagain.net*

3M Ergonomic Mouse has a vertical-grip handle design that keeps your arm in a more neutral position to reduce wrist and hand stress when using a computer. $58.57. *amazon.com*

Contour RollerMouse sits directly in front of the computer keyboard, giving you the ability to control the cursor with your fingertips, eliminating the reaching and gripping of a traditional mouse. $199.95 to $265. *rollermouse.com*

Never Forget to Take a Pill

Jim Miller, an advocate for older Americans, writes "Savvy Senior," a weekly information column syndicated in more than 400 newspapers nationwide. Based in Norman, Oklahoma, he also offers a free senior news service at SavvySenior.org.

To help yourself (or a loved one) keep up with medication regimens, there's a wide variety of pillboxes, medication organizers, vibrating watches and beeping dispensers that can help anyone stay organized and be reminded. To find these types of products, visit *epill.com* (800-549-0095), where there are dozens to choose from.

One popular option is the Cadex 12 Alarm Medication Reminder Watch for $100. It provides up to 12 daily alarms and displays a message of what medication to take at scheduled times throughout the day.

And there is the monthly MedCenter System ($80), which comes with 31 color-coded pillboxes, each with four compartments for different times of the day and a four-alarm clock for reminders.

There also are a number of web-based services that can notify you when it's time to take a medication.

Examples: MyMedSchedule (908-234-1701, *mymedschedule.com*) and Remember ItNow (925-388-6030, *rememberitnow.com*) offer free text-message and e-mail reminders. OnTimeRX (201-558-7929, *ontimerx.com*) provides phone call reminders in addition to text messages and e-mails for all types of scheduled activities, including daily medications, monthly refills, doctor appointments, wake-up calls and other events. These charge between $10 and $30 per month depending on how many reminders you need.

Another option is CARE Call Reassurance (602-265-5968, extension 7, *call-reassurance.com*), which provides automated call reminders to your loved one's phone. If he fails to answer or acknowledge a call, the service will contact a family member or a designated caregiver via phone, e-mail or text message. The cost is $15 per month if paid in advance for a year.

If you or your loved one needs a more comprehensive medication-management system, consider the MedMinder Automated Pill Dispenser (888-633-6463, *medminder.com*). This is a computerized pillbox that flashes when it's time to take a medication and beeps or calls your phone with an automated reminder if you forget. It will even alert you if you take the wrong pill.

This device also can be set up to call, e-mail or text a family member and caregiver if you a dose, take the wrong medication or don't refill the dispenser. The MedMinder rents for $40 per month.

Another good medication dispensing system is the Philips Medication Dispensing Service (855-681-5351, *managemypills.com*), a countertop appliance that dispenses medicine on schedule, provides verbal reminders and notifies caregivers if the pills aren't taken. Monthly rental and monitoring fees for the Philips service run $60 with an $99 installation fee.

Having Trouble Reading the Small Print?

Jim Miller, an advocate for older Americans, writes "Savvy Senior," a weekly information column syndicated in more than 400 newspapers nationwide. Based in Norman, Oklahoma, he also offers a free news service for seniors at SavvySenior.org.

With more than 25 million Americans living with some form of uncorrectable vision impairment today, more and more high-tech devices for low-vision problems are available, ranging in price from less than $40 to several thousand dollars. These devices can help you read menus, books, magazines and newspapers...make phone calls...work on your computer...and even get around your neighborhood more easily. *Here, some of the best...*

TALKING PHONES

Cell phone that speaks: The Samsung Haven from Verizon Wireless is able to "speak" everything that appears on the display screen, including caller-ID names and numbers, text messages and keypad presses when you dial a number. It also lets you make calls and send text messages by speaking the name of the person that you want to contact. (Of course most iPhones and androids allow you to "speak" your text message into your phone.) The Haven has extra-large, high-contrast text and big touch keys. Phones are available on Amazon.com and can be activated on a month-by-month basis. 800-256-4646, *www. verizonwireless.com*.

Telephone that speaks: The all-purpose ClearSounds WCSC600 Amplified Telephone has big buttons with a backlit keypad that "speaks" the numbers as you dial and a caller-ID that speaks and displays the name and number of the person who is calling. It also has a talking phonebook that allows you to record a name for each phonebook entry. It amplifies incoming speech up to 50 decibels (dB), compared with the standard 12 dB to 13 dB. It has one-touch voicemail that allows you to retrieve messages instantly. Phonebook has 39 name and number directory that easily stores frequently called numbers...plus one large one-touch emergency dial button. Hearing-aid compatible. $149.95. The ClearSounds CSC500 has eight framed buttons that include photos for easy recognition speed dialing: $89.95. 800-965-9043, *clearsounds.com*.

BOOK READERS

Low-vision eReader: For instant access to thousands of books, the Apple iPad Pro tops the list as the best eReading device for the visually impaired. It provides a large 9.7- or 12.9-inch high-resolution screen and a variety of built-in accessibility features, including font magnification up to 56 points, contrast adjustment and super color intensifier. Its VoiceOver feature is able to read text on the screen out loud. VoiceOver includes a systemwide Braille keyboard that supports 6 and 8 dot Braille. It also comes with a feature that allows you to find your iPad using GPS, should you lose it. $599 to $799, and up to $1,100 for models that work with your cellular network. 800-692-7753, *apple.com*.

For a low-tech alternative, the Library of Congress Talking Books program offers a free tape player and unlimited free books on tape to the legally blind—those whose vision is 20/200 or worse in the better eye. 888-657-7323, *nlstalkingbooks.org*.

Alternatives: For iPhone users, the new ZoomReader application developed by Ai Squared uses the built-in iPhone camera to take a picture of text and then reads it aloud. $19.99. 802-362-3612, *aisquared.com*.

CURRENCY READER

To protect yourself from being shortchanged or making mistakes when you pay for things with cash and receive change in bills, the iBill made by Orbit Research identifies all US bills by voice or by a series of tones or vibrations for privacy. You just insert the bill into a slot in the battery-operated device, which is small enough to fit on a key ring. Most bills are identified in less than a second, and it has just two buttons for operation. $119. 888-606-7248, *orbitresearch.com.*

Alternatives: The LookTel Money Reader, a free application for the iPad and some models of the iPhone and iPod Touch, also identifies US currency out loud. It does not require an Internet connection, so it can read money from any location. *looktel.com*

The free EyeNote application from the Bureau of Engraving and Printing works similarly and is compatible with the iPad and some iPhones and iPod Touch models. *eyenote.gov*

SMALL PRINT

Portable electronic magnifier: For reading small print, including food labels, prescriptions, bills and menus, the Ruby handheld video magnifier by Freedom Scientific provides clarity, contrast and magnification up to 14 times, far beyond an ordinary magnifying glass. It offers four high-contrast reading modes that let you change the text and background colors for comfortable reading on a 4.3-inch full-color video screen. It also has a freeze-frame option that allows you to capture an image on the screen and bring it close for better viewing and further magnification. It's small enough to fit in your pocket or purse. $545. 800-444-4443, *freedomscientific.com.*

Computer magnifier/reader: To customize a Microsoft Windows personal computer for low-vision, Ai Squared offers a software application called ZoomText Magnifier/Reader that lets you magnify everything on your computer up to 36 times. It provides technology for clear text at all magnification levels, a wide variety of screen color enhancements and eight different zoom window types that allow you to choose which part of the screen is magnified. It even speaks all program controls, including menus and list views. And when you want to give your eyes a rest, Zoom-Text can read your documents, web pages and e-mail to you through your computer's speakers. It also can speak each key or word that you type and read any text that you point your mouse at. These features are far superior to the Microsoft accessibility features that are built into Windows software. $599. 802-362-3612, *aisquared.com.*

DIRECTIONS

Talking GPS: The Trekker Breeze helps you keep your bearings. The small handheld GPS navigator announces the names of streets, intersections and landmarks such as favorite restaurants as you're walking (or riding in a vehicle). With the press of one of the extra-large buttons, it tells you your location. It provides much more detailed step-by-step information than a standard GPS does, such as how far you are from the intersection, how to retrace your steps if you get lost and which landmarks, public services and businesses are around you. It also allows you to record walking routes when you learn them with sighted people so that you can use them again without assistance. $799. 800-722-3393, *humanware.com.*

Easiest TV Remotes

Jim Miller, an advocate for older Americans, writes "Savvy Senior," a weekly information column syndicated in more than 400 newspapers nationwide. Based in Norman, Oklahoma, he also offers a free senior news service at SavvySenior.org.

It seems like most television remote controls today come with dozens of unnecessary buttons that make them very confusing to operate. Add in the fact that many people use at least two or three remotes to operate their home-entertainment equipment—TV, cable or satellite box, DVD player, etc.—and the complexity of remotes gets very frustrating.

Much better: There are a number of simplified universal TV remotes that are specifically designed for people with dexterity or vision problems and those who shy away from technology. These remote controls can make things simpler for anyone, with bigger buttons and fewer options that make them much easier to see and use. *Some top options…*

Flipper: This single remote works with all major-brand TVs plus cable, satellite and digital over-the-air receiver boxes. Available for $29.95 at *flipperremote.com*, it offers a tapered design that makes it easy to hold, and for simplicity it has only six large color-coded buttons that are exposed (On/Off, Channel Up and Down, Volume Up and Down and Mute). All other buttons used to program and control the remote are hidden behind a sliding panel so that they won't get in the way during day-to-day TV watching. Flipper also has an optional feature that lets you program up to 30 of your favorite channels for quick access.

URC SR3 Super Remote: Sold online for around $13, the SR3 can control TVs, cable and satellite boxes and DVD players. It is lightweight and has a long, tapered design that makes it comfortable to hold and operate…large easy-to-see numeric buttons, each in the shape of the number it represents…and a centrally located "My Button" that gives you the ability to turn on the TV and set the tuner to your favorite channel with a single press. It also provides four "Favorite" buttons for one-touch access to your favorite channels and an "All Off" button that lets you shut down the entire home-entertainment system with a single button press.

SUPERSIZED REMOTES

For people with vision problems, there are a number of excellent oversized remotes offered by Bay Products (813-871-0389, *bigbuttonremotes.com*), including…

Tek Partner: At 5½ inches wide and 8½ inches long, this $39.95 supersized remote offers big, brightly lit buttons with big readable characters and a narrowed center that makes it easy to handle. It also contains only the essential functions, making it easy to use and program. It operates any combination of TVs, VCRs, DVD players, cable boxes and satellite dishes.

Big Button: If you're looking for something a bit smaller (2½ inches x 9½ inches), the $24.95 rectangular-shaped Big Button remote has the same large, lighted buttons as the Tek Partner and the same features.

Tek Pal: This basic, compact remote (2¾ inches x 5½ inches) for the TV comes with just six large buttons (On/Off, Mute, Channel Up and Down, and Volume Up and Down) that light up when pushed. Available for $21.95, the Pal works only with televisions that have cable service connected directly to the TV—it does not control cable or satellite boxes.

Best Home Phones for Seniors

Jim Miller, an advocate for senior citizens, writes "Savvy Senior," a weekly information column syndicated in more than 400 newspapers nationwide. Based in Norman, Oklahoma, he also offers a free senior news service at SavvySenior.org.

For people with hearing loss, weak vision or arthritis, using a standard telephone can be challenging. Fortunately, there are phones on the market today that can help. *Here are some of the best…*

Telephone that speaks: The all-purpose ClearSounds WCSC600 Amplified Telephone has big buttons with a backlit keypad that "speaks" the numbers as you dial and a caller-ID that speaks and displays the name and number of the person who is calling. It also has a talking phonebook that allows you to record a name for each phonebook entry. It amplifies incoming speech up to 50 decibels (dB), compared with the standard 12 dB to 13 dB. It has one-touch voicemail that allows you to retrieve messages instantly. Phonebook has 39 name and number directory that easily stores frequently called numbers…plus one large one-touch emergency dial button. Hearing-aid compatible. $149.95. The ClearSounds CSC500 has eight framed buttons that include photos for easy recognition speed dialing: $89.95. 800-965-9043, *clearsounds.com*.

For emergencies: Geemarc Ampli600. This remote-controlled emergency response phone comes with a neck pendant and SOS buttons on a wristband that you press to automatically dial the phone's preprogrammed emergency numbers if you can't get to the phone. It offers 50 dB of amplification, caller ID, a speakerphone and one-touch emergency dial buttons. $199.95. 888-515-8120, *teltex.com.*

For owners with soft voices: Serene HD-40S. For seniors with difficult-to hear voices, the HD-40S can amplify the outgoing voice by as much as 40 dB. This phone also provides photo-memory dialing (you simply press a picture of the person you wish to call) and 18-dB amplification for incoming calls. $129.95. 800-825-6758, *harriscomm.com.*

For limited mobility: Clarity XLC2. This is a loud, simple and easy-to-use amplified cordless phone featuring up to 50dB amplification and a loud and clear speakerphone for hands-free conversation. Large, high contrast buttons are easy to press (especially for those with disability, such as arthritis) and see, and speak the numbers as they are dialed. Talking Caller ID announces the phone number of the incoming caller. $143. 800-426-3738, *clarity products.com* (and click on "Products").

For severe hearing loss: CapTel 840. This captioned phone lets you listen to the caller and read word-for-word captions of what he/she is saying on the phone's display window. Many states have programs that offer these phones for free to qualified residents. Visit *captel.com*, and click on your state to learn more, or call 800-233-9130.

Cordless phone: Serene CL-60A. The CL-60A offers big "talk-back" buttons that announce the numbers you dial, up to 50 dB of amplification, tone controls, amplified talking caller ID and an amplified slow-play answering machine that makes messages easier to understand. $169.95. 800-825-6758, *harriscomm.com.*

Free phones: Many states offer specialized programs that give free amplified telephones to residents in need. Check with your phone company.

The Three Simplest Smartphones

Jim Miller, an advocate for older Americans, writes "Savvy Senior," a weekly information column syndicated in more than 400 newspapers nationwide. Based in Norman, Oklahoma, he also offers a free senior e-news service at SavvySenior.org.

People have grown to depend on their smartphones for a variety of elaborate and impressive uses. But what if you want a smartphone to be as simple as possible for common functions, such as making and receiving phone calls, text messages and e-mails...and accessing the Internet?

There are free apps that can convert an existing smartphone into a simple-to-use one—and a variety of new smartphones that offer bigger icons and text, along with features that make them less confusing and easier to navigate. *Here are the best options now...*

SIMPLIFY YOUR PHONE

If you already have a smartphone but find it confusing to use or difficult to see, you can install a launcher app—a software application that transforms the appearance and functionality of most smartphones. For example, on the home screen, you can get big, well-labeled buttons for commonly used features such as phone calls, text messaging, contact lists and picture taking, along with an SOS button that—with one tap of the screen—can call your emergency contacts and pinpoint your location to them on their smartphones. Most launcher apps can be customized to prioritize features that you want on your home screen. If you change your mind, you can switch back to the phone's original appearance and functionality by adjusting its settings.

For Android phones, free launcher apps include the Simple Senior Phone (SeniorsPhone.mobi) and Necta Launcher (Launcher.Necta.us). Or for a onetime $10 fee, there's the Big Launcher (*biglauncher.com*), which is particularly helpful to visually impaired people because of the extra-large font sizes and different screen-color themes that make the screen easier to read.

For an iPhone with iOS 6.0 or later, you can use the free Silverline Mobile (Silverline.mobi) launcher app.

SIMPLE NEW SMARTPHONES

If you want to purchase a simple smartphone, here are models that stand out...

•**Jitterbug Touch3.** Offered by GreatCall Wireless, the Touch3 has a four-inch, high-definition touch screen and enhanced features that make it better than the previous GreatCall model. It starts with a simplified, large-font menu on the home page that lets you access often-used features such as the phone, messages, the camera, photos, e-mail and the Internet, along with one-touch access to your contacts and favorite apps.

It also offers a variety of optional health and safety features that appeal to many seniors, such as MedCoach, which reminds you to take medications and refill prescriptions, and Urgent Care, which provides unlimited access to registered nurses and board-certified doctors, day or night, to answer your health questions. At the touch of a button, its 5Star medical-alert service lets you speak to a live emergency-alert agent around the clock. These trained agents have your health and personal information and contact information for your loved ones and nearby emergency services. Agents will confirm your location via GPS tracking technology and dispatch help as needed.

Available at *greatcall.com*, the Touch3 sells for $150 with a onetime $35 activation fee and does not require a contract. Calling plans cost $15 per month for 200 minutes and up to $50 per month for unlimited talk and text. Data plans run from $2.50 for 40 megabytes (MB) up to $30 per month for 2.5 gigabytes (GB). The optional health-and-safety package costs an additional $20 to $35 per month.

•**Samsung Galaxy Note5.** If you want a bigger smartphone that makes it even easier to see the functions, the new Note5 is a popular mainstream Android phone that has a huge 5.7-inch, high-definition touch-screen display. The unique "Easy" mode in the phone's Settings boosts the size of the app icons and font size throughout the device and scales down the phone's home-screen layout to provide only essential features, which makes for easier, straightforward navigation.

With Easy mode turned on, your home screen will display only the time, date and local weather, and six functions you use the most, such as the phone, camera, messages, Internet, music and pictures. To access your 12 most important contacts, you simply swipe the home screen to the right...and to access your 12 favorites apps, swipe to the left.

The Note5 also offers the S Voice application that lets you navigate the phone by voice...and large fonts, screen magnification and text-to-speech options for users with weak vision. It also comes with a stylus that lets you jot down a quick note or number on the screen even when the screen is off.

The Note5 is available with 32 or 64 GB of storage capacity from the major carriers (AT&T, Sprint, Verizon, T-Mobile) and some smaller carriers for $670 to $740 (32 GB) or $770 to $840 (64 GB) without a contract. Monthly service plans for talk, text and data start around $50. The phone may be offered at a lower price if you are willing to sign a contract.

•**Apple iPhone 6 Plus or 6s Plus.** With a spacious 5.5-inch, high-definition touch-screen display, both the iPhone 6 Plus and newer 6s Plus offer a variety of features for customization that makes these phones less intimidating for tech novices. By going to the Accessibility menu in the Settings menu under General, not only can you make the text larger and bolder, which is a standard feature on most smartphones, you also can make the navigation controls more prominent by turning on the Button Shapes feature. And you can increase the size of the app icons by activating the Display Zoom feature in the Display & Brightness section of the main Settings menu.

If you have impaired vision or hearing or problems with dexterity, there's a variety of other helpful accessibility features such as the Zoom screen magnifier...VoiceOver screen reader...closed captions...LED flash to signal the arrival of a text message or call...phone noise cancellation that reduces ambient background noise for better hearing when on a call…and the improved Siri personal assistant that lets you navigate the phone with your voice and can remind you to perform certain tasks based on the time and your location. To make the home screen less cluttered, you can move the icons of your favorite apps to the home page and stack the rest in a folder in the corner.

The 6 Plus is available through most wireless providers for $649 without a contract for the 16 GB version or $749 for the 64 GB version. The 6s Plus costs $749 for 16 GB, $849 for 64 GB and $949 for 128 GB. Monthly service plans for talk, text and data start at around $50. The phones may be available at lower prices if you are willing to sign a contract.

WHEN A LESS-SMART PHONE IS ENOUGH

If a smartphone is more than you need, consider a basic cell phone. These are used primarily for making and receiving phone calls and sending and receiving text messages—they have no e-mail or Internet capabilities. They come with big buttons, menus that are easy to navigate, SOS emergency buttons and enhanced sound—and they are compatible with hearing aids. *Here are three of the best…*

•**Jitterbug5.** Offered by GreatCall (*greatcall.com*), this is a custom-designed Samsung flip-phone that offers a backlit keypad with big buttons, large text on a brightly colored screen and "YES" and "NO" buttons to navigate the phone's menu of options without confusing icons. It also offers voice dialing, a powerful speakerphone, a built-in camera, GPS technology that can locate the device and the optional health and safety features that are offered with the Jitterbug Touch3 such as MedCoach, 5Star medical alert and Urgent Care (see the previous page).

The Jitterbug5 sells for $99 with a onetime $35 activation fee, no-contract and calling plans that range from $15 to $40 per month. The health and safety package options cost $20 to $35 per month, and text options range between $3 and $15 per month.

•**Doro PhoneEasy 626.** Sold through Consumer Cellular (*consumercellular.com*), this black, silver or burgundy flip-phone offers a backlit keypad with raised black buttons on a white background that makes it easy to see and operate.

It also has a big color display screen that offers large text with different color themes—including white text on a black screen or yellow text on a blue screen—that can be easy to read for those with vision problems.

Other handy features include two speed-dial buttons, shortcut buttons to texting and the camera, a powerful two-way speakerphone, video-recording capabilities and an ICE (in case of emergency) button on the back of the phone that will automatically dial one preprogrammed number. It also uses GPS technology, so if you call 911, it may be able to pinpoint your location. This phone sells for $50 with service plans that range between $10 and $50 per month and no contract.

•**Snapfon ezTWO.** Made and sold by SeniorTech (*snapfon.com*), this simple budget-friendly phone is free other than a onetime $35 phone-activation fee. Service plans range from $10 to $30 per month with no contract. If you don't want the Snapfon service plan, you can choose AT&T or T-Mobile service instead and pay $80 for the phone.

This open-faced rectangular phone has big raised buttons, a color screen, enhanced volume with a speaker phone and a speaking keypad that tells you the number you just pushed. A big red SOS emergency alert button on the back of the phone can sound a siren-like alert when pushed and held down for five seconds (that feature can be disabled). The phone then sends a text message to as many as five emergency contacts and calls those contacts (one of which could be 911) in order until the call is answered.

Or, for an additional $15 per month, you can subscribe to the "sosPlus" mobile monitoring service, which will connect you to a call center manned by trained agents who have access to your health and personal information and the contact information of your loved ones and nearby emergency services.

Hiring an In-Home Caregiver—What You Must Know

Jullie Gray, LICSW, CMC, principal of Aging Wisdom, a geriatric-care-management company based in Bellevue, Washington. AgingWisdom.com

The vast majority of Americans would rather remain in their homes than move to an assisted-living facility, according to surveys by AARP. Hiring an in-home caregiver could make it possible to remain at home even after you no longer can live fully independently—but it's a trade-off in challenges compared with a nursing home–type facility. The experience can be pretty horrible, in fact, if you don't take the right steps.

Here's how to select and manage an in-home caregiver…

ASSESSING YOUR NEEDS

As a first step, it is very worthwhile to have a professional geriatric care manager assess the senior's needs. For example, does the senior mainly need companionship during the day? Housekeeping? Meals prepared and served? Medication doled out? Does he/she need help with activities of daily living, such as toileting, bathing and dressing? Are there health issues that require trained assistance, such as giving injections to a person with diabetes or assistance with physical therapy exercises? Do you need an aide who can drive—on outings, errands and to doctor appointments…and will you provide a car or will you require the use of the aide's car? (The care manager also can recommend caregiver agencies and/or caregivers.)

This assessment usually takes about two hours at $100 to $150 an hour. Aging Life Care Association (*aginglifecare.org*) can help you find a care manager in your area. Or ask local senior centers, Area Agency on Aging offices or the senior's doctor if he/she can recommend agencies or care providers.

HIRE THROUGH AN AGENCY

In-home caregivers can be hired directly or through an agency, but agencies are the safer and simpler option.

Hiring in-home help directly might save you a few dollars an hour, but in general, the savings are significant only for people who hire an undocumented immigrant and/or don't pay the required taxes. Doing either of these things could lead to legal problems for both of you. (If you hire someone directly, that person will be your employee, creating insurance and tax obligations—you are required to pay payroll taxes, obtain the worker's liability insurance and file employer tax forms with the state and federal governments.)

Hiring directly also means that you will have to conduct a background check on this person yourself and find a replacement on short notice if he/she is sick, needs time off, quits or is fired. Hiring an undocumented immigrant also makes it virtually impossible to run a full background check on the caregiver. That's a big risk when you consider that this person essentially will be unsupervised in the senior's home.

A reputable agency should handle all of these issues for you.

When you speak with an agency, ask the following…

• **Are you licensed by the state?** Some, though not all, states require licensing—your local Area Agency on Aging office should know if yours does.

• **Are you a member of the American Association for Homecare?** Belonging to this professional association suggests a commitment to professionalism (*aahomecare.org*).

Also ask about the process for requesting a new caregiver if the first one assigned doesn't work out or is sick. You should be able to do this relatively quickly and easily.

Make sure the senior meets any potential caregivers during the interview process so that he will be more welcoming when you actually make a hire.

MAKING THE CAREGIVING RELATIONSHIP WORK

• **Be very clear with the caregiver about your expectations.** Explain precisely what you want him/her to do. Are there specific household or personal tasks that should be prioritized? Is social interaction for the senior a priority?

Lack of communication about needs and expectations is a common cause of problems. If you want something done, ask. If you don't like how something is being done, give instructive feedback.

•**Lock up all valuables, or move the valuables to the home of a trusted relative before allowing a caregiver to work in the home.** Secure any checkbooks, credit cards and documents containing Social Security numbers or other personal data, too, and keep a close eye on accounts and credit reports for any signs of identity theft. These measures are important even if you eventually come to know and trust a caregiver.

•**Plan ahead for backup.** It is best to hire multiple caregivers on a rotating schedule—possibly one for weekdays and one for weekends—if your caregiving needs are truly full-time. Even if you hire a live-in, no one can work 24/7. And even if the caregiver tells you that he wants to work every day to make more money, everyone needs days off for vacation, sick days and doctor visits. It will be easiest on your senior, both physically and emotionally, if his care is consistently provided by caregivers he knows and who are adequately trained in his needs.

•**Visit randomly.** Close friends and relatives of the senior should drop in without warning occasionally when the caregiver is working to make sure that he is doing his job and that the senior is happy and safe in his care.

WHAT WILL THIS COST?

Extensive in-home support is expensive. In-home care costs an average of $18 an hour—around $19 if "personal care" such as help bathing, dressing and/or using the bathroom is required. These hourly rates vary by region and can easily reach $25 or more per hour in high cost-of-living areas. Agencies typically have four-hour minimums per day. Round-the-clock live-in assistance averages around $350 a day, nearly three times the price of the typical assisted-living facility. There might be

additional onetime costs associated with remaining in the home as well, such as modifying the house to allow wheelchair access, installing an easy-access bathtub and grab bars throughout the home or adding a bedroom for a live-in caregiver. Julie Gray is past-president of this organization.

Low-Cost Ways to Make Your Home Easier and Safer to Live In

Tom Kraeutler, a former professional home inspector and contractor in New York City. He is host of *The Money Pit*, a nationally syndicated radio show on home improvement broadcast to more than three million listeners. MoneyPit.com

Ella Chadwell, a home-safety consultant, Brentwood, Tennessee, and president of Life@Home, a web-based company that provides information on home-accident prevention and markets products for home safety.

Wendy A. Jordan, a Certified Aging-in-Place Specialist (CAPS), designated by the National Association of Home Builders.

Remodeling a house to make it safer and more user-friendly can run tens of thousands of dollars. *But here are ways* to improve and update your home without spending much…*

THROUGHOUT THE HOME

•**Replace round doorknobs,** which are difficult to grasp and turn, with lever-style handles that you push down to open. Most of the time, the lever handles can be attached to the existing latch mechanism already on the door. You can do the job yourself with just a screwdriver. Also, consider replacing cabinet door and drawer knobs with easy-to-grasp C- or D-shaped handles.

*Most of these items are widely available at home-improvement and plumbing-supply stores. For proper installation, consult an occupational therapist or Certified Aging-in-Place Specialist (CAPS)—architects, designers, contractors and health-care consultants with special training in modifying homes for older individuals. To find a CAPS in your area, go to nahb.org/capsdirectory.

Cost: About $30/lever and $10/handle. Available at home-improvement centers.

• **Install better lighting.** Vision inevitably deteriorates with age. Adequate lighting throughout the house helps prevent falls and run-ins with walls, corners and doors. Central ceiling fixtures, wall sconces with translucent shades and skylights are all good choices. Motion-activated lighting is helpful during middle-of-the-night trips to the bathroom. Task lighting in the bathroom, kitchen and reading nooks should be directed from the side, versus overhead, to avoid glare.

Cost: Average $95 to $1,500, depending on scope of work done.

• **Switch to rocker light switches.** They are on/off switches that rock back and forth when pressed. They are larger and easier to operate, and many people find them more attractive than the standard, small flip switches used in most homes. Rocker switches let you turn on a light with your elbow or fist if you're entering a room when your hands are full, and they're easier to find in the dark.

Cost: About $5 per light switch. Available at home-improvement centers.

• **Raise the position of some electrical outlets.** Wall outlets that are close to the floor can be hard to reach and inconvenient for plugging in appliances that you use intermittently, such as vacuums, heating pads and chargers for phones and laptops. Use those low outlets for lamps and other devices that you rarely unplug. Hire an electrician to raise other outlets at least 27 inches off the floor. They'll still be inconspicuous but much more accessible.

Cost: Typically $250 and up to move about half a dozen outlets.

• **Use remote controls for more than TVs.** They can operate window coverings, such as drapes and blinds, so you avoid stretching and straining, and let you control interior and exterior lights from your car or from within the home to prevent you from tripping in the dark.

My favorite: Lutron AuroRa (888-588-7661, *www.lutron.com*).

Cost: The AuroRa entry system starts at around $225 and provides wireless house lighting control for up to five dimmers that can be operated from the car or the bedside. Online retailers, such as *amazon.com* offer it.

• **Create "wider" doorways.** Residential building codes and home builders don't consider the needs of older people who may need more than the standard 32-inch doorway, especially if they use a wheelchair or walker. Actually widening a doorway can be expensive and impractical, especially if it's along a weight-bearing wall.

Instead: Replace your standard door hinges with expandable "offset" hinges. These special hinges allow the door to close normally. But upon opening, they swing the door clear of the door frame by an extra two inches. This lets you use the entire width of the doorway when you enter or exit.

Cost: About $20 for a set of two door hinges. Available at home-improvement stores. A handy person can install these hinges because they fit in the existing holes in your door frame. Otherwise, a carpenter may charge about $100/hour.

• **Add a second handrail to staircases.** It's easier and safer to climb and descend when you can use both hands. Adding an extra handrail is an inexpensive and easy way to increase safety. Make sure both handrails are at the same height and between 30 and 34 inches above the front edge of the step. Also, for maximum safety, handrails should extend about six inches beyond the top and bottom steps if possible.

Cost: About $60 to $400 for each new handrail plus carpenter installation. Available at home-improvement stores.

• **Getting up from the couch.** Even young, healthy people can easily lose their balance when they stand up after being in a sitting position for a long time.

Solutions: Stand up slowly while grabbing on to the arm of the couch or chair before taking a step. If the arm isn't high enough to be of help, consider a CouchCane, a stabilizing device that adjusts in height from 29 to 32 inches.

Cost: About $100 at stores that sell wheelchairs, canes and other products for the physically impaired.

KITCHEN

•**Lower your microwave.** Many home builders, contractors and home owners like to save space by mounting microwave ovens above the stove or high on a wall. This position is hazardous because it requires you to reach above your head to get hot foods or forces you to balance on a stool.

Better: If your existing microwave is on the wall, build a shelf under it where you can rest hot foods after they finish cooking. Or choose a new model with a tray feature that slides out and is easier to reach.

Example: The Sharp Insight Pro Microwave Drawer Oven installs just beneath your countertop. The entire oven slides open, drawer-style, giving you access to the cooking compartment from above.

Cost: About $950 for the microwave and $150 and up for carpenter installation.

•**Install a pullout kitchen faucet.** Lugging heavy pots of water to the stove can be difficult and even dangerous. Many plumbing manufacturers now offer kitchen faucets featuring high-arc, pullout spouts. You can remove the spout and use it as a sprayer hose to fill pots within three to five feet of the stove.

Cost: Starts at about $150 plus plumber installation. Available at home-improvement stores.

•**Install a pull-down shelving system inside your kitchen wall cabinets.** Top shelves in cabinets are difficult to reach. This simple device rests in your upper cabinet until you grab a handle on the shelf frame. A set of three or four shelves swings out of the cabinet and down toward you. The shelves lock in place so you can get the item you need.

Afterward, the whole unit swings back into place.

My favorite: Rev-A-Shelf's chrome pull-down shelving system for 24- and 36-inch cabinets. You can do the installation yourself.

Cost: $466 (800-626-1126, *rev-a-shelf.com*).

•**Kitchen tasks.** As we grow older, we often lose strength and agility, making it riskier to use knives and handle hot food.

For cutting food, consider semicircular cutting tools, such as the Rocking T Knife, that let you slice meat, bread and other foods by rocking the blade back and forth. Semicircular knives require less strength and are usually considered safer than standard butcher knives.

Cost: About $30 from kitchen appliance stores.

To make handling hot food easier, consider a "push-pull stick." These devices grip the oven rack so you can easily slide it in or out from a safe distance.

Cost: About $15 at kitchen speciality stores.

BATHROOM

•**Add upscale grab bars near toilets and tubs.** Some people have avoided installing grab bars in their bathrooms because they look too institutional. Now, there are much more attractive versions. Brushed nickel or oil-rubbed bronze grab bars by Moen are designed to match other Moen bath accessories and faucets for a coordinated look. The grab bars meet all federal government guidelines. They have a stainless steel core and are 1¼ inches in diameter, making them easy to hold.

Cost: About $25 to $70 for the bar. Available at home-improvement stores. You can install them yourself, but it requires drilling holes in the wall.

Note: A towel bar is not the same thing as a grab bar—the latter is designed to be weight bearing and must be anchored into blocking (a secure mount). If they are in the right location, your contractor can attach grab bars to wall studs. Otherwise, a contractor can open the wall and install mounts for grab bars.

•**Elevated toilets.** At 17 to 19 inches high (a few inches higher than a standard toilet), "comfort height" or "chair height" toilets are often more comfortable for anyone to use, regardless of health condition. For people with painful joints or arthritis, they require less bending at the knee, and wheelchair users find them easier to get on and off of. They come in a range of designs, from utilitarian to trendy, and need not cost more than standard-height models.

What You Need to Bathe Safely

Wendy A. Jordan, a Certified Aging-in-Place Specialist (CAPS), designated by the National Association of Home Builders.

Wheelchair users need a wide entry and turnaround space in the shower. A flat entry promotes safe access for anyone who has balance, vision or mobility concerns. With no raised threshold to avoid overflow, the floor of the shower should be gently angled toward the drain. To guard against slipping, the floor should have a nonskid surface. Honed-finish ceramic tiles and tiles with nonslip coating are good choices. Small tiles (four inches or smaller) are preferred—the extra grout lines also help prevent skids.

An aging-in-place shower needs a bench or seat…and multiple showerheads (an overhead fixture plus a handheld), ideally with heat-control function to avoid accidental burns. The faucet, handheld showerhead and grab bar should be reachable from the seat. These accessories come in a range of prices and styles and don't take up as much room as you would think.

For people who prefer baths, wide, flat tub ledges provide seating for safe transfer into the tub. And faucets can be offset for easier transition in and out of the tub. Another option is a walk-in tub, with a hinged door for easy, safe entry. Walk-in tubs come in a variety of sizes—compact, standard and oversized. Prices vary widely.

ing demand for accessibility features now that the baby boom generation is reaching retirement age. *These include…*

•**No-threshold showers.** Stepping over a high tub wall onto a slick surface can be dangerous for aging home owners with hip, leg or balance problems. Easy-access showers that don't require this big step are becoming a popular choice.

Other shower features gaining momentum: Handheld showerheads…doorless shower stalls…and even two-person showers.

•**Residential ramps and elevators.** These are no longer just for public buildings. Older home owners are adding ramps to their entryways, and they even are installing in-home elevators when stairs become too much of a physical challenge.

•**Single-level layouts.** Stairs and elevators are not necessary when all the rooms in a home are on one level. When small lot size makes a single-story layout impractical, today's home owners still like to locate the master bedroom on the first floor, with the other bedrooms upstairs.

Additional feature for an aging population…

•**Locations close to urban centers.** Living near cities and public transportation is becoming more popular. Many older home owners like these locales because they trim car usage (sometimes making it possible to live completely without a car).

Renovations That Pay Off Big Now…

Kermit Baker, PhD, chief economist, American Institute of Architects (AIA), Washington, DC, and senior research fellow, Joint Center for Housing Studies, Harvard University, Cambridge, Massachusetts. AIA.org

Older home owners tend to prefer residences that are easy to get around. It's no surprise that we're seeing increas-

House Problems You Must Fix Now and Those You Can Let Slide

Danny Lipford, who has worked as a contractor for more than 30 years. Based in Mobile, Alabama, he hosts the nationally syndicated TV program *Today's Homeowner with Danny Lipford*, airing on more than 200 stations nationwide. DannyLipford.com

Houses sometimes develop problems in bunches, and there isn't always enough money or time to tackle all the needed repairs at once. *Here's how to decide which projects must take priority...*

PRIORITY #1: Leaky roof. If water is dripping into your home, it must be stopped immediately. Delay would almost certainly lead to mold, mildew, rotted wood and/or water-damaged ceilings. A small roof leak might drip into an attic for months before it shows through the ceiling of the living space below. Take a bright flashlight into your attic during heavy rainstorms a few times each year to scan for leaks. Pay special attention to the areas around chimneys and roof vents.

Related: Dripping pipes and plumbing fixtures also should be treated as a top priority if the water is dripping into the home, not into a drain. If you can't stop the drip, turn off the water main—or at least position a bucket to catch the drip—and call a plumber immediately.

PRIORITY #2: Electrical issues. If your circuit breakers often trip...or turning on power-hungry electrical devices causes your lights to dim...or some of your home's switches or outlets work sporadically or become hot to the touch, call an electrician to evaluate your system very soon. Your home might have serious electrical issues that could cause a fire. The $100 to $300 or so that an electrician will charge to evaluate your home and perhaps replace a breaker or an outlet is worth it for the peace of mind alone. If the electrician finds serious shortcomings in your electrical system, it might cost $2,000 to $3,000 to upgrade your electrical service or $4,000 to $8,000 or more to rewire the home.

PRIORITY #3: Slip-and-fall risks. A slippery step might seem like a mild annoyance—until someone has a serious fall. Do not wait until that happens. Eliminating household slip-and-fall risks usually is an inexpensive do-it-yourself project. *Common danger spots...*

• Slick concrete porches. Paint these with a textured antislip paint to reduce the risk. Expect to pay around $30 per gallon, which covers 300 square feet.

• Slick or steep stairs. Apply antiskid tape to the steps, especially near the front edge of each step.

Example: A two-inch-by-five-yard roll of 3M Safety Walk Indoor/Outdoor Tread costs less than $15. Or install carpeting.

• Loose or weak handrails. A handrail that isn't strong enough to support someone leaning on it is a fall waiting to happen. If the loose rail is attached to wood, remove the screws and reattach the rail using wood screws that are at least one inch longer than the existing screws. Screw these into studs or floor joists, not just drywall or flooring. If the handrail is attached to concrete, sink lead anchors into the concrete, then screw stainless or coated steel bolts into these. If the concrete is cracked or crumbling where the handrail attaches, use a concrete repair product, such as concrete repair epoxy, to hold the lead anchor in place.

PRIORITY #4: Foundation cracks. The longer a foundation crack is left unrepaired, the larger that crack is likely to grow—and the more expensive it will likely be to correct. Meanwhile, this foundation crack will serve as a path for water and insects to enter the home, and it could cause shifting, settling and cracking in the house.

Helpful: Hairline cracks usually are not big problems, but horizontal cracks and wide cracks often are.

For $150 or so, a structural engineer or home inspector should be able to take a quick look and tell you how serious the problem is. You might be able to patch a minor crack yourself with a tube of mortar repair caulk, available for less than $10. This caulk should at least stop more water from entering, preventing the problem from becoming worse. If major foundation repairs are needed, they could cost anywhere from $1,500 to $10,000 or more.

PRIORITY #5: Loose or damaged shingles or roof flashing...or tree limbs that rub against the roof during storms. These problems might not be causing water leaks through your roof yet, but they eventually will if allowed to linger. Use binoculars to scan for shingle or flashing problems if you're not comfortable climbing onto your roof. A roofer should be able to fix minor shingle or flashing issues for $200 to $400. Hiring a professional tree trimmer to cut back branches rubbing against the roof could cost $250 to $500 or more.

PRIORITY #6: **Peeling exterior paint.** This isn't just an aesthetic issue. It lets water penetrate your wood siding or trim, leading to rot. If your paint is peeling in only a few spots that are accessible, you could sand, prime and paint these areas yourself. This won't look perfect, but it should prevent further water damage to the siding. If the peeling is widespread, a new paint job is needed relatively soon. A quality job is likely to cost $8,000 to $12,000.

PRIORITY #7: **Aged heating and air-conditioning components.** If your furnace or boiler, air conditioner and water heater still are working, you can safely put off replacing them. Still, updating old heating, ventilation and air-conditioning (HVAC) systems and water-heating components should be somewhere on your to-do list—today's high energy costs make it expensive to operate inefficient equipment. Once these heating and cooling components pass their twelfth birthday, it is wise to replace them rather than repair them when they break down.

The New Way to Declutter Your Home (Do It the Japanese Way)

Marie Kondo is a cleaning consultant based in Japan and author of *The Life-Changing Magic of Tidying Up: The Japanese Art of Decluttering and Organizing*, from which this article is adapted. The book has sold more than two million copies worldwide. TidyingUp.com

Tidying up your home can dramatically improve your life. Yes, dramatically. Tidying—clearing away clutter—can help you let go of the past…increase your confidence in your decision-making abilities…reduce stress…clarify what's truly important in your life…and make it easier to see where you should focus your energies in the future.

Unfortunately, tidied homes often degenerate back into clutter. But Marie Kondo, a cleaning consultant in Japan, has come up with ways to declutter a home so that it stays decluttered. In Japan, where apartments are small, tidiness is a philosophy of living. Her personal neatness education began at age five, when she learned feng shui principles from her mother. At age 18, she worked at a Shinto shrine keeping order for the shrine elder. *She has taken what she's learned and created her own life-changing method for creating order…*

•**Tidy up in one big push.** The usual advice is to tidy a very cluttered home a little at a time so that the task does not seem overwhelming. This slow-and-steady method does not work.

If you completely declutter your entire home within a short period—in perhaps a few days—the transformation is jarring and unforgettable. You feel happier and calmer…and are truly inspired to continue to live this way. If you tackle the task of tidying a little at a time, there is no jarring transformation and, likely, no fundamental change in mind-set. The bad habits that led to clutter in your past likely will recur. In fact, you might already be recluttering parts of your house before you declutter other parts.

Helpful: The best time to start decluttering is first thing in the morning. That's when the mind is clear and sharp. If you struggle to begin this big job—or struggle to see it through—visualize what it will be like to live in a clutter-free home. That will help motivate you.

•**Tidy by category rather than by room.** It seems natural to clean first one room, then the next. Trouble is, most people have similar items stored in more than one room in their homes. Clothes might be in multiple closets and in the attic…books might be spread throughout the house. If you tidy room by room, you could easily fail to notice that you have more of something than you need. Tidying category by category avoids this problem.

Start with categories that hold little sentimental value, such as clothes, books and paperwork. Leave the category of family mementos for last—these are especially challenging to give away.

•**Keep things that bring you joy, and get rid of the rest.** Hold a possession that is not in regular use in your hands. Ask yourself,

Does this spark joy? If it does not, you're better off without it. It is cluttering your life, and that is keeping you from joy. Repeat this with every rarely used item in your home.

Warning: It can be difficult to get rid of items that still are in good condition—it feels wasteful. Thank these items for the joy they gave you in the past...or for teaching you that items like them do not truly bring you the joy you expected. These objects cannot hear you, of course, but you will hear these words. Hearing this could help your mind understand that these objects have served their purpose, so it is not wasteful to get rid of them.

• **Honor the past by discarding items that have sentimental value.** People often hang onto things from the past because they think throwing them away would dishonor a treasured memory. In fact, it's leaving these items untouched in boxes that dishonors memories. Discarding sentimental items—for example, family photos—involves picking them up, holding them and reliving the memories, which is likely more honor than has been bestowed upon these things in years. It also lets you identify the small percentage of your sentimental items that spark the greatest joy. These few items can then be truly treasured rather than left untouched in boxes.

• **Don't buy organizing products.** Home stores are full of storage bins, shelving systems and other organizing products that claim to contain the clutter. Do not buy these—they're a trap, especially when you are just beginning the tidying up process. No matter how many storage bins you buy, they soon will be filled to overflowing. The primary solution is not putting things away more efficiently...it's getting rid of the things that you don't need.

• **Do not badger other members of your household to tidy with you.** This will only sour them on the task. Instead, quietly go about decluttering your own spaces and your own possessions. You might find that the other people in your household start to tidy, too, as if by magic—tidying can be contagious.

• **Do not put out-of-season clothing into storage.** Organizing professionals often recommend freeing up closet space by stashing winter clothes in bins during summer and summer clothes in bins during winter. This is a mistake.

People who free up closet space this way often end up filling that space by buying more clothes—including duplicates of garments they already own, because they forget what's in storage. Packing and unpacking seasonal clothes twice a year is a time-consuming task that's often delayed until deep into a season. Clothes look wilted after months in bins. And this system makes it difficult to access warm clothes on unseasonably cold summer days and light clothes on unseasonably warm winter days.

Stash out-of-season clothes in bins only if your closet is extremely small.

DUMP IT!—SEVEN MORE THINGS TO THROW AWAY

These items almost always should be disposed of during the tidying up process...

• **Unwanted gifts and old greeting cards.** The purpose of gifts and greeting cards is to convey the giver's feelings. Once they are received, they have served this purpose and can be discarded if they do not spark joy.

• **Unidentified electrical cords and plugs.** These will remain unidentified. Most probably are for products that you stopped using long ago.

• **Broken appliances.** These will never be fixed.

• **Electronics packaging.** This is unlikely to ever be needed again.

• **Promotional giveaways.** Companies often give out free items bearing their logos. Most are never used.

• **Credit card statements and old check registers.** Once you have paid credit card bills and balanced your checking account, these no longer serve any purpose. If you later need to track down some spending detail, you can do so through your bank or credit card issuer's website.

• **User manuals.** Most people never refer to the manuals that come with the products they purchase, at least not after the first few days of ownership. User manuals typically are available online if they are needed.

6

Secrets to Staying Steady On Your Feet: Balance, Bone Health and More

Fall-Proof Your Life

Every year in the US, about one-third of people age 65 and older fall, with 1.6 million treated in emergency rooms and 12,800 killed. But falling is not an inevitable result of aging.

Falling is associated with impairments (such as from stroke, gait or vision problems, or dementia) that are more common with age. But risk for falling is also increased by poor balance and muscle strength and by side effects of certain drugs, especially those prescribed for sleep and depression.

RISKY MEDICATIONS

Several types of widely prescribed drugs have been linked to an increased risk for falls, including...

• **Sleep medications,** such as the new generation of drugs heavily advertised on TV, including *eszopiclone* (Lunesta) and *zolpidem* (Ambien).

• **Antidepressants,** including selective serotonin reuptake inhibitors, such as *citalopram* (Celexa)...selective serotonin-norepinephrine reuptake inhibitors, such as *duloxetine* (Cymbalta)...and tricyclic antidepressants, such as *amitriptyline.*

• **Benzodiazepines** (antianxiety medications), such as *alprazolam* (Xanax).

• **Anticonvulsants,** such as *pregabalin* (Lyrica), a class of drugs that is prescribed not only for epilepsy but also for chronic pain problems, such as from nerve damage.

• **Atypical antipsychotics,** such as *quetiapine* (Seroquel), which are used to treat bipolar disorder...schizophrenia...and psychotic episodes (such as hallucinations) in people with dementia.

• **Blood pressure medications,** including diuretics, such as *furosamide* (Lasix)...and

Mary Tinetti, MD, director of the Program on Aging and the Claude D. Pepper Older Americans Independence Center at the Yale School of Medicine in New Haven, Connecticut.

calcium channel blockers, such as *nifedipine* (Procardia).

Important: Taking five or more medications also is linked to an increased risk for falls.

LOW BLOOD PRESSURE

Side effects of several medications (including drugs for Parkinson's disease, diuretics and heart drugs such as beta-blockers) may increase the risk of falling by causing postural hypotension (blood pressure drops when you stand up from lying down or sitting). Not enough blood flows to the heart to keep you alert and stable, and the body's normal mechanism to counteract this fails.

What to do: Ask your doctor to test you if you have symptoms, including feeling lightheaded or dizzy after standing. He/she will have you lie flat for five minutes, and then check your blood pressure immediately when you stand up. You will remain standing and have your pressure checked one or two minutes later. If systolic (top number) blood pressure drops at least 20 mmHg from lying to standing, you have postural hypotension.

If this is the case, ask about reducing your dosage of hypertensive, antidepressive and/or antipsychotic medications—the three drug types most likely to cause this condition.

Also: Drink more water—at least eight eight-ounce glasses a day. Dehydration can cause postural hypotension and is common among older people, who have a decreased sense of thirst.

Helpful: When you wake up in the morning, take your time getting out of bed. Sit on the edge of the bed for a few minutes while gently kicking forward with your lower legs and pumping your arms. This will move more blood to your heart and brain. Then stand up while holding on to a nearby stable object, such as a bedside table.

VITAMIN D

Vitamin D promotes good muscle strength, so people with low blood levels of vitamin D may be at increased risk for falls. If your level is below 30 ng/mL, ask your doctor about taking a daily vitamin D supplement.

Why Seniors Fall

Stephen Robinovitch, PhD, professor, kinesiology and engineering science, Simon Fraser University, British Columbia, Canada. His study was published in *The Lancet*.

You've probably already heard that falling is the most frequent cause of injury among people age 65 and older. *But here's a question to ponder...*

Why do most seniors fall?

You might think that most falls are due to tripping or slipping, but a new study points to a different, more surprising cause.

It's something that most of us do every day without even thinking—and it's something that can be easily avoided.

FALLS CAUGHT ON VIDEO

In the first study of its kind, Canadian researchers set up shop at two long-term-care facilities for the elderly that had video cameras installed in common areas (dining rooms, lounges, hallways, etc). Whenever an elderly resident fell on camera, researchers analyzed the video footage to determine what caused the fall. *Here are the problems that caused the falls and the percentage of falls that each problem caused...*

- **Unknown cause: 2%**
- **Slipping: 3%**
- **Bumps or hits: 11%**
- **Loss of support: 11%**
- **Collapse: 11%**
- **Trips or stumbles: 21%**
- **Incorrect weight-shifting (more on this below): 41%!**

So something the researchers called "incorrect weight-shifting" was, unexpectedly, the top cause of falls. Now, what does that mean exactly? Incorrect weight-shifting is when you abruptly change your center of gravity so that the bulk of your weight isn't aligned between your feet—it's thrown off to one side, which can cause your body to tilt off balance. This is different from tripping, for example (when your balance is thrown off by some external object)—this problem is internal or self-induced, due to the way you move around.

GUARD AGAINST TUMBLES

You can fall at any age, of course, but the rate of falls during normal daily activities increases with age, said lead study author Stephen Robinovitch, PhD. So the older you get, the more careful you need to be. And age isn't the only risk factor—certain conditions also can play a role, such as vision impairment, cognitive problems and reduced muscle strength, to name just a few.

To help protect yourself (or a loved one) from taking a spill, focus on the number-one form of prevention, according to this study— try not to shift your center of gravity outside the base of support provided by your feet while moving around. *Here are some tips from Dr. Robinovitch, which may help you avoid doing exactly that…*

• **When standing**—Keep your body weight evenly distributed between your feet—don't lean too far sideways or on the heels or balls of your feet.

• **When walking**—Avoid abrupt turns— turn slowly, with your whole body at once (don't swivel your head and torso around without moving your lower half, too, for instance).

• **When reaching**—Instead of grasping for high items that are near the limit of your reach (such as the door of a kitchen cabinet that's above the refrigerator) and causing your body to lurch awkwardly, use a wide, low step stool or call someone taller to help.

• **When bending**—If you've dropped, say, your car keys, instead of leaning down with your upper body while keeping your legs straight (which causes your center of gravity to shift forward), lower yourself by bending your knees and moving into a squatting position.

Wearing New Eyeglasses Increases Fall Risk

When new glasses are stronger than the old ones—or when older adults are switched from single-vision glasses to bifocals or progressive lenses—falls are twice as likely. They are common when an older person navigates steps, stairs and curbs—which may seem closer, farther away, smaller or bigger than before. Before getting new glasses, tell the optometrist about medical conditions, disabilities or weak muscles that might increase your risk for falls. When using bifocals or progressive lenses, tuck your chin in to view stairs or steps through the distance-vision area of the lenses.

David B. Elliott, PhD, professor of clinical vision science, University of Bradford, UK, published in *Optometry and Vision Science*, reported in *Johns Hopkins Medical Letter: Health After 50.*

Beware: Bifocal and Multifocal Glasses and Contacts Increase Risk for Dangerous Falls

Stephen Lord, PhD, senior principal research fellow, Falls and Balance Research Group, Prince of Wales Medical Research Institute, University of New South Wales, Sydney, Australia.

Could it be that the glasses meant to help you see better actually put you in danger of a potentially fatal or disabling accident? It could, according to findings that have linked bifocals and trifocals with an increased likelihood of falls in older adults.

WHAT'S THE PROBLEM?

It's not hard to see the root of the danger. The common vision problem called presbyopia, caused by a hardening of the lens of the eye, typically arises around age 40. Presbyopia makes it more difficult to see images close at hand, which is why middle-aged people have difficulty reading without glasses. If this is your only vision problem, the solution is easy—to read, you wear glasses that magnify. But for those with additional vision problems that also need correction, the usual solution is multifocal glasses or contact lenses (bifocals, trifocals or progressive lenses)—and this is where people, quite literally, run into trouble.

A growing body of research, much of it originating at the Falls and Balance Research Group at the Prince of Wales Medical Research Institute in Sydney, Australia, has demonstrated that when older folks wear multifocal lenses while walking and also performing a secondary task—like reading a sign—they tend to "contact more obstacles" (as in, trip or bump into something). The glasses focus differently for near and far, which means that the wearer's ability to see obstacles near his/her feet gets compromised. The fact that falls are the leading cause of death from injury among older adults in the US makes this especially worrisome.

A SIMPLE SOLUTION

There's an easy solution to this problem. People who wear multifocal glasses or contact lenses should also keep with them a pair of single-focal glasses—with a prescription for distance vision only—to wear when walking outside their homes. Easy enough and worth doing, I think—far better to spend the money on an additional pair of glasses than on a ride in an ambulance.

Keep an Eye on Pets Below

Pets cause more than 86,000 people to fall and injure themselves each year. The main causes are tripping over the animals or being pulled or pushed by them. Dogs are responsible for 88% of the injuries, and often the most severe ones. Most accidents occur in the home. Children age 14 and younger and adults ages 35 to 54 are the most likely to get hurt.

Self-defense: Be aware of fall hazards caused by pets, and have dogs professionally trained.

Centers for Disease Control and Prevention, Atlanta.

Stress Could Trigger Falls

In a new study, about one-third of nearly 5,000 men over age 65 who had experienced at least one stressful event, such as the death of a loved one or serious financial problems, fell significantly more often within the following year than those who didn't have a life shock.

Possible reason: Stress may trigger negative neurohormonal responses, which could affect balance and vision.

If you have had a life shock within the past year: Talk to your doctor about ways to reduce your risk for falls.

Howard Fink, MD, MPH, staff physician, Minneapolis VA Medical Center.

Hearing Loss Increases Risk for Falls

Researchers tested the hearing of 2,017 adults (ages 40 to 69) and asked them about recent falls.

Finding: Those with even mild hearing loss were three times more likely to have fallen within the previous year than those with normal hearing. Each 10-decibel loss of hearing raised risk of falling 1.4-fold.

Theory: Hearing loss may overwork the brain, leaving fewer resources to maintain gait and balance.

Frank R. Lin, MD, PhD, assistant professor of otolaryngology and epidemiology, The Johns Hopkins University, Baltimore.

Walkers and Canes Can Cause Serious Injury

Walkers and canes can cause serious falls, a recent study warns. An average of 129 Americans age 65 and older are treated in emergency rooms every day for injuries from falls involving these devices.

Example: Many people tripped over their walkers or canes while moving about.

Important: Learn how to use your walker or cane properly. Be carefully fitted for it and thoroughly trained in its use by a physical therapist or an occupational therapist.

Judy A. Stevens, PhD, senior epidemiologist, National Center for Injury Prevention and Control, Centers for Disease Control and Prevention, Atlanta, CDC.gov.

Urinary Problems a Hidden Fall Danger

In a recent four-year study of 5,872 men (age 65 or older), those who reported moderate lower urinary tract problems, such as urgency to urinate or urinary frequency, were 21% more likely to fall at least twice within a one-year period than those without urinary problems.

Theory: Falls may occur when a man is rushing to the bathroom—during the day or at night.

If you have urinary tract symptoms: Ask your doctor about treatment.

J. Kellogg Parsons, MD, assistant professor of surgery, Cancer Prevention & Control Program, Moores Cancer Center, University of California, San Diego.

Falls More Likely for Sleep-Deprived Women Over 70

A new study shows that women over age 70 who get five hours of sleep or less on a regular basis are 47% more likely to fall than those women who get seven to eight hours of sleep. Talk to your doctor if you have trouble getting enough sleep—there are several treatment options, including medication and environmental changes, such as darkening the room, eliminating noise, etc.

Katie L. Stone, principal investigator, California Pacific Medical Center Research Institute, San Francisco.

Better Antidepressant Choice for Older Adults

Researchers analyzed the use of antidepressants in 60,746 depression patients (age 65 and older).

Result: Those who took selective serotonin reuptake inhibitors (SSRIs), such as *citalopram* (Celexa), were at increased risk for several adverse events (including death, stroke, falls and fractures) compared with those who took older tricyclic antidepressants (TCAs), such as *amitriptyline.*

If you're 65 or older and your doctor prescribes an SSRI: Be sure to ask about the risks and benefits—and discuss perhaps taking a lower dose.

Carol Coupland, PhD, associate professor, medical statistics, The University of Nottingham, UK.

"Test" Your Flexibility and Balance...Plus Easy Fixes

Marilyn Moffat, PhD, PT, a professor of physical therapy at New York University in New York City and a former president of the American Physical Therapy Association. She is coauthor of *Age-Defying Fitness.*

We all know that exercise is good for us, but some ways of exercising are particularly effective...and they don't require time-consuming maneuvers or expensive equipment.

Are you out of breath after walking up a flight of stairs? Do you feel discomfort or pain when looking over your shoulder as you back up a car? Is it becoming difficult to reach the top shelves of closets? Or after having sat through a movie, do you feel pain or stiffness when you stand up? Any "yes" answer means that exercise would be especially beneficial for you.

TO INCREASE FLEXIBILITY

Test: Put one arm over your shoulder, and reach behind your back. Then bring your other arm up behind your back, and try to touch the fingers of the hand that went over your shoulder.

Goal: To increase the flexibility of your arms, especially your shoulders.

Exercise: The "test" is also an exercise. Perform it several times a day, holding the stretch 30 seconds, then reversing your arms. Soon your fingers will easily touch. At that point, it's OK to reduce the frequency until you reach a level where you can consistently touch fingers.

Exercise for lower back and hamstring muscles: Sit toward the front of a chair with one leg stretched out straight with toes pulled toward you, and the other leg bent to a right angle at the hip and knee. With one hand on top of the other, reach your hands toward the toes of the straight leg.

Important: If you have osteoporosis or have had an upper-back fracture, do not do this exercise.

FOR BETTER POSTURE

Test: Stand with your back as flush as possible against a wall and both heels touching it. When you're in that position, does your head easily touch the wall? If it doesn't, you could use some work on posture, which can be vital to overall physical health.

Goal: To improve posture as quickly as possible.

Exercise: Once or twice daily, sit in a supportive chair, chin tucked in toward your chest. Breathe in as you bend your elbows at your sides and close your fingers in a relaxed fist. Gently press your elbows back into the chair. Stay in that position for 10 seconds as you continue to breathe deeply. Do not move. Breathe in again as you release the position slowly. Begin with three repetitions and build to 10 or 20.

Once your head effortlessly touches a wall when you stand against it, you'll know that your posture has improved. At that point, reduce the number of times you perform the exercise.

By experimenting with the frequency of the exercise, you can determine how many times you need to do it in order to maintain good posture. Keep in mind, however, that as you age, the number of times required will nearly always increase slightly from year to year.

FOR MORE STRENGTH

Test: In 30 seconds, how many times can you stand up from and sit down in a chair with your arms crossed on your chest?

Goal: Women between the ages of 60 and 64 should be able to stand and sit 12 to 17 times in 30 seconds. Men of that age should be able to perform the task 15 to 20 times. The benchmark drops slightly as your age increases.

Exercise: Perform the test two or three times a day until you can easily stand and sit within the benchmark range. Then do the exercise once every other day to keep in shape.

Also helpful: Unless you have problems with your hips and knees, walk up and down a flight of stairs two or three more times a day than you normally would.

To strengthen the arms, weighted dumbbells may be used. You should seek the guidance of a physical therapist before you start any weight training so that you perform the motions correctly and also use the correct amount of weight. An alternative to using weights is using elastic bands that can be cut into appropriate lengths for both arm and leg exercises. (See my book *Age-Defying Fitness* for many exercises with weights and elastic bands.)

Advantages of elastic bands: Unlike weights, there's no danger in dropping an elastic band when you exercise. Also, you can easily take an elastic strip with you when you travel.

Thera-Band strips, about six inches wide, are available from many retailers that sell exercise equipment and from distributors (800-321-2135, *thera-band.com*).

Price: About $50 for 25 yards.

How to do it: Run the elastic band under the seat of an armless chair from side to side. Sit in the chair, and hold one end of the band in each hand. Then raise your arms high over your head, stretching the band as you do so and also breathing out. Cut the Thera-Band strip to a length that lets you perform a set of eight to 12 stretches before tiring. Perform one or two sets of these exercises three times a week.

FOR BETTER BALANCE

Test: Cross your arms on your chest, then see how long you can stand on one leg. Then test the other leg.

Goal: To remain standing for at least 30 seconds. If you can't, your balance needs improving.

Exercise: Hold on to the counter with one hand and stand on your toes. Then, bend one knee back so that you're standing on your toes with one leg. After doing it only a few times, you may not need to hold on to the counter with your hand. Also try to rise up and down on your toes five to 10 times while standing on one leg.

TO INCREASE ENDURANCE

Test: Assuming that you do not have any heart or lung problems, try to march in place for two minutes, bringing your knees about halfway up to the level of your hips. Count only the number of times you bring your right knee up.

Goal: In two minutes, women ages 60 to 64 should be able to bring up the right knee between 75 and 107 times. For men of that age, the benchmark is between 87 and 115 times.

Exercise: March in place several times a week, slowly increasing the number of steps you take in each two-minute period. Traditional exercises, such as walking, running and bicycling, are also effective in building up endurance. Or use a treadmill or stationary bike. Whatever your choice of endurance exercise, you should gradually build up to 30 to 45 minutes each session anywhere from three to seven days a week.

GETTING STARTED

Note: If you're new to exercise, consult a physical therapist who will guide you through an appropriate exercise program. If you have heart, blood pressure or lung problems, also consult your physician before starting the program. To find a physical therapist, contact the American Physical Therapy Association (800-999-2782, *www.apta.org*) or contact your state's physical therapy association.

Fix Your Footwear, Protect Yourself from Falls

Hylton Menz, PhD, deputy director of the Musculoskeletal Research Center at La Trobe University in Victoria, Australia. Currently a Fulbright Senior Scholar at the Institute for Aging Research at Harvard Medical School in Boston, he is the author of the textbook *Foot Problems in Older People: Assessment and Management.*

Each year, about one in every three people over age 65 suffers a fall, a mishap that is far more dangerous than most people realize.

Important new research: In a 20-year study of nearly 5,600 women ages 70 and older, breaking a hip doubled the risk for death in the following year. Men who suffer a broken hip after a fall are also at increased risk for an untimely death.

Most people know the standard recommendations to reduce their risk for falls—get medical attention for balance and vision problems…improve the lighting in and around their homes…and eliminate loose carpets, cords and other obstacles.

What often gets overlooked: Painful feet…foot deformities such as bunions…weak foot and ankle muscles…and improper footwear also can significantly increase one's risk for falls.

Recent scientific evidence: In a 2011 study in the *British Medical Journal*, a comprehensive program of foot care reduced falls by one-third among a group of older people with assorted foot problems.

GET A FIRM FOUNDATION

With age, the muscles that support our ankles and feet often become weak—a common problem that contributes to foot pain and reduced activity levels. Structural abnormalities in the feet, such as bunions and hammertoes, undermine stability. And conditions that blunt sensations in the feet, such as nerve damage commonly caused by diabetes, may impair the ability of one's feet to react quickly and adjust to potentially hazardous conditions.

BASIC FALL-PREVENTION WORKOUT

Stretching and strengthening exercises can reduce foot pain—and lower your risk for falls. *Basic exercises to perform daily...*

To increase your ankles' range of motion: Sit in a chair with one knee extended. Rotate your foot in a clockwise, then counterclockwise direction. Repeat 10 times with each foot, in each direction.

To strengthen your toe muscles: Place small stones or marbles on the floor in front of you. While seated, pick up the stones with your bare toes and place them in a box, one by one. Pick up 20 stones with each foot, then repeat.

To stretch your calf muscles: Stand about two feet from a wall, then lean into it with one leg slightly bent at the knee about three inches in front of the other. Then reverse the position of your feet and lean forward to stretch the muscles of the other calf. Hold the stretch for 20 seconds, three times for each leg.

PROPER FOOTWEAR

The right shoes are essential for everyone, but especially those with problem feet.

Most women know to avoid high heels, which make it more difficult to maintain balance. But many people opt for flimsy slip-on footwear, such as flip-flops, which may be comfortable but often become loose or come off the foot altogether, creating a balance hazard. It's far better to wear shoes that fasten to your feet with laces, Velcro or buckled straps.

Surprising fact: Most people assume that thick, cushiony soles, such as those found on most sneakers, help prevent falls because they tend to provide good support for your feet. But thinner, harder soles, such as those on some walking shoes, are safer because thin-soled shoes allow your feet to feel the sensations that help you maintain balance. A trade-off between comfort and safety may be necessary—you may have to wear less cushiony shoes that optimize balance.

Also, be sure that your shoes are the right size. Your feet may slide around in shoes that are too loose, while tight footwear won't allow your toes to respond to variations in the ground to help maintain stability while walking.

Remember: Shoe size often changes with age, as feet swell and spread. So have your feet measured every time you buy shoes.

Slightly more falls occur indoors than outdoors, and the proportion increases with age. Therefore, even when you're at home, proper footwear is crucial.

Important recent finding: When researchers at Harvard's Institute for Aging Research followed a group of older adults for more than two years, they found that more than half of those who fell indoors were barefoot, in their stocking feet or wearing slippers. These injuries tended to be more serious than those of people who were wearing shoes when they fell.

Best to wear at home: Sturdy, thin-soled shoes that have more structural integrity than the average slipper.

DO YOU NEED ORTHOTICS?

Many adults over age 65 could benefit from wearing orthotics—inserts that fit inside the shoe—to help prevent falls by providing additional support.

Properly made orthotics may improve the way your feet move as you walk, distribute your weight more broadly to reduce pressure on sensitive spots and help convey sensory information to your feet, all of which may lessen the risk for falls.

If you have structural foot problems due to diabetes or rheumatoid arthritis, you may need customized orthotics from a podiatrist.

Typical cost: About $400. Insurance coverage varies. But over-the-counter versions (made with firm material, not just a soft cushion) may work as well if your feet are relatively normal and your foot pain is fairly mild. Good brands include Vasyli and Langer. Usually, you will be able to transfer orthotics between shoes.

Most people find that full-length orthotics are less likely to slip inside the shoe than the half-length variety. Full-length orthotics also may feel more comfortable, especially if you have corns or calluses under the toes or on the ball of your foot.

GETTING HELP

If you have foot problems, seek care from a podiatrist or other health professional—and be sure to mention any concerns about falling. Also ask for exercises, in addition to the ones described here, to address your specific foot issues.

Catch Your Balance Problem Before It's Too Late

Jason Jackson, MSPT, a physical therapist in the outpatient rehabilitation department at Mount Sinai Hospital in New York City, where he specializes in balance training, along with prosthetic training, manual therapy and neuromuscular disease.

No one expects to get seriously injured—or even die—from a fall. But it happens all the time. And while older adults are at greatest risk for falls, there are no age requirements for taking a tumble.

Surprising statistic: Even among adults in their 30s, 40s and 50s, falls are the leading cause of nonfatal injuries (more than 3 million each year) that are treated in US hospital emergency departments. For adults age 65 and older, falls are the leading cause of fatal injuries.

Certain "fall hazards" are well known—electrical cords and area rugs…slippery floors…medications such as sleeping pills and blood pressure drugs…vision problems…and even poorly fitting shoes.

What often gets overlooked: Subtle changes in the neuromuscular system (the nervous system and muscles working together), which helps keep us upright. Regardless of your age, exercising and strengthening this system before you get unsteady (or fall) is one of the best steps you can take to protect your health. *Here's how…*

WHY OUR BALANCE SLIPS

Does your foot or ankle feel a little wobbly when you stand on one leg? Some of that is probably due to diminished strength and flexibility. After about age 40, we begin to lose roughly 1% of our muscle mass every year. As we age, we also become more sedentary and less flexible. These factors make the body less able to adapt to and correct a loss of balance.

The nervous system also gets less sensitive with age.

Example: Sensory receptors known as proprioceptors are found in the nerve endings of muscles, tendons, joints and the inner ear. These receptors make us aware of our bodies in space (proprioception) and can detect even the slightest variations in body positions and movements. But they don't work well in people who don't exercise them (see suggestions on next page)—and these people find it harder to keep their balance.

The other danger: Muscle weakness, even when it's slight, can lead to apprehension about losing your balance. You might then start to avoid physical activities that you feel are risky—walking on uneven pavement, for example. But avoiding such challenges to your balance actually accelerates both muscle and nervous system declines.

ARE YOU STEADY?

If you're afraid of falling or have a history of falls, a professional balance assessment, done by your doctor or a physical therapist, is the best way to find out how steady you are on your feet. *The assessment usually includes tests such as the following (don't try these tests on your own if you feel unsteady)…*

• **Sit-to-stand.** Sit in a straight-backed chair. If your balance and leg strength are good, you'll be able to stand up without pushing off with your hands.

• **Stand with your feet touching.** You should be able to hold this position for 15 seconds without any wobbling.

• **The nudge test.** Ask someone to gently push on your hip while you're in a normal stance. If you stagger or throw out your hands to catch yourself, your balance is questionable. If you start to fall, your balance needs improvement.

BOOST YOUR BALANCE

Balance, like strength and endurance, can be improved with simple workouts. Incorporate the exercises below into your daily routine—while at the grocery store, in the office, while watching TV, etc. Do them for about 15 minutes to 30 minutes a day, three to four days a week (daily if you have the time). *What to do…**

• **One-legged stands.** You don't have to set aside time to do this exercise. You simply stand on one leg as you go about your daily activities—while waiting in line, for example. Lift your foot about six inches to 12 inches off the floor to the front, side and back. Try to hold each position for about 15 seconds, then switch legs. This strengthens the muscles in the ankles, hips and knees—all of which play a key role in one's balance.

• **Heel raises.** This move is good for balance and strength. While standing, rise up on your toes as far as you can. Drop back to the starting position, then do it again. Try for 10 repetitions. You can make this exercise more difficult by holding weights. Start with three-pound weights, gradually increasing weight as you build tolerance.

FOR MORE BENEFITS

Once you have become comfortable with the exercises described earlier, you can up your game with the following to keep you even safer from falling…

• **Balance on a Bosu ball.** It's a rubberlike half-ball (about two feet in diameter) that you can use for dozens of at-home workouts, including balance and abdominal exercises.

Cost: About $100, on *amazon.com* and in some sporting-goods stores.

Example: With the flat side on the floor, start by standing with both feet on the ball. Your muscles and joints will make hundreds of small adjustments to keep you balanced. When you get better at it, try to stand on one leg on the ball. When you're really comfortable, have someone toss you a basketball or tennis ball while you maintain your balance.

JUST FOR FUN

You don't always need formal balance exercises. *Try this…*

• **Walk barefoot.** Most of us spend our days in well-padded shoes that minimize the

---

*Check with your doctor before beginning any exercise program.

"feedback" between our feet and the ground. Walking without shoes for at least a few minutes each day strengthens the intrinsic muscles in the feet and improves stability. If you prefer to wear socks, be sure to use nonslip varieties that have treads to avoid slipping on wood or tiled floors.

Also helpful: Minimalist walking/running shoes. They're made by most major footwear companies, such as New Balance, Adidas and Nike, as well as by Vivobarefoot. Because they have a minimal amount of heel cushioning and arch support, they give the same benefits as barefoot walking but with a little extra protection.

• **Do these exercises next to a stable object,** such as a countertop, if you feel unsteady. Also, they are more easily done while wearing shoes. When you feel comfortable doing these moves, you can perform them barefoot to add difficulty.

Functional Fitness: Easy-to-Do Moves That Keep You Young

Barbara Bushman, PhD, a professor in the department of kinesiology at Missouri State University in Springfield, a fellow of the American College of Sports Medicine (ACSM) and editor of *ACSM's Complete Guide to Fitness & Health.*

N eed to sit down to put on socks? That's a common sign of what happens as we age—balance, coordination and agility fade. Fortunately, we can boost those skills with simple moves that fit into the fancy-sounding category of neuromotor exercise training. The point is to reduce the risk for falls and injury and enhance "functional fitness," or the ability to go about our daily business.

Update: Newest guidelines from the American College of Sports Medicine (ACSM) recommend doing 20 to 30 minutes of neuromotor exercise training two or three days per week, for a total of about 60 minutes weekly.

Tai chi and yoga are good examples—but you don't need to take a class to become more functionally fit. "Lots of neuromotor exercises can be done at home. All it takes is a bit of creativity and some time," said Barbara Bushman, PhD, a professor in the department of kinesiology at Missouri State University and editor of *ACSM's Complete Guide to Fitness & Health*. Ideally, you'll add neuromotor activities to your existing workout regimen without sacrificing cardio, resistance training or stretching time.

As with any new exercise routine, get your doctor's OK first. Then try the activities below, starting with a minute or two per exercise and gradually increasing your time, Dr. Bushman recommended. Activities can be done in any order and spread throughout the day, if desired. If balance is a challenge, do the exercises while standing near a countertop or other sturdy object that you can grasp for support if necessary.

• **Box Step.** On the floor, line up half a dozen empty boxes of varying sizes, positioning them about 12 to 15 inches apart, then practice stepping up and over them.

As you improve: Increase the height and width of the boxes…step over the boxes sideways…or design your own more complex stepping pattern.

If you're a beginner: Skip the boxes and simply practice walking backward and shuffling from side to side.

• **Sock Stand.** Barefoot, stand on your right foot. Bending your left knee, lift your left foot and put on a sock without sitting or using any other support…then, left foot still lifted, remove the sock. Repeat several times, trying not to touch your left foot to the ground, then switch legs.

As you improve: Try putting on, tying and then removing a shoe as you stand on one leg.

If you're a beginner: Just practice standing on one leg for 20 to 30 seconds, then rest and repeat several times…then switch legs.

• **Chair Squat.** Stand in front of a sturdy chair, facing outward, and hold your arms straight out in front of you. Slowly bend your knees and stick your rear end out, lowering yourself toward the chair as if about to sit. Allow your rear end to touch the chair seat only very lightly—without resting—then slowly rise to standing again. Repeat. This activity builds strength as well as balance.

• **Paper Towel Tube Pickup.** Place the empty cardboard tube from a roll of paper towels on the floor about 12 inches in front of you. Stand on your right foot, lifting your left foot out behind you. Carefully lean forward, bending your right knee…reach down to pick up the roll…then stand up straight. Repeat several times without touching your left foot to the ground, then switch legs.

As you improve: Use a smaller object, such as a pencil, instead of the paper towel tube.

If you're a beginner: Standing on your right foot, lift your left foot slightly. With the toes of the left foot, touch the floor in front of you…then touch the floor to your left side…then touch the floor behind you. Repeat several times, then switch legs.

• **Ball Toss.** Sit or stand and toss a tennis ball repeatedly back and forth from one hand to the other.

As you improve: Toss the ball higher…hold your hands farther apart…use a larger, heavier ball (such as a softball)…and/or stand on one leg while you toss. Try not to drop the ball!

Better Balance for Parkinson's Patients

Dancing the tango improved balance and functional mobility in 40 Parkinson's patients who took twice-weekly classes for 12 weeks. Dancers also reported better cognitive function and less fatigue.

Why: The rhythmic forward-and-backward steps of the tango stimulate cognitive functioning and promote better balance.

Silvia Rios Romenets, MD, clinical research fellow, McGill University, Montreal, Canada.

Inner-Ear Dizziness Can Cause Balance Problems

Jack J. Wazen, MD, vice president and director of research, Silverstein Institute Ear Research Foundation, Sarasota, Florida.

Yuri Agrawal, MD, resident, department of otolaryngology-head and neck surgery, Johns Hopkins University School of Medicine, Baltimore.

I've begun to feel that I'm not walking quite as straight as I used to, and I sometimes sway a little when I'm standing still. What's going on?

You could have a balance disorder. The inner ear is the main organ of balance. The eyes and the proprioceptive system (components of muscles, joints and tendons) also send signals to the brain, which processes muscle coordination. A disruption in any one of these systems can cause a feeling of being off-balance. The risk increases with age, with the condition affecting 85% of people over age 80.

Common causes of inner-ear dizziness include infections of the middle or inner ear, fluid buildup in the middle ear and floating inner-ear calcium crystals. Other important causes include Ménière's disease, which can result from a fluid imbalance in the inner ear, and acoustic neuroma, a benign tumor on the auditory nerve. Vision changes, low blood pressure, medication side effects, low blood sugar and neurological disorders, such as multiple sclerosis, also can result in dizziness and lack of balance.

A neuro-otologist (a medical doctor who specializes in disorders of the ear) or an otolaryngologist (ear, nose and throat specialist) can evaluate your condition and recommend treatment, which may include antibiotics or diuretics. Your doctor may also refer you to physical therapy to improve balance and stability.

Best Tests for Osteoporosis (for Women and Men)

Felicia Cosman, MD, clinical director of the National Osteoporosis Foundation, NOF.org, and professor of clinical medicine at Helen Hayes Hospital in West Haverstraw, New York, an affiliate of Columbia University College of Physicians and Surgeons in New York City. She is the author of *What Your Doctor May Not Tell You About Osteoporosis.*

What you don't know could lead to a life-threatening bone fracture. By now, most people know that osteoporosis isn't just a female disorder. While one in two women over age 50 will experience a fracture related to the bone-thinning disease, as many as one in four men in this age group will as well.

This potentially debilitating disease is preventable and treatable—yet few people know all they should about the most effective screening methods for the disease.

Key facts for women and men...

SHOULD YOU BE SCREENED?

In women and men, bone loss occurs with age. In women, bone loss is accelerated by menopause (due to declines in estrogen levels).

The National Osteoporosis Foundation recommends that average-risk women be screened by age 65 and men by age 70. *But due to a number of factors that hasten bone loss, earlier testing is advisable (at menopause for women and age 50 for men)...*

•**Broken bones.** Screening is recommended when a fracture occurs for any reason—fractures that occur from falls are often misinterpreted as being related to trauma, when osteoporosis may play a role.

•**Medical history.** Diseases that can accelerate bone loss include diabetes, rheumatoid arthritis, inflammatory bowel disease, celiac disease and neurologic disorders (such as stroke or Parkinson's disease). These diseases may lead to the release of certain hormones, poor nutrition (low calcium and vitamin D) or a sedentary lifestyle, all of which promote bone loss.

•**Use of certain medications.** Oral cortico-steroids, such as prednisolone, and androgen deprivation drugs used by prostate cancer patients may lower bone mass substantially. Other medications that may cause bone loss include certain aromatase inhibitor drugs taken for breast cancer, such as *anastrozole* (Arimidex)…and some antidepressants, such as *fluoxetine* (Prozac).

People who are age 50 or older and are taking—or about to start taking—any of these medications should have a bone density test.

•**Low body weight or recent weight loss.** This is generally defined as a body mass index (weight to height ratio) of less than 20 or weight loss of 10% or more from healthy adult body weight over a period of months or years.*

•**Vitamin D insufficiency.** Only recently have doctors come to appreciate that vitamin D is at least as important as calcium in maintaining bone health. A blood test is used to measure vitamin D levels. For adults age 50 and older, the National Osteoporosis Foundation recommends 1,200 mg of calcium and 800 international units (IU) to 1,000 IU of vitamin D daily.

•**Lifestyle factors.** Smoking and excessive alcohol intake (more than two drinks a day for men and one for women) also cause bone loss.

MOST ACCURATE TESTING

The best bone test is dual-energy X-ray *absorptiometry* (DEXA or DXA), which uses minute amounts of radiation to measure bone density. The standard procedure, central DXA (cDXA), measures the lower spine, hip and narrowest part of the hip bone (the femoral neck).

What it involves: While you are clothed and lying on your back on a table, a machine takes images of your spine, hip and femoral neck. The test lasts about five minutes, costs about $80 and is virtually risk-free.

If you have osteoporosis or are at risk: Get tested every one to two years. If an initial screening shows that your bones are well preserved, get tested every two to four years.

*To calculate your body mass index, go to the website of the National Heart, Lung and Blood Institute, *nhlbi.nih.gov*, and search "BMI calculator."

Most insurers cover the cost of cDXA when it is ordered by a doctor.

Results of cDXA testing give an accurate estimate of how likely you are to sustain a fracture of the hip or spine (the most common sites) or elsewhere in the body. Hip fractures, in particular, can be life-threatening—long-term immobility that occurs during recovery can allow pneumonia to develop or blood clots to form in the leg veins or lungs.

OTHER TESTS TO CONSIDER

When cDXA isn't readily available (the equipment is expensive), other options include…

•**Peripheral DXA (pDXA).** This test uses the same technology to examine bone density in the heel, wrist or finger. These measures are useful, but hip measurements are better—hip fracture is the most important fracture to try to prevent.

•**Quantitative ultrasound densitometry (QUD).** With this test, sound waves are used to estimate bone density in the heel, kneecap or shin. No radiation is used.

If either of these tests shows possible deficiencies, the results should be confirmed with cDXA, which is more accurate and reliable.

WHAT YOUR NUMBERS MEAN

Bone test results are usually expressed as a T-score, which compares your bone mineral density to someone with optimal bone density. What the results mean…

•**A score of -2.50 or lower means bone density is substantially below optimal (osteoporosis).** The risk for fracture is sufficiently high to require some sort of therapy, such as osteoporosis medication, including *alendronate* (Fosamax) or *risedronate* (Actonel). These drugs have been linked to an unusual thigh-bone fracture when used for an average of seven years. However, the drugs' benefits outweigh their risks for most osteoporosis patients.

•**BMD of -1.0 or higher is considered normal.**

•**Between -1.0 and -2.5 means "low bone mass" or osteopenia, which indicates high risk for osteoporosis.** How likely you are to suffer a fracture and whether you need treatment to prevent osteoporosis will depend on such factors as your personal medical history, family history, age and weight.

WHEN YOU'RE AT VERY HIGH RISK

If you're likely to have already had a spinal fracture due to certain other risk factors (such as advanced age—70 and older for women, and 80 and older for men...loss of height—1.6 inches from past height for women, and 2.4 inches from past height for men...and/or long-term steroid treatment—three or more months), your doctor may add a vertebral fracture assessment test.

This test identifies fractures in the spine (which often cause no symptoms). The test involves a closer examination of DXA pictures of the spine. Even small and previously unnoticed spinal fractures greatly increase the risk for additional fractures—in the spine and elsewhere.

Low Testosterone Can Cause Falls

Men with low testosterone are prone to falls.

Recent finding: Older men with the lowest levels of the hormone testosterone had a 40% greater risk of falling than those with the highest levels. It is too soon to say whether testosterone replacement would help prevent falls. Testosterone declines naturally with age. Older men can lower the risk of falling by increasing leg strength and coordination and by avoiding alcohol and sedatives, which may increase the risk of falls.

Eric Orwoll, MD, professor of medicine, associate vice president and associate dean for research, School of Medicine, Oregon Health & Science University, Portland. He is leader of a study of 2,587 men, published in *Archives of Internal Medicine*.

Guidelines on Bone Testing: What It Means

Bruce Ettinger, MD, an emeritus clinical professor of medicine at the University of California Medical Center, San Francisco, and an adjunct investigator in the Division of Research at Kaiser Permanente Medical Care Program for Northern California.

Guidelines from the US Preventive Services Task Force (USPSTF) recommend bone density testing for women age 65 and older as well as for "younger women whose fracture risk is equal to or greater than that of a 65-year-old white woman who has no additional risk factors." Confusing? *Here's some help...*

• **Women are at significantly higher risk than men for osteoporosis,** the disease that weakens bones and leads to fractures. Risk increases with age. The old USPSTF guidelines, set in 2002, recommended bone density testing to screen all women age 65 and older (that part has not changed), plus women ages 60 to 64 who were at increased risk for osteoporotic fractures. Those guidelines were recently revised to more specifically define the level of risk that merits bone density testing for the 60-to-64 age group and to address the needs of younger women by utilizing an updated online fracture risk assessment tool called FORE FRC. The FORE FRC closely aligns to the United States FRAX™ version 3.0 from the World Health Organization, with few exceptions.

• **FORE FRC prompts you to input your status with regard to various risk factors.** These include age...height and weight...ethnicity (since genetic influences put Caucasians at higher risk than Asians, Blacks or Hispanics)...alcohol and tobacco use...diseases or drugs that can affect bones...and personal and family history of fractures. Then the web-based program instantly calculates your 10-year probability of experiencing a fracture due to osteoporosis.

To use FORE: Visit *riskcalculator.fore.org/,* enter the pertinent information and answer simple yes/no questions. The calculator gives you two percentages. The main number to consider is your risk of having a fracture at any of the four major osteoporotic fracture sites—hip, spine, wrist or upper arm/shoulder—within the next 10 years. Once this risk reaches 9.3%, which is the risk level of a healthy 65-year-old white woman, bone density screening is recommended. (The other percentage given is your 10-year risk of fracturing a hip specifically. Hip fractures are singled out because they are the most serious of the osteoporotic fractures—but since these are rare before age 70 to 75, for younger women it is more useful to consider the combined risk at all four major sites.)

A fair number of women in their 50s do have a FRAX score higher than that of the hypothetical 65-year-old. Dr. Ettinger explained, "If you are 55 and you smoke, are thin and have a parent who had a hip fracture, then you're more like a typical 65-year-old in terms of osteoporosis risk."

Bottom line: If your major fracture site FRAX score is…

• **Below 9.3%**—continue to follow your doctor's recommendations on diet, exercise and lifestyle habits that protect bones… and complete the FRAX questionnaire again in three to five years. Fracture risk typically doubles every seven to eight years, Dr. Ettinger said, so you can estimate when in the future your score might cross the threshold for bone density testing.

• **9.3% or higher**—the recommendation is for your doctor to order a dual-energy X-ray absorptiometry (DEXA) test to measure your bone density. Those results can be entered into the FORE calculator to further refine your risk level. If your bone density is right at the expected level for your age, your score won't change much. But if your bone density is much lower than expected, this new factor could easily double your risk, Dr. Ettinger said. Your doctor will take this into account in determining the next appropriate step in your care.

Are Your Bone-Building Drugs Bad for You?

Harris H. McIlwain, MD, founder of the Tampa Medical Group and an adjunct professor at the University of South Florida College of Public Health, both in Tampa. He conducts clinical research on osteoporosis, arthritis and related conditions. Dr. McIlwain is coauthor of 26 books, including *Reversing Osteopenia* and *The Osteoporosis Cure*.

When bone-building medications known as bisphosphonates were introduced 17 years ago, they were hailed as near-miracle drugs for people with thinning bones. Studies showed that these drugs—first, *aldendronate* (Fosamax) and later, *risedronate* (Actonel), *ibandronate* (Boniva) and *zoledronic acid* (Reclast)—significantly reduced the incidence of hip and spine fractures in people with osteoporosis and osteopenia (bone loss that is less severe than osteoporosis).

Now: Despite the established benefits of bisphosphonates, the medications are increasingly coming under fire for having potentially serious side effects. For example, studies have shown that the drugs may increase risk for various conditions, such as breakage of the femur (thigh bone)…osteonecrosis (death of bone tissue) in the jaw…and even esophageal cancer. Two FDA advisory panels recently wrote in a report that, due to the potential risks associated with long-term use of bisphosphonates, bisphosphonate therapy could be safely discontinued in some cases—but did not specify when or for how long to discontinue the drug.

Studies on the safety of bisphosphonates are ongoing. Thus far, the research is mixed on the benefits of taking the drug for more than five years. For example, research has shown that women who took Fosamax for another five years (for a total of 10 years) had the same rate of femur fractures as those who took a placebo. The risk for spine fracture, however, was higher in the group taking a placebo.

FINDING THE BEST TREATMENT

The decision to take bisphosphonates (or any medication) requires balancing benefits against risks. People at high risk for fractures should not stop taking these medications but instead work with their doctors to determine the duration of treatment. This includes people who have had previous fractures or a family history of fractures…and those with rheumatoid arthritis, which can increase bone loss. Other high-risk individuals include those who take the corticosteroid prednisone for a chronic condition…women who weigh under 127 pounds…people who lead a sedentary lifestyle (weight-bearing exercise strengthens bones)…and smokers (their risk for bone loss is twice that of a nonsmoker).

Women and men who have a high risk for fracture but who have other health concerns may want to talk to their doctors about taking a nonbisphosphonate bone-strengthening medication. *Examples…*

•**Denosumab (Prolia),** a monoclonal antibody that reduces the body's bone-breakdown mechanism. If you have gastroesophageal reflux disease, this drug, which is delivered via an injection, may help you avoid the gastrointestinal side effects common with bisphosphonates. However, in a few rare cases, osteonecrosis of the jaw has been reported.

•**Teriparatide (Forteo),** a type of parathyroid hormone that builds bone. This injectable drug increases bone thickness, so if you have a history of periodontal disease, you may be better off with this drug.

HOW BONES AGE

Bones are living tissue in a constant state of flux. Children and teenagers generally produce more bone than they lose until they reach peak bone mass in their mid-20s. By the time women and men reach their early 30s, the amount of bone loss is about the same as the amount that is created.

After that, as estrogen levels start to decline in women, the rate of bone loss slowly begins to exceed the amount that is built. During menopause, when estrogen levels decline even more sharply, bone loss accelerates markedly. In fact, according to the National Osteoporosis Foundation, women can lose as much as 20% of their bone mass in the first five to seven years of menopause. Men in their 50s do not rapidly lose bone mass the way women do after menopause, but by age 65, men and women lose bone mass at the same rate.

KEYS TO BETTER BONE HEALTH

Women at low risk for fracture but who have osteopenia are the best candidates for discontinuing (or not starting) bisphosphonates, but they should talk to their health-care providers first to discuss benefits versus risks and continue having regular bone mineral density tests. *They should also talk to their doctors about the following steps to promote bone health…*

•**Eat a diet rich in calcium.** Calcium is the main mineral in bone. Low-fat dairy foods, such as skim milk, yogurt and cheese, are excellent sources of calcium. If you don't like dairy or are unable to tolerate it, try eating leafy greens, tofu, almonds and salmon. Aim to get 1,200 mg to 1,500 mg of calcium a day through a combination of diet and supplements.

Note: Also talk to your doctor about magnesium. Adequate levels of this mineral are needed for optimal calcium absorption.

•**Get your vitamin D through a combination of diet and supplements.** Fortified milk, salmon and cod-liver oil are good dietary sources of vitamin D. Talk to your doctor about getting a blood test to measure your vitamin D level (nearly half of people with osteoporosis have low vitamin D levels)…and about taking 1,000 international units (IU) of vitamin D a day to maintain a vitamin D blood level of 32 ng/mL or higher.

•**Don't forget vitamin K.** It helps the bones absorb calcium. Aim for 65 micrograms (mcg) to 80 mcg a day. Good sources include leafy greens, broccoli, beef liver and soybean oil. Vitamin K is also available in supplement form.

Do 30 minutes of weight-bearing exercise every day, such as walking, hiking, yoga, tai chi or jogging, to stimulate the body to produce new bone. If it's been awhile since you exercised, start slowly and work your way up to a half hour a day.

•**Add back exercises.** Back exercises typically involve strengthening the abdominal (core) muscles, which support the spine.

• **Ask your doctor about strontium.** Strontium is a natural element that is prescribed in Europe for osteoporosis. It works by slowing bone resorption and increasing bone production. Strontium supplements are available at health-food stores. Ask your doctor what dosage of strontium would be best for you.

Men Get Osteoporosis, Too!

Up to one in four men over age 50 will break a bone due to osteoporosis.

Problem: A recent analysis that looked at 439 patients' medical records found that men are less likely than women to be screened for osteoporosis and far less likely to be treated for the condition after a fracture.

Why it matters: Treating the fracture but not the underlying cause puts patients at risk for future breaks.

Tamara D. Rozental, MD, associate professor of orthopedic surgery, Harvard Medical School, Boston.

Hidden Bone Loss Danger

Low bone density is known to boost fracture risk, but a recent study shows that it also impairs balance and hearing. Participants age 65 and older with low bone density were almost four times more likely (and those 40 and older twice as likely) to fail a balance test than those with normal density.

Explanation: Bone loss affects the entire body, including bones in the skull that house the organs for balance and hearing.

Angelico Mendy, MD, MPH, researcher in epidemiology, The University of Iowa College of Public Health, Iowa City.

Way Beyond Calcium: Minerals Your Bones Need Most

Mao Shing Ni, PhD, DOM (doctor of oriental medicine), LAc (licensed acupuncturist), is chancellor and cofounder of Yo San University in Los Angeles and codirector of Tao of Wellness, an acupuncture and Chinese medicine clinic in Santa Monica, California. He is author of *Secrets of Longevity: Hundreds of Ways to Live to Be 100.* TaoOfWellness.com

A recent study has us worried that getting too much calcium from supplements increases our risk for heart attacks. That's why many of us are cutting back on calcium supplements to protect our hearts… and, hopefully, boosting our consumption of calcium-rich foods (which are not linked to cardiovascular problems), such as dairy products and dark green leafy vegetables, to protect our bones.

But: This makes it more important than ever to guard against osteoporosis. An excellent strategy, according to Mao Shing Ni, PhD, DOM, LAc, author of *Second Spring: Dr. Mao's Hundreds of Natural Secrets for Women to Revitalize and Regenerate at Any Age,* is to be sure to get enough of four other essential, yet less familiar, minerals that our bones need to stay strong. These minerals are especially vital for women given that we are four times more likely than men to develop osteoporosis.

The ideal way to get these minerals is through food because foods contain complementary components that enhance nutrient absorption, Dr. Mao said. For a mineral-rich, bone-building diet, follow the guidelines below. For serving sizes, see "Amounts that constitute one serving of…" at the end of this article.

Boron helps the body use calcium, vitamin D and other nutrients vital to bone formation.

Be sure to eat: At least three servings per day of nuts (almonds, hazelnuts, peanuts) or nut butters…or fruits (apples, avocados, bananas, grapes, oranges, pears, tangelos).

Added boost: Dried fruits are especially rich in boron—but don't overdo it on these, as they also are high in sugar. Onions are another good source.

Manganese is essential for the proper formation and maintenance of bone, cartilage and connective tissue.

Be sure to eat: Two or more daily servings of legumes (chickpeas, lentils, lima beans)... nuts (chestnuts, hazelnuts, pecans, pine nuts)...or whole grains (barley, brown rice, bulgur, couscous, oats).

Added boost: For extra manganese, have some pineapple, blackberries, raspberries or strawberries.

Silicon assists calcium with bone growth and increases collagen, the protein component of bones. A study published in the *Journal of Bone and Mineral Research* showed that silicon was particularly helpful for premenopausal women.

Be sure to eat: Four or more servings per week of whole grains (barley, brown rice, oats)...or fruits (apples, bananas, cherries, grapes, mangoes, pineapples, plums).

Added boost: Silicon also is found in cabbage, celery, cucumbers, green beans and tofu.

Zinc produces enzymes that recycle worn-out portions of bone protein and help heal injured bones.

Be sure to eat: Two servings a week of shellfish (crabs, lobster, oysters)...lean meat (beef, lamb, pork, veal)...poultry (chicken, duck, turkey)...legumes (black-eyed peas, chickpeas, lentils, lima beans, navy beans)...or seeds (pumpkin, sesame, squash, sunflower).

Added boost: Other good sources include barley, bulgur, cashews, pine nuts, ricotta cheese and yogurt.

Amounts that constitute one serving of...

•*Fish, meat, poultry or a soy product:* Three to four ounces.

•*Cooked grains or whole-grain cereal:* One-half cup...or one slice of whole-grain bread.

•*Chopped raw or cooked vegetables or legumes:* One-half cup.

•*Fruit:* One whole small fruit...one-half cup of berries or diced fruit...or one-quarter cup of dried fruit.

•*Nuts or seeds:* Two ounces...or one tablespoon of peanut butter or other nut butter.

How Much Vitamin D Do Bones Need? Probably More Than You Think

Bess Dawson-Hughes, MD, director of the Bone Metabolism Laboratory at the Jean Mayer USDA Human Nutrition Research Center on Aging at Tufts University in Boston and coauthor of an article on vitamin D supplementation and fracture risk in *The New England Journal of Medicine*.

The Institute of Medicine currently recommends getting 600 IU of vitamin D daily for most Americans and 800 IU for those over age 70. But a huge recent study suggests that those levels are still too low to keep our bones from breaking as we age.

Researchers pooled data from 11 clinical trials involving a total of 31,022 seniors ages 65 and up, 91% of whom were women. The trials focused on the effects of vitamin D supplements taken with or without calcium. Rather than looking at how much vitamin D participants were given as part of a study, as is typically done, the researchers zeroed in on how much vitamin D people actually did take. Based on that, participants were divided into four groups, or quartiles, ranging from the highest to the lowest levels of actual vitamin D intake.

Findings: In the highest quartile, vitamin D supplementation averaged 800 IU (and ranged from 792 IU to 2,000 IU) per day. People in this quartile were 30% less likely to break a hip and 14% less likely to suffer a nonvertebral fracture, such as in a wrist or forearm, than people in all of the other quartiles. In fact, the results showed no benefit in terms of fracture prevention from taking less than 800 IU daily.

Take-home message: Talk to your doctor about supplementing with at least 800 IU of vitamin D daily. (Note that many multivitamins provide only 400 IU of vitamin D.) But don't fall into a "lots more is lots better" mind-set— the evidence for benefit from higher doses is not there yet, researchers said…and excessive vitamin D can lead to high blood levels of calcium, which can cause kidney damage and blood vessel calcification.

Potassium—The Mineral Calcium Needs to Keep Your Bones Strong

Janet Brill, PhD, RDN, dietitian and fitness expert, Allentown, Pennsylvania. She is author of *Blood Pressure Down: The 10-Step Plan to Lower Your Blood Pressure in 4 Weeks Without Prescription Drugs* and *Cholesterol Down: Take Control of Your Cholesterol—Without Drugs.* DrJanet.com

You've probably been led to believe that if you just drink enough milk, eat enough yogurt and cheese, get some broccoli and maybe take a calcium supplement, you will be assured of having healthy bones that are resistant to osteoporosis. Wrong! The truth is, if you're not getting enough of another essential nutrient, potassium, you won't get the benefit from all that calcium. *Here's how to make sure you get the amount of potassium you really need for healthy bones…*

IT'S NOT ABOUT CALCIUM ANYMORE

With all the constant hoopla about calcium, you would never guess that numerous studies have shown that potassium is just as important for bone health. So why does calcium get all the publicity? Maybe even doctors don't realize how important potassium is…and maybe the supplement industry is just too hooked on its calcium profits to put the spotlight somewhere else. But the fact is, a lot of people who think they're doing good for their bones are consuming too little potassium. And their bones are suffering for it.

Strong proof of the importance of potassium: Researchers recently analyzed 14 high-quality studies on the effects of potassium supplements on bone health and found that people who had higher intakes of potassium excreted less calcium in their urine and had markers in their blood that showed less bone loss. The reason? Potassium aids calcium absorption.

Thus, diets higher in potassium might be a way to improve bone strength and help prevent bone weakening and osteoporosis.

Potassium has been shown to slow down a process called bone resorption, which happens in our bodies all the time as a natural process. In the bone-resorption process, small cells called osteoclasts break down bone to make room for new bone growth. However, as we age, new bone formation slows down and can be outpaced by bone resorption. The result is thin and brittle bones that can easily fracture.

High intake of potassium has been shown to significantly reduce the excretion of calcium in the urine. Furthermore, potassium neutralizes the excess acid from the metabolism of a heavy meat-eating diet.

Aim to get 4,700 milligrams (mg) of potassium a day, an amount in line with the recommendation of the Institute of Medicine of the National Academy of Sciences, which helps set US health policy. Stay away from potassium supplements, which do not deliver nutrition as efficiently as nutrition-rich food. Besides, potassium supplements can cause intestinal problems such as diarrhea, stomach upset and flatulence in some people.

And people on diuretics or other blood pressure medications and those with kidney disease need to be extra cautious about potassium supplementation. Certain diuretics, such as Aldactone, Midamor and Dyrenium, and many other blood pressure medications, such as Avapro, Cozaar, Diovan and Vasotec, and also NSAIDs, when taken with potassium supplements can lead to potassium excess in the body. This condition, called hyperkalemia, can cause symptoms of tingling extremities, muscle weakness or irregular heart beat that can result in cardiac arrest. If you're taking any medication, particularly the ones mentioned above, it is strongly advised that you don't take a potassium supplement without first consulting an MD or a naturopathic doctor.

FINDING POTASSIUM IN YOUR FOOD

So where does safe, natural potassium come from? Think 'P' for potassium and produce.

Of course not all produce is created equal. Some is more chock-full of potassium than others. In addition to the best-known potassium sources—bananas and white potatoes—a "hot list" of high-potassium foods might include spinach, kale, beet greens (and other dark, leafy green vegetables), cantaloupe, kidney beans and avocado.

Also recommended: Low-sodium V-8 juice, a cup of which offers 820 mg of potassium. If you eat at least eight servings of such foods each day, you'll be sure to reach your 4,700 mg of potassium quite easily.

And if you would like a mouthwatering, potassium-rich dinner recipe for inspiration, check out this salmon dish from *Blood Pressure Down*. *It packs about 2,000 mg of potassium per serving…*

OVEN-ROASTED SALMON WITH POTATOES AND TOMATOES

This recipe serves four. *The ingredients you'll need are…*

Four 6-ounce salmon fillets (you can substitute cod, which contains about the same amount of potassium as salmon)
3 tablespoons olive oil, divided
1 teaspoon salt-free seasoning blend
½ teaspoon freshly ground black pepper
2 pounds small red potatoes, washed and quartered
4 cloves garlic, peeled and halved
½ teaspoon dried rosemary
½ teaspoon dried thyme
2 cups grape tomatoes, halved
Juice of one lemon plus extra slices of lemon to squeeze to taste on the finished dish
¼ cup minced parsley

Preheat oven to 450°F. Drizzle the salmon with one tablespoon olive oil and sprinkle with salt and pepper. Refrigerate until ready to use.

On a rimmed baking sheet, toss potatoes with garlic, rosemary, thyme, salt-free seasoning blend, pepper and the remaining two tablespoons olive oil. Turn cut sides of the potatoes down. Bake for about 20 minutes, just until the potatoes start to brown. Remove baking sheet from the oven. Add the tomatoes to the potatoes, and push them to the side to make room for the salmon fillets. Return the pan to the oven, and bake until the fish is cooked through and the potatoes are brown and tender…about 20 minutes. Remove from the oven, transfer to plates, sprinkle with fresh chopped parsley and drizzle with lemon juice.

Vitamin K Strengthens Bones

Vitamin K strengthens bones. Older people who consumed the most broccoli, spinach and other leafy green vegetables rich in vitamin K had higher bone mineral density than those who consumed the least vitamin K. Supplements of vitamin K also improve bone quality, but it is best to get the vitamin from food sources, which have other nutrients as well.

Caution: If you are taking a blood-thinning medication, such as warfarin, talk to your doctor before increasing your intake of vitamin K.

Study of 365 people by researchers at Universitat Rovira i Virgili, Reus, Spain, published in *Bone*.

DHEA Supplements Build Better Bones

Older women (not men) who supplemented daily with the hormone dehydroepiandrosterone (DHEA) plus calcium and vitamin D had a 4% average increase in spinal bone density after two years—enough to reduce spinal fracture risk by up to 50%. Women who took only calcium and vitamin D had no bone density increase. Ask your doctor about taking 50 mg of DHEA daily. Avoid DHEA if you have a history of breast or endometrial cancer.

Edward Weiss, PhD, associate professor of nutrition and dietetics, Doisy College of Health Sciences, Saint Louis University.

Prunes Help Prevent Osteoporosis

As we age, our bones break down faster than they are built. Prunes suppress the rate at which people's bones break down.

Recent finding: Women who ate about 10 prunes per day for 12 months had higher bone mineral density than women who ate dried apples. These women also took 500 milligrams of calcium and 400 international units of vitamin D daily.

Bahram H. Arjmandi, PhD, RD, chair, department of nutrition, food and exercise sciences, The Florida State University, Tallahassee, and leader of a study published in *British Journal of Nutrition*.

Soy Helps Strengthen Bones

Genistein, a compound in soy, increases bone mineral density and strengthens bones. Genistein resembles the bone-protecting hormone estrogen, which declines after menopause. The FDA recommends that women get 25 grams of soy protein per day.

Best sources: Tofu, soy milk and tempeh.

Caution: Women at risk for endometrial or breast cancer should talk to their doctors before increasing soy intake.

Francesco Squadrito, MD, professor of pharmacology, University of Messina, Italy, and researcher in a study of 389 women, published in *Annals of Internal Medicine*.

Ice Cream Can Hurt Your Bones

Cream and products made from cream are linked to lower overall bone mineral density (BMD) and increased risk for bone fractures.

Reason: Cream is surprisingly low in calcium and vitamin D.

Better choices: Milk and yogurt, both of which improve BMD.

Study of 3,212 people by researchers from Institute for Aging Research at Hebrew SeniorLife, the largest elder-care provider in the Boston area, published in *Archives of Osteoporosis*.

Stop Flushing Your Calcium Down the Drain

Elson M. Haas, MD, founder and director of the Preventive Medical Center of Marin in San Rafael, California. He also is the author of numerous books, including *Staying Healthy with Nutrition: The Complete Guide to Diet and Nutritional Medicine*. PMCMarin.com

Are you conscientiously eating calcium-rich foods and following your doctor's orders about calcium supplement use? That's good—but not good enough to ensure that your bones benefit.

Reason: Some foods contain substances that interfere with calcium absorption, so whatever else you eat along with your calcium influences how much of the mineral goes to your bones...and how much literally gets flushed away when you go to the bathroom.

To tip this balance in your favor, it helps to allow a few hours to elapse between eating the foods that you rely on for calcium and eating the types of foods that reduce calcium absorption, So just what kinds of foods are we talking about?

Calcium-rich foods: These include beans (great northern, navy, white)...Chinese cabbage...dairy products...fortified cereals...leafy greens (beet greens, collards, dandelion greens, kale, turnip greens)...nuts...okra...rice...seafood (crab, salmon, ocean perch, sardines, shrimp)...seeds...and soy products.

Here's what interferes with calcium...

• **Sodium.** When you eat too much sodium, the excess is excreted in your urine—but when that sodium leaves your body, it drags calcium with it.

Best: Limit daily consumption of sodium to no more than 2,300 mg or about the amount in one teaspoon of salt. What if you do go overboard on salt? Potassium helps limit sodium-induced calcium excretion, so have a high-potassium food (banana, cantaloupe) with your calcium.

● **Caffeine.** Do you often have calcium-rich yogurt for breakfast or take your calcium pill with your morning meal—then wash it down with a big mug of coffee or tea? Caffeine from any source works against strong bones by interfering with calcium absorption and causing more of the mineral to be lost through the urine.

Better: Have your morning yogurt with a glass of orange juice instead, since its vitamin C and magnesium improve calcium absorption…or take your supplement in the afternoon or evening, after you've finished drinking coffee for the day.

● **Phytates.** Found in high-fiber foods such as berries, corn, nuts, oatmeal, rye and especially wheat bran, phytates are substances that bind calcium, reducing its absorption. Fiber-rich foods have many health benefits, so of course you don't want to shun them…but if you're increasing your fiber intake (for instance, to help regulate digestion), be sure to increase your calcium intake, too.

● **Phosphorus.** This mineral, which is plentiful in meat and poultry, has many important functions in the body. But for proper bone density, a delicate balance must be maintained between phosphorus and calcium—which means that as phosphorus intake increases, the need for calcium increases, too.

Problem: Ideally, people should eat more calcium than phosphorus, but the typical meat-focused Western diet contains roughly two to four times more phosphorus than calcium. Also, because both phosphorus and calcium require vitamin D for absorption, phosphorus-rich foods compete with calcium-rich foods for the available vitamin D.

Bone smart: Ask your doctor about supplementing with vitamin D. Also, cut back on

meat and focus more on plant foods…and be aware that carbonated beverages such as colas have as much as 500 mg of phosphorus in one serving—so say "so long" to soda.

Nighttime note: Has your doctor recommended calcium supplements? Choose a brand that also includes magnesium for maximum absorption…and take half of your daily dose at bedtime, Dr. Haas suggested—it may even help you relax and sleep better.

Running Good for Bones

Running is more effective for building bones and lowering risk for osteoporosis than weight lifting or cycling.

Reason: The impact of a runner's feet hitting the ground stimulates bones to grow stronger.

Pam Hinton, PhD, associate professor, department of nutrition and exercise physiology, University of Missouri, Columbia, and coauthor of a study of cyclists, runners and weight lifters, published in *Journal of Strength and Conditioning Research*.

Yoga for Bone Health

Carol Krucoff is a yoga therapist at Duke Integrative Medicine, which is part of the Duke University Health System in Durham, North Carolina (HealingMoves.com). She is author of the *Healing Yoga for Neck and Shoulder Pain* and the DVD *Relax Into Yoga: Finding Ease in Body and Mind*.

If yoga makes you think of stretching and improving your flexibility, think again. The ancient practice of yoga actually has something in common with walking, running, dancing and weight training—all are weight-bearing exercises. So, if you need to do weight-bearing exercises to protect your bones, consider yoga—especially if you don't have access to weights or want a form of exercise that's easier on your joints than an activity like running. Carol Krucoff, a yoga therapist at Duke Integrative Medicine and author of *Healing Yoga for Neck and Shoulder Pain*, shares some of the yoga positions that can improve bone health...

One of the benefits of yoga for bone health: Many yoga positions require that you support your body weight with your legs and/or arms. In some positions, such as downward dog or plank, both your arms and legs support your body weight. These postures provide a boost to bones in both the upper and lower body, a claim that can't be made by activities such as running or walking, which just involve the lower body. A recent study by researchers at University of California at Los Angeles found that yoga reduced the curvature of the spine in adults with hyperkyphosis (also known as "dowager's hump), a condition that often is caused by bone loss. Another study by researchers based in Bangkok found that postmenopausal women who practiced yoga had significantly lower levels of bone degradation than those who didn't practice yoga.

Here are a few simple yoga poses that help to build bones. For best results, do each pose three times a week. (For details on how long to hold each pose, see below.)

Bone-building yoga poses...

CHAIR POSE

What it does: Strengthens the bones of the legs and hips.

How to do it: Stand with feet hip-distance apart. Extend your arms forward at shoulder height. (To make the move more difficult, you can put your arms over your head with your upper arms parallel to your ears.) Bend your knees, bow forward at the hips, stick your bottom out and lower it down as if you were going to sit in an invisible chair. Make sure that your back is straight, not rounded, and that your knees are not in front of your toes. Hold the position for two or three slow, deep breaths, then return to standing. Repeat five times, working your way up to 10 times.

SPINAL BALANCE

What it does: Strengthens bones in the arms, shoulders and thighs.

How to do it: Come onto all fours—with your knees directly under your hips and your wrists directly under your shoulders. Moving slowly, extend the left leg out behind you and raise it to hip height, toes toward the floor. Next, extend your right arm forward and raise it to shoulder height. Hold for one full, easy breath. Then return to the starting position and switch sides. Repeat three times on each side, working up to holding the pose each time for three breaths.

WARRIOR II

What it does: Strengthens bones of the lower body.

How to do it: Step your feet about three to four feet apart. Extend your arms out to both sides and parallel to the floor, palms facing down. Turn your left foot 90 degrees to the left and angle the toes of your right foot toward the left. Bend your left knee (make sure that your left knee is over your left ankle) and align the arch of your right foot with the heel of your left foot. Straighten your right leg, pressing the outer heel into the floor. Gaze out over the left fingertips. Hold for three to five breaths, then switch sides and repeat.

PLANK

What it does: Strengthens bones in the arms, shoulders and legs.

How to do it: Come onto all fours with your palms flat against the floor under your shoulders, fingers spread wide. Extend your right leg out behind you, toes tucked under. Next, extend your left leg out behind you, toes tucked under, so that your body forms a straight line from the top of your head to your heels. Stay here, balanced on your hands and toes, for three full breaths. If you can't breathe easily with your legs straight, bring your knees to the floor and perform the pose with your knees on the floor. This version of the pose is easier to do but still strengthens the arm bones.

When starting any new physical activity, including yoga, it's a good idea to speak to your doctor to ensure that it is safe for you. To learn the postures accurately, you can take a class with a registered teacher. The Yoga Alliance, a national yoga education organization, which maintains a national registry of teachers who have completed at least 200 hours of yoga teacher training, can help you find a teacher in your area.

Don't Get Hurt When Working Out at Home

Barbara Bushman, PhD, a professor in the department of kinesiology at Missouri State University in Springfield, a fellow of the American College of Sports Medicine (ACSM) and editor of *ACSM's Complete Guide to Fitness and Health*.

Exercising in the comfort of your own home is convenient and can save a bundle in gym fees over time. But there's a potential downside, too, and it has to do with safety—because unlike at a good gym, at home there's no professional trainer correcting your improper technique or making sure damaged equipment gets repaired. When it comes to treadmills, multistation home-gym machines and stationary bikes, the risks can be substantial.

What you need to know about using a...

• **Treadmill.** The treadmill causes more injuries than any other type of exercise equipment, according to the Consumer Product Safety Commission.

• **If your treadmill has a safety cord that clips to your clothing,** be sure to use it (and if your unit does not have this feature, consider upgrading to one that does). At one end of the cord is a key that plugs into the treadmill. If you lose your footing and fall, the cord disengages from the machine, shutting off the treadmill automatically.

• **Familiarize yourself with your treadmill's speed and grade options.** Incorrectly manipulating the controls could cause the treadmill to speed up or raise its incline when you were expecting to go slower or lower, Dr. Bushman warned—and that could send you flying.

• **Use caution when placing towels,** magazines, water bottles or other objects on the console at the front of the treadmill. An object that drops onto the treadmill could wind up underfoot, causing you to trip.

• **Multistation Home-Gym Machine.** Any multistation unit should be installed professionally. Even with all the nuts and bolts in the right places, inattention can lead to accidents—so stay alert and keep hands and other body parts well clear of the multistation's moving weight stacks, leverage arms, pulleys and cables.

• **Examine your unit's pulleys,** connections and other moving parts at least once a month for signs of wear, including fraying or other damage. Follow the manufacturer's directions for lubricating and tightening the unit's components and replacing worn parts promptly.

• **Stationary Bicycle.** These are relatively safe, but you'll still want to exercise caution.

• **Avoid wearing pants that flare at the ankle**—depending on your bike's style, the fabric could get trapped in the spinning mechanism and wrench your leg. The same goes for untied or unnecessarily long shoelaces.

• **A seat that is too low puts strain on your knees.**

Best: Adjust the seat height so that there's a slight bend in the knee when your foot is at the far reach of the pedal stroke.

How to Fall Down: Tricks from an Oscar-Winning Stuntman

Hal Needham, who appeared as a stuntman in more than 4,000 television episodes and more than 300 feature films. He is author of *Stuntman! My Car-Crashing, Plane-Jumping, Bone-Breaking, Death-Defying Hollywood Life.*

When we fall, our natural instinct is to reach out for the ground with our hands. Unfortunately, that only increases our odds of injury—our hands, wrists and arms are full of small bones that are easily broken. *Instead, when you realize you are falling...*

1. Buckle your knees. This can in essence lower the height that your upper body falls by as much as a foot or two, significantly reducing the impact when you hit the ground. In a forward fall, it might result in bruised knees, but that's better than a broken bone in the upper body.

Helpful: In a backward fall, tuck your head into your chest as you buckle your knees—try to turn yourself into a ball.

2. Throw one arm across your chest whether you're falling forward or backward. Do this with enough force that it turns your body to one side. It doesn't matter which arm you use.

3. Rotate the rest of your body in the direction that you threw your arm, increasing your spin. If you can rotate enough, you can come down mainly on your backside, a well-padded part of the body unlikely to experience a serious injury.

Trouble is, while stuntmen know exactly when and where they're going to fall, real-world falls usually take people by surprise. It can be difficult to overcome instinct and put this falling strategy into action in the split second before hitting the ground.

Practice can help. If you have access to a thick gym mat and you don't have health issues that make it risky, try out this falling technique until it feels natural.

Jewelry That Can Save Your Life

Richard O'Brien, MD, associate professor of emergency medicine at The Commonwealth Medical College of Pennsylvania in Scranton. Dr. O'Brien, who died in 2015, was also a spokesperson for the American College of Emergency Physicians, ACEP.org.

Medical ID jewelry has evolved. Those simple and basic necklaces and ID bracelets that people used to wear to alert others to medical problems, such as a heart condition or a seizure disorder, have gone high-tech, offering an array of data-sharing options so emergency responders can gain instant access to your comprehensive medical information. The new generation of medical-emergency bracelets and tags uses portable computer memory devices (typically a USB drive) or an Internet component to store and share your medical information. *Here's a sampling of what's available...*

•**The CARE medical history bracelet** is basically a USB drive you wear strapped to your wrist. It holds software and forms. It alerts emergency personnel that you have a medical condition and, once plugged into a computer (it works on both PC and Mac), downloads a detailed medical history. The waterproof bracelet comes in five colors. (*care memoryband.com*, 210-681-3840, $19.99)

Similar in appearance to a traditional dog tag, the American Medical ID is a USB drive that carries a summary of medical information. It is easy to use and update. The tag can be engraved with four lines summarizing your critical medical information, such as food or drug allergies or a seizure disorder. (*americanmedical-id.com*, 800-363-5985, $39.99)

•**ICEdot band,** a web-based service supported by the American Ambulance Association, assigns each wearer a personal identification number (PIN) that first responders use to trigger a text message detailing critical medical information, emergency contacts or whatever other data you choose to provide.

How it works: Your $10/year membership buys six stickers displaying the PIN (to be displayed in convenient places, for instance on your driver's license) that allows emergency responders to access your information. The bracelet is $20. (*icedot.org*, 918-592-3722)

•**Road ID Interactive is an ID band,** tag or pouch you can wear on your wrist, ankle or shoe. It is engraved with two lines of personal information (name, address) and a toll-free phone number, web address and PIN that responders can use to get more details. (*roadid. com*, 800-345-6336, $19.99 to $29.99, including free online access for a year, then $9.99/year thereafter)

• **Medic Alert** is the classic line of jewelry, now in an updated variety of attractive styles (for instance, made with Swarovski "pearls" or sterling silver), including bracelets, necklaces, sports bands, shoe tags and even a watch. These pieces can be engraved with medical info and also provide phone access to a 24-hour emergency service that provides more detailed information. The service notifies anyone you designate that you've had an emergency and provides information on where you're being treated. (*medicalert.org*, 800-432-5378, $19.95 and up for the jewelry, plus a membership fee starting at $15/year).

HOW TO CHOOSE

If you're not into flash drives, at minimum, write down your information on an index card, having it laminated (you can do this at many office-supply stores) and storing it in your wallet, as EMTs know to look there.

A "wish list" of information that emergency physicians would like to get from every patient in order to deliver the best possible emergency care…

• **Name, date of birth, address(es).**

• **Your phone numbers, contact for next of kin or significant other(s), identifying features—moles, tattoos, scars, etc.—that can positively distinguish you from others.**

Contact information for your primary care physician and relevant specialists, including name, phone number, location.

A list of all known allergies.

An up-to-date list of medications and any supplements you take.

Information on previous surgery or planned elective surgery (such as an upcoming gallbladder surgery or a scheduled biopsy).

Current immunization information, including flu and other vaccines, along with the date of your most recent tetanus shot and others as appropriate.

List of other medical problems such as diabetes, cancer, etc.

List of any medical devices that you have or use: Pacemaker, prosthesis, cochlear implant, etc.

Whether it is recorded on a flash drive, a bracelet, an index card or elsewhere, putting this information together and keeping it with you can make all the difference—at the very least, by expediting treatment in the event of an emergency and quite possibly even saving your life.

Help and Natural Healing for Broken Bones

Amy Rothenberg, ND, naturopathic physician in private practice in Enfield, Connecticut. AmyRothenberg.com

Mark Stengler, NMD, founder and medical director of the Stengler Center for Integrative Medicine in Encinitas, California, and adjunct associate clinical professor at the National College of Natural Medicine in Portland, Oregon. MarkStengler.com

A homeopathic preparation called Symphytum officinale, derived from the herb comfrey (also called "bone knit"), is ultradiluted and completely safe for children and adults. It helps to heal bones as well as the periosteum (a fibrous sheath that covers the bone). For a new fracture, I recommend taking two pellets of the 30C potency four times daily for two weeks. If a follow-up X-ray (typically taken about a month after a bone is broken) shows that the bone is healing slowly, take two pellets of a 30C potency twice daily for two more weeks. This homeopathic remedy is available in health-food stores.

Except as a homeopathic remedy, symphytum should not be taken orally, because it can damage the liver. However, symphytum cream or ointment is safe to apply topically to reduce swelling.

A high-potency multiple vitamin-mineral supplement with calcium and magnesium can help the healing process. Many nutrients are needed for healing, such as vitamins A, C, E and K, as well as zinc, iron and copper. Proper nutritional intake and absorption are key to timely and complete bone healing.

How NOT to Die of a Broken Hip

John E. Morley, MD, Dammert Professor of Gerontology and director of the Division of Geriatric Medicine at Saint Louis University School of Medicine. He is director of geriatric research at St. Louis Veterans Affairs Medical Center and is coauthor, with Sheri R. Colberg, PhD, of *The Science of Staying Young*.

About 25% of hip-fracture patients 65 years and older die within six months of the fracture...two-thirds die within two years.

Surgery is almost always necessary to repair a hip fracture. Generally, the better your health before a hip fracture, the better your chances for a complete recovery. But for elderly patients, especially those with health problems, a hip fracture can be deadly.

How not to die of a broken hip—plus how to prevent one in the first place...

BASICS TO PREVENT AND HEAL

These measures can help prevent a hip fracture and aid in recovery...

• **Vitamin D.** We've seen a significant increase in hip fractures over the last 20 to 30 years. During this same period, people have been increasingly avoiding the sun or using sunscreen to reduce their risk for skin cancer.

What's the connection? The body synthesizes vitamin D from exposure to the sun's ultraviolet radiation. People who get little sun often are deficient in vitamin D. Low vitamin D decreases bone and muscle strength, increasing the risk for falls as well as fractures.

What to do: Have your vitamin D measured now and also if you suffer a hip fracture. The level shouldn't be less than 30 nanograms per milliliter. Many Americans, including younger adults, have a significant vitamin D deficiency. You can supplement with vitamin D—the recommended dose is 400 international units (IU) to 800 IU daily—but I usually advise patients just to get more sun. About 20 to 30 minutes of sun exposure daily without sunscreen—new research shows that noon is best—will provide adequate vitamin D without increasing the risk for skin cancer.

• **More protein and calcium.** Poor nutrition can impair balance, cognitive abilities and bone and muscle strength. It also can delay healing by impairing tissue repair after surgery.

Recommended: Ask your doctor about taking a balanced amino acid (protein) drink one to three times daily after a hip fracture. I also advise patients to eat eight ounces of yogurt a day. Most yogurts supply about 400 mg of calcium. Combined with the calcium in a normal diet, that's usually enough to promote stronger bones.

MORE HEALING HELP

The following can keep a hip fracture from becoming a death sentence...

• **Zoledronic acid.** It was discovered recently that an intravenous medication called *zoledronic acid* (Zometa, Reclast), typically used to treat cancer, can aid in recovery from a hip fracture. A 2007 study in *The New England Journal of Medicine* showed that zoledronic acid reduced hip-fracture mortality by about 28%. Similar to drugs used to treat osteoporosis, it's a bisphosphonate that inhibits bone breakdown and increases bone strength.

Patients who have fractured one hip have a fivefold increased risk of fracturing the other. This means that their mortality risk is doubled. Zoledronic acid helps to prevent future fractures of the hip as well as the spine.

The drug is given as a five-milligram (mg) infusion once a year. Some patients experience fatigue, muscle aches or fever after the first injection. Subsequent injections are unlikely to cause significant side effects.

• **Treatment for depression.** Depression is extremely common after a hip fracture, partly because patients often feel helpless and dependent.

Why it matters: Patients who are depressed are less likely to exercise and follow through with a rehabilitation program. They also are more likely to get a subsequent fracture because depression increases the body's production of cortisol, a substance that depletes bone calcium.

Most patients with depression do best with medication, alone or in combination with talk therapy.

Caution: Drugs in the SSRI class of antidepressants, such as *paroxetine* (Paxil), can impair alertness and coordination and increase the risk for falls. These drugs also pull calcium from the bones. Some of the older antidepressants, such as *nortriptyline* (Pamelor), are a better choice for hip-fracture patients because they are less likely to impair alertness and balance.

• **Pain relief.** Postsurgical pain is normal—chronic pain that lasts months or years after hip surgery is unacceptable. Chronic pain interferes with exercise and rehabilitation. It also is a leading cause of depression. You should never have chronic pain after hip surgery. Some patients do fine with over-the-counter pain relievers, such as ibuprofen, but others need stronger painkillers. If you're hurting, tell your doctor.

Helpful: The Wong-Baker FACES Pain Rating Scale. Patients look at illustrations of facial expressions (which are accompanied by a number) and choose the one that reflects their pain. During rehabilitation, no one should experience pain greater than a three or four. During daily life, pain should be rated no higher than a one or two.

• **Prevention of clots and pneumonia.** Hospital patients have a high risk of developing deep vein thrombosis, a life-threatening condition in which blood clots in the legs travel to the lungs and cause a pulmonary embolism. They also have a higher risk for pneumonia, partly because being sedentary can allow mucus to collect in the lungs, providing a breeding ground for bacteria.

What to do: In the hospital, move as much as you can, even if it is nothing more than regularly flexing your legs or sitting up in bed.

Patients who have had hip surgery are routinely referred to a physical or occupational therapist. After that, they should continue to be active—ideally, by walking or doing other forms of exercise for 20 to 30 minutes most days.

7

Drive Safer Longer... or Live Independently Without a Car

You Don't Have to Give Up Those Car Keys

Driving may be the most hazardous thing that most of us do each day, but simply growing older—or having a chronic medical condition, no matter what your age, that affects your vision, thought process or physical abilities—doesn't mean that you can't continue to be independent.

To drive safely as long as possible: It's crucial to proactively avoid problems that can limit your car-handling competence. *Here's how...*

PREEMPT PROBLEMS

Beyond commonsense imperatives such as getting regular medical, vision and hearing checkups, a few simple steps will help ensure that your driving abilities are intact.

At your checkup with your primary care doctor, have a candid talk to discuss any med-

ical conditions you may have that could affect your driving now or in the future.

For example, a stroke may result in lingering visual or movement problems...diabetes might be causing neuropathy in your feet, making it difficult to feel the gas or brake pedals...and cataracts, macular degeneration or glaucoma may limit vision if it's not carefully treated. A conversation with your doctor can help you minimize these issues and prevent them from becoming a bigger problem down the road. *Also...*

MANAGE YOUR MEDS

Some prescription or over-the-counter medications can impair your ability to drive by triggering drowsiness, cutting concentration, inducing shakiness or uncoordinated move-

Patrick Baker, an occupational therapist, certified low-vision therapist and certified driver-rehabilitation specialist at the Cleveland Clinic in Cleveland, Ohio.

Richard A. Marottoli, MD, associate professor of medicine at Yale School of Medicine and medical director of the Dorothy Adler Geriatric Assessment Center at Yale-New Haven Hospital, both in New Haven, Connecticut.

ments, or increasing your reaction time. Taking multiple drugs—a common practice among older adults and those coping with chronic medical problems—can make matters even worse by amplifying medication side effects. Certain dietary supplements, such as melatonin or valerian, may also have an effect.

What to find out: Show your doctor or pharmacist a list of all the medications (prescription and over-the-counter) and dietary supplements you take and ask how they interact and may affect your driving abilities.

Also: Ask if the timing of when you take any drugs or supplements that may affect cognition or coordination can be altered—for example, taken before bedtime instead of in the morning.

Important: If you are on painkillers or narcotics, also ask your spouse or a trusted friend if the medication makes you "loopy"—an effect that you may not notice but is perhaps obvious to another person.

CUSTOMIZE YOUR CAR

Age can compromise your eyesight and bring physical changes that make it more difficult to see the road while driving—for example, many people lose one to three inches of height due to bone loss and spinal compression. Or a stroke or eye condition (such as cataracts) may affect your peripheral vision, interfering with your ability to spot traffic alongside your car. To address these changes, it helps to customize your car. *Here's how...*

•**Set power seats at the highest level.** Also, consider adding a firm cushion (such as the durable type used for outdoor furniture) to the driver's seat so that your chin is at least three inches higher than the top of the steering wheel.

•**Use extra (or bigger) mirrors inside and/or outside your car to increase your field of vision.** For example, you can get a mirror that attaches to your rearview mirror to expand your view to the rear. Or you can get bigger mirrors or extra mirrors that can be bolted onto existing side mirrors or the side of the car itself. Check with your car dealer for details for your make and model.

•**Keep your headlights clean.** Also, consider replacing the bulbs—even before they burn out. The bulbs get dimmer before they've completely burned out.

•**Opt for automatic.** If you're buying a new car, be sure to get one with automatic transmission, power steering and power brakes, which don't require as much strength to operate. Also, consider a car with backup alert sensors, which detect objects in your blind spots.

SPRUCE UP YOUR SKILLS

A driving refresher course (ideally taken every three to five years) will keep you up to date on the newest traffic rules and can reduce road mishaps.

Good news: Some car insurance companies even lower premium rates if you take one of these courses, which usually lasts four to eight hours.

Good choice: A course such as those offered by AAA or AARP is likely to have an instructor who is well versed in issues facing older adults—as well as classmates who are true peers. If you are interested in taking a driver course because of a medical condition, consult The Association for Driver Rehabilitation Specialists (*aded.net* and search "CDRS provider") to find a program near you.

Avoid dangerous situations...

•**Use routes that minimize left turns—** they are more dangerous than right turns. When waiting to turn left, keep your wheels straight so you won't be pushed into oncoming traffic if hit from behind.

•**On the highway, stay in the right lane whenever possible.** There's less risk of being tailgated, and you probably won't need to change lanes to exit.

•**Minimize travel on congested or poorly lit roads.**

•**Do not drive in rain or snow or when you feel tired or stressed.** Stay home or call a taxi.

See and be seen...

•**To determine if you're tailgating, pick a spot that the car in front of you passes, then count the seconds until you reach that** spot. If it's less than three seconds—or six seconds in rain or fog—back off.

• **Use your window defroster on high heat to clear window fog quickly**...then switch to cool air (not cold) to keep fog from coming back. This works in all weather.

• **Keep your windows clean inside and outside.**

• **Be on the watch for distracted drivers.** Stay focused yourself, too—don't talk on the phone or eat or fiddle with the CD player or have emotional conversations with your passengers.

• **Keep headlights on, even during the day**—it makes you more visible to others. Clean headlights often.

• **If you have poor night vision, drive only in daylight.**

Master new car technology...

• **Put your seat as far back as you comfortably can to avoid being injured by the air bag if it deploys.**

• **Tilt the steering wheel so that the air bag points toward your chest, not your head.** If your steering wheel telescopes, move it closer to the dashboard to lessen air bag impact.

• **If you skid, do not "pump" anti-lock brakes**—just brake steadily.

FOCUS ON FOOTWEAR

When it comes to hitting the gas and brake, what's on our feet can be just as important as our ability to see and react. *Consider these important footwear-related issues...*

• **Choose the right sneaker.** Running-style sneakers with soles that are thick, chunky and/or beveled can catch on pedals as you move your foot, so opt for a flat sole, such as a tennis-style or walking sneaker.

• **Go for thin soles.** People with diabetic neuropathy or limited foot sensation should wear thinner-soled shoes while driving. Thin soles, which don't have much padding between the bottom of the feet and the car pedals, give you a better sense of how hard you are pushing the brake and accelerator.

Important: Be sure to choose a car that "fits" you well—with good sight lines to the

sides and rear...controls that are easy to reach...and a model that is easy for you to get in and out of.

Over 50? These Gadgets Make Driving Safer, Easier...and More Fun

Jim Miller, an advocate for senior citizens, writes "Savvy Senior," a weekly information column syndicated in more than 400 newspapers nationwide. Based in Norman, Oklahoma, he also offers a free senior news service at SavvySenior.org.

While age doesn't make someone a bad driver, it typically does bring about physical and cognitive changes that can make driving more challenging. Fortunately, to help keep aging drivers safe, there is a wide variety of affordable devices and tools that you can purchase today and add to your vehicle to help with many different needs.

ENTRY AND EXIT

Each year in the US, an estimated 37,000 seniors are injured simply entering or exiting vehicles. *If a mobility problem or limited range of motion is hampering your ability to get in and out of your auto, here are some items that can help...*

• **Metro Car Handle** is a small portable support handle (made of steel with a non-slip grip for your hand) that inserts into the U-shaped hooklike striker plate on the door frame. (The striker plate is the piece of metal that holds the door closed in the event of a side collision.) $25.* 435-755-0453, *stander. com.*

• **CarCaddie Mobility Aid** is a nylon handle that hooks around the top of the door window frame. $15. 435-755-0453, *stander.com.*

• **Swivel Seat Cushion** is a round portable pad that turns 360 degrees to help drivers and passengers rotate into and out of a ve-

*Prices in this article are recent figures from manufacturers or *amazon.com.*

hicle. Works best on flat car seats. $15. 800-247-2343, *briggscorp.com*.

VISION HELPERS

Many older drivers are especially sensitive to glare and/or have difficulty turning to look over their shoulders. *Products that can help...*

• **Glare Guard Polarized Sun Visor** is a plastic tinted visor that clips onto your existing sun visor to remove sun glare without obstructing vision. It also incorporates a sliding shield that lets you further block extra-bright glare spots. $36. *amazon.com*.

• **Wireless Back-up Camera System** is a small camera with night vision that attaches to your rear license plate so that you can see what's behind you without turning around. It comes with a 3.5-inch LCD color monitor that mounts to your dash or windshield and is powered by the car's cigarette lighter. $79. *amazon.com*.

ARTHRITIC HANDS

Drivers who have arthritic or weak hands may find turning the ignition key, twisting open the gas cap, and other tasks difficult. *Tools that can help...*

• **Easy-to-Grasp Key Holder.** For $30, this plastic handle device attaches to car keys to provide additional leverage when turning the key in the ignition. Or for car keys with thick plastic head covers, there's a Key Lever for $35. 888-940-0605, *liveoakmed.com*.

• **Gas Cap Tool.** To help at the pump, this long-handled device fits onto most gas caps and works like a wrench to help open the gas tank with ease. $16. 877-785-8326, *lifesolutions plus.com*.

SMALL DRIVERS

Most people shrink a little as they get older...and for those who were small to start with, it can be difficult to see over the steering wheel or to reach a vehicle's pedals without being too close to the airbag. *Solutions include...*

• **Ortho Wedge Cushion.** This seat cushion supports the back and elevates you a few extra inches to help you see. $15. 800-231-5806, *wagan.com*.

• **Foot pedal extensions** allow you to reach the pedals while keeping you 10 to 12 inch-

es from the steering wheel. Costs for a gas and brake pedal range from $128 to $220, depending on length. They should be installed by a mechanic to ensure safety. 888-372-0153, *pedalextenders.com*.

SEAT BELT AIDS

Products that help enhance seat belt comfort and functionality without sacrificing safety...

• **Easy Reach Seat Belt Handle** is a six-inch rubber extension handle that attaches to your seat belt strap to make it easier to reach. $18. 888-940-0605, *liveoakmed.com*.

• **Eboot Seatbelt Shoulder Pad** fits around the shoulder strap to protect your neck and shoulder from rubbing and chafing. $9. 888-940-0605, *amazon.com*.

• **Seat Belt Adjuster.** This small plastic clip, which attaches to the shoulder strap and lap belt, allows you to adjust the seat belt shoulder strap between shoulder and neck for greater comfort and safety. $7 for a set of two. 855-202-7391, *easycomforts.com*.

Hands Free Is NOT Distraction Free

Voice-controlled car systems distract drivers. Drivers who use hands-free systems to dial phone numbers, change music, send texts and do other tasks remain distracted for up to 27 seconds after talking to the systems. At a slow speed—25 miles per hour—a driver distracted for 27 seconds travels nearly the length of three football fields before returning full attention to the road.

Self-defense: Use the systems for as short a time as possible while driving and only to support elements of driving, such as navigation or climate control—not for entertainment purposes such as e-mail and web access.

Two studies of voice-activated car systems by researchers at University of Utah, Salt Lake City, done for the AAA Foundation for Traffic Safety, a nonprofit charitable organization based in Washington, DC.

Hazards of Car Backup Cameras

Karl Brauer, senior director for insights into automotive trends with *Kelley Blue Book*, which provides information about new and used cars. KBB.com

Backup-camera systems that give drivers a view behind the car are becoming increasingly common on new cars, and studies suggest that they do indeed reduce the odds of accidentally backing into things. But paradoxically, they can present their own dangers. *What you need to know to use your car's backup camera safely...*

•**A glance is not enough.** The display screen—in the dashboard or rearview mirror—usually is small, so you must pay close attention to spot all but the largest obstacles. And don't neglect to also look back over your shoulder to check whether there is anything just out of the viewing area of the camera.

The view varies greatly from vehicle to vehicle. Some backup cameras show a full 180-degree span behind the vehicle...others as little as 130 degrees. The narrower field of view could miss an obstacle...but the wider view distorts the image, making things look farther away than they really are. Take special care when driving a vehicle, such as a rental car, that has a different field of view than your own vehicle.

•**You can become too dependent.** Once you drive a car with a backup camera for a while, it's easy to forget how to safely back up if, say, your car's camera is covered by dirt or snow. Clean an obstructed lens as soon as possible.

"Around View" systems are available in some new vehicles, especially Infiniti and Nissan models, with more on the way. They have cameras arrayed all around the vehicle, showing potential hazards on all sides. Consider choosing a vehicle equipped with this sort of system.

Safe-Driving Strategies for Small-Car Owners

William Van Tassel, PhD, manager of driver training operations at AAA's national office in Heathrow, Florida, AAA.com. He is a member of the Transportation Research Board's Committee on Operative Regulation and Education and a sports car racer with the Sports Car Club of America.

Small cars can be major money savers, trimming gas bills by 50% or more compared with full-size sedans and SUVs. However, small cars also tend to be riskier than larger vehicles, with fatality rates more than twice as high as those of gas guzzlers. *To make small-car driving as safe as possible...*

•**Select the safest small car.** When buying a car, look for...

•Side-impact air bags. These greatly improve your odds of survival if your small car is hit on the side.

•Electronic stability control. This computerized safety system detects when your vehicle is skidding and helps you get the vehicle under control quickly.

•High scores in crash tests. Crash-test ratings from the National Highway Traffic Safety Administration (NHTSA) are available at *safer car.gov.* Ratings from the Insurance Institute for Highway Safety (IIHS) can be found at *iihs.org/ratings.*

•Bright color. Select a brightly colored car —red and yellow are particularly visible. Avoid black, silver and gray.

•**Turn on your headlights during the day to increase visibility.** If your car doesn't have daytime running lights (low-beam headlights that turn on when the car does), put on the headlights.

•**Wait a bit before entering intersections when the light turns green.** A driver in a larger vehicle could be barreling through the other way trying to beat the red light.

•**Avoid driving in packs with larger vehicles.** When possible, drop back or speed up slightly to create a bubble of open space around you. If a vehicle is tailgating you, look for an opportunity to pull aside and let it pass.

• **Think ahead.** Consider in advance what you would do if a vehicle fails to notice you and pulls into your path. Preselect an "emergency escape," an open area into which you could safely maneuver. Wide shoulders usually make the best emergency escapes, so it's usually safest to drive in a lane adjacent to a shoulder.

• **Learn your car's capabilities.** Your small car probably can stop and swerve more quickly than larger vehicles. That maneuverability can help you stay out of collisions if you know what your car is capable of before an emergency occurs. Take your small car to an empty parking lot, and practice hard stops and sharp swerves.

When You Should Give Up Driving…

Red flags that you may need to give up driving…You are having trouble seeing cars or pedestrians at night, as well as trouble braking quickly when needed…reacting slowly to sirens or flashing emergency lights…receiving frequent traffic tickets…getting honked at by other drivers…or you have been involved in any crash or near-misses during the last two years.

Also: If you have conditions such as angina, severe arthritis, cataracts or cognitive problems, ask your doctor to assess whether or not your condition is affecting your ability to drive.

University of California, Berkeley Wellness Letter. *BerkeleyWellness.com*

Driving Mistakes You Don't Know You're Making

John Kennedy, executive director of defensive driving courses at the National Safety Council, 1121 Spring Lake Dr., Itasca, Illinois 60143, *nsc.org.*

Driving mistakes can be very costly. A serious collision can end your life, but even a minor one can wipe out your savings unless you're well insured.

Serious road crashes are common in the US, causing some 2.4 million disabling injuries and 44,700 deaths a year. Many of these crashes are the result of poor driving habits. These errors are hard to spot because they're often the result of physical changes that occur gradually over many years. In some cases—visual acuity, for instance—even a slight change can create serious risks.

Even worse: When you catch yourself making one kind of mistake, you may be distracted from noticing your other driving errors. People with hearing problems, for example, may concentrate so hard on listening to road sounds that they neglect to look for hazards at intersections.

Costly driving mistakes that are easy to overlook…

• **Putting up with daytime glare.** As we grow older, we may have difficulty with bright light, which often causes a glare that's a serious risk on the road.

Self-defense: If adjusting your car's sun visor doesn't work, try wearing lightly tinted sunglasses when you drive. And of course, talk with your eye doctor, who may recommend medical procedures, such as cataract surgery, if needed.

• **Putting up with nighttime glare.** Glare is more common at night. If you experience it, the best solution is simply not to drive when it's dark. Also, people who are susceptible to daytime glare are often distracted at night by their dashboard lights.

Self-defense: When you drive at night, try dimming the dashboard lights. When oncoming traffic approaches, avoid looking directly at the bright headlights and instead glance toward the right side of the road.

• **Driving after dark if your nighttime vision isn't as good as it used to be.**

Self-defense: When you visit your eye doctor, ask about your nighttime vision. If the doctor finds a problem that can't be corrected, restrict your nighttime driving.

• **Failing to compensate for loss of peripheral vision.** Peripheral vision loss can result from many medical conditions, including high blood pressure and migraine headaches.

Self-defense: Have your eye doctor check your peripheral vision at least once a year.

If you've lost peripheral vision, ask your doctor if the amount is enough to warrant giving up driving. If you've lost only a small amount, you may be able to compensate by turning your head very, very slightly from time to time as you drive.

• **Overlooking drug effects.** Since medication is intended to make us feel better mentally or physically, it's often difficult to anticipate problems it may cause.

In fact, prescription drugs can interact with each other and with over-the-counter (OTC) medication in ways that aren't always predictable, causing drowsiness, disorientation and other conditions that impair your driving ability.

Warning: If you drive while impaired from a drug interaction, you can be charged with "driving under the influence" just as you would if you had been drinking alcohol. The charge can result in a hefty fine, increased insurance premiums, possible loss of your driver's license—and even jail.

Self-defense: Give each doctor who prescribes drugs for you a list of other medications you're taking, including OTC drugs and herbal supplements. Ask the physician to check on possible interactions, and before taking a new OTC medication, check again with your doctors.

• **Turning up the radio while you drive.** Many of us enjoy listening to music or keeping up with the news, but a car radio can be dangerously distracting.

Self-defense: If you have the radio on, keep the volume just high enough so you can hear it.

Smart move: Whether the radio is on or not, keep a window open just a crack so you're more aware of outside sounds, especially horns and sirens.

• **Keeping your foot on the accelerator when there's a chance you'll soon need to use the brakes.**

Self-defense: Put your foot over the brake pedal every time you take it off the accelerator—you'll be able to stop a fraction of a second faster, often a lifesaving margin.

Also helpful in improving reacton time: Regular physical exercise (with the approval of your physician). Also, when on the road, taking frequent breaks when on a long driving trip—at least once every couple of hours.

• **Not showing caution when approaching intersections.**

Self-defense: Even when there's little traffic, drive defensively by slowing down at intersections, where a high percentage of collisions occur. Scan ahead to anticipate problems, such as a car that runs a red light from either your right or left. If there's a particularly treacherous intersection on your route, consider taking another road.

ON TOP OF YOUR GAME

Driving well—like playing a sport well—is a skill that takes continual practice. AARP, the American Automobile Association and the National Safety Council are three nationwide organizations that offer low-cost refresher driving courses—both online and in the classroom.

Courses from the three groups vary from state to state but usually take six to eight hours and cost less than $65. All courses emphasize defensive driving, including techniques for judging distance and making evasive maneuvers.

Added benefit: Most insurance companies reduce premiums for liability and collision coverage—typically by 10%—for drivers who complete a refresher course. *To find a course in your area, contact your state motor vehicle bureau or...*

• **American Automobile Association** (407-444-7000, *aaa.com*).

• **AARP** (888-227-7669 and 800-350-7025, *aarp.org/families/driver_safety*).

• **National Safety Council** (630-285-1121, *nsc.org*).

Adults More Likely to Text While Driving Than Teens

Almost half of all adults report texting while driving, versus 43% of teens.

Comparison of two surveys of more than 1,000 adults and 1,200 teens ages 15 to 19 by AT&T.

Night Driving Strategies

William Van Tassel, PhD, manager of driver-training operations at AAA's national office in Heathrow, Florida. He holds a doctorate in safety education. AAA.com

Fatal car crashes are three times more likely at night than during the day, per mile driven. The dark makes it more difficult to spot trouble on the road, and the late hour makes it more likely that we share the road with drunk or drowsy drivers.

Older drivers in particular often have trouble at night. Our eyes' ability to see in limited light declines steadily starting in our 30s. This happens so gradually that many older drivers don't realize how much night vision they have lost.

Fortunately, minor adjustments to our driving habits and vehicles can make a major difference in our night time driving risks. Five things drivers can do to see and drive better at night...

Shift your gaze down and to the right to avoid being blinded by approaching headlights. Use the edge of the road or the line marking the outside of your lane as a reference point until the headlights have passed.

If you are blinded by oncoming headlights, drive conservatively until your eyes readjust to low light—that typically takes around six seconds—but resist the urge to brake if there are cars close behind you. The drivers behind you might have been temporarily blinded by the oncoming headlights, too, and not notice that you've slowed.

Increase your following distance. In clear daytime conditions, three seconds is considered a safe following distance—pick a fixed object along the roadside and count off the seconds from when the car in front of you passes it until you do. At night, five or six seconds is more appropriate, since, among other things, our reaction times are slowed if we're drowsy.

Check your mirrors frequently. This increases your awareness of what's happening outside the beams of light cast by your headlights. It also keeps your mind active and attentive while you are driving.

Also: Avoid using cruise control after dark, and alter your speed periodically. This, too, keeps the brain more engaged, combating drowsiness.

Tap your brakes a few times before stopping if there are cars behind you. This makes your brake lights flash—and flashing lights grab the attention of drowsy or drunk drivers much better than steady lights.

Also: Use your blinkers well before you slow to turn. Use your hazard lights if you must stop on the side of a dark road.

If you wear glasses, choose ones that have an anti reflective (AR) coating. This clear coating cuts down on lens glare, improving your ability to see at night despite oncoming headlights.

AUTOMOTIVE ADJUSTMENTS

Five ways to prep your car for safer night driving...

• **Adjust your side mirrors so that you can almost, but not quite, see the outside of your own car in them.** Most drivers angle their side mirrors a bit too far to the inside, which allows the headlights of vehicles behind them to reflect into their eyes, reducing their night vision. Side mirrors angled too far inside also increase drivers' "blind spots" behind and to the side of the car at night and during the day.

Also, don't forget to switch your center rearview mirror to its night setting after dark to avoid headlights reflecting into your eyes. If your car has a self-dimming rearview mirror, double-check to make sure this function is turned on and working.

•**Clean your windshield, windows, headlights and taillights frequently.** Windshield and window smudges and grime that are barely noticeable during the day can cause tremendous glare when hit by other vehicles' headlights at night. Remember to clean the inside of the glass, not just the outside.

Dirt also builds up on headlights and taillights, dramatically reducing their brightness over time.

Consider installing enhanced replacement headlight bulbs on your car. These may help you see more of the road ahead for perhaps just $10 or $20 extra per bulb.

•**Dim your interior gauges slightly.** The glow from a bright dashboard can detract from your eyes' ability to see outside the vehicle at night. Turn gauge brightness down a bit, even if this means that you must strain a little to read the gauges—seeing what's outside your car is more important than reading dashboard gauges. Also, don't allow any passengers to have lights on inside the car when you're driving.

•**Turn on your headlights at dusk, or use them all the time.** Headlights won't provide much help seeing the road until it's quite dark—but they do help other drivers see you at all hours, which reduces the odds of collisions.

Using your high-beam headlights can further improve your vision at night. Just be sure to dim them when you detect another vehicle, either coming toward you or traveling ahead of you in the same direction.

Exercise Your Night Vision

Marc Grossman, OD, LAc, holistic developmental/behavioral optometrist, licensed acupuncturist and medical director, Natural Eye Care, New Paltz, New York. He is coauthor of *Greater Vision* and *Natural Eye Care.* NaturalEyeCare.com

This won't speed up the eyes' process of adjusting to the dark, but may encourage a mental focus that helps the brain and

eyes work better together—thus improving your ability to perceive objects in a darkened environment.

What to do: For 20 minutes four times per week, go into a familiar room at night and turn off the lights. As your eyes are adjusting, look directly toward a specific object that you know is there...focus on it, trying to make out its shape and details and to distinguish it from surrounding shadows. With practice, your visual perception should improve. For an additional challenge, do the exercise outdoors at night...while looking at unfamiliar objects in a dark room...or while using peripheral vision rather than looking directly at an object.

When driving at night, avoid looking directly at oncoming headlights. Shifting your gaze slightly to the right of center minimizes the eye changes that would temporarily impair your night vision, yet still allows you to see traffic.

Also: Use the night setting on rearview mirrors to reduce reflected glare.

•**Clean car windows and lights.** When was the last time you used glass cleaner on the inside of your windshield...or on rear and side windows...or on headlights and taillights? For the clearest possible view and minimal distortion from smudges, keep all windows and lights squeaky clean.

Safer Winter Driving: Products That Help

Michael Clark, cohost of The Road Trip, a weekly car show on CJOB Winnipeg, 68 AM. (Saturday mornings at 10:30 central time. Listen online at cjob.com.) He writes about cars for CanadianDriver.com and previously wrote for the automotive section of the *Winnipeg Free Press.*

Ice and snow can make for difficult, dangerous winter driving across much of North America. And cold temperatures can turn engine oil into molasses...add to the stress on a vehicle's electrical system...make a car hard to start...cause fogged windows, limiting visibility...and reduce tire pressure.

Michael Clark, who has worked in the automotive industry for 20 years, identifies products that can keep cars running well this winter. As cohost of a car radio show in Winnipeg, Manitoba, one of the continent's coldest cities, he often addresses winter-weather–related issues. *Clark's recommendations…*

●**High-quality winter tires.** What most people call "snow tires" really should be called "winter tires," because they help drivers in all cold-weather situations, not just when there is snow on the ground. In fact, they are the single most important product for winter driving.

The "all-season" tires found on most cars today are marketed as appropriate for winter, but they're made from compounds that get less than optimal traction in subfreezing temperatures, even on dry roads.

Best tires for winter conditions: Gislaved NordFrost (*gislaved-tyres.com*), which are great in snow…and Michelin X-Ice (866-866-6605, *michelin-us.com*), which perform well in both icy and snowy conditions. Snow tires cost between $100 and $200 per tire.

Important: Buy four snow tires. People often think that they need just two—for their front wheels if the vehicle has front-wheel drive or for their rear wheels if the vehicle has rear-wheel drive. But snow tires provide traction when you brake, not just when you accelerate. Without a full set of four, it will take longer for the car to stop. Even all-wheel-drive vehicles can benefit from snow tires. Just because you have traction doesn't mean that you will have the grip to stop.

Drive very conservatively for at least a week after putting on new snow tires. Even the best tires do not provide optimal traction until they're broken in.

Alternative: Tire chains aren't as effective as snow tires on slick winter roads, but they are a reasonable emergency option in regions where snow and ice are rare. Chains are illegal in some states. Check state law regarding chain use.

New products, such as Spikes-Spider (800-227-5260, *spikes-spiders.com*), provide do-it-yourself kits complete with chains (sold in pairs) and accessories to install them. You can easily attach the chains to your car tires, and they center themselves when you drive the car. You pay extra for this convenience—they cost $300 to $500 per pair, several times more than traditional chains, which can be found for less than $100 per pair.

●**Steel wheels.** Today's cars often come with alloy wheels. These look nice and weigh less than steel wheels, but they are a poor choice for winter driving. Road salt can cause pitting in alloy wheels, detracting from their appearance, and may cause tires to deflate if pitting occurs where the wheel and tire meet. Alloy wheels also tend to crack when they take a sharp blow and often must be replaced after sliding into a curb on winter ice. A steel wheel would only dent and might be repairable.

Helpful: If your vehicle has alloy wheels, have your snow tires mounted on a separate set of steel wheels. Then simply swap wheels when winter arrives, rather than having your snow tires remounted to your alloy wheels each winter and removed each spring. You will have to pay to balance your wheels each time they're changed, but that is less costly than remounting tires.

Steel wheels are less expensive than alloy wheels. (Average price is $100 per wheel, compared with several hundred per wheel for alloy.) Internet companies, such as TireRack. com (888-541-1777, *tirerack.com*), sell snow tires premounted on steel wheels for less than local dealers are likely to charge, depending on the model.

●**Synthetic winter oil.** If your car won't start on cold days, the problem could be your motor oil. Traditional oils thicken at low temperatures, forcing your battery to work harder to start the car. Synthetic oils specifically designed for winter temperatures remain more fluid, easing the battery's burden.

Best: Mobile 1 Synthetic Motor Oil, which costs about $8 to $10 per quart (800-662-4525, *mobiloil.com*).

Warning: Check your vehicle's owner's manual for guidelines before putting motor oil in your car. Don't worry about switching back and forth between synthetic and traditional oil—it won't damage your engine.

• **Windshield water repellent/antifogger.** You can improve winter visibility by applying chemical water repellents to the exterior of your windshield—in many cases, the rain and snow will roll off before freezing onto the glass.

Best: Rain-X Glass Treatment. It typically costs less than $10 for a 16-ounce spray bottle that can treat a typical windshield about 20 times (855-888-1990, *rainx.com*). Chemical antifoggers also can be applied to the interior of auto glass to further improve winter visibility.

Best: Rain-X Anti-Fog, which costs less than $7 for a 3.5-ounce bottle. Apply both products every few weeks in the winter.

• **New cabin air filter.** If your vehicle's heater no longer keeps you warm in the winter… or your defogger no longer clears your windshield, the culprit could be a clogged cabin air filter. Filters should be replaced every year or so. Consult your vehicle's owner's manual for cabin-air-filter replacement instructions and schedules. Replacement filters cost about $10 to $30 plus labor, depending on the vehicle.

Alternative: If a new cabin air filter does not improve heater or defogger performance, take your vehicle for a coolant flush (when the fluid from the radiator is drained and replaced). Automotive heater cores have relatively narrow passages, so they tend to clog before the rest of the coolant system.

Cost: $50 to $145, though dealerships often charge more.

• **Winter windshield wipers.** When wipers ice up, they can't flex with the curves of the windshield, leaving large areas uncleared. Winter wipers typically have plastic or rubber covers enclosing their structural elements. This keeps out water and makes wiper freeze-ups rare, aiding visibility. Winter wipers made by well-known companies, such as Bosch or ANCO, typically cost $10 to $20 per wiper in auto-parts stores.

Don't pay extra for a wiper that claims to be tough enough to remove winter ice. No wiper can do this effectively.

• **Chemical coatings for door locks.** If you often park outdoors in subfreezing temperatures, applying a lubricant or grease to the accessible parts of your vehicle's door locks can reduce the odds that they will ice shut. Coat the latch and striker (the striker is the piece of metal in the door frame that the latch grasps), and inject a small amount into the keyhole.

Best: Eureka Fluid Film (888-387-3522, *fluid-film.com*) or white lithium grease (made by many companies). Both are widely available in auto-parts and home stores. Both cost about $10 for 12 ounces.

• **All-weather floor mats.** If you live in a very snowy climate and you track in a lot of snow, ice and road salt, consider replacing your factory floor mats with heavy-duty all-weather rubber floor mats. These mats have a high lip to contain melting snow and ice and to protect the metal floor pan under your car's carpeting from water.

Best: Factory all-weather floor mats, which are precisely molded to your specific car model.

Clean All the Ice and Snow Off

Remove all snow and ice from your car before starting to drive. Driving with only a small amount of the windshield cleared is not only dangerous, it is illegal in some areas. Failing to clear the entire car completely also increases the chance that snow or ice will come off while you are moving and hit another car or a pedestrian.

Sgt. Scott Kristiansen, Buffalo Grove Police Department, Illinois.

Driving in Fog

Since it's difficult to see oncoming cars when you're driving in a thick fog, keep your window open. Chances are, you'll hear the cars coming toward you before you can see them.

Lydia Wilen and Joan Wilen are folk-remedy experts based in New York City. The sisters are coauthors of many books, including *Bottom Line's Household Magic* and *Secret Food Cures*.

Drugs That Increase the Risk for Car Crashes

Hui-Ju Tsai, MPH, PhD, associate investigator, division of biostatistics and bioinformatics, Institute of Population Health Sciences, National Health Research Institutes, Taiwan. She is lead author of a study published in *British Journal of Pharmacology*.

If you are among the millions of people taking any of these drugs, then you'll definitely want to know whether or not you're at increased risk...

WHICH DRUGS WERE STUDIED?

Researchers looked at two groups of data on people age 18 or over. One group was made up of people who had a record of being in a car accident (as a driver, not a passenger) at some point over a recent 10-year span, and the other group comprised people of similar ages who had no record of being in a car accident (as a driver, not a passenger) over the same 10-year span. (The researchers couldn't be sure that the accident was the driver's fault—there was no way to tell, based on the data. And determining blame in accidents is sometimes subjective.) *Then researchers analyzed who in the accident group had taken any of the following drugs within one month of the accident...*

- **Antipsychotics**
  - *chlorpromazine*
  - *loxapine*
  - Zyprexa (*olanzapine*)
  - Seroquel (*quetiapine*)
  - Risperdal (*risperidone*)

- **Antidepressants**

SSRIs (selective serotonin reuptake inhibitors)...
  - Prozac (*fluoxetine*)
  - Paxil (*paroxetine*)
  - Zoloft (*sertraline*)
  - Celexa (*citalopram*)
  - Lexapro (*escitalopram*)

Tricyclic antidepressants...
  - Trofanil (*imipramine*)
  - *amitriptyline*

"Others"...
  - Wellbutrin (*bupropion*)
  - Effexor (*venlafaxine*)
  - Cymbalta (*duloxetine*)

- **Benzodiazepines**

Hypnotics...
  - Halcion (*triazolam*)
  - *flurazepam*

Anxiolytics...
  - Xanax (*alprazolam*)
  - Klonopin (*clonazepam*)
  - Valium (*diazepam*)
  - Ativan (*lorazepam*)

- **"Z-drugs" or sleeping pills**
  - Ambien (*zolpidem*)
  - Sonata (*zaleplon*)

Then researchers compared people of the same age and gender in both groups to see whether those who had taken any of the drugs mentioned above were more likely to have been in car accidents.

IMPAIRED DRIVING SKILLS

Only two categories of drugs—antipsychotic drugs and "other" antidepressants—were not associated with a higher risk of having a car accident while every other category was.

It is, of course, possible that the underlying medical conditions that caused people to take the drugs—depression, anxiety and insomnia—contributed to the car accidents. Future research will need to address that. But there is some evidence that the drugs themselves may have played a role.

Many psychotropic drugs impair cognitive and psychomotor abilities—and of course, cognitive and psychomotor abilities are crucial for driving. While on these drugs, you might feel more drowsy or more confused, and your reflexes might be slower. All of these things may negatively impact your judgment and coordination.

Researchers aren't exactly sure why antipsychotic drugs and "other" antidepressants weren't shown to be associated with car crashes. It could be due to the smaller number of subjects taking these drugs in the study…or it could be that people on these particular drugs drive less often…or it could be that these drugs impair cognitive and psychomotor abilities less than the other drugs mentioned above.

PROTECT YOURSELF ON THE ROAD

If you take any of the types of drugs listed above that were associated with having car accidents, here's some advice from Dr. Tsai…

For those who take the medication in the morning, ask your doctor whether you can take it at night instead. The effects of many psychotropic drugs are strongest after you first take them, and since people tend to drive most in the daytime, this simple switch might help.

Ask your physician if you can take a lower dosage of the drug or possibly be weaned off the drug altogether. Perhaps you can use a natural treatment or make a lifestyle change instead.

If you have to stay on the drug and there is someone else who can drive you places (such as a spouse, sibling, child or friend), see if it's possible to become a passenger for at least the time being.

People who must drive: Stay extra alert while you're on the road, drive slowly and, of course, wear your seatbelt. And be sure not to drive if you are tired or upset.

One Drink Too Many…

Even small amounts of alcohol may be too much if you're driving. Adults over age 55 who drank roughly the equivalent of one glass of wine had worse driving skills—such as more difficulty controlling the wheel—in a simulated test than sober peers and younger drivers who drank the same amounts of alcohol.

Reason: Alcohol is more potent in older adults.

Sara Jo Nixon, PhD, chief, division of addiction research, University of Florida College of Medicine, Gainesville.

Early Alzheimer's Harms Driving Skills

Jeffrey Dawson, ScD, departments of biostatistics and neurology, University of Iowa, Iowa City, and leader of a study of 155 older people, including 40 with early-stage Alzheimer's, funded by the National Institute on Aging and published in *Neurology*.

Warning signs include loss of memory and cognitive abilities, such as needing more help than before with directions or a new route… getting lost on once-familiar roads…having trouble making turns, especially left turns… becoming confused when exiting a highway… being honked at frequently by other drivers… drifting in and out of the proper lane.

What to do: If you notice these signs in yourself or a family member, talk to a doctor.

Also: Consider consulting a driver-rehabilitation specialist who can provide a comprehensive evaluation to determine one's ability to drive and/or provide rehabilitation to strengthen driving skills—find one through the American Occupational Therapy Association, 301-652-2682, *aota.org/olderdriver*.

Stare at Drivers

Staring at drivers keeps pedestrians safer. When study subjects stared at drivers in approaching cars, the cars were more likely to stop for the pedestrians to cross the street—instead of driving past them—than when the subjects looked only in the general direction of the car.

Possible reason: Eye contact may trigger a driver's desire to make a good impression on a pedestrian by stopping.

Study led by researchers at Université de Bretagne-Sud, France, published in *Safety Science*.

Want an Extra $8,000 a Year? Living Car-Free Is Easier Than You Think

Chris Balish, an award-wining writer, reporter and broadcast journalist in Santa Monica, who has lived without a car since 2003. He is author of *How to Live Well Without Owning a Car: Save Money, Breathe Easier, and Get More Mileage Out of Life.*

Most car owners have no idea how much their vehicles actually cost them. Add up car payments, insurance, gas, repairs, maintenance, depreciation and other assorted expenses, and we paid an average of $8,876 in 2015 to own a car (which is actually less than previous years because of declining gas prices), according to AAA.

This expense might not be necessary. You can live happily in the US without a car. Going car-free tends to be easier in cities than in less densely populated areas, as well as for those without young children than for those with families—but it's a viable option for virtually everyone.

Another option: If you own two cars, cut back to one.

Helpful: The average debt per American household with at least one credit card is over $15,000, according to *nerdwallet.com*. By eliminating a second car, a family might be able to pay this off in less than two years.

I became car-free by accident in 2003, when I was living in St. Louis, and I found a buyer for my SUV before I got a new car. Once I saw how much I was saving and how easily I could get around without a car, I decided my days as a car owner were over.

ALTERNATIVE TRANSPORTATION

Before you sell your car, spend a few weeks trying to live without it. No single alternative transportation option can take the place of a car, but by combining two or three of the following alternatives, you'll always have a way to get wherever you need to go.

•**Public transit.** Approximately 50% of Americans live within a quarter mile of a public transit stop. Buses and trains are reliable, and fares are reasonable. During rush hour in metro areas, public transit can be faster than a car. Even if public transit takes a little longer in off hours and/or less congested areas, you will get more done during your transit time, because you won't have to focus on the road. Work or read during your ride, and you'll gain productive hours. Public transit is very safe. Accident rates are much lower for buses and trains than for cars, and there are far more carjackings every year than violent crimes against bus and train patrons.

Helpful: The average person can comfortably walk one mile in 10 to 20 minutes. If the nearest transit stop is too far for you to walk, you might want to bike. Most public transit systems let passengers bring bikes on board or provide bike racks at the stop or on the front of the bus. I can get just about anywhere in the Los Angeles area—I now live in Santa Monica—by combining my bicycle with mass transit.

•**Carpools.** The Internet makes carpooling easier than ever. Websites, such as *carpool world.com* and *erideshare.com*, match riders with potential rides. Your regional *craigslist. com* website also has carpool listings under the "Rideshare" heading. If you work outside your home, ask coworkers who live in your area if they would be willing to carry a passenger. Offer to chip in for gas, parking and tolls, and everyone wins.

•**Walking and biking.** Forty percent of all car trips taken in this country are two miles or less, meaning that they could have been bike trips or walks instead. Trips up to six miles on relatively flat terrain can be biked without extreme effort. Walking and biking take longer than driving, but they're great for your health and usually enjoyable.

•**Car sharing.** Car-sharing programs let members borrow vehicles on an hourly or daily basis at very reasonable rates, generally less than $10 an hour or $70 a day—gas, insurance and parking included. (There's a membership fee, starting at $7.) Check with Zipcar (866-494-7227, *zipcar.com*) for more information.

• **Rental cars.** Renting a car can be relatively inexpensive if you book online and use a vehicle mostly on weekends. To get the best rates, log onto rental company websites and sign up to receive e-mails about special deals in your region.

See page 143 for more car services, including volunteer driving programs for seniors.

MAKING THE CAR-FREE LIFE WORK

People often are concerned that they will feel isolated without a car. In fact, a car-free life offers an opportunity to be more social. You will meet more people biking, walking and carpooling than you would if you drove everywhere on your own.

Arrange joint errands and shopping trips with friends who have cars, and these once solitary tasks become shared and enjoyable experiences. Your friends might appreciate the company, too—particularly if you pay for gas or lunch, so they don't think you're taking advantage of them.

If you prefer to shop alone, rent a car, join a car-sharing service or call a taxi every few weeks to stock up on nonperishables. For smaller shopping trips, a bike or a scooter with saddlebags can carry three grocery bags with ease.

If there's no way you can live without a car in your rural or suburban location, consider the advantages of moving to town. Living in a more urban environment is likely to offer more social options than living in the country.

10 Affordable Cities Where You Don't Need a Car

Matt Lerner, cofounder of Walk Score, a website that calculates walk times to nearby amenities, then uses this data to evaluate how convenient areas are for people on foot. WalkScore.com

Walkable cities tend to be vibrant, interesting places to live. When people are able to run their errands or enjoy a day out without getting in a car, they feel more connected to their communities. And property values in walkable areas with good public transit systems tend to be particularly resilient. Houses in these locations hold their value very well.

Trouble is, America's most famous walkable cities—New York, San Francisco and Boston—are also among its most expensive places to live. However, there are places in the US that are walkable… affordable…safe…and well served by public transit. Locating these requires a bit more digging because rather than choosing a city well known for its walkability, you must seek out specific neighborhoods in cities that are not highly acclaimed for their walkability. These can be great places to live. *Ten of the best…*

• **Baltimore.** Baltimore's Mount Vernon neighborhood is very walkable—most everyday errands, such as grocery shopping and picking up dry cleaning, can be handled on foot. This neighborhood also is the home of the Walters Art Museum, the Maryland Historical Society, several theaters and many excellent restaurants. Other walkable Baltimore neighborhoods include Charles Village, home to Johns Hopkins University, the Baltimore Museum of Art and lots of attractive 19th-century architecture…and Seton Hill, a historic neighborhood that is home to the beautiful St. Mary's Park. All three neighborhoods have affordable homes and apartments and good public transit. And unlike some sections of Baltimore, their crime rates are not especially high by urban standards.

• **Buffalo.** The Buffalo neighborhoods of Allen, Bryant and Front Park are very nice places to live without a car. They are well served by Buffalo's very good public transit system—which comes in handy in the winter when this famously frigid city is too cold or snowy for long strolls. Rents and home prices are extremely affordable in Buffalo even in desirable neighborhoods such as these.

• **Chicago.** Chicago is your best option if you want to live in a very large US city where you do not need a car but you cannot afford New York. Chicago has one of America's best public transit systems and some very appealing walkable neighborhoods. And while it is not inexpensive, it is possible to find decent apartments for less than $1,000 a month. These include Lake View, home of Wrigley Field...Uptown, home of the Uptown Entertainment District...and Hyde Park, home to the University of Chicago.

•**Cleveland.** Cleveland can be a great place to live affordably without a car, but only if you live downtown...it is virtually on par with San Francisco in terms of walkability and public transit quality—and Cleveland is much, much less expensive. There's plenty worth walking to in downtown Cleveland these days, including a wide range of museums, sporting venues, theaters and shopping districts—plus more than 300 bars, restaurants and coffee shops.

•**Dallas.** Sections of Dallas near the city center are surprisingly appealing places to live without a car. Dallas's Main Street District has become a wonderfully walkable area with abundant shopping, dining and nightlife, plus Main Street Garden Park. The nearby Farmer's Market District and Government District are walkable, too. Public transit is very good in these downtown areas, and affordable condos and apartments are available.

•**Milwaukee.** Milwaukee's Juneau Town neighborhood (also known as East Town) is walkable, relatively affordable and well served by public transit. The neighborhood features more than 200 dining and drinking establishments...the indoor Milwaukee Public Market... and Juneau Park. The Milwaukee Art Museum and the Bradley Center, home of the NBA's Bucks, are both within walking distance. Other walkable Milwaukee neighborhoods with good public transit include the Lower East Side...Yankee Hill...and Murray Hill.

•**Minneapolis.** Minneapolis's cosmopolitan downtown is extremely walkable...its public transit system is very good...and the city has many miles of bike lanes and an extensive bike-sharing program. Minneapolis's relatively hill-free terrain is a big plus for walkers and bikers, too.

•**Pittsburgh.** Pittsburgh has been transformed in recent decades into a vibrant place, with river views, interesting restaurants and abundant cultural and entertainment options. Yet it remains affordable. Many parts are not great options for people who lack cars—steep hills make walking and biking a challenge, and the city's public transit system is only average. But certain neighborhoods including the Central Business District, Shadyside and Southside Flats are relatively level, walkable and bikeable and well served by public transit.

•**Rochester, New York.** Rochester's Central Business District remains fairly walkable even in the depths of the upstate New York winter because of the Rochester Skyway, a network of enclosed walkways. The neighborhood is well served by bus lines as well. The Pearl-Meigs-Monroe neighborhood (also known as the Garden District) is another nice part of town for people without cars. Homes and apartments are very affordable in Rochester.

•**St. Louis.** Sections of this engaging city are very walkable and relatively affordable. The Downtown neighborhood, for example, features Busch Stadium, home of baseball's Cardinals...the Peabody Opera House...about 150 restaurants, bars and coffee shops...and plenty of park space, including the famous Gateway Arch. Central West End is another walkable, affordable St. Louis neighborhood.

Getting Around When You No Longer Drive

Jim Miller, an advocate for older Americans, writes "Savvy Senior," a weekly information column syndicated in more than 400 newspapers nationwide. Based in Norman, Oklahoma, he also offers a free senior e-news service at SavvySenior.org.

Have you thought about what would happen if you or someone close to you could no longer drive? What now seems simple, such as getting to the doctor, the grocery store and other activities, could suddenly become difficult.

It's a common problem—about 600,000 older adults stop driving each year in the US, usually because of vision problems or some other physical or cognitive impairment, according to the National Association of Area Agencies on Aging.

Smart move: Take a little time now to learn what the transportation options are for you—or for a loved one—if you or he/she ever need to give up the car keys. This will give you peace of mind and make life easier if that day comes.

Bonus: You may decide that it's quite nice to not have to drive yourself everywhere even if you could and start using these services just for convenience!

Keep in mind that transportation options vary widely by community. While most urban areas offer a variety of different services, the options may be few for people living in some suburbs, small towns and rural areas.

Here's a rundown of possible transportation solutions that could help you or a loved one get around, along with some resources to help you locate them...

• **Family and friends.** For most people, this is the first option, but don't make the common mistake of limiting the people who can help to the most obvious ones. Include all the possible candidates you might call on for rides including your children, grandchildren, siblings, cousins, nieces and nephews, friends and neighbors. Determine their availability and contact information. It's always best to give drivers plenty of advanced notice, and if you're reluctant to ask for rides or feel as though you're imposing, offer to reimburse them for their gas and time so that they feel appreciated.

• **Volunteer-driver programs.** These types of programs—usually sponsored by nonprofit organizations that serve seniors and people with disabilities—typically offer flexible transportation to and from doctor's appointments, shopping and other activities, and many provide door-to-door service or something called "door-through-door service," in which the volunteer driver also helps you by opening doors and providing physical support as needed.

Drivers are usually part-time volunteers or paid workers that drive their own vehicle or the program's vehicle, which may be a car or van. Many volunteer-driver programs charge a nominal fee for rides or suggest donations for rides, though some are free.

Examples: The Eldercare Locator at *eldercare.gov* is a public service of the U.S. Administration on Aging connecting you to local services for older adults and their families. You can also call 800-677-1116. The Independent Transportation Network (*itnamerica.org*) includes transportation programs in about 20 areas across the US and has more in development. It charges riders age 60 and older and visually impaired adults of any age annual membership dues of around $50, plus a $4 pick-up fee and a mileage fee of around $1.50 per mile. Rates will vary slightly by program.

Independent Transportation Network programs also offer a car-trade program that lets you convert your car into a fund to pay for future rides...and a car-donation program that provides a tax deduction if you itemize on your tax returns.

Paratransit services, also called "dial-a-ride" or "elderly and disabled transportation services," typically are government-funded programs that provide door-to-door or curb-to-curb services. Most paratransit services use mini-buses or vans and offer accessible services for riders with disabilities. They typically require reservations a day or two in advance and charge a small fee ranging anywhere between $0.50 and $10 on a per-ride basis. However, some services may be free for those who can't afford to pay.

To locate a paratransit service in your area, contact your Area Aging Agency. Call 800-677-1116 or visit *eldercare.gov* to find your agency's phone number.

Public mass transit is a wonderful option in some cities, and people who haven't used it in a long time are often surprised to find that it is pleasant and reliable. Of course, that doesn't describe packed trains or buses at rush hour! But bus, rail and subway services in some cities are quite useful for many people who no longer drive. Reduced fares usually are available for seniors and people with disabilities. For information on options in your area, contact your public transit agency or visit the

American Public Transportation Association at *publictransportation.org*.

●**Taxi/car services.** These private services provide flexible transportation options but are more expensive than the previously listed options. Trips usually can be scheduled in advance or on the spot. Some taxis/cars are wheelchair-accessible and meet ADA standards. Taxi and car services in some areas offer senior discounts.

●**Ride-sharing services.** This is a rapidly growing alternative to taxis. The two biggest ride-sharing services are Uber (*uber.com*) and Lyft (*lyft.com*), which operate in major cities across the US.

With a ride-sharing service, you can request a ride anytime from an independent driver who uses his/her privately owned vehicle to transport you. Ride requests with Uber are made using the Uber smartphone app or at the Uber mobile website (*m.uber.com*)...with Lyft, you use its smartphone app only. However, New York City Medicaid residents who are members of the National MedTrans Network now can request a Lyft ride to non-emergency medical appointments via phone by calling 844-714-2219.

Rates for all ride-sharing services vary greatly by city, the time of day you ride and the type of service you pick, but costs generally are comparable to taxi fares. Uber and Lyft drivers are required to undergo a driving check and criminal background check, although critics have complained that the process is not thorough enough, and Lyft does driver vehicle inspections, too.

●**Private transportation services.** Some hospitals, health clinics, senior centers, adult day centers, malls and other businesses offer free transportation for program participants or customers. And some nonmedical home-care agencies that provide companionship, household chores and errand running offer fee-based transportation services. It's worth asking any business or institution that you deal with (or that you might deal with) whether it provides transportation or has an arrangement with a service that does.

●**Drivers for hire.** If you live in an area where there are limited or no transportation services available, another option is to pay someone to drive you. Consider hiring a neighbor, retiree or high school or college student who has a flexible schedule and wouldn't mind making a few extra dollars. But before hiring someone, make sure you see a driver's license and proof of insurance, and check references.

Two excellent resources for finding local transportation options include your local Area Agency on Aging (call 800-677-1116 or visit *eldercare.gov* to find your agency's phone number)...and a nonprofit service called Rides in Sight (855-607-4337 or *ridesinsight.org*).

8

Stay Safe from Crime and Scams

Don't Believe These Myths About Crime

Some of the things that people do to avoid crime actually increase their odds of becoming victims. *Here, the truth about common misconceptions about crime—plus important safety strategies…*

MYTH: **If you're mugged, throw your wallet or purse at the assailant and run.** The mugger will stop to pick up your valuables rather than pursue you.

REALITY: Many street criminals value respect above all else. Throwing your valuables could be taken as a form of disrespect. The mugger might use violence against you for this.

Better: Politely hand over your valuables without making eye contact. Follow the mugger's directions, and do not say anything beyond, "Take my money…it's all yours."

Exception: If you hand over your valuables and the mugger continues issuing instructions, such as "get down on your knees" or "walk into that alley," it is time to run away. Muggers who do not leave quickly after obtaining a victim's possessions often intend to commit murder or sexual assault.

MYTH: **The best way to fight back against a male assailant is with a kick to the groin.**

REALITY: Attempts to disable assailants with kicks or punches to the groin almost always fail. Men usually experience an adrenaline rush when they commit assaults or muggings. One consequence of this adrenaline rush is that their testicles retreat up close to their bodies, making the testicles a very difficult target to hit. Most men also are quite adept at protecting their groin area when they realize that an attack might be coming. Even if

Dale Yeager, a criminal analyst who is CEO of SERAPH Corporation, a security consulting and training company based in Phoenixville, Pennsylvania.

an assailant's testicles are struck, the onset of pain is not instantaneous. An assailant might have enough time to seriously injure or kill you before feeling the full effects.

Better: If you do attempt a physical attack on an assailant, go for a kidney. The kidneys are located on our sides, just above the waist—roughly where the thumbs rest when we stand with our hands on our hips. Kidneys are extremely sensitive. If an attacker comes at you, hit or slap the kidney or stab a pen in the area.

MYTH: **If you act confident, you are less likely to be targeted by criminals**.

REALITY: Criminals could mistake your show of confidence for arrogance and target you to take you down a peg. When a man acts very confidently, a male criminal might target him for assault to prove that the criminal is the top dog. When Americans abroad act confidently, they sometimes are targeted by criminals who consider the US their enemy. Rape-prevention groups often recommend that women walk and act with exaggerated confidence when they feel threatened, but this can increase the risk for sexual assault.

Better: It is fine to feel confident, but don't act cocky. Arrogance can make you a target. Also, feigned confidence often seems unnatural and makes us stand out from crowds. Acting the way we actually feel helps us blend in, a far better way to avoid unwanted criminal attention.

MYTH: **The least safe areas are "bad neighborhoods" at night.**

REALITY: In my experience, the highest-risk areas for physical attacks by strangers are not bad neighborhoods but near nightclubs. The perpetrators typically are nightclub patrons who have had too much to drink.

Better: Stay out of nightclubs, and advise your adult children to do the same. If you do go to nightclubs in any kind of neighborhood, leave before midnight—most attacks happen later, when patrons have been drinking for many hours. If you feel at all threatened when leaving a nightclub, ask a doorman or bouncer to keep an eye on you as you walk to your car. Avoid parking near nightclubs if you will be returning to your car after midnight.

MYTH: **Burglars won't come in if they know you're home.**

REALITY: Most break-ins happen between 2 pm and 9 pm, partly because this is when people are likely to have their doors unlocked. Burglars target homes that appear easy to break into and move on to other homes if the first one selected proves challenging.

Better: Determine what your neighbors do for home security, then do that and a little more in your own home. Dogs, motion-detecting lights, deadbolts and alarm systems all can be effective deterrents. And be sure to lock doors.

Crime Can Happen Anywhere: Be Your Own Bodyguard

Irene van der Zande, cofounder, executive director and instructor at Kidpower Teenpower Fullpower International, a nonprofit organization that has taught personal safety and self-defense techniques to children, adults and seniors since 1989, Santa Cruz, California. KidPower.org

W e all need to become our own bodyguards when we're out and about. Most of us know the basic safety advice, such as always being aware of our surroundings. *Here are more tactics to stay safe when you're out in public...*

• **Program your cell phone with the local police number on speed dial in case there's trouble.** Police have told me that this often yields a faster officer response than 911 because a 911 operator has to route the call to a police officer. Check with your local police department to find out which would be faster in your region.

• **Always lock your car.** This seems like a no-brainer, but you would be surprised at how many people forget to do it. Lock your car even if you're just sitting in it for a few moments in a parking lot before you drive off.

• **Carry mugger's money if you are in a high-risk locale, such as a bad neighborhood or a tourist spot in a foreign country.** Keep a wallet with $20 to $50 in small bills that's easily accessed, separate from your other valuables.

• **Press the panic button on your car key to set off the car alarm if someone frightens you.** Many alarms can be triggered from at least 45 feet away, sometimes 100 feet or more. The loud noise can deter would-be attackers.

• **Put your valuables down and move away if you are asked to give up your wallet or purse.** This increases the distance between you and the assailant.

• **Yell orders if you feel your life is being threatened.** If you give up your valuables, but the person says, "You're coming with me," or starts to attack or pull you, yell clear messages, such as, "Stop," and "Leave me alone," to the attacker. Then, if there are others around, yell, "Call the police," or "Call 911." Don't yell, "Help." The word "help" makes people afraid for their own safety and unsure of what to do.

Example: Late one night, an elderly woman's car broke down in a bad neighborhood. While she was waiting for the tow service, five young men got out of their cars and started threatening her. She screamed to a woman she saw, "Call the police." She then yelled at her attackers, "Stop right there! Get back in your cars and leave. The police are on their way." The men took off.

• **Know simple moves targeted at the most vulnerable spots on the body in case you must physically defend yourself.** Yelling, "No!" while you perform these moves helps give you more power…

• The Eye Strike. Squeeze your fingers together (like a bird's beak), and jab them hard into the attacker's eyes. You also can claw your fingers like a rake across the eyes.

These moves aren't meant to disarm or overpower an attacker, which is difficult to do. You just want to buy yourself enough time to break away from his grasp. If you can manage to get a few feet away from him—all the while screaming—chances are high that he will flee to avoid being caught rather than chase you.

Why Big Trees Reduce Crime

Neighborhoods with large trees tend to have less crime than areas with smaller trees.

Theory: Large trees indicate to criminals that an area is well cared for.

Geoffrey H. Donovan, PhD, research forester, Portland Forestry Sciences Laboratory, Oregon, and coauthor of a study of 431 crimes, published in *Environment and Behavior*.

How to Travel Safely

Peter V. Savage, vice president and cofounder of Passport Health, a leading provider of low-cost immunizations and travel-related services to businesses and tourists, Baltimore. PassportHealthUSA.com. He is author of *The Safe Travel Book*.

When you're on vacation, the last thing you want to worry about is your safety, but it's wise to be prepared. *Important travel advice…*

• **Contact the embassy.** Before you book a trip, call the American embassy in the country you will be visiting and ask for the Regional Security Officer (RSO). You can get the number by contacting the State Department at 888-407-4747 (202-501-4444 outside the US) or *travel.state.gov*.

The RSO should be able to answer questions about disease outbreaks, high-crime areas, weather issues, where to get the best exchange rates and problems American travelers have had recently.

Example: A few years ago, I called the RSO in Ottawa, Canada, and asked about Montreal. The RSO told me that if I rented a sport utility vehicle (SUV) during my stay, I should keep it parked in a garage. Criminals were stealing SUVs off the streets, quickly stripping them and shipping the parts to China.

• **Don't dress like an American.** I shake my head when I see Americans in foreign countries wearing clothing that announces where they're from or where they went to college. I even saw an American oilman in Venezuela wearing cowboy boots and a cowboy hat with a turkey feather. Letting others know that you're an American may prompt crooks to assume that you are a wealthy tourist worth robbing or, even worse, worth kidnapping for a ransom.

• **Keep watches and jewelry—even costume jewelry that looks real—at home.** If you must bring jewelry or other valuables, make sure they are insured. Also, avoid using expensive luggage. Keep cameras hidden when not in use.

• **Outsmart pickpockets.** I keep money, my passport and credit cards in a wallet that attaches to my belt and is concealed under my clothes. You can buy these at *magellans.com.*

If you use a fanny pack, keep the pouch in front. (A common trick of pickpockets is to bump into you front and back—pickpockets usually work in teams—and quickly slice the bottom of the fanny pack and catch the valuables as they drop.) Women should carry purses football fashion. Don't bother getting traveler's checks—these days, credit cards have wider acceptance. In your purse or pocket, carry enough cash to satisfy a mugger.

• **Keep important information with your passport.** Write down the phone numbers of the American embassies in the countries that you intend to visit. Also, include your blood type and whether your blood's Rh factor is positive or negative. Make copies of your passport and keep them with you in case you lose your original. Leave copies with friends or relatives at home as well.

Sneaky New Tricks from Identity Thieves—How to Protect Yourself

Steve Weisman, an attorney and a member of the National Academy of Elder Law Attorneys. He is author of 50 *Ways to Protect Your Identity in a Digital Age: New Financial Threats You Need to Know and How to Avoid Them.* Scamicide.com

Identity thieves have developed new ways to gain access to our credit card accounts, bank accounts, Social Security numbers and other sensitive data. *Here, the sneakiest threats and ways to protect yourself...*

HOTEL WI-FI

In decades past, criminals who targeted hotel guests typically broke into rooms and stole valuables from luggage. These days, identity thieves can steal from hotel guests without ever setting foot in their rooms. They do this by setting up Wi-Fi networks that appear to be official hotel Wi-Fi networks, then stealing private data from hotel guests who log on. All public Wi-Fi networks should be treated with caution, but hotel Wi-Fi is particularly dangerous because guests tend to feel secure in the privacy of their rooms, making them more likely to access financial accounts, enter credit card details or reveal other super-sensitive information. *To protect yourself...*

• **Update your laptop, tablet or smartphone security software immediately before staying at a hotel (see below under "Smartphones").** This maximizes the odds that the security software will identify threats.

• **Never use hotel Wi-Fi for online banking, credit card account management or investment management.** Don't use a hotel lobby computer for such things, either. "Keyloggers" that track every keystroke and report things such as passwords to identity thieves often are loaded onto public computers. Consider using your smartphone's network instead for these functions, because it is somewhat safer. Or at least check with the hotel to confirm that you are logging in to the authentic hotel Wi-Fi.

• **If you're prompted to update software or download a program while accessing the Internet through a hotel Wi-Fi system, decline to do so.** Downloading this "update" actually might load malware (malicious software) onto your computer. If you feel that you must update your software as directed, at least don't click a link in a pop-up window to do so. Instead, visit the software provider's official website, and download the update from there.

• **Don't call the phone number provided on a restaurant menu slipped under your hotel room door.** In one new scam, identity thieves print phony delivery menus, then slip them under hotel room doors. When guests call to place orders, they're asked for credit card information, which then is used for fraudulent purchases. If you wish to order from such a menu, look up the restaurant's number on your own.

SMARTPHONES

Smartphones essentially are portable computers, yet many people don't take smartphone security as seriously as they do home computer security. *To protect yourself…*

• **Load antivirus software onto your smartphone,** and keep this software updated. Options for phones that use the Android operating system include Kaspersky Internet Security for Android (*usa.kaspersky. com*, $14.95)…ESET Mobile Security (*eset. com*, $19.95)…BullGuard Mobile Security (*bull guard.com*, $29.95)…and AVG AntiVirus FREE (*avgmobilation.com*, free). They are available at the websites and at app stores.

For iPhones, iPads and iPods, quality antivirus software is harder to find and less of a necessity because hackers have not gone after them yet, although they probably will before long. Still, Apple smartphone, iPad and iPod users should consider downloading AVG Safe Browser, a free web browser that will warn them away from unsafe sites (download it through iTunes or the App Store on your device). While Apple smartphones currently are at low risk for computer viruses, that eventually will change. Apple computers once were

very safe from viruses, too, but now are essentially as vulnerable as Windows PCs.

• **Download apps only from usually reliable sources.** If you download an app from the wrong site, you might unknowingly load malicious software onto your phone as well. Trustworthy app sources for iPhones include Apple's App Store.

Trustworthy sources for Android include Google Play (*play.google.com*) and Appstore for Android on *amazon.com* (select "Appstore for Android" from the "Shop by Department" menu).

• **Set a pass code on your smartphone.** A simple four-digit PIN (or longer pass code) will make it much more difficult for a thief who steals your smartphone to access the data you have stored in it…or for someone who has access to your home or office to load malware onto your phone when you're not watching. The procedure for setting a pass code varies from phone to phone.

CREDIT CARDS

The merchant you buy from might not properly protect your credit card data or the merchant himself could be a thief. Many card issuers now offer two smart ways to reduce this danger. *Contact your card issuers for details and availability…*

• **Ask the issuer to supply a single-use authorization number.** This number is tied to your credit card account but is valid only for a single transaction and would be provided to an Internet merchant in place of the actual credit card number. It's worth considering when buying from Internet merchants that you are not sure you can trust. Even if a crook obtained it, he couldn't use it for additional purchases.

• **Set up a password for online card use through the card issuer.** A box will pop up requesting the password whenever the card is used online. Even online merchants never see this password.

SOCIAL NETWORKS

It isn't news that identity thieves prey upon Facebook users, pretending to be online friends in order to gather personal data. But many users of Facebook and other social networks don't realize that this is not the only way that identity thieves might target them. *To stay safe...*

• **Don't provide any details about yourself on your Facebook** page that could be used to answer the personal security questions you've set up for accounts. If you forget the password for one of your accounts—anything from an e-mail account to a financial account that can be accessed online—that account provider's website likely will ask you a personal question to confirm your identity before providing access. The personal question might involve your mother's maiden name, the name of your childhood best friend or some other personal detail that strangers are unlikely to know. Trouble is, people often supply these personal details on their Facebook pages or elsewhere.

Much better: Choose personal security questions that cannot be answered using information available on your Facebook page or elsewhere online. Or adjust your answers to personal security questions in a way that you can remember but that no one else is likely to guess. You could tack your favorite number or color onto each response, typing "Larryblue" rather than "Larry" when asked your childhood best friend's name, for example.

• **Don't click links in messages you receive through social networks—even when those messages come from close friends.** When an identity thief breaks into a victim's Facebook account, he/she often will send messages to all of that person's Facebook friends pretending to be this person. These messages typically include a link that, when clicked, secretly loads malware onto the friends' computers, allowing the thief to steal their identities, too.

Identity Scams Are Growing

Criminals pose as someone you know or trust to get personal data for identity theft.

Examples: The grandchild scam involves sending an instant Facebook message from a supposed grandchild, asking for immediate help because his/her money was stolen or he has been wrongly imprisoned. The sender actually is a thief who has hacked into a Facebook account. Another scam uses online links—supposedly from friends—to send you to sites that install malware.

What to do: Never respond to money requests immediately—take the time to check out the claims. Do not click on links to sites recommended in an e-mail unless you call the sender and are sure his/her account has not been hacked.

Federal Trade Commission Consumer Alert. FTC.gov

Aging Brains Are More Vulnerable to Fraud

The anterior insula, an area of the brain that helps interpret the trustworthiness of people, does not function as efficiently in people over age 55 as it does in younger people. This may explain why older people are more likely to fall for financial scams.

Study by researchers at University of California, Los Angeles, published in *Proceedings of the National Academy of Sciences.*

Prepaid-Funeral Scams

Joshua Slocum, executive director of Funeral Consumers Alliance (FCA), a nonprofit consumer-rights organization based in South Burlington, Vermont. The FCA has served as an independent funeral-industry watchdog since 1963. Funerals.org

Some well-meaning people purchase prepaid-funeral contracts so that when they die, their heirs won't have to pay their funeral expenses. The contracts might cover everything from the burial or cremation to the casket, embalming, death notices, use of the funeral home, limousines and flowers. But these contracts sometimes don't work as well as expected.

Example: National Prearranged Services, which sold prepaid-funeral service contracts for up to $10,000 to about 150,000 customers from 1992 to 2008, failed to place its customers' payments in insurance policies or trusts as required by law, according to federal prosecutors. This left the company without enough money to fund the agreements they sold.

This was hardly the first prepaid-funeral contract problem. Scammers have disappeared with prepaid-funeral customers' money or taken advantage of grieving heirs by delivering lower-quality funeral services than promised, such as cheaper caskets and smaller flower arrangements.

In fact, prepaid-funeral contracts are almost always a bad idea, even if you manage to avoid the outright scams. As much as 30% of your prepayment might go to the salesperson and/or the prepayment-services company rather than toward your funeral costs. Some or all of the money you prepay is likely to be lost if you die in a different part of the country than anticipated. And the money you prepay won't earn interest for your heirs.

Better: If you don't want your heirs to have to pay for your funeral, instead put sufficient money to finance this expense into a bank payable-on-death account or another savings or investment account. Name a trusted heir as this account's beneficiary so that the money doesn't become tied up in probate. Instruct this heir to use the money to pay your funeral costs—you also might offer guidance about the kind of funeral you want—and let other heirs know of this arrangement as well. (Expect a simple cremation without ceremony to start at $1,000. A full funeral with a casket burial can run as high as $10,000, though prices vary.)

Exception: It might be worth buying a prepaid-funeral contract if you must spend down your assets to qualify for Medicaid.

Package-Delivery Scam

Victims receive an e-mail that appears to be from the US Postal Service stating that a package could not be delivered. The e-mail says to click on a link in the message to arrange delivery or pickup—but clicking on this link loads a malicious virus that can steal information from the victim's computer. Forward spam e-mails to *spam@uspis.gov.*

Note: If there is a package for you, the postal service will leave a notice in your mailbox rather than send an e-mail.

Margaret D. Williams, national public information representative with the US Postal Inspection Service. PostalInspectors.uspis.gov

How to Avoid ID Theft on the Internet

James Christiansen, former senior vice president of information security at Visa International and former chief information security officer at General Motors. He is author of several books on Internet security, including *Internet Survival Guide: Protecting Your Financial Information.*

High-tech thieves can use the Internet to gather the account numbers and other personal data they need to steal your identity. You could be at risk if you shop, pay bills or access your bank accounts online—or even if you store personal data, such as your Social Security number or credit card numbers, on your own computer.

Here's how to steer clear of the Internet missteps that can lead to identity theft. *These include…*

MISTAKE: **Sending e-mails that contain confidential information.**

Even if the recipient of your e-mail is reliable enough to be trusted with your sensitive information (Social Security number, driver's license number, credit card number, date of birth, mother's maiden name), others could gain access to your message as well. E-mails do not transfer instantly from our computer to our recipient's computer. They make stops at several points along the way, where they could be read.

Alternately, if a criminal gained access to your computer or the message recipient's computer, he/she could find your e-mail stored in memory.

Self-defense: Convey sensitive information over the phone, not the Internet.

MISTAKE: Providing personal details on social networking websites or chat groups.

The Internet is a great place to converse with people who share your interests, but sharing too much information could put you in danger. A criminal might decide that you make a good target for identity theft—or worse.

Self-defense: Keep personal details to a minimum when online. Never mention your address, phone number or financial institutions with which you have accounts. Use a nickname. Withhold personal information even in private e-mail exchanges with people you meet through the Internet. These people might not be what they seem.

MISTAKE: Downloading free programs from the Internet or clicking on pop-ups.

When you download a program from the Internet, you could unknowingly load spyware onto your computer in the process. This spyware could give a scammer access to any information you type into or save on your computer. Clicking on a pop-up could create similar problems. (There often is no way to tell the safe pop-ups from the unsafe ones, so the best policy is to skip them all.)

Self-defense: Download software from the Internet only if you're confident in the integrity of the site providing the program.

Best: Ask your Internet service provider if access to an Internet security program is included in your monthly fee.

MISTAKE: Assuming e-mail messages are from who they seem to be from.

Scammers can make e-mail messages appear to have been sent by anyone, including people and businesses you know.

Examples: You receive an e-mail that appears to be from your bank. It asks whether you made a particular transaction and warns that you must respond immediately if you did not. Or, you receive an e-mail that appears to come from the IRS. It says you will be audited if you do not reply to the message quickly, then asks for your Social Security number or other personal information.

Self-defense: Be very suspicious of e-mails claiming to be from financial institutions or the IRS, particularly if these messages ask you to enter passwords, account numbers or Social Security numbers (or steer you to websites that ask for any of these things). These messages are likely to be from scammers. Instead, look up the phone number of the company or agency that the e-mail claims to be from (do not trust the phone number that might be included in the e-mail) and call to confirm the validity of the message.

If you receive an e-mail message that seems to be from a friend featuring an Internet link or picture and a simple message such as "you have to see this," it might have been sent by a scammer. If you click the link, it could load spyware onto your computer, opening the door to identity theft. Do not click the link or open the picture until you have contacted your friend and confirmed that he sent the note.

MISTAKE: Entering important data or passwords into a public computer.

The public computers in libraries and coffeehouses are often contaminated with spyware.

Self-defense: Assume that everything you type on these computers is being recorded. Never use public computers to make online purchases or to do online banking. Do not even check your e-mail—a scammer could learn your user name and password and gain access to personal information stored in your e-mail files.

MISTAKE: Trusting websites that have weak security.

Most Internet companies that accept credit card numbers or other sensitive data work very hard to keep this information secure. Unfortunately, some sites' security measures fall short, increasing the odds that a criminal could be monitoring your transaction and stealing your information.

Self-defense: Do not enter your credit card number or any other important data into a website unless its web address begins "https," not just "http." The "s" indicates an added level of security. A small picture of a closed lock should appear on the web address line as well.

Note: Never enter confidential information onto a site if you clicked on it from an e-mail, even if it has "https." Always type in a URL.

MISTAKE: **Picking obvious passwords.**

Scammers have software that can help them guess common passwords. If your password is a date, a name, a word or a repeating or progressive series of letters or numbers, such as "zzzz" or "2468," it could be cracked if a high-tech criminal targets you. If you use the same password for many accounts, this could give the criminal wide access to your personal and financial information.

Self-defense: The most secure passwords are multiple-word phrases. If the site permits, these should include numbers or symbols, such as "my2dogsareyellow" or "Ilikeham$alad."

Select phrases that are memorable to you. Use different ones for each account, and don't write them down near your computer. A program called RoboForm (*roboform.com*) provides an encrypted computer "password safe" that can remember several passwords for you for free.

Identity Thieves Search Obituaries to Set Up Scams

D o not include in an obituary the deceased's specific birth date and date of death. These can make it easier for con men to obtain a copy of the death certificate, which often has the deceased's Social Security number. Also, consider leaving out the person's hometown and

state—including these may help thieves obtain vital records from the county clerk's office.

Karen Barney, program director, Identity Theft Resource Center, San Diego. IDTheftCenter.org

---

Quick and Free Cybersecurity

Greg McBride, chief financial analyst for Bankrate. com.

T here are all kinds of things we can do to prevent identity theft—ranging from the simple (not giving out your Social Security number) to the complicated (separate passwords for every account) to the expensive (hundreds of dollars for credit-monitoring services).

All of these can be effective, says Greg McBride, chief financial analyst for *bankrate.com*. But there are two quick, easy and free things we can do that most of us don't do that are truly worth our trouble…

Log onto bank and investment accounts every week or so rather than wait for month-end statements. Skim for withdrawals that you don't recall authorizing. If you find any, immediately inform the financial company even if the amount is very small. (Crooks sometimes make small, probing withdrawals before stealing larger amounts…or remove small amounts repeatedly in the hope that the tiny thefts will go unnoticed.) You can bookmark your financial companies' websites in your Internet browser to save time. Never use public Wi-Fi to access financial accounts.

Examine your credit report every few months. You might already know that you can receive a free credit report from each of the three major credit bureaus (Experian, Equifax and TransUnion) once each year through *annualcreditreport.com*. Now you also can get a free EquiFax credit report as often as once each month through his site, *mybankrate.com*. If you find a credit account that is not yours on your report, contact both the lender listed and the credit bureau.

Watch Out for "Friendship Fraud"

Watch out for "friendship fraud" on social-networking sites. Scammers invade on-line groups by finding members who easily accept requests to join their group. Then the scammers participate in group discussions for a while...and introduce a scam—often a phony investment idea—after people become used to interacting with them.

What to do: Avoid any investment that lacks publicly available information...promises high returns with little or no risk...comes with a sense of urgency—scammers often say that they can hold an opportunity only for a day or a week...is sold largely on the basis of testimonials from supposedly satisfied investors.

Jack Herstein, president, North American Securities Administrators Association, Washington, DC, and assistant director of the Nebraska Department of Banking and Finance, Bureau of Securities, Lincoln.

Biggest Tax Scams Now

Be alert for some of these prevalent tax scams...

Phone scams involving aggressive, threatening calls from criminals claiming to be IRS agents...phishing scams using phony e-mails or fake websites to try to steal personal information...identity theft by criminals who file returns using other people's Social Security numbers...and return-preparer fraud, in which preparers misrepresent refunds or use their knowledge of personal information to steal identities.

If you are suspicious about any issues involving taxes, contact the IRS, *irs.gov/identity theft*.

Internal Revenue Service. IRS.gov

Safeguard Your Social Security Payments

John Sileo, president of The Sileo Group, a think tank based in Denver that helps organizations protect critical data. He is a keynote speaker and author of *Privacy Means Profit: Prevent Identity Theft and Secure You and Your Bottom Line.* Sileo.com

Block scammers from stealing your Social Security payments electronically. Anyone who uses a bank account with direct deposit is vulnerable.

Thieves first obtain personal information including your Social Security and bank account numbers. Then the scammers use that information electronically to have the Social Security Administration (SSA) reroute your monthly benefits to a different direct-deposit account.

Example: An 86-year-old man received a letter telling him that he won $3.5 million and asking him to submit personal information by phone—after which he became a victim of diverted Social Security payment fraud.

There have been thousands of reports of this type of scheme involving millions of dollars in diverted payments, and several culprits have been arrested and convicted.

Self-defense: Never give out financial information to callers, even if they say that they are from a bank or the government. Always check the real phone number of the institution, and call it before divulging any information.

You can contact Social Security at 800-772-1213 and arrange to block anyone from making changes electronically or by phone to your account or establishing new online access to your account.

You also can use that number to report missing direct-deposit payments and open a fraud investigation. You will be reimbursed by the SSA, but it may take several weeks.

Warning: Cyber Thieves May Have Your Social Security Number

John Sileo, president and CEO of The Sileo Group, a Denver-based data-security think tank that has worked with the Department of Defense and Federal Reserve Bank of New York, among other clients. He is author of *Privacy Means Profit: Prevent Identity Theft and Secure You and Your Bottom Line.* Sileo.com

Massive data breaches at giant companies have become so commonplace that consumers now tend to shrug them off. But high-tech criminals have ratcheted up the danger—and the steps required to safeguard consumer finances and identities—to a whole new level.

The biggest and most recently revealed example of a much more dangerous hacking incident involves the health insurance provider Anthem—although similar, less publicized invasions have occurred at other companies—and it makes the possible fallout from incidents of credit card and password theft seem mild in comparison.

We asked security expert John Sileo to explain why the dangers are so high now and what consumers can do to protect themselves...

SOCIAL SECURITY NUMBERS ARE KEY

Unlike the hacking incidents at such companies as Target and The Home Depot, the Anthem breach could lead to long-lasting and even life-altering identity theft for many of the up to 80 million current and former customers potentially affected. That's because the hackers who invaded Anthem's computers stole data including names, employment and contact information, health insurance IDs, addresses, birth dates and Social Security numbers.

Social Security number breaches are especially dangerous because they don't just help crooks gain access to your accounts, the way a credit card breach does. Social Security breaches allow the crooks to pose as you in myriad ways that could wreck your life. Victims might spend the rest of their lives fending off bill collectors about purchases they never made...fighting to remove inaccurate and potentially lethal information from their medical files...explaining to police that it was really someone else who was arrested and skipped bail...and praying that no one steals their tax refunds.

That's far worse than having your credit card information stolen—credit cards can be quickly canceled, passwords can be changed and any losses usually are covered by the issuer.

If you become a victim of a corporate data breach, don't be fooled into thinking that you're safe just because...

•**Months have passed and your credit reports remain fine.** A 2012 survey by consulting company Javelin Strategy & Research found that 22.5% of people who receive a notice informing them that they were the victim of a data breach later become victims of identity theft—but it doesn't always happen fast. Data thieves sometimes wait years to use stolen data.

•**You have never been an Anthem customer.** There have been other comparable data breaches, and more are sure to follow.

Examples: Community Health Systems, a network of more than 200 hospitals across 29 states, had approximately 4.5 million patient records breached. Experian, which maintains confidential credit files, was breached, exposing an unknown number of files.

Possible consequences for victims of the Anthem breach—and other similar breaches—and what to do about each...

PHONY DEBTS IN YOUR NAME

An identity thief who has your Social Security number might open new credit accounts in your name or even borrow against the value of your home. You would not be held legally responsible for these debts ultimately, but it could take decades to clear up the mess. In the meantime, your damaged credit score could mean higher interest rates on loans... higher auto insurance rates...and even rejections from potential employers.

What to do: Place a security freeze on your credit files. The usual advice is to put a fraud alert on your files, but that does not provide sufficient protection. Alerts generally expire in 90 days, and while lenders are supposed to take added precautions when an alert is in place, these precautions can fail. A freeze completely blocks your credit report from being accessed and credit from being issued until the freeze is lifted.

• **Contact all three credit bureaus** by phone or online to establish this freeze (*experian.com*, *equifax.com* and *transunion.com*). You will have to contact the bureaus again and provide a password whenever you wish to temporarily lift the freeze to apply for credit. Costs vary by state, but expect to pay $3 to $10 to each reporting agency each time the freeze is lifted. In some states, there also is a fee to establish or reestablish a freeze.

Helpful: Ask lenders and credit card issuers which credit-reporting agency or agencies they use, and then lift the freeze only with those—generally only mortgage lenders check all three. In some states, you will be exempt from the fees cited above if you are 65 or older (62 or older in Louisiana and North Carolina) and/or can provide a police report showing that you are a victim of ID theft.

If you are unwilling to place a security freeze on your credit—perhaps because you are in the process of applying for loans or jobs—at least sign up for an ID-theft-monitoring service. These services do not prevent ID theft, but they can notify you quickly of certain signs of trouble and help you navigate the often frustrating recovery process.

Warning: The ID-theft-monitoring services provided to the victims of large-scale data breaches for free usually are badly lacking, possibly monitoring credit reports with only one of the three major credit bureaus, for example.

Instead, consider spending around $250 per person a year for a high-quality ID-theft-monitoring service. Choose one that monitors credit reports from all three credit-reporting agencies plus address-change requests, court records, driver's license activity, payday loan applications and websites where stolen identities are bought and sold. Services that use the underlying monitoring technology of a company called CSID tend to be among the most robust. These include IDT911 and LifeLock.

PHONY DEBTS IN KIDS' NAMES

If your children are covered through your health insurance, they also could be at risk for identity theft if your insurer or one of your medical providers is breached. This wasn't a risk with retailers such as Target and The Home Depot that do not normally have minors' confidential information on file.

ID theft can be especially troublesome for minors because it often isn't noticed for years. One frustrating twist for parents—you generally cannot place a fraud alert or a security freeze on a young child's credit file. If the child doesn't yet have credit, he/she probably doesn't yet have a credit file. If you try to set up a fraud alert or credit freeze for such a child, it could trigger the creation of a credit file, which in some ways makes it easier to steal the child's identity.

What to do: An ID-theft-monitoring service that includes family protection can monitor databases for signs that the child's Social Security number is being used by identity thieves. Even the free monitoring product being offered by Anthem likely can do this, though a higher-quality service offered by a pay service probably could do it better.

PHONY HEALTH INSURANCE BILLS

Someone could use your health insurance ID number to obtain health services in your name, leaving you to battle health-care providers and bill collectors about co-pays and other fees that you don't owe. What's more, your medical records could become corrupted with someone else's information, leading to a potentially lethal misdiagnosis.

What to do: Read every "Explanation of Benefits" statement you get from your insurer. If any don't correspond to a medical visit you made or treatment you had, contact the provider and the insurer immediately to alert them to potential medical identity theft. If you have access to your medical records through a health-care provider's online patient portal, check this every month or so.

STOLEN TAX REFUNDS

An identity thief who has your Social Security number and date of birth could file a phony tax return in your name to claim a tax refund. Not only could this greatly complicate your own tax filing, it might mean that you can't receive the refund you are due until the situation is cleared up, which could take years.

If you filed taxes last year in Florida, Georgia or Washington, DC—the places with the highest rates of tax-refund identity theft—you can apply for an identity-protection personal identification number, or IP PIN, through the IRS website. On *irs.gov*, enter "IP PIN" into the search box, then select "The Identity Protection PIN (IP PIN)." Once you receive your six-digit IP PIN, enter it on your tax return to confirm that the return actually is from you. IP PINs also are available to the approximately 1.7 million taxpayers who received a letter offering them this safeguard because the IRS identified what it considered suspicious activity in their accounts. IP PINs cannot be used on state tax returns, however. For more information on eligibility and rules, go to *irs.gov/individuals/the-identity-protection-pin-ip-pin*.

SHOULD YOU GET A NEW SOCIAL SECURITY NUMBER?

The Social Security Administration allows people to request new Social Security numbers when other measures fail to stop identity thieves. To request this, complete form SS-5, Application for a Social Security Card (*socialsecurity.gov/forms*) and bring proof of your identity and proof of a serious ID-theft problem—such as letters from bill collectors or credit-reporting agencies—to your local Social Security office.

But this generally is worth doing only in the most extreme cases. Replacing a Social Security number inevitably leads to years of headaches as lenders and other legitimate companies try—and often fail—to make sense of the unusual situation. Worse, it won't necessarily solve your problem. Every company that has your current Social Security number on file will add a note in its system linking your new Social Security number to it. The old number could continue to be abused—and perhaps the new one, too.

Three Major Social Security Scams

1 An identity thief contacts you by phone, e-mail or letter and claims to be a Social Security employee checking records and asks for personal data such as your Social Security number and mother's maiden name. 2) A scammer claims to be able to get you a higher benefit if you pay a filing fee. 3) Someone claims that you will get a lump-sum payment to compensate for the recent lack of Social Security cost-of-living adjustments if you pay to file a new tax return.

What to do: Before providing any personal information or responding to a suspicious offer, call the Social Security Administration at 800-772-1213 to make sure that the contact is legitimate.

AARP.org.

Do Not Pick Up Calls from Unknown Numbers

City area codes favored by scammers, in addition to toll-free numbers starting with 800, 855, 866, 877 and 888: Detroit, 313...Houston, 713...Fort Lauderdale, 954...Atlanta, 404...Eastern and Southeastern Pennsylvania, 484...Orlando, 407...Dallas, 214 and 972...Washington, DC, 202...Birmingham, 205. Numbers that you do not recognize—especially from these area codes—may be from thieves. Do not pick up calls from unknown numbers, and never return a call to a number you do not know.

Research by WhitePages.com, reported at ClickOn Detroit.com.

Missed-Call Phone Scam

Roundup of experts on telephone scams, reported at TechCrunch.com.

Crooks use computers to call thousands of numbers per hour, letting each phone ring only once. The computer hangs up before you can answer, but your phone will notify you that you've missed a call. The number looks like a US number but is a disguised international one. If you call back, you will be charged several dollars to connect the call and several more for each minute you are on hold or remain in conversation with a scammer.

Self-defense: Do not call back a number that you do not recognize. If you are unsure, Google the number and be sure that the area code is a legitimate US one. Watch your phone bill, and request reversal of any scam-related charges.

What's Hidden in Your Cell-Phone Bill?

Susan Grant, director of consumer protection at Consumer Federation of America, a Washington, DC–based association of nonprofit consumer organizations. ConsumerFed.org

Companies you've never heard of might be slipping charges for services you never ordered onto your cell-phone bill. These added charges might be relatively small—perhaps $10 or less—but they're likely to recur every month, adding up to substantial amounts over time.

This scam, known as "cramming," has long been common with landline phone bills.

Here's how it works: An unethical provider of services, such as voice mail, fax or sports or horoscope information, or memberships (to discount buying clubs, campgrounds, etc.) tells a phone company that you signed up for its service even though you didn't. The phone company adds this service to your phone bill without bothering to confirm anything with you, then takes a cut of the charge for itself.

Cramming has become common with cell phones, with consumers' annual losses believed to be in the hundreds of millions of dollars. Through these cramming cases, the FCC and its partners brought a total of $353 million in penalties and restitution against the four largest wireless carriers...so phone companies are attempting at more vigilance, but false charges still slip through.

Example: A recent study of Vermont cell-phone users found that a staggering 60% of third-party charges on mobile phone bills had been put there by crammers. Yet cell-phone bills are so difficult to interpret—and so rarely scrutinized—that most victims don't even realize that they are being scammed.

First line of defense: Look at your bill closely before paying it. Charges often are described in intentionally vague terms such as "enhanced services" or "service fee" to escape notice.

If you find charges that you don't understand, call your cellular provider and ask for an explanation. If you're told that one or more of these is a charge from an outside company for an unfamiliar download or service, explain that you didn't order this and ask that it be canceled and the charge removed. Providers almost always will do this when confronted.

Next, ask if this is a recurring charge that has appeared on your bill in prior months (or go back through your old bills to check). If it is, ask to be credited for these earlier charges, too. There may be a limit to how far back your service provider is willing to refund, so it is important to catch problems early.

If you are told to contact the third party directly, don't bother—you probably will just get the runaround there. Instead, ask to speak to the cellular service rep's supervisor.

Online Selling Tips

Take precautions when selling online... When using sites such as Craigslist or eBay, insist on being paid through PayPal or with a

159

cashier's check for deals of more than $100. Don't include your address or phone number in posts offering items for sale. If shipping an item, require a signature on delivery so that the recipient cannot claim it never arrived. Consider buying shipping insurance for further protection. To guard against swap-out scams—in which someone orders an item identical to an already broken one, then returns the broken one and claims the shipment arrived damaged—take detailed photos of the item and any distinguishing marks it has. If you're concerned about safety, meet a buyer at a neutral, busy location, such as a supermarket parking lot that has video surveillance.

Roundup of experts on online selling and scams, reported at Bankrate.com.

Scammers Target Online Daters

Barbara Sluppick, founder of RomanceScams.org, a support group for victims of dating scams.

Scams targeting people who use online dating websites and social-media sites are on the rise—and very profitable for the scammers. In the second half of 2014 alone, online dating scammers robbed Americans of an estimated $82 million. Both men and women are targeted—and often the victims are seniors.

Scammers might ask victims for financial support during a fabricated emergency…or for help with travel costs for a visit that eventually will be canceled…or to deposit a check for them and send them the cash (the check will bounce).

Five red flags that your "date" may be a scammer…

•**He/she claims to be an American who is temporarily abroad.** In one common variation, the scammer claims to be in the military temporarily deployed overseas. A scammer wants his/her victims to believe that the scammer's permanent residence is close to the victim's so that the victim can imagine a

life together. But most scammers actually are based in foreign countries—western Africa is the most common location.

•**You notice strange language quirks.** These scammers often speak and write English very well, but they might not be familiar with expressions common in the US. One woman noted that her "American" beau seemed confused by the expression "See you later, alligator."

•**His/her photo matches someone else's.** Scammers pass off other people's photos as their own. Load any pictures you have of this person into both *tineye.com* and Google Image Search (*images.google.com*, then click the camera icon in the search bar). It's a very bad sign if these sites find these images elsewhere on the Internet with someone else's name on them.

•**Video chats never work properly.** Perhaps the sound works but not the picture when you try to video chat with your new love interest…or perhaps the picture works but not the sound.

•**You are asked for money and/or to engage in unusual banking activities.** If someone you have never met in person is asking for these things, you almost certainly are being scammed.

When Buying Meds Online…Beware

Connie T. Jung, RPh, PhD, acting associate director for policy and communication, Office of Drug Security, Integrity and Recalls, Office of Compliance, Center for Drug Evaluation and Research, US Food and Drug Administration, Rockville, Maryland.

Have you ever bought a prescription medication online? If you have, you're in good company. A recent FDA survey showed that almost one-quarter of Internet users have. The majority of these respondents used an online service associated with their health insurance.

It's easy to see why many people go online—it's convenient. You press a few buttons on your computer, and without having to leave your home, your prescription is delivered to your doorstep.

But if you're thinking about purchasing prescription medications from an online source that isn't affiliated with your health insurance or a local pharmacy, there are many unregulated, fraudulent companies that want you to think that they are legitimate, legal pharmacies—and they may even have websites that look very professional. But if you use one, you may not receive what you paid for. There's no way to know for sure whether the product that you receive contains the right amount (or any) of the active ingredient. Plus, the medicine could be contaminated or expired. *Here's how to safely buy prescription medications online...*

RED FLAGS

Many people don't realize how important it is to research an online pharmacy before using it. For example, the FDA survey showed that 15% of the respondents said that they would consider buying medication from an online pharmacy based outside the US. But the FDA doesn't regulate pharmacies that are located outside the US. So the first rule of thumb is to make sure that an online pharmacy is licensed in the US state where it is operating. This ensures that the pharmacy will be held to following state laws. To find out whether your Internet pharmacy is licensed by the state that it's operating in, don't just go by a statement on the site (because that could be fake). Check with your state's licensing organization by clicking here.

Here are more questions to ask yourself before you commit to using a particular online pharmacy, from Connie Jung of the US Food and Drug Administration...

•**Does the pharmacy require that you send in your prescription?** If it doesn't, don't use the pharmacy. Any legit pharmacy will require a prescription. Depending on the pharmacy, the pharmacist will either ask you to mail in the prescription or he or she might contact your doctor directly.

•**Does the pharmacy send you spam?** If you start getting spam or weird e-mails from the pharmacy that offer deep discounts and push you hard to buy medications, don't use the pharmacy. That's a sign that the "pharmacy" and its website may be a sham.

•**Does the pharmacy offer prices that are too good to be true?** There's no way to know exactly what's "too good to be true," but if, say, one pharmacy typically charges $32 for a bottle of a brand-name (nongeneric) medication, and another charges $30, but an online pharmacy is charging just $5, that's suspicious.

•**Does the pharmacy have pharmacists who are available to talk to you?** If the store doesn't allow you to speak with any pharmacists over the phone, don't use it. It may be an indication that real pharmacists aren't running the pharmacy.

Scammers Are Targeting People with Diabetes

Thieves pretending to be from a diabetes association or with the government or Medicare call with offers of supposedly free diabetic supplies in exchange for the patient's financial or Medicare information...or they ask you to confirm your personal information.

What to do: Get the person's contact information, then report the call immediately to the Office of the Attorney General at 800-HHS-TIPS.

Also: Periodically check your Medicare summary to make sure that you have not been charged for items you did not request.

Office of Inspector General, US Department of Health and Human Services, Washington, DC. OIG. HHS.gov

Don't Fall for These Medical Scams...

Charles B. Inlander, a consumer advocate and health-care consultant based in Fogelsville, Pennsylvania. He founded the nonprofit People's Medical Society, a consumer advocacy organization, and is the author or coauthor of more than 20 consumer-health books.

Not long ago, a neighbor of mine was persuaded by a telemarketer to buy $50 worth of vitamins over the phone. She then began receiving the same vitamins every month along with a $50 charge on her credit card. When she called to complain, the company told her that she had enrolled in a two-year program with an unbreakable contract. It was only after she called her state's attorney general's fraud division that the monthly charges stopped. This is just one example of the health frauds that are costing consumers and health insurers more than $80 billion each year. *My advice on how to avoid getting taken in by these common scams...*

• **Identity-theft scams.** Since passage of the ACA (also known as "Obamacare"), con men have been taking advantage of people's confusion surrounding the recent law. For example, imposters (claiming to be from the federal government) contact individuals and demand proof of health insurance. These crafty individuals ask for insurance numbers and subsequently steal identity.

Be smart: Never give any insurance, Social Security or other personal numbers to anyone who knocks on your door or calls you on the phone.

• **False billing by medical providers.** Most health fraud is actually committed by unscrupulous doctors, nurses, nursing home operators and home-care agencies. They often bill insurers, in patients' names, for services never rendered. This affects patients in the form of steeper copayments and/or deductibles.

Be smart: Keep a record of your medical appointments, and carefully read statements of claims submitted to your insurer (including Medicare). Call your insurer if you suspect something is amiss. And never sign a blank insurance claim form handed to you by a provider.

• **Medical-equipment fraud.** You've no doubt seen TV ads for "free" medical equipment, such as electronic scooters. While some of these companies are legitimate, others are deceiving customers. The truth is, the equipment is not free. Medicare or your private health insurer pays the bill—but only if your doctor has certified that you need the equipment and that you cannot get by with a manual wheelchair without a motor. This important detail is not revealed when the company asks for your insurance ID number and the scooter is sent to you. If the bill for the scooter is then rejected by the insurer—and it often is—then you are responsible for full payment.

Be smart: Before ordering any medical equipment, get a prescription from your doctor and check with Medicare or your insurer to make sure that it is covered and that the vendor is eligible for payment. To avoid this type of fraud, insurers now preapprove vendors.

PART 3

Long-Term Health Care

9

Get the Best Medical Care

The Epidemic of Overdiagnosis—Is the Pursuit of Health Making You Sick?

There's a dangerous epidemic out there. It's called overdiagnosis—when you are diagnosed with a condition that will never hurt your health.

Overdiagnosis can lead to potentially harmful medical care, as you undergo invasive tests, take medications or have surgery—all for a condition that is harmless. Medical care also can be expensive, time-consuming and anxiety-producing. *Here, the conditions that are frequently overdiagnosed...*

HIGH BLOOD PRESSURE

There is tremendous value in treating moderate-to-severe hypertension—a reading of 160/100 or higher—because it can prevent heart attack, heart failure, stroke and kidney failure. But below that range (very-mild-to-mild hypertension), overdiagnosis is likely. In statistical terms, almost everyone treated for severe hypertension will benefit, but 18 people with mild hypertension have to be treated for one person to benefit.

And all that unnecessary treatment can involve added expense, hassle (doctor appointments, lab tests, refills, insurance forms, etc.) and drug side effects such as fatigue, persistent cough and erectile dysfunction.

My viewpoint: Don't automatically take medication to lower mild high blood pressure. Losing weight and getting more exercise generally are the way to go.

TYPE 2 DIABETES

More than 20 million Americans have type 2 diabetes, which can cause complications such as heart disease, kidney failure, blind-

---

H. Gilbert Welch, MD, MPH, professor of medicine at The Dartmouth Institute for Health Policy and Clinical Practice and general internist at the White River Junction VA in Vermont. He is author of *Overdiagnosed: Making People Sick in the Pursuit of Health* and *Should I Be Tested for Cancer? Maybe Not and Here's Why.*

ness, nerve pain and leg infections that lead to amputation.

However: Like high blood pressure, type 2 diabetes has a range of abnormality, from the asymptomatic to the severe. Some people with diabetes will never develop complications.

That's even more likely nowadays because the medical definition of type 2 diabetes—and therefore, the criteria for who should and should not be treated—has changed. The definition of type 2 diabetes used to be a fasting blood sugar level higher than 140 mg/dL. Today, it is a fasting blood sugar level higher than 126 mg/dL—turning millions of people into diabetics. A newer test—hemoglobin A1C, a measurement of long-term blood sugar levels that detects the percentage of red blood cells coated with glucose (blood sugar)—defines diabetes as a level of 6.5% or higher.

My viewpoint: Physicians should use medication to reduce blood sugar in patients with an A1C of 9% or higher...discuss treatment with patients between 8% and 9%...and typically not treat patients under 8%.

In a randomized trial designed to test the effect of aggressive blood sugar reduction, more than 10,000 people with type 2 diabetes and A1C levels above 8% were divided into two groups. One group received intensive glucose-lowering therapy aimed at reducing A1C to less than 6%. The other group received standard therapy, targeting a level of 7% to 7.9%. After three years, the intensive-therapy group had about 25% increased risk for death, and because of that, the trial was stopped.

PROSTATE CANCER

In 2012, the US Preventive Services Task Force recommended against screening for prostate cancer with the prostate-specific antigen (PSA) test, concluding that "many men are harmed as a result of prostate cancer screening and few, if any, benefit."

Recent research shows that 1,000 men need to have a PSA test annually for a decade to prevent one death from prostate cancer. However, between 150 and 200 of those men will have a worrisome PSA test (a level higher than 4) that will lead to a biopsy of the prostate—an invasive procedure that

can cause blood in the urine, infections and a high rate of hospitalization in the month after the procedure. Of those biopsied, 30 to 100 will be treated for a cancer that was never going to bother them. As a result, between one-third and one-half of those men will become impotent and 20% to 30% will become incontinent.

My viewpoint: I am a 57-year-old man—I have not had a PSA test, nor do I intend to. I understand that I may develop symptoms of prostate cancer (such as trouble urinating and bone pain), that I may die from prostate cancer (as about 3% of men do) and that lifelong screening might reduce my risk (maybe down to as low as 2.5%). But I also recognize that most men (about 97%) will die from something else, and I don't want to spend my life looking for things to be wrong. Most prostate cancers found by the PSA test are slow-growing and not life-threatening, but because there is no way to determine which prostate cancers are dangerous and which are nonthreatening, most of them are treated. Given the limited benefits in saving lives and the terrible risks of overtreatment, I don't recommend PSA testing.

BREAST CANCER

Diagnostic mammography—testing a woman when a new breast lump is found to see if she has cancer—is an absolute must. Screening mammography—for early detection of breast cancer—is not.

Recent scientific research: A study I co-authored, published in *The New England Journal of Medicine*, links three decades of mammographic screening for breast cancer to a doubling in the number of cases of early-stage breast cancer, from 112 to 234 cases per 100,000 women. Our study estimated that over those 30 years, 1.3 million American women have been overdiagnosed—tumors that were detected on screening would never have led to clinical symptoms.

The result is more tests...more anxiety from "suspicious" findings...and more harsh anticancer treatments, including more mastectomies.

My viewpoint: It is probably true that some women will die of breast cancer if they don't get screened for it. But it is much more common to be hurt by screening than helped by it. Mammography is a choice, not an imperative.

Better Time for Doctor Appointments

In a recent study involving 21,867 patients with acute respiratory infections, doctors were 26% more likely in the fourth hour of their shifts to give patients an antibiotic prescription—whether it was needed or not—than in the first hour.

Takeaway: Doctors are human, too, and may experience "decision fatigue" over the course of the day.

What to do: Schedule doctor appointments early in the day whenever possible, and always be sure to ask your doctor if an antibiotic is really needed.

Jeffrey Linder, MD, associate professor of medicine, Harvard Medical School, Boston.

---

6 Common Medical Tests That Most People Don't Need

Tanveer P. Mir, MD, chair of the Board of Regents of the American College of Physicians and medical director of palliative care and ethics at Florida Hospital, Orlando. She is board-certified in internal medicine, geriatrics and hospice and palliative medicine.

You expect your doctor to order tests during routine checkups or to investigate unexplained symptoms. But do you need all of those tests?

Maybe not.

The American College of Physicians and other groups have joined a project called Choosing Wisely that uses evidence-based medicine to identify tests, treatments and medical screenings that most people don't need. *Common offenders...*

CT SCANS FOR HEADACHES

If you start getting migraines or pounding headaches, you'll want to know why. So will your doctor. Result: About one in eight patients who sees a doctor for headaches or migraines winds up getting scans.

Yet CT scans find abnormalities in only 1% to 3% of cases—and many of those abnormalities will be harmless or have nothing to do with the headaches. The scans are highly unlikely to change your diagnosis or affect your treatment options. But doctors order them anyway.

The tests create their own problems. Excess radiation is one concern. So is the likelihood that a scan will reveal "incidentalomas," a somewhat tongue-in-cheek name for unimportant abnormalities that can lead to additional (and unnecessary) tests.

Bottom line: CT scans are rarely needed because doctors can readily diagnose headaches just by talking with patients and taking detailed medical histories.

Who might need it: You might need a scan if your headaches are accompanied by neurological symptoms (such as a seizure or fit, change in speech or alertness or loss of coordination) or if you suffered from an accident that involved a sharp blow to the head.

PREOPERATIVE CHEST X-RAY

If you've ever had an operation, you almost certainly had one or more chest X-rays. Many hospitals require them to "clear" patients for surgery.

What are the X-rays for? No one really knows. They have become a part of the presurgical routine even though a study published in *JAMA* found that only 2% of the X-rays provided useful information for the surgeon/anesthesiologist. Most patients don't need them.

Bottom line: If you're generally healthy, tell your doctor you don't want the X-ray.

Who might need it: Patients who have been diagnosed with heart or lung disease or who are having surgery on the heart, lungs or other parts of the chest should get the X-ray. So should those who are older than 70 and haven't had a chest X-ray within the last six months (the likelihood of an abnormal X-ray is higher in these people).

HEART DISEASE STRESS TEST

If you're between the ages of 40 and 60, there's a chance that you've had (or been advised to have) an exercise stress test to determine your risk for heart disease and heart attack. A 2010 study that looked at nearly 1,200 people in this age group found that nearly one out of 10 had been given a stress test.

Unless you're having symptoms of heart disease—such as chest pain and shortness of breath—a stress test will probably be useless. The cost is considerable—you can expect to spend $200 to $300.

Stress tests tend to produce unclear results. This can lead to additional tests, including coronary angiography—an expensive test that exposes you to as much radiation as 600 to 800 chest X-rays.

Bottom line: You're better off reducing your particular risks—giving up smoking, controlling hypertension and lowering cholesterol—than getting a stress test.

Who might need it: Agree to an exercise stress test only if you're having symptoms of heart disease or your doctor suspects that you already have heart disease.

IMAGING FOR BACK PAIN

There's a good chance that your doctor will order an MRI or a CT scan if you complain of sudden back pain. Yet 80% to 90% of patients will improve within four to six weeks. You might need an imaging test when symptoms are severe or don't improve, but there's no reason to rush it—or to expose yourself to unnecessary radiation from a CT scan.

Bottom line: Don't agree to a test that's unlikely to change your diagnosis or treatment options. Since most back-pain patients will recover with physical therapy, over-the-counter painkillers and other "conservative measures," imaging tests usually are unnecessary.

Who might need it: A scan typically is warranted if your doctor suspects a compression fracture from osteoporosis...you have burning pain down a leg that doesn't improve...or you're also having numbness, muscle weakness, a loss of bowel/bladder control or other neurological symptoms.

PELVIC EXAM

Some gynecologists and primary-care physicians believe that a pelvic exam is a good way to detect ovarian cancer or problems with the ovaries, uterus, vulva or other pelvic structures. It's usually combined with a Pap test to screen for cervical cancer.

A study published in *JAMA* concluded that routine pelvic exams are unlikely to detect ovarian cancer. Nor are they likely to help women with uterine fibroids or cysts.

Bottom line: The routine pelvic exam is a low-yield test that should be discontinued, particularly because it makes women anxious and uncomfortable.

Important: Don't forgo regular Pap smears—you can get them without having a pelvic exam. Women 30 years old and older should have a Pap smear—along with testing for the human papillomavirus (HPV), which is done at the same time—every five years. For those with a family history of cervical cancer or other risk factors, the Pap test should be repeated every three years.

PSA TEST

For a long time, men were routinely advised to have this blood test, which measures prostate-specific antigen (PSA) and screens for prostate cancer. Now the American Cancer Society and some other groups advise against it.

The test can't differentiate harmless cancers (the majority) from aggressive ones. Studies have shown that men who test positive are only marginally less likely to die from prostate cancer than those who were never tested... and they're more likely to have biopsies, surgeries and other treatments that will make no difference in their long-term health, that pose serious risks of their own and that cause unnecessary anguish.

Bottom line: Men between the ages of 50 and 74 should discuss the test and the possible risks and benefits with their doctors.

Who might need it: Those with a family history of prostate cancer—particularly a cancer that affected a close relative, such as a sibling or parent—may want to get tested.

Testing Guidelines Miss Cancers

Prostate cancer screening guidelines may miss aggressive cancers, warns Daniel Barocas, MD, MPH. The guidelines—in place since 2011—recommend against routine PSA tests to avoid overdiagnosis and overtreatment. But while it is true that many prostate cancers are slow-growing and not life-threatening, the "screen-none" guidelines can miss important cancers, especially among men with a family history of prostate cancer and men of African descent.

Daniel Barocas, MD, MPH, assistant professor of urologic surgery and medicine, Vanderbilt University Medical Center, Nashville, and leader of an analysis of data on new prostate cancer diagnoses, published in *The Journal of Urology*.

Don't Let Your Doctor Get It Wrong

Helen Haskell, MA, president of Mothers Against Medical Error, a nonprofit patient-safety organization, MAME MomsOnline.org. She serves on the board of directors of the National Patient Safety Foundation and is a board member of the Institute for Healthcare Improvement and the International Society for Rapid Response Systems. In 2015, she was named one of the top 50 patient-safety experts in the country by *Becker's Hospital Review*.

Fifteen years ago, my teenage son Lewis went to the hospital for an elective surgical procedure. After the operation, his doctors failed to notice that he was suffering from an undetected infection and blood loss from an ulcer caused by pain medication. They believed his symptoms were an indication of constipation from other pain medications he was taking. This mistake cost my son his life— he died four days after entering the hospital.

Now: I teach patients skills that can help them avoid a similar tragedy.

A "BLIND SPOT" IN MEDICINE

A groundbreaking new report from the prestigious Institute of Medicine (IOM) concluded that most Americans will experience at least one diagnostic error—that is, an inaccurate, missed or delayed diagnosis, as determined by later definitive testing—at some point in their lives.

The IOM report called diagnostic errors a "blind spot" in the delivery of quality health care. Each year, about one in 20 patients who seek outpatient care will suffer from a wrong or delayed diagnosis. According to autopsy studies, diagnostic mistakes contribute to about 10% of patient deaths. Unfortunately, diagnostic errors haven't gotten as much attention as treatment and surgical errors—for example, operating on the wrong body part—partially because the latter are easier and quicker to identify. Now patient-safety experts are taking steps to better understand why diagnostic errors occur. *Key reasons…*

•**Tests help—and hurt.** Patients may be given a staggering number of tests—X-rays, blood tests, biopsies and more. The process of ordering, conducting and conveying the results of a test, however, can be complex and poorly organized.

•**Poor communication.** Can you count on the internist to talk to the nurse? Will the radiologist convey all of the pertinent information to the surgeon? Don't count on it. Patients also play a role. They should tell their doctors about all the symptoms they're having and whether they're getting better or worse after starting a new treatment.

•**Snap judgments.** Doctors often develop a working diagnosis within the first few minutes of hearing the patient's reported symptoms. The danger is that doctors can develop a so-called anchoring bias that leads them to cling to their initial diagnosis and prevents them from fully considering new information or looking for other possibilities.

HOW TO MAKE SURE YOUR DOCTOR GETS IT RIGHT

Major medical groups, including the Society to Improve Diagnosis in Medicine, have identified a number of institutional factors—such as stronger teamwork—to reduce errors. But no one has more at stake in these situations than the patients themselves. Four steps you can take to avoid a misdiagnosis…

STEP 1. Organize your thoughts. Most of the time, doctors have only 15 minutes with each patient, so you need to make the most of your time together. Plan ahead: Your medical history—including a description of symptoms and when the problem started—is the most important part of an exam. Describe the nature and context of your symptoms in as much detail as you can. When do you feel them? What makes them worse or better? Why are you worried? Keep it concise and on topic, but include your own thoughts so the doctor can address the issues that concern you.

My advice: If possible, before you see the doctor, use the Internet to investigate your symptoms and the likely causes. Your findings should not be used to challenge your doctor, but rather as a way to have a more informed conversation. If you don't have confidence in your own abilities to do research, take advantage of a service like Expert HealthSearch (*ImproveDiagnosis.org/ ?page=ExpertHealthSearch*), a free service that puts you in touch with a medical librarian who can search the literature for you.

STEP 2. Don't be afraid to question test results. They are more prone to error than most people imagine. In one study, experts who reviewed biopsies of more than 6,000 cancer patients concluded that 86 had been given a wrong diagnosis. Samples can be too small or even contaminated…technicians can make mistakes…and there can be false-negatives or false-positives. Results can be misinterpreted, or even more often, they can go unreported to the patient.

My advice: If a test result seems to fly in the face of the symptoms you are experiencing, consider asking to repeat the test or have a second doctor review it. And never assume that no news is good news. Follow up to be sure that your test results have been received and reviewed and that you know what they are.

STEP 3. Ask about alternatives. Many common symptoms—such as fatigue, muscle aches and abdominal pain—are known as nonspecific symptoms. They can be caused by dozens of conditions.

My advice: To help understand your doctor's thinking, ask him/her this question: Could you please explain your differential diagnoses? This is a list of possible diagnoses ranked in order of likelihood. It's a thought process that helps a diagnostician avoid overlooking any likely possibilities. The most serious conditions on the list should be ruled out before settling on a less serious diagnosis, and the doctor should be looking for causes and not just treating symptoms.

What to ask: If there is any question about a diagnosis, patients can help assess the "fit" by asking three important questions: Does this diagnosis match all my symptoms? What else could it be? Could there be more than one thing going on?

STEP 4. Don't skip the second opinion. I cannot stress this enough. In the study of cancer patients cited earlier, Johns Hopkins University researchers found that one to two of every 100 who got a second opinion with definitive testing after a tumor biopsy had gotten a wrong diagnosis the first time.

My advice: It's not always possible to get a second opinion—sometimes in medicine you have to move fast. But if you can, a second (or even a third) opinion is smart when symptoms seem severe…if your doctor is recommending surgery…or if you are told that you have a rare or fatal condition. Check first, but usually insurance will pay for a second opinion. Outside of emergencies, most of the time a brief delay in treatment while you get a second opinion will not affect your outcome.

When to Think Twice About Medical Advice

H. Gilbert Welch, MD, MPH, an internist at White River Junction VA Medical Center, Vermont, and a professor of medicine at The Dartmouth Institute for Health Policy & Clinical Practice, where he specializes in the effects of medical testing. He is author of *Less Medicine, More Health: 7 Assumptions That Drive Too Much Medical Care.*

It's natural to assume that more health care is better than less—that checkups, tests and treatments make people healthier. But that isn't always the case.

Obviously, people who are sick need to see doctors and get the necessary tests. Those who are healthy may benefit from preventive medicine. But many of the assumed benefits of medicine don't always pan out.

Here are four common but false assumptions about medical care...

False: **It never hurts to get more information.**

It would seem that getting as much medical information as possible would be a good thing. Not necessarily.

Example: A colleague's father was 85 years old and in good health when his doctor noticed an abdominal bulge during a checkup. He ordered an ultrasound, which showed that the bulge wasn't a problem—but the test did reveal a possible problem with the pancreas. To check it out, the doctor ordered a CT scan. The pancreas was normal, but the test showed a possible nodule on the liver. A biopsy showed that the liver was healthy, but the biopsy caused serious bleeding and other complications, necessitating a week in the hospital.

More data can produce more problems, which require more tests, which can create problems of their own. And all this can cost you real money—yet not improve your health.

More data also can distract your doctor. Minor laboratory abnormalities identified during a routine visit—such as slightly elevated cholesterol or slightly depressed thyroid function—often draw physicians away from the problems you want to talk about.

My advice: Expect more and more opportunities to get tested for a variety of conditions. Know that while all these tests may serve the financial interests of their manufacturers, they may not serve your interests. Before agreeing to any test, ask your doctor what he/she is looking for. Is there a specific problem you are likely to have? Or is it a fishing expedition? Avoid the latter—it's too easy to catch trash fish (meaningless abnormalities). Also, ask your doctor whether more information will change what you should do. If not, don't seek more information.

False: **It's always better to fix the problem.**

All medical treatments are a bit of a gamble. You might improve when a problem is "fixed." Or things could go wrong and you could get worse. It's often better to manage a problem than to bring out the big guns.

Consider coronary artery disease. It's potentially life-threatening, so it needs to be treated. Many doctors recommend balloon angioplasty, a procedure to expand the arterial opening and restore normal blood flow. It can eliminate symptoms almost immediately, but it also carries significant risks to the patient.

With medical management, on the other hand, your doctor will treat the problem with medications and advice for a healthier lifestyle. You'll still have the underlying problem, but you'll learn to live with it.

How do the approaches compare? One large study found that patients with stable angina who had balloon angioplasty were no less likely to die or have a heart attack than those who depended on lower-risk medical management.

My advice: When you're faced with a medical decision—scheduling a test, having surgery, starting medications—tell your doctor that you want to take a stepwise approach. Start with the easiest, safest treatments first. You can always add more aggressive treatments later.

Think about upper-respiratory infections. Sure, you could get pneumonia, and you might eventually need antibiotics. But most people can just wait it out. Don't get tests or treatments unless your doctor convinces you, with good evidence, that you need them.

***False:* It's always better to find it sooner.**

The argument for cancer screening seems obvious. If you had cancer, wouldn't you want to know as soon as possible? Screening (looking for disease in large populations) does turn up a lot of cancers. Does this save lives? Less often than you might think.

Take mammography. It's been used for widespread screening for 30 years, yet the number of women who are diagnosed with metastatic breast cancer is about the same now as it was before. For every 1,000 women who get the screenings, at most three (likely closer to less than one) will avoid dying from breast cancer as a result. The numbers are roughly the same for men who are screened for prostate cancer.

The benefits are huge if you happen to be in one of these small groups, but what about the rest? They're faced with the cost and inconvenience of the initial test. Many will be advised to get biopsies or other follow-up tests. Some will have surgery or radiation for cancers that probably would have done nothing.

I'm not saying that screening tests are all bad—just that they aren't all good.

My advice: Ask your doctor if he/she is confident that you, as an individual, will benefit from screening tests.

***False:* Newer treatments are always better.**

There's a saying in medicine, "When you have a new hammer, everything looks like a nail." When doctors discover a new treatment, such as a drug or a particular surgery, they tend to want to use it again and again.

Some new drugs really are superior to old ones—but not that often. Vioxx is a good example. It's an aspirin-like arthritis drug that got a lot of attention because it was somewhat less likely than similar drugs to cause stomach bleeding. But a few years after it was approved by the FDA, it was removed from the market because it was found to increase the risk for heart attack and stroke.

New drugs are tested in relatively small numbers of people. It can take many years before their benefits and risks become fully apparent.

My advice: Unless you have to take a new, breakthrough drug, tell your doctor that you would prefer something tried and true—preferably a drug that's been on the market for seven years or more.

Did You Know That TV Doctors Often Give Wrong Advice?

Only 43% of recommendations on the *Dr. Oz Show* are supported by evidence…and only 63% of those on *The Doctors*. And 15% of the *Dr. Oz* recommendations—along with 14% of those on *The Doctors*—contradict available medical evidence.

Study of 80 major recommendations made on the two shows by researchers at University of Alberta, Canada, published in *BMJ*.

When You Should See a Specialist…

Dennis Gottfried, MD, an associate professor of medicine at the University of Connecticut School of Medicine, Farmington, and an internist with a private practice in Torrington, Connecticut. He is the author of *Too Much Medicine: A Doctor's Prescription for Better and More Affordable Health Care*.

You might assume that you will get better care when you spend extra time and extra money to see a medical specialist. But is that really true?

Not always. Generalists—such as internists, general practitioners and family physicians—have a broader, more holistic view of the patient's condition and provide integrated care, but they lack the in-depth knowledge that specialists have in their area of medicine. Specialists may provide more fragmented care and order unnecessary tests and more procedures that are risky, studies show.

So when does the benefit of a specialist's added expertise outweigh the problem of sometimes disjointed medical care and excessive testing?

Rule of thumb: Specialists are generally preferable when a single medical condition that requires expert knowledge dominates all other medical concerns, such as a cardiologist treating an acute heart attack or an oncologist prescribing chemotherapy. Generalists, however, are usually more suitable when multiple chronic conditions, such as hypertension, diabetes and high cholesterol, are present.

How to get the best care for specific medical problems...

ARTHRITIS

Where to start: If you have osteoarthritis, you'll probably do better in the care of a general physician.

Osteoarthritis, a condition in which the cartilage in joints gradually wears down, often occurs with aging. Most patients do well with basic approaches: Regular exercise, physical therapy, glucosamine supplements and/ or the use of *naproxen* (Aleve) or *ibuprofen* (Motrin).

See a specialist when: The pain is constant or severe and is not relieved by any of the above treatments. Orthopedists (specialists who often treat arthritis patients) frequently advise joint replacement for arthritic hips, knees and shoulders.

For rheumatoid arthritis: A specialist (rheumatologist) is needed. Rheumatoid arthritis is an autoimmune disease that causes widespread swelling and pain in the joints.

Patients frequently are treated with powerful anti-inflammatory and immune-modulating medications, such as *etanercept* (Enbrel), *adalimumab* (Humira) or *cyclophosphamide*. These and other related drugs have serious side effects, including depressed immunity and an increased risk for infection and cancer. They are best administered by a rheumatologist who has experience in their use.

DIABETES

Where to start: A primary care physician. Type 2 diabetes is largely a lifestyle disease caused by obesity and inactivity. It is initially managed with diet, exercise and oral medications, although insulin may be required as the disease progresses. Cardiovascular risk factors, such as high blood pressure, as well as lifestyle factors and blood sugar levels need to be monitored. Because of the comprehensive care that they require, people with type 2 diabetes should optimally be cared for by a generalist.

Diabetes specialists, or diabetologists, endocrinologists who specialize in diabetes, often take a narrow view. For example, they emphasize the importance of lowering blood sugar, frequently with insulin or oral medications.

Overall blood glucose control is monitored by the A1C blood test, which measures average blood sugar levels over the past two to three months. The major health risks for type 2 diabetics are heart disease and stroke, but lowering blood sugar too much (more than a full point in those at high risk) can actually increase risk for heart attack.

See a specialist when: Your A1C level is consistently above 8. (A normal level is below 6.3.) Elevated A1C increases the risk for some diabetes complications, including kidney disease. A specialist might be better able to lower consistently elevated A1C to healthier levels.

For type 1 diabetes: These patients should almost always see a diabetologist. Type 1 diabetes occurs more commonly in young adults and requires insulin shots from the onset. Also, the use of insulin and insulin pumps, which is recommended for type 1 diabetes patients, requires specialized knowledge.

HEART ATTACK

Where to start: People who have had heart attacks always need to see a cardiologist. The first hours (even minutes) after a heart attack are critical, and an emergency room physician will work with a cardiologist. A cardiologist will know what medication should be rapidly administered to minimize long-term damage to the heart and what tests (such as an angiogram) or procedures (such as stenting) need to be ordered. This specialist also will have significant experience prescribing the best drugs for common problems such as dissolving clots and restoring normal heart rhythms.

Most patients who have had a heart attack should see a specialist once or twice a year for the rest of their lives. The patient will be monitored to determine whether treatment such as surgery or stenting is necessary.

See a generalist when: Your condition is stable—that is, you are not having symptoms, such as shortness of breath or heart irregularities. Patients who have fully recovered from a heart attack may want to seek care from an internist or family doctor who has good communication with the cardiologist.

Example: Cardiologists often prescribe multiple medications to aggressively treat heart patients with high LDL "bad" cholesterol by lowering levels from, say, 100 mg/dL to 70 mg/dL. Yet there's little evidence that reducing LDL that much improves life expectancy. The medication needed to achieve such a low level may increase the risk for muscle pain and memory loss.

Primary care doctors often give a lower dose of the same medication to slightly improve cholesterol and minimize the risk for memory loss and muscle pain.

For heart failure: People with this condition, in which the heart is too weak to efficiently pump blood throughout the body, are best managed jointly by a cardiologist and a generalist. However, people with cardiac risk factors, such as hypertension or elevated cholesterol, but no history of heart attack, are best cared for by a generalist.

MENTAL HEALTH

Where to start: Almost 20% of patient visits to primary care doctors are for psychiatric problems. Primary care doctors can prescribe antidepressants and antianxiety medications and, if necessary, provide referrals to therapists and support groups. This is appropriate and sufficient for most psychiatric disorders.

See a psychiatrist when: The treatment isn't working. A psychiatrist will have the knowledge to recommend other medications or medication combinations. Patients with more severe psychiatric problems, such as bipolar disorder or schizophrenia, should always be treated by a psychiatrist.

STROKE

Where to start: A neurologist should treat anyone who has suffered an acute stroke. If carotid artery disease is the suspected cause of the stroke, a vascular surgeon should be seen to monitor and treat the patient's risk for blood clots.

An analysis of 10 randomized clinical trials found that patients who were treated in hospital stroke units (with a neurologist on call 24 hours a day) had better survival rates than those who were treated in general hospital wards. Similarly, patients who were treated by neurologists were more likely to maintain brain function than those who were treated by nonspecialists.

See a generalist when: A neurologist has identified and treated all of the possible causes of stroke, such as hypertension and atrial fibrillation. Once a patient has recovered from the stroke itself, a general physician can manage the anticlotting and blood pressure medications.

Do You Really Need That Surgery?

Dennis Gottfried, MD, an internist with a private practice in Torrington, Connecticut, and an associate professor of medicine at the University of Connecticut School of Medicine in Farmington. He is also the author of *Too Much Medicine: A Doctor's Prescription for Better and More Affordable Health Care.*

Before you agree to undergo a surgical procedure, ask yourself if it really needs to be done. Based on some of the latest research, there's a good chance that it doesn't.

Shocking statistic: Nearly one-third of all health-care dollars are spent on unnecessary medical services, including tens of thousands of surgeries. This alarming statistic is a good reminder that everyone should get a second opinion.

Procedures you should question—and possible alternatives...

NECK SURGERY

It's one of the most commonly performed orthopedic procedures in the US.

Problem: A herniated disk in the neck that presses on a nerve can cause severe pain and sometimes numbness and tingling that extends down an arm and into the hand. However, the bulging or rupturing of a disk herniation usually corrects itself over weeks to months.

Important finding: A recent study found that 23% of patients with neck problems had been advised to have surgery, even though they didn't meet the commonly accepted criteria of MRI or CT evidence of a spinal nerve root with pain and weakness throughout that nerve.

Disk surgery has serious potential risks, including nerve damage, infection and chronic postoperative pain.

Who does need neck surgery: People with persistent, severe pain that interferes significantly with their daily lives…or those with significant muscle weakness in the arm or hand that's caused by pressure on the nerve.

Who doesn't need neck surgery: Individuals whose only symptoms are pain, tingling or numbness. They often do well with nonsurgical measures such as anti-inflammatory medications, physical therapy, localized steroid injections and massages. Symptoms for the majority of people with a ruptured cervical disk will improve in time.

GALLBLADDER SURGERY

About 35% to 40% of older Americans have gallstones, lumps of cholesterol, calcium salts and other substances that can be as small as a grain of salt or as large as a golf ball. In about 90% of cases, the stones cause no symptoms at all.

Problem: Doctors often recommend a cholecystectomy, the removal of the gallbladder, for cholecystitis, an inflammation of the gallbladder characterized by pain in the upper-right quadrant of the abdomen along with fever, nausea and vomiting. Cholecystitis is usually caused by gallstones blocking the outflow from the gallbladder.

Surgery to remove the gallbladder presents risks. The traditional open cholecystectomy and the more commonly done laparoscopic technique carry such risks as infection…peritonitis (inflammation of the peritoneum, the thin tissue that lines the inner wall of the abdomen)…bile leakage…and even death.

Who does need gallbladder surgery: People who have acute cholecystitis with blockage in the pancreatic or common bile duct almost always have surgery. Other people with acute cholecystitis, who are otherwise healthy, usually have their gallbladders removed.

Who doesn't need gallbladder surgery: Twenty percent of Americans have vague abdominal pains. Many of them coincidentally also have gallstones. A cholecystectomy in those people rarely provides any benefit and subjects them to the risks of the procedure.

Isolated acute cholecystitis without involvement of the common bile duct usually resolves in days. However, it may recur months or years later. Although a person who is otherwise healthy usually has his/her gallbladder removed, it may be better not to remove the gallbladder in someone who is not in good health, since acute cholecystitis is often an isolated event.

COLONOSCOPY

This is the most accurate test to detect and prevent cancer of the colon and rectum. Most people are advised to have a colonoscopy every 10 years, starting at age 50. Regular screenings can reduce death from colorectal cancer by about 50%. Colorectal cancer screening is an essential part of cancer prevention.

Problem: A study of Medicare patients who had a colonoscopy found that 46% repeated the test within seven years, and nearly half didn't need a follow-up test that soon.

Colonoscopy is expensive, inconvenient— and sometimes risky. Its major complications are bleeding and perforations. Colonoscopy is technically considered surgery, since anesthesia is used and biopsies are often performed.

Who needs more frequent colonoscopies: Overall, about 30% of Americans over age 50 have colon polyps found during colonoscopy, with polyps coming in different types and sizes.

If you have had polyps, ask the doctor what size and type they were. People with a villous adenoma polyp or multiple and/or large tubular adenoma polyps have an increased risk of developing colon cancer and may need a colonoscopy every three to five years. Those with a parent, sibling or child who had colon cancer (or an adenomatous polyp before age 60) are screened every five years.

Who doesn't need frequent colonoscopies: People without any polyps...with one or two small (less than 1 cm) tubular adenoma polyps...or with hyperplastic polyps in the descending colon or rectum are at no increased risk and can be screened every 10 years, unless they have other risk factors.

For people over age 75, the risk of routine colonoscopy outweighs its benefit and no further screening is indicated.

KIDNEY STONE REMOVAL

Many people with kidney stones never have symptoms. Symptoms generally occur when a stone migrates into the ureter, one of the two tubes that carry urine from the kidneys to the bladder. A "passing" stone can cause severe groin or side pain, blood in the urine, a burning sensation when urinating, nausea, vomiting and/or chills.

Problem: Doctors often recommend procedures to remove kidney stones that are causing no problems. Stones passing through the ureter will frequently pass on their own with medication, fluid and time.

Who does need kidney stone removal: People who develop an infection in the kidney from an obstructing ureteral stone. When the blockage is affecting the function of the kidney or the pain is severe and persists for more than two weeks, surgery is recommended.

Typically, the doctor will insert a tube via the urethra into the bladder and then thread a small instrument into the ureter until it reaches the stone. The stone can often be removed or repositioned to be broken up by shock waves (lithotripsy).

Stones in the kidney that are greater than 2 cm can usually be treated with lithotripsy. The procedure requires anesthetic but is done on an outpatient basis.

Who doesn't need kidney stone removal: People whose stones are asymptomatic or those who have only occasional mild pain. Most stones less than 5 mm in diameter may hurt while they pass through the ureter, but they will pass (sometimes it takes weeks). I advise patients not to worry about asymptomatic stones and to give a ureteral stone, if appropriate, time to pass.

Future stone formation can often be prevented, depending on the type of kidney stone, by drinking lots of water, limiting sodium intake and taking medications if indicated by your doctor.

What Doctors Know Now That They Wish They Knew Then

Dennis Gottfried, MD, an assistant clinical professor of medicine at the University of Connecticut School of Medicine, Farmington, and an internist with a private practice in Torrington, Connecticut, DrDennisGottfried.com. He is the author of *Too Much Medicine: A Doctor's Prescription for Better and More Affordable Health Care.*

What if your doctor had advised you for years to follow a certain treatment or lifestyle practice but later told you that the advice had been found to be harmful or outdated? That's exactly what has happened numerous times over the past several years.

Science is always changing. Dennis Gottfried, MD, is a leading expert on medical research. He identified some of the most significant and interesting medical advances that have occurred during the past quarter century.

Some represent frightening realizations. For example, millions of women had been treated for decades with hormone replacement therapy (HRT) for hot flashes and other menopausal symptoms. Then, in 2002, a Women's Health Initiative study showed that HRT increased a woman's risk for life-threatening conditions such as heart attack, stroke and breast cancer.

But there were other developments that received far less fanfare. *For example...*

CATARACT FIX IN ONE DAY

By age 80, more than half of all Americans either have a cataract or have had cataract surgery.

By the late 1960s, surgeons had developed techniques to remove the damaged lens of the eye. But patients who had cataracts removed could see only if they wore thick, Coke bottle–style glasses. They also had to stay in the hospital—and lie almost completely still—for five or six days. In 1981, the FDA approved the first implantable lens so that thick glasses were no longer needed after surgery.

Now: Cataract surgery is one of the most common surgical procedures in the US—and it's almost always done at outpatient centers.

The lens of the eye is removed via an incision that's usually no longer than one-eighth inch. An artificial lens is slipped through the opening. The incision then usually closes on its own, without stitches. Vision in the corrected eye is typically improved within two weeks. Implantable lenses continue to evolve—even bifocal implants are now available.

"KEYHOLE" SURGERIES

A few decades ago, most surgeries were "open" procedures, requiring large incisions and lengthy hospital stays and recovery times.

Now: Most surgeries are done using laparoscopes, which allow the area being operated on to be seen through a telescope-like tube that is connected to a video camera. Such minimally invasive "keyhole" surgery is routinely performed for gallbladder removal, appendectomies, hernia repairs, gynecological surgery and many orthopedic procedures. The incisions can be as small as five millimeters in length and generally result in reduced blood loss, less pain and shorter hospital stays—or no hospital stay at all.

CT DANGERS

Computed tomography (CT) scans, which were introduced in 1972, have revolutionized our ability to detect tumors and other abnormalities in virtually every part of the body.

However, the precision offered by CT scans has come with an unexpected cost—Americans are now exposed to more radiation from medical diagnostic tests than people anywhere else in the world.

The National Cancer Institute estimates that radiation exposure from CT scans done in 2007 alone eventually will result in 29,000 cancers and 15,000 cancer deaths.

Now: Because the diseases caused by medical radiation take decades to develop, we're just beginning to see the consequences of excessive testing with radiation-producing imaging scans such as CTs.

Important: Don't assume that you need a scan just because your doctor ordered it. Question every scan. Ask if the diagnosis can be made in some other way.

Also important: Ask the imaging center for a digital copy of your scan. It's usually free of charge. Having a copy may help you avoid unnecessary duplicate scans if you later get treated at a different hospital.

"KILLER" EGGS

For decades, it was widely believed that eating eggs would increase one's cholesterol levels. It's true that eggs (or, more specifically, yolks) contain a significant amount of cholesterol—213 mg in one large egg. So it seemed logical that eating eggs would greatly increase blood-cholesterol levels.

Now: We know that you do not have to avoid eggs to protect your heart. In fact, some doctors now frequently recommend that their patients eat eggs as a good source of protein and other nutrients. For the majority of people, most of the cholesterol in the body is not affected by diet. Most of the cholesterol that comes from diet is converted in the liver from the saturated fats and trans-fatty acids in our food.

Most importantly, no studies have found any connection between eggs and the development of heart disease. Exception: People with existing cardiovascular disease or hard-to-control cholesterol should limit their egg consumption to no more than a few eggs a week or eat egg whites only.

BETTER THAN BUTTER?

Margarine was initially developed as a low-cost alternative to butter. By the mid-1970s, the consumption of margarine worldwide was about 25% greater than that of butter. Later, when manufacturers touted margarine's health benefits—the trans fat in margarine was supposedly healthier than the saturated fat in butter—sales rose even more.

Now: Nutritionists agree that margarines with high levels of trans fat are linked to various health risks. For example, such margarines elevate LDL "bad" cholesterol just as much as saturated fat and promote inflammation in the body, one of the underlying causes of heart disease.

Stick margarine contains the most trans fat, while many soft-tub margarines contain less than 0.5 g trans fat per serving, which appears as "zero trans fat" on the label.

Best: Benecol spread or Promise activ Light Spread. They contain modified plant extracts that can reduce cholesterol by about 15%.

THREE EXTRA YEARS OF LIFE

Perhaps the greatest medical advance in the past 25 years has been our successful effort against cardiovascular disease. Although cardiac disease is still the leading cause of death in the US and stroke is the third, the death rate from these diseases has dramatically declined. According to the American Heart Association, cardiac deaths dropped 36.4% from 1996 to 2006, and over the past 25 years, death from strokes has been cut in half. The average American has gained more than three years of added life expectancy from these advances!

Sophisticated cardiac surgeries and procedures have played a role, but prevention has been the overwhelming reason for our improved cardiovascular statistics. Fewer adults now smoke, and blood pressure drugs are more effective and more widely taken. Research has shown that cholesterol-lowering statins—beginning with the first FDA-approved statin, *lovastatin*, in 1987—decrease cardiac death by 35%.

Caution: About one-third of Americans are obese—a known risk factor for many serious conditions, including diabetes. Ultimately, the increased cardiac deaths related to diabetes could erase the advances of the last few decades.

Doctor House Calls— They're Back!

Thomas Cornwell, MD, president of the American Academy of Home Care Medicine based in Edgewood, Maryland. Dr. Cornwell has made 31,000 house calls during his 20 years in practice. Based in Wheaton, Illinois, he specializes in family medicine and geriatrics. AAHCM.org

The image of a doctor visiting sick patients at home, black bag in hand, is no longer a part of our past.

What's new: Advances in portable medical equipment, a rapidly aging population and increased payments from Medicare for in-home doctor visits mean that house calls are back. In fact, the number of house calls made to Medicare patients more than doubled in recent years, and private insurers are beginning to cover them as well.

To find out more about the recent upswing in house calls and how they can benefit you, we spoke with Thomas Cornwell, MD, a national leader in home-care medicine who has made 31,000 in-home visits throughout his career.

WHY THE COMEBACK?

Until recently, most major tests, like X-rays and ultrasounds, required a visit to a hospital or other medical facility. Now, technology makes possible diagnostic and therapeutic equipment that's portable and accurate. Even a chest X-ray can be done in the comfort of the home. And house-call physicians currently have an arsenal of tools that they can use on the road—such as an ultrasound machine that fits in a pocket…a smartphone case that turns into an EKG machine…and an app for checking drug interactions.

Another driving factor: Most older adults would prefer to remain in their homes as they age and avoid expensive nursing homes. For many, this would not be possible without house calls.

What's more: Studies have shown that doctors visiting patients in the home reduce hospital admission rates, readmission rates and overall costs. In fact, a recent study of Medicare patients found that those cared for at home had 17% lower health-care costs.

The types of doctors most likely to make house calls include family physicians, internists, geriatricians and palliative-care doctors.

THE MANY BENEFITS

Some patients are too sick to come into the doctor's office but don't need to go to an emergency room. Or they simply refuse to go to the doctor's office…or don't have anyone to take them.

Additionally, house calls are typically much longer than the usual office doctor visit. By going into the home, the doctor can assess much more than the current health issue affecting a patient. If the patient is frail, the need for in-home medical equipment, such as grab bars in a shower or bath, can be identified. Plus, safety risks like electrical cords or rugs can be pointed out to help prevent falls.

Patients are encouraged to bring all of their medicines to a doctor appointment, but this is not always done, and often a drug or supplement is forgotten. A home visit is more likely to uncover all the prescriptions and supplements that are being taken. And by investigating other factors like diet and living conditions, a physician can better treat chronic conditions, such as diabetes or heart disease, or determine if the patient should be getting additional at-home assistance.

Finally, by remaining in their homes for medical care, patients are not exposed to the viruses and bacteria common in doctors' offices. This is particularly helpful for those who have weakened immunity.

WHO SHOULD CONSIDER HOUSE CALLS

•**Frail older patients.** For older patients who have difficulty getting out of the house, a home visit can be a literal lifesaver. Home-based primary care for frail older patients can help delay institutionalization or admission to the hospital and allow physicians to assess the quality of help caregivers are able to provide. For patients who are terminally ill, home visits provide palliative care and reduce the chances of dying in a hospital.

•**Patients who have certain disorders/ diseases.** Among patients of all ages, house calls are extremely helpful for those who suffer from neuromuscular diseases like muscular dystrophy, Lou Gehrig's disease or paralysis. With these conditions, getting to an appointment can be an arduous task, and home visits keep the doctor up-to-date on the patient's needs.

OTHER HOUSE-CALL OPTIONS

Some doctors' offices now offer medical concierge services (the patient pays an annual fee or retainer to a primary care doctor). These services may include house calls. Costs range from less than one hundred to several thousand dollars a year. Some employers also offer home visits as part of their employee insurance.

HOW TO ARRANGE A HOUSE CALL

For Medicare recipients and many with private insurance, there needs to be a medically necessary reason for the house call. The patient must also find it physically difficult to leave his/her home in order for Medicare or private insurance to cover some portion of the visit. Medical concierge services may not have this requirement.

To find a doctor who makes house calls: First, check with your primary care doctor to see if he can provide this service or give you a referral. You can also go to the website of the American Academy of Home Care Medicine, *aahcm.org*, and click on "Locate a Provider."

GETTING THE MOST OUT OF YOUR HOUSE CALL

The length of a house call depends on the patient's specific needs and whether it's a first-time visit or a follow-up. *How to prepare…*

•**As with any doctor appointment,** write down all your questions and concerns beforehand.

•**Before the doctor arrives,** arrange all of your prescription medications, over-the-counter medications and supplements in one place so that they can be reviewed by the doctor.

•**Make sure any family members who help out with your care** are present so the doctor can get an accurate picture of the home environment.

Also: Don't be afraid to reach out to your doctor between visits. Doing so, even if the problem seems minor, such as a lingering cough, may prevent an unnecessary ER visit or hospitalization down the road.

---

5 DIY Tests That Could Save Your Life

David L. Katz, MD, MPH, an internist and preventive medicine specialist. He is cofounder and director of the Yale-Griffin Prevention Research Center in Derby, Connecticut, and clinical instructor at the Yale School of Medicine in New Haven, Connecticut. Dr. Katz is also president of the American College of Lifestyle Medicine and the author of *Disease-Proof: The Remarkable Truth About What Makes Us Well*.

If you're conscientious about your health, you probably see your doctor for an annual physical…or perhaps even more often if you have a chronic condition or get sick.

But if you'd like to keep tabs on your health between your doctor visits, there are some easy, do-it-yourself tests that can give you valuable information about your body. These tests can sometimes tip you off that you may have a serious medical condition even though you don't have any symptoms.

Here are self-tests that you can do at home—repeat them once every few months, and keep track of results. See your doctor if you don't "pass" one or more of the tests…*

TEST #1: STAIRS TEST

Why this test? It helps assess basic lung and heart function.

The prop you'll need: A single flight of stairs (about eight to 12 steps).

What to do: Walk up the steps at a normal pace while continuously reciting "Mary had a little lamb" or some other simple verse.

Watch out: You should be able to talk easily while climbing the stairs and when at the top—without feeling winded. If you cannot continue to talk, or if you feel discomfort or tightness in your chest at any time during this test, see your doctor as soon as possible.

*These self-tests are not a substitute for a thorough physical exam from your doctor. Use them only as a way to identify potential problem areas to discuss with your physician.

Beware: If the small stress of climbing one flight of stairs causes physical problems, it could be a sign of hardening of the arteries (arteriosclerosis) or heart disease.

For some individuals, being out of breath could mean that they have asthma or bronchitis…chronic obstructive pulmonary disease (COPD), including emphysema…or even lung cancer.

TEST #2: GRAVITY TEST

Why this test? It measures how well your body adapts to changes in position, which can signal a variety of health problems, ranging from anemia to medication side effects.

The prop you'll need: Either a stopwatch or clock that measures seconds.

What to do: Lie down on a bed or the floor, and rest there for a minute or two. Then, start the stopwatch and stand up at a normal pace with no pauses (it's OK to use your hands).

Watch out: If you feel dizzy, make note of this. Most people can go from lying down to standing up within five seconds—and feel perfectly normal. In a healthy person, the body responds to the change in posture by pumping blood more strongly to the head.

Beware: Dizziness can signal any of the following…

• **Low blood pressure.** With orthostatic hypotension, your body doesn't pump enough blood to counteract the effects of gravity when you stand up.

• **Medication side effects,** especially from diuretics, such as *furosemide* (Lasix)…beta-blockers, such as *atenolol* (Tenormin) or *propranolol* (Inderal)…drugs for Parkinson's disease, such as *pramipexole* (Mirapex) or *levodopa* (Sinemet)…tricyclic antidepressants, such as *imipramine* (Tofranil) or *amitriptyline*…or drugs to treat erectile dysfunction, such as *sildenafil* (Viagra) or *tadalafil* (Cialis).

• **Dehydration.**

• **Anemia.**

• **Atherosclerosis,** in which blood flow is partially blocked by fatty deposits in blood vessels, or other vascular problems.

TEST #3: PENCIL TEST

Why this test? It checks the nerve function in your feet—if abnormal, this could indicate diabetes, certain types of infections or auto-immune disease.

The prop you'll need: A pencil that is freshly sharpened at one end with a flat eraser on the other end…and a friend to help.

What to do: Sit down so that all sides of your bare feet are accessible. Close your eyes, and keep them closed throughout the test.

Have your friend lightly touch your foot with either the sharp end or the eraser end of the pencil. With each touch, say which end of the pencil you think was used.

Ask your friend to repeat the test in at least three different locations on the tops and bottoms of both feet (12 locations total). Have your friend keep track of your right and wrong answers.

Watch out: Most people can easily tell the difference between "sharp" and "dull" sensations on their sensitive feet. If you give the wrong answer for more than two or three locations on your feet, have your doctor repeat the test to determine whether you have nerve damage (neuropathy).

Beware: Neuropathy is a common sign of diabetes…certain autoimmune disorders, including lupus and Sjögren's syndrome…infection, such as Lyme disease, shingles or hepatitis C…or excessive exposure to toxins, such as pesticides or heavy metals (mercury or lead).

TEST #4: URINE TEST

Why this test? It helps evaluate the functioning of your kidneys.

The prop you'll need: A clear plastic cup or clean, disposable clear jar.

What to do: In the middle of the day (urine will be too concentrated if you do this first thing in the morning), urinate into the cup or jar until you have caught at least an inch of urine. Throughout the day, note how often you urinate (about once every three waking hours is typical).

Watch out: The urine should be a pale, straw color—not deep yellow, brown or pinkish. Urine that's discolored could indicate dehydration, abnormal kidney function or another health problem.

Next, smell the urine. It should have nothing more than a very faint urine odor (unless you recently ate asparagus).

Beware: While dark-colored or smelly urine could simply mean that you are dehydrated, there are too many other potentially serious causes to ignore the signs.

Some of the disorders that can affect urine include…

• **Kidney or bladder infection,** which can cause discolored urine and frequent urination.

• **Kidney disease,** which can cause smelly, discolored urine. Interestingly, both too frequent urination and infrequent urination are signs of kidney disease.

• **Diabetes or enlarged prostate,** which can cause frequent urination.

TEST #5: "RULE OF THUMB" TEST

Why this test? It can help identify hearing loss.

The prop you'll need: A perfectly quiet room.

What to do: Rub your right thumb and index finger together continuously to create a kind of "whisper" sound. Raise your right arm so that it's level with your ear and your arm is roughly forming a right angle. Continue rubbing your thumb and index finger together. Can you still hear the sound? If not, move your hand toward your right ear, stopping when you can just hear the sound. Repeat on the left side.

Watch out: You should be able to hear this "finger rub" when your hand is six inches or more away from your ear.

Beware: If you need to be closer than six inches to hear the sound in either ear, you may have hearing loss. See an audiologist or otolaryngologist (ear, nose and throat specialist) for an evaluation.

While many people dismiss hearing loss as a mere inconvenience, it can have serious repercussions, such as getting into a car wreck because you can't hear the sound of a car approaching from the side.

When Hospitals Make Mistakes

E. Wesley Ely, MD, MPH, professor of medicine and critical care, Vanderbilt University Medical Center, Nashville. Dr. Ely is the founder of Vanderbilt's ICU Delirium and Cognitive Impairment Study Group and associate director of aging research for the VA Tennessee Valley Geriatric Research and Education Clinical Center (GRECC).

You research the pros and cons and shop around before you buy a car—so why not compare local hospitals in case you, or someone close to you, becomes ill or has an accident? Lack of accessible information may have discouraged you from taking a close look in the past, but the Centers for Medicare & Medicaid Services (CMS) now reports hospital error rates on its website. The information is right there at *hospitalcompare.hhs.gov*, making it easy to see how the various medical centers in your area stack up against each other. So what can you find out?

ADVERSE EVENTS: MORE COMMON THAN YOU THINK

Hospital-acquired conditions (HACs) are also called "never events"—because they are serious problems that people develop in the hospital that should seldom, if ever, happen as long as proper procedures are followed. As an example, according to the Department of Health and Human Services' Office of the Inspector General, 13.5% of hospitalized patients on Medicare experience preventable adverse events such as falls and infections. That's clearly way more than "never"…and way too many.

The CMS tracks hospitals' rates on these eight "never events"…

• **Foreign objects.** Yes, it really is true—sometimes surgeons accidentally leave a sponge or clamp in a patient's body.

• **Air embolism.** Without proper care and attention, a dangerous air bubble may develop in your bloodstream. This can happen with a central IV line and during vascular procedures.

• **Mismatched blood.** Hospitals occasionally administer the wrong type of blood in a transfusion.

• **Severe pressure sores.** If you can't move around independently and caregivers don't help you shift position frequently, you can develop painful and potentially life-threatening pressure sores, what most people call bedsores.

• **Falls and injuries.** Without proper assistance, a simple trip to the bathroom may result in a fall and a debilitating injury.

• **Vascular catheter-associated infection.** This is a blood infection from catheters—small tubes that are used to treat heart disease or other disease and carry a risk for sepsis.

• **Catheter-associated urinary tract infections.** Catheters also are used to help patients urinate, and infections are a common complication.

• **Uncontrolled blood sugar.** Signs of poorly controlled blood sugar range from confusion, anxiety and sweating (low blood sugar or hypoglycemia) to headaches, blurred vision and fatigue (high blood sugar or hyperglycemia). This is a concern for hospital patients with diabetes and also for others—for instance, those for whom the stress of hospitalization is too much. Pregnancy can cause short-term hyperglycemia as well.

After reading through that list, are you ready to take yourself to just any old hospital? I didn't think so. It's clearly a good idea to track error rates, notes E. Wesley Ely, MD, MPH, a professor and specialist in pulmonary and critical care medicine at Vanderbilt University Medical Center—but, he adds, it's something that needs to be done very carefully for the benefit of both patients and the hospitals themselves. For example, it's reasonable and helpful to hold hospitals responsible for mistakes such as transfusing the wrong blood type or leaving a foreign object in a patient during a surgical procedure—but it's not helpful to automatically blame hospitals when patients develop delirium after surgery, as the CMS originally proposed, because delirium is not always preventable. Fortunately, the CMS reversed its position on this condition, says Dr. Ely.

WHAT YOU NEED TO KNOW BEFORE YOU GO

To increase your odds of a safe and successful hospital stay, become an educated consumer…

• **Check hospital ratings.** Visit CMS's website and read about hospital errors. You'll find the incidence rate for each of the eight HACs in the nation's 4,700 hospitals. That is how many times an HAC has occurred per 1,000 discharges. At *hospitalcompare.hhs.gov*, you also can learn how satisfied other people were with their hospital stays...how closely hospitals followed best practices of care...how many people died within 30 days of hospitalization for a heart attack, heart failure or pneumonia...and 30-day readmission rates for these conditions.

• **Don't pay for their mistakes.** Medicare does not pay for treatment of conditions that result from hospitals' mistakes, and you don't have to either. If you develop any of the eight above conditions in the hospital, you can't be charged for the resulting necessary treatment, according to the Deficit Reduction Act of 2005.

• **Work with caregivers as a team.** For best results, Dr. Ely urges families to communicate closely with doctors, nurses and other healthcare professionals. Provide caregivers with a complete list of all prescription and over-the-counter medications and supplements that the patient takes so that nothing gets overlooked in an emergency. This is particularly important so that doctors can avoid drug interactions with new medications they might prescribe. Ask questions about the risks and potential benefits of treatment options, and speak up about any other concerns, such as a patient being sedated too deeply or for too many days. As well-meaning as most healthcare professionals are, the demands of their jobs mean that a patient's quality of care isn't necessarily automatic.

• **Safer at home.** Dr. Ely also encourages you to keep talking to your hospitalized loved ones so they remain as oriented and aware as possible...so that they get out of bed sooner...recover and come back home where they belong. It's much safer there!

How to Find Out If Your Hospital Is Safe

Marty Makary, MD, MPH, a surgeon at Johns Hopkins Hospital and an associate professor of health policy at the Johns Hopkins School of Public Health. He is the author of *Unaccountable: What Hospitals Won't Tell You and How Transparency Can Revolutionize Health Care*. UnaccountableBook.com

When you're admitted to a hospital, you probably don't stop and wonder what your chances are of getting out alive. But the odds are worse than you might imagine—and you can literally save your own life (or that of a loved one) by knowing how to investigate a hospital's record before you're checked in.

Frightening statistics: An estimated 98,000 hospital patients die from medical errors in the US annually. That's more than twice the number of Americans killed in car crashes each year. Many other hospital patients will suffer from serious—and preventable—complications.

Examples: About one of every 20 hospital patients will develop an infection...and surgeons operate on the wrong body part up to 40 times a week.

Getting the information you need: Because few hospitals publish statistics about their performance, it's difficult for patients to know which ones are worse—in some cases, much worse—than average.

For advice on avoiding the most common threats to hospital patients, we spoke to Marty Makary, MD, MPH, one of the country's leading experts on hospital safety.

WHAT YOU CAN FIND OUT

When I've asked patients why they chose a particular hospital, they typically say something like, "Because it's close to home." Others might say, "That is where my doctor has privileges." But those are bad answers. Before you get any medical care in a hospital, you should find out everything you can about the track record of the hospital. *Five clues to consider...*

CLUE #1. Bounceback rate. This is the term that doctors use for patients who need to be rehospitalized within 30 days. A high bounceback rate means that you have a higher-than-average risk for postsurgery complications, such as infection or impaired wound healing. Patients also can look up bounceback rates for conditions such as heart attacks and pneumonia. The rate for a particular procedure should never be higher than the national average.

Why this matters: A high bounceback rate could indicate substandard care or even a lack of teamwork in the operating room. It could also mean that the hospital is discharging patients too soon or that patients aren't getting clear discharge instructions that tell them what to do when they get home.

What to do: Check your hospital's rating on the US Department of Health and Human Services' website Hospital Compare (*hospitalcompare.hhs.gov*), where the majority of US hospitals are listed. You can see if the bounceback rate is better than, worse than or the same as the national average for the procedure you need.

Hospitals that are serious about reducing readmissions go the extra mile. For example, they will provide patients with detailed instructions on such issues as medication use and proper wound-cleaning procedures. Some even give patients a 24-hour hotline number to call if they have symptoms that could indicate a problem.

CLUE #2. Culture of safety. My colleagues and I at Johns Hopkins recently surveyed doctors, nurses and other hospital employees at 60 reputable US hospitals and asked such questions as, "Is the teamwork good?" "Is communication strong?" "Do you feel comfortable speaking up about safety concerns?"

We found a wide variation in the "safety culture" at different hospitals—and even within different departments at the same hospital. At one-third of the hospitals, the majority of employees reported that the level of teamwork was poor. Conversely, up to 99% of the staff at some hospitals said the teamwork was good.

Why it matters: Hospitals with a poor safety culture tended to have higher infection rates and worse patient outcomes.

What to do: Few hospitals that have conducted this type of survey make the findings public. Patients have to find other ways to get similar information. To do this, I suggest that before you choose a hospital you ask employees—including nurses and lab technicians—if they'd feel comfortable getting medical care where they work. Even if some hospital employees put a positive spin on their answers, you can generally tell a lot from their demeanor and comfort level when they respond.

CLUE #3. Use of minimally invasive procedures. Compared with "open" surgeries, minimally invasive procedures—such as knee arthroscopy and "keyhole" gallbladder surgery—require shorter hospitalizations. They're also less painful, less likely to result in an infection and less likely to lead to the need for subsequent surgery.

In spite of this, some surgeons still prefer open procedures. During my training, for example, I worked with a surgeon who was not skilled at minimally invasive surgery. His procedures were always open and involved large incisions—his wound-infection rate was about 20%. But his colleagues, who had trained in the newer minimally invasive techniques, had infection rates that were close to zero.

Why it matters: For the reasons above, you should usually choose a minimally invasive procedure if it's appropriate for your condition.

What to do: When discussing surgery, ask your doctor if there's more than one approach…the percentage of similar procedures that are done in a minimally invasive way…and the percentage that he/she does that way versus the percentage done each way nationwide.

Important: Get a second opinion before undergoing any ongoing or extensive treatment, including surgery. About 30% of second opinions are different from the first one.

CLUE #4. Volume of procedures. "See one, do one, teach one" is a common expression in medical schools. The idea is that new doctors have to start somewhere to learn how to perform medical procedures. Don't let them start on you.

Why it matters: Surgical death rates are directly related to a surgeon's experience with that procedure. The death rate after pancreas surgery, for example, is 14.7% for surgeons who average fewer than two procedures a year. It is 4.6% for those who do four or more. A survey conducted by the New York State Department of Health found that hospitals with surgeons who did relatively few procedures had patient-mortality rates that were four times higher than the state average.

What to do: Ask your doctor how often he does a particular procedure. For nonsurgical care, ask how many patients with your condition he treats.

Helpful: If 50% or more of a doctor's practice is dedicated to patients with exactly your condition, he will probably be a good choice.

CLUE #5. The availability of "open notes." Doctors make detailed notes after every office visit, but many patients have never seen these notes. Hospitals may not make them easily available, or the office/hospital can make it difficult (or expensive) to get copies.

Why it matters: Transparency builds trust. Patients who know what's in their medical records will not have to wonder what the doctor is writing about them.

Patients who read the notes will remember details about treatment advice…ask questions if they are confused…and often correct errors that can make a difference in their diagnosis and/or treatment. Also, these records are needed for a second opinion.

I purposely dictate notes while my patients are still in my office sitting next to me. Once, I was corrected when I said that a prior surgery was on the left side—it was actually on the right side. Another patient corrected me when I noted a wrong medication dose. Another reminded me to mention a history of high blood pressure.

What to do: Get copies of all of your medical records, including test results. If your doctor or hospital refuses to share them, ask to speak to an administrator. The records are yours—you have a right, under federal law, to see them and get copies. Fees range from a few dollars for a few pages to hundreds of dollars for extensive records.

Hospital Self-Defense: Take a Walk, Leave Sooner

To leave the hospital sooner, take a walk.

New study: Researchers interviewed 485 former hospital patients (ages 70 and older) who were treated for acute illnesses, such as pneumonia, or chronic conditions, such as congestive heart failure or chronic obstructive pulmonary disease.

Finding: Patients who walked varying distances in their rooms and/or in the hallways during their stays went home a day and a half earlier, on average, than those who spent their time in bed or seated next to it.

Anna Zisberg, PhD, assistant professor of nursing, University of Haifa, Mount Carmel, Israel.

Protect Yourself

Print your name on a large piece of brightly colored poster board, and hang it over your hospital bed so that everyone who enters can easily identify you. Bring antiseptic wipes or sprays, and use them from time to time on everything you touch. Bring shoes or slippers with rubber soles to use when walking to the bathroom or into the hall. Take a cell phone programmed with the number for the hospital's front desk or emergency department—if you need urgent help and your call button does not produce a response, you can use the phone.

Trisha Torrey, hospital advocate, Baldwinsville, New York, and author of *You Bet Your Life! The 10 Mistakes Every Person Makes: How to Fix Them to Get the Health Care You Deserve.* EveryPatientsAdvocate. com

Make Sure You Get This Test

All hospital patients should have their blood glucose levels checked, according to new guidelines issued by the Endocrine Society.

Reason: Between 32% and 38% of hospitalized patients have hyperglycemia (high blood glucose), which increases risk for longer hospital stays, infections and death in those who are not critically ill.

If you are hospitalized: Be sure to get this test.

Guillermo E. Umpierrez, MD, professor of medicine, division of endocrinology, metabolism, Emory University School of Medicine, Atlanta.

Germy Doctors

Physicians wash their hands before examining their patients (or certainly should!). But what about their stethoscopes? In a new study, the parts of stethoscopes used to examine 71 patients were found to be contaminated with more bacteria (including dangerous MRSA) than every part of the physician's hand except the fingertips.

Before your doctor uses a stethoscope: Ask him/her to clean it with an alcohol wipe.

Didier Pittet, MD, director, infection control program, University of Geneva Hospitals, Switzerland.

10

Medication Smarts

5 Medication Mistakes You Never Want to Make

Chewing a pill when it is meant to be swallowed might taste pretty bad, but it wouldn't necessarily be dangerous, right? Wrong—it can be fatal if too much of the active ingredient is released at one time.

This is just one of the preventable medication errors that occurs regularly in our country—in fact, at least 100,000 Americans are hospitalized from such mistakes every year. How could something as simple as taking a medication go so wrong?

Here's how some of the most common medication mistakes can occur—*and how to avoid them...*

MISTAKE #1: Not verifying the instructions on e-prescriptions. Prescription pads are quickly becoming a thing of the past. Instead, your doctor now may enter your prescription into a computer, which electronically transmits it to your pharmacy. The good news is e-prescriptions solve the problem of illegible handwriting and help stop errors. For example, if your doctor enters a dose of a drug that is too low or too high for any patient, the computer will flag it. In hospitals, computerized prescribing has reduced medication errors by up to 85%. But mistakes still happen.

How errors can occur: Let's say that your doctor wants you to take a long-acting diabetes medication only once a day, but the computer's default setting, which comes up automatically, calls for twice-daily dosing. If he/she does not notice, the computer will send that information to the pharmacy. The level of medication in your body could become too high, and blood sugar could drop dangerously low.

Albert W. Wu, MD, MPH, an internist and a professor of medicine, surgery and health policy & management at The Johns Hopkins Bloomberg School of Public Health and the director of the Center for Health Services and Outcomes Research, both in Baltimore. He was a member of the committee formed by the Institute of Medicine to identify and prevent medication errors.

My advice: Always ask your doctor how to take medication—how much…how frequently…what time of day…and with or without food. Write all this information down. Then check this information on the drug label when you pick up the prescription. If there's any discrepancy between what the doctor told you and what the label says, the pharmacist should contact your doctor.

MISTAKE #2: Not discussing the name of the drug with the doctor. There are more than 10,000 prescription drugs and some 300,000 over-the-counter (OTC) medications. Many have similar-sounding—and similarly spelled—names that are easily confused.

How errors can occur: Your doctor might inadvertently key in *clonazepam* (an anti-anxiety drug) instead of *clonidine* (for high blood pressure).

My advice: Ask your doctor to pronounce and/or write down for you the name of the drug he is prescribing. Repeat the name to make sure you have it right. When you pick up the drug, say the name aloud to the pharmacist and/or show him the paper so you can double-check that you're getting the right medication.

MISTAKE #3: Accepting an "average" dose. When prescribing a drug, most doctors choose an average dose that would cover people of various sizes and ages. It's approximate, not precise.

How errors can occur: Suppose that you need a 10-mg dose of Lasix (a diuretic), based on your body weight, gender and age. If the lowest dose from the manufacturer is 20 mg, that's probably what you'll get (you could be instructed to cut the pill in half, but that may not happen). Too-high doses increase the risk for side effects and other complications.

My advice: Tell your doctor that you'd like to start low. Ask for the lowest possible effective dose. You and your doctor can increase it later.

MISTAKE #4: Splitting pills that should never be split. Some people split their pills in half to save money. But some pills can be safely split…others can't.

How errors can occur: Splitting a time-released medication could cause all of the active ingredient to be released at once. Or the pill's protective coating may be damaged, causing the drug to be broken down in the stomach rather than in the intestine, so it is not properly absorbed.

My advice: If cost is an issue, tell your doctor. There might be a lower-priced medication that will work as well. For example, a generic antiviral can cost $9, while a brand-name option could be as much as $65.

MISTAKE #5: Taking double doses. This happens a lot—mainly because people don't realize what the active ingredients are in the various drugs they're taking.

How errors can occur: Let's say that you take OTC acetaminophen for joint pain. But maybe you are taking a cold medicine that also contains acetaminophen. Then your doctor or dentist gives you a prescription for Tylenol with codeine (which contains even more acetaminophen). You could wind up getting a double or even triple dose.

Too much acetaminophen can cause liver damage, particularly when combined with alcohol.

My advice: Even though the active ingredients are listed on package inserts or packaging for all drugs, ask your pharmacist about this when you pick up a medication. If any active ingredients are found in more than one of the drugs you take, ask your pharmacist and/or doctor if the combined dosage is safe.

VITAL QUESTIONS FOR YOUR PHARMACIST

Do yourself a favor—the next time you pick up a prescription talk to your pharmacist. This is one of the best ways to avoid medication errors. *Key questions to ask your pharmacist…*

•**What is the active ingredient in this medicine?**

•**Should I avoid any other medicines, supplements, foods or drinks when taking this drug?***

•**Is there anything I should watch for—such as allergic reactions or other side effects?**

•**Should I take this medication on an empty stomach or with food?**

•**What should I do if I miss a dose...or use too much?**

•**Will I need any tests to check on the medicine's effectiveness—such as blood tests?**

•**How and where should I store this medicine?**

*You also can check for interactions at *pdrhealth. com.*

Medication Mix-Ups Can Be Deadly

Milap C. Nahata, PharmD, a professor and chairman of pharmacy practice and administration in the College of Pharmacy at Ohio State University and associate director of pharmacy at the Ohio State University Medical Center, both in Columbus.

When you take a drug, you expect it to ease your symptoms or cure your medical problem. However, the drugs you take can sometimes cause serious harm—or even death—if there is a medication "error" (such as taking a wrong dose or an inappropriate drug).

Frightening statistic: Each year, up to 1.5 million Americans are affected by preventable errors involving both prescription and over-the-counter (OTC) drugs, according to the Institute of Medicine. Most of these errors are minor and unlikely to cause serious problems—with dangerous exceptions.

Example: A baby in one hospital needed 0.5 mg of morphine for sedation and/or pain relief. The doctor who wrote the prescription didn't put a "0" before the decimal point. A nurse who didn't see the decimal point gave the child 5 mg. This tenfold error was doubled when the child, who later died as a result of the overdose, was given an additional excessive dose.

WHAT'S GOING WRONG?

Medication errors can occur in several ways. Often, patients skip doses, stop a drug without medical advice or neglect to tell their doctors about other drugs and/or supplements they are taking, exposing themselves to the possibility of a dangerous interaction.

But health-care professionals also can play a role in medication errors. *Common reasons for medication errors that occur in doctors' offices and at pharmacies and hospitals...*

•**Incorrect doses.** Most prescription drugs come in standard doses, such as 10 mg or 100 mg. On occasion, doctors may accidentally omit a "0" or jot down a decimal point that's difficult to see.

Self-defense: When your doctor hands you a prescription, confirm the dose (the specific number of milligrams, for example) before leaving his/her office.

ABBREVIATIONS

When writing prescriptions, doctors use abbreviations that can be easily misread by pharmacists.

Example: The abbreviation "QOD" means every other day..."QD" means every day..."BID" means twice a day...and "QID" is four times a day. If the pharmacist reads "QD" as "QID," the patient will be taking four times the recommended dose, which can lead to side effects.

Self-defense: Make sure you understand the intended dosing instructions (for example, once or twice daily) before leaving your doctor's office. Then confirm the drug and dose with the pharmacist before leaving the pharmacy to ensure that you're receiving both the correct medication and dose.

WRONG DRUGS

There are more than 10,000 prescription drugs and as many as 300,000 OTC medications on the market. Some of these drugs have similar names that are easily confused—either by the doctor who is writing the prescription or by the pharmacist who's filling it.

Example: It's easy to confuse *bupropion,* an antidepressant, with *buspirone,* an antianxiety drug.

189

Self-defense: Know the exact name of the drug you're supposed to be taking (both the generic name and the brand name)...why you're taking it...and what it looks like—consult the *Physicians' Desk Reference* online at *pdrhealth.com* to view photographs of commonly prescribed drugs.

Check the drug name before you leave your doctor's office. Repeat the name out loud when you order the drug at the pharmacy. In the example above, bupropion is the generic name for the brand-name drug Wellbutrin. Buspirone is the generic name for Buspar.

Helpful: Prescription tablets and capsules are imprinted with numbers that are specific to particular drugs and doses from specific manufacturers. When you first fill a prescription, write down the manufacturer's number and keep it in a safe place. When you get the prescription refilled, double-check to ensure that it has the same number.

OTHER PRECAUTIONS TO TAKE

If you take medication...

• **Consult the pharmacist.** About 95% of patients don't ask questions about how to use their medication, according to research published by the California Board of Pharmacy and other groups. These patients may not understand not only how much of the medication to take or when and how often to take it, but also what side effects might occur or how to tell if the drug is working.

Self-defense: Consult with the pharmacist every time you start a new prescription—particularly if you're also taking other drugs with which it might interact.

Important: Many people who work behind the counter are pharmacy technicians. When asking questions about a medication, make sure that you're talking to a pharmacist. Look for the title "Pharmacist" or "RPh" (Registered Pharmacist) on the person's jacket (or nameplate)—or ask the person's title.

Helpful: A patient who takes multiple drugs can prevent many errors by buying them all at the same pharmacy. Virtually all pharmacies now have computers that track medications and will automatically give an alert if a patient adds a new drug that might interact with others that he is taking.

• **Tell your doctor about everything you take.** Adults over age 65 account for 13% of the US population but take one-third of all prescription drugs. Anyone taking numerous drugs may experience side effects and/or drug interactions—many of which could be avoided if patients periodically reviewed medication use with their doctors and/or pharmacists.

Doctors usually ask patients what medications they're currently taking. They don't always ask about—or patients fail to mention—supplements and/or OTC drugs.

Self-defense: Every time you see your doctor, bring a list that includes everything you're taking. Don't assume that supplements, including herbs, don't count. Many of these products can interact with prescription drugs.

Example: The husband of one of our employees was admitted to the hospital with a bleeding disorder. The condition had developed because he was taking the blood thinner *warfarin* (Coumadin) to prevent clots but hadn't told his doctor (or pharmacist) that he also was using the herbal supplement ginkgo biloba, which increases the risk of bleeding—especially when combined with warfarin.

Accidental Addicts—5% of Seniors Abuse Drugs

Ihsan M. Salloum, MD, MPH, professor, department of psychiatry and behavioral sciences, chief, Division of Alcohol and Drug Abuse: Treatment and Research, and director, Addiction Psychiatry and Psychiatric Comorbidity Programs, University of Miami Miller School of Medicine, Miami, Florida.

According to a recent government report, about 4.3 million Americans over age 50 are drug abusers, and this number is expected to double by 2020. While it is true that many are ex-hippies who never stopped smoking pot or using other illicit drugs, many other middle-aged and senior drug abusers slid into their habits unwittingly. And for a variety of reasons, these "accidental addicts" may be in even greater danger than the aging groovesters, in part because they might not even realize that they are addicted... nor be aware of the very serious risks.

JUST SAY NO?

The older we get, the more sensitive our bodies are to drugs, notes Ihsan M. Salloum, MD, a professor at the University of Miami Miller School of Medicine and chief of its division of alcohol and drug abuse. So as you age, it's better to completely avoid potentially addictive drugs such as certain pain killers, sleeping pills and antianxiety medications. If you must take them to recover from surgery or to get through a stressful period, keep it short-term—meaning take as low a dose as you can for the least time possible.

Prescription drug abuse often begins when a doctor prescribes an antianxiety benzodiazepine (such as *alprazolam*/Xanax) to help a patient relax or an opioid pain medication (such as *oxycodone*/OxyContin) following major surgery, such as a hip or knee replacement. Use of such drugs over long periods can develop into tolerance (when your body adapts to a drug and you need larger and larger doses to achieve the same effect) or addiction—especially in those with a genetic predisposition or personal history of substance abuse.

SERIOUS RISKS

Dr. Salloum warns that older people in particular face a variety of increased risks from drugs, whether they are illicit or prescribed...

• **Older people metabolize drugs differently**—the kidneys and liver don't function as effectively, so the drugs remain in the system longer. Other age-related changes (such as lower levels of lean body mass) mean that drugs affect older people differently across the board, making them more sensitive to the effects of drugs.

• **Drug-to-drug interactions are more common in older people.** If you have multiple chronic diseases, you likely take multiple medicines. The more drugs you take, the greater the chance of dangerous interactions.

• **More prone to falls already, older people are more likely to be dangerously injured**

when they tumble. If age has already left you a bit unsteady, side effects of drugs may easily worsen balance and cause a fall.

• **Older people are more likely to have heart attacks or strokes caused by medications.** Stimulants, in particular, are more likely to cause heart attacks or strokes in older people.

RECOGNIZING AND COPING WITH A PROBLEM

The line between use and abuse can be a fine one, but generally speaking, addiction is what you call it when you lose control over the use of a substance and/or it begins to interfere with daily life. *Signs to watch for in yourself or someone close to you include...*

• **Missing professional, financial or social obligations.**

• **Changes in personality or behavior.**

• **Neglecting personal hygiene or appearance.**

• **Irritability and restlessness.**

• **Driving under the influence or getting into accidents.**

• **Preoccupation with getting and using a drug, and inability to stop using it.**

• **Feeling that you need the drug to deal with your problems.**

If you suspect that you have become dependent on any drug, visit your primary care doctor and share your concern—he/she can help you evaluate the problem and assess what can and should be done from a medical perspective. *You can also learn more, for yourself or to help a friend or loved one, by visiting websites such as...*

• **The Partnership for a Drug-Free America** at *drugfree.org/Intervention/*.

• **Drug and Alcohol Addiction Support Groups** at *recoveryconnection.org/support_groups/drug-alcohol-addiction-support-groups.php*.

• **Hazelden Betty Ford Foundation** at *hazelden.org*.

• **Mayo Clinic** at *mayoclinic.com/health/drug-addiction/DS00183/*.

Are You Overdosing On OTC Drugs?

Suzy Cohen, RPh, a licensed pharmacist in Boulder, Colorado, and the author of the "Dear Pharmacist" syndicated column, which reaches 20 million readers nationwide, *The 24-Hour Pharmacist* and *Diabetes Without Drugs and Drug Muggers*. SuzyCohen.com

Painkillers, heartburn drugs and laxatives are among the worst offenders.

We hear a lot about overuse of prescription drugs. That's because every year, more than 20,000 Americans die from a prescription drug overdose. About 75% of those fatalities are from painkillers such as *oxycodone* (OxyContin) and *hydrocodone* (Vicodin). But there's another unexpected threat—and that's overdosing on over-the-counter (OTC) painkillers.

Believe it or not, the main culprit is acetaminophen—the common pain reliever in Tylenol and other brands. It hospitalizes 30,000 people annually, many of whom develop acute liver failure.

Studies show that one-half to two-thirds of acetaminophen overdoses are the result of victims' poor understanding of the product's dosing instructions. One study published in the *Journal of General Internal Medicine* tested 500 people to determine their knowledge about and use of acetaminophen.

By their answers, many of the study participants showed that they would overdose—24% by using one product and unknowingly taking more than the safe limit of 4,000 mg (4 g) every 24 hours...and about 46% by using two acetaminophen-containing products at the same time without realizing the combined dosage would be an overdose.

The same misuse of medications and misunderstanding of labels occurs with other types of OTC medications described throughout this article—with potentially disastrous long-term consequences for health. *Here's how to make sure that you don't overdose on or overuse OTC drugs...*

ACETAMINOPHEN

Acetaminophen is the most commonly used OTC drug in the US—every week, one out of every five adults takes it. And for good reason—the drug works fast to reduce pain and fever. In fact, acetaminophen works so well, it's the main pain-relieving, fever-lowering ingredient in many OTC products for headache, arthritis, back pain, colds, coughs, sinus problems and more. But the effectiveness and availability of the ingredient is a setup for overdosing.

Fortunately, a few simple precautions can help prevent an acetaminophen overdose...

• **Read the labels and do the math.** Read the ingredient list on every OTC drug you take and know which contain acetaminophen and how much. Keep careful track of your daily intake—and don't ever take more than 1,000 mg at any one time or exceed 4,000 mg in a day. The more acetaminophen-containing products you take, the more likely it is you'll overdose.

Example: In the *Journal of General Internal Medicine* overdose study, three drug combinations were most likely to cause an overdose—a pain reliever and a PM pain reliever...a pain reliever and a cough and cold medicine...a sinus medication and a PM pain reliever.

• **Know if you are at high risk—and be extra-cautious if you are.** In the overdose study, people who were "heavy users" of acetaminophen (taking it a couple of days a week or more) were more likely to underestimate their intake—and to overdose.

Important: If you suffer from chronic pain, see your primary care physician or a pain specialist, and ask for a stronger medication that is taken once or twice a day. That way, you won't have to take as many OTC painkillers.

• **Know the signs of an overdose.** An overdose of acetaminophen typically causes nausea and vomiting, sweating, yellowing of the skin and eyes and a general feeling of flulike illness. Within one to three days, it causes pain in the upper right quadrant of the abdomen (the location of the liver). If you develop those symptoms after regular use of acetaminophen (or after a single dose that is excessive)—seek immediate medical care.

Self-defense: Call 911 or go to a hospital emergency department if you have severe symptoms, such as gasping for air. The standard treatment for acetaminophen overdose is *n-acetyl-cysteine* (NAC), an antioxidant that reverses liver toxicity, often given intravenously. Although NAC capsules are available at health-food stores, it's best to be treated by medical personnel since an overdose is a serious medical condition. If you suspect that you may be experiencing symptoms of an overdose, you can call a 24-hour poison control center such as the National Capital Poison Center at 800-222-1222.

PROTON PUMP INHIBITORS (PPIS)

These popular drugs work by slowing down your body's production of stomach acid, preventing and relieving the symptoms of heartburn. They also are used to treat indigestion (dyspepsia), ulcers and other upper gastrointestinal (GI) problems. Two kinds are available OTC—*lansoprazole* (Prevacid 24HR) and *omeprazole* (Prilosec OTC, Zegerid OTC).

The danger: These drugs, if taken daily, should not be used for more than two weeks without a doctor's approval, according to label instructions. Studies show that overuse can increase risk for hip, wrist or spine fractures in adults over age 50…and cardiac arrhythmias, intense diarrhea, colds, flu and pneumonia, and vitamin and mineral deficiencies in users of all ages. In addition, when you stop taking one of these drugs abruptly, it can trigger rebound acid hypersecretion—a surge of stomach acid that worsens symptoms, forcing you back on the drug for relief.

Self-defense: Slowly wean yourself off long-term use of a PPI. Speak to your doctor about the best way to do this. Afterward, treat heartburn with OTC antacids, a much safer choice (follow label instructions).

NASAL DECONGESTANTS

Many people suffer from rhinitis medicamentosa (RM)—a chronically stuffy nose caused by overuse of nasal decongestant spray.

For example, you might use a spray, such as Afrin or Neo-Synephrine containing the ingredient oxymetazoline or phenylephrine, during a cold or allergy season. It provides relief, but there is "rebound congestion" when the spray wears off. You use it again…there is rebound congestion…and you use it again. Soon, you have RM—and are addicted to the nasal spray for "relief."

Self-defense: If you are addicted to a nasal spray, wean yourself off slowly. (*Examples*: Alternate nostrils with each use, rather than spraying both nostrils. Or use the spray only at bedtime to get you through the night.) As you decrease use, try a nonmedicated saline spray or a menthol nasal spray and a humidifier or steam vaporizer. You might also ask your doctor for a short-term prescription for nasal corticosteroids, which will relieve congestion while you withdraw from the spray. Plus, address underlying health problems that may cause nasal congestion, such as food allergies or structural problems in the sinuses.

LAXATIVES

Constipation is a common problem, and daily use of OTC laxatives, such as Miralax and Milk of Magnesia, is frequently the "solution."

The danger: Laxative overuse can lead to abdominal cramping, nausea and vomiting, blood in the stool, mineral deficiencies, electrolyte imbalances that cause heart and kidney damage—and, in rare cases, death.

Self-defense: Wean yourself slowly off laxatives. For example, start by switching from daily use to every-other-day use.

As you're reducing use, add more fiber to your diet, with fruits, vegetables, whole grains and beans—and, if necessary, take a daily fiber supplement—to help ensure regular bowel movements. Take a probiotic, a supplement of "friendly" bacteria that aids digestive health. Other digestive aids that can help cure constipation include aloe vera, essential fatty acids and digestive enzymes. Talk to your doctor about which of these digestive aids might work best for you. Drink water throughout the day and exercise regularly, which stimulates bowels.

STAY SAFE

Keep all your prescriptions at the same pharmacy. That way, your pharmacist has your complete medication profile and can accurately advise you about your OTC medications.

When buying an OTC product, ask your pharmacist to check for interactions between your prescription drugs and your OTC choices. You are not being a "pest"—the pharmacist wants to help keep you safe.

Why Your Dentist Should Know About the Supplements You Take

Mark Donaldson, PharmD, director of pharmacy services, Kalispell Regional Medical Center, Kalispell, Montana, and clinical professor, Skaggs School of Pharmacy, University of Montana, Missoula.

You're health-savvy enough to know that it's important to tell your doctor about any dietary or herbal supplements you take—because some supplements can cause big problems in people who take certain medications, and vice versa.

But do you also tell your dentist about all the supplements you take? You should...for the exact same reason. After all, oral-health-care providers—dentists, periodontists, orthodontists, endodontists and oral surgeons—all may prescribe or administer medications before, during and after dental procedures.

And certain supplements are especially likely to cause problems if combined with the particular types of medications dental patients most often are given. Fortunately, there's an easy way to avoid this, a new study suggests.

RISKY COMBINATIONS

The study was led by Mark Donaldson, PharmD, a clinical professor at the University of Montana's Skaggs School of Pharmacy in Missoula. He reviewed various drug-interaction databases looking for evidence of interactions between supplements and drugs that

are commonly used in dental practice. *Here's what he discovered about...*

•**Ginkgo biloba and evening primrose.** These herbs can reduce your blood's ability to clot, possibly leading to excessive bleeding during and/or after your dental procedure—particularly if you also take another anticoagulant, such as aspirin or *ibuprofen* (Advil).

Recommended: Ginkgo's half-life (the time it takes for the substance's concentration in your body to be reduced by half) is about seven hours, and it takes about four half-lives for 90% of the drug to be eliminated from your system—so you should stop taking ginkgo at least 28 hours before a dental appointment to reduce your risk for excessive bleeding. Evening primrose doesn't linger in the body quite as long, so stopping it 24 hours before your appointment should give enough time to clear it from your body.

•**St. John's wort.** The most potential interactions are found with this herb, which often is used to help reduce anxiety, ease depression or aid sleep. St. John's wort can increase your sensitivity to sunlight, potentially leading to severe sunburn—and its likelihood of doing so is increased when it is combined with other drugs that are frequently administered or recommended by dentists. These include ibuprofen...the antibiotics *azithromycin*, *doxycycline* and *tetracycline*...and the antihistamine *diphenhydramine* (Benadryl), given in the event of an allergic reaction or simply during the allergy season.

St. John's wort also can interfere with the metabolism of antianxiety benzodiazepines such as *alprazolam* (Xanax), *diazepam* (Valium) and *lorazepam* (Ativan)...sedatives such as *zaleplon* (Sonata) and *zolpidem* (Ambien)...the antibiotics *clarithromycin*, *clindamycin*, *erythromycin*, *doxycycline* and *tetracycline*...and the anti-inflammatory drugs *prednisone* and *dexamethasone*. All these drugs can be rendered less effective when combined with St. John's wort.

Finally, narcotics such as *codeine*, *hydrocodone* (Vicodin) and *oxycodone* (OxyContin) can become even more intoxicating when taken with St. John's wort. This can lead to sleepiness, lethargy and dizziness in some patients, greatly reducing their ability to function normally for the rest of the day or even longer, Dr. Donaldson cautioned.

Best: The half-life of St. John's wort is up to 25 hours, so discontinue it four days before your dental appointment. Unlike with antidepressants, which must be tapered off gradually, there is no risk in abruptly stopping St. John's wort because the herb's long half-life basically makes it "self-tapering," Dr. Donaldson said.

•**Valerian.** This herb has mild sedative effects—and that's where the real problems can occur. Dentists may prescribe benzodiazepine drugs to help anxious patients relax in the chair…or they may prescribe strong painkillers containing codeine for after a procedure. "Any time you use something that depresses the central nervous system in combination with another drug that does the same, they are going to have an additive effect. And if the two substances work by different mechanisms, they could produce a synergistic effect, so that the end result is even greater than the sum of the substances' individual effects," Dr. Donaldson said. For some patients, this can lead to significant sleepiness, lethargy and dizziness that can persist into the next day.

Important: Valerian use should be stopped at least 24 hours before your dental appointment.

•**Calcium and magnesium.** Certain antibiotics commonly used in dentistry, particularly doxycycline and tetracycline, bind to these minerals—which means that the antibiotic won't be properly absorbed, compromising your ability to fight off infection.

What to do: If you supplement with either or both of these minerals and your dentist prescribes antibiotics, allow at least two hours between the time you take the drug and the time you take the supplement. Remember that these minerals often are found in dairy products, multivitamins and antacids, so the same guidelines would apply, Dr. Donaldson noted.

•**Fish oil or another omega-3–rich oil.** These very popular supplements weren't included in the review, so I asked Dr. Donald-

son if there were any concerns. He said, "One potential issue is that fish oil might interfere with the absorption of drugs. However, since none of the drugs commonly used in dentistry that we reviewed are particularly fat-soluble, the fish oil should not markedly increase or decrease the effectiveness of those drugs. However, high doses of fish oil can have anticlotting effects, so there could be a problem with bleeding, particularly if the patient also is taking aspirin."

What to do: "If you normally take more than three grams a day of omega-3–rich oil, consider reducing your daily dose to three grams at least 24 hours ahead of your dental appointment. The day after your appointment, you can return to your usual higher dose," Dr. Donaldson said.

SAFEST BETS

Certain medications used by dentists have better safety profiles than others in the same class, so if your dentist is unsure about a potential interaction, it's best to opt for the drug with the least chance of becoming half of a bad combination, Dr. Donaldson said. *Talk to your dentist about the options for…*

•**Pain relief.** *Acetaminophen* (Tylenol) is probably the safest pain reliever for most people who take supplements, Dr. Donaldson said, because it's not associated with major drug-supplement interactions (though at high doses or if taken with alcohol it can damage the liver). Do not exceed the maximum dosage listed on the product label.

If acetaminophen alone does not provide sufficient relief (for instance, after serious drilling or other major dental work), the best bet is to combine acetaminophen with a nonsteroidal anti-inflammatory medication, such as ibuprofen. As always, your goal should be to use the lowest possible dose for the shortest period of time necessary to achieve the needed effect.

•**Antibiotics.** Safest for supplement users are usually *amoxicillin, cephalexin, metronidazole* and *penicillin*. If your dentist says that you need an antibiotic, ask whether one of these four would be appropriate.

• **Sedatives.** For dental patients who need a sedative or antianxiety medication, nitrous oxide gas is typically a safe choice, Dr. Donaldson said, because it is not metabolized by the body. Instead it is inhaled, usually through a nasal mask, and diffused through the lungs before entering the brain and triggering relaxation. This happens quickly, typically within three deep breaths...and the nitrous oxide exits the system within minutes once the gas is turned off. Its effect is easily modified, so if you're already taking valerian, for example, your dentist can simply "dial down" the concentration of nitrous oxide you inhale.

OPEN WIDE AND SPEAK UP

Considering that more than one-third of all Americans now take supplements, all health-care providers should be asking every patient about their use. But according to a recent survey by AARP and the National Center for Complementary and Alternative Medicine (a part of the National Institutes of Health), 67% of the adults surveyed did not speak with their health-care providers about any supplement use. Of those who did, the majority said that they themselves—and not their health-care providers—brought up the topic.

Takeaway message: If your dentist doesn't ask you about all of the drugs you use, including over-the-counter medications and supplements, take the initiative and bring up the subject. If your dentist is not well versed in drug-supplement interactions, show him this article—he may learn quite a bit!

The Overdose Danger

Jack E. Fincham, PhD, RPh, a registered pharmacist and professor in the division of pharmacy practice and administration at the University of Missouri, Kansas City, where he is also an adjunct professor in the Bloch School of Management. Dr. Fincham is also a former panel member of the FDA Non-Prescription Drugs Advisory Committee.

W hen you get a new prescription, the first thing your doctor does (after choosing the drug) is decide on the dose.

What most people don't think about: Your doctor's dosing decision is crucial—getting even slightly more of a medication than you need can greatly increase your risk for side effects. Correct dosing, however, can lessen (or even eliminate) side effects.

Each year in the US, drug side effects are estimated to cause more than one million hospitalizations and more than 100,000 deaths. Yet many doctors reflexively prescribe "average" doses without checking recommendations for optimal dosing based on such factors as age, sex and body weight.

For example, a 100-pound woman might be given the same dose as a 200-pound man... and a 75-year-old may be given the same dose as a healthy college student. It's not hard to guess who is more likely to have preventable side effects. While many people know that taking a blood thinner in a dose that's too high can have devastating consequences, recent research is focusing on other drugs that can also have dangerous side effects.

Important new finding: With blood pressure drugs and diabetes medication, in particular, excessive doses can increase risk for dizzy spells, confusion, falls and even death—especially among adults age 70 and older, according to recent research in *JAMA Internal Medicine.*

DOSING DANGERS

Common drugs to watch out for...*

• **Blood pressure drugs.** About 25% of patients who take one or more of these medications stop using them within six months because of side effects, and up to half quit taking them within a year. The majority of people who take blood pressure drugs will initially suffer from dizziness, unsteadiness, falls or other side effects. Alert your physician if you experience any of these side effects. Even though the discomfort typically wanes over time, it can often be prevented altogether by starting with a lower dose of medication.

Beta-blockers, such as *metoprolol* (Lopressor) and *propranolol* (Inderal), are particularly dose-sensitive. So are alpha-blockers, such as *prazosin* (Minipress). Women who take these

*Never change a medication dose without consulting your doctor.

drugs tend to have a greater drop in blood pressure/heart rate than men, so they typically need a lower dose. The same may be true of patients who have both high blood pressure and lung disease, who often suffer shortness of breath when they take excessive doses. People who take multiple blood pressure medications are also more likely to have side effects.

My advice: Tell your doctor that you would like to start with one drug. Emphasize that you'd like to take the lowest possible dose—and that you're willing to be retested (or check your own blood pressure at home with an automated blood pressure monitor) to make sure that the treatment is working.

• **Diabetes medications.** The risks for diabetes complications—such as nerve damage, blindness, stroke and heart attack—are so great that doctors tend to treat it aggressively. But oral diabetes drugs given in high doses can easily cause blood sugar to fall too low.

Example: Patients who take *glyburide* or *repaglinide* (Prandin) often develop hypoglycemia, excessively low blood sugar that can cause dizziness, confusion and other symptoms. Even if the initial dose was correct, physiological changes as you age and/or changes in your lifestyle could make that starting dose too potent. For example, suppose that you start exercising more and eating a healthier diet. You'll probably need a lower drug dose than you did before, but your doctor might not think (or know) to change the prescription.

My advice: Tell your doctor right away about any lifestyle changes that could affect your blood sugar levels, such as exercise frequency (or intensity), changes in meal timing, etc. Keep careful tabs on your blood sugar with home tests. If your blood sugar is consistently testing at the lower end of the recommended range (or below it), call your doctor and ask whether you should switch to a lower drug dose.

• **Painkillers.** Aspirin, *ibuprofen* (Motrin) and other nonsteroidal anti-inflammatory drugs (NSAIDs) are widely available and ef-

fective. But they're also dangerous at high doses. One study found that more than 70% of people who take these drugs daily on a regular basis suffer at least some damage to the small intestine. Like the blood thinner *warfarin* (Coumadin), they're a common cause of excessive bleeding.

My advice: Take the lowest possible dose… use painkillers as rarely as possible…and always take them with food. People assume that over-the-counter drugs are safe, but none of these medications are meant to be used long term (more than four weeks).

If you can, switch to one of the many brands of acetaminophen (such as Tylenol). It has about the same pain-relieving effects, but even with its increased risk for liver damage, acetaminophen (taken at the recommended dosage) is less likely than an NSAID to cause side effects.

• **Sedatives.** Valium and related drugs, known as benzodiazepines, are commonly prescribed sedatives in the US, but the standard doses can be much too high for women as well as older adults.

Medications such as *diazepam* (Valium), *triazolam* (Halcion) and *zolpidem* (Ambien) accumulate in fatty tissue. Since women have a higher percentage of body fat than men, the drug effects can linger, causing next-day drowsiness or a decline in alertness and concentration. In older adults, the drugs are metabolized (broken down) more slowly, causing unacceptably high levels to accumulate in the body.

My advice: Women who are given a prescription for one of these drugs should always ask if the dose is sex-specific. They can ask something like, "Do I need a lower dose because I'm a woman?"

Also, in my opinion, people age 65 or older should avoid these drugs altogether unless they have to take them for a serious problem, such as a seizure disorder. If your doctor says that you need a sedative, ask if you can use a shorter-acting drug such as *lorazepam* (Ativan)…if you can take it for a short period of time (less than a month)…or if you can get by with a lower dose.

Important: These drugs should never be combined with alcohol. The combination increases the sedative effects.

To read more about a drug you're taking: Go to *drugs.com*.

What Your Doctor May Not Tell You About High Blood Pressure Drugs

Mark C. Houston, MD, associate clinical professor of medicine at Vanderbilt University School of Medicine and director of the Hypertension Institute at Saint Thomas Medical Group, both in Nashville. He is the author of four books, including *What Your Doctor May Not Tell You About Hypertension* and the upcoming *What Your Doctor May Not Tell You About Heart Disease.* HypertensionInstitute.com

---

A woman—let's call her Naomi—was diagnosed with high blood pressure and went on medication prescribed by her doctor. Within a few months, she was back at the doctor's office, her blood pressure heading up instead of down. It turned out that she was not taking her medication properly—and that the drug she had been given was not the most appropriate one for her.

Naomi is hardly alone. Nearly one-third of US adults have hypertension (blood pressure higher than 140/90), a symptomless disease that, if not appropriately managed, can result in a heart attack or stroke.

Mark C. Houston, MD, is director of the Hypertension Institute at Saint Thomas Medical Group in Nashville and author of *What Your Doctor May Not Tell You About Hypertension.* He explained that failure to take medication properly is one primary reason why high blood pressure is often so hard to get under control.

Another problem is that finding the right medication or combination of medications can be tricky, and often doctors have resorted to a "try this, try that" approach.

Good news: Recent research has helped clarify which types of drugs are likely to work best for certain patients. So if you have recently been diagnosed with hypertension or if your medication is not working, it's time to talk to your doctor about...

• **Your levels of the blood pressure-modulating enzyme renin.** A recent study showed that people with different blood levels of renin responded differently to various hypertension drugs—and that taking the wrong kind of medication actually made blood pressure go up.

• **Patients with high-renin hypertension responded best to...**

• Angiotensin-converting enzyme (ACE) inhibitors, which reduce blood pressure by blocking an enzyme that produces angiotensin II (a hormone that causes blood vessels to narrow)...dilating arteries...and reducing inflammation and oxidative stress. They also decrease clotting, further protecting against heart attack and stroke.

• Angiotensin receptor blockers (ARBs), which work by blocking receptors for angiotensin I (the precursor to angiotensin II). They also dilate blood vessels and ease inflammation and oxidative stress.

• Direct renin inhibitors, which reduce angiotensin I and relax blood vessels.

• Beta-blockers, which reduce blood pressure by reducing nerve signals to the heart and blood vessels and slowing the heart rate.

• **People with low-renin hypertension responded best to...**

• Calcium channel blockers, which combat high blood pressure by preventing calcium from moving into arteries and heart muscle cells and allowing arteries to dilate.

• Diuretics, which cause kidneys to remove excess sodium and water from the body and dilate blood vessel walls.

• **How your blood pressure is being measured.** The blood pressure cuff in your doctor's office may not be reliable if you are prone to "white-coat hypertension" (blood pressure that rises from the anxiety of being in the doctor's office) or "masked hypertension" (lower blood pressure numbers in the doctor's office but consistently higher numbers at other times).

Ask your doctor if you might benefit from using a high-quality home blood pressure monitor (sold over the counter in pharmacies and online for $50 to $150) to keep track of your readings every day. Also discuss the option of using a 24-hour ambulatory blood pressure monitor. A cuff worn on your arm and a small device clipped to your belt record your pressure every 15 to 30 minutes for 24 hours…then your doctor analyzes that data.

• **How consistently you take your medicine.** The different types of hypertension drugs can cause a variety of side effects, such as fatigue, memory problems and sexual dysfunction. If you experience these or other problems, do not suffer in silence—and certainly do not keep silent if you sometimes skip doses to avoid side effects. Tell your doctor and discuss alternative drugs.

But if you are conscientious about taking your meds, be sure your doctor knows that, too. Otherwise he or she may wrongly assume that any lack of effectiveness is due to your noncompliance rather than to a need for a different medication.

• **When to take your medication.** Since blood pressure medications are effective for only 24 hours, it is important to take them at the same time every day. Don't drive yourself crazy if you are an hour early or an hour late, but do not be off by several hours.

Very important: Most heart attacks and strokes happen between 3 am and 10 am, which is when blood pressure typically is highest. That's why the new recommendation generally is to take your medicine at night, Dr. Houston said—to block that early morning blood pressure spike.

Prescription Drugs That Make You Sick

Armon B. Neel, Jr., PharmD, a certified geriatric pharmacist and coauthor of *Are Your Prescriptions Killing You? How to Prevent Dangerous Interactions, Avoid Deadly Side Effects, and Be Healthier with Fewer Drugs.* MedicationXpert.com

When your doctor pulls out his/her prescription pad, you probably assume that your health problem will soon be improving. Sure, there may be a side effect or two—perhaps an occasional upset stomach or a mild headache. But overall you will be better off, right?

Not necessarily. While it's true that many drugs can help relieve symptoms and sometimes even cure certain medical conditions, a number of popular medications actually cause disease—not simply side effects—while treating the original problem.

Here's what happens: Your kidney and liver are the main organs that break down drugs and eliminate them from your body. But these organs weaken as you age. Starting as early as your 20s and 30s, you lose 1% of liver and kidney function every year. As a result, drugs can build up in your body (particularly if you take more than one), become toxic, damage crucial organs such as the heart and brain—and trigger disease.

Older adults are at greatest risk for this problem because the body becomes increasingly less efficient at metabolizing drugs with age. But no one is exempt from the risk. *To protect yourself—or a loved one…*

DEMENTIA

Many drugs can cause symptoms, such as short-term memory loss, confusion and agitation, that patients (and physicians) frequently mistake for dementia. The main offenders are anticholinergic medications, which treat a variety of conditions by blocking the activity of the neurotransmitter acetylcholine.

Hundreds of medications are anticholinergic, and it's likely that any class of drugs beginning with anti- is in this category—for example, antihistamines and antispasmodics.

Cholesterol-lowering statins also can cause dementia-like symptoms.

Other offenders: Beta-blockers (for high blood pressure or cardiac arrhythmias)…benzodiazepines (for anxiety)…narcotics…tricyclic antidepressants…anticonvulsants…muscle relaxants…sleeping pills…fluoroquinolone antibiotics…heartburn drugs (H2 receptor antagonists and proton-pump inhibitors)…antipsychotics…nitrates (for heart disease)…and sulfonylurea derivatives (for diabetes).

My advice: If you or a loved one has been diagnosed with dementia, the patient should immediately undergo a comprehensive medication review—drug-induced dementia usually can be reversed by stopping the offending drug (or drugs). A competent physician or consultant pharmacist can always find an alternative drug to use.

Surprising threat: Even general anesthesia can cause weeks or months of dementia-like confusion (and an incorrect diagnosis of Alzheimer's) in an older person as the drug slowly leaves the body.

The anesthesia is collected in the fat cells in the body, and normal cognition may take months to return. The longer a person is under anesthesia, the longer it takes to recover.

CANCER

Medications known as biologics are frequently used to treat autoimmune diseases such as inflammatory bowel disease, or IBD, (including Crohn's disease and ulcerative colitis) and rheumatoid arthritis.

This class of drugs includes *adalimumab* (Humira), *certolizumab* (Cimzia), *etanercept* (Enbrel), *golimumab* (Simponi) and *infliximab* (Remicade).

Important finding: The use of biologics was linked to more than triple the risk for lymphoma, breast, pancreatic and other cancers in a study that was published in *The Journal of the American Medical Association*.

The danger: While these medications may have a role in the treatment of autoimmune diseases, they often are carelessly prescribed by primary care physicians. For example, a biologic that is intended for IBD may be mistak-enly prescribed for irritable bowel syndrome (IBS), a far less serious digestive disorder.

If you are prescribed a biologic for IBD: Before starting the drug, ask for a comprehensive workup to confirm the diagnosis. This may include lab tests, imaging tests (ultrasound, CT or MRI), a biopsy and a stool analysis (to rule out C. difficile and other bowel infections that would require an antibiotic). Do not take a biologic for IBS.

If you are prescribed a biologic for rheumatoid arthritis: Before starting the medication, ask your doctor for a comprehensive workup to confirm the diagnosis, including lab tests and imaging tests (X-ray, ultrasound or MRI). Do not take a biologic for osteoarthritis. Besides increasing cancer risk, the suppression of the immune system opens the door for serious bacterial and viral infections.

DIABETES

Many commonly prescribed drugs increase risk for type 2 diabetes. These medications include statins…beta-blockers…antidepressants…antipsychotics…steroids…and alpha-blockers prescribed for prostate problems and high blood pressure.

Safer alternatives to discuss with your doctor, consultant pharmacist or other health-care professional…

If you're prescribed a beta-blocker: Ask about using a calcium-channel blocker instead. *Diltiazem* (Tiazac) has the fewest side effects. The 24-hour sustained-release dose provides the best control.

If you're prescribed an antidepressant: Ask about *venlafaxine* (Effexor), a selective serotonin and norepinephrine reuptake inhibitor (SSNRI) antidepressant that treats depression and anxiety and has been shown to cause fewer problems for diabetic patients than any of the older selective serotonin reuptake inhibitor (SSRI) drugs.

If you're prescribed an alpha-blocker: For prostate problems, rather than taking the alpha-blocker *tamsulosin* (Flomax), ask about using *dutasteride* (Avodart) or *finasteride* (Proscar). For high blood pressure, ask about a calcium-channel blocker drug.

HEART DISEASE

Nonsteroidal anti-inflammatory drugs (NSAIDs), frequently taken to ease pain due to arthritis, other joint problems or headaches, are widely known to damage the digestive tract. What's less well known is that NSAIDs have been found to increase the risk for cardiovascular disease.

My advice: No one over the age of 50 with mild-to-moderate pain should use an NSAID.

Fortunately, there is an excellent alternative. A daily dose of 50 mg of the prescription non-narcotic pain reliever *tramadol* (Ultracet, Ultram) and/or 325 mg of *acetaminophen* (Tylenol) works well and has less risk for adverse effects. Acetaminophen, taken in appropriate doses (less than 3,000 mg daily) without alcohol use, is safe and effective. I also recommend 3 g to 4 g of fish oil daily—it has been shown to effectively treat joint pain. Talk to your doctor first because fish oil may increase risk for bleeding.

THE VERY BEST DRUG SELF-DEFENSE

If you're over age 60—especially if you take more than one medication or suffer drug side effects—it's a good idea to ask your physician to work with a consulting pharmacist who is skilled in medication management. A consulting pharmacist has been trained in drug-therapy management and will work with your physician to develop a drug-management plan that will avoid harmful drugs. These services are relatively new and may not be covered by insurance, so be sure to check with your provider.

To find a consulting pharmacist in your area, go to the website of the American Society of Consultant Pharmacists, *ascp.com*, and click on "Find a Senior Care Pharmacist."

Also helpful: Make sure that a drug you've been prescribed does not appear on the "Beers Criteria for Potentially Inappropriate Medication Use in Older Adults." Originally developed by Mark Beers, editor of *The Merck Manual of Medical Information*, the list has been recently updated by The American Geriatrics Society. To download the list for free, go to *americangeriatrics.org* and search "Beers criteria."

Surprisingly Dangerous Medicines

Robert Steven Gold, RPh, hospital pharmacist and affiliate instructor of clinical pharmacy at Purdue University, West Lafayette, Indiana. He is author of *Are Your Meds Making You Sick? A Pharmacist's Guide to Avoiding Dangerous Drug Interactions, Reactions and Side Effects.*

Some medicines are obviously risky. Most people know that codeine and driving don't mix…and that you might bleed too much when taking a blood thinner such as warfarin.

What people don't realize is that every drug, including over-the-counter medications, potentially can cause serious side effects. A study in *The Journal of the American Medical Association* reported that adverse drug reactions were responsible for 700,000 emergency room visits in just one year.

Here, medicines that seem safe but have unexpected risks…

MINERAL OIL

It's been used for generations for treating constipation. It's inexpensive, effective and available in supermarkets and pharmacies.

The danger: Lipoid pneumonia, a type of lung inflammation caused by inhaling an oil-based substance.

It's common to inhale (aspirate) substances into the lungs. This often happens when we eat or drink. The natural response is to cough—but mineral oil soothes the throat and calms the cough reflex.

Result: Particles of oil stay in the lungs and cause irritation that can lead to pneumonia. The symptoms include a persistent cough or difficulty breathing…and the irritation can increase your risk for a bacterial infection in addition to pneumonia.

To be safe: Don't exceed the recommended dose of one to three tablespoons daily. The more you take, the more you increase your risk for aspirating some of the oil.

Also important: Don't swallow mineral oil when you're lying down—it's more likely to get into the lungs. Consuming mineral oil after you've been drinking alcohol also is risky because alcohol impairs the body's ability to swallow normally.

I advise patients who need a laxative to use newer, safer products, such as Metamucil or Colace.

CALCIUM CARBONATE ANTACIDS (ROLAIDS, TUMS)

People don't believe me when I tell them that antacids can be risky. Believe it. Up to 10% of patients who frequently use calcium-based antacids to relieve heartburn or increase calcium intake experience side effects.

The danger: High doses of calcium carbonate can lead to hypercalcemia, elevated blood calcium, which can cause heart problems.

Warning signs: Nausea, abdominal and/or lower back pain, increased urination and/or impaired thinking.

To be safe: Follow the dosing instructions on the label, and don't take the tablets for more than two weeks without a doctor's supervision.

Also, ask yourself if you really need an antacid. People who frequently use aspirin or *naproxen* (Aleve), for example, may experience gastrointestinal (GI) irritation that feels like heartburn. *Acetaminophen* (Tylenol) may be less likely to cause GI problems.

Alternative: For relief from heartburn, you occasionally can substitute other, noncalcium types of antacids, such as Maalox or Alka-Seltzer.

THE DIURETIC FUROSEMIDE (LASIX)

It's among the most frequently prescribed diuretics—"water pills" that remove excess fluid from patients with cardiovascular problems such as hypertension and heart failure.

The danger: Hearing loss. Drugs in this class, known as loop diuretics (others include bumetanide and ethacrynic acid), affect the concentration of potassium and other electrolytes in the inner ear. When given at high doses, usually in intravenous treatment, they're estimated to cause hearing loss in up to 100,000 patients a year.

To be safe: Talk to your doctor if you notice hearing loss in both ears soon after starting the medication. You might need to take a lower dose…or your doctor might switch you to a different medication that doesn't affect hearing.

Hearing usually returns once the dose and/or medication is changed—but the risk for permanent damage increases the longer you take the medication.

THE DIURETIC SPIRONOLACTONE (ALDACTONE)

This drug is used to reduce edema (fluid retention) in patients with heart, liver or kidney disease. It also can be used to treat hypertension.

The danger: It sometimes causes a dangerous increase in blood potassium, a condition known as hyperkalemia, which can cause an irregular heartbeat that is potentially deadly.

To be safe: Patients who take this drug must undergo frequent testing for blood potassium. When you are first prescribed it, you will need to have an electrolyte panel two to four weeks later…a follow-up test after three months…and regular tests about every six months.

If your potassium is elevated, your doctor might advise you to stop taking the drug. This will allow potassium levels to drop back to normal.

Also helpful: Don't combine this medication with supplements—such as energy drinks or multinutrients—that contain potassium.

METFORMIN FOR DIABETES

Metformin improves the body's sensitivity to insulin and decreases production of glucose (blood sugar) in the liver.

The danger: It can cause lactic acidosis, a rare but potentially deadly complication that occurs when a metabolic by-product, known as lactate, accumulates in the body. Only about five in 100,000 patients who take metformin will develop lactic acidosis, but it's fatal in up to 50% of cases.

To be safe: Know the signs. The onset of lactic acidosis often is subtle and accompanied by symptoms such as fatigue, muscle pain and respiratory distress.

Patients with kidney or liver disease usually are advised not to take metformin—or, if they do take it, to undergo frequent (every three to six months) blood and urine tests.

Also don't combine metformin with *cimetidine* (Tagamet), a medication used for heartburn and ulcers. It can increase the amount of metformin in the body by up to 40%. Other GI-protecting drugs, such as *famotidine* (Pepcid), don't have this effect.

SEROTONIN FOR DEPRESSION

Millions of Americans take selective serotonin reuptake inhibitors (SSRIs), the most frequently used medications for depression. SSRIs such as *escitalopram* (Lexapro) and *paroxetine* (Paxil) increase brain levels of serotonin, a neurotransmitter that affects mood.

The danger: Some people retain too much serotonin, a condition known as medication-induced serotonin syndrome. It can cause muscle twitches, loss of coordination, agitation, heavy sweating and other symptoms, including shivering or diarrhea. It is fatal in rare cases.

To be safe: Ask your doctor to review all your medications before starting treatment with an SSRI antidepressant. The risk for serotonin syndrome increases when SSRIs are combined with other medications, including dextromethorphan (an ingredient in cough medications), the antibiotics *linezolid* (Zyvox) and *ritonavir* (Norvir), and narcotic painkillers such as codeine.

Important: Don't take the herbal supplement St. John's wort if you're also taking an SSRI. St. John's wort increases serotonin.

Popular Drugs That Have Surprising Side Effects

Robert Steven Gold, RPh, a hospital pharmacist and affiliate instructor of clinical pharmacy at Purdue University in West Lafayette, Indiana. He is the author of *Are Your Meds Making You Sick? A Pharmacist's Guide to Avoiding Dangerous Drug Interactions, Reactions and Side Effects.*

Medication is given to patients to help them, not harm them, which is why it is so hard to comprehend that the side effects and interactions from medications cause more deaths annually than homicides, car accidents and airplane crashes combined. This means that, every year, approximately 100,000 deaths in the US are caused, in part, by dangerous drug reactions.

Some medication side effects are easy to recognize, such as an upset stomach after taking aspirin or confusion from sedatives. Other side effects—as well as drug interactions—may be unexpected and harder to recognize.

For example…

IRREGULAR HEARTBEAT

Culprit: *Levofloxacin* (Levaquin), a broad-spectrum antibiotic given for infections. The fluoroquinolone class of antibiotics, which includes *levofloxacin* and ciprofloxacin (Cipro), has been linked to torsades de pointes, a rare but dangerous heart irregularity (arrhythmia) that can cause instant death in some cases.

Warning: Patients who take one of these antibiotics along with a thiazide diuretic, such as *hydrochlorothiazide* (Microzide), may have a higher risk for heart irregularities.

New development: A study published in *The New England Journal of Medicine* has found that *azithromycin* (Zithromax and others), an antibiotic used to treat bacterial infections, may increase risk for irregular heartbeat and sudden death in patients with, or at risk for, heart disease.

Solution: If you take any of these antibiotics and experience a change in your heart's rhythm (a feeling of fluttering in the heart or a heart rate greater than 100 beats per minute), go to the emergency room. Episodes that last for more than about 10 seconds can cause a loss of consciousness and sometimes seizures.

BURNING RASH ON UPPER BODY

Culprit: *Sulfamethoxazole and trimetho prim* (Bactrim), a sulfonamide antibiotic, used to treat intestinal and urinary tract infections and pneumonia. This class of antibiotics can lead to Stevens-Johnson syndrome (SJS), an immune reaction that causes flulike symptoms, including fever, followed by a painful, itchy rash that spreads, blisters and can become infected. Sores in the mouth and mucous membranes also are common.

SJS is rare, affecting one to three patients per 100,000, but it can be life-threatening. About 25% to 35% of patients who have an extensive rash (covering 30% or more of the body) die from it.

Solution: If you take sulfamethoxazole and trimethoprim or another sulfonamide antibiotic and experience any of the side effects described earlier, go to the emergency room. Patients with SJS are hospitalized and given the same treatments as burn victims.

UNEXPLAINED BRUISES

Culprit: *Warfarin* (Coumadin), a "blood thinner" that inhibits blood clotting and often is prescribed to patients with heart disease or who have had a heart attack. Warfarin, as well as other anticlotting drugs, can make the blood so thin that bleeding occurs from the stomach, intestine or gums. And since bleeding can take longer to stop, blood can leak from a capillary and cause a bruise without an injury.

An article by Canadian researchers published in *Annals of Internal Medicine* analyzing the results of 33 previous studies, found that patients taking warfarin had about a one in 39 chance of serious bleeding. About one in eight patients with major bleeding episodes died.

Solution: Warfarin can be a life-saving drug if you need it, but you should work closely with your doctor to find the dosage that is best for you. Also, it's crucial to be aware that other medications, supplements and even foods can thin your blood. These medications include nonsteroidal anti-inflammatory drugs (NSAIDs), such as aspirin and *ibuprofen* (Motrin), and *clopidogrel* (Plavix), an antiplatelet drug—all of which have bleeding as a side effect. Before taking any other drug, let your doctor know that you're also taking warfarin.

Caution: Many herbs and supplements, such as fish oil, licorice, ginseng and coenzyme Q10, can increase/worsen the effects of warfarin.

Also important: Foods that are high in vitamin K, such as spinach and kale, affect the rate at which your blood clots and could require a change in your dose of warfarin. If you take a blood thinner, speak to your doctor about the effects of other medications, supplements and foods on your blood.

STOMACH OR ESOPHAGUS ULCERS

Culprit: *Alendronate* (Fosamax), taken to prevent/treat osteoporosis. Alendronate is known to cause stomach ulcers in about 1% of patients and ulcers in the esophagus in up to 2%. These are small percentages, but the risk rises when patients also take an NSAID, such as *ibuprofen* or *naproxen* (Aleve).

Solution: If you need a drug such as alendronate to preserve bone strength, changing how you take the medication can reduce the side effects.

Examples: Take alendronate first thing in the morning when your stomach is empty, washing it down with six to eight ounces of plain water. Taking it with some beverages or foods, particularly orange juice or acidic foods, increases the risk for ulcers. Don't lie down for 30 minutes after taking it—this can cause stomach acids to reach, and damage, the esophagus.

Also important: Avoid NSAIDs. Take *acetaminophen* (Tylenol), a non-NSAID painkiller.

PERSISTENT MUSCLE PAIN

Culprit: *Gemfibrozil* (Lopid), a fibrate medication that's used to reduce triglycerides and increase HDL "good" cholesterol, taken with a statin drug.

Doctors routinely tell patients that cholesterol-lowering statins, such as *atorvastatin* (Lipitor) or *simvastatin* (Zocor), may cause muscle pain. But they often neglect to mention that other cholesterol medications can have the same effect. Up to 30% of patients who take a statin experience some degree of muscle pain. The risk is higher when patients also take gemfibrozil or another fibrate drug because this medication decreases levels of liver enzymes that are needed to break down statins.

Result: Statin levels gradually rise in the body, which increases the risk for muscle pain.

Solution: If you're taking both a fibrate and a statin, ask your doctor if the statin dose is low enough to prevent side effects.

TREMORS

Culprit: *Metoclopramide* (Reglan), a medication for heartburn, plus *prochlorperazine*, a medication to relieve nausea.

Metoclopramide causes Tardive dyskinesia (uncontrolled muscle movements, especially in the face) in about 20% of patients who take it for three months or longer. It blocks the effects of dopamine, a brain chemical that plays a role in cognition and movement, the loss of which also occurs in Parkinson's patients. Prochlorperazine also blocks the effects of dopamine. When these drugs are taken together, the risk for movement disorders is much higher.

Solution: Switch to a different heartburn drug—for example, an antacid or a medication such as *cimetidine* (Tagamet), an H2 blocker, that does not typically block dopamine.

Important: Tremors caused by medication may not appear for up to six months. If you are experiencing any kind of movement disorder, ask your doctor to review all of your medications, not just the ones that you've recently started.

STEPS TO PROTECT YOURSELF

Speak to each of your physicians about all the medications you are taking. Alert your prescribing doctor if you experience any side effects when starting a new drug. Doctors often can find an effective substitute.

Very important: It's best to always use the same pharmacy or pharmacy chain. Every medication that you take, or have taken, is stored in the pharmacy's computer, which identifies potential drug interactions. Ask the pharmacist to look up your record when you are picking up a prescription.

Are Statin Drugs Destroying Your Muscles?

Mark A. Stengler, NMD, naturopathic medical doctor and author of *The Natural Physician's Healing Therapies.* Dr. Stengler is also founder and medical director of the Stengler Center for Integrative Medicine in Encinitas, California. MarkStengler.com

According to research published several years ago in *Clinical and Investigative Medicine,* microscopic signs of muscle damage often occur in people within one week of starting to take statins. I believe that statins exacerbate the normal age-related loss of muscle known as sarcopenia. In your 60s, you lose about 1% of muscle mass each year, and the percentage of muscle loss doubles with each subsequent decade. Who gets the majority of statin prescriptions? Middle-aged and elderly people—the very same people who are at the greatest risk for age-related muscle loss.

Remember, too, that the heart is your body's most active muscle. It's no surprise that there is a strong relationship between the use of statins and the development of cardiomyopathy, a life-threatening disease of the heart muscle.

NUTRIENTS THAT PROTECT YOUR MUSCLES

Several dietary supplement regimens can help protect muscles.

If you take a statin, then take the first two nutrients for as long as you are on the statin…

•**Coenzyme Q10 (CoQ10).** While reducing the body's production of cholesterol, statins also interfere with the body's manufacture of CoQ10, a vitamin-like nutrient. Many side effects of statins appear to be related to low levels of CoQ10. CoQ10 supplements can significantly reduce statin-induced muscle myopathy. Considerable research supports the use of CoQ10 in treating statin side effects. Take 100 milligrams (mg) to 200 mg of CoQ10 daily.

•**Vitamin D.** Vitamin D is needed for the normal synthesis of muscle tissue. Current medical thinking is that weak muscles, not weak bones, lead to most falls and fractures. Add statins to the picture, and connect the dots. Statins disrupt the biochemical process that makes vitamin D in your body, and it's likely that statins will significantly increase the incidence of sarcopenia and fractures. Take at least 2,000 international units (IU) of vitamin D daily. Have your vitamin D level checked by a physician and take a higher dose if necessary.

If you have stopped taking a statin because of muscle pain, try either of the following (in addition to the two nutrients above)…

• If the muscle pain is bearable, try one or two of the supplements below for one month and then evaluate how you feel. If you still feel pain, try different supplements from the group below.

• For severe pain, take a more aggressive approach and use all the supplements below until your muscle pain subsides.

• **Magnesium.** Your body uses this essential mineral to help break down food and make adenosine triphosphate (ATP), the chemical form of energy in the body. Take 300 mg to 400 mg daily of magnesium citrate, aspartate or amino acid chelate.

• **Amino acids.** You need these protein building blocks to make muscle. Best: Take an amino acid supplement that contains eight to 10 amino acids.

Most important amino acids to supplement: The three branched-chain amino acids (BCAA), which are L-leucine, L-isoleucine and L-valine. Studies have shown that these supplements increase muscle synthesis in seniors. They are made by many companies. Take 5 grams (g) to 10 g daily of a multi–amino acid blend or 3 g daily of BCAAs.

• **Methylsulfonylmethane (MSM).** MSM supplements are rich in the sulfur and chemical methyl groups, both important building blocks of tissue and biochemicals. MSM supplements are a safe, natural anti-inflammatory that can help muscles recover from statin-related damage. Take 3,000 mg to 4,000 mg daily.

• **Turmeric extract.** Rich in curcumin, turmeric is an anti-inflammatory that aids muscle healing. Curcumin blocks dozens of different inflammatory processes in the body.

Brand to try: Terry Naturally's CuraMed (*EuroPharmaUSA.com*). Take 600 mg three times daily.

If you have muscle pain and continue to take a statin…

I believe that anyone taking a statin who experiences muscle pain should stop taking the statin (under a doctor's supervision)—and I think that most conventional physicians would agree with me. If you do continue to take the statin, you can take all of the remedies described above indefinitely.

OTC Painkillers That Can Be Deadly

Lynn R. Webster, MD, vice president of scientific affairs with PRA Health Sciences, a research organization, Salt Lake City, and past president of the American Academy of Pain Medicine. He is author of *The Painful Truth: What Chronic Pain Is Really Like and Why It Matters to Each of Us.* ThePainfulTruthBook.com

---

The Food and Drug Administration recently strengthened an existing label warning that non-aspirin nonsteroidal anti-inflammatory drugs (NSAIDs) increase the risk for heart attack and stroke. Popular over-the-counter medications including *ibuprofen* (Advil and Motrin) and *naproxen* (Aleve) are among the products affected. Taking these regularly for as little as a few weeks can put people's lives at risk…as could exceeding recommended dosages.

What to do: If you take an NSAID, keep your dose as low as possible and your duration of use as short as possible. People who have a history of heart disease, kidney disease or stroke should be especially careful to limit NSAID use.

Hidden danger: When you take a cold medication or sore throat medication, check the ingredients on the label for NSAIDs. If you see these, avoid extended use and do not take these medications if you also are taking a painkiller that contains any NSAID—the combined dose could put you in danger.

If you must take a painkiller for more than a week or so or if you have a history of stroke, heart problems or kidney issues, speak with your doctor about options other than NSAIDs. Acetaminophen could be a safer choice in certain circumstances, for example. Also, acupuncture and mindfulness meditation can help.

The Painkiller Trap

Jane Ballantyne, MD, a professor in the department of anesthesiology and pain medicine at the University of Washington School of Medicine in Seattle, where she serves as director of the UW Pain Fellowship. She is coauthor of *Expert Decision Making on Opioid Treatments* and has editorial roles on several journals and textbooks, including *Bonica's Management of Pain, 4th Edition.*

If you have ever suffered from severe pain, you probably know that a strong pain pill can seem like the holy grail. In fact, with chronic pain affecting about one-third of Americans—or roughly 100 million people—it's perhaps no surprise that the most commonly prescribed medication in the US is a painkiller, *hydrocodone* (Vicodin).

Frightening trend: Hydrocodone and the other prescription opioid painkillers (also known as narcotics) have now overtaken heroin and cocaine as the leading cause of fatal overdoses, according to the Centers for Disease Control and Prevention.

Why the shift?

Until recently, prescription opioids were used to treat only acute (severe, short-lived) pain, such as pain after surgery or an injury or pain related to cancer.

Now: As doctors have stepped up their efforts to better control pain in all patients, opioids are much more widely prescribed. These powerful medications are now being used to treat chronic painful conditions such as low-back pain, chronic headaches and fibromyalgia.

What pain sufferers need to know...

DANGERS OF OPIOIDS

Each day, an estimated 4.3 million Americans take hydrocodone or other widely used opioids, such as *oxycodone* (Oxycontin), *hydromorphone* (Dilaudid), codeine and morphine. For some patients, opioids are prescribed as an alternative to nonsteroidal anti-inflammatory drugs (NSAIDs), which are notorious for causing gastrointestinal bleeding and other side effects, including increased risk for heart attack and kidney disease.

Opioids work by mimicking natural pain-relieving chemicals in the body and attaching to receptors that block the transmission of pain messages to and within the brain. These drugs can be highly effective pain relievers, especially for arthritis patients who can't tolerate NSAIDs.

But opioids also have potentially serious side effects, especially when they're used long term (usually defined as more than 90 days). While the effectiveness of the medications often decreases over time (because the patient builds up a tolerance to the drug), the risk for side effects—including constipation, drowsiness or even addiction—increases due to the higher and more toxic doses used to overcome tolerance.

Continuous use of these pain medications also can have far-reaching health effects that can include a heightened risk for falls and fractures...slowed breathing...concentration problems...and vision impairment. And these drugs can compromise the immune system, resulting in susceptibility to infection.

Men who take opioids long term are five times more likely to have low testosterone levels, which can curb libido and result in erectile dysfunction. Even at low doses, such as 20 mg of morphine, opioids can diminish alertness and have been shown to increase risk for car accidents by 21%.

BEST NONDRUG ALTERNATIVES

If your doctor suggests taking an opioid for back pain, chronic headaches or migraines, or fibromyalgia, ask him/her about trying the following nondrug treatments first. Opioids should be considered only as a last resort.

•**Back pain.** For long-term low-back pain, exercises that strengthen the abdomen and back (or "core") muscles are the most effective treatment. If the pain is so severe that you can't exercise, over-the-counter painkillers sometimes can alleviate the pain enough to start an effective exercise regimen.

Bonus: Exercise can ease depression, which is common in back pain sufferers. Yoga may also be effective because it stretches the muscles and ligaments in addition to reducing mental stress.

Other possible options: If the approaches described above don't provide adequate relief, you may be a candidate for steroid injections into the spine or joints...a spinal fusion...or disk-replacement surgery. In general, these treatments have less risk for adverse effects than long-term use of opioids.

• **Chronic headaches or migraines.** With chronic headaches or migraines, opioids can worsen pain by causing "rebound" headaches that occur when the drug is overused. Try lifestyle changes, such as daily meditation, and the sparing use of mild painkillers, such as NSAIDs. Supplements, including magnesium and feverfew, also have been shown to relieve headache pain.

• **Fibromyalgia.** With this condition, which has no known cure, opioids have been found to intensify existing pain.

Much better: A review of 46 studies has found aerobic exercise, such as brisk walking or pool aerobics (done two to three times a week for an hour), may reduce system-wide inflammation, making it an effective treatment for fibromyalgia.

If you're in too much pain to do aerobic exercise, a mild painkiller or a nondrug approach, such as massage, may allow you to start.

Cognitive behavioral therapy is another good choice. With this treatment, a therapist can help you reframe negative thoughts that may be fueling fibromyalgia pain.

Additional nondrug approaches that may help all of these conditions: Acupuncture, relaxation exercises and heating pads.

208

WHAT'S YOUR RISK FOR ADDICTION?

Some people who take opioids are more likely to become addicted than others. *Risk factors include...*

• **Depression, anxiety or some other psychiatric condition (current or in the past).**

• **Substance abuse.** This includes alcohol or other drugs (current or in the past).

• **Poor coping skills.** Those with "catastrophizing" personalities—they tend to imagine the worst possible outcomes in trying situations—are more likely to develop chronic pain and drug dependence.

Before using an opioid, discuss your potential for addiction with your physician. You want a doctor who understands the risks and benefits of the drug...who is aware of your potential for dependence and addiction...and who will take you off the drug if he/she notices problematic behavior. See your doctor often—at least monthly when you first start taking the drug.

Medications That Hurt Your Eyes

Jeffrey R. Anshel, OD, optometrist and founder of Corporate Vision Consulting, which addresses visual demands in the workplace. He has written six books on computer vision concerns and nutritional influences on vision, the latest being *The Ocular Nutrition Handbook.*

Are your eyes dry or sensitive to light? Do you have blurred vision or "floaters"? These and other eye problems could be side effects of common medications.

Few people make the connection between changes in their eyes and medications they take—yet the truth is that many prescription and over-the-counter drugs cause ocular side effects. *Here are common symptoms and the drugs that could be causing them...*

Important: Contact your physician (eye doctor or primary care) if you have any of these symptoms. Most are not dangerous, and minor eye problems may be a reasonable trade-off for a potentially lifesaving drug. Always bring with you to the doctor a complete list of the medications you take—prescription and over-the-counter—and the doses. Stopping the medications can reverse the symptoms in many cases.

• **Abnormalities in pupil size.** Discrepancies in how your pupils react to light (called aniscoria) can be caused by a variety of medications, including Catapres (for hypertension), Donnatal (irritable bowel syndrome/ulcers), Humulin (diabetes) and Tavist (allergies).

If your pupils aren't always the same size—especially if only one pupil is abnormally enlarged—it's important to go to the emergency room immediately. The brain controls pupil size, so a disturbance there can cause pupils to be different sizes.

• **Cataracts.** If you live long enough, you eventually will develop cataracts (lenses that have clouded over, making it more difficult to see). Certain drugs may speed the process, including Coumadin (for heart disease), Plaquenil (malaria, rheumatoid arthritis and lupus) and most steroids.

• **Difficulty focusing.** The medical term for this condition is "accommodative insufficiency." It grows more common with age and also is a side effect of some medications. These include Adipex (for obesity), *methyclothiazide* (hypertension), Norpramin (depression) and Xanax (anxiety).

• **Double or blurred vision.** There are many potential causes for seeing double or for vision that suddenly blurs. Medications that can cause this include Adipex (for obesity), Celebrex (inflammation), Lamictal (seizures), *lovastatin* (elevated cholesterol), Tylenol (pain relief) and Zantac (ulcers).

If your blurred or double vision is sudden, severe and unrelenting, go to the emergency room immediately. This visual impairment is not only unsafe (for instance, when you are driving), but it could be a sign of a serious medical problem such as a stroke or brain lesion.

• **Dry eyes.** Many factors (including computer use, wearing contact lenses and allergies) can reduce tear production and cause dry eyes—and so can certain medications, such as Actifed (for allergies), Catapres (hypertension), Detrol (bladder control) and Paxil (depression).

Until you see your doctor, self-treatment options for dry eyes include blinking as often as possible…use of artificial tear solutions (available in drugstores and chain stores)…avoiding irritants, including eye makeup and air pollution…and wearing sunglasses. Or try an oral gamma-linolenic acid (GLA) product such as BioTears.

• **Eye irritation.** Redness in the whites of your eyes or irritations on your eyelids can be caused by medications such as Aricept (taken to improve cognitive loss), Cardizem (heart disease), *methyclothiazide* (heart disease) and Voltaren (rheumatoid arthritis, osteoporosis).

• **Floaters and other visual disturbances.** Flashes of light or color, floaters and other visual disturbances can occur for a host of reasons, including as a side effect of a drug. Medications linked to visual disturbances include Benadryl (for allergies), Cardizem (heart disease), and Xanax (anxiety).

The causes of visual disturbances can range from inconsequential to potentially serious, so they should be checked out by your eye doctor as quickly as possible. This is especially true if you suddenly see flashes of light or if numerous new floaters appear—that could be a sign of a retinal detachment.

• **Light sensitivity.** Though there are other possible causes, light sensitivity may be a side effect of drugs (including recreational drugs such as cocaine and amphetamines). Drugs linked with light sensitivity include Diabinese (for diabetes), Dilantin (epilepsy), Lipitor (high cholesterol/heart disease), Pepcid (gastric ulcers) and Viagra (erectile dysfunction). If light sensitivity is severe and your pupils are enlarged—especially if only one pupil is enlarged—go to the ER. It could be a sign of stroke or a brain tumor.

• **Yellowed eyes.** Several conditions can cause the white parts of the eye to turn yellow, including illness, sun exposure and drugs such as Diabinese (for diabetes), and Librium (anxiety). Yellowing may be a sign of cirrhosis or hepatitis. It is important to see your doctor quickly to have this checked out.

Drugs That Work Against Each Other

David Lee, PharmD, PhD, assistant professor in the College of Pharmacy at Oregon State University in Portland. Dr. Lee is also a coauthor of a recent paper on therapeutic competition that was published in the journal *PLOS ONE*.

Cynthia Kuhn, PhD, professor in the department of pharmacology at Duke University School of Medicine, Durham, North Carolina, and codirector of Brainworks, a Duke program that develops education programs about the brain. She is a coauthor of *Buzzed: The Straight Facts About the Most Used and Abused Drugs from Alcohol to Ecstasy*.

Most people who have a chronic health problem such as osteoarthritis, high blood pressure or diabetes are accustomed to taking medication to help control their symptoms.

But if you have more than one chronic condition—and take medication for each of them—you could be setting yourself up for other problems.

The risk that often goes undetected: Taking medication prescribed for one disease may actually worsen another health problem. This situation, known as "therapeutic competition," has received surprisingly little attention from the medical profession.

According to the federal Substance Abuse and Mental Health Services Administration, emergency room visits involving adverse reactions to pharmaceuticals increased 82.9% between 2005 and 2009 (from 1.2 million to over 2.2 million), particularly among patients 65 and older.

Caution: The risk for drug interactions is highest among the elderly. They tend to use the most drugs, and their bodies metabolize (break down) drugs more slowly than younger adults.

HOW INTERACTIONS HAPPEN

Patients who use medications appropriately—taking the prescribed doses for only particular conditions and regularly reviewing drug use with a physician—are unlikely to have serious problems.

Main risks: Different drugs prescribed by more than one doctor…using drugs to treat conditions for which they weren't originally prescribed (many people stockpile leftover drugs and use them later, possibly for unrelated conditions)…or using a drug that was appropriate initially but might be dangerous when combined with drugs a patient has subsequently started taking.

Protect yourself by frequently updating a list of the drugs and supplements you take. Review the list with every doctor at every office visit and whenever a new drug is prescribed.

ARE YOU AT RISK?

Therapeutic competition can occur at any time in a person's life. But the risk increases with age—the older we get, the more likely we are to have chronic medical conditions and use more medications. Because our bodies metabolize medication less efficiently as we age, we're also more likely to develop side effects that can worsen other health problems.

Modern medicine has not done very much to help the situation. For one thing, polypharmacy—the use of multiple medications—has become more common than ever before.

For people with more than one chronic medical condition, frequent conflicts occur if you have…

HIGH BLOOD PRESSURE

If you also have chronic obstructive pulmonary disease (COPD), drugs that you take to ease your breathing, such as the beta-adrenergic agonist *albuterol* (Proventil) or a corticosteroid, may raise your blood pressure.

If you are also being treated for depression, an antidepressant such as *venlafaxine* (Effexor) or *duloxetine* (Cymbalta) could push your blood pressure higher. COX-2 inhibitors such as *celecoxib* (Celebrex), commonly used for osteoarthritis, also may increase blood pressure.

DIABETES

Corticosteroids taken for COPD can raise blood sugar levels, worsening diabetes. If you have an enlarged prostate and take an alpha-blocker such as *tamsulosin* (Flomax) or a beta-blocker such as *atenolol* (Tenormin) for high blood pressure, the drug can mask symptoms of low blood sugar, such as shakiness.

COPD

If you also have high blood pressure or angina and take a non-selective beta-blocker such as *propranolol* (Inderal), the drug could worsen lung symptoms.

HEART DISEASE

COPD drugs, including albuterol…tricyclic antidepressants such as *imipramine* (Tofranil), taken for depression…and COX-2 inhibitors for osteoarthritis also can make heart disease worse.

ATRIAL FIBRILLATION

Osteoporosis drugs, including bisphosphonates such as *alendronate* (Fosamax)…and Alzheimer's drugs, including cholinesterase inhibitors such as *donepezil* (Aricept), may worsen atrial fibrillation.

OSTEOPOROSIS

Corticosteroids used to treat COPD often lead to significant bone loss. Glitazones taken for diabetes and proton pump inhibitors such as *omeprazole* (Prilosec), commonly prescribed for gastroesophageal reflux disease (GERD), can accelerate bone loss.

GERD OR PEPTIC ULCERS

Warfarin (Coumadin) or *clopidogrel* (Plavix), often prescribed for atrial fibrillation or heart disease, as well as nonsteroidal anti-inflammatory drugs (NSAIDs), can cause bleeding that worsens GERD and ulcers. Bisphosphonates taken for osteoporosis may aggravate esophageal damage that commonly occurs with GERD and ulcers.

OPIOID PAINKILLERS/SEDATIVES

Opioid painkillers, such as hydrocodone and oxycodone, have powerful effects on the central nervous system. Even on their own, they can suppress breathing when taken in high enough doses. The risk is much higher when they're combined with sedating drugs, such as those used to treat anxiety or insomnia. These include the benzodiazepine class of medications, such as *diazepam* (Valium) and *alprazolam* (Xanax).

Many people take these drugs in combination. For example, someone might take alprazolam for chronic anxiety, then add hydrocodone following an injury. The drugs often are prescribed by different doctors who don't know the patient's drug history.

What to do: Never combine prescription painkillers and sedatives without your doctor's okay.

WARFARIN/ANTIBIOTICS/NSAIDS

The blood thinner *warfarin* (Coumadin) is notorious for interacting with other drugs. It has a narrow "therapeutic index," the difference between a helpful and a toxic dose. Drugs that increase the effects of warfarin can lead to uncontrolled bleeding.

Many antibiotics and antifungal drugs, including *erythromycin, ciprofloxacin* and *ketoconazole*, are broken down by the same liver enzyme that metabolizes warfarin. Taking warfarin and any of these drugs together may deplete the enzyme, leading to higher levels of warfarin in the body.

What to do: If you have an infection, your doctor can prescribe an antibiotic that is less likely to interact with warfarin. Antibiotics that are less likely to cause an interaction include penicillin, amoxicillin, ampicillin and tetracycline.

Caution: Warfarin may cause gastrointestinal bleeding when combined with aspirin, ibuprofen or other nonsteroidal anti-inflammatory drugs (NSAIDs). If you take warfarin and need a painkiller, *acetaminophen* (Tylenol) might be a better choice.

MULTIPLE ANTIDEPRESSANTS

Patients who combine selective serotonin reuptake inhibitor (SSRI) antidepressants, such as *fluoxetine* (Prozac) and *sertraline* (Zoloft), or who combine an SSRI with another type of antidepressant may experience serotonin syndrome, a rare but potentially fatal reaction.

Many antidepressants increase brain levels of serotonin, a chemical produced by some neurons (nerve cells). Patients who combine antidepressants or take too much of one can accumulate toxic levels of serotonin. This can cause dangerously elevated blood pressure, known as a hypertensive crisis.

Serotonin syndrome usually occurs when patients switch from an SSRI antidepressant to a monoamine oxidase inhibitor (MAOI), an older type of antidepressant, without allowing time for the first drug to wash out of the body.

What to do: Follow your doctor's instructions exactly when discontinuing an antidepressant. Most of these drugs have to be tapered—slowly decreasing the dose over a period of weeks—before starting a new drug.

VIAGRA/NITRATES

Men who take nitrate drugs (such as nitroglycerine) for heart problems should never take *sildenafil* (Viagra) without a doctor's supervision.

Viagra and similar drugs for treating erectile dysfunction cause blood vessels to relax. Nitrate drugs do the same thing. Combining them can cause a dangerous drop in blood pressure.

What to do: Men who take nitrates for heart problems can talk to their doctors about safer alternatives for treating erectile dysfunction, including vacuum devices or penile injections.

ACETAMINOPHEN FROM MULTIPLE PRODUCTS

Taken in excessive doses, the pain reliever *acetaminophen* (Tylenol) can cause liver damage.

Main risk: Combining acetaminophen—for treating arthritis pain, for example—with unrelated products (such as cold/flu remedies) that also contain acetaminophen.

What to do: When using acetaminophen, don't exceed the dose listed on the product label—and check labels to ensure that you don't take another product that contains acetaminophen simultaneously.

HOW TO PROTECT YOURSELF

If you have more than one chronic condition and take two or more medications to treat them, it is crucial that you watch for signs of therapeutic competition, such as new symptoms that are unexplained or begin soon after a new medication is started. Any new health condition actually may be an adverse effect of medication.

Important steps to avoid therapeutic competition…

● **Try to cut back on the drugs you take.** The less medication you're on, the less likely one of your drugs will adversely affect another condition. Ask your doctor whether it's advisable to reduce the overall number of prescriptions you take. A drug you have been taking for years may no longer be necessary. You may also be able to make lifestyle changes—such as getting more exercise—that will allow you to cut back on blood pressure or diabetes medication.

● **Get the right medication.** If it seems that a drug is worsening another condition, ask your doctor about less harmful alternatives. Some medications are more selective—that is, their effects on the body are more focused on the target illness, making unintended consequences for other conditions less of a danger.

Example: Nonselective beta-blockers, such as propranolol, often worsen COPD symptoms, but medications with more selective action, such as *metoprolol* (Lopressor), are usually just as effective for the heart problem they're prescribed for without adversely affecting your lungs.

GET A YEARLY MEDICATION CHECK

If you suffer from multiple ailments, you need to tell all your doctors about the medications you take. Also, talk to your pharmacist each time you pick up a new prescription to make sure your drugs aren't working against each other.

To ensure that no drug-related problems develop: Once a year, have a pharmacist (ask one at your drugstore) review all your medications. This service includes a discussion of side effects, interactions and alternatives. For many people, Medicare Part D and some private health plans will pay for this service. If not, it usually costs less than $100.

The Wrong Antibiotic Can Be Life-Threatening

B. Joseph Guglielmo, Jr., PharmD, professor and chair of the department of clinical pharmacy at the University of California, San Francisco (UCSF), and founder of the Antimicrobial Management Program at UCSF Medical Center. He is a coauthor of *Applied Therapeutics: The Clinical Use of Drugs*.

Antibiotics are among the most frequently prescribed drugs in the US.

What most people don't realize: Because drug companies generally do not make much profit by developing oral antibiotics, there are few new options available. That's why it's especially important that the available drugs be used correctly. Taking the wrong antibiotic can allow infections to linger—and sometimes become life-threatening. *What you need to know...*

WHEN TO TAKE AN ANTIBIOTIC

The immune system in healthy adults is very effective at eliminating minor infections—even ones caused by bacteria. Antibiotics are needed only when an infection overwhelms the immune system's ability to stop it or when an infection is too dangerous (or too painful) to be allowed to clear up on its own.

Examples: A bacterial infection of the lungs can be fatal, so it is almost always treated with antibiotics. Bacterial ear infections generally will go away without treatment, but antibiotics may decrease the duration of symptoms.

Good rule of thumb: Most infections of the ears, sinuses and respiratory tract are viral and don't require antibiotics.

How to tell: Viral infections of the respiratory tract usually start to improve in five to seven days. If you get worse after that time, there's a good chance that the infection is bacterial and may require antibiotics.

SHOULD YOU GET A CULTURE?

Doctors usually can guess which organism is causing an infection—and choose the right antibiotic—just by reviewing a patient's description of his/her symptoms.

However, cultures (taken from a throat swab, for example) should be used when it's unclear what's causing an infection—or when previous antibiotics weren't effective. In otherwise healthy adults, antibiotics start to ease symptoms of an infection within 24 hours. Symptoms that don't improve within two days may indicate that the initial diagnosis or antibiotic choice was incorrect.

BEWARE OF SIDE EFFECTS

Nearly every antibiotic may cause diarrhea, intestinal cramps or yeast infections in the mouth or vagina. That's because the drugs not only kill harmful microbes, but also reduce the numbers of "good" bacteria that keep harmful bacteria and fungi in check.

Besides the general side effects, each antibiotic also has other risks. *For example...*

•**Amoxicillin** plus *clavulanate* (Augmentin), commonly used for certain respiratory tract infections, may cause skin rashes and hives.

•**Doxycycline** (Doryx), for chronic eye infections and Lyme disease, increases sensitivity to sunlight.

•**Ciprofloxacin** (Cipro), for urinary tract infections, can cause headache, abdominal pain and vomiting.

WHAT TO TAKE FOR COMMON INFECTIONS

Most effective antibiotics for common medical conditions...

•**Bacterial pneumonia.** Most cases are caused by an organism called Streptococcus pneumoniae, but some patients are infected with multiple and/or "resistant" organisms.

Main treatment: Hospitalized patients with community-acquired pneumonia usually are given an intravenous antibiotic, such as *ceftriaxone* with *azithromycin* (Zithromax), or a "respiratory" fluoroquinolone, such as *levofloxacin* (Levaquin).

•**Ear infections.** Even doctors have difficulty differentiating viral from bacterial ear infections. Antibiotics often are used "just in case." If the infection is bacterial, the symptoms will start to abate within 24 hours of starting an antibiotic.

Main treatment: Amoxicillin for seven to 10 days. Patients with a history of antibiotic use for ear infections may have resistant organisms and will probably be given a broad-spectrum cephalosporin antibiotic, such as *cefdinir*. Similarly, patients who are allergic to amoxicillin may be given a cephalosporin antibiotic if the allergy is mild—or a fluoro-quinolone, such as levofloxacin, if the allergy is severe.

• **Sinus infections.** Recent research by the Cochrane Collaboration, which reviews health-care practices and research evidence, found that about 80% of patients with sinus infections recover within two weeks without antibiotics.

However, a viral sinus infection can sometimes progress to a more serious, secondary bacterial infection. Patients with sinus pain that lasts for more than a week to 10 days—or who have a period of recovery followed by a painful relapse—probably need antibiotics.

Main treatment: The same as that used for ear infections.

• **Skin infections** are usually due to Staphylococcus aureus or Streptococcus pyogenes, common bacteria that can enter the skin through a cut or scrape.

Recent danger: A virulent, drug-resistant form of staph, known as methicillin-resistant Staphylococcus aureus (MRSA), can cause cellulitis, a life-threatening infection even in healthy adults.

What to look for: Although most localized skin infections will clear up on their own, an area of skin that is red and feels warm and tender and might spread rapidly could be cellulitis. In severe cases, the center area will turn black as the tissue degenerates. Treatment of MRSA usually requires consultation with an infectious-disease specialist.

• **Urinary tract infections** (UTIs) usually occur when fecal bacteria enter the urethra. Women get UTIs more often than men because of the close proximity of the urethra to the anus.

Mild UTIs often will clear up on their own. In studies, about two-thirds of women who take a placebo will recover within seven to 10 days, compared with 80% to 85% of those taking antibiotics. However, antibiotics are usually recommended both for symptom relief and to prevent a UTI from progressing to pyelonephritis, a dangerous kidney infection.

Main treatment: *Trimethoprim plus sulfamethoxazole* (Septra or Bactrim), a combination treatment usually taken for three days.

Important: If you get two or more UTIs a year, you may have resistant organisms. Your doctor may perform a urine culture to identify the organism, which will determine the appropriate antibiotic.

Caution: Don't combine ciprofloxacin with antacids or iron supplements—both can interfere with the absorption of this antibiotic.

Drugs Plus Supplements: Proceed with Caution

Leo Galland, MD, internist and director, Foundation for Integrated Medicine, New York City, MDHeal.org. Dr. Galland publishes a free newsletter, which includes more information about supplements and drugs, and free access to Dr. Galland's interaction database at PillAdvised.com.

About 40% of Americans now take dietary supplements in the form of a vitamin, mineral, herb or other substance—and those 50 and older are more likely than younger folks to use supplements and, as a group, to take more medications. The sicker and more fragile you are, the greater the impact of an interaction. But in truth, anyone combining drugs and supplements is at risk for interactions—and the more drugs and supplements that you take, the greater the danger.

WHEN INTERACTIONS CAUSE HARM

Leo Galland, director of the Foundation for Integrated Medicine in New York City, explained that there are certain common pathways for negative interactions. Specifically, interactions often occur because the supplement interferes with the way the drug is absorbed into the bloodstream, metabolized by the liver or excreted by the kidneys—in this way, the remedy you turn to for help with one problem may bring about others that are far worse. Sometimes drugs and supplements have a similar action in the body, so that taking both magnifies the effect of the drug—while other supplements can block the effect of a drug so that the drug doesn't work. In either case, the effect can be lethal.

According to Dr. Galland, the supplement that causes the greatest number of interactions is St. John's wort. "It can have a profound effect on the enzymes that metabolize drugs, decreasing their activity and drastically changing the level of a drug in the body," he said. The commonly prescribed drug that causes the greatest number of dangerous interactions is the blood thinner warfarin, which is often prescribed to prevent blood clots. "Warfarin has a very narrow safety margin," Dr. Galland explained—meaning that the dose you take must be precisely right or the effect could be dangerous.

Next most dangerous: Statin drugs, used to control cholesterol, also affect liver enzymes and muscle function in ways that can be magnified when taken with certain supplements.

SURPRISINGLY COMMON INTERACTIONS

Dr. Galland went through some of the more common medications people take and what supplements might cause dangerous interactions...

•**Blood-thinning drugs.** If you take warfarin or another blood-thinning drug (including aspirin), don't take ginkgo biloba, and ask your doctor about the advisability of taking vitamin E, since even the amount in a multivitamin can increase your risk for hemorrhage.

Two others to beware of: Ginseng and St. John's wort also can be dangerous for those on blood-thinning drugs, as they may prevent warfarin from working properly and increase risk for blood clots.

•**Statins.** If you take a statin drug, don't take vitamin E or St. John's wort because they may reduce the drug's effectiveness and leave you vulnerable to heart attack. It's well known that grapefruit can increase blood levels of some statin drugs to dangerously high levels, increasing the risk for liver or muscle damage, but you may not know that pomegranate and pomegranate extract can have the same effect.

•**Diuretics.** Anyone who takes a thiazide drug (such as *hydrochlorthiazide*) on its own or in combination with another blood pressure medication (such as an ACE inhibitor) should avoid the supplements white willow bark and ginkgo biloba—these can prevent the drugs from working properly, so patients may end up with elevated blood pressure. Horsetail, senna, cascara, licorice and uva ursi (all typically taken for bloating and water retention) boost the diuretic effect of thiazide drugs and can lead to dehydration and potassium depletion.

•**Antihypertensives.** People on ACE inhibitors for blood pressure, a category that includes *captopril* and *lisinopril* (Zestril and Prinivil), should avoid taking iron supplements within two hours of taking the medication because iron can interfere with absorption of the drug. Iron naturally present in food does not have the same effect. Also problematic is the supplement cayenne (sometimes referred to as capsicum or capsaicin), used as a digestive aid or for control of inflammation, which increases the side effects of ACE inhibitors, especially cough.

•**Oral diabetes medications.** If you are taking diabetes medicines such as *metformin* (Glucophage) or *glyburide* (Glynase), avoid ginkgo biloba because it can interfere with the effects of insulin and raise your blood sugar. Also use caution with the supplements vanadium, gymnema, chromium, ginseng and bitter melon, as these can dangerously depress blood sugar levels in sensitive individuals.

•**Antiarrhythmia drugs.** Patients who take the antiarrhythmia drug *digoxin* should never take supplemental forms of licorice (often used for cough or sore throat) because it can bring on severe—even fatal—arrhythmia. Others to avoid include pectin, a stool-bulking agent, because it reduces absorption of the digoxin, and ginseng, which binds with the digoxin, making it unavailable. Also avoid horsetail, senna and cascara, which can bring about dangerous reductions of potassium levels, which increase the risk for digoxin toxicity.

• **Antibiotics.** If you are on tetracycline or the antibiotic class known as quinolone antibiotics, which includes Cipro and *levofloxacin* (Levaquin), do not take minerals or eat mineral-rich foods within two hours of taking the drug—minerals such as calcium, magnesium, iron and zinc bind to these drugs and prevent their absorption. Dairy products and calcium-fortified juices should also be avoided within two hours of antibiotics because the calcium can block drug absorption.

• **Thyroid medications.** If you take a thyroid medication such as *levothyroxine* (Synthroid), do not take any iron, calcium or aluminum (found in antacids) within four hours because they interfere with absorption of the drug.

ASK AN EXPERT

Dr. Galland notes that supplements should be used with the same care as drugs. It's best to take them under the supervision of a doctor (such as a naturopath) who is specially trained in their use or to ask your pharmacist for advice.

---

4 Supplements That Can Impair Your Brain

Cynthia Kuhn, PhD, professor of pharmacology, cancer biology, psychiatry and behavioral sciences at Duke University School of Medicine in Durham, North Carolina. Dr. Kuhn is also coauthor, with Scott Swartzwelder, PhD, and Wilkie Wilson, PhD, of *Buzzed: The Straight Facts About the Most Used and Abused Drugs from Alcohol to Ecstasy.*

It's hardly news that supplements—just like drugs—can have physical side effects.

Recent development: Researchers are now learning more and more about unwanted mental changes that can occur when taking popular supplements (such as herbs and hormones).

These supplements can be a hidden cause of depression, anxiety, mania and other mental changes because patients—and their doctors—often don't realize how these products can affect the brain.

Supplements that may cause unwanted mental changes…

MELATONIN

Melatonin is among the most popular supplements for treating insomnia, jet lag and other sleep disorders. Melatonin is a natural hormone that's released by the pineal gland at night and readily enters the brain. Unlike many sleep aids, it doesn't render you unconscious or put you to sleep—it causes subtle brain changes that make you "ready" for sleep.

Studies have shown that people who take melatonin in the late afternoon or early evening tend to fall asleep more quickly when they go to bed. The amount of melatonin used in scientific studies ranges from 0.1 mg to 0.5 mg. However, the products in health-food stores typically contain much higher doses—usually 1 mg to 5 mg. Supplemental melatonin also may become less effective over time, which encourages people to increase the doses even more.

Effects on the brain: In people with depression, melatonin may improve sleep, but it may worsen their depression symptoms, according to the National Institutes of Health.

What to do: Melatonin can help when used short term for such problems as jet lag. It is not particularly effective as a long-term solution for other causes of insomnia.

ST. JOHN'S WORT

St. John's wort is probably the most studied herb for treating depression. Researchers who analyzed data from 29 international studies recently concluded that St. John's wort was as effective as prescription antidepressants for treating minor to moderate depression.

St. John's wort appears to be safe, particularly when it's used under the supervision of a physician. However, it can cause unwanted mental changes.

Effects on the brain: St. John's wort may increase brain levels of "feel good" neurotransmitters, including serotonin and dopamine. But unwanted mental changes that may occur in anyone taking St. John's wort include anxiety, irritability and vivid dreams. It may also lead to mania (a condition characterized by periods of overactivity, excessive excitement and lack of inhibitions)—especially in individuals who are also using antipsychotic drugs.

Caution: This supplement should never be combined with a prescription selective serotonin reuptake inhibitor (SSRI) antidepressant, such as *sertraline* (Zoloft) or *paroxetine* (Paxil). Taking St. John's wort with an SSRI can cause serotonin syndrome, excessive brain levels of serotonin that can increase body temperature, heart rate and blood pressure—conditions that are all potentially fatal. It also can interact with certain drugs such as oral contraceptives and immunosuppressant medications.

What to do: If you have depression, do not self-medicate with St. John's wort. Always talk to your doctor first if you are interested in trying this supplement.

TESTOSTERONE

Older men whose testosterone levels are declining (as is normal with aging) are often tempted to get a prescription for supplemental "T," which is advertised (but not proven) to improve their ability to get erections. Some women also use testosterone patches or gels (in much lower doses than men) to increase sexual desire and arousal.

Effects on the brain: If your testosterone is low, taking supplemental doses may cause a pleasant—but slight—increase in energy. However, with very high doses, such as those taken by bodybuilders, side effects may include aggression and mood swings. Men and women may experience withdrawal symptoms—such as depression and loss of appetite—when they stop taking it.

Testosterone replacement for men is FDA approved only for those with a clinical deficiency—defined as blood levels under 300 nanograms per deciliter (ng/dL).

What to do: Testosterone has been shown to increase sexual desire in women—it is not FDA approved for women but may be prescribed "off-label." The evidence supporting testosterone's ability to improve sexual function and well-being in normally aging men is weaker—unless they have been proven on more than one occasion to have low testosterone and related symptoms. Both men and women should take testosterone only under the supervision of a doctor.

WEIGHT-LOSS SUPPLEMENTS

Two ingredients that are commonly used in weight-loss supplements, *beta-phenylethylamine* (PEA) and *P-synephrine*, are said to increase metabolism and burn extra calories.

Effects on the brain: Both PEA and P-synephrine (a compound found in supplements made from bitter orange) can make you feel jittery and anxious, particularly when they are combined with stimulants such as caffeine.

Many weight-loss products are complicated cocktails of active ingredients that haven't been adequately studied—nor have they been approved by the FDA. They've been linked to dangerous increases in blood pressure.

Important: There is little evidence that these products work as a weight-loss aid.

What to do: Don't rely on weight-loss supplements. To lose weight, you need to decrease your food intake and increase your exercise levels—no supplement can accomplish that!

How to Avoid Dangerous Herb-Drug Interactions

Catherine Ulbricht, PharmD, senior attending pharmacist at Massachusetts General Hospital in Boston. She is coeditor of *Natural Standard Herb & Supplement Handbook: The Clinical Bottom Line.*

An increasing number of American adults now take herbs or nutritional supplements for a wide range of ailments, including arthritis, depression and nausea.

Problem: Unlike prescription drugs, herbal supplements are not regulated by the FDA, so there are no labeling requirements regarding potential interactions with prescription or over-the-counter (OTC) drugs.

Whether they are used in capsules, extracts, liquid, cream or tea, many herbal products can be harmful when combined with prescription or OTC medication.

What happens: Some herbs can interact with medications by affecting their absorption, metabolism or by other mechanisms. As a result, drug levels may become too high or too low.

Catherine Ulbricht, PharmD, a pharmacist at Massachusetts General Hospital and one of the country's leading experts on herb-drug interactions offers her advice on commonly used herbs...*

CAYENNE

Cayenne is also known as chili or red pepper. Cayenne's active component, capsaicin, which is used as a spice in food, is commonly used as a pain reliever in prescription medicine, often for osteoarthritis, rheumatoid arthritis and diabetic neuropathy (nerve pain resulting from diabetes).

Possible interactions: When combined with aspirin, *ibuprofen* (Advil) or any other nonsteroidal anti-inflammatory drug (NSAID), cayenne may increase these drugs' side effects, especially gastrointestinal (GI) upset. In some people, cayenne also may enhance the pain-relieving action of NSAIDs.

Like NSAIDs, cayenne can have a blood-thinning effect, increasing the risk for bleeding. (When used topically, this risk is lessened because lower doses of cayenne are absorbed.) Do not use cayenne if you take a monoamine oxidase (MAO) inhibitor antidepressant, such as *phenelzine* (Nardil).

Caution: Avoid getting cayenne (in any form) in your eyes, nose, etc., where it can cause burning or stinging.

GINGER

Ginger is a popular antidote for nausea and/or vomiting. Research suggests that ginger also may help prevent blood clotting and reduce blood sugar levels.

Possible interactions: If you take an NSAID or antiplatelet drug, such as *clopidogrel* (Plavix), ginger may further increase bleeding risk.

Caution: Although there's strong evidence that it is particularly effective for nausea and/or vomiting in pregnant women, high-dose supplemental ginger (more than 1 g daily) is

*Check with your doctor or pharmacist before taking any herbal product.

not recommended during pregnancy because of possible fetal damage and/or increased bleeding risk. Because of the lack of long-term studies on ginger, consult your doctor before taking it for an extended period of time.

GREEN TEA

As scientific evidence has revealed the disease-fighting benefits of antioxidant-rich green tea, an increasing number of Americans have begun drinking it—or, in some cases, taking it in capsules or extracts. Although new research questions the health benefits of green tea, some studies have found that it may help prevent cancer, especially malignancies of the GI tract, breast and lung. More investigation is needed to confirm these findings. To read more about clinical trials on green tea, go to the National Institutes of Health's website, *clinicaltrials.gov.*

Possible interactions: Most forms of green tea contain caffeine, which may intensify the effect of any medication that increases blood pressure and/or heart rate, such as the decongestant *pseudoephedrine* (Sudafed). Decaffeinated green tea is available, but this form still contains some caffeine and may not have the same health benefits.

Caution: People with arrhythmia (abnormal heart rhythm) should consume no more than moderate amounts of green tea, determined by their personal sensitivity to caffeine.

LICORICE

Licorice contains a compound known as glycyrrhizin, which has antiviral properties. For this reason, licorice is often used to treat the common cold and herpes infections (including cold sores). However, some studies have shown that topical licorice cream does not help genital herpes.

Possible interactions: Licorice can interact with diuretics, such as *chlorothiazide* (Diuril) and *furosemide* (Lasix), and any medication that affects hormone levels, such as birth control pills.

Caution: It also may increase blood pressure and bleeding risk.

MILK THISTLE

This popular herb is used for liver problems, including cirrhosis and hepatitis. These benefits are well documented by research.

Possible interactions: Milk thistle may interfere with how the liver breaks down certain drugs, such as antibiotics and antifungals. Milk thistle also may interact with the anticonvulsant *phenytoin* (Dilantin). The herb may lower blood sugar and cause heartburn, nausea and vomiting or other GI upset.

Caution: If you take diabetes medication, do not use milk thistle unless you are supervised by a health-care professional.

ST. JOHN'S WORT

St. John's wort is commonly used for depression. Several studies show that it may work as well as a prescription antidepressant, such as *paroxetine* (Paxil), for mild to moderate depressive disorders. More research is needed before St. John's wort can be recommended for severe depression.

Possible interactions: St. John's wort may interact with drugs that are broken down by the liver, including birth control pills, the blood thinner *warfarin* (Coumadin) and migraine medications. People who take St. John's wort may experience stomach upset, fatigue, sexual dysfunction, dizziness or headaches.

Caution: St. John's wort should not be taken with prescription antidepressant medication.

Vitamins and Herbs That Don't Mix with Common Medications

George T. Grossberg, MD, the Samuel W. Fordyce Endowed Chair in Geriatric Psychiatry in the department of neurology and psychiatry at St. Louis University School of Medicine in St. Louis, Missouri. He is the author, with Barry Fox, PhD, of *The Essential Herb-Drug-Vitamin Interaction Guide.*

Most doctors warn their patients about the potential dangers of combining some medications, but few take the time—and some are not well informed enough—to offer guidance on the harmful effects of taking certain vitamins and/or herbs with prescription drugs.

Recent study: Among 132 pharmacists surveyed, 47% had seen a patient with a suspected side effect from a vitamin-drug or herb-drug interaction, according to research published in the *Annals of Pharmacotherapy.*

Hidden danger: The problem is particularly common among Americans over age 65, who comprise about 14% of the US population but take 40% of all drugs, vitamins and herbs. Older people also are more sensitive to the side effects of vitamin-drug or herb-drug interactions due to changes in metabolism and the brain.

HARMFUL INTERACTIONS

When some vitamins and/or herbs are taken with certain drugs, the supplement can...

- **Weaken the effectiveness of the drug.**

Example: The herb astragalus, which is used to boost immunity, may reduce the immunosuppressive effects of such drugs as cortisone.

- **Strengthen** the effectiveness of the drug, causing a type of drug overdose.

Example: Black cohosh, an herb used to control the symptoms of menopause, can lower blood pressure. If taken with an antihypertensive medication, it can cause *hypo*tension (severely low blood pressure) with symptoms such as dizziness and fatigue.

VITAMIN-DRUG INTERACTIONS

Vitamins that are among the most likely to cause dangerous interactions with drugs...*

- **Vitamin A** promotes immunity, proper bone growth and healthy skin. It also plays a role in night vision and the growth and maintenance of cells of the gastrointestinal tract.

Recommended Dietary Allowance (RDA): 2,300 international units (IU) for women...3,000 IU for men.

Supplemental vitamin A may interact with drugs including: The anticoagulant

---

*Multivitamins or individual supplements containing nutrients that exceed the RDA may cause interactions.

warfarin—vitamin A can increase the risk for bleeding and bruising.

• **Vitamin B-6** is involved in digestion, the production of red blood cells and the maintenance of a healthy brain and nervous system.

RDA: 1.3 mg for all adults ages 19 to 50…1.5 mg for women over age 50…1.7 mg for men over age 50.

Supplemental vitamin B-6 may interact with drugs including: Amiodarone (Cordarone), taken for heart arrhythmias—B-6 may increase skin sensitivity to sunlight…*carbidopa* and *levodopa* (Sinemet), taken for Parkinson's disease—B-6 may interfere with the medication's effectiveness…*theophylline* (Elixophyllin), taken for asthma—B-6 may increase the risk for seizures induced by theophylline.

• **Vitamin C** is important for immunity and helps the body manufacture and repair blood vessels, skin, muscles, teeth, bones, tendons, ligaments, hormones and neurotransmitters.

RDA: 75 mg for women…90 mg for men.

Supplemental vitamin C may interact with drugs including: The anticoagulants *heparin* or *warfarin,* taken for cardiovascular disease—vitamin C may reduce the effectiveness of these drugs.

• **Calcium** helps build strong bones and assists in wound healing, blood clotting, cellular metabolism and muscle contraction.

*Adequate intake (AI):*** 1,000 mg for adults ages 19 to 50…1,200 mg for adults over age 50.

Supplemental calcium may interact with drugs including: Digitalis drugs, such as *digoxin* (Lanoxin), which improve the heart's strength and efficiency—calcium can decrease digitalis levels…aminoglycoside antibiotics—calcium can increase the risk for kidney failure.

HERB-DRUG INTERACTIONS

Herbs that are among the most likely to cause dangerous interactions with drugs…

• **Valerian,** a mild sedative, is used to treat insomnia and anxiety.

Lowest effective dose: 400 mg, up to two hours before bedtime.

**AI is sometimes used in place of RDA.

Valerian may interact with drugs including: A selective serotonin reuptake inhibitor (SSRI), such as *sertraline* (Zoloft), or tricyclic antidepressant, such as *desipramine* (Norpramin)—valerian can cause excessive sedation, depression and mental impairment.

• **Grapeseed extract** is rich in powerful antioxidants called procyanidolic oligomers (PCOs). It is used to treat high blood pressure, heart disease, varicose veins and macular degeneration.

Lowest effective dose: 75 mg daily.

Grapeseed extract may interact with drugs including: A blood-thinning medication, such as aspirin or warfarin—grapeseed extract can increase the risk for bleeding and bruising.

• **Yohimbe** is an African herb that improves blood flow. It is sometimes prescribed for men who have erectile dysfunction.

Lowest effective dose: 5.4 mg daily.

Yohimbe may interact with drugs including: The allergy medication phenylephrine, found in over-the-counter products, such as Vicks Sinex Nasal Spray…or the asthma medication *albuterol* (Proventil)—yohimbe can cause a potentially dangerous increase in heart rate and blood pressure.

• **Apple cider vinegar** is a popular folk remedy that has been used to treat arthritis, high blood pressure and leg cramps.

Lowest effective dose: One tablespoon daily.

Apple cider vinegar may interact with drugs including: Medication for congestive heart failure and/or high blood pressure, such as digoxin, *furosemide* (Lasix) and *hydrochlorothiazide* (Microzide)—apple cider vinegar can increase the risk for hypokalemia (low potassium levels), which can further complicate heart disease.

• **Evening primrose oil** is derived from the seed of the evening primrose plant. This herbal supplement delivers high levels of gamma-linolenic acid (GLA), an essential fatty acid. It is used to treat premenstrual syndrome, hot flashes, high blood pressure (during pregnancy) and rheumatoid arthritis.

Lowest effective dose: 540 mg daily.

Evening primrose oil may interact with drugs including: Antiseizure medications, such as *clonazepam* (Klonopin)—evening primrose oil can lower the effectiveness of such drugs, making a seizure more likely.

When Drugs and Juices Don't Mix

Beverly J. McCabe-Sellers, PhD, RD, who was a professor of dietetics and nutrition at the University of Arkansas for Medical Sciences in Little Rock for more than 20 years. She continues to serve as an adjunct professor of nutrition at the university's School of Public Health and is a coeditor of the *Handbook of Food-Drug Interactions*.

If you take any kind of prescription or over-the-counter (OTC) medication, you may be unwittingly reducing its benefits and/or increasing its risks by drinking certain beverages when you swallow the drug. The potentially harmful interactions also may occur if you drink the beverage hours before or after taking the medication.

For example...

DANGERS OF GRAPEFRUIT JUICE

Grapefruit juice has long been known to alter the effects of certain medications, but not all doctors warn their patients about these potential dangers.*

Grapefruit juice contains compounds that inhibit an important enzyme called CYP3A4, which is found in the liver and intestines. CYP3A4 is one of several enzymes that help break down up to 70% of all medications.

Grapefruit juice that is made from concentrate usually contains the entire fruit, including the rind—the primary source of the compound that affects drug metabolism. Grapefruit juice that is not made from concentrate contains less of this compound. However, to be safe, it's best to avoid grapefruit juice (and grapefruit itself) altogether if you take certain medications.

Among the drugs that can interact with grapefruit juice...

*As a general guideline, it is best not to drink any juice at the same time that you take medication. Instead, use water to swallow pills.

• **Anti-arrhythmic medications,** such as *amiodarone* (Cordarone), *quinidine* and *disopyramide* (Norpace), which are taken for abnormal heart rhythms.

Risks: Heart arrhythmias as well as thyroid, pulmonary or liver damage.

• **Blood pressure–lowering calcium channel blockers,** such as *felodipine*, *nifedipine* (Procardia) and *verapamil* (Calan).

Risks: A precipitous drop in blood pressure, as well as flushing, swelling of the extremities, headaches, irregular heartbeat and, in rare cases, heart attack.

• **Cholesterol-lowering drugs,** such as *atorvastatin* (Lipitor), *lovastatin* (Mevacor) and *simvastatin* (Zocor).

Risks: Headache, stomach upset, liver inflammation and muscle pain or weakness.

• **Sedatives** such as *diazepam* (Valium) and *triazolam* (Halcion).

Risks: Dizziness, confusion and drowsiness.

DANGERS OF APPLE JUICE AND ORANGE JUICE

New research shows that apple juice and orange juice can decrease the absorption of some drugs if the juice is swallowed at the same time as the pill. Grapefruit juice is also believed to have this effect.

Specifically, researchers found that apple, orange and grapefruit juice decrease the absorption of...

• **Allergy medication** *fexofenadine* (Allegra).

• **Antibiotics,** such as *ciprofloxacin* (Cipro) and *levofloxacin* (Levaquin).

• **Antifungal drug** *itraconazole* (Sporanox).

• **Blood pressure–lowering beta-blockers,** such as *atenolol* (Tenormin).

• **Chemotherapy drug** *etoposide* (Toposar).

If you are taking any of these drugs, it is probably safe to drink apple or orange juice (and eat whole fruits) at least two hours before or three hours after taking the medications. Check with your doctor first. Avoid grapefruit juice (and grapefruit itself) altogether.

DANGERS OF COFFEE

Coffee can interact with certain medications in a variety of ways. Do not drink coffee at the same time that you take any medication. *Limit daily consumption of coffee to one to two cups if you take…*

•**Antacids.** Because coffee contains acid, it counteracts the effectiveness of OTC antacids such as *calcium carbonate* (TUMS) and Maalox.

•**Aspirin or other nonsteroidal anti-inflammatory (NSAID) medications,** such as *ibuprofen* (Advil) or *naproxen* (Aleve). Because coffee increases stomach acidity, combining it with these drugs may increase risk for gastrointestinal side effects, including stomach irritation and bleeding.

•**Bronchodilator theophylline (Elixophyllin),** used to treat asthma or emphysema. Consuming coffee with the bronchodilator can slow the breakdown of the drug, leading to higher blood levels and an increased risk for nausea, vomiting, palpitations and seizures.

•**Monoamine oxidase inhibitor (MAOI) antidepressants,** such as *phenelzine* (Nardil) and *selegiline* (Eldepryl). The combination may increase anxiety.

•**Osteoporosis drug alendronate (Fosamax).** Studies show that coffee (and orange juice) can inhibit absorption of Fosamax by 60%. If you take Fosamax or any other osteoporosis medication, ask your pharmacist about foods or other beverages that may interact with the drug.

DANGERS OF CRANBERRY JUICE

In the United Kingdom, there have been at least eight recent reports of bleeding in patients (one of whom died) after they drank cranberry juice with the blood-thinning medication *warfarin* (Coumadin).

Health officials were unable to definitively link the bleeding to the combination of cranberry juice and warfarin, but it's probably safest to avoid cranberry juice altogether if you're taking this medication. Cranberry juice has been shown to inhibit a key enzyme that is responsible for warfarin metabolism, but more research on this interaction is needed.

If you take another drug with blood-thinning effects, such as aspirin, you can probably drink cranberry juice occasionally (no more than four ounces—at least two hours before or three hours after taking the medication). Consult your doctor.

DANGERS OF MILK

The calcium in milk can interact with certain medications. *Drink milk at least two hours before or three hours after taking…*

•**Antacids,** such as calcium carbonate products (Rolaids) or sodium bicarbonate products (Alka-Seltzer and Brioschi). Drinking milk with these antacids can cause milk-alkali syndrome, a condition characterized by high blood calcium levels that can lead to kidney stones or even kidney failure.

•**Antibiotics,** such as tetracyclines and *ciprofloxacin* (Cipro). Calcium blocks absorption of these drugs, decreasing their effectiveness. Calcium-fortified juices are believed to have the same effect.

BETTER DRUG METABOLISM

Our bodies need nutrients to properly metabolize most medications. Chief among these nutrients is protein. Though we tend to eat less protein as we age—due to a variety of reasons, such as dental problems that make it harder to chew meat—we actually require more of this nutrient, since our bodies become less efficient at digesting and utilizing it.

Because the lining of the small and large intestines—where drugs are absorbed—regenerates every three to seven days, you need a continual supply of protein to maintain healthy levels of the enzymes that promote metabolism of medications.

To facilitate drug metabolism: Aim to eat about half a gram of protein daily for every pound of body weight.

Good sources: Fish, meats, eggs, peanut butter and soybeans.

B vitamins also play a key role in drug metabolism. Food sources rich in B vitamins include meats, fortified cereals, bananas and oatmeal.

Helpful: If you skip breakfast and aren't much of a meat eater, consider taking a multivitamin supplement containing the recommended daily intake of B vitamins.

Food-Drug Dangers

Eric R. Leibovitch, MD, senior attending physician and coordinator of internal medicine education at Ventura County Medical Center in Ventura, California. He's the lead author of "Food-Drug Interactions," published in the medical journal *Geriatrics*.

Many of the same foods that are recommended for a healthful diet can make a variety of commonly prescribed medications less effective or, in some cases, cause life-threatening side effects.

Ordinarily, when you take a drug, molecules of the active ingredient pass through the intestinal wall into the blood. The molecules then are broken down in the liver or the kidneys.

Problem: When certain foods and drugs are taken together, the food can alter the way the drug works in the body, or it can affect the absorption, distribution or excretion of the drug.

Potential food interactions involving commonly used drugs…*

• **Antibiotics.** These drugs are used to treat many different types of bacterial infections.

Dietary danger: Blood levels of tetracyclines, such as *tetracycline* (Achromycin V), and fluoroquinolones, such as *ciprofloxacin* (Cipro) and *levofloxacin* (Levaquin), decline when patients eat high-calcium foods (milk, cheese, yogurt, etc.) or calcium-fortified foods (orange juice and cereal) or take calcium supplements. Most antacids also inhibit absorption of these antibiotics, either because they contain calcium or they bind to the drug, making it less effective.

Self-defense: Don't eat calcium-rich foods and/or take calcium supplements or antacids two hours before or after taking the drugs.

Also: Fiber binds to penicillin antibiotics, including *amoxicillin* (Amoxil), and prevents their absorption into the blood. Don't eat high-fiber foods (particularly high-fiber cereals,

*Always read the information insert included with your medications, and consult your pharmacist about any foods (as well as drugs or herbs) that may interact with the drug you are taking.

bran and beans) or take a fiber supplement two hours before or after taking the drugs.

• **Anticoagulants.** *Warfarin* (Coumadin) is used to prevent blood clots from forming in blood vessels.

Dietary danger: Foods or supplements high in vitamin K block warfarin's anticlotting effects. Patients who start eating more leafy, green vegetables (spinach, kale, bok choy, etc.) or other vitamin K–rich foods, such as dairy products and eggs, after starting warfarin can eliminate all of the drug's effects.

Self-defense: Don't alter your diet or start taking supplements that contain vitamin K after starting warfarin therapy. Your dose of warfarin is determined by your prothrombin time (PT), a measure of blood clotting.

If you do eat more vitamin K–rich foods, tell your doctor. He/she will need to recheck your PT and possibly adjust your dose of warfarin.

• **Antihistamines.** *Diphenhydramine* (Benadryl), *clemastine* (Tavist) and *loratadine* (Claritin) are used to treat congestion, itchy eyes and other common allergy symptoms.

Dietary danger: The body's absorption of these drugs declines significantly when they're combined with any food.

Self-defense: Take them on an empty stomach, at least two hours before or after meals.

• **Calcium channel blockers.** Drugs in this class, such as *felodipine*, *nifedipine* (Procardia) and *isradipine*, often are used to treat high blood pressure.

Dietary danger: Grapefruit juice (or a whole grapefruit) greatly increases your body's absorption of the drugs. Combining the two results in greater blood levels of the drug and could cause a dangerous drop in blood pressure.

Self-defense: If you usually drink grapefruit juice or eat grapefruit, tell your doctor—and continue consuming the same amount while taking a calcium-channel blocker. If you start consuming more or less, your doctor may need to adjust your drug dose. Your doctor may suggest not consuming grapefruit at all.

• **Congestive heart failure drugs.** *Digoxin* (Lanoxin) helps control heart-beat irregularities (arrhythmias).

Dietary danger: High-fiber foods (beans, whole grains, vegetables, etc.) and fiber supplements bind to the drug and prevent its absorption.

Result: Lower-than-expected drug concentrations that increase the risk for life-threatening heart problems.

Self-defense: Don't change your diet once you start taking digoxin. If you do start eating more fiber, tell your doctor. He will need to re-check levels of digoxin in the blood and possibly increase your dose of the drug.

Also important: Don't take a fiber supplement or eat high-fiber food two hours before or after taking digoxin.

• **Diabetes drugs.** *Metformin* (Glucophage) and *glipizide* (Glucotrol) are taken by some people with diabetes for blood sugar control.

Dietary danger: Taking metformin with dietary fiber decreases drug levels in the blood and can reduce its effectiveness. Taking glipizide with any food decreases absorption.

Self-defense: Both drugs work best when taken on an empty stomach, at least two hours before or after meals.

• **Sedatives.** *Diazepam* (Valium) and *triazolam* (Halcion) are members of a family of sedatives known as benzo-diazepines, which are commonly used to treat insomnia and anxiety.

Dietary dangers: A high-fat diet increases blood levels of the drugs and can cause prolonged sedation. Grapefruit juice or grapefruit increases absorption of the drugs into the bloodstream, which enhances their effects.

Self-defense: Avoid grapefruit when taking diazepam or triazolam. Also, if you start including more high-fat foods in your diet, report any side effects to your doctor. He may need to lower your dose of sedative medication.

HOW MUCH WATER DO YOU NEED?

Most patients take drugs with just a swallow of water. That's not enough. You need at least eight ounces of water when taking drugs, to protect the stomach lining and promote their absorption through the intestine into the blood.

Don't substitute caffeinated beverages or grapefruit or other juices for water when swallowing drugs. Any of these beverages can decrease or increase absorption of certain medications.

Green Tea May Interfere With Blood Pressure Medication

Study titled "Green Tea Ingestion Greatly Reduces Plasma Concentrations of Nadolol in Healthy Subjects," published in *Clinical Pharmacology and Therapeutics.*

We've all gotten used to thinking of green tea as a veritable fount of good health because it's a great source of antioxidants that reduce cholesterol, triglycerides and the risk for cancer, cardiovascular disease and Parkinson's disease.

But: For certain people, green tea actually may do more harm than good—by interfering with a type of blood pressure medication called a beta-blocker. *Here's the news from a recent study…*

TEA TEST

For two weeks, one group of participants drank 24 ounces of green tea every day...a second group avoided green tea and drank water instead. After the two weeks were up, all participants were given a single 30-mg dose of the beta-blocker *nadolol* (sold in the US as Corgard and also used in the combination drug Corzide). Then, numerous times over the next 48 hours, blood and urine samples were collected from the participants so that researchers could measure the amount of the drug that was circulating in the blood and the amount excreted in urine. Participants' blood pressure and pulse rates also were measured.

After a two-week break, the process was repeated but with the participants switching beverages—so that the former green-tea-drinking group stuck to water, and the former water group drank the three cups of green tea each day for two weeks. Then, as before, everyone took a dose of the beta-blocker drug and gave blood and urine samples. *Results…*

• **Compared with the test results after participants drank water,** the two weeks of daily tea-drinking resulted in an average 85% reduction in the blood concentration of the blood pressure drug…and an average 82% reduction in the amount of the drug excreted in the urine. Because of the way nadolol is processed in the body, the portion of the drug that does get absorbed by the body is mostly excreted unchanged in the urine—so both the reduction in the drug's blood concentration and the reduction in the urine concentration suggested that green tea seriously interfered with the absorption of the blood pressure medication.

• **In addition,** the participants' blood pressure dropped significantly less after drinking green tea than after drinking water—meaning that the green tea kept the beta-blocker from properly doing its job of reducing blood pressure.

Explanation: Based on laboratory experiments, the researchers suspect that a compound in green tea, epigallocatechin-3-gallate (EGCG), inhibits the ability of specialized transporter cells to move the blood pressure drug across the intestinal wall and into the bloodstream. Ironically, EGCG is the same antioxidant compound credited with giving green tea many of its health-boosting effects.

What we still don't know: This was a small study, and many questions remain. For instance, does green tea interfere with the absorption of all types of beta-blockers or just nadolol? Might green tea extract, a popular supplement, also interfere with beta-blocker medication in the same way that the beverage does? (The amount of green tea consumed per day in this study provided 322 mg of EGCG, which is less than the amount of EGCG found in many green-tea-extract supplements.) Clearly, more research is needed.

What to do in the meantime: If you're taking nadolol or another beta-blocker and you're accustomed to drinking green tea, discuss these study findings with a nutrition-oriented doctor. If your blood pressure is well controlled, your doctor may say it's OK to carry on as you are. However, if your blood pressure is not well controlled, you may be advised to reduce or cut out green tea to see whether this helps control your blood pressure better. Either way, of course, it's best to follow a healthful diet that helps keep blood pressure down.

11

Healthful Eyes, Ears, Nose and Mouth

Save Your Sight

Vision problems in the US have increased at alarming rates, including a 19% increase in cataracts and a 25% increase in macular degeneration since 2000.

Why the increase? Americans are living longer, and eyes with a lot of mileage are more likely to break down. But not getting the right nutrients plays a big role, too—and the right foods and supplements can make a big difference.

Of course, people with eye symptoms or a diagnosed eye disease should work closely with their doctors. I also recommend medical supervision for people who are taking multiple supplements.

But here are common eye problems and the foods and supplements that can fight them...

DRY EYES

The eyes naturally get drier with age, but dry-eye syndrome—a chronic problem with the quantity and quality of tears—often is due to nutritional deficiencies. Poor nutrition can permit damaging free radicals to accumulate in the glands that produce tears.

What to do: Take one-half teaspoon of cod liver oil twice a week. It's an excellent source of DHA (docosahexaenoic acid, an omega-3 fatty acid) and vitamins A and D, nutrients that improve the quality of tears and help them lubricate more effectively.

Also helpful: BioTears, an oral supplement that includes curcumin and other eye-protecting ingredients. (I am on the scientific advisory board of BioSyntrx, which makes BioTears and Eye & Body Complete, see next page, but I have no financial interest in the company.) I have found improvement in about 80% of patients who take BioTears. Follow the directions on the label.

Jeffrey R. Anshel, OD, founder of the Ocular Nutrition Society. He is author of *What You Must Know About Food and Supplements for Optimal Vision Care: Ocular Nutrition Handbook.* SmartMedicineForYourEyes.com

CATARACTS

Cataracts typically are caused by the age-related clumping of proteins in the crystalline lens of the eyes. More than half of Americans will have cataracts by the time they're 80.

What to do: Eat spinach, kale and other dark leafy greens every day. They contain lutein, an antioxidant that reduces the free-radical damage that increases cataract risk. (Lutein and zeaxanthin, another antioxidant, are the only carotenoids that concentrate in the lenses of the eyes.)

Important: Cook kale or other leafy greens with a little bit of oil…or eat them with a meal that contains olive oil or other fats. The carotenoids are fat-soluble, so they require a little fat for maximal absorption.

I also advise patients to take 500 milligrams (mg) of vitamin C three or four times a day (cut back if you get diarrhea). One study found that those who took vitamin C supplements for 10 years were 64% less likely to have cataracts.

The supplement Eye & Body Complete contains a mix of eye-protecting compounds, including bioflavonoids, bilberry and vitamins A and D. Follow instructions on the label.

COMPUTER VISION SYNDROME

The National Institute of Occupational Safety and Health reports that 88% of people who work at a computer for more than three hours a day complain of computer-related problems, including blurred vision, headaches, neck pain and eye dryness.

What to do: Take a supplement that contains about 6 mg of astaxanthin, a carotenoid. It reduces eyestrain by improving the stamina of eye muscles.

Also helpful: The 20/20/20 rule. After every 20 minutes on a computer, take 20 seconds and look 20 feet away.

REDUCED NIGHT VISION

True night blindness (nyctalopia) is rare in the US, but many older adults find that they struggle to see at night, which can make night driving difficult.

What to do: Take a daily supplement that includes one-half mg of copper and 25 mg of zinc. Zinc deficiencies have been associated with poor night vision—and you'll need the extra copper to "balance" the zinc. Zinc helps the body produce vitamin A, which is required by the retina to detect light.

Also helpful: The foods for AMD (below).

AGE-RELATED MACULAR DEGENERATION (AMD)

This serious disease is the leading cause of blindness in older adults. Most people with AMD first will notice that their vision has become slightly hazy. As the disease progresses, it can cause a large blurred area in the center of the field of vision.

What to do: Eat several weekly servings of spinach or other brightly colored vegetables, such as kale and yellow peppers, or egg yolks. The nutrients and antioxidants in these foods can help slow the progression of AMD. The National Eye Institute's Age-Related Eye Disease Study (AREDS) reported that patients who already had macular degeneration and had adequate intakes of beta-carotene, zinc, copper and vitamins C and E were 25% less likely to develop an advanced form of the disease.

Also helpful: The Eye & Body Complete supplement, mentioned earlier. It contains all of the ingredients used in the original AREDS study—plus many others, including generous amounts of lutein and zeaxanthin that were included in a follow-up study, known as AREDS2—and was found to have positive effects.

Eye Symptoms Never to Ignore—They Could Mean a Medical Emergency

Neil Shulman, MD, associate professor in the department of internal medicine at Emory University School of Medicine, Atlanta, and Jack Birge, MD, medical director for performance improvement at Tanner Medical Center in Carrollton, Georgia. They are authors, with Joon Ahn, MD, of *Your Body's Red Light Warning Signals.* RedLightWarningSignals.com.

M any serious health problems are first diagnosed from changes in the eyes. Never ignore these eye symptoms…

SUDDEN EYELID DROOP

What it may mean: If you notice that one of your eyelids has abruptly drooped lower than the other (possibly accompanied by double vision), it could indicate an aneurysm—a ballooning-out of a blood vessel in the brain. This is particularly likely when a patient's pupils are unequal in size. An aneurysm can press against nerves that control both eyelid position and pupil size.

Aneurysms aren't always dangerous, but those that rupture can cause brain damage or death. It's estimated that up to 5% of Americans have a brain aneurysm.

Causes: Most brain aneurysms are due to a natural weakness in an artery wall. Less often, they're caused by head trauma.

What to do: Get to an emergency room immediately.

Treatment: Aneurysms that are large and/or are causing symptoms are typically clipped—a neurosurgeon uses a metal clip to prevent blood from flowing through the aneurysm. Small aneurysms often are best left alone.

CHRONIC EYELID DROOP IN BOTH EYES/DOUBLE VISION

Chronic eyelid droop sometimes is accompanied by blurred or double vision, jaw fatigue or general weakness that gets worse as the day progresses.

What it may mean: These are common symptoms of myasthenia gravis, a condition in which nerves are unable to communicate effectively with muscles.

Causes: Myasthenia gravis is an autoimmune disease. The immune system creates antibodies that damage cellular receptors for acetylcholine, a neurotransmitter involved in nerve/muscle communication.

It's not clear what triggers this condition, although it has been linked to disorders of the thymus gland.

What to do: Get to a doctor as soon as possible (ideally within a week). If your symptoms are accompanied by breathing problems, you should get to an emergency room immediately.

Treatment: Most patients are treated with medications, such as *pyridostigmine* (Mestinon), which improve the transmission of nerve signals. Other medications, including steroids, may be used. The thymus gland may be removed in patients with tumors if medication fails. This may or may not improve symptoms—it is mainly done to reduce the risk for a future cancer.

EYEBALL PAIN (OFTEN SUDDEN)

What it may mean: In the absence of trauma, eye pain can be due to glaucoma, a build-up of pressure within the eye. (Other causes of eye discomfort are inflammation in the eye or dry eyes.)

Causes of glaucoma: The different forms of glaucoma all cause an increase in intraocular pressure. This usually is due to impairments in drainage, which increase fluid levels within the eye.

Important: Glaucoma is the second-leading cause of blindness among American adults (behind macular degeneration). Eye pain may be the only early symptom.

What to do: If you have severe pain and/or vision loss, get to an ophthalmologist within a day.

Treatment: Medications that reduce pressure by improving drainage and/or reducing fluid production.

Examples: Medicated eyedrops, such as *timolol* (Timoptic) or *brimonidine* (Alphagan). Less often, surgery may be needed to improve eye drainage.

A HAZE, BLUR OR DARKNESS IN THE FIELD OF VISION

What it may mean: A clot in a blood vessel may be blocking circulation to the retina, optic nerve or brain. Patients with this type of clot may be suffering from a stroke or be at high risk for a subsequent stroke—possibly within hours or days. (Other conditions that can cause these symptoms include inflammation in the blood vessels, a retinal detachment or inflammation of the optic nerve.)

Causes of stroke: The same risk factors for cardiovascular disease, such as diabetes, high blood pressure and smoking, also increase the risk for stroke. The optic nerve and retina are very sensitive to changes in blood flow. Even a partial blockage can cause visual changes—and these changes may occur long before an actual stroke.

Important: Small clots that cause visual changes often dissolve on their own. Symptoms disappear—but the stroke risk still is there. Also, if you're having a stroke, you may not be aware of any symptom—an onlooker may be the one to alert you to a shift in behavior.

What to do: Get to an emergency room, even if the symptom is fleeting.

Treatment: Patients with clots (or a history of getting them) usually are treated with clot-dissolving (or clot-preventing) therapies. These include aspirin, heparin, warfarin or tissue plasminogen activator (TPA).

A procedure called carotid endarterectomy may be recommended for patients with large amounts of plaque in the carotid arteries. Fatty buildups in these arteries, which run from the neck to the brain, increase the risk for subsequent strokes. A test called the carotid doppler can be used to detect and measure the plaque.

SWARMS OF FLOATERS OR FLASHING LIGHTS

What it may mean: We all see drifting specks, or "floaters," from time to time. They occur when the clear jelly inside the eyeball (the vitreous humor) releases strands of cells that are briefly visible.

Occasional floaters are harmless—but a dramatic swarm of floaters or flashing lights can indicate a developing retinal tear or detachment, which, without immediate surgery, can cause blindness.

Causes: The retina, a light-sensitive structure at the back of the eye, can separate from the blood vessels behind it. This often happens when the vitreous humor leaks through a small tear in the retina, weakening the supportive bonds. A tear in the retina may be caused by age-related changes, trauma or extreme nearsightedness. The longer the retina remains detached, the less oxygen it receives—and the greater the risk for subsequent blindness.

What to do: See your ophthalmologist promptly—the sooner, the better. Don't wait longer than 24 hours.

Treatment: Surgery to repair the tear often is effective, but it can take months for vision to improve—and some people don't ever fully regain their normal vision.

Note: A swarm of floaters also can be caused by bleeding in the eye due to other conditions, such as abnormal blood vessel growth. This usually occurs in patients with diabetes, hypertension or sickle-cell disease.

EYE SYMPTOMS THAT ARE ALWAYS AN EMERGENCY

- **Sudden drooping of one or both eyelids.**
- **Pupils that are suddenly of unequal size.**
- **Severe pain within the eyeball.**
- **Rapid vision changes, such as blurred vision or swarms of floaters or flashing lights.**

Beware of Eye Floaters

Adam Wenick, MD, PhD, assistant professor of ophthalmology in the Retina Division at the Wilmer Eye Institute at The Johns Hopkins School of Medicine in Baltimore. He is board-certified by the American Board of Ophthalmology, with special expertise in retinal tears and detachment as well as other diseases of the retina.

If you have ever noticed a few tiny dots, blobs, squiggly lines or cobweblike images drifting across your field of vision, you are not alone. These visual disturbances, called floaters, are common, and most people simply dismiss them as a normal part of growing older. But that's not always the case.

When it could be serious: In about 15% of cases, floaters are a symptom of a harmful condition known as a retinal tear, which can, in turn, lead to a vision-robbing retinal detachment in a matter of hours to days.

HOW DOES THIS HAPPEN?

The retina, which is an extremely thin, delicate membrane that lines the inside of the back of the eye, converts light into signals that your brain recognizes as images. However, with age, a jelly like material called the vitreous that fills much of the eyeball commonly shrinks a bit and separates from the retina. If the shrinkage or some other injury exerts enough force, the retina can actually tear.

You might notice a sudden shower of new floaters or flashes of light that look like shooting stars or lightning bolts. What you're seeing when this occurs are actually shadows that are being cast on the retina by the tiny clumps of collagen fibers that comprise the floaters. The flashes of light are caused by the tugging of the vitreous on the retina, which stimulates the photoreceptors that sense light.

Why floaters and/or flashes are a red flag: The retina lacks nerves that signal pain, so these visual disturbances are the only way you will be alerted to a tear. Left untreated, fluid can leak through the retinal tear, and the retina can detach like wallpaper peeling off a wall. A retinal detachment is an emergency—if it's not treated promptly, it can lead to a complete loss of vision in the affected eye.

ARE YOU AT RISK?

Changes in the eye that increase risk for a retinal tear or detachment begin primarily in your 50s and 60s—and continue to increase as you grow older.

In addition to age, you can also be at increased risk for a retinal tear or detachment due to…

• **Nearsightedness.** People of any age with nearsightedness greater than six diopters (requiring eyeglasses or contact lenses with a vision correction of more than minus six) are five to six times more likely to develop a retinal tear or detachment. That's because nearsighted eyeballs are larger than normal. Therefore, the retina is spread thinner, making it more prone to tearing.

Important: If you're nearsighted, don't assume that corrective eyewear or LASIK surgery decreases your risk for a retinal tear or detachment. Neither does.

• **Cataract surgery.** This surgery alters the vitreous jelly, increasing the risk that the vitreous will pull away from the retina, possibly giving way to a retinal detachment.

Cataract surgery has been known to double one's detachment risk, but a new Australian study suggests that improvements in technology, such as phacoemulsification, which uses an ultrasonic device to break up and remove the cloudy lens, have cut the risk from one in 100 to one in 400.

• **Diabetes.** Because it impairs circulation to the retina over time, diabetes leads to a higher risk for a severe type of retinal detachment that is not associated with floaters and flashes and can be initially asymptomatic.

Individuals who have diabetes should be sure to have annual eye exams with dilation of the pupils to check for this and other ocular complications of diabetes. The Optomap test provides a wide view of the retina, but you also need pupil dilation for a thorough screening.

THE DANGER OF A RETINAL TEAR

Anyone who experiences a sudden burst of floaters or flashes, especially if they are large or appear in any way different from how they have in the past, should contact an ophthalmologist right away for advice.

If an eye exam confirms a retinal tear, it can be treated in an eye doctor's office, using either lasers or freezing equipment to "spot-weld" the area surrounding the tear. (Anesthetic eyedrops are used to numb the eye, but the procedure can still be uncomfortable.)

The resulting scar tissue will seal off the tear so the fluid doesn't leak behind the retina and pull it away. The good news is that both laser photocoagulation and freezing are more than 90% effective in preventing detachment. There is a small risk for tiny blind spots.

WHEN A DETACHMENT OCCURS

If you suffer a retinal tear but don't get treatment within a day or two, the fluid can seep through the tear, detaching the retina.

Red flag for detachment: A gradual shading in your vision, like a curtain being drawn on the sides or top or bottom of your eye, means that a retinal detachment may have occurred. If your central vision rapidly changes, this also may signal a retinal detachment or even a stroke.

Retinal detachment is an emergency! When your doctor examines you, he/she will be able to see whether the center of your retina is detached. When the center is involved, vision often cannot be fully restored.

If you have suffered a retinal detachment, your doctor will help you decide among the following treatments…

•**Vitrectomy.** This one- to three-hour surgery is performed in a hospital operating room, usually with sedation anesthesia plus localized numbing of the eye. The vitreous is removed, tears are treated with lasers or freezing, and a bubble (typically gas) is injected to replace the missing gel and hold the retina in place until the spot-welding treatment can take effect. (The bubble will gradually disappear.)

Important: It is necessary to keep your head in the same position for seven to 14 days in order to "keep the bubble on the trouble," as doctors say. Therefore, you will need a week or two of bed rest at home. You may have to keep your head facedown or on one side.

•**Scleral buckle.** With this procedure, a clear band of silicone is placed around the outside of the eyeball, where it acts like a belt, holding the retina against the wall of the eyeball.

Also performed in a hospital operating room, scleral buckle involves freezing the retina or treating it with a laser to create localized inflammation that forms a seal, securing the retina and keeping fluid out.

Scleral buckle takes from one to two hours and is sometimes combined with vitrectomy to improve the outcome. It is frequently used for younger patients and those who have not had cataract surgery.

•**Pneumatic retinopexy.** Depending on where the retinal detachment is located, a 20-minute, in-office procedure called a pneumatic retinopexy is an option for patients with smaller tears. With this procedure, a gas bubble is injected, and retinal tears are frozen or treated with a laser.

This is followed by up to two weeks of bed rest. Your head may need to be held in a certain position, such as upright at an angle, depending on the location of your tear.

With pneumatic retinopexy, the reattachment success rate is lower than that of scleral buckle or vitrectomy (70% versus 90%), but it is less invasive and no hospital visit is required. In addition, pneumatic retinopexy costs less than a hospital-based procedure, which could range from $5,000 to $10,000.

Even with a successful procedure, 40% of patients who suffer retinal detachments see 20/50 or worse afterward even when using glasses. The remainder have better vision.

Daily Aspirin Use May Be Linked to Vision Loss

Wet late-stage aging macular disorder (AMD)—also called age-related macular degeneration—is twice as common in people who take aspirin daily as in people who never use aspirin.

Caution: Do not stop aspirin therapy without talking with your physician. Eat a healthful diet, rich in vitamins C and E, beta-carotene and omega-3 fatty acids.

Paulus de Jong, MD, PhD, emeritus professor of ophthalmic epidemiology at the Netherlands Institute for Neuroscience and Academic Medical Center, Amsterdam, and first author of a study of 4,691 people, age 65 and older, published in *Ophthalmology*.

Superfoods for Healthy Eyes

Jennifer Adler, MS, CN, a certified nutritionist, natural foods chef in the Puget Sound area. PassionateNutrition.com

Spirulina can help prevent cataracts and age-related macular degeneration. Taking spirulina can double blood levels of zeaxanthin, an antioxidant linked to a reduced risk for cataracts and age-related macular degeneration, reported researchers in *British Medical Journal*.

How to add it to food: There are many ways to include spirulina in your daily diet…

•**Put it in smoothies.** Add between one teaspoon and one tablespoon to any smoothie or shake.

•**Add to juice.** Add one teaspoon or tablespoon to an eight-ounce glass of juice or water, shake it up and drink it.

•**Sprinkle it on food.** Try spirulina popcorn, for instance—a great conversation starter at a potluck. To a bowl of popcorn, add one to two tablespoons of spirulina powder, three to four tablespoons of grated Parmesan cheese, two or three tablespoons of olive oil, one-half teaspoon of salt and one-eighth teaspoon of cayenne pepper.

•**Add it to condiments.** Put one-quarter teaspoon in a small jar of ketchup, barbecue sauce, mustard or salad dressing. This way you'll get a little each time you use these products.

Broccoli Helps the Eyes

Broccoli also is rich in the carotenoid antioxidants lutein and zeaxanthin. Both are important in preventing ultraviolet light damage to the eyes and can help prevent cataracts and age-related macular degeneration, the leading cause of blindness in people age 65 and older.

Recommended: Eat one-half cup of raw or lightly steamed broccoli daily (buying frozen broccoli is fine). Avoid boiling—it diminishes its nutritional value. Broccoli sprouts, which are the newly sprouted seeds of broccoli, can be added to sandwiches or salads. They contain 30 to 50 times the concentration of protective phytonutrients found in mature broccoli plants. Broccoli sprouts are especially rich in sulforaphane. Because broccoli sprouts can be contaminated with bacteria, people with weak immune systems should check with their doctors before consuming them.

Mark A. Stengler, NMD, a naturopathic medical doctor, founder and medical director of the Stengler Center for Integrative Medicine in Encinitas, California. MarkStengler.com

Exercises to Improve Eye Strength

Marc Grossman, OD, LAc, holistic developmental/behavioral optometrist, licensed acupuncturist and medical director, Natural Eye Care, New Paltz, New York. He is coauthor of *Greater Vision* and *Natural Eye Care.* NaturalEyeCare.com

When it comes to signs of aging, different people have different pet peeves. Some of us really don't like those gray hairs…others sigh over a lost silhouette…still others hate needing reading glasses to see what's on the menu.

Since exercise improves the strength, flexibility and function of our bodies, it makes sense that eye exercises could improve our ability to see close up. Yet this is a controversial topic. Though various studies have found no clear benefit from eye exercises, many holistic practitioners and their patients say that vision can indeed be improved.

The challenge with aging eyes: Many people first become farsighted—meaning that nearby objects look blurry even though more distant objects are clear—starting in their 40s. This is due to presbyopia, a condition in which the aging lens of the eye becomes too stiff to focus clearly up close.

Detractors of eye exercise say that it won't restore lens elasticity. But that's not the point. Eye exercises can improve the strength, flexibility and adaptability of muscles that control eye movement and encourage a mental focus that helps the brain and eyes work better together. This can slow the progression of farsightedness and possibly improve vision.

So can eye exercises help us say good riddance to reading glasses? The answer is yes for some people—and it certainly can't hurt to try.

The four exercises below will help you improve close-up vision. While you do the exercises, remember to keep breathing and keep blinking. And smile! Smiling reduces tension, which helps your muscles work optimally and your brain focus on what's around you.

Try to do the exercises while not wearing any reading glasses—or if your close-up vision is not good enough for that, wear weaker reading glasses than you normally do. If you usually wear glasses or contacts for distance vision, it is OK to wear those while doing the exercises.

How long to practice: Do each exercise for three to four minutes, for a total practice time of about 15 minutes per session, at least three times weekly. If you get headaches while exercising your eyes, reduce the time spent on each exercise—and see your eye doctor if the problem persists.

•**Letter reading**—for better scanning accuracy and conscious eye control when reading or using a computer.

Preparation: Type up a chart with four rows of random letters, just large enough that you can read them while holding the page at a typical reading distance (type size will vary depending on an individual's vision). Leave space between each row. In row one, type all capitals, one space in between each letter...row two, all lowercase, one space in between each letter...row three, all lowercase, no spaces...row four, wordlike groups of random letters arranged as if in a sentence.

Exercise: Hold the chart with both hands. Looking at row one, read each letter aloud left to right, then right to left. Then read every second letter...then every third letter. If your mind wanders, start over.

Over time: When you master row one, try the same techniques with row two...then row three...then row four. If you find that you have memorized parts of the chart, make a new one using different letters.

•**Near and far**—for improved focus and focusing speed when switching your gaze from close objects to distant objects (such as when checking gauges on a car as you drive).

Preparation: Type a chart with six to eight rows of random capital letters, each letter about one-half inch tall (or as tall as necessary for you to read them from 10 feet away). Tack the chart to a wall and stand back 10 feet.

Exercise: Hold a pencil horizontally, with its embossed letters facing you, about six inches from your nose (or as close as possible without it looking blurry). Read any letter on the pencil, then read any letter on the chart. Keep doing this, switching back and forth as fast as you can without letting the letters blur.

Over time: Do this with one eye covered, then the other.

•**Pencil pushups**—to promote eye teamwork. All you need is a pencil.

Exercise: Hold a pencil horizontally at eye level 12 inches from your face (or as far as necessary to see the pencil clearly). With both eyes, look at one particular letter on the pencil...keep looking while bringing the pencil closer to your face. If the letter blurs or doubles, it means that one eye is no longer accurately on target—so move the pencil back until the letter is clear once more...then try again to slowly bring the pencil closer while keeping the letter in focus.

•**The "hot dog"**—for improved flexibility of the muscles within the eye that allow the lens to change shape. No props are needed.

Exercise: With your hands at chest height about eight inches in front of you, point your index fingers and touch the tips together, so that your index fingers are horizontal. Gaze at any target in the distance and, without changing your focus, raise your fingers into your line of sight. Notice that a "mini hot dog" has appeared between the tips of your fingers. Still gazing at the distant object, pull your fingertips apart slightly—and observe that the hot dog is now floating in the air. Keep the hot dog there for two breaths...then look directly at your fingers for two breaths, noticing that the hot dog disappears. Look again at the distant object and find the hot dog once again. Continue switching your gaze back and forth every two breaths.

As your close-up vision improves, you may find that you need less-powerful reading glasses—or none at all—for your day-to-day activities.

Secrets to Choosing the Best Glasses for You

Melvin Schrier, OD, FAAO, an optometry consultant based in Rancho Palos Verdes, California. A fellow of the American Academy of Optometry and past president of the New York Academy of Optometry, he operated a private optometry practice in New York City for more than 40 years and has written numerous journal articles and book chapters on eye health.

With all the lenses that are available today—from sophisticated progressives to drugstore readers—and an array of contacts and fashionable frames to choose from, you might think that selecting your eyewear has never been easier.

The truth is, there now are so many choices out there—each with its own quirks and pitfalls—that you really need to know what you're doing to avoid making costly, potentially eye-damaging mistakes.

How to guard against the most common mistakes…

MISTAKE #1. Assuming that progressives are always the best choice. Those nifty lenses known as "progressives," which offer a continuum of clear vision from near to far (close-up, midrange and distance) within a single pair of glasses or contacts, may seem like the ideal solution for aging eyes. Unlike bifocals and trifocals, progressives have no line separating the different viewing zones.

But for many people, progressives are not all they're cracked up to be. Stationary objects may sometimes appear to be moving because the edges of the optical zones are somewhat blurred by design. This also can make driving tricky—for example, you must move your head to the right or left rather than glancing to the sides, where the edges will be blurred.

On top of that, progressives are more expensive than traditional bifocals and trifocals—about $400 and up versus about $200 to $300 for bifocals or trifocals, which have separate viewing zones separated by lines.

If your eye doctor agrees that progressives are a good choice for you, ask about lenses from manufacturers that are pulling out all the stops to try to address some of the common pitfalls.

Two progressive lenses you may want to discuss with your doctor…

• **Varilux S Series.** To help do away with blurry peripheral vision, these new lenses use a patented design that is intended to even out the magnification across the lens. For more information, go to *varilux-s-series.com*.

• **Shamir Golf glasses.** These progressive lenses are designed to provide sharp focus for the distances that are most important to golfers—for the scorecard in their hands…the ball at their feet when putting or teeing off…and the green in the distance. For more details, go to *shamirlens.com*.

MISTAKE #2. Expecting one set of eyewear to do the trick. Even if you can get by with a pair of progressives, you may want to have more than one set of eyewear to get the best possible vision correction for different tasks.

For example, if you spend long hours in front of a desktop or laptop computer, you may need a prescription for single-vision glasses designed specifically for the distance between you and the screen. These glasses will help reduce eyestrain and fatigue, dry eyes and blurred vision.

Very helpful: Measure the distance from the bridge of your nose to your computer screen (laptop or desktop), and take this measurement to your eye exam. The American Optometric Association recommends that the computer screen be placed 20 to 28 inches from the user's eyes.

So-called "computer glasses" can even be made with lenses that selectively filter out harmful blue light, also known as high-energy visible (HEV) light. In the blue and violet part of the light spectrum, HEV is a particularly intense light wave that is emitted from electronic devices, including computers, tablets and smartphones. (Certain bands of blue light, such as blue-turquoise, are found in the sun's UV rays and are beneficial, aiding in color perception and vision sharpness.)

Studies published in the *Archives of Ophthalmology* show that chronic exposure to harmful blue light may damage the retina, the light-sensitive tissue of the eye, and may increase risk for eye disorders such as age-related macular degeneration and cataracts.

Single-vision eyeglasses designed specifically for computer work usually offer the best correction for heavy computer users. If you're over age 40, however, you may want to consider using bifocal computer glasses. This allows you to see the computer screen clearly and read written material on your desk.

For eyeglasses that are designed to block out harmful blue light and glare, you may want to talk to your eye doctor about the following high-quality lenses: Crizal Prevencia

• **No-Glare blue-light lenses,** *crizalusa. com.*

If you are a computer user and prefer progressives, ask your doctor about these well-crafted lenses: Zeiss Business and Gradual RD, *vision.zeiss.com*…and Seiko PCWide, *seikoeyewear.com.*

MISTAKE #3. Opting for fashion over function. Lots of people accept less than excellent vision in exchange for chic eyewear, but this can set you up for trouble.

Examples: If the frames are too big for you, your eyes will not be optimally centered, which could cause visual distortion…if you favor the look of small frames, there may not be enough room for the bifocal or progressive lenses you need.

Either way, you are increasing your risk for blurry vision, headaches and neck pain.

MISTAKE #4. Not getting the right fit. No matter what your prescription and frames, your eyes should sit precisely in the center of the eyeglass (this may not be the center of the frame) to see clearly.

Progressive lenses have the least room for error. If they're off by even a millimeter, you may have trouble seeing at all three distances.

Important: A precise fit is something online retailers can't offer. Sure, purchasing glasses online may save you money, but this could also prevent you from having clear and comfortable vision.

Better approach: Get your exam from an eye-care professional (optometrist or ophthalmologist), and purchase your glasses there for easy follow-up in case there are any problems.

Also: There is no reason to accept thick, "Coke-bottle" type lenses these days. The technology now is available for even very strong prescriptions to be made in relatively thin lenses.

MISTAKE #5. Not getting double-checked. Many people never revisit their eye-care specialists even if they suspect there's a problem.

Good rule of thumb: It may take up to three days to get used to a new prescription and frames—but if you're uncomfortable after that time, go back to the eye-care doctor who gave you the prescription.

Sometimes all it takes is a simple adjustment to your frames. In many people, for example, one ear sits slightly higher than the other, so such an adjustment is needed.

MISTAKE #6. Getting hooked on drugstore readers. You can't beat the price! And these simple reading glasses do offer various levels of magnification.

However, because these readers provide identical magnification in both lenses, they're a viable option only for people who need the same level of vision correction in both eyes—something that rarely occurs.

Many adults have a condition known as anisometropia, in which the eyes require significantly different prescriptions. In fact, a new study has found that nearly one-third of people over age 75 have the condition.

If you have anisometropia and try to get by with drugstore readers, your vision will not be as clear as it would be if you wore prescription readers—not to mention the ill effect it will have on your ability to complete your weekly crossword puzzle!

New Ways to Cope with Low Vision

Ronald Siwoff, OD, an optometrist who works exclusively in the field of low vision. He is director of the Siwoff Low Vision Center, which offers cognitive vision rehabilitation, in Denville, New Jersey, SiwoffLowVision. com.

If you have "low vision," chances are your eye doctor has told you that there's nothing more that he/she can do for you. People who suffer from this condition have difficulty reading street signs or recognizing familiar faces even when they're wearing their glasses (or contact lenses) and there is plenty of light. Images may appear blurry and distorted, for example. Low vision, which affects about 2.4 million Americans, according to the National Eye Institute, typically results from macular degeneration, glaucoma, retinal tears or diabetes-related vision loss.

Good news: If you have low vision, you may be able to significantly improve your eyesight with vision rehabilitation, which includes specialized training and the use of visual devices, such as special glasses or magnification aids.*

Low-vision therapies are offered by some optometrists and specially trained occupational therapists. Check your health plan to find out whether these services are covered.

Low-vision therapy may help you if you have vision loss due to…

MACULAR DEGENERATION (MD)

This condition destroys central (straight-ahead) vision and is a leading cause of vision loss in Americans age 60 and older. People with high blood pressure, elevated cholesterol or obesity are at greater risk for MD. With "wet" MD, vision decreases as a result of swelling caused by leaky blood vessels behind the retina (the light-sensitive tissue located at the back of the eye). "Dry" MD occurs when cells in the macula, which is located in the center of the retina, slowly break down, gradually causing blurriness or a blind spot in your central vision in the affected eye. Dry MD is the more common and less severe form of the disease.

How low-vision rehab can help: If you have low vision caused by MD, the images produced by your eye fall on scar tissue that has accumulated on your retina, making your central vision distorted or blurry. With a new therapy known as retinal image translocation (RIT), a low-vision specialist uses high-quality digital images to locate healthy areas of the retina, where a person has the greatest potential for eyesight.

Through the use of customized lenses with prisms that are placed in your eyeglasses, the retinal image is moved to an area containing healthy retinal tissue and away from scar tissue. This sets a new retinal focal point in a different location. About six weeks after receiving these RIT lenses for your glasses, your brain learns to connect to a different area of the retina and eyesight improves. RIT, which costs about $1,000 for the therapy and glasses if not covered by insurance, is currently available from approximately 30 low-vision specialists in the US. To find an RIT specialist, consult the website of the manufacturer of the RIT testing device, Diopsys, *diopsys.com*, and click on "Patients," then "Find a Doctor" or call the manufacturer at 973-244-0622.

If you do not have access to RIT, telescopic lenses that mount on top of your eyewear, such as those made by Designs for Vision (800-345-4009, *designsforvision.com*)…or Ocutech, Inc. (800-326-6460, *ocutech.com*) may help with seeing things at a distance. Telescopic lenses can also help with near vision. For example, the Ocutech VES-Sport and the Designs for Vision telescopic spectacles can be modified to focus at any distance. Telescopic lenses from Designs for Vision cost $1,000 to $3,000… Ocutech's are $1,300 to $1,800.

GLAUCOMA

This condition is caused by an increase in pressure within the eye that can gradually damage the optic nerve, resulting in vision loss or blindness. (The optic nerve transmits vision information from the eye to the brain.) Catching and treating an increase in eye pressure in the early stages of glaucoma can prevent the loss of peripheral vision that commonly occurs.

How low-vision rehab can help: Because glaucoma can reduce peripheral vision, optical aids are needed to expand the visual field and allow one to see further to the side. Field-expanding reverse telescopic lenses are one option to give a wider field of vision. A second option is conventional prism glasses, which are used for binocular visual problems that produce double vision. A third possibility is a handheld reverse telescopic lens that can be worn around the neck. Reverse telescopes are like the peepholes in most front doors—the field of view is wider but things appear slightly smaller and farther away. These help with seeing distant objects, such as a street sign or bus number.

Glare is a problem for people with glaucoma, so certain types of tinted or polarized lenses will reduce light and sharpen contrast. Amber-, yellow- or brown-tinted lenses are best for blocking glare.

New product: While micro-coated polarized lenses have been available for a long time, polarized lenses, now available in various colors, offer the best of both worlds—the tint to cut glare and the polarized lens to filter light. The color of the lens can improve contrast. Colored polarized lenses are available from KBco (800-722-8776, *kbco.net*).

DIABETIC RETINOPATHY

Diabetic retinopathy, a leading cause of blindness, occurs when high blood sugar over time damages the blood vessels that nourish the retina and also cause the lens of the eye to swell, which blurs vision.

How low-vision rehab can help: Microscopic spectacles help magnify images so people with diabetic retinopathy can see at very close distances, such as reading small print.

Another option is the Clear Image Lens made by Designs for Vision, which fuses together two lenses of different materials that both magnify and can be used for reading and close work. Fused lenses can be used by people who wear eyeglasses or contacts. A third option is telescopic spectacles, which mount on top of your glasses and reduce the visual field—they can be used for reading.

RETINAL DETACHMENT

An injury to the eye, advanced diabetes and/or inflammatory disease can lead to retinal detachment and a loss of sight in that eye.

What happens: When the vitreous (jelly-like) substance in the eye separates from the retina, it may create a retinal tear through which eye fluids may leak. The retina may then pull away from the layer of blood vessels that supply oxygen and nutrients.

A retinal detachment is an emergency. If diagnosed promptly so that the retina can be surgically repaired, vision loss can be prevented. A retinal detachment is almost always preceded by early warning signs that include seeing showers of spots or flashes of light in one eye...or feeling like a shade is being drawn on your vision in one eye. When these signs occur, you must seek emergency treatment to avoid permanent vision loss.

Prism lenses and new prescriptions can improve vision after the retina is attached.

*To find a low-vision specialist in your area, contact Lighthouse International, a nonprofit organization dedicated to fighting vision loss, at 800-829-0500 or *lighthouse.org*.

More from Dr. Siwoff...

High-Tech Aids for Low Vision

Reading on an e-reader, such as a Kindle, or a tablet, such as an iPad, can help people with low vision because these handheld devices allow the user to magnify text on the screen and improve the contrast so type is clearer. If you worry about being able to correctly read street signs while you are walking, you can use a "smartphone" with an app that lets you know when you are approaching key landmarks or traffic lights. This can greatly ease your travel by public transportation—and you can even control certain phones with voice commands so you don't have to use the keyboard. Check with your local cell-phone service providers. Text-enlarging computer software, such as ZoomText, makes letters on your monitor larger than those enlarged by built-in software systems. ZoomText with Speech and Jaws read on screen text aloud.

Nutrients That Reverse Cataracts

Marc Grossman, OD, LAc, holistic developmental/behavioral optometrist, licensed acupuncturist and medical director, Natural Eye Care, New Paltz, New York. He is coauthor of *Greater Vision* and *Natural Eye Care*. NaturalEyeCare.com

Are cataracts no big deal? Cataract surgery has become so quick and effective that many people now ignore opportunities to protect themselves from getting cataracts in the first place. They assume that their eyes can be made good as new one day with some simple surgery—so why worry about it now?

Please don't think that way. While cataract surgery has been well perfected, there is always potential for problems—including retinal detachment. The good news is that there are very simple ways to ward off the cloudiness of cataracts.

Cataracts begin forming in the eyes shortly after you pass the age of 50 and currently affect some 22.3 million Americans. One of the keys to cataract prevention is a combination of diet and supplements that boost the body's level of glutathione, a powerful antioxidant that is distinguished by its ability to interfere with the development of cataracts.

Several studies show that glutathione can prevent the further formation of cataracts and in my own experience, I've seen glutathione reverse the development of cataracts that have already formed. That's pretty extraordinary.

A CLOSER LOOK

To appreciate how glutathione works, it's important to understand how cataracts develop. The lenses in your eyes are made up of proteins arranged in a very orderly way so that light passes easily through them. But as we age—especially if we lapse into poor diets, smoking or too much alcohol or develop diabetes or other chronic diseases—oxygen interacts with these proteins, creating highly reactive free radicals that cause the proteins to clump together. As they do, it becomes more difficult for light to pass through the lenses,

238

and the result is cataracts and vision that's increasingly blurry.

Here's where antioxidants come into play. These substances can protect cells against the effects of free radicals. Vitamins A, C and E are antioxidants that we all know about. Those that are somewhat less well known include beta-carotene, lutein, lycopene and selenium. All of these help to slow the development of cataracts, but when it comes to the eye lens, the most powerful antioxidant is glutathione.

If glutathione—which is made up of three amino acids (cysteine, glycine, glutamic acid)—were easy for the body to absorb, preventing cataracts would be a simple matter of taking regular supplements. Unfortunately, we have the opposite scenario—glutathione is far more difficult to absorb than the more familiar antioxidants.

The solution is twofold. First, eat foods that boost your body's ability to create glutathione, primarily in your liver. The list includes asparagus, eggs, broccoli, avocados, garlic, onions, cantaloupe, watermelon, spinach and strawberries. However, it's doubtful that diet alone can raise glutathione to sufficient levels for preventing the formation of cataracts. I also suggest that you eliminate, or at least reduce, the amount of refined sugar in your diet (including milk sugar, which is found in dairy products) and take supplements, not of glutathione itself but of substances known to encourage production of the body's level of glutathione—N-acetyl cysteine (NAC), alpha lipoic acid and vitamin C. Alpha lipoic acid is particularly effective. You can buy it and NAC at some drugstores, many health-food outlets and online. One brand is DeTox Formula made by Vital Nutrients (800-383-6008, *pureformulas.com*).

NAC and alpha lipoic acid are generally OK for everyone as long as the safe dosage is not exceeded—up to 300 mg for alpha lipoic acid and up to 600 mg for NAC. However, it's best to talk to your doctor before taking either supplement, because they may lower thyroid hormone levels, adversely affect people with certain kidney conditions as well as strengthen the effects of certain medications—including ACE inhibitors for high blood pressure and immunosuppressive drugs.

Ultraviolet light encourages the proteins in the lens to clump together. So in addition to increasing levels of glutathione by eating the foods above and taking supplements, be sure to wear quality sunglasses that block UV light and a wide-brimmed hat whenever you're out on a sunny day.

Questions to Ask Before Cataract Surgery

Brett Levinson, MD, ophthalmologist, Specialized Eye Care, Baltimore. Dr. Levinson is an expert in diseases of the conjunctiva and cornea.

Unlike LASIK surgery, where you can try on a pair of contacts or glasses to simulate what your "new" vision will look like, it is impossible to do this with cataract surgery—so it's important to have an in-depth conversation with your doctor about how you really use your eyes in daily life before you have the surgery.

There are three sorts of artificial lenses—and which you choose determines the kind of vision you will have after surgery. It doesn't matter how good your near or far vision is before surgery, because your eye lens is being replaced, so you have a choice to make about which kind of vision you'd prefer. The good news is that your "new" vision will last forever, because unlike a natural lens, an artificial lens isn't vulnerable to age-related vision changes.

WHICH LENS TO CHOOSE?

If you want cataract surgery, make sure that your doctor offers these three lenses. *Then discuss the pros and cons of each…*

• **Monofocal lens.** This is the most basic and most commonly used lens because it is covered by medical insurance. It is a single-focus lens, meaning that it allows your eye to focus sharply either near or far—your choice. So with this sort of lens, you can opt to improve distance vision only, which means that you will probably still need glasses for up-close vision…or, if having sharp up-close vision without glasses is more important to you, you can have your eyes focused for near vision, but you'll probably still need glasses for distance.

A third option: You could put a near-focused artificial lens in one eye and a distance-focused artificial lens in the other—then your brain can blend the two together to improve both your up-close and distance vision (but the experience can be annoying for some). This is called monovision, but perfect 20/20 vision can't usually be achieved. Also, monofocal lenses do not correct astigmatism. So if you have a moderate or severe amount of astigmatism (usually due to an irregularly shaped cornea) before cataract surgery and choose a monofocal lens, you may still need to wear glasses after surgery—two pairs, one for distance and one for reading.

• **Toric lens.** This lens is similar to the monofocal lens—the only difference is that it corrects astigmatism for one type of vision (distance or up-close). You'll still need glasses—but only one pair, for the other type of vision that is not corrected. This type of lens carries an additional out-of-pocket cost—typically about $750 to $1,500 per lens.

• **Multifocal lens.** This is the most advanced type of lens—the design is only about 10 years old—and not all doctors offer it. So if it interests you, be sure to ask about it. This lens corrects both up-close and distance vision (but does not correct astigmatism). Multifocal lenses work by splitting light entering the eye into a near and distance focus. The brain then learns to interpret these images, creating the ability to see well at a distance and close.

The big advantage: Most people with the multifocal lens will not need glasses for most situations. But your eye has to be completely healthy for you to be a candidate—for instance, if you have macular degeneration, the lens won't work properly. And the surgery to implant a multifocal lens demands high precision—there is little room for error, or else your vision could end up blurry or with glare or halos—so make sure you are choosing an experienced eye surgeon who is board-certified. Also, ask how many surgeries he has performed and if you can speak to past patients. Insurance plans don't cover these expensive lenses, which run about $2,500 per eye. If your vision does end up blurry and it bothers you, you can have laser vision-correcting surgery or wear glasses or contacts.

Bottom line: Cataract surgery can leave you very happy with your vision...but for the best chance of that, you've got to really talk thoroughly to your doctor about the options that are open to you and the compromises that they involve. This is one place where you do not want to be surprised!

Better Cataract Surgery Prep

If you're planning to get cataract surgery, you may not need all those pre-op tests. A new study of more than 400,000 patients found that 53% had at least one test, such as blood work, chest X-ray or electrocardiogram, in the month before surgery, even though such health tests are usually not necessary for this common outpatient procedure.

If your doctor orders these tests before cataract surgery: Ask him/her if they are really necessary for you.

Catherine L. Chen, MD, MPH, resident physician, University of California, San Francisco School of Medicine.

No-Stitch Cataract Surgery

The FDA recently approved the first gel sealant for the corneal incision that's required after cataract surgery. In clinical studies, ReSure was more effective than a single suture in preventing eye fluid from leaking through the incision. There were no significant differ-

ences between the gel sealant and suture in eye pain, corneal swelling or inflammation.

James J. Salz, MD, eye surgeon in private practice in Los Angeles.

How to Prevent Glaucoma Vision Loss Before It's Too Late

Harry A. Quigley, MD, A. Edward Maumenee Professor of Ophthalmology and director, Glaucoma Center of Excellence, Wilmer Eye Institute, Johns Hopkins University, Baltimore. HopkinsMedicine.org. Proceeds of the book sales will go to glaucoma research.

Imagine that, as you read this on your computer, the many pixels on the screen begin to stop working, a few at a time...not right in the center, but in clusters all around the screen. It happens slowly, eventually wiping out all but a tiny central spot...which eventually drops out, too. The screen is blank then.

That's a pretty close analogy of what happens when glaucoma runs its course. You'll start losing your peripheral vision first, one eye at a time, and you likely won't even realize that it's happening until much of the damage has been done. The damage is irreversible, but the process can be stopped with early detection and treatment.

ARE YOU AT RISK?

Glaucoma is the second-leading cause of blindness in the world after cataracts, and it mostly affects people as they age past 60. The disease is characterized by dying ganglion nerve cells in the retina, the light-sensitive tissue at the back of the eye that catches the images we see. Once these cells die, they are never replaced, which makes early detection of glaucoma critical.

Among the many different types of glaucoma, the most common is open-angle glaucoma, caused by clogging of the eyes' drainage canals in people who have a wide angle between the iris and cornea. Besides older age, risk factors include genetic predisposition, nearsightedness, higher eye pressure, high and low blood pressure, diabetes and hypothyroidism.

DETECTION

The lack of symptoms is a major reason why glaucoma is often not detected early. And the idea that glaucoma always has something to do with high eye pressure is a prime reason why diagnosis is often missed by eye specialists during regular eye exams. Although high eye pressure is a hallmark of a condition called angle-closure glaucoma, it is not necessarily present in the more common open-angle glaucoma.

Annual eye exams are recommended for people who are over age 60 and anyone with a first-degree relative (parent, sibling or child) who has or had glaucoma. People younger than 60 should consider getting eye exams, including glaucoma screening, every two years.

To ensure that your exams are thorough enough to detect glaucoma, make sure that, besides having eye pressure measured, you receive a side vision test, which examine speripheral vision, or a visual field test, which examines both peripheral and central vision. The optic nerve head or optic disc (a part of the eye where ganglion cells enter the optic nerve) should also be examined by the eye specialist to evaluate the health of those ganglion cells.

TREATMENT

If glaucoma is detected, treatment can prevent further damage by restoring eye-fluid drainage and/or relieving eye pressure. This is accomplished by use of daily eyedrops or a combination of eyedrops and oral medication. Many different types of eyedrops—some known as prostaglandin analogs (such as Xalatan, Lumigan and Travatan Z)...some alpha agonists (such as Alphagan P)...and some carbonic anhydrase inhibitors (such as Trusopt)—are prescribed, depending on glaucoma symptoms that need to be managed. Laser eye surgery or traditional types of eye surgery that relieve pressure and correct blocked drainage ducts are options for people who don't get adequate relief from eyedrops or who experience allergy or severe side effects from medications—but these people still may need to continue using

some form of medication after surgery until eye pressure and drainage aright themselves.

Side effects of eyedrops can include change in color of the iris and eyelid skin, stinging and burning of the eye, blurred vision and related problems. But most people who become lax about eyedrop use don't do so because of side effects. They do so because they forget to use them, sabotaging their fight against glaucoma symptoms.

In a study in which we electronically monitored people who were using eyedrops for glaucoma management. We discovered that, under the best of circumstances, patients were taking their eyedrops only 70% of the time. Of course, eyedrops can't help relieve glaucoma unless they are consistently used.

Helpful: Set up a reminder system. For example, set your cell-phone alarm to alert you when to use the drops.

As for alternative treatments for prevention of open-angle glaucoma beyond early detection and management, scientific evidence shows no association between glaucoma and a person's personal habits, such as diet, use of vitamins and supplements, alcohol consumption and caffeine intake. Altering these behaviors, unfortunately, will not decrease your chances of getting glaucoma or prevent it from getting worse. However, aerobic exercise (20 minutes four times a week) can increase blood flow and reduce eye pressure, which can keep glaucoma from worsening.

WHERE TO GET TREATMENT

Optometrists can diagnose glaucoma and treat it with eyedrops. Ophthalmologists can diagnose it and treat it with a wider range of therapies—eyedrops as well as laser treatments and eye surgery. But whichever type of specialist you consult, make sure that he is up-to-date on how best to detect glaucoma during an eye exam. To find optometrists and ophthalmologists in your area who have specialized training in glaucoma diagnosis and treatment and have been given by glaucoma experts, visit the American Glaucoma Society website at *glaucoma.org*.

Prevent Glaucoma with a Folate Supplement

Study titled "A Prospective Study of Folate, Vitamin B-6, and Vitamin B-12 Intake in Relation to Exfoliation Glaucoma or Suspected Exfoliation Glaucoma," published in *JAMA Ophthalmology*.

Glaucoma is an insidious disease—literally happening before your very eyes undetected, having virtually no symptoms until, in a blink, you've got eye surgery on your plate and you may even be going blind. You may think that, nowadays, glaucoma is easily treatable, but one form of glaucoma, pseudoexfoliation glaucoma (called "PEX" or sometimes just exfoliation glaucoma) is much harder to fix than others. Research from Harvard Medical School, though, is showing that the more folate you get each day, the less likely PEX will develop.

ARE YOU AT RISK?

PEX is caused by pressurized buildup of debris that clogs the eye's ability to drain, and it can lead to cataract formation, destruction of the optic nerve and blindness. PEX can happen because it's in your genes or because your eyes have been exposed to too much of the sun's ultraviolet (UV) light. People who live in some northern parts of the world, such as Scandinavia (possibly because of genes) and higher altitudes (where the thin air encourages more UV-radiation exposure) are also more at risk for this eye disease. People with PEX also have high levels of an amino acid called homocysteine in their blood, tears and eye fluid. Because B vitamins can help keep homocysteine levels in check, some researchers thought that getting enough B vitamins was the key, but the team from Harvard Medical School discovered that it's not quite that simple—it appears that you must get a certain B vitamin in a certain specific way.

UNCOVERING THE PRECISE NUTRITIONAL LINK

To get a clearer picture, the Harvard researchers analyzed information from about 120,000 people from two very large, long-term health study databases, the Nurses' Health Study and the Health Professionals Follow-up Study, with a specific focus on people who were 40 years old or older, were free of glaucoma at the start of the study, had had eye exams within a certain two-year period and had provided information about their dietary habits. They discovered that people who ultimately got PEX were deficient in one particular B vitamin, folate. They also found that, although the amount of folate gotten only from food had little impact on prevention of PEX, getting enough from a supplement made a big difference.

FOLATE IS AN EYE-SAVER

People with the highest intake of folate—at least 335 micrograms (mcg) per day for women and 434 mcg for men—from vitamin supplements had an 83% reduced risk of PEX compared with people who did not take such supplements. The good news is that any high-quality B complex vitamin supplement, which will generally contain 400 mcg of folate, together with a diet rich in green leafy vegetables, fortified whole grains, beans and peas and especially beef liver (if you have a taste for it) will supply you with enough folate to protect you from PEX. You can even find folate supplements that contain 800 mcg or more, but be aware that the daily tolerable upper limit of supplemental folate for adults, according to the Institute of Medicine, is 1,000 mcg. Also, be aware that folate supplements can interfere with the anticancer effectiveness of the drug methotrexate. Speak with your doctor if you take that drug. Folate supplements also aren't well absorbed in people taking antiepileptic drugs or *sulfasalazine* (Azulfidine, used to treat ulcerative colitis), so guidance about folate supplement dosage, in these instances, also should be discussed with a doctor.

We're increasingly being told by medical experts to ditch vitamin supplements and get our nutrients from whole foods. Although I think this is generally sound advice over pill-popping, even if those pills are vitamins, I also think it's important to pay heed to studies like this one that show that a supplement is exactly what's needed to stave off a serious condition. And sight-robbing glaucoma is serious enough in anyone's book!

Glaucoma Care

My ophthalmologist has given me eyedrops to treat my glaucoma. Is there any kind of supplement I also can take? —R.F., Pittsburgh.

Glaucoma occurs when fluid does not drain properly from the inner chambers of the eye, causing a buildup of pressure that can lead to vision loss. Oral supplements can be taken in addition to eyedrops. Magnesium (250 mg twice daily) and vitamin C (1,000 mg twice daily) have both been shown to be effective in treating glaucoma. Reduce the dose if stools become loose.

Mark A. Stengler, NMD, a naturopathic medical doctor and author of *The Natural Physician's Healing Therapies*. He is also founder and medical director of the Stengler Center for Integrative Medicine in Encinitas, California. MarkStengler.com

Medical Marijuana for Glaucoma

Donald I. Abrams, MD, a professor of clinical medicine at the University of California, San Francisco, School of Medicine, chief of hematology and oncology at San Francisco General Hospital and president of the Society for Integrative Oncology.

Marijuana has been found to help reduce eye pressure caused by glaucoma and is approved for this purpose in several of the states that permit its use.

Currently, 20 states and Washington, DC have approved medical marijuana for patients with chronic or debilitating diseases that cause pain, nausea, vomiting, loss of appetite and other serious symptoms.*

Marijuana is unlikely to cause serious side effects—but, like any drug, it's not appropriate for everyone. *Marijuana may…*

•**Lower blood pressure and increase heart rate.** For this reason, it may not be ap-

*Marijuana is approved for medicinal use in Alaska, Arizona, California, Colorado, Connecticut, Delaware, Hawaii, Illinois, Maine, Massachusetts, Michigan, Montana, Nevada, New Hampshire, New Jersey, New Mexico, Oregon, Rhode Island, Vermont, Washington and Washington, DC.

propriate for people with a history of heart problems.

•**Cause unwanted sedation.** The use of marijuana might increase confusion in older adults with cognitive difficulties. Similarly, it shouldn't be used when driving or operating machinery.

Many people wonder about the potential health risks of smoking marijuana, but there's no evidence that the small amounts used for medicinal purposes are likely to increase the risk for lung cancer or serious respiratory diseases.

Consider using a "vaporizer" to take marijuana. Some patients use devices that heat, but don't actually burn, marijuana. Vapors go into a bag and can be extracted only through the mouthpiece. We've found in studies that fewer noxious gases are inhaled when marijuana is vaporized as opposed to smoked.

Be cautious with dosing. Go slowly. Because the potency varies by plant, marijuana can't be standardized in the same ways that medications are standardized in a laboratory. In addition, a patient's sensitivity to marijuana will partly depend on his/her genetic makeup. I recommend patient-titrated dosing—try a small amount…see how you feel…then increase/decrease the dose as needed.

New Ways to Slow, Stop and Perhaps Even Reverse Vision-Robbing Macular Degeneration

Stephen Rose, PhD, chief research officer of the Foundation Fighting Blindness. Dr. Rose is the former director of the Division of Clinical Recombinant DNA Research at the Office of Biotechnology Activities of the National Institutes of Health. Blindness.org

Age-related macular degeneration (AMD), the most common cause of vision loss in people over age 55, has always been considered a difficult—if not impossible—condition to treat.

Now: There is more reason than ever before to be hopeful that this dreaded eye disease, which affects about 10 million Americans, can be slowed, stopped or even reversed.

Exciting new scientific findings…

BREAKTHROUGHS FOR DRY AMD

Dry AMD, which affects about 90% of people with AMD, occurs when the light-sensitive cells in the macula slowly break down, gradually blurring central vision—which is necessary for reading and driving.

There is no treatment for dry AMD, though many drugs are in clinical trials. In the meantime, we now have evidence that certain nutrients can help control the disease, and exciting advances are taking place in stem cell therapy.

•**Nutrients that can help.** The Age-Related Eye Disease Study (AREDS), landmark research conducted by the National Eye Institute, found that a supplement containing high levels of antioxidants and zinc reduced the risk for advanced dry and wet AMD (the latest stages of AMD) in people with vision loss in one or both eyes.

The daily regimen: 500 mg of vitamin C…400 international units (IU) of vitamin E…15 mg of beta-carotene…80 mg of zinc… and 2 mg of copper. People with all stages of AMD were studied. With early-stage AMD, there may be no symptoms or vision loss. The condition is detected when an eye-care professional can see drusen (yellow deposits under the retina) during a dilated eye exam.

Scientists also are studying other nutrients for dry AMD, and there have been several positive reports. For example…

•**Zeaxanthin and lutein.** When 60 people with mild-to-moderate dry AMD took 8 mg a day of zeaxanthin for one year, they reported a marked improvement in vision (more "visual acuity" and a "sharpening of detailed high-contrast discrimination") along with visual restoration of some blind spots, researchers reported in the journal *Optometry*. A group receiving 9 mg of lutein daily along with zeaxanthin also had improvements in vision.

Many supplements that contain all of the nutrients mentioned earlier are available over-the-counter (OTC). But these should not be taken without a diagnosis of large drusen and

monitoring by a doctor—some of these nutrients could be harmful for certain individuals, such as current and former smokers.

•**Stem cell therapy.** Perhaps one of the most remarkable findings ever reported in the literature of AMD treatment occurred earlier this year when new retinal cells grown from stem cells were used to restore some of the eyesight of a 78-year-old woman who was nearly blind due to a very advanced form of dry AMD.

The breakthrough therapy involved the use of human embryonic stem cells, which are capable of producing any of the more than 200 types of specialized cells in the body. New retinal cells grown from stem cells were injected into the patient's retina. Four months later, the patient had not lost any additional vision and, in fact, her vision seemed to improve slightly.

For more information: Go to *clinicaltrials.gov* and search "advanced dry age-related macular degeneration and stem cells."

BREAKTHROUGHS FOR WET AMD

Wet AMD, which affects about 10% of people with AMD, is more severe than the early and intermediate stages of the dry form. It occurs when abnormal blood vessels behind the retina start to grow. This causes blood and fluid to leak from the vessels, and the macula to swell. Because the condition progresses quickly, it requires prompt treatment for the best chance of saving your vision. You are at an increased risk for wet AMD if you have dry AMD in one or both eyes…or you have wet AMD in one eye (the other eye is at risk).

The two standard treatments for wet AMD are the injection of a medication directly into the eye to block the growth of the abnormal blood vessels…and photodynamic therapy, in which a drug that's injected into the arm flows to the abnormal blood vessels in the eye and is activated there by a laser beam that destroys the vessels.

What's new…

•**More affordable drug choice.** The drugs *ranibizumab* (Lucentis) and *bevacizumab* (Avastin), which are injected into the eye, halt or reverse vision loss. However, these drugs have a huge price disparity. Lucentis, which is FDA-approved as a treatment for wet AMD, costs $2,000 per injection, while Avastin, a cancer drug that is used "off-label" to treat AMD, costs $50.

New finding: In a two-year study, both drugs worked equally well, with two-thirds of patients having "driving vision" (20/40 or better).

Another option: Aflibercept (Eylea), also injected into the eye, was approved by the FDA for wet AMD in November 2011. Research shows that every-other-month injections of Eylea (about $1,800 per injection) can be as effective as monthly injections of Lucentis.

Bottom line: You now have three safe and effective AMD treatment options to discuss with your doctor.

• **At-home monitoring.** Monthly monitoring by an ophthalmologist or optometrist for the subtle visual changes that herald wet AMD (or indicate a diagnosed case is worsening) is impractical for many.

New: An at-home system, the ForeseeHome AMD Monitoring Program, was recently approved by the FDA. You look into this lightweight and portable monitor for a few minutes daily. If results indicate a problem, you and your doctor are alerted to schedule an eye appointment.

WHAT IS MACULAR DEGENERATION?

Age-related macular degeneration (AMD) causes progressive damage to the macula, the part of the eye that allows us to see objects clearly. With "dry" AMD, there is a thinning of the macula, which gradually blurs central vision but generally does not cause a total loss of sight. With "wet" AMD, a more severe form of the disease, abnormal blood vessels grow beneath the macula, leaking fluid and blood. Wet AMD often progresses rapidly, leading to significant vision loss or even blindness.

A Diet to Fight Eye Disease

Vitamins reduce risk of macular degeneration, the leading cause of severe vision loss in Americans age 60 and over. A diet rich in vitamins C and E, beta-carotene and zinc lowers risk for the disease. Vitamin E and zinc are especially effective. Vitamin E is found in whole grains, eggs, nuts and vegetable oil... zinc in meat, poultry, fish, whole grains and dairy...vitamin C in citrus fruits and juices, broccoli, green pepper and potatoes...beta-carotene in carrots, spinach and kale.

Redmer van Leeuwen, MD, PhD, Erasmus Medical Center, Rotterdam, The Netherlands, and leader of an eight-year study of more than 4,000 residents of Rotterdam, published in *The Journal of the American Medical Association.*

Calcium and AMD

Calcium supplements are linked to age-related macular degeneration (AMD), we hear from Shan Lin, MD. In a recent study, adults (age 68 and older) who took more than 800 mg of calcium a day were twice as likely to have AMD, a leading cause of blindness in people age 50 and older, as those who didn't take calcium.

Possible explanation: Drusen, fatty yellow deposits beneath the retina that can be a sign of AMD, may accumulate around tiny specks of calcium. If you have risk factors for AMD, such as family history, smoking or age (60 or older), talk to your doctor about the risks and benefits of using calcium supplements.

Shan Lin, MD, professor of ophthalmology, University of California, San Francisco.

Revolutionary Nutrient Therapy For Macular Degeneration

Mark A. Stengler, NMD, licensed naturopathic medical doctor in private practice, Stengler Center for Integrative Medicine, Encinitas, California.

Imagine sitting back in a comfortable chair in your holistic physician's office and providing your body with such a boost of nutrients that you are able to see more clearly after the one-and-a-half-hour treatment session than you could before it. That was what happened to Lou, an 83-year-old patient who had age-related macular degeneration (AMD), a disease in which the macula (part of the retina) degenerates, causing vision loss. Lou had "wet" AMD, the more severe form of the disease in which abnormal blood vessels form, leaking fluid into the macula.

The treatment that helped Lou was intravenous (IV) nutrient therapy, a technique in which vitamins and other nutrients are delivered directly into the bloodstream in an IV solution, flooding the body's cells with higher levels of the nutrients than they would get from ingesting them. IV nutrient therapy can help both wet and "dry" AMD, a less severe form of the disease.

I also use IV nutrient therapy to treat patients with chronic fatigue and heavy metal poisoning. IV nutrient therapy has been found to help viral hepatitis C…heart arrhythmias caused by nutritional imbalances…and neurological diseases, such as Parkinson's. AMD responds particularly well to IV nutrient therapy.

One of the leading practitioners of IV nutrient therapy in the country is Paul Anderson, ND, a professor of naturopathic medicine at Bastyr University near Seattle. He created the IV nutrient therapy for AMD. I trained with Dr. Anderson and now use his protocol with my patients. I spoke to Dr. Anderson about this treatment…

HOW IT WORKS

The eyes' tissues are extremely responsive to nutrients—which is why holistic physicians tell their patients to take antioxidants such as lutein, which has been found to slow the progression of AMD. So just consider what nutrients can do for eye tissue when administered intravenously at up to 100 times the concentration of antioxidants taken orally. While there have been no studies yet on IV nutrient therapy for AMD, patients who have had the treatment report extremely positive results that include restoration of most—but not all—of the vision that had been lost. The therapy can be effective at stopping the disease from progressing further.

First, a patient is cleared for IV nutrient therapy based on a medical exam and blood tests to ensure that the liver and kidneys can handle the treatment. (Patients also are monitored throughout the treatment.) The infusion for AMD includes vitamin C (for its antioxidant properties) and selenium and zinc (minerals that help the body absorb antioxidants), chromium (an element that strengthens blood vessels) and l-carnitine (for its neuroprotective benefits). Dr. Anderson gives patients at least six infusions, usually two a week for the first three weeks. If the patient is age 75 or older or has advanced AMD, he may recommend as many as 12 infusions. Each infusion takes about one-and-a-half to two hours and typically costs $150 to $200. Check to see if your insurance plan covers this type of treatment.

After a patient's nutrient levels have gotten this boost, the patient can maintain any improvement in vision by following a therapeutic regimen of oral supplements combined with a diet high in flavonoids, plant nutrients that have antioxidant properties. This regimen also can be used to help prevent AMD.

Flavonoids are important to eye health because they can neutralize inflammation in the eye. Foods high in flavonoids include beans (red kidney beans, pinto beans), dark-colored fruits (blueberries, cranberries, blackberries) and vegetables (cabbage, onions, parsley, tomatoes). Make these foods a regular part of your diet. *Recommended maintenance supplements include…*

• **A multivitamin** to ensure that patients get many vitamins and minerals that are in the IV treatment.

• **Fish oil that contains the omega-3 fatty acids DHA and EPA.** These help to maintain the healthy structure and function of ocular tissue and keep eye cell membranes fluid and flexible.

Dose: At least 1,000 milligrams (mg) to 2,000 mg daily. Some patients need even more.

• **Eye-health supplement.** These supplements contain nutrients that support eye health.

Brand to try: Eye-Vite (made by KAL and available at health-food stores and online), which contains zinc, beta-carotene, vitamin E and bilberry fruit extract (a rich antioxidant) and other nutrients.

• **Lutein and zeaxanthin,** two carotenoids that benefit macular tissue. The best way to ensure that you get the appropriate amounts of carotenoids is to take them in supplement form.

Dose: 15 mg daily of lutein and 3 mg daily of zeaxanthin with a meal.

• **Taurine and l-carnitine.** These amino acids are beneficial to eye health because they help nerve tissue in the brain conduct impulses needed for vision.

Dose: 500 mg daily of taurine and 1,500 mg daily of l-carnitine.

• **A high-density bioflavonoid supplement.** To ensure that you get enough flavonoids, it is recommended that you take a supplement such as Cruciferous Complete (made by Standard Process, 800-558-8740, *standardprocess.com*), which contains phytochemicals from plants in the Brassica family (vegetables such as kale and brussels sprouts). These vegetables protect against free radicals (disease-causing molecules), help eye function and stimulate the body's cleansing systems. Follow label instructions.

When patients are properly screened for IV nutrient therapy by a physician trained in this treatment, IV therapy is safe. To locate a physician who administers IV nutrient therapy, contact International IV Nutritional Therapy for Physicians (503-805-3438, *ivnutritionaltherapy.com*). This organization helps people find IV nutrient therapists in their areas.

Two New Meds for AMD

A new medication for macular degeneration costs less and works as well as Lucentis, reports Abdhish R. Bhavsar, MD. The medication Eylea (*aflibercept*) treats the wet form of age-related macular degeneration—the major cause of blindness in those over age 55. Eylea can be given once every two months after an initial series of three monthly doses. Eylea costs about $1,850 per dose, compared with $2,000 per dose for Lucentis (which is administered monthly). Both drugs are injected into the eye with a tiny needle.

Abdhish R. Bhavsar, MD, a retina surgeon and director of clinical research, Retina Center of Minnesota, Minneapolis, and a clinical correspondent for the American Academy of Ophthalmology.

Long-Term Treatment for Occlusion

S teroid unblocks retinal veins, restoring vision. Central retinal vein occlusion (vein blockage in the retina) destroys vision. Patients who got an average of two injections into the eye with the steroid triamcinolone were five times more likely to have regained vision after one year than patients who got no injections.

Breakthrough: This is the first long-term treatment for this condition.

Michael S. Ip, MD, associate professor of ophthalmology, University of Wisconsin, Madison, and chair of a study of 271 people.

New Way to Prevent Diabetes-Related Blindness

A fter a year of treatment, almost half of patients with diabetic macular edema (diabetes-related swelling of the central part of the retina) treated with lasers and the injectable drug *ranibizumab* (Lucentis) showed substantial visual improvement—versus 28% of patients treated with lasers alone.

Neil M. Bressler, MD, retina division chief and professor of ophthalmology, Wilmer Eye Institute, Johns Hopkins University School of Medicine, Baltimore, and coauthor of a study of 691 patients with diabetic macular edema, published in *Ophthalmology.*

Diabetes Drug Linked to Vision Loss

Adiabetes drug may be linked to vision loss. The glitazone class of oral medication, which includes *pioglitazone* (Actos), helps control blood sugar. Taking these drugs more than doubled patients' risk for diabetic macular edema (DME), in which fluid buildup in the retina causes progressive vision loss.

Self-defense: If you take a glitazone, see an ophthalmologist yearly to check for DME.

Donald S. Fong, MD, director, clinical trials research, Kaiser Permanente Southern California, Pasadena, and leader of a study of 170,006 diabetes patients.

Color Vision Changes as We Age

Marilyn Schneck, PhD, research scientist, Smith-Kettlewell Eye Research Institute, San Francisco and University of California, Berkeley. Her study was published in *Optometry and Vision Science.*

Do flowers seem less beautiful and rainbows less vibrant than they used to be? Do clothes you used to love seem a little more ho-hum? If your world seems drabber today, you may worry about your attitude—and hey, who knows, maybe you are turning into a curmudgeon!

But there's probably something else going on. It's not that you're getting crabbier with age. Instead, it's likely that your color vision is changing.

That's right. A surprising proportion of seniors experience a marked decrease in the ability to perceive subtle differences in color. This doesn't just affect people's enjoyment of the visual world—it can affect their safety, too, especially since they often do not realize what's happening. *Here's what you should know...*

TWO TESTS FOR AGING EYES

Earlier research suggested that the ability to discriminate among colors decreases with age, but those studies excluded people over age 70 and people who had eye problems normally associated with aging, such as cataracts—meaning that they ignored a significant portion of the population. To address that oversight, the new study included 865 adults who ranged in age from 58 to 102 years old... and the only people excluded were those with a known congenital color-vision deficiency (the red-green color blindness that about 8% of males and 0.5% of females are born with).

The researchers used two proven tests to screen for color-vision changes. First, all the participants completed a test that can detect subtle errors in color discrimination. About one-third of the participants had perfect scores on that test. The remaining two-thirds went on to complete a second test, called the Farnsworth D-15, which was designed to detect color-vision defects severe enough to affect some activities of daily life. (It was assumed that participants with perfect scores on the tougher first test would also get perfect scores on the easier Farnsworth D-15 test.)

Both tests require participants to arrange colors of very slight variations in a particular order. The number and type of errors made is translated into a "color confusion score." A perfect score is zero...a failing score is 30 or higher.

Here's how the study participants did...

• **Overall, 36% of people failed the first test, 21% failed the second test and 18% failed both tests**—much higher percentages than the "up to 8%" usually cited when talking about congenital red-green color blindness.

• **Across the board, failure rates increased markedly as the participants' ages rose.** For instance, on the Farnsworth D-15 test, less than 8% of people under age 65 failed...but more than one-quarter of those in their mid-to-late 70s failed...and nearly half of those age 90 and up failed.

• **The most common problem by far,** accounting for nearly 80% of the abnormalities, was the blue-yellow defect, which makes it hard to distinguish between colors in the blue-yellow section of the spectrum. For instance, blues are easily confused with blue-greens, especially pale ones...and for people with more severe problems, yellows may be confused with violets.

Explanation: This study was not designed to explain why people lose their ability to discern certain colors as they age. However, the researchers noted that most common age-related vision diseases, including macular degeneration, glaucoma and diabetic eye disease, all produce blue-yellow anomalies. Also, with age comes pupillary miosis (a decrease in the size of the pupil), which lets less light into the eye… and yellowing of the lens of the eye (associated with cataracts), which blocks the wavelengths that allow us to perceive blue correctly.

SEE FOR YOURSELF

Why is failing color vision a concern? People who have trouble distinguishing colors may have difficulty carrying out important everyday tasks—such as distinguishing between different-colored medications! And often people are unaware that their color vision has diminished, so they don't know that they need to be on guard against such hazards.

Online test: At your next eye checkup, ask your eye doctor to test you for color-discrimination problems. In the meantime, you can try this online test. The goal is to arrange the colored squares in order by dragging each square into a line, placing each one next to the color it's most similar to. If your score indicates diminished color vision, talk to your doctor about ways to compensate for problems this might cause—for instance, by carefully noting the size and shape (and not just the color) of your various medications, so you don't mix them up.

The Crucial Test Missing from Most Checkups

Katherine Bouton, author of *Living Better with Hearing Loss: A Guide to Health, Happiness, Love, Sex, Work, Friends…and Hearing Aids* as well as *Shouting Won't Help.* She is a member of the board of trustees of the Hearing Loss Association of America, HearingLoss.org, and has had progressive bilateral hearing loss since she was 30.

If you get an annual checkup, you probably assume that you're doing everything you need to do to take good care of your health. But chances are your physicals have not included a test that's crucial to your physical and mental well-being.

Shocking fact: Only about 30% of primary care physicians do a basic screening of their patients' hearing. In fact, most adults haven't had their hearing tested since they were in grade school! For most people with hearing loss, this means their problem (or the severity of their deficiency) can go undetected.

KEEPING IT SIMPLE

Testing for hearing loss is painless and easy. My advice…

•**Start now!** No matter what your age, ask your primary care physician to do a hearing screening during your annual physical. Professional guidelines vary on the frequency for such testing, but I believe that it's important enough to get screened every year—subtle changes can easily go unnoticed if you wait too long between testing.

As an initial screening, your primary care doctor will likely ask you a series of questions such as: "Does your spouse complain that the TV is too loud?" and "Do you find that people often say, 'Oh, never mind. It's not important.'?" The doctor may also snap his/her fingers behind your head or rub his fingers together next to your ear. If you seem to be having trouble hearing, he'll refer you to an audiologist for diagnostic testing. (An otolaryngologist, or ear, nose and throat specialist, may also employ an audiologist who gives hearing tests.)

•**Go to a true professional.** Try to stick to your doctor's referral. Lots of hearing-aid shops employ people who may not have adequate training to accurately diagnose hearing loss. You want to be sure to see an audiologist. They're trained to diagnose, manage and treat hearing and/or balance problems. An audiologist can also fit you with hearing aids.

THE BEST TESTING

When you go to an audiologist, you'll be asked about your general health history, work history, exposure to noise and use of certain medications—drugs such as nonsteroidal anti-inflammatory drugs (NSAIDs), certain antibiotics and loop diuretics (commonly used to treat heart failure) can cause temporary hearing loss...and repeated doses of other drugs, including the cancer drug *cisplatin* (Platinol), can cause permanent hearing loss. *The audiologist will then take you to a soundproof room for the following tests...*

• **Pure-tone test.** This test provides a baseline of the softest level at which you can hear sounds.

What happens: You put on headphones, and the audiologist activates tones at different pitches and loudness. You respond by raising a finger or pressing a button when the tone is heard. The test is given in one ear at a time. If the test is normal, the audiologist will probably send you home. If not, other tests follow.

• **Bone-conduction test.** This test helps identify whether hearing loss originates from the inner, middle or outer ear.

What happens: You will be fit with a headset that has a vibrator placed on the bone behind the ear. This bypasses the ear canal (outer and middle ear) and sends vibrations directly to the cochlea (inner ear). Again, the audiologist will activate tones at different intervals.

If the result is normal or better than the pure-tone test, it suggests the problem is in the middle or outer ear—sound is not getting through to the cochlea. If the result is worse than the pure-tone test, it points to a problem in the cochlea.

• **Speech perception test.**

What happens: While hiding his mouth (so there's no cheating by lipreading), the audiologist reads a list of common two-syllable words (or a recording is played) to determine the lowest level at which you can correctly identify 50% of the words spoken. If you cannot hear 50% of the sounds, the volume is turned up until you can. The test is given in quiet or with noisy background sounds. It helps to determine the extent of hearing loss and the need for a hearing aid.

• **Tympanometry test.** This test helps detect problems in the middle ear. It can reveal tumors, fluid buildup, impacted earwax or a perforated eardrum—all of which can lead to hearing loss.

What happens: The audiologist uses a probe that changes the air pressure in the ear canal and causes a healthy eardrum to easily move back and forth.

Important: While you're being tested, stay still and do not speak or swallow to make sure your results are accurate.

WHAT'S NEXT?

If your audiologist recommends hearing aids, don't panic. Unlike the bulky devices you may have seen in the past, today's hearing aids are comfortable, highly effective—and most are small enough to not be seen when looking at the wearer's face. But they are also expensive—up to $4,000 per aid—and are not covered by insurance.

For people with mild-to-moderate-hearing loss, personal sound amplification products (PSAPs) are a less expensive option (up to $700 a pair). They help in specific situations, such as a noisy restaurant, crowded airport or large lecture hall.

Surprising Ways to Improve Your Hearing

Michael Seidman, MD, director of the Otolaryngology Research Laboratory and the Division of Otologic/Neurotologic Surgery at the Henry Ford Health System in Detroit. Dr. Seidman is coauthor, with Marie Moneysmith, of *Save Your Hearing Now.*

Aside from protecting your ears from blasting stereos and jackhammers, there's not much you can do to control what happens to your hearing, right? Wrong!

It's true that genetic and environmental factors (such as loud noises) are usually what cause hearing loss. But most people have far more ability to prevent hearing loss—or even improve their hearing—than they realize.

Here's why: Most problems with hearing begin when the hair cells located in the cochlea, or inner ear, don't work well or stop functioning and die. Improving blood supply to the inner ear and tamping down inflammation within the body are among the strategies that may help keep your hearing sharp.

At first glance, you wouldn't think that the steps below would have anything to do with your hearing. But they have a lot to do with it.

Here's my advice for improving your hearing or keeping it intact…

CHECK YOUR MEDS

If you're having trouble hearing, see an otolaryngologist (ear, nose and throat specialist) or audiologist for an evaluation—and ask your doctor about the medications you take. Among the many medications that are "ototoxic"—that is, they can lead to hearing loss…

• **Antidepressants** such as *fluoxetine* (Prozac) and *amitriptyline*.

• **Antibiotics,** such as erythromycin, gentamicin and tetracycline.

• **Nonsteroidal** anti-inflammatory drugs (NSAIDs), such as aspirin and *ibuprofen* (Motrin).

If medication is causing your hearing loss, stopping the drug or switching to a new one, under your doctor's supervision, may improve your hearing.

For a list of drugs that can cause hearing loss: Go to the hearing loss resource website, nvrc.org (click on Hearing Loss, then Ototoxic Drugs for a downloadable PDF).

GET THE RIGHT NUTRIENTS

Certain nutrients are known to promote blood flow and help fight inflammation throughout the body—including in the ears.

To ensure that you have adequate levels of such nutrients, consider taking targeted supplements to protect your hearing. Among those that are beneficial are alpha lipoic acid, acetyl-L-carnitine, L-glutathione and CoQ10. Taking these supplements may help slow hearing loss and protect against damage from loud noises.

What to do: To determine which supplements (including doses) are best for you, consult an integrative physician. To find one near you, contact the Academy of Integrative Health and Medicine at aihm.org.

LOOK AT YOUR LIFESTYLE

Other ways to increase your odds of keeping your hearing sharp as long as possible…

• **Chill out.** If you're late for a meeting and stuck in traffic, your stress levels will probably climb. But what's that got to do with your hearing? Quite a lot, actually.

Research has now shown that brain chemicals called dynorphins respond to stress by triggering inflammation in the brain—and in the inner ear. Inflammation not only exacerbates hearing loss but also hearing-related problems such as tinnitus.

What to do: Setting aside time each day for anything that alleviates tension—be it daily meditation, yoga or listening to restful music—may reduce your stress levels…and improve your hearing or help prevent hearing loss.

Surprising new research: Chewing gum may curb hearing loss in some cases—perhaps by distracting the brain from stress that may be interfering with the brain's processing of sound.

• **Keep off the pounds.** Evidence is continuing to mount that the more a person is overweight, the greater his/her risk for hearing loss. What's the link? Factors closely related to obesity, such as high blood pressure, are believed to restrict blood flow to the inner ear.

What to do: Both men and women should aim for a body mass index (BMI) of 18.5 to 24.9.

• **Get enough exercise.** In recent research, women who walked at least two hours a week had a 15% lower risk for hearing loss, compared with those who walked less than one hour a week. The hearing protection conferred by exercise is also believed to apply to men.

What to do: To protect your hearing—and perhaps even improve it—spend at least two hours a week doing exercise, such as brisk walking.

• **Avoid cigarette smoke.** Smoking is bad for the lungs, the heart and many other parts of the body. But the ears? Absolutely! In a study of adults ages 48 to 92, smokers were more likely than nonsmokers to have hearing impairment. And though it's not well known, even nonsmokers who live with smokers (this includes cigar and pipe smokers, too) are more likely to have hearing loss, suggesting that secondhand smoke can cause damage that impairs hearing.

What to do: Kick the tobacco habit—and encourage family members to do the same.

GETTING ENOUGH ZS

Sleep apnea, a disorder marked by chronic breathing pauses during sleep, has been recently linked to a 90% increased risk for low-frequency hearing loss (difficulty hearing conversation on the phone is a hallmark) and a 31% increased risk for high-frequency hearing loss (this often makes it hard to understand higher-pitched sounds, such as a woman's voice).

The results are preliminary, but some researchers believe that sleep apnea may trigger hearing loss due to poor blood flow to the cochlea, or inner ear.

What to do: If you snore (a common symptom of sleep apnea), see a doctor to determine whether you have sleep apnea and ask whether you should also have your hearing tested. If you have sleep apnea, it's possible that treating it will improve your hearing.

Self-Test for Hearing Loss

David Foyt, MD, associate professor of clinical surgery in the divisions of otolaryngology and neurosurgery, Albany Medical Center.

Nora Perkins, MD, department of surgery, division of otolaryngology, Albany Medical Center.

Suddenly not being able to hear as well as usual is frightening. Does it mean you are going deaf or becoming hard of hearing? Not always—in fact, not usually, and now new research has identified an easy way to get reassurance without having to visit a doctor.

Here's how the test works. If you have a plugged ear or experience sudden difficulty hearing in one ear, hum a note. If you hear the hum in the "sick" ear, this indicates you probably have a conductive hearing loss that will likely get better on its own. Hearing it

in the other side may indicate a more serious nerve hearing loss—if this condition lasts longer than just a few days, schedule a visit with your doctor for evaluation. Hearing it in the midline means hearing is similar in both ears and should be normal.

Common Vitamin Protects Against Hearing Loss

In an 18-year study of 51,529 men, those age 60 and older with the highest intake of the B vitamin folate (folic acid) had a 21% lower risk for hearing loss than men of the same age who consumed the least folate.

To protect your hearing: Eat folate-rich foods, such as spinach, chickpeas, sunflower seeds and fortified cereals, daily.

Caution: Consuming more than 800 mcg of folate daily has been linked to higher risk for colon cancer. Researchers do not know why folate appears to protect hearing nor whether the nutrient would help prevent hearing loss in women.

Josef Shargorodsky, MD, otolaryngologist, Massachusetts Eye and Ear Infirmary, Boston.

This Drug Could Be Causing Your Hearing Loss

Robert Steven Gold, RPh, a hospital pharmacist and affiliate instructor of clinical pharmacy at Purdue University in West Lafayette, Indiana. He is the author of *Are Your Meds Making You Sick?*—a book that examines several adverse drug reactions.

Sudden hearing loss could actually be caused by a drug you're taking...*

You might notice that you're having trouble hearing high frequencies (high music notes, women's voices, etc.) or that everything sounds a little "muddy."

Possible cause: *Furosemide* (Lasix), a diuretic that's often used to treat high blood pressure and swelling in the feet and/or legs. At high doses, it can cause a loss of potassium, which can impair the hair cells in the inner ear and the nerves that transmit sounds to the brain.

Most cases of ototoxicity (damage to the inner ear) occur in patients who take the drug intravenously. But it can also occur with standard oral doses, particularly when furosemide is paired with other drugs (such as the painkillers Celebrex and Advil) that also have hearing loss as a side effect.

My advice: If you're taking furosemide and notice any degree of hearing loss—or you suddenly develop tinnitus (ringing sounds in the ears)—see your doctor right away. Hearing loss is a rare side effect, but the damage can be permanent if the drug isn't stopped quickly enough. Careful monitoring is crucial, especially when using a high dose.

*Never stop taking a prescribed drug or change your dose without consulting your doctor.

Say What? A Surprising Link to Hearing Loss for Women

Derek J. Handzo, DO, an otolaryngology resident, and Kathleen Yaremchuk, MD, the chair of the department of otolaryngology–head and neck surgery at Henry Ford Hospital in Detroit. They are coauthors of a study on diabetes and hearing loss presented at a recent Triological Society Combined Sections Meeting.

Needing to turn up the volume on the TV or radio yet again…straining to catch a dinner companion's words in a crowded restaurant…having trouble identifying background noises. It's normal to notice an increase in such experiences as we get older.

But: A new study has highlighted an important and often overlooked risk factor that can make age-related hearing loss among women much worse than usual—diabetes that was not well controlled.

Researchers reviewed the medical charts of 990 women and men who, between 2000 and 2008, had had audiograms to test their ability to hear sounds at various frequencies…participants also were scored on speech recognition. Study participants were classified by age, gender and whether they had diabetes (and, if so, how well controlled their blood glucose levels were).

Results: Among women ages 60 to 75, those whose diabetes was well controlled were able to hear about equally as well as women who did not have diabetes—but those with poorly controlled diabetes had significantly worse hearing. (For men, there was no significant difference in hearing ability between those with and without diabetes, no matter how well controlled the disease was, though this finding could have been influenced by the fact that men generally had worse hearing than women regardless of health status.)

Now hear this: Diabetes also increases the risk for heart disease, vision loss, kidney dysfunction, nerve problems and other serious ailments…so this new study gives women with diabetes yet one more important motivation for keeping blood glucose levels well under control with diet, exercise and/or medication.

If you have not been diagnosed with diabetes: If your hearing seems to be worsening, ask your doctor to check for diabetes—particularly if you have other possible warning signs, such as frequent urination, unusual thirst, slow wound healing, blurred vision and/or numbness in the hands and feet.

Painkillers Can Harm Your Hearing

In a recent finding, women who regularly took *ibuprofen* (such as Advil or Motrin) or *acetaminophen* (Tylenol) at least twice a week had up to a 24% higher risk for hearing loss than women who used the painkillers infrequently. Other studies have found similar effects in men. These pain relievers may damage the cochlea in the inner ear by reducing blood flow or depleting antioxidants.

Self-defense: Limit painkillers to occasional short-term use—but talk to your doctor before making any changes in your medications.

Study of more than 62,000 women by researchers at Harvard Medical School, Boston, published in *American Journal of Epidemiology*.

Don't Feel Ready for a Hearing Aid?

Barbara E. Weinstein, PhD, a professor of audiology and head of the Audiology Program at The City University of New York Graduate Center, where she specializes in hearing loss in older adults, hearing screening, disability assessment and evidence-based practice. She is the author of the textbook *Geriatric Audiology*.

I f you are reluctant (or can't afford) to use a hearing aid, there are dozens of personal sound amplification products (PSAPs), over-the-counter devices that can help you hear a little better but don't cost as much as hearing aids, which run up to $3,000 each.

NOT QUITE A HEARING AID

Hearing aids are recommended for those who have been diagnosed with hearing loss by an audiologist. PSAPs, which come in many shapes and sizes, often resembling a Bluetooth headset, are meant to amplify sounds in situations where hearing is difficult, such as large gatherings or noisy restaurants.

In reality, it's not an either-or choice. Only 20% to 25% of people who could benefit from a hearing aid actually use one. PSAPs, with their lower price and availability on the Internet, in pharmacies and in stores such as RadioShack, can serve as "training wheels" for people who want to hear better but hesitate to shell out big bucks for a hearing aid.

Important: The hearing aids sold by audiologists are approved by the FDA as medical devices and must meet certain standards

related, for example, to frequency ranges and distortion. PSAPs, on the other hand, are classified as electronic products. They aren't subject to FDA review, so you can't assume that they'll work for you. However, some PSAPs already rival the quality of "official" hearing aids and will keep getting better as technology improves.

KNOW WHAT YOU NEED

Before you look into PSAPs, get tested by an audiologist. About 14% of adults in their 50s, one-quarter in their 60s and more than one-third of those age 65 and older have some degree of age-related hearing loss. But do not assume that your hearing is normal—or that hearing loss is inevitable.

You may think that your hearing is becoming impaired because of your age when, in fact, it may be due to a medical issue, such as infection, abnormal bone growth, an inner-ear tumor or even earwax—all of which can be treated and sometimes reversed.

If your hearing loss is not related to a medical issue, a PSAP may be appropriate in the following situations…

• **You have trouble hearing the TV.** It is a common complaint but fairly easy to overcome. Inexpensive earbuds or a headset that merely amplifies the sound may be all that you need. Some products are wireless or have long cords that plug directly into the TV.

• **You have trouble hearing in quiet environments.** Speech can sound muffled or be entirely unintelligible if you have age-related hearing loss. Even if you can easily hear background sounds (such as music), you might struggle with the high-frequency sounds that are characteristic of speech.

If you plan to use a PSAP mainly at home or in other quiet settings (such as a museum or a hushed restaurant), look for a device that amplifies high frequencies more than low ones. You'll hear voices more clearly without being overwhelmed by the volume of sounds.

Warning: Some inexpensive products boost both high and low frequencies indiscriminately—avoid them. Your best choice will be a product that allows you to make adjustments and fine-tune it in different settings.

• **You have trouble hearing in noisy environments.** Even mild hearing loss can make it hard to hear voices over the din of clattering plates, a chattering crowd and background music. A simple amplifier won't work because it will make all of the sounds louder.

Better: A device that amplifies the sounds you want to hear while filtering out the rest. Look for a PSAP that has a directional microphone that will pick up speech while muting noise…noise cancellation to filter out low-frequency background sounds…volume control…and multiple channels that are suitable for different sound environments.

• **You're on the fence.** It's common for people to put off getting a hearing aid because of embarrassment or cost. (Hearing aids aren't covered by Medicare or most insurance plans.) You might be telling yourself, "Maybe I'll get one when I'm a lot older."

Important: Don't wait too long. The parts of the brain associated with hearing become less active when they aren't used. You need to hear sounds to keep this brain circuitry working and actively processing speech.

You might want to use a PSAP while you're making up your mind about hearing aids. Even if you get a PSAP that just boosts volume, it will keep the brain signals firing. In my opinion, it's reasonable to use one of these devices for a few months or even a few years. You can always buy a hearing aid later.

GREAT PSAP MODELS

Personal sound-amplification products you may want to consider…

• **For TV listening.** Sennheiser Wireless RS Headphones look like old-fashioned stereo headsets, but they let you turn up the sound. $100 to $450, *sennheiser.com.*

• **For more volume in loud environments.** Able Planet Personal Sound 2500 AMP is packed with high-end electronics to reduce background noise while amplifying sounds you want to hear (such as voices). $900 a pair, $500 for one, *ableplanet.factoryoutletstore.com.*

• **For more volume in both loud and quiet places.** The Bean Quiet Sound Amplifier by Etymotic provides amplification of soft speech without distorting sounds. $550 a pair, $300 for one, qsabean.com.

• **For more volume at a low cost.** Dozens of affordable products mainly increase volume without other features.

Example: Sonic SE5000 SuperEar Personal Sound Amplifier, a handheld amplifier you can attach to a pocket, belt, hat or purse strap. About $50, *sonictechnology.com.*

All of the PSAP manufacturers listed here offer a money-back guarantee if the product is returned within 30 days.

Fish Reduces Risk for Age-Related Hearing Loss

People over age 50 who eat at least two five-ounce servings of fish per week have a 42% lower risk of developing hearing loss, compared with people who eat less than one serving of fish per week.

Possible reason: Omega-3s may help preserve circulation in the inner ear. Fish that are high in omega-3 fatty acids, such as salmon, sardines and mackerel, provide the greatest benefit.

Paul Mitchell, MD, professor, department of ophthalmology, University of Sydney, Australia, and coauthor of a study of 2,956 people, published in *American Journal of Clinical Nutrition.*

Ignoring Hearing Loss Is Dangerous, Can Lead to Dementia, Depression and More

Virginia Ramachandran, AuD, an audiologist at Henry Ford Hospital in Detroit, and president-elect of the Michigan Academy of Audiology. She is coauthor of *Basic Audiometry Learning Manual.*

For most people, age-related hearing loss, also known as presbycusis, happens so slowly that they don't notice it at first.

In fact, hearing loss actually begins in our late 20s and early 30s, when we lose the ability to hear high pitches, such as that of a buzzing mosquito. And by the time we reach our 70s, about half of us have diagnosable hearing loss.

What you may not know: Despite the high incidence of hearing loss, only about two in every five adults over age 65 with hearing loss use hearing aids. Plenty of people resist getting a hearing aid because they fear that it will make them look old, be too complicated to use and/or cost too much money.

Now: Based on recent research, people with untreated hearing loss have more reason than ever before to consider getting a hearing aid.

HEALTH HAZARDS

While most people consider hearing loss a mere annoyance, researchers are now discovering that it may increase one's risk for…

•**Dementia.** In a study of 639 men and women (ages 36 to 90) published in the *Archives of Neurology*, the risk of developing dementia was two, three and five times higher in those with mild, moderate and severe hearing loss, respectively, than in those with normal hearing.

Researchers do not have an explanation for the association between hearing loss and dementia—and they point out that the link does not prove cause and effect.

However, it's possible that damage to the cells involved in hearing may be a sign that damage has also occurred to nerve cells that are responsible for cognitive functions, including memory. Hearing loss also can cause social isolation, which contributes to the risk for dementia.

•**Depression.** Significantly more older adults with hearing loss who did not wear hearing aids reported feelings of sadness and depression for two or more weeks during a one-year period than their peers who wore hearing aids, according to a study from the National Council on Aging.

Possible reason: Depression may be caused or worsen in people with hearing loss who withdraw from social interactions.

•**Injury.** Hearing loss is a safety hazard, especially for pedestrians who may have trouble hearing oncoming traffic and for drivers who rely on their ability to hear to prevent collisions. It also affects a person's ability to hear a phone, doorbell and smoke detector alarm.

DO YOU NEED A HEARING AID?

If you have hearing loss, a loved one may be the first to notice it. *In addition, if any of the statements below applies to you, it may mean that you have hearing loss…*

•**You frequently ask, "What?"** in conversations.

•**You have trouble following conversations.**

•**Everyone around you seems to mumble.**

•**You're always turning up the volume on the TV.**

•**You can hear someone talking,** but not what the person is saying.

•**It's especially difficult for you to hear women and children,** both of whom have higher-pitched voices and generally speak with a lower volume than men. Higher-pitched voices are the most difficult to hear.

BEST HEARING AID OPTIONS

Many of today's hearing aids are highly sophisticated. *For example…*

Cutting-edge product: One of the newest hearing aids available is the SoundBite Hearing System, which allows sound to travel via the teeth to the inner ear. A small microphone in the ear canal transmits sounds to a wireless unit behind the ear, which sends a signal to a device that fits over the back teeth. The device converts the signals into vibrations, rerouting sound to the inner ear. SoundBite is especially helpful for people with hearing loss in one ear or who have conductive hearing loss—a problem in the middle or outer ear.

Main types of hearing aids…

•**Behind-the-ear (BTE) hearing aids,** which are generally larger than other types of hearing aids, are the traditional kind that hooks over the top of your ear and sits behind it. The hearing aid picks up sound, amplifies it and carries the amplified sound to an ear mold that fits inside your ear canal. The large size allows for directional microphones and easier adjustment of volume and battery changing.

The BTE hearing aid is appropriate for almost all types of hearing loss and does the best job of amplifying sound for people with severe hearing loss. Siemens offers a couple of rechargeable BTE hearing aids for mild-to-moderately severe hearing loss.

Typical cost: $500 to $2,000 per ear.

• **Open-fit models are among the newer aids available today.** They are smaller than BTE aids and suitable for mild-to-moderate hearing loss. Generally placed behind the ear, these aids leave the ear canal mostly open and are less visible than BTE models. Sound travels from the open-fit hearing aid through a small tube or wire to a tiny dome or speaker in the ear canal.

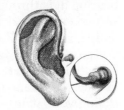

Typical cost: $1,000 to $2,500 per ear.

• **In-the-ear (ITE) hearing aids are custom-made to fit in the outer ear.** ITE devices may pick up background sounds such as wind, since the microphone sits at the outermost portion of the ear. But the batteries tend to last longer than other types of hearing aids and are easier to change, especially if you have arthritis in your fingers.

Typical cost: $1,200 to $2,500 per ear.

• **In-the-canal (ITC) hearing aids** fit farther into the ear canal than ITE aids. This style is best for mild-to-moderate hearing loss. It is hardly visible and is easy to use with the telephone. The small size makes adjustments, including battery changes and volume control, difficult for some people. The device may not fit well in smaller ears.

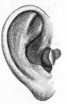

Typical cost: $1,300 to $2,500 per ear.

• **Completely-in-the-canal hearing aids** are custom-molded and best for mild-to-moderate hearing loss. This is the least noticeable type of hearing aid and the least likely to pick up background noises such as wind. It also works well with telephones. But the small batteries require frequent replacement.

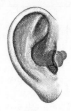

Typical cost: $1,300 to $3,000 per ear.

Main hearing aid manufacturers: Oticon, Phonak, Starkey, ReSound, Widex and Siemens.

Important: There are many over-the-counter devices that simply amplify sound. However, hearing aids are usually preferable because they are customized for an individual's specific degree and type of hearing loss, allowing them to be programmed for optimal hearing improvement.

If you are having difficulty hearing: See an audiologist. You can find one at the American Academy of Audiology consumer website at *howsyourhearing.org*. An audiologist can help you select the best hearing aid for you and explain how to properly use and maintain it. If the audiologist suspects that you may have an undetected medical condition that is causing your hearing loss, you will be referred to a physician.

WHAT ABOUT COST?

Some people don't get hearing aids because of their high cost—about $500 to $3,000 per ear.

Recent finding: People who have insurance plans that cover the entire cost of hearing aids purchased them seven years earlier, on average, than those who had partial or no insurance, according to a study conducted at Henry Ford Hospital in Detroit.

But only about one-third of health insurance policies cover the cost of hearing aids. Medicare does not. Health insurance from the Veterans Administration does cover the cost, and the Lions Club has a program that provides hearing aids to people who can't afford them.

You can use a health savings account or flexible spending account to pay for hearing aids with pretax funds, or you can deduct the cost on your tax return (check with your tax preparer for details).

Hearing Aid Bargains

Jim Miller, an advocate for older Americans, writes "Savvy Senior," a weekly information column syndicated in more than 400 newspapers nationwide. Based in Norman, Oklahoma, he also offers a free senior e-news service at SavvySenior.org.

H earing aids have become very expensive. *But you can reduce or even eliminate the cost...*

• **Hearing aid bargains.** Most Costco stores sell top brands of hearing aids for 30% to 50% less than other warehouse chains, hearing aid dealers and audiologist offices. They offer high-quality devices under the brands Kirkland Signature (the Costco house brand), Rexton, ReSound, Bernafon and Phonak at prices ranging from $500 to $1,800 per ear. This includes an in-store hearing test, fitting by a specialist and follow-up care.

Also, websites including *embracehearing. com* and *audicus.com* sell high-quality hearing aids directly from the manufacturer for as little as $400 or $500. But you will need to get a hearing evaluation from a local audiologist first, which can cost between $50 and $250.

• **Check your insurance.** Most private health insurers don't cover hearing aids, but a few do. UnitedHealthcare, for example, offers custom-programmed hearing aids through hi HealthInnovations (*hihealthinnovations.com*) for $599 to $899 each to people enrolled in its employer-sponsored individual or vision plans.

Some other insurers contribute a specified amount toward hearing aids, typically $500 or $1,000, or give a discount if you purchase hearing aids from a contracted provider.

Three states—Arkansas, New Hampshire and Rhode Island—require insurers to cover hearing aid costs for adults, and 20 states require it for children. Eligibility and amounts vary by state, and certain insurance plans are exempt.

Original Medicare (Parts A and B) and Medigap supplemental policies do not cover hearing aids, but some Medicare Advantage (Part C) plans, which are obtained through private insurers, include hearing aids. To find a plan that covers hearing aids, call 800-633-4227 or go to *medicare.gov/find-a-plan*.

If you are a current or retired federal employee or if a member of your family is enrolled in the Federal Employees Health Benefits Program, some insurers provide coverage, including a Blue Cross and Blue Shield plan that covers up to $2,500 every three years.

Medicaid programs in most states cover hearing aids. Contact your state's Medicaid program or visit *medicaid.gov*.

• **Benefits for veterans.** The Department of Veterans Affairs provides hearing aids and replacement batteries free of charge to veterans if their hearing loss is connected to military service or linked to a medical condition treated at a VA hospital. Veterans also can get free hearing aids through the VA if hearing loss is severe enough to interfere with activities of daily life. Call 877-222-8387 or visit *va.gov*.

Assistance programs: If your income is low, there are various programs that provide financial assistance for hearing aids. Check by calling your state vocational rehabilitation department (see *parac.org/svrp.html* for contact information). Also contact Sertoma (*sertoma. org*), a civic service organization that provides a list of state and national hearing aid assistance programs. Or call the National Institute on Deafness and Other Communication Disorders at 800-241-1044, and ask for a list of financial resources for hearing aids.

Ear Implants Help Depression

C ochlear implants help more than hearing. A cochlear implant is a small electronic device that boosts hearing in someone who is deaf or severely hard of hearing. Seniors with the implants reported better quality of life, lower rates of depression and improved thinking skills. The number of patients free of depression was 59% before receiving a cochlear implant and 76% one year after receiving the device.

Study led by researchers at Assistance Publique-Hôpitaux de Paris, France, published in *JAMA Otolaryngology–Head & Neck Surgery*.

Finally...Real Relief for Tinnitus

Murray Grossan, MD, an ear, nose and throat specialist in private practice in Los Angeles with more than 30 years of experience in treating tinnitus and hearing loss. Dr. Grossan is the author of *The Whole Person Tinnitus Relief Program*, an e-book available at DrGrossanTinnitus.com.

It's estimated that about one in 10 Americans hears noise—ringing, buzzing, roaring, hissing, whooshing or clicking sounds—when no external sound is present. This condition, known as tinnitus, can be a minor annoyance, or the sound can be loud enough or persistent enough to make concentration, sleep and communication impossible. The torment even drives some sufferers to suicide.

About 20% of people with tinnitus seek medical help. But far too many are told there's nothing that can be done and they should "learn to live with it"—a hopeless prognosis that only compounds their suffering.

Recent development: A panel of leading experts from the American Academy of Otolaryngology—Head and Neck Surgery Foundation has developed new diagnostic and treatment guidelines, which will help tinnitus sufferers get much better care. *What you need to know...*

DETERMINING THE CAUSE

When you see a doctor for tinnitus, he/she should start with a physical examination and detailed medical history to determine if it's caused by a treatable condition, such as...

• **Ménière's disease.** Intense vertigo is the most dramatic symptom of this condition, but hearing loss and tinnitus can be symptoms as well. Diuretics or steroids, taken as needed, may help the disease and relieve the tinnitus.

• **Cochlear hydrops.** This condition, caused by increased fluid pressure in the inner ear, is like Ménière's disease but without the vertigo. It can often be cured by reduced intake of salt and use of a diuretic, taken as needed, to eliminate fluid, which in turn alleviates the tinnitus.

• **Temporomandibular joint (TMJ) syndrome,** whiplash or head or shoulder muscle injury. These issues can activate nerve signals

that the brain interprets as sound. Physical therapy, chiropractic treatment and/or orthodontia may help these problems and the tinnitus.

• **High blood pressure.** Elevated blood pressure alters the inner ear chemistry to cause tinnitus in some people. Effective treatment of hypertension may stop the tinnitus.

• **Anxiety and depression.** Tinnitus aggravated by anxiety and depression may be alleviated by therapy for these conditions.

• **Excessive earwax.** Removal of the wax stops the tinnitus.

• **Medications.** Most commonly, nonsteroidal anti-inflammatory drugs (NSAIDs), such as aspirin, *ibuprofen* (Advil, Motrin) or *naproxen* (Aleve), can cause tinnitus and should be stopped if suspected.

Note: Low-dose aspirin (81 mg), often used for heart health, is not known to cause tinnitus.

What a physical exam should include: A hearing test (audiometry). Hearing loss is common with tinnitus, and a hearing aid sometimes makes it better (see "Sound therapy" below).

More advanced tests like magnetic resonance imaging (MRI) are usually not required. But when tinnitus and hearing loss are limited to one side, such tests may be needed to rule out a benign tumor on the acoustic nerve—a rare condition known as acoustic neuroma.

Many tinnitus cases, however, are "idiopathic"—there's no identifiable underlying disease.

TREATMENTS THAT HELP

The expert panel approved the following two therapies for idiopathic tinnitus. *Patients can try both at the same time or do them individually...*

• **Cognitive behavioral therapy (CBT).** This type of therapy aims to alter negative thinking about tinnitus and its effects on your life. When the patient understands tinnitus better (for example, "It's not my fault"), it takes away some of the mystery and reduces associated distress. To find a CBT therapist, go to the website of the American Tinnitus Association.

• **Sound therapy.** Just as the ticking of a clock in a quiet room becomes inaudible when there's traffic in the street outside, background sound can reduce or relieve tinnitus. This masking effect is the simplest form of sound therapy. To mask the tinnitus sound, the patient wears earbuds that deliver white noise, nature sounds or low-volume music. In other forms of sound therapy, enjoyable sounds or music is mixed with the sound that mimics a patient's tinnitus.

Simply getting a hearing aid to correct hearing loss is also a type of sound therapy—restoring normal perception of external sound often makes the phantom noise much less noticeable.

According to recent sound therapy research, such treatments reduce tinnitus over time, possibly by retraining the brain circuits that generate the perceived sound.

You can develop your own sound therapy program by using apps such as Nix Tinnitus Ear Amp at *bxtel.com* ($9.99, iOS)...and Tinnitus Balance at *phonak.com* (free, iOS and Android).

Important: Stress does not cause tinnitus, but sufferers will tell you that it can worsen it. Do all you can to keep stress levels in check.

Helpful: Counting breaths.

What to do: As you inhale slowly, count from one to four. Then, as you exhale, count from one to six. The longer exhale makes this exercise particularly relaxing. Repeat these breaths for about a minute, every waking hour for several weeks, to establish the habit. Then you can use these exercises any time you need to de-stress.

WORTH TRYING?

The evidence is limited or mixed for the following treatments, and the recent guidelines advise against most of them. *But some people report that these approaches help, so you may want to consider trying them...*

• **Supplements.** Numerous studies suggest possible benefits of supplements for tinnitus. For example, magnesium may improve hearing loss, and alpha-lipoic acid may protect the ears against damage from loud noise or drug toxicity. Also, some research has shown an association between tinnitus and low levels of B vitamins or other nutrients. In practice, some clinicians report improvements in patients

who take the supplements described above as well as coenzyme Q10, zinc, selenium and/or other antioxidants that are important for hearing chemistry.

• **Alternative and experimental approaches.** Acupuncture has been used for tinnitus since the fifth century BC, but scientific reviews have found no conclusive evidence that it works (the panel made no recommendation for or against this treatment). Repetitive transcranial magnetic stimulation (rTMS), in which external magnetic fields are applied in an attempt to change brain function, is now being offered for tinnitus in some clinics, but the FDA has not approved the treatment for this condition and research has not yet shown evidence that it offers long-term benefit.

If you start experiencing tinnitus after starting a new medication, talk to your doctor. In most cases, the tinnitus will go away when you stop taking the drug, lower the dose or switch to a different medication.

EAR PROTECTION

Loud noise is not only the main cause of tinnitus, it also can increase the risk that existing tinnitus will get worse.

Use some form of ear protection, such as earmuffs or earplugs, when you are in any very noisy environment. This includes any time you are around noisy outdoor equipment, such as lawn mowers, leaf blowers and snowblowers, as well as household appliances, such as vacuum cleaners and blenders.

Safe Earwax Removal for Better Hearing

Murray Grossan, MD, an otolaryngologist at Tower Ear, Nose & Throat in Los Angeles. GrossanInstitute.com

Richard M. Rosenfeld, MD, MPH, professor and chairman of otolaryngology, Long Island College Hospital and State University of New York-Downstate, both in Brooklyn, and editor-in-chief of Otolaryngology—Head and Neck Surgery.

Earwax lubricates the ear's delicate skin and traps germs and debris. When you talk or eat, jaw motion pushes excess wax out of the ear canal to the point where it is visible. It can then be wiped away with a damp cloth or swab.

Headphones that fit over the ear do not stimulate earwax production, but small ear-buds that slide into the ear canal could. Any-thing that is worn in the ear canal, such as earbuds or hearing aids, can cause earwax to accumulate.

Warning: Using a cotton swab to clean in-side ears can also push wax deeper into the ear canal.

Plus: Sometimes the ear gets clogged as wax builds up. Do not try to dig wax out of the ear canal—this could abrade the skin, inviting infection…compact wax further…or puncture the eardrum. *Better…*

•**Wax may get stuck if it's too dry.** To soft-en it, once a week use an eyedropper to place two drops of unscented baby oil in each ear.

•**Clogs may occur if you secrete excess wax or have narrow ear canals.**

To unclog: Tilt your head sideways, clogged ear up, and drip an eyedropperful of body-temperature water into the ear. Wait five min-utes…tilt to the other side to drain…suction out the ear with an infant nasal aspirator. Re-peat twice daily for up to three days. If you want, you can try an over-the-counter product that dissolves earwax—but usually this is un-necessary because earwax is water-soluble.

See a doctor if…the above methods don't help, hearing is impaired or you hear ringing. Your doctor can remove excess wax with ir-rigation, suction and/or a tiny looped instru-ment using a magnifier for guidance. Also, to minimize infection risk, leave earwax removal to a doctor if you have a perforated eardrum or diabetes.

Cautions: Never irrigate an ear with a den-tal device, such as Water Pik—the pressure could rupture the eardrum. Never try ear can-dling, a procedure that involves placing one end of a hollow candle in the ear and light-ing the other, supposedly to create suction—it does not work and can cause burns even if done professionally.

Urgent: How Good Is Your Sense of Smell?

Jayant Pinto, MD, associate professor of otolaryngolo-gy–head and neck surgery in the department of surgery at The University of Chicago Medicine, where he specializes in sinus and nasal diseases and olfactory dysfunction.

Alan Hirsch, MD, founder and neurological director of the Smell & Taste Treatment and Research Foundation in Chicago. He is a neurologist and psychiatrist, and author of *Life's a Smelling Success.* SmellAndTaste.org

Can you smell the rose that's under your nose? What about the odor of burn-ing toast? Or the foul smell of spoiled food?

Just as it's common to have fading vision or diminished hearing as you age, many people lose at least some of their ability to smell. In fact, about 25% of adults over the age of 53 have a reduced sense of smell, and the percentage rises to more than 60% in those age 80 and older.

AN EARLY ALERT

You're probably well aware that a decreased sense of smell can affect appetite. People who can't smell and/or taste their food tend to eat less and may suffer from weight loss or nutri-tional deficiencies. *But you might not know that a diminished sense of smell could also be an early indicator of a serious health problem…*

Surprising finding: In a recent study, peo-ple ranging from ages 57 to 85 who lost their ability to smell were more than three times more likely to die within five years than those with a normal sense of smell—the risk of dying was even higher than for individuals diagnosed with lung disease, heart failure or cancer.

This study didn't uncover the exact link be-tween smelling loss and earlier-than-expected deaths. But the risk for neurodegenerative diseases could be a factor. For example, peo-ple who eventually develop Parkinson's or Alzheimer's disease may notice a diminished sense of smell long before they have neuro-logical symptoms.

It's also possible that cellular senescence, the age-related reduction in cell regeneration, affects the olfactory bulb or other parts of the olfactory system before it becomes apparent in other parts of the body.

TEST YOURSELF

Even if you think your sense of smell is fine, some basic testing might show otherwise. In the study mentioned earlier, some individuals who thought they had a good sense of smell actually didn't, while some people who thought they had a problem with their sense of smell actually did well on the smell tests.

How to test yourself…

• **The alcohol test.** Hold an alcohol-swab packet near your belly button and open it up. If your sense of smell is perfect, you will detect the odor. If you can't smell it, raise it higher until you can. Some people won't detect the odor until it's just a few inches from the nose—or not even then. You can do the same test with anything that's strongly scented. The closer the item needs to be for you to smell it, the worse your sense of smell is.

• **Compare yourself to others.** Suspect that you have a problem if you're the only one in the family who doesn't notice the wonderful smell of brownies in the oven. Or if you say "Huh?" when your spouse mentions that the fireplace is smoking or that there's a nasty smell in the refrigerator.

If you think you have a diminished sense of smell: Get evaluated by an otolaryngologist or a neurologist. He/she can determine if your impairment is due to aging or a more serious problem that may have a better outcome if it is detected early.

WHAT YOU CAN DO

So far, a reduced sense of smell can't be restored.* *What can help…*

• **Practice smelling.** German scientists report that it may be possible to improve your sense of smell by smelling more. Spend a few minutes every day sniffing a variety of scents—spices, perfumes, aromatic foods, etc. This approach hasn't been proven, but it could be helpful for some people.

• **Eat a well-balanced diet and take a multivitamin,** which will provide the necessary micronutrients that help slow aging of the olfactory system and promote regeneration.

*Exception: If your loss of smell is due to nasal inflammation—from allergies, chronic sinusitis, etc.—intranasal steroid sprays and antihistamines may restore it.

If you have appetite loss due to a reduced sense of smell…

• **Kick up the seasoning.** Food will not be very appealing if you can't smell or taste it. To make your dishes as flavorful and aromatic as possible, use plenty of strong spices, such as pepper, garlic, cilantro, ginger, etc., in your cooking.

• **Focus on preparation and presentation.** *Chefs have a saying:* "The eyes eat first." Use brightly colored fruits and vegetables and other colorful ingredients, and add garnishes to your plate. Also, vary the textures of the foods you eat.

Exception: If your loss of smell is due to nasal inflammation—from allergies, chronic sinusitis, etc.—intranasal steroid sprays and antihistamines may restore it.

Often, when the underlying problem is corrected, the sense of smell returns. People who quit smoking usually regain all or most of their sense of smell, but this can take years. *Also…*

• **The nutrients thiamine** (100 milligrams daily) and phosphatidylcholine (9 grams daily) can elevate levels of neurotransmitters that improve the sense of smell. In one study, about 40% of patients improved significantly after taking phosphatidylcholine for three months. The success rate with thiamine is somewhat lower.

• **Sniff therapy.** People who expose themselves to the same scent 20 to 50 times a day for several weeks will have an increase in scent receptors and will sometimes regain their ability to smell that particular scent.

Keep Your Nose Happy

Murray Grossan, MD, an otolaryngologist and head and neck surgeon with the Tower Ear, Nose and Throat Clinic at Cedars-Sinai Medical Center in Los Angeles. He is the author of the newly released *Free Yourself From Sinus and Allergy Problems—Permanently.*

I f you suffer from hay fever (allergic rhinitis), you may dread the arrival of spring. As billions of pollen spores are released into the air, it's likely that your nose will start running or become stuffy, your eyes will itch, you won't be able to stop coughing and your head will ache.

At least 30% of people who suffer from hay fever go on to develop a related condition known as sinusitis (inflammation of the sinus cavities, usually due to a bacterial or viral infection). But airborne allergens aren't the only culprit.

If you're exposed to air pollution, smoke or dry or cold air, or even if you have a common cold, you also are at increased risk for sinusitis. In all of these instances, the mucous glands secrete more mucus to dilute the offending material. Unless the cilia (tiny hairs on the cells of the mucous membrane) move the mucus out, this creates an ideal breeding ground for infection.

When you have cold like symptoms that last for at least 12 consecutive weeks, you are likely to have chronic sinusitis, the most commonly diagnosed chronic illness in the US. Most of the 37 million Americans who suffer from sinusitis each year turn to decongestants, antihistamines and antibiotics.

What most sinusitis sufferers don't know: You will have the best chance of preventing sinus problems in the first place if you take care of the cilia. *My secrets to improving the health of your cilia...*

Cilia: The Missing Link

The cilia play a crucial—though underrecognized—role in keeping the respiratory tract healthy. These tiny hairs wave rhythmically to carry tiny airborne particles and bacteria out of the nasal passages. When allergy symptoms persist for many days or even weeks, however, the cilia become overworked and quit moving.

Cilia also can be damaged if you regularly take antihistamines or breathe dry air—both of which decrease the liquid component of mucus that traps bacteria and is needed for good cilia movement. When the cilia no longer do their job, bacteria multiply, setting the stage for infection.

To test the health of your cilia: Many ear, nose and throat specialists (otolaryngologists) use the so-called saccharin test. With this test, the doctor places a particle of saccharin in

your nose and times how long it takes you to taste it.

Normally, the patient tastes the saccharin in five to eight minutes. If the cilia are damaged, however, it may take 25 minutes or longer for the patient to taste it. If the damage is severe, special treatment, such as breathing exercises, may be required.

KEEP YOUR CILIA HEALTHY

When allergy or cold symptoms persist or when nasal discharge becomes colored (usually yellow or green)—a symptom of sinusitis—there are some surprisingly simple steps you can take to ensure the health of your cilia. *Favorite methods...*

•**Drink hot tea with lemon and honey.** Compounds found in black and green tea help block the body's allergic response to pollen by inhibiting the production of histamine, the substance that causes nasal stuffiness and dripping due to a cold or hay fever.

Drinking five cups of hot tea a day helps the body mount its natural defenses against infection, scientific studies have shown. The moist heat stimulates the cilia, while lemon and honey thin mucus, allowing for better cilia movement.

•**Sing "oooommmmm" in a low tone.** You might feel a little silly at first, but singing the "oooommmmm" sound, which was used by the ancient yogis as a form of meditation, causes a vibration of air that stimulates the cilia. Make this sound often throughout the day. As an alternative, buy a toy kazoo and hum into it for 10 minutes daily.

•**Use pulsatile irrigation.** This highly effective strategy involves rapidly but gently rinsing your nose with a stream of saltwater (saline solution) that pulses at a rate matching the normal pulse rate of healthy cilia—hence the name pulsatile irrigation.

Clinical trials involving thousands of patients have shown that pulsatile irrigation increases blood flow to the nasal passages and helps restore function to damaged cilia.

Several pulsatile irrigation devices are available from websites specializing in allergy or medical products, such as National Allergy (*natlallergy.com*, 800-522-1448) or Health Solutions Medical Products (*pharmacy-solutions. com*, 800-305-4095). The typical cost is around $100 to $140. For best results, use this form of irrigation twice daily, as needed.

Nose Getting Bigger

With age, your nose can thicken, getting wider and bulkier as nasal pores plug with oil that solidifies. To prevent this, cleanse oily skin on the nose twice daily. Cleansing facials also help.

Also: Fatty tissue under the skin of the nose thins with age and can no longer support the nose's heavy tip. The tip then starts to droop, moving closer to the upper lip and possibly blocking breathing at night. If you experience this, use one-half-inch-wide medical tape to hold the tip up while you sleep. Start the tape between the nostrils, then gently lift the tip by pulling the tape up along the main nasal bridge, stopping between the eyes.

Murray Grossan, MD, otolaryngologist, Cedars Sinai Medical Center, Los Angeles.

Don't Pluck Those Nose Hairs!

Most men love a good head of hair, but not necessarily flowing from their nose. It's fine to trim (not remove) nose hairs that visibly protrude beyond the nostrils, using an electric trimmer or scissors designed for this purpose. Aggressive removal or "plucking" can cause painful ingrown hairs or a skin infection that may require antibiotics.

If your husband gets redness or tenderness after trimming, he should apply an antibiotic ointment twice daily to the inner skin of the nasal passage for a few days to reduce the chance of infection.

Nose hairs are necessary to filter airborne particles, so he should leave enough to avoid compromising this important function.

Richard M. Rosenfeld, MD, MPH, professor and chairman of otolaryngology, SUNY Downstate Medical Center, Brooklyn, New York.

Reduce Allergy Symptoms by Changing Your Eating Habits

If you are allergic to tree pollen, don't eat almonds, apples, carrots, cherries, pear, kiwifruit, parsley, celery, hazelnuts, peaches and plums. These may cause oral allergy symptoms, including itchiness/swelling of the lip, tongue and mouth. If you are sensitive to ragweed, ingestion of cantaloupe, watermelon, honeydew, banana, zucchini, echinacea and chamomile tea can aggravate symptoms. Effects differ from person to person—but if your allergies are bothersome or allergy medications appear not to be effective, eliminating possible food triggers can be worth trying.

Clifford Bassett, MD, medical director, Allergy and Asthma Care of New York, New York City. AllergyRelief NYC.com

Cure Allergies The Natural Way

Richard Firshein, DO, director of the New York City—based Firshein Center for Comprehensive Medicine. He is the author of *Reversing Asthma* and *The Vitamin Prescription*. DrFirshein.com

Seasonal allergies are most commonly associated with springtime. But the flare-ups that occur in the summer can be just as bad—if not worse—due to the added discomfort caused by unpleasant climate conditions, such as heat and humidity.

Interesting new fact: Allergy symptoms may be lasting even longer due to extended pollen seasons brought on by climate change, according to a recent analysis.

That's why it's more important than ever for the 40 million Americans who suffer from seasonal allergies to use the most effective therapies—with the fewest side effects.

Good news: You don't have to fill your medicine cabinet with powerful drugs that simply temporarily relieve your allergy symptoms and potentially lead to side effects ranging from headache and drowsiness to difficulty breathing. Instead, you can get relief from the natural remedies described in this article.

THE ROOT OF THE PROBLEM

Most doctors treat allergies with a regimen that includes oral antihistamines, such as *loratadine* (Claritin) or *cetirizine* (Zyrtec), to block the release of histamine so that runny noses and itchy eyes will be reduced…and/or inhaled steroids, such as *triamcinolone acetonide* (Nasacort) or *flunisolide*, to reduce inflammation, mucus production and nasal congestion.

Problem: Aside from the side effects these drugs can cause, many allergy sufferers experience a "rebound effect"—that is, when the drug wears off, the histamine that has been suppressed by the medication explodes, causing an even bigger allergic reaction.

Important: To transition from medication to the natural regimen described here, first take the natural remedy with the medication, then slowly wean yourself off the medication over a few weeks.

Try these three simple natural approaches…*

STEP 1—SUPPLEMENTS

Mother Nature has tools that work with your body to stop allergy symptoms. The following naturally occurring substances have few side effects and often are just as effective as over-the-counter and prescription allergy medications.

My advice: Try quercetin, then add others in severe cases.

• **Quercetin is a bioflavonoid,** a type of plant pigment that inhibits histamine-producing cells. It's found in citrus fruits, apples and onions but not in amounts that are sufficient

*Consult a doctor before trying this regimen if you are pregnant or have a medical condition.

to relieve allergy symptoms. For optimal relief, try quercetin tablets.

Typical dose: Up to 600 mg daily depending on the severity of your symptoms. Quercetin also can be taken as a preventive during allergy season. Discuss the dose with your doctor. Quercetin is generally safe. Rare side effects may include headache and upset stomach. People with kidney disease should not take quercetin—it may worsen the condition.

Good brand: Quercetin 300, *allergyresearchgroup.com*

• **Stinging nettle is a flowering plant that,** when ingested, reduces the amount of histamine that the body produces in response to an allergen. Look for a product that contains 1% silicic acid (the key ingredient).

Typical dose: 500 mg to 1,000 mg once or twice a day depending on the severity of symptoms.

Caution: Some people are allergic to stinging nettle. In rare cases, oral stinging nettle may cause mild gastrointestinal upset.

Good brands: Nature's Way Nettle Herb, *naturesway.com*…or Solgar Stinging Nettle Leaf Extract, *solgar.com*.

• **Fish oil.** The same potent source of omega-3 fatty acids that is so popular for preventing the inflammation that leads to heart disease also helps with allergies. Look for the words "pharmaceutical grade" and "purified" or "mercury-free" on the label. This ensures that the product is potent enough to have a therapeutic effect and has undergone a manufacturing process that removes potential toxins. Choose a brand that provides at least 500 mg of *eicosapentaenoic acid* (EPA) and 250 mg of *docosahexaenoic acid* (DHA) per capsule.

Typical dose: Take 2,000 mg of fish oil per day. Consult your doctor if you take a blood thinner.

Good brands: Nordic Naturals Arctic Omega, *nordicnaturals.com*…or VitalChoice fish oils, *vitalchoice.com*.

STEP 2—NASAL CLEANSING

Inflammation in the nasal passages due to allergies prevents the sinuses from draining and can lead to sinus infection.

Self-defense: Nasal cleansing once daily during allergy season reduces the amount of pollen exposure and can prevent the allergic reaction in the first place.**

One option: Flush your nasal passages with a neti pot. A neti pot looks like a miniature teapot with an elongated spout (available at drugstores for $8 to $30). Add one tablespoon of aloe vera gel and a pinch of salt to the warm distilled water you place in the pot.

What to do: While standing over a sink, tilt your head horizontally, left ear to ceiling, and gently insert the spout into your left nostril. As you slowly pour the mixture into the nostril, it will circulate through the nasal passages and out the right nostril. Continue for 10 seconds, breathing through your mouth, then let the excess water drain. Repeat on the other nostril. Be sure to run your neti pot through the dishwasher or clean with soap and hot water to disinfect it after every use.

Alternative: If using a neti pot feels uncomfortable, try using a syringe bulb…or cup warm water (mixed with salt and aloe) in your hand and breathe it in slowly.

Even better: Use a nasal irrigator, which is more thorough and takes less effort than a neti pot. This instrument forcibly expels water—and uses the same aloe/salt/water mixture as you would in a neti pot.

Recommended: The Hydro Pulse, developed by ENT doctor Murray Grossan, *hydro medonline.com*, $78…or SinuPulse Elite Advanced Nasal Irrigation System, *sinupulse. com*, $80.

STEP 3—ACUPRESSURE OR ACUPUNCTURE

Acupuncture and acupressure can relieve allergies by stimulating certain pressure points to encourage blood flow, reduce inflammation and release natural painkilling chemical compounds known as endorphins.

•**Acupressure.** For 30 to 60 seconds, push (with enough pressure to hold your head on your thumbs) each thumb into the area where each brow meets the nose. Then, press your thumbs just below your eyebrows and

**Nasal cleansing may be irritating for some people. If you experience any irritation, discontinue it immediately.

266

slide along the ridges. Finally, press beneath both cheekbones, moving outward with both thumbs toward the ears. Do this sequence three times daily.

•**Acupuncture.** While acupressure helps relieve allergy symptoms, acupuncture is generally more effective. I recommend six to 10 sessions with a licensed acupuncturist during allergy season.

OTHER REMEDIES

•**Allergy shots and drops.** These traditional approaches are in many ways quite natural. Small amounts of an allergen extract are injected. After a number of treatments, you build up a natural resistance to the allergen. Allergy drops (placed under the tongue) are an alternative to allergy shots and work in much the same way.

•**Speleotherapy and halotherapy.** Used for centuries in Europe, these treatments are gaining popularity in the US. With speleotherapy, patients spend time in salt caves. Halotherapy uses man-made salt rooms that simulate caves. The salt ions combined with unpolluted air seem to improve lung function in those with respiratory and sinus ailments as well as allergies.

Salt mines and salt rooms are not always easy to find. Search online under "salt therapy."

Recommended: During allergy season, four to 12 speleotherapy or halotherapy sessions may be helpful. A 45- to 60-minute session typically costs $10 to $15.

A New Key to Longevity: Good Oral Health

Robert J. Genco, DDS, PhD, distinguished professor in the department of oral biology, School of Dental Medicine, and in the department of microbiology, School of Medicine and Biomedical Sciences at the State University of New York at Buffalo.

Until recently, most people who took good care of their teeth and gums did so to ensure appealing smiles and to perhaps avoid dentures. Now, a significant body of research shows that oral health may play a key role in preventing a wide range of serious health conditions, including heart disease, diabetes, some types of cancer and perhaps even dementia.

Healthy teeth and gums also may improve longevity. Swedish scientists recently tracked 3,273 adults for 16 years and found that those with chronic gum infections were significantly more likely to die before age 50, on average, than were people without gum disease.

What's the connection? Periodontal disease (called gingivitis in mild stages…and periodontitis when it becomes more severe) is caused mainly by bacteria that accumulate on the teeth and gums. As the body attempts to battle the bacteria, inflammatory molecules are released (as demonstrated by redness and swelling of the gums). Over time, this complex biological response affects the entire body, causing systemic inflammation that promotes the development of many serious diseases. *Scientific evidence links poor oral health to…*

• **Heart disease.** At least 20 scientific studies have shown links between chronic periodontal disease and an increased risk for heart disease. Most recently, Boston University researchers found that periodontal disease in men younger than age 60 was associated with a twofold increase in angina (chest pain), or nonfatal or fatal heart attack, when compared with men whose teeth and gums are healthy.

• **Diabetes.** State University of New York at Buffalo studies and other research show that people with diabetes have an associated risk for periodontitis that is two to three times greater than that of people without diabetes. Conversely, diabetics with periodontal disease generally have poorer control of their blood sugar than diabetics without periodontal disease—a factor that contributes to their having twice the risk of dying of a heart attack and three times the risk of dying of kidney failure.

• **Cancer.** Chronic gum disease may raise your risk for tongue cancer. State University of New York at Buffalo researchers recently compared men with and without tongue cancer and found that those with cancer had a 65% greater loss of alveolar bone (which sup-

ports the teeth)—a common measure of periodontitis. Meanwhile, a Harvard School of Public Health study shows that periodontal disease is associated with a 63% higher risk for pancreatic cancer.

• **Rheumatoid arthritis.** In people with rheumatoid arthritis, the condition is linked to an 82% increased risk for periodontal disease, compared with people who do not have rheumatoid arthritis.

Good news: Treating the periodontitis appears to ease rheumatoid arthritis symptoms. In a recent study, nearly 59% of patients with rheumatoid arthritis and chronic periodontal disease who had their gums treated experienced less severe arthritis symptoms—possibly because eliminating the periodontitis reduced their systemic inflammation.

• **Dementia.** When Swedish researchers recently reviewed dental and cognitive records for 638 women, they found that tooth loss (a sign of severe gum disease) was linked to a 30% to 40% increased risk for dementia over a 32-year period, with the highest dementia rates suffered by women who had the fewest teeth at middle age. More research is needed to confirm and explain this link.

STEPS TO IMPROVE YOUR ORAL HEALTH

Even though the rate of gum disease significantly increases with age, it's not inevitable. To promote oral health, brush (twice daily with a soft-bristled brush, using gentle, short strokes starting at a 45-degree angle to the gums) and floss (once daily, using gentle rubbing motions—do not snap against the gums). *In addition…*

• **See your dentist at least twice yearly.** Ask at every exam, "Do I have gum disease?" This will serve as a gentle reminder to dentists that you want to be carefully screened for the condition. Most mild-to-moderate infections can be treated with a nonsurgical procedure that removes plaque and tartar from tooth pockets and smooths the root surfaces. For more severe periodontal disease, your dentist may refer you to a periodontist (a dentist who specializes in the treatment of gum disease).

Note: Patients with gum disease often need to see a dentist three to four times a year to prevent recurrence of gum disease after the initial treatment.

Good news: Modern techniques to regenerate bone and soft tissue can reverse much of the damage and halt progression of periodontitis, particularly in patients who have lost no more than 30% of the bone to which the teeth are attached.

• **Boost your calcium intake.** Research conducted at the State University of New York at Buffalo has shown that postmenopausal women with osteoporosis typically have more alveolar bone loss and weaker attachments between their teeth and bone, putting them at substantially higher risk for periodontal disease. Other studies have linked low dietary calcium with heightened periodontal risk in both men and women.

Self-defense: Postmenopausal women, and men over age 65, should consume 1,000 mg to 1,200 mg of calcium daily to preserve teeth and bones. Aim for two to three daily servings of dairy products (providing a total of 600 mg of calcium), plus a 600-mg calcium supplement with added vitamin D for maximum absorption.

Helpful: Yogurt may offer an edge over other calcium sources. In a recent Japanese study involving 942 adults, ages 40 to 79, those who ate at least 55 grams (about two ounces) of yogurt daily were 40% less likely to suffer from severe periodontal disease—perhaps because the "friendly" bacteria and calcium in yogurt make a powerful combination against the infection-causing bacteria of dental disease.

• **Control your weight.** Obesity is also associated with periodontitis, probably because fat cells release chemicals that may contribute to inflammatory conditions anywhere in the body, including the gums.

• **Don't ignore dry mouth.** Aging and many medications, including some antidepressants, antihistamines, high blood pressure drugs and steroids, can decrease saliva flow, allowing plaque to build up on teeth and gums. If you're taking a drug that leaves your mouth dry, talk to your doctor about possible alternatives. Prescription artificial saliva products—for example, Caphosol or Numoisyn—also

can provide some temporary moistening, as can chewing sugarless gum.

• **Relax.** Recent studies reveal a strong link between periodontal disease and stress, depression, anxiety and loneliness. Researchers are focusing on the stress hormone cortisol as a possible culprit—high levels of cortisol may exacerbate the gum and jawbone destruction caused by oral infections.

• **Sleep.** Japanese researchers recently studied 219 factory workers for four years and found that those who slept seven to eight hours nightly suffered significantly less periodontal disease progression than those who slept six hours or less. The scientists speculated that lack of sleep lowers the body's ability to fend off infections. However, more research is needed to confirm the results of this small study.

Supplements That Help Prevent Gum Disease

Mark A. Breiner, DDS, an authority on holistic dentistry with a practice in Fairfield, Connecticut. Dr. Breiner is the author of *Whole-Body Dentistry: A Complete Guide to Understanding the Impact of Dentistry on Total Health.* WholeBodyDentistry.com

If you're over age 65, the odds of getting gum disease jump to 64%. Even people who brush and floss and avoid sugar can fall victim because some risk factors (such as aging and having certain genes) are unavoidable. And as you know, oral health is connected with overall health—gum disease raises your risk for systemic health issues, such as stroke, diabetes and cancer. *Here are natural strategies you need to know...*

KEEP YOUR GUMS IN THE PINK

Here are Dr. Breiner's natural ways to prevent and/or treat gum disease.

1. Rinse with an herbal mouthwash. Herbs such as echinacea, eucalyptus, lavender and thyme are good at killing harmful bacteria, so they help prevent gum disease and help heal gum tissue if gum disease has already developed. So look for a mouthwash that lists at least one of those herbs on the label (ideally all of them). While you're checking the ingredient list, make sure that the mouthwash is alcohol-free, because some studies have found an association between alcohol-based mouthwash and oral cancer. For example, you could try a brand called PerioWash ($9 for 16 ounces at Drugstore.com) after brushing and flossing each morning and night—it contains all four herbs mentioned above and no alcohol.

2. Take certain supplements.

• **Vitamin C.** Whether you have gum disease or not, ask your doctor about taking 500 milligrams (mg) daily of vitamin C because the nutrient builds collagen, a connective protein that is the foundation of gum tissue.

• **Coenzyme Q10.** This supplement is good for those who already have gum disease because it provides cellular energy that helps repair gum tissue. Ask your doctor what the best amount for you is—standard daily dosages range from 30 mg to 200 mg daily.

• **Magnesium.** Grinding your teeth can worsen existing gum disease (and cause all sorts of other dental problems, such as tooth decay, even if you don't have gum disease). So ask your dentist whether you should also take 50 mg to 100 mg of magnesium one hour before bedtime to relax your muscles—this helps lots of his patients who are grinders, said Dr. Breiner.

Dry Mouth Isn't Just Uncomfortable...It's Dangerous...Here Are the Best Solutions

Louis Mandel, DDS, an associate dean, a clinical professor and director of the Salivary Gland Center at Columbia University College of Dental Medicine in New York City.

Mouth dryness, known as xerostomia, is commonly thought of as a normal part of aging. But that's not true. Healthy adults continue to produce adequate amounts of saliva, but some medical conditions and certain medications can lead to dry mouth—and that can be more dangerous than you might think.

What most people don't realize: Dry mouth is more than a mere annoyance. It significantly increases risk for infection (including gum disease) and severe tooth decay. And treating the teeth does not solve the problem of dry mouth.

LOW-SALIVA SYMPTOMS

Saliva is mostly water, but it also contains enzymes that break down food particles. It inhibits the growth of bacteria that can damage tooth enamel and is crucial for preventing fungal infections in the mouth. Saliva also lubricates the mouth so that we can speak and swallow.

If you don't produce enough saliva, you will, of course, notice mouth dryness. Other symptoms include cracks in the lips or the corners of the mouth, bad breath, burning of the mouth, a dry feeling in the throat and an increase in tooth decay and/or gum disease.

Self-test: You're probably producing normal amounts of saliva if you can chew a dry cracker and swallow it easily. People who consistently struggle to eat and swallow dry foods have a problem.

If you have dry mouth, your physician or dentist may want to measure your output of saliva with a Lashley cup, a device that fits over the opening of the parotid duct (the primary duct of the major salivary gland). Salivary flow is stimulated with a citric acid solution that is applied to the borders of the tongue with a cotton swab. Saliva is then collected. A healthy adult should produce between 0.5 cc and 1.2 cc of saliva (about one-tenth to one-quarter of a teaspoon) per minute per gland when stimulated.

WHAT CAUSES MOUTH DRYNESS?

Sjögren's syndrome, an autoimmune disorder, is a common cause of mouth dryness. This disease damages the glands that produce saliva and can cause swelling and pain in the joints.

Other causes of xerostomia ...

• **Radiation treatments** for oral or neck cancers can permanently damage cells in the salivary glands.

Example: Radiotherapy that's used to treat oral cancer kills saliva-producing cells as the beam passes through the salivary glands.

• **Medication use.** According to the Surgeon General's report on oral health in America, more than 400 prescription and over-the-counter (OTC) drugs cause mouth dryness as a side effect.

Common offenders: Antihistamines, antidepressants, decongestants and diuretics and other blood pressure drugs.

It's rare for a single medication to cause significant dryness (though it can happen). The risk multiplies when patients are taking multiple medications that have mouth dryness as a side effect.

To find out if a medication you are taking may cause mouth dryness: Check the website for the Physicians' Desk Reference, *pdrhealth.com.*

• **Mouth-breathing.** Some people tend to breathe through their mouths, which can cause dryness even if they produce normal amounts of saliva. This usually occurs in those who have some kind of nasal obstruction, such as a deviated septum, or the breathing disorder sleep apnea.

To check yourself for mouth-breathing at night: Notice whether your mouth feels dry in the morning. People who mouth-breathe tend to experience the most dryness when they first wake up.

• **Dehydration.** You need adequate amounts of fluids to produce saliva. Most people get enough water from beverages and food, but older adults often forget to drink enough water.

Other causes of dry mouth include uncontrolled diabetes. Frequent urination (a symptom of diabetes) may lead to dehydration and dry mouth.

Interesting: Some people who believe they have dry mouth actually produce normal amounts of saliva but may, in fact, suffer from depression or anxiety. That's why it's important to discuss your symptoms with your doctor and perhaps get tested.

BEST TREATMENT OPTIONS

If you and your doctor determine that your mouth dryness is caused by medication, ask about switching to a drug and/or dose that doesn't have this side effect. *Also helpful...*

• **Try a saliva substitute that contains carboxymethylcellulose or hydroxyethylcellulose.** Such products, which are sold OTC at most drugstores in solutions, sprays, gels and lozenges, can be used as needed to replace moisture in the mouth. Good choices include Optimoist...Biotene Moisturizing Mouth Spray...and Entertainer's Secret.

• **Chew sugarless gum and suck on sugarless hard candies to help increase saliva flow.** Hard lemon drops are a good choice because the sourness stimulates more saliva.

• **Drink more water or suck on ice cubes to moisten your mouth and increase your fluid intake.**

• **Use a dry-mouth toothpaste such as Biotene.** It doesn't increase saliva, but it may relieve burning sensations caused by mouth dryness and is less likely to irritate dry tissues in the mouth than other toothpastes. It also has mild antiseptic properties, which can help prevent tooth decay or gum infections.

• **Avoid mouthwashes with alcohol.** Some products contain more than 25% alcohol. Alcohol is a desiccant that dries tissues in the mouth. If you use a mouthwash, buy an alcohol-free version—and use it only once a day.

• **Protect your teeth with fluoride.** I advise patients who are scheduled for—or have already had—radiation treatments of the head or neck to apply fluoride gel to the teeth. Your dentist can make plastic dental trays and provide the gel. Applying fluoride for five to 10 minutes daily will help prevent tooth decay that may result from excessive mouth dryness.

Little-Known Dangers to Teeth

Chlorine from swimming pool water can cause dental abrasion—so swim in salt-water whenever possible. Acidic beverages such as lemonade and sports drinks can weaken tooth enamel, so drink water instead—or at least have a glass of water after consuming one of these acidic drinks. White wine is more acidic than red wine and can erode tooth enamel, so drink water or eat bread between sips of wine. Berry juices and smoothies can discolor teeth—drink them with a straw to help liquid pass to the back of your mouth, avoiding your teeth.

EveryDayHealth.com.

How Long Should You Brush Your Teeth?

It is generally recommended that you spend two to three minutes brushing all surfaces of your teeth in a methodical manner. However, depending on one's dexterity with the brush, different people can spend the same amount of time brushing and have different levels of success in removing bacterial deposits and food particles from the teeth. Your dentist and hygienist can evaluate how well you're brushing. If you're not getting good results due to limited dexterity, an electric toothbrush may help. However, the time you need to devote to brushing with an electric toothbrush is not significantly different from that required for a manual toothbrush. And don't forget to floss at least once daily!

Sheldon Nadler, DMD, dentist in private practice, New York City.

A Tooth-Friendly Snack

Are raisins good for your teeth? New finding: Oleanolic acid, a plant chemical found in raisins, was shown to inhibit the growth of two species of oral bacteria, Streptococcus mutans, which causes cavities, and Porphyromonas gingivalis, which is associated with gum disease. This finding refutes the long-standing belief that raisins promote tooth decay.

Christine D. Wu, PhD, professor, periodontics department, University of Illinois at Chicago College of Dentistry.

Root Canal May Help Your Teeth But Harm Your Health

Mark A. Stengler, NMD, naturopathic medical doctor and founder and medical director of the Stengler Center for Integrative Medicine in Encinitas, California. MarkStengler.com

When I'm taking a patient's medical history and he/she mentions having had a root canal procedure, I take note—especially if the patient has a chronic illness that began weeks to months after the procedure.

There is a growing concern among holistic health-care professionals that root canal procedures are making people sick.

Reason: Bacteria and other microbes can live on in the treated tooth and release toxic by-products that damage the immune system, leading to all kinds of health problems. Infection also can occur years after the procedure if the sealant material on the tooth breaks down.

The irony of this: The main function of root canal (technically known as endodontic therapy) is to enable people to avoid having a tooth extracted because it is infected, cracked or decayed. But I have seen many cases in which fatigue, weak immunity or a chronic illness, including sinusitis, fibromyalgia or an autoimmune condition such as rheumatoid arthritis, sets in after root canal. Some doctors think that there even may be a link between root canal and increased cancer risk.

More than 20 million root canal procedures are performed annually in the US. Not all root canal procedures go wrong. Many procedures save teeth that have been damaged by trauma, for instance, or when an infection is treated early. But not all root canal proce-

271

dures are harmless either. To find out how you can protect yourself, our editors spoke to Tom McGuire, DDS, a leading authority on mercury-safe, holistic dentistry in Sebastopol, California (*dentalwellness4u.com*).

Here's what you need to know…

INSIDE THE TOOTH

Root canal is a way to "save" the bony shell of the tooth while removing the infected living tissue inside it. During the procedure, the dentist removes the pulp, which is the tissue, including nerves and blood vessels, in the center of the tooth, and the tissue in the roots. The tooth is then cleaned and sealed.

When you understand what is going on inside a tooth, you understand why bacteria can be a problem. Within the inner layer of a tooth's enamel coating are millions of microscopically small canals called tubules that transport nourishing fluid throughout the dentin (the area between the pulp and the enamel coating). During a root canal procedure, the main root canal area is packed with a filling material, but the tubules are too small to fill. As a result, bacteria often remain inside the tubules after the tooth is sealed up, out of reach of antibiotics or immune system antibodies.

A key variable is the individual's own immune system. If yours is strong, then you can probably tolerate a chronic, low-level flow of toxic bacteria into your system without any noticeable ill effects. Over time, as people age and experience declines in immune function, it becomes harder for the body to handle this toxic stress.

What can go wrong: The infection can progress to the bone surrounding the root tips. There is a big difference between bacteria contained within a tooth and bacteria in bone, which has its own blood supply. Now the infection is not contained within the tooth but is in the body.

The body may be able to wall this off and form a protective cyst, but the body's own bacteria fighters can get access to the cyst or infection only on its outer edges, leaving the bacteria with a safe haven to produce virulent toxins. If the body cannot maintain control of the cyst and it breaks or leaks, the blood supply will receive a massive dose of highly toxic bacteria.

This can dramatically affect the overall health of someone with an already compromised immune system.

Microorganisms that can cause chronic infection after a root canal procedure include enterococci, streptococci, peptostreptococci and candida, among others. Some people feel pain from the remaining living nerves in the affected area or the nerves of the jawbone from a developing abscess, but not all do.

At this point, even if the root canal procedure has been done correctly, the only way to treat the existing infection in the bone is to have the tooth extracted and the infected area cleaned. Once the infection has been eliminated, the onslaught on the immune system stops and healing begins.

HOW TO PROTECT YOURSELF

As Dr. McGuire does, I advise patients who need to have a root canal procedure about the possible risks and urge them to make sure that a root canal procedure is really what they need. Many root canal procedures shouldn't be done in the first place. Several other oral health issues, such as chronic mercury poisoning from amalgam fillings and gum disease, can severely weaken the immune system. Impaired immunity makes it harder for these patients to fight off infection. These oral health issues should not be overlooked when deciding if a root canal should be performed. I also advise patients about the option of having the tooth extracted and replaced with a metal-free bridge.

If you do choose to have a root canal, it is best to have the treatment done by a root canal specialist (endodontist) who is willing to take as long as needed to give repeated antimicrobial treatments if necessary.

The reality, however, is that no endodontist can tell for sure whether all the bacteria is gone.

Endodontists may perform follow-up X-rays to see how the tooth is healing. If the infection worsens, it will dissolve bone in that area—and this will show up on an X-ray.

If you've already had a root canal treatment, monitor your health carefully, especially if other infection-related illnesses occur and don't respond to treatment. That may be the main way to know if you have this type of festering infection. A blood test can reveal chronically low white blood cells, another indication of this type of infection.

If you suspect that you have a health problem caused by a root canal procedure, the tooth can be retreated by an endodontist or you can have the treated tooth extracted. I've had many patients whose conditions clear up as soon as the tooth is extracted.

Chronic Heartburn's Unexpected Target: Teeth

Daranee Versluis-Tantbirojn, DDS, MS, PhD, associate professor, restorative dentistry, The University of Tennessee Health Science Center, Memphis. The study was published in *The Journal of the American Dental Association*.

The tingling pain in the throat from chronic heartburn may make you concerned about your increased risk for esophageal cancer, but a new study points to yet another health problem worth worrying about—tooth erosion.

Unfortunately, chronic heartburn (a.k.a. gastroesophageal reflux disease, or GERD) can cause dental damage due to the acid that's constantly washing around in your mouth—even if you're taking antacids.

And there's one particular type of dental damage that it's very important to keep an eye on, as it turns out…

ALARMING OBSERVATIONS

Researchers analyzed participants with GERD and healthy people, looking at how much tooth enamel (the outer layer) was lost over six months, and determined whether the erosion was due to normal wear-and-tear or the effects of regurgitated stomach acid.

To learn about the results, we spoke with study author Daranee Versluis-Tantbirojn, DDS, MS, PhD, an associate professor of restorative dentistry at the University of Tennessee Health Science Center in Memphis.

Findings: On average, compared to the control group, GERD patients had more tooth damage—and some had much more. In fact, two GERD patients had five times the damage, two had seven times the damage and one

even had nine times as much. These patients had tooth surfaces with deeper "craters" and/or had thinner teeth.

The researchers were surprised to see just how much tooth erosion was measured in some patients, considering that most were taking medications to combat GERD. This means that the level of tooth damage may be even worse in patients who forgo medicating the problem, she said.

TONS OF TOOTH TIPS

Just the thought of pitted, thinning teeth is enough to turn my stomach. Aside from the fact that it's aesthetically displeasing, tooth erosion can also lead to poor chewing ability and sensitivity to cold food and drinks (ouch!). Plus, Dr. Versluis-Tantbirojn said, people with severe damage often need expensive dental crowns or caps to restore the form and function of their choppers.

If you or someone you know has GERD, Dr. Versluis-Tantbirojn offered these tips for preventing dental damage…

• **Don't brush at the wrong time.** After a reflux episode, don't brush your teeth right away—wait at least one hour—because brushing acid-softened teeth will sweep away the softened surface, resulting in more erosion. But keep brushing as you normally would twice a day.

• **Use a fluoride mouthwash.** Rinsing with a fluoride mouthwash immediately after a reflux episode can enhance saliva's ability to restore damaged tooth surfaces. Be careful not to swallow it, as over time it may be toxic to your system. (Fluoride mouthwashes are available in any drugstore, but don't use brands containing alcohol, which can make the mouth feel like it's burning and dry it out.)

• **Use "dental cream".** Ask your dentist about obtaining a prescription dental cream containing fluoride, calcium and phosphate ions, which enhances repair of softened enamel more than saliva or fluoride mouthwash alone. (It costs about $15 to $20 for a 1.8-ounce tube, which will last about one month.) Dental cream can be used anytime after an acid reflux episode, and applying it with your finger is more effective than with a toothbrush.

What's Causing Your Tongue Problems?

Jordan S. Josephson, MD, an endoscopic sinus surgeon and director of the New York Nasal and Sinus Center in New York City. He is the author of *Sinus Relief Now*, as well as multiple textbook chapters on endoscopic sinus surgery and facial cosmetic surgery. SinusReliefNow.com

It's a good idea to examine your tongue at least once a week.

What to do: When you first wake up, stand in front of a mirror close to a window with natural light shining into your mouth. Do not brush your teeth or tongue first, since doing so may remove signs of problems.

Important: If you notice that your tongue has a new or unusual coating, color or texture or you have an unexplained taste in your mouth, see an otolaryngologist—an ear, nose and throat (ENT) doctor—for an evaluation.

Common tongue problems that can signal health issues elsewhere in the body...

•**Slimy or patchy white tongue.** Surprisingly, this condition, commonly known as thrush, could be a red flag for a sinus infection or gastroesophageal reflux disease (GERD). Thrush, which is typically caused by a fungal infection, can be a tip-off that a patient's sinuses are inflamed or infected or that stomach acid is flowing back into the mouth and/or sinuses—this causes irritation and increases risk for infection.

While most sinus infections are caused by viruses or bacteria, fungi (especially mold) can also lead to inflammation/infection in the nose and sinuses.

Recent finding: The number of cases of fungal sinusitis has significantly increased over the past three decades, due in part to inappropriate use of antibiotics and the use of new immunosuppressive drugs, such as those prescribed to treat rheumatoid arthritis and given after organ transplant.

Treatment for thrush needs to be aggressive, including prescription topical antifungal medications (swishes and lozenges). Treating fungal sinusitis or GERD will also help thrush. Reduc-

ing alcohol and sugar intake may help starve the fungi, which feed on sugar and yeast.

•**White or red sores.** If you have a stubborn white or red sore or patch (or a lump, bump or an ulcer) on or under your tongue that doesn't go away within a week or two, be sure to see your dentist or doctor.

There could be several possible causes for such sores or patches—the most serious being tongue cancer. Other symptoms of this type of malignancy may include chronic tongue pain, a sore throat and trouble swallowing, chewing or moving your tongue. If your dentist or doctor is concerned, he/she should refer you to an otolaryngologist who will perform a biopsy. You may need surgery to remove a tumor (minimally invasive techniques are used whenever possible, especially if diagnosed early), along with radiation and/or chemotherapy for larger and more advanced tumors.

Recent research: Oropharyngeal cancers (affecting the back of the tongue, throat, soft palate and/or tonsils) are on the rise in both men and women in the US—largely due to the increasing prevalence of human papillomavirus (HPV), which can be spread through oral sex. Researchers think that an increase in people having oral sex, especially with many partners, could be behind the rise in oropharyngeal cancers. Smoking and alcohol consumption are also risk factors.

•**Burning mouth.** A fiery sensation in the tongue (and sometimes lips, gums and throat), known as burning mouth syndrome, typically occurs out of the blue, but upper respiratory tract infections, sinus infections, dental work and stress have been known to trigger it. For unknown reasons, postmenopausal women are also at increased risk.

Other culprits: Too little vitamin B-12, riboflavin, folate, zinc or iron.

What helps: The first step is a complete physical examination that includes blood tests and a comprehensive medical history. You'll likely also need a consult with a nutritionist or integrative health practitioner who can help assess you for nutritional deficiencies and work with you to improve your diet and recommend supplements.

12

Help for Chronic Conditions*

Don't Let Age-Related Diseases Catch You Off-Guard

Few situations could be more tragic for older adults than being treated as if they have Alzheimer's disease when they really have a treatable health issue, such as a drug side effect or depression. Equally alarming is not knowing what is happening or where to turn if debilitating arthritis, Alzheimer's or a movement disorder, such as Parkinson's disease, is setting in. This is especially true for older people who live alone and away from family. It happens every day to thousands of mature adults. They end up malnourished and living in squalor, forgotten in suboptimal nursing facilities—or on the street.

Help is available—help that can ensure you get the right diagnosis and treatment. And, just like estate planning, it can assist you in making arrangements in advance for health and physi-

cal needs if you have the beginnings of an incurable and progressive age-related disease.

WHEN DAILY LIVING BECOMES A CHALLENGE

The doorway to help is through a process called a geriatric assessment. Besides physical and psychological health, a geriatric assessment evaluates whether activities of daily living are becoming challenging. Activities include ordinary tasks such as eating, bathing and dressing as well as taking medications, keeping appointments, paying bills and getting around.

The first step is to make an appointment with your primary care physician for a geriatric assessment. The doctor will give you a physical exam and interview you to assess activities

*Chronic conditions, such as arthritis, diabetes and lung disease, are the primary causes of disability and nursing home attendance, according to the Centers for Disease Control and Prevention.

Jullie Gray, MSW, LICSW, CMC, co-owner of Aging Wisdom, a life-care management firm in Seattle, president National Academy of Certified Care Managers, and past president, National Association of Professional Geriatric Care Managers.

of daily living. If an age-related health issue is found, the doctor may act as the point person for a team of specialists who will take care of your health needs and help you plan for the future, whether that be making arrangements for physical therapy, optimizing your home to help you live there safely, getting transportation or a visiting nurse service or home-delivered meals, or arranging for nursing home care. Or the doctor may refer you to a geriatric specialist to assess your health and act as the point person for multispecialty care.

KNOW WHEN TO GO

A recent health alert by the division of geriatrics and palliative medicine at University at Buffalo, The State University of New York, gave guidance about when to arrange for a geriatric assessment of a parent, spouse or sibling by observing how that person manages the activities of daily living. It's easy to see when someone close to you is becoming frail and physically or mentally challenged—but what about when you have to make that decision about yourself? *A geriatric assessment may be wise if you answer yes to even one of these questions…*

• **Are you more forgetful, distracted and irritable than usual,** and are you worried that your memory is failing?

• **Do you feel not as steady on your feet, resulting in having a fall?**

• **Is taking care of your house, paying your bills and taking care of your health becoming more challenging?**

• **Do you have more than one chronic health problem?**

• **Are you worried about changes in your health and feel confused about what to do or who to turn to for help?**

PREPARING FOR AGING

Whether or not you decide to have a geriatric assessment, there are ways to ease age-related challenges that you can do on your own, such as optimizing your living space with better lighting, grab rails, easy-to-reach cabinets and drawers, elevated toilets and open showers. (See chapter 5, "Live at Home Forever," for affordable solutions.)

A Hidden Cause of Chronic Disease

Bennett Lorber, MD, a professor of microbiology and immunology and the Thomas M. Durant Professor of Medicine at Temple University School of Medicine in Philadelphia, where he specializes in anaerobic infections, the interaction of society and infectious diseases and the infectious causes of "noninfectious" diseases.

Everyone gets infections from time to time—a swollen cut…a tooth abscess…or simply a common cold. Most infections come on quickly, cause a brief period of discomfort and then disappear, either on their own or with medication.

What research is now finding: The acute illnesses that we get from infections might be just the tip of the iceberg. Experts now believe that some of the most serious chronic diseases are actually old infections in disguise.

SIMMERING DAMAGE

If you're struck with a nasty infection, you probably assume that once you start feeling better, everything is fine. But that may not be true. Even after your symptoms are gone, some bacteria and viruses have the ability to linger almost indefinitely—you can have a subclinical infection that persists months or even years after the initial illness is gone.

WHEN INFECTION LINGERS

Some infections, such as those caused by the human papillomavirus (discussed on the next page), have a proven link to chronic diseases. Others may be part of a constellation of risk factors that may also include genetics or immune system vulnerabilities. *Examples…*

• **Atherosclerosis.** Up to half of those with atherosclerosis (the accumulation of cholesterol and other fats on artery walls) have none of the usual risk factors, such as smoking or high blood pressure. Yet something causes the fats to accumulate.

Arterial inflammation is a known trigger for atherosclerosis—and inflammation is often due to infection. When researchers examined the blood vessels of patients with atherosclerosis, they repeatedly discovered *Chlamydophila pneumoniae* (a bacterium that causes pneumonia and bronchitis), *Helicobacter pylori* (a bacterium that causes ulcers) and other infection-causing organisms. This doesn't prove that the organisms were responsible for the atherosclerosis. Some bacteria or viruses may have been innocent bystanders that just happened to be there.

What's more, if the microbes caused atherosclerosis, eliminating them should have been helpful—but heart attack patients who were treated with antibiotics were just as likely to have a second heart attack as those who weren't given the drugs. It's possible, however, that the bacteria were eliminated after the arterial damage was done.

What is known: It's been proven that patients with periodontal disease (a gum infection) are more likely to get heart disease. So are people with high levels of C-reactive protein (CRP), an inflammatory "marker" that may be elevated by any type of infection.

My advice: Since CRP is a heart disease risk factor—one that may be caused by infection—it's worth getting it checked. Ask your doctor for advice on the frequency of CRP testing. People who test high might be motivated to take better care of themselves—stopping smoking, eating a healthier diet, lowering blood pressure, etc. Be sure to get regular dental checkups, too.

Also helpful: If you have been diagnosed at any time with C. pneumoniae, H. pylori or another serious infection, tell your doctor so that he/she can consider this as a potential risk factor for atherosclerosis.

• **Rheumatoid arthritis.** It occurs when the immune system attacks the membrane that lines the joints, usually in the hands and feet. Periodontal disease appears to increase risk for rheumatoid arthritis.

What may happen: One of the bacteria (Porphyromonas gingivalis) that causes virtually all periodontal disease produces enzymes that allow the infection to survive in crevices between the teeth and gums. These enzymes then trigger a chemical reaction that produces immunogens, molecules that activate an immune response in the body's joints.

Scientific evidence: A study of more than 6,600 men and women found that those with moderate-to-severe periodontitis were more than twice as likely to have rheumatoid arthritis as those with no or only mild periodontitis.

Even though not everyone with periodontal disease will develop rheumatoid arthritis (or have worse symptoms if they've already been diagnosed), there's strong evidence that the two are related.

My advice: In addition to daily brushing and flossing, get your teeth checked at least once a year. Periodontal disease can be treated with professional care. It will help you save your teeth—and possibly your joints as well.

• **Cervical and anal cancers.** Virtually all of these malignancies—along with many cancers of the oral cavity—are caused by the human papillomavirus (HPV), the most common sexually transmitted infection in the US.

HPV is so common that most sexually active men and women will get at least one form of the virus. Most people will never know they're infected (your immune system usually eliminates the virus with time), and there's no blood test to detect it. Most HPV viruses have oncogenic (cancer-causing) potential. Two of the highest-risk strains, types 16 and 18, account for the majority of cervical cancers. (The viruses that cause genital warts do not cause cancer.)

My advice: The HPV vaccine is recommended for young men and women before they start having sex, but it's effective for anyone who hasn't yet been exposed. Even if you've already been infected with HPV, the vaccine may protect you against a strain that you haven't yet been exposed to. Talk to your doctor for advice.

Also important: Women between the ages of 21 and 29 should have a Pap test every three years, and starting at age 30, they should have a Pap and HPV test at least every five years until age 65. (The HPV test may detect the virus before cell changes can be seen with the Pap test.) A form of the Pap test can also be done for men and women who engage in anal sex.

5 Myths About Arthritis

C. Thomas Vangsness, Jr., MD, professor of orthopaedic surgery and chief of sports medicine at Keck School of Medicine at University of Southern California, Los Angeles. He is author, with Greg Ptacek, of *The New Science of Overcoming Arthritis: Prevent or Reverse Your Pain, Discomfort and Limitations.*

About one in six Americans will have to cope with osteoarthritis* during their lifetimes. But even though so many people have it, there's still a lot of misinformation about it. *What's true about osteoarthritis—and what's not…*

MYTH: Running causes arthritis.

It would seem likely that the pounding the body receives during running could damage cartilage and increase the risk for arthritis. Not true.

A study that followed nearly 75,000 people for seven years found that those who ran 1.2 miles a day were 15% less likely to develop osteoarthritis and 35% less likely to need a hip replacement than those who merely walked.

Even though runners strike the ground with a force that equals eight times their body weight, they take longer strides (and require fewer steps) than walkers. The cumulative jolts caused by running actually appear to be similar to the slower-speed impacts among walkers.

That said, if you have, say, an arthritic knee, you should consult with a medical professional before beginning a running program. The joint stress from running could increase the progression in an already-damaged joint.

MYTH: Don't move when you're hurting.

The traditional arthritis advice is to give your joints total rest during flare-ups. Don't believe it.

You obviously don't want to overdo it when a joint is inflamed. But gentle movements keep joints mobile, flush out inflammatory chemicals and improve the flow of oxygen and nutrients to damaged tissues.

On "good" days, you could swim, lift weights, jog, etc. Yoga is an excellent exercise because it strengthens muscles and joints in a controlled fashion. Tai chi is another excellent form of gentle exercise.

Important: If you have more pain than usual, talk to your doctor or physical therapist before starting—or continuing—exercise. You might need to adjust your workouts, including stopping/starting particular exercises.

MYTH: It's an age-related disease.

This is one of the most pervasive myths. Over the last few decades, people have begun to get osteoarthritis at younger and younger ages. Today, the average age at which symptoms start is 45—and the downward trend is likely to continue.

Experts aren't sure how to explain the increase in younger adults. Americans are heavier than they used to be, and obesity is strongly associated with arthritis. Also, injuries to joints during sports can lead to joint pain down the road. Ongoing inflammation increases cartilage destruction in the joint.

Important: If you have had a joint injury—a torn meniscus in the knee, for example—at any age, there's a good chance that you eventually will develop arthritis in the same joint. Work with a physical therapist to strengthen the muscles and tendons that surround the joint before symptoms start.

MYTH: A little extra weight is OK.

Studies have shown that people who are obese have more inflammation, less joint mobility and more cartilage damage than those who are lean. But what if you're just a few pounds overweight?

It's still a problem. People tend to exercise less when they're overweight. Reduced movement leads to less joint mobility—and more pain. Also, even a small amount of extra weight increases pressure on the joints. Every 10 pounds that you add above the waist generates an extra 70 to 100 pounds of pressure on the knees when you walk.

Research has shown that women who lose about 11 pounds can reduce their risk of developing arthritis symptoms by more than 50%.

MYTH: You can't stop it.

Arthritis may be persistent, but it's rarely hard to treat. Most patients get good relief

---

*The advice in this article may help with rheumatoid arthritis, too. Talk to your doctor.

without high-tech treatments or expensive medications.

My advice: Take one of the NSAIDs (non-steroidal anti-inflammatory drugs) such as aspirin, ibuprofen or naproxen. They reduce pain as well as inflammation. Follow the dosing directions on the label, or ask your doctor for advice.

Helpful: To reduce stomach irritation (a common side effect of all the NSAIDs), take an anti-ulcer medication, such as *cimetidine* (Tagamet). I also have been prescribing a newer medication, *misoprostol* (Cytotec), for stomach irritation. Ask your doctor whether either of these might help you.

(For natural remedies, see the following article.)

Arthritis—Easy Ways to Beat the Pain

Peter Bales, MD, a board-certified orthopedic surgeon and member of the clinical staff in the department of orthopedic surgery at the University of California at Davis Health System. A research advocate for the Arthritis Foundation (Arthritis.org), he is the author of *Osteoarthritis: Preventing and Healing Without Drugs.*

Osteoarthritis has long been considered a "wear-and-tear" disease associated with age-related changes that occur within cartilage and bone.

Now: A growing body of evidence shows that osteoarthritis may have a metabolic basis. Poor diet results in inflammatory changes and damage in cartilage cells, which in turn lead to cartilage breakdown and the development of osteoarthritis.

A recent increase in osteoarthritis cases corresponds to similar increases in diabetes and obesity, other conditions that can be fueled by poor nutrition. Dietary approaches can help prevent—or manage—all three of these conditions.

Key scientific evidence: A number of large studies, including many conducted in Europe as well as the US, suggest that a diet empha-sizing plant foods and fish can support cartilage growth and impede its breakdown. People who combine an improved diet with certain supplements can reduce osteoarthritis symptoms—and possibly stop progression of the disease.

A SMARTER DIET

By choosing your foods carefully, you can significantly improve the pain and stiffness caused by osteoarthritis. *How to get started…*

• **Avoid acidic foods.** The typical American diet, with its processed foods, red meat and harmful trans-fatty acids, increases acidity in the body. A high-acid environment within the joints increases free radicals, corrosive molecules that both accelerate cartilage damage and inhibit the activity of cartilage-producing cells known as chondrocytes.

A Mediterranean diet, which includes generous amounts of fruits, vegetables, whole grains, olive oil and fish, is more alkaline. (The body requires a balance of acidity and alkalinity, as measured on the pH scale.) A predominantly alkaline body chemistry inhibits free radicals and reduces inflammation.

What to do: Eat a Mediterranean-style diet, including six servings daily of vegetables… three servings of fruit…and two tablespoons of olive oil. (The acids in fruits and vegetables included in this diet are easily neutralized in the body.) Other sources of healthful fats include olives, nuts (such as walnuts), canola oil and flaxseed oil or ground flaxseed.

Important: It can take 12 weeks or more to flush out acidic toxins and reduce arthritis symptoms after switching to an alkaline diet.

• **Limit your intake of sugary and processed foods.** Most Americans consume a lot of refined carbohydrates as well as sugar-sweetened foods and soft drinks—all of which damage joints in several ways. For example, sugar causes an increase in advanced glycation endproducts (AGEs), protein molecules that bind to collagen (the connective tissue of cartilage and other tissues) and make it stiff and brittle. AGEs also appear to stimulate the production of cartilage-degrading enzymes.

What to do: Avoid processed foods, such as white flour (including cakes, cookies and crackers), white pasta and white rice, as well as soft drinks and fast food. Studies have shown that people who mainly eat foods in their whole, natural forms tend to have lower levels of AGEs and healthier cartilage.

Important: Small amounts of sugar—used to sweeten coffee or cereal, for example—will not significantly increase AGE levels.

•**Get more vitamin C.** More than 10 years ago, the Framingham study found that people who took large doses of vitamin C had a threefold reduction in the risk for osteoarthritis progression.

Vitamin C is an alkalinizing agent due to its anti-inflammatory and antioxidant properties. It blocks the inflammatory effects of free radicals. Vitamin C also decreases the formation of AGEs and reduces the chemical changes that cause cartilage breakdown.

What to do: Take a vitamin C supplement (1,000 mg daily for the prevention of osteoarthritis…2,000 mg daily if you have osteoarthritis).* Also increase your intake of vitamin C–rich foods, such as sweet red peppers, strawberries and broccoli.

•**Drink green tea.** Green tea alone won't relieve osteoarthritis pain, but people who drink green tea and switch to a healthier diet may notice an additional improvement in symptoms. That's because green tea is among the most potent sources of antioxidants, including catechins, substances that inhibit the activity of cartilage-degrading enzymes. For osteoarthritis, drink one to two cups of green tea daily. (Check with your doctor first if you take any prescription drugs.)

•**Eat fish.** Eat five to six three-ounce servings of omega-3–rich fish (such as salmon, sardines and mackerel) weekly. Omega-3s in such fish help maintain the health of joint cartilage and help curb inflammation. If you would prefer to take a fish oil supplement rather than eat fish, see the recommendation below.

*Check with your doctor before taking any dietary supplements.

SUPPLEMENTS THAT HELP

Dietary changes are a first step to reducing osteoarthritis symptoms. However, the use of certain supplements also can be helpful.

•**Fish oil.** The two omega-3s in fish—docosahexaenoic acid (DHA) and eicosapentaenoic acid (EPA)—block chemical reactions in our cells that convert dietary fats into chemical messengers (such as prostaglandins), which affect the inflammatory status of our bodies. This is the same process that's inhibited by nonsteroidal anti-inflammatory drugs (NSAIDs), such as *ibuprofen* (Motrin).

What to do: If you find it difficult to eat the amount of omega-3–rich fish mentioned above, ask your doctor about taking fish oil supplements that supply a total of 1,600 mg of EPA and 800 mg of DHA daily. Look for a "pharmaceutical grade" fish oil product, such as Sealogix, available at FishOilRx.com, 888-966-3423, *fishoilrx.com*…or RxOmega-3 Factors at *iherb.com*.

If, after 12 weeks, you need more pain relief—or have a strong family history of osteoarthritis—add…

•**Glucosamine, chondroitin and MSM.** The most widely used supplements for osteoarthritis are glucosamine and chondroitin, taken singly or in combination. Most studies show that they work.

Better: A triple combination that contains methylsulfonylmethane (MSM) as well as glucosamine and chondroitin. MSM is a sulfur-containing compound that provides the raw material for cartilage regrowth. Glucosamine and chondroitin reduce osteoarthritis pain and have anti-inflammatory properties.

What to do: Take daily supplements of glucosamine (1,500 mg)…chondroitin (1,200 mg)…and MSM (1,500 mg).

Instead of—or in addition to—the fish oil and the triple combination, you may want to take…

•**SAMe.** Like MSM, S-adenosylmethionine (SAMe) is a sulfur-containing compound. It reduces the body's production of TNF-alpha, a substance that's involved in cartilage destruction. It also seems to increase cartilage production.

In one study, researchers compared SAMe to the prescription anti-inflammatory drug *celecoxib* (Celebrex). The study was double-blind (neither the patients nor the doctors knew who was getting which drug or supplement), and it continued for four months. Initially, patients taking the celecoxib reported fewer symptoms—but by the second month, there was no difference between the two groups.

Other studies have found similar results. SAMe seems to work as well as over-the-counter and/or prescription drugs for osteoarthritis, but it works more slowly. I advise patients to take it for at least three months to see effects.

What to do: Start with 200 mg of SAMe daily and increase to 400 mg daily if necessary after a few weeks.

Stay-Well Secrets for People with Diabetes or Prediabetes

Theresa Garnero, advanced practice registered nurse (APRN), certified diabetes educator (CDE) and clinical nurse manager of the Center for Diabetes Services at the California Pacific Medical Center in San Francisco. She is the author of *Your First Year with Diabetes: What to Do, Month by Month.*

Many people downplay the seriousness of diabetes. That's a mistake. Because elevated glucose can damage blood vessels, nerves, the kidneys and eyes, people with diabetes are much more likely to die from heart disease and/or kidney disease than people without diabetes—and they are at increased risk for infections, including gum disease, as well as blindness and amputation. (Nerve damage and poor circulation can allow dangerous infections to go undetected.)

And diabetes can be sneaky—increased thirst, urination and/or hunger are the most common symptoms, but many people have no symptoms and are unaware that they are sick.

Despite these sobering facts, doctors rarely have time to give their patients all the information they need to cope with the complexities of diabetes. Fortunately, diabetes educators—health-care professionals, such as registered nurses, registered dietitians and medical social workers—can give patients practical advice on the best ways to control their condition.*

Good news: Most health insurers, including Medicare, cover the cost of diabetes patients' visits with a diabetes educator.

SAVVY EATING HABITS

Most doctors advise people with diabetes or prediabetes to cut back on refined carbohydrates, such as cakes and cookies, and eat more fruits, vegetables and whole grains. This maximizes nutrition and promotes a healthy body weight (being overweight greatly increases diabetes risk). *Other steps to take…*

• **Drink one extra glass of water each day.** The extra fluid will help prevent dehydration, which can raise glucose levels.

• **Never skip meals—especially breakfast.** Don't assume that bypassing a meal and fasting for more than five to six hours will help lower glucose levels. It actually triggers the liver to release glucose into the bloodstream.

Better strategy: Eat three small meals daily and have snacks in between. Start with breakfast, such as a cup of low-fat yogurt and whole-wheat toast with peanut butter or a small bowl of whole-grain cereal and a handful of nuts.

Good snack options: A small apple or three graham crackers. Each of these snacks contains about 15 g of carbohydrates.

• **Practice the "plate method."** Divide a nine-inch plate in half. Fill half with vegetables, then split the other half into quarters—one for protein, such as salmon, lean meat, beans or tofu…and the other for starches, such as one-third cup of pasta or one-half cup of peas or corn. Then have a small piece of fruit. This is an easy way to practice portion control—and get the nutrients you need.

Ask yourself if you are satisfied after you take each bite. If the answer is "yes," stop eating. This simple strategy helped one of my clients lose 50 pounds.

*To find a diabetes educator near you, consult the American Association of Diabetes Educators, 800-338-3633, *diabeteseducator.org.*

• **Be wary of "sugar-free" foods.** These products, including sugar-free cookies and diabetic candy, often are high in carbohydrates, which are the body's primary source of glucose. You may be better off eating the regular product, which is more satisfying. Compare the carbohydrate contents on product labels.

GET CREATIVE WITH EXERCISE

If you have diabetes or prediabetes, you've probably been told to get more exercise. Walking is especially helpful. For those with diabetes, walking for at least two hours a week has been shown to reduce the risk for death by 30% over an eight-year period. For those with prediabetes, walking for 30 minutes five days a week reduces by about 60% the risk that your condition will progress to diabetes. *But if you'd like some other options, consider...***

• **Armchair workouts.** These exercises, which are performed while seated and are intended for people with physical limitations to standing, increase stamina, muscle tone, flexibility and coordination. For DVDs, go to *arm chairfitness.com* or call 800-882-7432.

• **Strength training.** This type of exercise builds muscle, which burns more calories than fat even when you are not exercising.*** Use hand weights, exercise machines or the weight of your own body—for example, leg squats or bicep curls with no weights. Aim for two to three sessions of strength training weekly, on alternate days.

• **Stretching**—even while watching TV or talking on the phone. By building a stretching routine into your daily activities, you won't need to set aside a separate time to do it. If your body is flexible, it's easier to perform other kinds of physical activity. Stretching also promotes better circulation. Before stretching, do a brief warm-up, such as walking for five minutes and doing several arm windmills. Aim to do stretching exercises at least three times weekly, including before your other workouts.

**Consult your doctor before starting a new exercise program.

***If you have high blood pressure, be sure to check with your doctor before starting a strength-training program. This type of exercise can raise blood pressure.

CONTROL YOUR BLOOD GLUCOSE

If you are diagnosed with diabetes, blood glucose control is the immediate goal. Self-monitoring can be performed using newer devices that test blood glucose levels.

Good choices: LifeScan's OneTouch Ultra... Bayer's Contour...or Abbott Laboratories' Free-Style.

The hemoglobin A1C test, which is ordered by your doctor and typically is done two to four times a year, determines how well glucose levels have been controlled over the previous two to three months.

If you have prediabetes: Don't settle for a fasting glucose test, which measures blood glucose after you have fasted overnight. It misses two-thirds of all cases of diabetes. The oral glucose tolerance test (OGTT), which involves testing glucose immediately before drinking a premixed glass of glucose and repeating the test two hours later, is more reliable. If you can't get an OGTT, ask for an A1C test and fasting glucose test.

If you have diabetes or prediabetes, you should have your blood pressure and cholesterol checked at every doctor visit and schedule regular eye exams and dental appointments. *In addition, don't overlook...*

• **Proper kidney testing.** Doctors most commonly recommend annual microalbumin and creatinine urine tests to check for kidney disease. You also may want to ask for a glomerular filtration rate test, which measures kidney function.

• **Meticulous foot care.** High glucose levels can reduce sensation in your feet, making it hard to know when you have a cut, blister or injury. In addition to seeing a podiatrist at least once a year and inspecting your own feet daily, be wary of everyday activities that can be dangerous for people with diabetes.

Stepping into hot bath water, for example, can cause a blister or skin damage that can become infected. To protect yourself, check the water temperature on your wrist or elbow before you step in. The temperature should be warm to the touch—not hot.

STAY UP TO DATE ON MEDICATIONS

Once diabetes medication has been prescribed, people with diabetes should review their drug regimen with their doctors at every visit. *Insulin is the most commonly used diabetes drug, but you may want to also ask your doctor about these relatively new medications...*

•**DPP-4 inhibitors.** These drugs include *sitagliptin* (Januvia), which lowers glucose levels by increasing the amount of insulin secreted by the pancreas. DPP-4 inhibitors are used alone or with another type of diabetes medication.

•**Symlin.** Administered with an injectable pen, *pramlintide* (Symlin) helps control blood glucose and reduces appetite, which may help with weight loss. It is used in addition to insulin.

If you have prediabetes or diabetes: Always consult a pharmacist or doctor before taking any over-the-counter products. Cold medicines with a high sugar content may raise your blood glucose, for example, and wart removal products may cause skin ulcers. Pay close attention to drug label warnings.

Reduce Diabetes Risk One Serving at a Time

Start by substituting just one serving a day of water or unsweetened tea or coffee for one serving of a sugar-sweetened soft drink or dairy beverage.

Reason: Each daily serving of a sweetened soft drink or milk drink, such as a milk shake, raises diabetes risk by 14% to 27%. Each additional 5% of total calories from sweetened drinks raises the risk by 18%.

Study of data on diet and diabetes incidence in more than 25,000 British men and women, ages 40 to 79, by researchers at University of Cambridge, UK, published in *Diabetologia*.

Supplements That Help Manage Diabetes

Mark A. Stengler, NMD, licensed naturopathic medical doctor in private practice, Stengler Center for Integrative Medicine, Encinitas, California...author of many books, including *The Natural Physician's Healing Therapies* and coauthor of *Prescription for Natural Cures*.

Lifestyle change has always been the cornerstone treatment for people with type 2 diabetes. Beyond that, natural approaches are rarely discussed. Mark Stengler, ND, author of several books on alternative health, recommends a number of plant-based remedies for those with diabetes, some of which date back hundreds, even thousands, of years...

According to Dr. Stengler, type 2 diabetes absolutely can be prevented and, in certain cases, even reversed with diet, exercise and appropriate dietary supplements. The following is some of his own "best practice" advice for prevention, maintenance and symptom management of this lifestyle-related disease.

To prevent diabetes...

•**Curb sugar cravings with gymnema sylvestre.** A staple of Ayurvedic medicine, this herb helps curb cravings for sugary foods that throw your blood glucose levels off balance. Scientists speculate that it works by positively influencing insulin-producing cells in the pancreas.

Dr. Stengler believes gymnema sylvestre works best when used in combination with other glucose-balancing herbs, such as bitter melon and fenugreek. Ask your doctor for advice on the best combination and dosage for you.

•**Chromium can normalize sugar levels.** Your body requires adequate levels of chromium to properly control blood glucose levels. This essential trace mineral aids in the uptake of blood sugar into the body's cells, where it can be used to generate energy more efficiently. It's also helpful in reducing sweet cravings.

Dr. Stengler advises up to 1,000 micrograms of chromium a day (under your physician's supervision). He adds that this is a good mineral to take with gymnema.

• **Regulate blood sugar with fiber and fiber supplements.** Soluble fiber helps prevent or control prediabetes and diabetes by slowing the rate at which intestines release glucose into the bloodstream, thus modulating fluctuations in blood sugar levels. Rich sources of soluble fiber include plant foods, such as legumes, oat bran, rye, barley, broccoli, carrots, artichokes, peas, prunes, berries and bananas. In a small study in Taiwan, scientists found that supplementation with glucomannan (a soluble dietary fiber made from konjac flour) lowered elevated levels of blood lipids, cholesterol and glucose in people with diabetes.

Most Americans eat too much junk food and too little fiber. For his patients who fall into that category, Dr. Stengler typically prescribes one glucomannan capsule 30 minutes before lunch and dinner, and another before bedtime with a large glass of water.

Managing symptoms and minimizing complications…

• **Boost antioxidant levels with alpha-lipoic acid.** This powerful antioxidant kills free radicals that damage cells and cause pain, inflammation, burning, tingling and numbness in people who have peripheral neuropathy (nerve damage) caused by diabetes. Studies also suggest that alpha-lipoic acid (ALA) enables the body to utilize glucose more efficiently.

Dr. Stengler says to take alpha-lipoic acid daily under a physician's supervision.

• **Decrease blood glucose levels with chamomile tea.** Drinking chamomile tea, a rich source of antioxidants, may help prevent diabetes complications, such as blindness, nerve damage and kidney problems, according to recent research by UK and Japanese scientists.

Drink chamomile tea along with antioxidant-rich black, white and green teas, says Dr. Stengler.

• **Take omega-3 fatty acids to reduce inflammation.** These healthy fats improve the body's ability to respond to insulin, reduce inflammation, lower blood lipids and prevent excessive blood clotting. Good dietary sources of omega-3 fatty acids include cold-water fish, such as salmon or cod (eat two or three times a week), olive or canola oil, flaxseed and English walnuts.

Dr. Stengler's advice: Unless you know you are getting sufficient omega-3 fatty acids in your diet, it's good to take a daily fish oil supplement that contains about 1,000 mg of the omega-3 fatty acid eicosapentaenoic acid (EPA) and about 500 mg of the omega-3 fatty acid docosahexaenoic acid (DHA).

Caution: Because many dietary supplements lower blood sugar, and fish oil supplements may alter the way anticoagulant therapy functions, it is critical to work closely with your doctor before and while taking any of the above supplements. He/she will prescribe the right doses for you and also may suggest that you alter other medications accordingly.

DON'T NEGLECT THE ABCS OF DIABETES SELF-CARE

When addressing a difficult disease such as diabetes, all the nutrients and vitamins in the world will do no good if you do not also follow the basics of diabetes self-care. Maintain a healthy weight…get 20 to 30 minutes of exercise most days of the week…follow a diet that emphasizes lean proteins and healthy fats and limits simple carbohydrates…monitor blood glucose levels…and take diabetes, blood pressure and cholesterol medicine as prescribed by your physician. Dr. Stengler adds that even as simple a measure as taking a 10-minute walk after each meal can keep blood sugar under control. Start today.

Diabetes: Make Your Life Easier by Avoiding These Mistakes

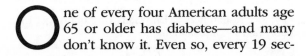

Gretchen Becker, a Halifax, Vermont–based science and medical writer who was diagnosed with type 2 diabetes in 1996. She is the author of *The First Year: Type 2 Diabetes.* GretchenBecker.com

One of every four American adults age 65 or older has diabetes—and many don't know it. Even so, every 19 seconds, an American is diagnosed with type 2 diabetes.

My story: After I was diagnosed with type 2 diabetes 20 years ago, I vowed to help people avoid some of the missteps that are commonly made when navigating the trickier aspects of this complex disease. *Mistakes you can avoid…*

MISTAKE #1: Assuming that you'll have obvious symptoms. You may be able to name a few of the classic diabetes symptoms, such as excessive thirst, frequent urination and blurred vision. But maybe you don't have any of these red flags.

Perhaps you do feel a little more tired than usual or have numbness or tingling in your hands or feet that you can't explain. These could be subtle signs that your blood glucose levels are out of whack. The symptoms that I initially dismissed were frequent bathroom breaks, increasing nearsightedness and scratches on my arms that wouldn't heal for more than a month.

Surprisingly, you could even be losing weight. Even though diabetes is commonly associated with being overweight, sometimes people drop a few pounds because they're losing water weight when they are urinating frequently and/or their metabolism is not allowing them to properly absorb calories.

What you should know: If you notice any changes—even if they seem minor—write them down and be sure to discuss them at your next doctor visit.

Important: If your doctor doesn't routinely test your blood glucose levels, ask him/her to do so at least every three years if you're past age 45. If you have any risk factors, such as a family history (in a parent, sibling or child) or being overweight, you may need more frequent testing…and perhaps starting at an earlier age.

Also: Be sure that you're not fighting a cold or some other infection when you're tested—such illnesses can elevate blood glucose levels.

MISTAKE #2: Worrying only about sugar. Lots of people assume that individuals with diabetes simply need to avoid sugar. The truth is, it's much more complicated than that. In fact, virtually everything you eat affects your blood glucose in one way or another.

Carbohydrates (which include starchy foods, such as bread, rice and potatoes, that turn into sugar when they are digested) as well as sugar itself actually have the greatest effect on your blood glucose. Fiber (both soluble fiber, the type that slows down digestion and is found in oat bran, barley, nuts, seeds and beans… and insoluble fiber, the type that adds bulk to your stool and is found in wheat bran and whole grains) also plays a role. It's soluble fiber that can be used to improve your blood glucose levels.

What you should know: Food labels are confusing. Because fiber is a healthy carbohydrate, food labels in the US include it in the total carbohydrate count—for example, a product with 34 g of carbohydrates and 14 g of fiber, has an actual carbohydrate content of 20 g. In other countries, such as those in Europe, the food label would list this same product as having 20 g of carbohydrates and 14 g of fiber. Understanding such quirks in food labeling will help ensure that you're not getting more or less carbs than you think.

MISTAKE #3: Not keeping close tabs on your numbers. If you are diagnosed with diabetes, your doctor will no doubt explain that the condition is largely a numbers game—with the prime target being your blood glucose level. Whatever advice your doctor gives you in terms of testing, take it seriously.

Especially in the first year, it's important for most people with diabetes to monitor these levels three to five times throughout the day. Don't try to cut corners. It's true that the test strips you use can be expensive if your insurance limits the number you receive, but the cost of diabetes complications is much greater. If you must economize on test strips, ask your doctor for advice on the best times to test during the day.

Frequent testing will help you understand what causes your blood glucose levels to become elevated. You can then develop strategies to keep them in the normal range—this is the single best way to prevent serious complications, such as kidney failure, diabetic neuropathy and amputation of lower limbs.

In addition to diet, there are other factors that affect blood glucose. Managing stress and increasing physical activity are also important. Aim for 30 minutes of aerobic exercise (such as brisk walking) at least five days a week, but be sure to add some weight lifting a few times a week—it also helps with blood glucose control.

What you should know: Even when your blood glucose levels improve, you can't revert back to old behavior. The improvement simply means that you're doing what you need to do to control your disease and now have the flexibility to make small modifications, such as adding a few more carbs to your diet if you've lost some extra weight. Be sure to keep testing to make sure you don't overdo it. And never stop taking your diabetes medication without consulting your doctor!

MISTAKE #4: **Settling for daily blood glucose testing alone.** Even though your daily blood glucose levels are the main number you need to focus on, other tests are helpful. For example, your doctor should also order (usually quarterly) a hemoglobin A1c test, which measures your average blood glucose for the past two to three months. This will tell you how well your overall diabetes treatment is working. Closely tracking your blood pressure and lipid levels (including cholesterol and triglycerides) is also important.

What you should know: No matter what test you are receiving, always insist on knowing the normal range for the lab. Just asking for the result (without knowing the lab's range) can be very misleading.

MISTAKE #5: **Going it alone.** Other diabetes patients can often provide crucial tips, insights and lifestyle advice that you won't hear from a physician who doesn't live with diabetes on a daily basis.

What you should know: You'll save yourself time and trouble by going online for practical tips. In addition to support groups such as *dlife.com* and the American Diabetes Association's online community at *diabetes.org*, there's an excellent resource that was founded by David Mendosa, a fellow diabetes patient—*mendosa.com/advice.htm*. His site is especially useful because he reviews other websites so you can go directly to the ones that offer the best information.

Diabetes Coach to the Rescue!

Lisa Foster-McNulty, RN, CDE, a registered nurse, certified diabetes educator and the director of patient care and education at Integrated Diabetes Services in Wynnewood, Pennsylvania, IntegratedDiabetes.com. She serves as cochair of the Education Committee for the local affiliate of the American Association of Diabetes Educators.

If you've got diabetes, whether you're prescribed medication or not, your doctor may well give you a daunting to-do list with items such as "lose weight"…"cut back on carbs"…"lower your blood sugar"…and "get more exercise."

The challenging part is that you are on your own in *reaching* those goals! Most doctors don't have time to give patients the support they need in managing the self-care of their disease. But help is available.

Many people now depend on health coaches. A coach—ideally a "certified diabetes educator" (CDE), a health-care professional, such as a registered nurse, pharmacist or registered dietitian, with specialized training—can help people with diabetes navigate the intricate day-to-day details that determine how effectively they will control their disease.

HOW IT WORKS

With diabetes coaching, patients usually meet their coaches in person (the frequency and number of visits often depend on insurance coverage). The meetings can be private or in group settings at a doctor's office or medical center. In some cases, coaches also stay in touch with patients with phone calls, e-mail or Skype. What kind of help will you get? It depends entirely on what you need. *Examples…*

•**Exercise for nonexercisers.** Regular exercise is among the best ways to lower blood sugar, improve insulin sensitivity and reduce diabetes-related complications.

However, the reality is that many people with diabetes have never exercised, and you can't expect someone to go from being totally sedentary to athletic just by saying that he/she should.

A coach looks for ways to ease people into exercise. For example, you might take a 10-minute walk after each meal—but even that might be too much, particularly for someone who's obese or has other health issues. How about standing up during TV commercials? Even this small step can make a difference. Marching in place is even better. Don't feel like standing? Try tapping your feet while you sit. From a health coach's perspective, *any* activity is better than none.

• **Investigating blood sugar spikes.** Let's say you take diabetes medication and check your blood sugar every day. The readings have generally been good, but lately your glucose has been consistently testing high. What changed?

It could be many things. For example, have you had a recent illness? A bacterial infection may raise glucose levels. Maybe you've gotten careless with your diet because you're not testing often enough.

Your coach can help you figure it out. He will look at *all* of the factors that affect blood sugar—not in general terms, but those that affect you personally.

• **Help with carb counting.** It's among the most effective ways to manage after-meal glucose levels. Counting carbohydrates is particularly important for people taking insulin—they often need a higher dose for a carbohydrate-rich meal.

But carb counting can be tricky. Carb plans are individualized, but generally patients are advised to have between nine and 13 carbohydrate choices a day, with each "choice" equaling 15 g of carbohydrate. A coach can help you fine-tune your carb plan when your glucose is running high.

Example: Many people depend on "eyeball estimates"—they look at the size of an apple or another food and make a quick mental calculation about the carbohydrates. You might be great at estimating...or not so great. If there's been an unexpected change in your readings, inaccurate carb counting could be to blame. Your coach might recommend that you take a more scientific approach, such as using a scale or measuring cups.

• **Real-life monitoring.** Many people don't realize that their glucose is high because they're not checking their blood sugar levels often enough (the full cost of test strips isn't always covered by insurance). A diabetes coach will *always* ask how often and when you're checking your glucose—and help you find a solution if cost is an issue.

Example: Maybe you should be checking your glucose level more than four times a day but can't afford it. A coach might advise you to check your glucose around breakfast time one day...around lunchtime another day... and at bedtime on a third day. After a few weeks, the coach will have enough information to identify, in general terms, your blood sugar trends. He can then recommend certain changes—such as eating more or less carbohydrates (see above)—to bring your readings into your target range.

• **Strategic eating.** To help keep your blood sugar levels under control, a coach may give advice not only on the foods you eat but also on the order in which they are consumed. That's because research shows that eating protein-rich foods first and saving carbs for the end of meals helps blunt blood sugar spikes. Using this strategy, a person with diabetes having a meal of, say, grilled chicken, broccoli and potatoes should consume those foods in that order to minimize the impact on his blood sugar.

HOW TO FIND A COACH

If you have diabetes, a certified diabetes educator (CDE) can give you the kind of attention you need to really get control of your disease. A CDE is a health-care professional, such as a nurse, pharmacist or dietitian, who has met the requirements of the National Certification Board for Diabetes Educators (NCBDE). This certification, which requires 1,000 hours of diabetes-management training, passing an exam and undergoing continuing education, greatly increases your chances of getting reimbursed for the cost of diabetes coaching services. Check with your insurer.

If the coaching is not covered by insurance, depending on where you live, you can expect to pay $30 (for a group) to $200 (one-on-one) for an initial consultation with a coach/diabetes educator, with an additional charge for a "service plan" that includes a certain number of visits, phone calls and/or e-mails. To find a certified diabetes educator near you, go to *ncbde.org*.

How to Use Insulin the Right Way

Richard K. Bernstein, MD, a diabetes specialist in private practice in Mamaroneck, New York. Dr. Bernstein is also the author of nine books on diabetes, most recently *Dr. Bernstein's Diabetes Solution: A Complete Guide to Achieving Normal Blood Sugars*. His free monthly teleseminars are available at AskDrBernstein.net.

Insulin injections are crucial for type 1 diabetes and often needed for type 2 diabetes. *To use effectively…*

•**Change with the seasons.** Most people need less insulin in summer than winter (or during a warm spell in colder months). Capillaries dilate when warm, and more blood containing insulin is delivered to peripheral tissues. Adjust your dose accordingly.

•**Prevent blood sugar spikes by correctly gauging how much insulin you need to cover each meal and when to inject it.** With Regular (a type of short-acting insulin), that's usually 30 to 45 minutes before the meal.

To determine your best timing: Inject an insulin dose, and check blood sugar after 25 minutes, then at five-minute intervals. When it has dropped by 5 mg/dL, it's time to eat. This may not work for people who have diabetic gastroparesis, which causes unpredictable stomach emptying.

Statins Can Help Diabetes Complications

In addition to lowering risk for heart attack and stroke, statins lowered risk for diabetes complications, according to a recent finding. People with diabetes taking statins were 34% less likely to be diagnosed with diabetes-related nerve damage (neuropathy)…40% less likely to develop diabetes-related damage to the retina…and 12% less likely to develop gangrene than diabetics not taking statins.

Børge G. Nordestgaard, MD, DMSc, chief physician at Copenhagen University Hospital, Herlev, Denmark, and leader of a study of 60,000 people, published in *The Lancet Diabetes Endocrinology*.

The Diabetes Complication That Kills More People Than Most Cancers

James M. Horton, MD, chair of the Standards and Practice Guidelines Committee of the Infectious Diseases Society of America, IDSociety.org. Dr. Horton is also chief of the department of infectious disease and attending faculty physician in the department of internal medicine, both at Carolinas Medical Center in Charlotte, North Carolina.

A foot or leg amputation is one of the most dreaded complications of diabetes. In the US, more than 65,000 such amputations occur each year.

But the tragedy does not stop there. According to recent research, about half of all people who have a foot amputation die within five years of the surgery—a worse mortality rate than most cancers. That's partly because people with diabetes who have amputations often have poorer glycemic control and more complications such as kidney disease. Amputation also can lead to increased pressure on the remaining limb and the possibility of new ulcers and infections.

Latest development: To combat the increasingly widespread problem of foot infections and amputations, new guidelines for the diagnosis and treatment of diabetic foot infections have been created by the Infectious Diseases Society of America (IDSA).

What you need to know…

HOW FOOT INFECTIONS START

Diabetes can lead to foot infections in two main ways—peripheral neuropathy (nerve damage that can cause loss of sensation in the feet)…and ischemia (inadequate blood flow).

To understand why these conditions can be so dangerous, think back to the last time you had a pebble inside your shoe. How long did it take before the irritation became unbearable? Individuals with peripheral neuropathy and ischemia usually don't feel any pain in their feet. Without pain, the pebble will stay in the shoe and eventually cause a sore on the sole of the foot.

Similarly, people with diabetes will not feel the rub of an ill-fitting shoe or the pressure of standing on one foot too long, so they are at risk of developing pressure sores or blisters.

These small wounds can lead to big trouble. About 25% of people with diabetes will develop a foot ulcer—ranging from mild to severe—at some point in their lives. Any ulcer, blister, cut or irritation has the potential to become infected. If the infection becomes too severe to treat effectively with antibiotics, amputation of a foot or leg may be the only way to prevent the infection from spreading throughout the body and save the person's life.

A FAST-MOVING DANGER

Sores on the foot can progress rapidly. While some foot sores remain unchanged for months, it is possible for an irritation to lead to an open wound (ulcer), infection and amputation in as little as a few days. That is why experts recommend that people with diabetes seek medical care promptly for any open sore on the feet or any new area of redness or irritation that could possibly lead to an open wound.

Important: Fully half of diabetic foot ulcers are infected and require immediate medical treatment and sometimes hospitalization.

Don't try to diagnose yourself—diagnosis requires a trained medical expert. An ulcer that appears very small on the surface could have actually spread underneath the skin, so you very well could be seeing just a small portion of the infection.

WHAT YOUR DOCTOR WILL DO

The first step is to identify the bacteria causing the infection. To do this, physicians collect specimens from deep inside the wound. Once the bacteria have been identified, the proper antibiotics can be prescribed.

Physicians also need to know the magnitude of the infection—for example, whether there is bone infection, abscesses or other internal problems. Therefore, all diabetes patients who have new foot infections should have X-rays. If more detailed imaging is needed, an MRI or a bone scan may be ordered.

The doctor will then classify the wound and infection as mild, moderate or severe and create a treatment plan.

HOW TO GET THE BEST TREATMENT

Each person's wound is unique, so there are no cookie-cutter treatment plans. *However, most treatment plans should include…*

•**A diabetes foot-care team.** For moderate or severe infections, a team of experts should coordinate treatment. This will be done for you—by the hospital or your primary care physician. The number of specialists on the team depends on the patient's specific needs but may include experts in podiatry and vascular surgery. In rural or smaller communities, this may be done via online communication with experts from larger hospitals (telemedicine).

•**Antibiotic treatment.** Milder infections usually involve a single bacterium. Antibiotics will typically be needed for about one week. With more severe infections, multiple bacteria are likely involved, so you will require multiple antibiotics, and treatment will need to continue for a longer period—sometimes four weeks or more if bone is affected.

If the infection is severe…or even moderate but complicated by, say, poor blood circulation, hospitalization may be required for a few days to a few weeks, depending on the course of the recovery.

• **Wound care.** Many patients who have foot infections receive antibiotic therapy only, which is often insufficient. Proper wound care is also necessary. In addition to frequent wound cleansing and dressing changes, this may include surgical removal of dead tissue (debridement)…and the use of specially designed shoes or shoe inserts—provided by a podiatrist—to redistribute pressure off the wound (off-loading).

• **Surgery.** Surgery doesn't always mean amputation. It is sometimes used not only to remove dead or damaged tissue or bone but also to improve blood flow to the foot.

If an infection fails to improve: The first question physicians know to ask is: "Is the patient complying with wound care instructions?" Too many patients lose a leg because they don't take their antibiotics as prescribed or care for the injury as prescribed.

Never forget: Following your doctors' specific orders could literally mean the difference between having one leg or two.

More from Dr. Horton…

Foot Care Is Critical If You Have Diabetes

To protect yourself from foot injuries…

• **Never walk barefoot, even around the house.**

• **Don't wear sandals**—the straps can irritate the side of the foot.

• **Wear thick socks with soft leather shoes.** Leather is a good choice because it "breathes," molds to the feet and does not retain moisture. Laced-up shoes with cushioned soles provide the most support.

In addition, pharmacies carry special "diabetic socks" that protect and cushion your feet without cutting off circulation at the ankle. These socks usually have no seams that could chafe. They also wick moisture away from feet, which reduces risk for infection and foot ulcers.

• **See a podiatrist.** This physician can advise you on the proper care of common foot problems, such as blisters, corns and ingrown toenails. A podiatrist can also help you find appropriate footwear—even if you have foot deformities.

Ask your primary care physician or endocrinologist for a recommendation, or consult the American Podiatric Medical Association, *apma.org.*

Also: Inspect your feet every day. Otherwise, you may miss a developing infection. Look for areas of redness, blisters or open sores, particularly in the areas most prone to injury—the bottoms and bony inner and outer edges of the feet.

If you see any sign of a sore, seek prompt medical care. You should also see a doctor if you experience an infected or ingrown toenail, callus formation, bunions or other deformity, fissured (cracked) skin on your feet or you notice any change in sensation.

Pycnogenol Helps Diabetic Retinopathy

Mark A. Stengler, NMD, licensed naturopathic medical doctor and founder and medical director of the Stengler Center for Integrative Medicine, Encinitas, California. He is author of *The Natural Physician's Healing Therapies.*

Pycnogenol (pronounced pic-noj-en-all), an extract from the bark of the French maritime pine, is known to improve circulation, reduce swelling and ease asthma. Now Italian researchers have found another use for it—it helps patients with diabetes who are in the early stages of diabetic retinopathy, a complication of diabetes in which the retina becomes damaged, resulting in vision impairment, including blurred vision, seeing dark spots, impaired night vision, reduced color perception and even blindness.

All people with diabetes are at risk for diabetic retinopathy—and it's estimated that as many as 80% of people with diabetes for 10 years or more will have this complication.

Participants in the Italian study had been diagnosed with diabetes (the researchers did not specify whether the patients had type 1 or 2 diabetes) for four years, and their diabetes was well controlled by diet and oral medication. Study participants had early-stage retinopathy and moderately impaired vision. After two months of treatment, the patients given Pycnogenol had less retinal swelling as measured by ultrasound testing. Most important, their vision was significantly improved. This was especially noticeable because the vision of those in the control group did not improve.

My view: If you have type 1 or 2 diabetes, undergo a comprehensive eye exam at least once a year. If retinopathy is detected, it would be wise to supplement with Pycnogenol (150 milligrams daily). Because retinopathy among diabetes patients is so prevalent, I recommend this amount to all my patients with diabetes to protect their vision. Pycnogenol has a blood-thinning effect, so people who take blood-thinning medication, such as warfarin, should use it only while being monitored by a doctor.

Dr. Terry Wahls's Brain-Boosting Diet Helped Her Conquer Multiple Sclerosis

Terry L. Wahls, MD, an internist and clinical professor of medicine at the University of Iowa Carver College of Medicine in Iowa City and president of the Wahls Foundation, TheWahlsFoundation.com, which provides education to the public about managing multiple sclerosis and other chronic diseases. She is the author of *Minding My Mitochondria: How I Overcame Secondary Progressive Multiple Sclerosis and Got Out of My Wheelchair.*

At age 44, I was diagnosed with multiple sclerosis (MS). Three years later, when I became dependent on a wheelchair, my MS was classified as "secondary progressive," meaning that the disease was steadily progressing with no periods of improvement. I kept getting weaker, even though I was receiving widely used treatments for MS including chemotherapy and immune-suppressing medications.

Now: Thanks to the regimen I designed, I haven't needed a wheelchair or even a cane for several years. I ride to work on my bicycle, my energy is good and I've stopped taking medication to treat my MS. What happened?

Here's what I credit for my dramatic turnaround—and a description of how it might help you, as well. Because MS is a neurological disease, this program is designed to also help people who are concerned about dementia or Parkinson's disease, have depression or have suffered a traumatic brain injury or stroke.

FINDING A SOLUTION

With the help of my medical training, I began poring over the medical literature and designed my own treatment protocol in 2007 based on my theories of what allowed MS to develop and progress.

In people with MS, immune cells damage the myelin sheath, protein and fatty substances that surround nerve cells in the brain and spinal cord. This results in slower nerve signals, which lead to muscle weakness, a lack of balance and muscle coordination, bladder or bowel spasms, blurred vision and other symptoms.

Medications can reduce symptoms, but they don't accelerate nerve signals. As a result, MS patients battle physical and neurological disability—experienced either episodically or in a steady, unrelenting course. The disease often continues to worsen despite therapy. Within 10 years of initial diagnosis, half of MS patients are unable to work because of disabling levels of fatigue, and one-third need a cane, scooter or wheelchair.

After thoroughly reviewing the research, I decided to put myself on a diet that increases the efficiency of mitochondria, units within cells that supply the energy that's needed for nerve activity. Although the effect of diet on MS was unproven, I firmly believed that this was my best hope for fighting MS.

My eating plan was designed to improve the balance of neurotransmitters and supply the mitochondria with the building blocks needed for healthy nerve activity.

MY BRAIN-HEALTH DIET

People who follow this diet typically notice improvements in neurological symptoms within weeks.*

Because natural foods contain a variety of nutrients that can work synergistically, I recommend taking supplements only when you are unable to get the following nutrients in your diet. Be sure to discuss the supplements (and dosages) with your doctor if you take blood-thinning medication—some supplements may have a blood-thinning effect.

In addition to taking such general steps as avoiding sugary and/or processed foods that are low in key nutrients, make sure you get enough…

• **Sulfur vegetables.** Cabbage, kale, collard greens and asparagus are excellent sources of sulfur, which is used by the body to produce gamma-aminobutyric acid (GABA). This "inhibitory" neurotransmitter counteracts the early brain-cell death that can occur if the neurotransmitter glutamate reaches excessive levels.

My advice: Consume three cups of greens each day, including one to three cups of sulfur-rich vegetables daily.

Also: To get other important nutrients, consume one to three cups of brightly colored vegetables or berries each day.

• **Coenzyme Q-10.** Exposure to environmental toxins, such as detergents, pesticide residues and mercury, has been linked to MS and other neurological conditions, such as dementia and Parkinson's disease. Coenzyme Q-10 is a fat-soluble compound that helps minimize the effects of these toxins while increasing the amount of energy produced by mitochondria.

Organ meats, such as calf liver and chicken liver, are among the best sources of coenzyme Q-10. I particularly recommend organ meats for older adults because coenzyme Q-10 pro-

*Consult your doctor before trying the diet and/or supplements described here—especially if you take any medication or have kidney or liver disease.

duction declines with age. It's also suppressed by cholesterol-lowering statin drugs.

My advice: Eat organ meats at least once a week. If you don't like organ meats, sardines, herring and rainbow trout are also high in coenzyme Q-10. Coenzyme Q-10 is available in supplement form, too.

• **Omega-3 fatty acids.** The omega-3 fatty acids in cold-water fish, such as salmon and sardines, are used by the body to produce the myelin that insulates brain and spinal cord cells. Myelin is also used to repair damage caused by MS. Omega-3s are concentrated in the brain and are necessary to help prevent depression and cognitive disorders.

My advice: To avoid concern about mercury and other toxins in cold-water fish, such as salmon, get your omega-3s from fish oil supplements that are purified.

Recommended dose: 1 g to 3 g daily.

• **Kelp and algae.** These detoxify the body by binding to heavy metals in the intestine and removing them in the stool.

My advice: Take supplements—one to two 500-mg to 600-mg capsules of kelp and one to four 500-mg capsules of algae daily. Or, as an alternative, add about a tablespoon of powdered algae—different types include Klamath blue green algae, spirulina and chlorella—to morning smoothies.

• **Green tea.** It's high in quercetin, an antioxidant that reduces inflammation. Green tea also changes the molecular structure of fat-soluble toxins and allows them to dissolve in water. This accelerates their excretion from the body.

My advice: Drink several cups of green tea daily.

Best choice: Finely milled Matcha green tea. It has more antioxidants than the typical tea brewed with dried leaves.

Note: Most types of green tea contain caffeine—on average, about 25 mg per cup.

Got MS? Parkinson's? Had a Stroke? Ballroom Dancing Can Help—Really

Alexander Ng, PhD, associate professor, Program in Exercise Science, Marquette University, Milwaukee. His study, "Dancing with MS: Benefits of Ballroom or Recreational Social Dance for Persons with MS," was presented at the Consortium of Multiple Sclerosis Centers 2015 Annual Meeting.

When you have a chronic condition, you may not feel like dancing the night away. But dancing with a partner actually may be the best thing you can do for body and mind. Studies show that partnered dancing offers tremendous benefits to people with Parkinson's disease, Alzheimer's and other forms of dementia, and those recovering from a stroke.

Here's a new condition to add to the list—multiple sclerosis (MS). The progressive chronic central nervous system disease, which can alternate between flare-ups and periods of remission, can cause fatigue, muscle weakness and balance problems. It often affects the ability to walk unaided.

Whether it's the waltz, fox-trot or salsa, partnered dancing is a perfect activity for people with MS. "If you're with a partner, you might be able to do movements that you wouldn't ordinarily be able to do if you have issues with balance or impaired movement," says study author Alexander Ng, PhD, a professor of exercise science—and a recreational ballroom dancer himself. The partner offers physical support and can be somewhat of a coach, encouraging the patient to push him or herself.

To test the theory, Dr. Ng included 12 people with MS who were able to walk at least 25 feet on their own and stand for at least five minutes without assistance. Some had no noticeable movement problems at all, while others needed the help of a cane or walker to get around. Six participated in hour-long dance classes…twice a week…for six out of eight weeks (to give participants flexibility around summer vacations). The other six people, the control group, didn't dance but received the same routine medical care as the dancers. Dances included the waltz, fox-trot, rumba and swing. (In the next study now in progress, they will also be including salsa, tango and merengue.) Before and after the dance program, both groups underwent a battery of tests such as walking unaided for 25 feet, getting up from a chair and walking three yards and then sitting down quickly (a measure of mobility), and tests for walking balance, which predicts the risk of falling.

The results: Dancers had higher scores on those tests for balance, mobility and endurance. They also had improvements in self-reported fatigue and depression (which tend to afflict people with MS) as well as cognitive benefits related to the ability to stay focused, while the control group did not.

It's a small, preliminary study, although another small study has found similar benefits when people with MS learn salsa dancing. As it turns out, there is a good body of research backing up partnered dancing for chronic conditions.

HOW SOCIAL DANCING WORKS AS THERAPY

At a minimum, dancing is aerobic exercise, which has been demonstrated to improve both physical and cognitive function in people with neurological disorders. Dance is also a complex activity that uses a combination of physical and mental tasks. Physically, dance requires balance, flexibility, speed and coordination—all skills that diminish in people with MS. And it calls on brain power—you have to remember and repeat steps, work with a partner and coordinate your movements together. Plus, it's social, which engages yet another part of the brain, and, last but not least, it's joyful. "When you're focused on dancing," says Dr. Ng, "troubles that may otherwise occupy your brain are shunted aside, so that you finish mentally refreshed."

Indeed, neuroimaging studies have shown that frequent dancing increases activity throughout the brain. When you're in the groove, it seems, your whole brain just lights up.

The strongest evidence for the benefits of partner dancing is in Parkinson's disease, another neurological condition in which movement is affected. Partner dancing actually echoes many of the key elements recommended in physical therapy for Parkinson's, such as responding to cues, learning new ways to move and engaging in balance exercises.

Studies show that partnered dancing helps people with Parkinson's develop a better gait while walking, have less rigidity in their movements, improve their ability to use their arms and hands and, in general, helps with functional mobility. One non-profit organization, Dance for Parkinson's, offers resources in more than 100 communities in 13 countries.

Perhaps its strongest appeal is that it's fun, creative and social. Says Dr. Ng, "People don't tend to view dance as exercise or physical therapy...so they're more likely to want to do it." Nor do you need to find special classes for people with MS or other chronic conditions. While it's a good idea to get lessons in ballroom dancing if you're unfamiliar with the steps, it's not a requirement. Says Dr. Ng, "Partnered dance for people with MS isn't re-habilitation per see but a fun option for physical activity."

DANCING FOR THE REST OF US

Partner dancing is great for healthy aging for everyone, actually. Combining physical training with cognitive demands, such as having to learn dance moves, results in better cognitive improvements in healthy older adults, compared with doing either physical exercise or cognitive training by itself. What's more, healthy older adults who are involved in amateur dancing score better on a list of motor and cognitive skills than their nondancing counterparts. Once you get good at it, you may even want to consider competitive ballroom dancing.

Bonus: It's said to make women feel more beautiful.

Early Signs of Parkinson's Disease

Long before people exhibit the tremors, slowness and stiffness of Parkinson's, they often

have other problems. Some of the potential risk factors for Parkinson's are loss of smell (about 80% of Parkinson's patients lose most of their sense of smell before they have problems with their motor skills)...chronic constipation...sleeping problems, in which patients act out violent dreams and may injure themselves or their bed partners...and feelings of fear and anxiety that develop for the first time in life.

Tanya Simuni, MD, associate professor of neurology, Northwestern University Feinberg School of Medicine, Chicago.

Natural Ways to Quiet Tremors

Monique Giroux, MD, a neurologist and medical director and cofounder of the Movement & Neuro-performance Center of Colorado in Englewood, CenterforMovement.org. She is the author of *Optimizing Health with Parkinson's Disease.*

Most people think of tremors—rhythmic trembling in your hands, voice, head or other parts of your body—as a red flag for neurological disorders such as Parkinson's disease and multiple sclerosis (MS).

That can be true. But this constant shakiness can also accompany a wide range of other conditions, including so-called essential tremor (ET), a chronic but harmless disorder that often is inherited and affects an estimated seven million Americans—a greater number than those affected by MS and Parkinson's disease. In some people, tremors also can occur as a side effect of common prescription drugs such as certain antidepressants, asthma inhalers, seizure medicines and immune-suppressing drugs. Even pain and anxiety can cause mild shaking or worsen tremors that are due to disease or medication.

If you suffer from tremors, there's no question how disruptive the problem can be to everyday life. Simple movements most of us take for granted—such as shaving, eating or simply writing a check—can turn into a shaky endurance test.

But quieting tremors is no small feat. Medications such as antiseizure drugs and mild tranquilizers are effective only about half of the time and can have troubling side effects, including drowsiness and confusion. Injections of botulinum toxin (Botox) can help head and voice tremors but are less effective for hand tremors because weakness can result as a side effect. An invasive procedure called deep brain stimulation (DBS) is reserved for the worst cases. This treatment, which can be quite effective, involves surgically implanting electrodes in the brain that are connected to a pacemaker placed under the skin near the collarbone. Electrical pulses are continuously delivered to block the impulses that cause tremors.

Good news: If drugs or surgery aren't for you or leave you with lingering symptoms, several natural therapies can help calm tremors by easing the stress and altering the brain chemicals and emotional responses that exacerbate the condition.

Important: Before trying natural remedies, be sure to avoid caffeine, smoking and/or excess alcohol—all of which can worsen tremors. Also, make regular exercise (especially strength training) a priority—tremors are more common when muscles become fatigued. Natural treatments to tame any type of tremor...*

AROMATHERAPY

Breathing in the aroma of certain flowers and herbs can reduce tremors by enhancing brain levels of gamma-aminobutyric acid (GABA), a widely circulated neurotransmitter with proven stress-fighting effects. Raising GABA levels helps calm the overexcited neurons that can worsen tremors. *What to try for tremors...*

• **Lavender.** This fragrant blue-violet flower has been shown in a number of small studies to produce calming, soothing and sedative effects when its scent is inhaled. Lavender essential oil is widely available and can be inhaled in the bath (add five to eight drops to

*Consult your doctor before trying these therapies to determine the cause of your tremors and for advice on the approaches best suited to your situation.

bath water for a long soak) or by dabbing a drop on your neck or temples.

SUPPLEMENTS

Certain supplements can ease tremors by enhancing muscle relaxation and/or reducing the body's overall stress levels or load of inflammatory chemicals, which can play a role in tremors caused by neurodegenerative diseases. *Check with your doctor to make sure these supplements don't interact with any medication you may be taking and won't affect any chronic condition you may have...***

• **Magnesium.** This mineral helps to regulate nerve impulses and muscle contraction. Magnesium-rich foods include sesame seeds, beans, nuts, avocados and leafy greens. To ensure that you're getting enough magnesium, consider taking a supplement.

Typical dose to ease tremors: 200 mg to 400 mg daily.

• **Fish oil.** The omega-3 fatty acids in fish oil offer proven anti-inflammatory effects—systemic inflammation is implicated in neurodegenerative diseases such as MS and Parkinson's disease. Fish oil is abundant in fatty fish such as salmon, albacore tuna, mackerel and herring. Aim for two servings per week. If you don't like fish, consider trying a supplement.

Typical dose to ease tremors: 1,000 mg to 1,500 mg daily.

• **Valerian, skullcap and passionflower.** These calming herbs have been successfully used as part of a regimen to ease tremors. The supplements can be found in combination products, including capsules, teas and tinctures. Follow instructions on the label.

BEAT TREMORS WITH YOUR MIND

If you suffer from tremors, it's common to think—Oh no...my arm (or other body part) is shaking again...this is so embarrassing! I hate this! While such thoughts are perfectly natural when tremors emerge, they are potentially destructive when trying to calm your condition.

**Because supplements aren't regulated by the FDA for purity, I advise looking for products that bear the "USP-verified" stamp on the label—this means they have met rigorous testing standards to ensure quality by the scientific nonprofit US Pharmacopeial Convention.

What helps: Mindfulness can reset this negative thought pattern so that you stop viewing tremors as a problem, which only leads to distress that often worsens the condition.

Mindfulness is more than just relaxation. Often done in conjunction with deep-breathing exercises, mindfulness helps you simply observe your thoughts, feelings and sensations and let them pass without judging them, labeling them or trying to control them. By reducing the distress you feel about the tremors, you are no longer fueling the condition.

You can learn mindfulness from CDs or books. My recommendations: Consult your local hospital to see if it offers mindfulness-based stress-reduction classes. Also consider trying other mind-body therapies that may help, such as hypnosis, biofeedback and breath work.

Better Treatment for Early Parkinson's Disease

In a recent study, 251 Parkinson's patients (average age 52) with early motor symptoms, such as tremors, were given either standard medical treatment (the drug levodopa) or neurostimulation (a therapy involving an implanted device that blocks brain signals that cause motor problems).

Result: Quality of life in the neurostimulation group improved by 26% over two years, compared with a 1% worsening of quality of life in the medical treatment group.

Conclusion: Neurostimulation is an established treatment for advanced Parkinson's but may be effective for early cases as well.

Gunther Deuschl, MD, professor of neurology, University of Kiel, Germany.

A Better Way to Treat Advanced Parkinson's Disease

John T. Slevin, MD, professor of neurology and molecular and biomedical pharmacology, department of neurology, University of Kentucky Medical Center, Lexington. His study appeared in the *Journal of Parkinson's Disease.*

The drug Sinemet relieves Parkinson's disease symptoms such as tremor, difficulty swallowing and an awkwardly shuffling gait, but it becomes less effective over time.

Breakthrough: There's a new way of getting Sinemet's active ingredient, levodopa, to last longer and more consistently to control Parkinson's symptoms. It has been available in Canada, Australia and throughout Europe for a few years and, finally, it is now available here in America.

IMPROVING A DRUG'S STAYING POWER

Parkinson's disease happens when certain brain cells degenerate and produce less dopamine, a chemical necessary to control muscle movement. Levodopa is meant to replace that lost dopamine, but it wears off within minutes. The pill Sinemet contains levodopa plus a drug called carbidopa that helps the levodopa last longer and get to where it needs to go—the brain. It is initially very effective in controlling Parkinson's symptoms, but within four to six years of starting treatment, its effectiveness wears off for roughly 40% of patients. By nine years, 90% of patients are showing troublesome symptoms again. And besides the Parkinson's symptoms, the body begins to react poorly to the unevenness of levodopa levels…erratic muscle movements (a condition called dyskinesia) begin to occur either when the level of levodopa peaks in the body after taking a dose or when it wears off between doses.

A better—albeit invasive—way to receive levodopa that minimizes these problems was finally approved by the FDA in January 2015 after being available for several years in many other countries around the world. The treatment is a process called carbidopa-levodopa enteral suspension (CLES), marketed as Duopa. It involves surgery to insert a tube through the abdomen into the small intestine. The tube is connected to an external portable pump that a person can carry in his or her pants pocket or some other wearable pouch while the pump delivers a constant flow of the carbidopa-levodopa during waking hours.

THE BENEFITS AND RISKS

Although studies have shown that the CLES system works well to control Parkinson's symptoms in people with advanced disease, how safe and tolerable is it over the long term? A team of researchers from three top medical institutions—University of Kentucky Medical Center, Cleveland Clinic and Northwestern University Feinberg School of Medicine—along with researchers associated with the drug's manufacturer, AbbVie Inc., closely examined symptoms and patient quality of life before and after beginning CLES. Side effects of CLES were also examined.

In the first part of the study, which lasted three months, patients on Sinemet were compared with patients receiving CLES. In the second part of the study, the patients who had been on Sinemet were switched to CLES, and all the patients—those who had been on CLES and those new to it—were followed for a year.

The results: Patients put on the CLES system during the first part of the study averaged 12 symptom-free hours a day, compared with an average of 10 hours for patients on Sinemet. Once patients on Sinemet were switched to the CLES system, they also improved to meet the sustained 12-hour window of symptom control. Symptoms were less severe, and dyskinesia—the main debilitating side effect of Sinemet—was much less common once the patients were switched to CLES.

Most side effects were related to surgery rather than CLES use. In fact, serious side effects, such as intestinal perforation during surgery, were common, occurring in 23% of patients. In addition, infection at the surgical site occurred in 18% but cleared up with antibiotic therapy.

Besides surgical side effects, the most common side effects for those new to CLES were abdominal pain, which affected 42% of the patients. Nausea was also common, as was skin redness at the site of the tube insertion, which cleared up in some patients over time.

Since CLES is relatively new, doctors don't yet know exactly how long, in terms of years, the therapy will provide symptom control for patients with Parkinson's disease. The lead author of the study, John T. Slevin, MD, from the University of Kentucky Medical Center, said that it is expected that, as the disease progresses and more brain cells that produce dopamine are lost, the benefits of CLES will eventually ebb. CLES simply helps extend symptom control and quality of life longer when other treatments lose their effectiveness.

If you or a loved one has an interest in CLES to control worsening Parkinson's disease, consult an experienced neurologist who specializes in movement disorders who will work with a gastroenterologist skilled in gastrointestinal surgery. You can find Parkinson's Disease Centers of Excellence through the National Parkinson Foundation.

Best Nondrug Approaches for Parkinson's

Michael S. Okun, MD, professor and chair of the department of neurology and codirector of the Center for Movement Disorders and Neurorestoration at the University of Florida College of Medicine in Gainesville. He is also the medical director at the National Parkinson Foundation and has written more than 400 medical journal articles. Dr. Okun's latest book is *10 Breakthrough Therapies for Parkinson's Disease.*

The telltale tremors, muscle stiffness and other movement problems that plague people with Parkinson's disease make even the mundane activities of daily living—such as brushing teeth, cooking and dressing—more difficult.

What's new: Even though medication—such as levodopa (L-dopa) and newer drugs including *pramipexole* and *selegiline*—have long been the main treatment to control Parkinson's symptoms, researchers are discovering more and more nondrug therapies that can help.

Among the best nondrug approaches (each can be used with Parkinson's medication)...

EXERCISE

For people with Parkinson's, exercise is like a drug. It raises neurotrophic factors, proteins that promote the growth and health of neurons. Research consistently shows that exercise can improve motor symptoms (such as walking speed and stability) and quality of life.

For the best results: Exercise 30 to 60 minutes every single day. Aim to work hard enough to break a sweat, but back off if you get too fatigued—especially the following day (this indicates the body is not recovering properly). Parkinson's symptoms can worsen with over-exercise. *Smart exercise habits...*

For better gait speed: Choose a lower-intensity exercise, such as walking on a treadmill (but hold on to the balance bars), rather than high-intensity exercise (such as running), which has a higher risk for falls and other injuries.

A recent study showed that a walking group of Parkinson's patients performed better than a group of patients who ran.

Important safety tip: Parkinson's patients should exercise with a partner and take precautions to prevent falls—for example, minimizing distractions, such as ringing cell phones.

For aerobic exercise: Use a recumbent bicycle or rowing machine and other exercises that don't rely on balance.

For strength and flexibility: Do stretching and progressive resistance training.

Excellent resource: For a wide variety of exercises, including aerobic workouts, standing and sitting stretches, strengthening moves, balance exercises and fall-prevention tips, the National Parkinson Foundation's Fitness Counts book is available as a free download at *Parkinson.org/pd-library/books/fitness-counts.*

For balance: Researchers are now discovering that yoga postures, tai chi (with its slow, controlled movements) and certain types of dancing (such as the tango, which involves rhythmic forward-and-backward steps) are excellent ways to improve balance.

COFFEE AND TEA

Could drinking coffee or tea help with Parkinson's? According to research, it can—when consumed in the correct amounts.

Here's why: Caffeine blocks certain receptors in the brain that regulate the neurotransmitter dopamine, which becomes depleted and leads to the impaired motor coordination that characterizes Parkinson's. In carefully controlled studies, Parkinson's patients who ingested low doses of caffeine—about 100 mg twice daily—had improved motor symptoms, such as tremors and stiffness, compared with people who had no caffeine or higher doses of caffeine.

My advice: Have 100 mg of caffeine (about the amount in one six-ounce cup of home-brewed coffee or two cups of black or green tea) twice a day—once in the morning and once in the mid-afternoon.

Note: Even decaffeinated coffee has about 10 mg to 25 mg of caffeine per cup.

SUPPLEMENTS

Researchers have studied various supplements for years to identify ones that could help manage Parkinson's symptoms and/or boost the effects of levodopa, but large studies have failed to prove that these supplements provide such benefits.

However, because Parkinson's is a complex disease that can cause about 20 different motor and nonmotor symptoms that evolve over time, the existing research may not apply to everyone. *Some people with Parkinson's may benefit from...*

•**Coenzyme Q10 (CoQ10).** This supplement promotes the health of the body's mitochondria ("energy generators" in the cells), which are believed to play a role in Parkinson's. In a large study, people with Parkinson's who took 1,200 mg per day showed some improvement in symptoms over a 16-month study period. However, follow-up studies found no beneficial effects.

•**Riboflavin and alpha-lipoic acid** are among the other supplements that are continuing to be studied.

Important: If you wish to try these or other supplements, be sure to consult your doctor to ensure that there are no possible interactions with your other medications.

MARIJUANA

A few small studies have concluded that marijuana can improve some neurological symptoms, but larger studies are needed to show benefits for Parkinson's patients, especially for symptoms such as depression and anxiety.

However: Marijuana is challenging for several reasons—first, it is illegal in most states. If you do live in a state that allows medical marijuana use, it has possible side effects—for example, it can impair balance and driving…it is difficult to know the exact dosage, even if it's purchased from a dispensary…and with marijuana edibles (such as cookies and candies), the effects may take longer to appear, and you may accidentally ingest too much.

If you want to try marijuana: Work closely with your doctor to help you avoid such pitfalls.

SEEING THE RIGHT DOCTOR

For anyone with Parkinson's, it's crucial to see a neurologist and, if possible, one who has advanced training in Parkinson's disease and movement disorders.

Important new finding: A large study showed that patients treated by a neurologist had a lower risk for hip fracture and were less likely to be placed in a nursing facility. They were also 22% less likely to die during the four-year study.

Better Parkinson's Treatment

In a recent finding, Parkinson's patients who received low-frequency (60 Hz) deep-brain stimulation (DBS), in which an implanted "brain pacemaker" sends electrical impulses to the brain, had significant improvements in swallowing difficulty and in their walking gait—problems that were not resolved with standard treatment, including high-frequency (130 Hz) DBS or medication, such as carbi-

dopa and levodopa. The patients in the study received daily low-frequency treatments for six weeks.

Tao Xie, MD, PhD, assistant professor of neurology, The University of Chicago.

Statin Drugs May Fight Parkinson's

An analysis of nearly 44,000 adults found that those who stopped taking lipophilic (fat-soluble) statin drugs, such as *simvastatin* (Zocor) and *atorvastatin* (Lipitor), after reaching their LDL "bad" cholesterol target were 58% more likely to develop Parkinson's disease than those who continued to take the drugs.

Theory: Lipophilic statins have anti-inflammatory properties that may help prevent or delay the degeneration of brain cells that occurs in Parkinson's patients.

If you're considering going off statins: Talk with your doctor about your risk for Parkinson's.

Chia-Hsuin Chang, MD, ScD, attending physician and assistant professor of internal medicine, National Taiwan University Hospital, Douliou City.

Yoga Fights Pain

Chronic pain sufferers should hit the yoga mat, says M. Catherine Bushnell, PhD. Chronic pain can cause loss of gray matter in the brain, which can lead to memory loss, cognitive impairment, emotional problems and reduced pain tolerance.

New finding: Practicing yoga can actually increase gray matter in the brain, including in the area related to pain tolerance.

M. Catherine Bushnell, PhD, scientific director, National Center for Complementary and Integrative Health, Bethesda, Maryland.

Device Stops Chronic Pain

A new device alleviates chronic pain, says C. Evers Whyte, MS, DC. The Calmare pain therapy treatment relieves chronic neuropathic pain from diabetes, shingles, herniated disks, chemotherapy, reflex sympathetic dystrophy (RSD) and other causes. The FDA-approved device uses electrodes applied to the skin to transmit "no-pain" messages to the brain. Patients usually undergo 10 to 12 daily treatments, each lasting less than one hour. For a list of centers that offer Calmare therapy, go to *calmarett.com/locations.html*.

C. Evers Whyte, MS, DC, a pain expert and founder and director of the New England Center for Chronic Pain, Stamford, Connecticut. Neccp.com

Simple Stretches That Really Do Relieve Pain

Ben Benjamin, PhD, a sports medicine and muscular therapy practitioner since 1963. He is the author of several books, including *Listen to Your Pain: The Active Person's Guide to Understanding, Identifying, and Treating Pain and Injury.* BenBenjamin.com

I f you suffer from pain or stiffness due to an injury, arthritis or even a neurological disorder, such as Parkinson's disease or multiple sclerosis, a type of bodywork known as Active Isolated Stretching (AIS) may give you more relief than you ever thought possible.

What makes AIS different: While most other stretching techniques recommend doing each stretch for 30 seconds or longer, AIS uses brief, two-second stretches that are done eight to 10 times each.

What's the advantage of quick, repeated stretches? This approach gives the muscle a full stretch without triggering its stretch reflex—an automatic defense mechanism that causes the muscle to contract and ultimately undo many of the stretch's benefits. The result is that muscles stretch more efficiently and avoid the buildup of waste products that lead to muscle soreness.

Developed by American kinesiologist Aaron Mattes about 35 years ago, AIS also stretches each muscle group at a variety of different angles, thus stretching all muscle fibers equally.

A MINI REGIMEN

To get a sense of AIS, try the stretches in this article. While doing each one, slowly count to yourself "one-one thousand, two-one thousand"—never any longer than two seconds. Always exhale while performing the stretch and inhale as you return to the starting position.

The first repetition of each stretch should be gentle...the second should go up to the point where you begin to feel resistance. Subsequent repetitions should push just beyond this point (with the help of your hands, a rope or other aid, if necessary) to go a few degrees further each time, thus providing a maximum stretch. If you feel discomfort during a stretch, stop the stretch at that point. If a stretch feels painful from the start, then skip it.

Daily AIS exercises that help relieve common types of pain...*

SHOULDER STRETCHES

Purpose: To help prevent muscle strain and joint sprain by increasing flexibility.

1. With your right elbow bent, position your right arm at a 90° angle in front of your body. Place your right palm on the back of your right shoulder. Exhale and extend your flexed arm upward as far as possible. Gently assist the stretch with your left hand. Repeat eight to 10 times on each side.

2. With your right elbow bent and your right arm positioned at a 90° angle in front of your body, place your right palm on the back of your right shoulder. Drop a two- to three-foot rope over your right shoulder and grasp the bottom of it with your left hand. Gently pull the rope to move your right arm upward behind your neck at a 45° angle for a maximum stretch. Return to the starting position after each repetition. Repeat eight to 10 times on each side.

*Check with your doctor before performing these movements.

NECK STRETCHES

Purpose: To help prevent neck injuries, relieve stiffness and improve range of motion.

1. Tuck your chin as close to your neck as possible. Put both your hands on the back of your head and, while keeping your back straight, gently bend your neck forward, bringing your chin as close to your chest as you can. Return to starting position. Repeat 10 times.

2. Gently bend your head to the right side, moving your right ear as close as possible to the top of your right shoulder. Exhale and place your right hand on the left side of your head to gently extend the stretch. Keep your left shoulder down. Focus your eyes on a point directly in front of your body to keep your head in an aligned position. Repeat 10 times on both sides.

GETTING STARTED

For people who are new to AIS, I advise working with an AIS practitioner for hands-on instruction. If the movements are done incorrectly, you will get no benefits and could even hurt yourself. To find a practitioner near you, go to *stretchingusa.com* and click on the "Practioner Directory" link. Sessions are not typically covered by insurance and usually range from $50 to $150 per session. The website also offers books, including *Specific Stretching for Everyone*, and DVDs if you prefer to learn a complete AIS regimen on your own.

5 Hidden Causes of Pain

Vijay Vad, MD, a sports medicine specialist at the Hospital for Special Surgery and assistant professor of rehabilitation medicine at Weill Cornell Medical College, both in New York City. He is also the founder of the Vad Foundation, VijayVad.com, an organization that supports medical research related to back pain and arthritis, and the author of *Stop Pain: Inflammation Relief for an Active Life.*

Do you have arthritis, backaches or some other type of nagging pain that just won't go away?

Why pain often persists: For a significant number of people who chalk up their pain to a creaky joint, muscle aches or some other common problem, the true culprit actually has never been properly diagnosed.

But don't give up. One of the following conditions may be at the root of your pain—or at least making it much worse. *The good news is that there's plenty you can do to treat these hidden causes of pain...*

VITAMIN D DEFICIENCY

What does your backache have to do with the amount of vitamin D in your body? More than you might think, according to recent research.

Here's why: Vitamin D is needed for normal bone metabolism. People who don't produce enough are especially susceptible to low-back pain, possibly because the vertebrae become weakened. Low vitamin D levels also have been linked to hip pain and knee pain.

My advice: Get your vitamin D level tested once a year, particularly if you live in the Northeastern US or the Pacific Northwest. Limited sun exposure in these areas can make it difficult for the body to synthesize enough vitamin D, and it is difficult to get adequate amounts of this vitamin from food.

If your vitamin D level is low (most experts put the optimal blood level between 20 ng/mL and 36 ng/mL), take a daily supplement that provides 1,000 international units (IU) to 2,000 IU...and continue to get tested annually.

LOW THYROID

Underactive thyroid gland (hypothyroidism) is more common than most people realize. Even though the condition is most often found in women, it can affect men, too. The blood tests used to detect the condition are simple and inexpensive, yet few doctors order the testing routinely, as they should.

Thyroid hormones are real workhorses in the body—for example, they help regulate how many calories you burn, your heart rate and body temperature. If you have low thyroid levels, you're likely to suffer from fatigue, sensitivity to cold and unexplained weight gain.

What's not so well known is that people with hypothyroidism tend to have nagging muscle and joint pain. This is because low thyroid can accelerate the loss of cartilage in those who already have a touch of arthritis.

My advice: If you have arthritis or any type of joint or muscle pain that has unexpectedly worsened, ask your doctor for a thyroid test. This advice applies to men, too. A thyroid function panel measures blood levels of thyroid stimulating hormone (TSH), along with levels of different thyroid hormones. A normal TSH level is typically between 0.4 mlU/L and 4.0 mlU/L.

Even if your TSH level is "borderline," your thyroid may be contributing to your pain, so ask your doctor about medication. Thyroid-replacement hormones, such as Synthroid, mimic the effects of natural thyroid hormone and can start to relieve symptoms, including thyroid-related arthritis pain, within a month.

NOT ENOUGH ESTROGEN

Women tend to experience more pain overall once they go through menopause—not necessarily because of pain-causing conditions, but because the body's drop in estrogen lowers their pain tolerance.

Example: Knee pain that you might have rated as a 5 (on a 1-to-10 scale) before menopause might now feel like an 8. Pain sensitivity is higher in postmenopausal women who also have low thyroid.

My advice: Try supplemental curcumin. This potent anti-inflammatory reduces pain and improves joint flexibility. Most postmenopausal women (and men, too!) notice an improvement when they take it.

Dose: 2,000 mg daily. This supplement is generally safe for everyone to use, but consult your doctor first, especially if you take any medication (it can interact with some drugs, such as anticoagulants)…or if you have gallstones, since it could increase painful symptoms.

Good product: Northeast Natural's Triple Curc, *activebodyactivemind.com.*

If this doesn't give you adequate pain relief, you may also want to consider estrogen replacement. It decreases pain sensitivity and reduces the loss of joint cartilage.

Important: Estrogen replacement can increase risk for heart disease, stroke and breast cancer in some women, so ask your doctor to help you sort out the pros and cons.

LYME DISEASE

This tick-borne illness can be easily treated (usually with a three-week course of antibiotics)—if it's detected early. But many people don't know they have it, in part because the test isn't always accurate.

What happens: The bacterium that causes Lyme can destroy joint cartilage. Many people with Lyme know that something's wrong, but it often takes months—and multiple visits with different specialists—to get an accurate diagnosis.

My advice: If you live in an area where ticks and Lyme disease are common, do not wait to get help. The symptoms might include muscle or joint pain, unexplained fatigue and/or a burning sensation that affects your whole body. Treating Lyme disease quickly reduces the risk of lingering joint pain and other symptoms.

If you test negative but still suspect that your pain may be caused by the disease, consider seeing a doctor who specializes in diagnosing Lyme for a second opinion. To find such a specialist near you, consult the International Lyme and Associated Diseases Society at *ilads.org.*

POOR SLEEP

People who have chronic pain often don't sleep well. But it also works the other way—less deep sleep lowers your tolerance to pain.

Even if you think that you sleep well, you may not be getting enough rapid eye movement (REM) sleep—the more time you spend in this stage of sleep, the better equipped your body will be at tolerating pain.

My advice: Get at least 30 minutes of aerobic exercise every day. This type of exercise increases levels of deep sleep, which is needed for you to get adequate REM sleep.

Another Reason to Quit

Surprising link to chronic back pain. An analysis of 160 people found that smokers are three times more likely than nonsmokers to develop chronic back pain.

Possible reason: Smokers have a stronger connection between two brain regions that play a role in addictive behavior and chronic pain.

Good news: Study participants who quit smoking showed a drop in this brain circuit activity, decreasing their vulnerability to chronic pain.

A. Vania Apkarian, PhD, professor of physiology, Northwestern University Feinberg School of Medicine, Chicago.

Is the Way You Walk Giving You a Warning?

Mary Harward, MD, a geriatrician in private practice in Orange, California. She specializes in the diagnosis and treatment of gait disorders and other diseases affecting older adults. She is editor of *Medical Secrets*.

Have you surprised yourself recently with a stumble or a fall? If you blamed it on your shoes…your eyesight…or an obstacle, such as a throw rug, you may not be getting at the root cause of why you stumbled or fell. The fact is, the real reason many people fall (and sometimes die from it) is the way that they walk.

A problem that goes undetected: Most people who have treatable abnormalities in their gait (the way in which a person walks) never even discuss it with their doctors.

Here's why: When you go to the doctor, odds are that you are taken to an exam room and asked to "have a seat" until the doctor arrives. The problem is, you'll probably stay seated during the entire visit, and your doctor may miss a symptom—a dangerous gait—that's just as important as abnormal X-rays or blood tests.

TAKE IT SERIOUSLY

It's never normal to shuffle, be off-balance or have an unusual posture. A gait disorder always means that something—or, in most cases, a combination of factors—is awry.

Problems with gait affect about 15% of adults age 60 and older and more than 80% of those age 85 and older. Gait disorders, which interfere with stability and balance, are not only among the most common causes of falls and subsequent hospitalizations, but also can be one of the first health problems that eventually leads to nursing home care.

My advice: Doctors should ask every patient if he/she has fallen in the last year. In addition, if you're age 65 or older, you should ask your doctor to check your gait at least once a year.

WHAT'S BEHIND IT?

Patients often assume that problems with one's gait are due to neurological disorders, such as Parkinson's disease or multiple sclerosis (MS). With Parkinson's disease, patients also experience a resting tremor or shaking of one hand, muscle rigidity and slow movements, while MS typically is accompanied by vision problems, dizziness and trouble speaking. *But there are other possible causes of gait problems…*

•**Arthritis.** Gait problems are common in patients with arthritis, particularly osteoarthritis of the knee or hip. If you have knee or hip pain, you may favor that side and use other muscles to compensate. This throws off your posture and body mechanics, which may cause you to limp or take tentative steps.

Helpful: Ask your doctor if it's appropriate to see a physical therapist for advice on exercises to strengthen the muscles around the arthritic joint—this will help you walk normally and with less pain.

Pain control is also very important. Apart from making you more comfortable, it will help you do the exercises that you need for a better gait. If you don't get adequate relief from over-the-counter pain relievers, talk to your doctor about stronger forms of pain control. Stretching, massage, heating pads, cold packs and/or acupuncture are helpful to some people.

• **Back problems.** A gait problem often is due to a painful back. Patients with lumbar stenosis, for example, will frequently experience nerve pressure from damaged vertebrae in the spine, affecting their ability to walk. Patients with sciatica (nerve pain that often accompanies lower-back problems) will have difficulty walking or standing. Suspect nerve problems if you have back or leg pain that gets worse when you walk or stand for more than a few minutes and gets better when you're off your feet. See your doctor for treatment advice.

• **Balance disorders.** If you sometimes feel as though you're about to fall (even when you're not), see a doctor right away. Problems with balance—often accompanied by dizziness, spinning sensations, etc.—are a major cause of falls. Potential causes include ear infections, inner-ear disorders, neuropathy (nerve damage) and circulatory problems.

Also: Ask your doctor to test your vitamin B-12 level. Older adults often have low levels of intrinsic factor, a protein that's needed for B-12 absorption. It's also common for vegetarians to be deficient in this vitamin because meat is a major source of B-12. Low B-12 can make you feel light-headed, cause numbness and/or tingling in the feet and make it difficult to walk.

Similar foot and leg symptoms are caused by diabetic neuropathy, nerve damage that may occur in patients with poorly managed (or undiagnosed) diabetes. Bunions and other foot conditions also can contribute to gait disorders.

• **Drug side effects.** It's not surprising that sedating medications such as *diazepam* (Valium) can increase fall risk. What many people don't realize is that nonsedating medications also can be an issue.

Example: Medications that lower blood pressure, such as diuretics, can cause orthostatic hypotension, a sudden drop in blood pressure that can make you dizzy or light-headed. Some blood pressure drugs also

decrease magnesium, which can cause leg weakness or cramps. Your doctor might advise changing medications. Alcohol or drugs that lower blood sugar or affect mood or sleep also can change one's gait.

Important: Be especially careful after eating. Studies have shown that dizziness and gait problems tend to get worse about 30 minutes after meals—blood travels to the digestive tract after meals, sometimes lowering blood pressure.

• **Reduced brain circulation.** Gait disorders are often the first sign of infarcts, areas of brain damage caused by impaired circulation. Infarcts occur in patients who have had a stroke or other problems that affect blood vessels in the brain, such as hypertension or high cholesterol.

A patient who has multiple infarcts might walk very slowly...take short steps...stand with his feet wider apart than usual...and/or hesitate when starting to walk or have trouble slowing momentum when stopping.

HOW'S YOUR GAIT?

If you've noticed changes in the ways in which you move, see your doctor for an evaluation. *He/she will give you tests that may include...*

The timed get-up-and-go test. This measures the time it takes you to get up from a chair (without using your hands to push off from the armrests), walk 10 feet, turn around and walk back to the chair. You should be able to complete the sequence safely in 14 seconds or less. If it takes longer than 20 seconds, your gait is seriously impaired.

Eat This to Breathe Better

A diet high in fiber—especially from fruits and vegetables—can protect against such lung conditions as chronic obstructive pulmonary disease (COPD) and asthma.

New study: Spirometry tests found that among more than 1,900 adults, those who ate the most fiber every day had the best lung function.

Possible reason: Inflammation underlies many lung diseases, and fiber has anti-inflammatory properties. Fiber also changes the composition of the gut microbiome, which may release lung-protective compounds.

Corinne Hanson, PhD, RD, associate professor of medical nutrition, University of Nebraska Medical Center, Omaha.

4 Secrets to Easier Breathing...Simple Ways to Help Yourself

Gerard J. Criner, MD, a professor of medicine and director of pulmonary and critical care medicine at Temple Lung Center at Temple University School of Medicine in Philadelphia. He is codirector of the Center for Inflammation, Translational and Clinical Lung Research.

If you can't catch your breath, walking, climbing stairs or simply carrying on a conversation can be a challenge.

When breathing is a struggle, you wouldn't think that exercise is the answer. But it can be a solution for people with chronic obstructive pulmonary disease (COPD) or heart failure or even for healthy people who occasionally become short of breath.*

Four better-breathing techniques that really help...

PURSED-LIP BREATHING

When you're feeling short of breath, inhale through your nose for two seconds, then pucker your lips as if you were going to whistle or blow out a candle. Exhale through pursed lips for four seconds.

How it helps: It prolongs the respiratory cycle and gives you more time to empty your lungs. This is particularly important if you have emphysema. With emphysema, air gets

*If you don't have COPD, you should see a doctor if you have shortness of breath after only slight activity or while resting, or if shortness of breath wakes you up at night or requires you to sleep propped up to breathe.

trapped in the lungs. The trapped air causes the lungs to overinflate, which reduces the amount of force that they're able to generate. This results in a buildup of carbon dioxide that makes it difficult to breathe.

You may need to do this only when you're more active than usual and short of breath. Or you may breathe better when you do it often.

CHANGING POSITIONS

Simply changing how you stand or sit can improve breathing when you're feeling winded.

How it helps: Certain positions (see below) help muscles around the diaphragm work more efficiently to promote easier breathing.

Examples: While sitting, lean your chest forward...rest your elbows on your knees...and relax your upper-body muscles. When standing, bend forward at the waist and rest your hands on a table or the back of a chair. Or back up to a wall...support yourself with your hips...and lean forward and put your hands on your thighs.

CONTROLLED COUGHING

Your lungs produce excessive mucus when you have COPD. The congestion makes it harder to breathe. It also increases the risk for pneumonia and other lung infections. A normal, explosive cough is not effective at removing mucus. In fact, out-of-control coughing can cause airways to collapse and trap even more mucus. A controlled cough is more effective (and requires less oxygen and energy). You also can use this technique to help clear mucus from the lungs when you have a cold.

How to do it: Sit on a chair or the edge of your bed with both feet on the floor. Fold your arms around your midsection...breathe in slowly through your nose...then lean forward while pressing your arms against your abdomen. Lightly cough two or three times. Repeat as needed.

Important: Taking slow, gentle breaths through your nose while using this technique will prevent mucus from moving back into the airways.

COLD-AIR ASSISTANCE

This is a quick way to breathe better. When you are short of breath—or doing an activity that you know will lead to breathlessness, such as walking on a treadmill—position a fan so that it blows cool air on your face. You also can splash your face with cold water if you become short of breath.

How it helps: Cool air and water stimulate the trigeminal nerve in the face, which slows respiration and helps ease shortness of breath. That's why the treadmills and exercise bikes used in respiratory-rehabilitation facilities are often equipped with small fans.

More from Dr. Criner

When to Get Breathing Help from a Professional

You can do many breathing exercises on your own without the help of a health professional. For the techniques below, however, it's best to first consult a respiratory therapist (ask your doctor for a referral) to ensure that you know how to do the exercise properly. You can then continue on your own.

•**Paced breathing for endurance.** This technique is useful for people who have COPD and/or heart failure, since it improves lung capacity and heart function.

How it helps: With practice, this technique can increase your cardiorespiratory endurance by 30% to 40%. To perform the exercise, a metronome is set at a rate that's faster than your usual respiratory rate. Your therapist will encourage you to breathe as hard and as fast as you can for, say, about 15 minutes. (Beginners might do it for only a few minutes at a time.)

Example: The metronome may be set for 20 breaths per minute to start, and you may eventually work up to 40 breaths per minute.

You'll notice that breathing becomes easier when you're doing various activities—for instance, when you're exercising, climbing stairs or taking brisk walks.

•**Inspiratory muscle training.** Think of this as a workout for your breathing muscles.

It is especially helpful for people with COPD or other lung diseases and those recovering from respiratory failure. People who strengthen these muscles can improve their breathing efficiency by 25% to 30%.

How it helps: For this breathing exercise, you'll use a device known as an inspiratory muscle trainer, which includes a mouthpiece, a one-way valve and resistance settings. When you inhale, the one-way valve closes. You're forced to use effort to breathe against resistance. Then, the valve opens so that you can exhale normally. This breathing exercise is typically performed for 15 minutes twice a day. You can buy these devices online.

Good choice: The Threshold Inspiratory Muscle Trainer, available at fitnessmart.com for $59.95.

Fun Way to Fight Lung Disease

Playing the harmonica promotes lung health, we hear from Dan Hamner, MD. Blowing into the instrument lowers air pressure in the airways and expands the air sacs in the lungs, reducing the risk that they will narrow or collapse, as occurs in patients with asthma or emphysema. It also forces you to frequently change the pace and depth of your breath, which strengthens the diaphragm (a muscle separating the lungs from the abdomen).

If you have asthma, chronic bronchitis or emphysema: Consider learning to play the harmonica.

Dan Hamner, MD, a physiatrist and sports medicine physician, New York City.

CART: A Better Way to Catch Your Breath If You Have Asthma

Study titled "Controlling Asthma by Training of Capnometry-Assisted Hypoventilation (CATCH) VS Slow Breathing: A Randomized Controlled Trial," by researchers in the department of psychology and the Anxiety and Depression Research Center at Southern Methodist University, Dallas, published in *Chest*.

Asthma. The very mention of the word can make you feel like you have a boa constrictor wrapped around your chest. If you have asthma, chances are that when you feel that squeezing, suffocating feeling of an attack, you take deep breaths—gasping for air—but this is actually wrong. Or maybe you have heard that taking deep, slow and paced breaths is the right way to go. But research shows that there really is a much better way to catch your breath.

WHEN LESS IS MORE

In an attempt to catch their breaths, asthmatics gulp air and breathe too rapidly during an attack. It's a natural reaction, but this can cause a decrease in the body's level of carbon dioxide (CO2), resulting in hyperventilation and its characteristic symptoms of dizziness, breathlessness and pins and needles. The lungs become hyper-reactive, stuffy and dry, making the asthma attack far worse and scarier than it needs to be.

Now consider this: Shallow breathing does the opposite...it increases CO2 levels. Knowing this and knowing that shallow breathing helps people with panic disorder (who also tend to hyperventilate), researchers from Southern Methodist University in Dallas decided to test the effectiveness of a shallow-breathing technique, successfully used in people with panic disorder, in adults with asthma.

They randomly assigned 120 asthma sufferers to receive either a standard breathing therapy called slow-breathing and awareness training (SLOW) or a therapy called capnometry-assisted respiratory training (CART). SLOW teaches asthmatics to take slow, full breaths through awareness and control of their respiratory rate (the number of breaths they take per minute). CART also trains its users to control their respiratory rate but encourages shallow breathing and control of CO2 levels through use of a device called a capnometer. The capnometer provides feedback about CO2 levels so that a person can practice how to breathe to prevent CO2 from dipping too low.

The study participants practiced their therapies for four weeks on their own and with respiratory therapists and used their asthma medications as needed. The researchers monitored asthma attacks, need for medication and various aspects of respiratory function during this time and for six months' follow-up—and patients kept journals of the impact of SLOW or CART therapy on their asthma.

The results? Whereas both techniques resulted in an 81% improvement in lung function, the CART group was in better shape six months down the road than the other group. Their airways had become more widened and their CO2 levels were more normalized than those of patients practicing SLOW, and that difference remained consistent throughout further follow-up. Patients practicing CART also coped better when under the stress of an acute asthma attack because they felt more in control of their symptoms and what exactly was happening in their bodies during attacks.

LEARNING TO BREATHE

If you have (or know someone who has) asthma and are unfamiliar with breath retraining therapies, such as SLOW and CART, it's a good idea to ask your doctor for a referral to a respiratory therapist—especially someone who knows about CART. These therapies are not a substitute for asthma medication, but they clearly work as add-ons and can help you improve lung function so that you can possibly rely less on medication. As for which therapy is better for long-term improvement, this study, at least, points to CART.

How Not to Let Chronic Lung Disease Sneak Up on You

Roger S. Goldstein, MD, a professor of medicine and physical therapy at the University of Toronto, Ontario, Canada. A respirologist (specialist in lung function) at West Park Healthcare Centre in Toronto, he is also chair of respiratory rehabilitation research at the National Sanitarium Association.

M ost people are only vaguely aware of chronic obstructive pulmonary disease (COPD)—even though the Centers for Disease Control and Prevention reports it's now the third-leading cause of death in American adults, after heart disease and cancer. Deaths due to heart disease and cancer have decreased, but that has not occurred with COPD.

An unexpected threat: Even though current or former smokers are at greatest risk for COPD, as many as one out of six people with the condition never smoked.

Good news: COPD can be managed with early diagnosis and treatment. Even those who have had the condition for years can minimize periodic flare-ups by taking the right medications. *What you need to know about COPD…*

ARE YOU AT RISK?

Approximately 80% to 90% of all cases of COPD in the US are caused by smoking—primarily cigarette smoking, but long-term cigar or pipe smoking also increases risk.

Secondhand smoke (known as passive smoking) increases the risk for COPD by 10% to 45%, depending on the level of exposure, according to estimates from The World Health Organization. Increased risk can occur with daily exposure to secondhand smoke when living with a smoker.

People with long-term exposure to severe air pollution (as occurs in some big cities) and those who work or worked in the presence of dust, chemical fumes and/or vapors also are at increased risk for COPD.

In addition, some research shows a link between gastroesophageal reflux disease (GERD) and COPD. The reflux-causing disorder can worsen COPD or, in rare cases, cause it, though researchers are unsure why.

DIAGNOSIS CAN BE DIFFICULT

Shortness of breath, a chronic cough, wheezing and excess sputum production (with or without cough) are the main symptoms of COPD.

However, most people with early-stage COPD don't even know that they have it. The symptoms come on so slowly—usually over decades—that people get used to them. They think that it's normal to get short of breath when climbing stairs or to wake up with a mucus-filled cough. Or they attribute the coughing and/or shortness of breath to smoking itself and not to an underlying disease, such as COPD.

Important: The key symptom to watch for is shortness of breath, particularly during exercise or any type of exertion. This often is the first sign of COPD. Other symptoms, such as a chronic cough, usually occur later in the course of the disease.

By the time most people with undiagnosed COPD realize that something's wrong, a significant amount of lung tissue has already been irreversibly damaged.

In the advanced stages of COPD, patients may find that even simple tasks, such as walking to the mailbox or rising from a chair, will leave them short of breath.

ASK FOR THIS TEST

I suggest that everyone age 45 or older get tested at least once for COPD. Those with COPD risk factors—current or former smokers, for example, or those who are (or have been) exposed to dust/chemicals in the workplace—should be tested annually.

Spirometry is the main test for COPD. It's inexpensive and painless and can be done in the doctor's office in a few minutes. Few doctors routinely test patients with spirometry, but you should insist on it.

What the test involves: You blow into a spirometer, which measures your forced vital capacity (the total amount exhaled) and forced expiratory volume (the amount exhaled in the first second).

A "normal" reading will vary, depending on your age, sex and height. For example, an average, healthy 50-year-old man should be able to exhale about four liters of air in one second. A person with COPD might exhale only about 2.5 liters per second, or less.

Asthma can cause symptoms similar to those caused by COPD. Therefore, if you have asthma, your doctor may have you use an inhaled bronchodilator, then repeat the spirometry test. The spirometry readings will improve immediately in people who have asthma. With COPD, the readings remain the same or improve only slightly.

Insurance typically covers the cost of spirometry.

BEST PREVENTION STRATEGIES

Not smoking is the most important step you can take to protect your lungs. Those at highest risk for COPD have accumulated 20 "pack years"—a measurement calculated by multiplying the number of packs of cigarettes smoked per day by the number of years that you've smoked.

People who quit smoking may regain close to normal lung function if they have very early-stage COPD. Those who quit later can preserve more of their normal lung function and slow the rate at which the disease progresses. Even if you quit smoking years ago, it's possible to have undetected COPD without symptoms.

Since occupational pollutants are the second-leading cause of COPD, people who work in industrial jobs, such as mining or welding, or livestock farming, should always wear the appropriate protective equipment, such as particulate (air- purifying) respirator face masks.

Even in nonwork settings, you should wear a mask if painting, spreading fertilizer or doing any task that may involve dust or fumes. Caution: Do not wear a mask if you have shortness of breath.

THE RIGHT TREATMENT

If you've already been diagnosed with COPD, your doctor will probably prescribe medications to reduce symptoms—coughing, difficulty breathing, wheezing and/or mucus production—during flare-ups.

Important: Such drugs should be taken at the first signs of a flare-up to minimize lung inflammation and help reduce long-term damage.

An alternative to medication may involve simple breathing exercises and supervised rehabilitation. As the condition progresses, it is customary to use medication and breathing exercises together.

Best COPD medications...

• **Bronchodilators that contain a short-acting beta-agonist,** such as *albuterol* (Proventil) or *tiotropium* (Spiriva), expand and relax muscles around the airways and make it easier to inhale and exhale. Side effects may include vomiting and muscle pain.

• **Inhaled steroids,** such as *fluticasone* (Flovent), reduce inflammation and may improve airflow when used in combination with other medications. Side effects of inhaled steroids may include headache, sore throat and, according to recent research, increased diabetes risk.

• **During flare-ups,** oral steroids may be used for a short course (about 10 days), especially if a bronchodilator alone is not sufficient.

Other treatments...

• **Supplemental oxygen** is sometimes needed to improve breathing and exercise tolerance in those with advanced COPD.

• **Lung volume reduction surgery may be recommended in rare cases of severe emphysema.** It involves removal of the damaged sections of the lungs to allow the remaining lung tissue to work more efficiently. This treatment is effective only when patients have sufficient amounts of healthy lung tissue left after surgery.

Important: If you have COPD, any respiratory illness increases the risk for lung damage and may cause a more rapid decline in lung function. That's why every person with COPD should get an influenza vaccination annually. Your doctor might also recommend a pneumococcal pneumonia vaccination every five years or so.

WHAT IS COPD?

Chronic obstructive pulmonary disease (COPD) is a progressive lung disease that blocks airflow and interferes with a person's ability to breathe. The declining lung function that characterizes COPD is most often caused by emphysema and/or chronic bronchitis.

More than 12 million Americans have been diagnosed with COPD. An additional 12 million may have the disease but not know it.

Best Exercise for COPD Patients

Renae McNamara, BAppSc (Phty), clinical specialist physiotherapist, pumonary rehabilitation, clinical and rehabilitation sciences, University of Sydney, and department of respiratory and sleep medicine and department of physiotherapy, Prince of Wales Hospital, New South Wales, Australia.

My friend's dad suffers from chronic obstructive pulmonary disease (COPD), as well as back pain, so it's hard for him to move around and breathe easily. Of all the types of workouts that he has tried, group aquatic exercise is the one that he has stuck with the longest.

Heading to an indoor pool isn't exactly convenient for him—he needs someone to drive him there…and then he has to change into his swimsuit…and afterward, he needs to shower and change…etc. It would be much easier for him to simply go for a walk around the block or putter around in a weight room!

But apparently there is just something about being in a pool with an instructor and other folks just like him. He says that he likes the social aspect, the heated water is soothing and he finds the activity more fun than working out on land—I suspect that it makes him feel like a kid again when he splashes around.

So I was pleased when I saw a new Australian study that shows that aquatic exercise builds more endurance and decreases fatigue and shortness of breath more substantially for people like him than land exercise—and this finding may apply to people with other sorts of respiratory problems and chronic conditions, too.

WATER WORKOUTS: LESS PAIN, MORE GAIN

The new research focused specifically on people who had both COPD, an all-too-common respiratory problem that is the third-leading cause of death in the US, and an additional chronic condition that makes exercise difficult—such as obesity, joint problems or back pain. But there's every reason to think that the study's results will apply to people with other sorts of medical issues, especially those with respiratory conditions, said lead researcher Renae McNamara, BAppSc (Phty), a respiratory physiotherapist in Australia. Future studies will need to examine that.

Researchers were interested in finding out which type of workout would help people find the most relief—land-based exercise (a mixture of walking, cycling, aerobics and dumbbell lifts) or water-based exercise (aquatic calisthenics done in chest-to-neck high water in a pool heated to 93°F).

The patients were split into three groups. One group did one-hour water exercises three times a week for eight weeks with a trained physiotherapist. Another group did land exercises for the same amount of time with the same trained physiotherapist. And a third group performed no exercise (the control).

At the end of the study, when each group was asked to perform a walking test to measure endurance, members of the water group could walk 118% farther than they could at the start of the study, on average…the land group's distance improved, too, but by only 53%…and the control group actually got weaker—their distance was 13% shorter.

Also, the people who had been exercising in a pool saw a 9% decrease in shortness of breath and a 13% decrease in fatigue by the end of the study…while the people who had been exercising on land saw only a 4% decrease in shortness of breath and a 3% decrease in fatigue.

CONTRA-CONVENTIONAL WISDOM

So why did water workouts come out on top? "Water may have helped more for a few reasons. First of all, you have the effect of buoyancy, which supports your weight and reduces impact on your joints," said McNamara. "Warm water also helps with pain control and increases blood flow to muscles. Plus, water offers resistance to all your movements, so your muscles work harder, and that strengthens them."

What's ironic is that it wasn't all that long ago that people with COPD were warned not to do water-based exercise. Doctors worried that the water would compress the chest and that the exertion would stress the heart. But studies that have analyzed COPD and water exercise under controlled conditions (as in, when patients were under the watchful eye of a health professional) have shown that these fears are unfounded, said McNamara.

GET YOUR GOGGLES ON!

Now that we have these study results, if you suffer from COPD as well as obesity, joint problems or back pain, you owe it to yourself to talk to your doctor or physical therapist about trying pool-based therapy with a trained health professional. (If you have COPD but none of those other conditions…or if you have one of the other conditions but not COPD…or if you suffer from a different type of respiratory problem…you may still find pool-based therapy to be more beneficial than land exercises, so it's worth a try, said McNamara.)

Group classes are usually easier to find than individual classes (plus, they tend to be cheaper and more fun). But either type of class is useful. To find one, call your local YMCA (*ymca.net)* or a community recreation center that has a pool or a hospital with an aquatic rehab center.

You might find, like my friend's dad, that all it takes is a little water to ease your pain and help you stay active.

Natural Relief from Asthma

Jamison Starbuck, ND, a naturopathic physician in family practice and a guest lecturer at the University of Montana, both in Missoula. She is a past president of the American Association of Naturopathic Physicians and a contributing editor to The Alternative Advisor: The Complete Guide to Natural Therapies and Alternative Treatments.

Asthma is a disease that begins in childhood, right? Well, not always. Though many adult asthma sufferers have struggled with the condition since childhood, research shows that up to 40% of new asthma patients are over age 40 when they have their first asthma attack. While patients with severe or unresponsive moderate asthma need conventional medical attention, natural medicine has a lot to offer.

First, it's important to recognize which adults are at increased risk of developing asthma. This includes people who suffer from frequent and recurrent upper respiratory infections, such as colds, sinusitis and the flu. When these illnesses occur too frequently (once a month or more often), inflammation can damage the respiratory tract—a perfect setup for asthma. Asthma is also closely linked to allergies (due, for example, to certain food preservatives, such as sodium bisulfate, and inhaled irritants, such as pollen and mold) as well as exposure to pollutants and toxins, including cigarette smoke. Research now shows that severe stress can also trigger an asthma attack.

There's no one-size-fits-all approach to treating asthma. In general, I recommend approaches for my patients that will reduce inflammation and enhance their lung and immune health. Asthma-fighting supplements that I recommend (all can be used with asthma medication, if needed)…*

•**Fish oil.** Research has found that these oils reduce bronchial inflammation that often accompanies asthma.

Typical dose: 2,000 mg daily.

•**Antioxidants.** Vitamin C—2,000 mg per day—and vitamin E—400 international units

*Consult your doctor to find out if this asthma-fighting protocol is right for you.

(IU) daily. Both improve immune health and reduce the allergic response that so often triggers an asthma attack.

- **Magnesium.** Use of this mineral (300 mg to 500 mg daily) can reduce bronchospasm (a tightening of the airways that makes breathing more difficult).

- **Botanicals.** One of my favorites is astragalus. It supports both lung and immune health. Typical dose: Use one-quarter teaspoon of tincture in two ounces of water, daily until asthma symptoms improve. Repeat when needed.

Also helpful: Deep-breathing exercises and/or yoga help prevent asthma attacks by calming the nervous system and increasing lung capacity.

Because all asthma patients have different needs, I recommend seeing a naturopathic doctor (ND) to help create a personalized natural regimen. To find an ND near you, consult The American Association of Naturopathic Physicians, *Naturopathic.org*. But remember, not all asthma can be well controlled with natural medicine. If you have more than mild-to-moderate asthma, you should also be under the care of an allergist or pulmonologist and not shirk any prescription drugs, such as inhalers, that he/she has prescribed for you.

Combining natural medicine with prescription medication (when needed) gives you the best chance of keeping your asthma well controlled!

Unusual Asthma Warning Signs

Itching at the front of the neck or an itchy feeling in the chest may indicate asthma. These unusual symptoms may precede the more common symptoms, which include coughing, chest tightness, shortness of breath and wheezing.

Stephen J. Apaliski, MD, an allergist and immunologist, Allergy & Asthma Centres of the Metroplex, Arlington, Texas, and author of *Beating Asthma: Seven Simple Principles.*

How to Survive an Asthma Attack Without an Inhaler

Richard Firshein, DO, board-certified in family medicine and certified medical acupuncturist and founder and director of The Firshein Center for Comprehensive Medicine, New York City. He is author of *Reversing Asthma: Breathe Easier with This Revolutionary New Program.*

If you have asthma, a rescue inhaler can be your best friend if you're gasping from a serious asthma attack. But what do you do if you don't have it?

First question: Emergency or not? People can die from severe asthma attacks. This won't happen if you get to an emergency room fast enough—but you have to make a quick decision about the severity of your symptoms.

What to look for: Feelings of panic…shortness of breath…a cough that won't quit…inability to speak…sudden exhaustion…or soreness/tightness around the ribs. If you have a peak-flow meter, use it. A reading that's 25% (or more) lower than usual means that you're in trouble. Get to an ER or call an ambulance.

- **Stop the attack.** If my patients are not in immediate danger, I advise them to do all of the following…

- **Take an oral medication.** Oral prednisone or theophylline will quickly improve breathing. Certain over-the-counter medications—including antihistamines, cough medicines and guaifenesin (an expectorant)—can help in a pinch.

Also helpful: Vitamin C (1,000 mg during an attack) reduces inflammation and is a mild antihistamine…magnesium (500 mg) opens airways…and quercetin (about 1,500 mg) has antihistamine and anti-inflammatory effects.

- **Change locations.** Do it as soon as you notice that your breathing is labored. Attacks often are triggered by irritants in your immediate environment such as traffic fumes, pet hair, pollen, etc. Going a short distance away can make a surprising difference.

- **Grab a cup of coffee or caffeinated tea.** The body metabolizes caffeine into theophylline, the same compound in some asthma medications—and the caffeine itself relaxes airways.

• **Relax.** During an attack, your body increases production of adrenaline and cortisol. You need these hormones to reduce inflammation and improve breathing…but anxiety depletes them. Breathing exercises will help keep the airways open. Inhale deeply through your nose for about four seconds, then exhale through your nose for a count of six. Keep breathing like this until you're feeling better.

Another relaxation tool is visual imagery. In your mind, see your lungs opening up. Or picture yourself in nature or another restful place. Fill the picture with as much detail as possible.

• **Press the "lung points."** You can use acupressure to stimulate the points that control breathing. One is the LU5 point at the outer part of the elbow crease when your elbows are bent. Another is the LU1 point, which is located at the intersection of your chest and your shoulder. If you get into trouble, press each of these points one at a time for one to three minutes, starting with light pressure and gradually increasing it.

• **Take a long shower or bath.** It will help you relax, and the steam will loosen mucus and make it easier to breathe.

Surgical Cure for Asthma

Sumita B. Khatri, MD, MS, codirector, Asthma Center, The Respiratory Institute, Cleveland Clinic Foundation, Cleveland, Ohio.

A relatively recent surgical procedure may be life-changing—even potentially life-saving—for people with chronic asthma who haven't been able to get relief from the standard treatments. Called bronchial thermoplasty, the procedure was approved by the FDA last April. It's being done at only 23 hospitals around the country, but it is worth exploring as a treatment if you or someone you are close to is suffering recurrent asthma attacks that have not been helped by traditional treatments. Thus far, the evidence suggests that this procedure, the first nondrug treatment for asthma, dramatically reduces the occurrence of asthma attacks and improves asthma-related quality of life.

It's estimated that more than 23 million Americans (including seven million children) suffer from asthma, a chronic disease that inflames and narrows airways. Some individuals are born with a predisposition to asthma due to allergies or develop it from exposure to secondhand smoke, while in others the causes may be more unpredictable, such as viral illnesses.

In people with asthma, the layer of smooth muscle that surrounds the airways becomes thicker and more reactive to certain triggers, explained Sumita B. Khatri, MD, codirector of the Asthma Center at the Cleveland Clinic's Respiratory Institute. When a person with asthma has an attack, the muscles around the airways constrict and go into spasms, narrowing the airways and leading to shortness of breath, tightness in the chest and other distressing symptoms.

REDUCES SWELLING IN AIRWAYS

In contrast to asthma medications that target inflammation and may secondarily reduce some of the muscle thickening, bronchial thermoplasty treats the airways directly with heat created by radio-frequency waves.

The treatment is apparently quite effective. A randomized, double-blind controlled study of about 300 patients found that those who underwent bronchial thermoplasty experienced vastly improved asthma-related quality of life in the 12 months afterward, including…

• **32% reduction in asthma attacks, on average.**

• **84% drop in visits to hospital emergency rooms.**

• **66% reduction in lost work or school days.**

• **73% decline in hospitalizations for respiratory problems.**

Dr. Khatri said that two years after the first clinical trials, the improvements are still in place—including not only a reduction in symptoms overall but also in the frequency of severe asthma flare-ups and hospitalizations. Many patients also have reduced their need for rescue/emergency medications as well, she said.

TREATMENTS AREN'T PAINFUL

Bronchial thermoplasty takes place over three one-hour sessions scheduled three weeks apart. In each procedure, the patient receives light sedation—many actually fall asleep. Each of the three treatments targets a different area of the lungs—in the first session, the airways of the right lower lobe...in the second, the left lower lobe...and in the third, the airways in both upper lobes.

What's involved: The pulmonologist threads a long, flexible tube called a bronchoscope down the mouth or through the nose and into an airway in the lung. Inside the bronchoscope, a special thermoplasty catheter contains electrodes that are heated with radio-frequency energy. This shrinks the muscle, which is believed to prevent the extreme airway muscle contractions during asthma attacks. "This result is expected to be permanent, but there is still not enough data yet to know for sure," Dr. Khatri said.

There are no pain-sensing nerves in the airways, so the application of thermal energy does not hurt, notes Dr. Khatri. Patients are monitored for several hours afterward because symptoms sometimes worsen in the short term. To reduce the likelihood that this will happen, patients take a five-day course of steroids before and after surgery. Though bronchial thermoplasty often is done as an outpatient procedure, Dr. Khatri said that the Cleveland Clinic keeps patients overnight as an added safety precaution. She added that in the immediate post-procedure period, some patients experience discomfort similar to an asthma flare-up, requiring use of rescue/symptom relieving medications. Also, many patients have a sore throat from the bronchoscope, while other possible transitory side effects are chest discomfort or pain, partial lung collapse (serious but treatable), headaches, anxiety and nausea.

ARE YOU A CANDIDATE?

Bronchial thermoplasty is FDA-approved only for people age 18 and older with severe ongoing symptoms from asthma that are not well controlled with regular asthma medications. It can't be performed on smokers, people with active respiratory infections or people who have heart arrhythmias or have implanted pacemakers, defibrillators or other electronic devices.

Bronchial thermoplasty is expensive—as much as $15,000 or more—and since it is still considered experimental, Medicare doesn't cover it and neither do most insurers. However, Dr. Khatri expects this to change as time goes on and more and more patients experience significant health benefits after bronchial thermoplasty.

13

Cures for Everyday Aches and Illnesses

How to Wreck Your Immune System

Nobody wants to spend time sick in bed feeling miserable with a cold, the flu or any other illness.

But here's the catch: Even if you stay well rested, exercise and eat healthfully, you still could be sabotaging your immune system. Most people are unknowingly making it harder for their bodies to fight off illnesses. *How to stop hurting your immune system…*

• **Skip the germ-killing soaps.** Studies now show that triclosan, the key ingredient in many antibacterial hand soaps (as well as some shaving gels, shampoos, cosmetics, deodorants and other personal-care items), fuels the growth of antibiotic-resistant bugs in the public at large. With frequent use, triclosan also can hurt you personally by setting up your body to develop a secondary "super-infection" that can occur as a complication of colds, the flu or viral pneumonia.

Among the best ways to prevent colds and the flu: Vigorous, frequent hand-washing with plain soap is all you need, but here's the key—you need to scrub long enough (count to 20).

If you like the reassurance offered by a hand sanitizer, products with at least 60% alcohol, such as Purell or Germ-X, are widely recommended. However, the alcohol in such hand sanitizers can lead to dry, cracked skin, which provides an entry point for bacterial or fungal skin infections. Alcohol-based products are supported by strong research, but if dry skin is a problem, rely on hand-washing and/or a hand sanitizer that contains natural antibacterial plant oils such as citrus, oregano, rosemary and/or thyme.

Robert Rountree, MD, a family physician in private practice and owner of Boulder Wellcare in Boulder, Colorado. He is coauthor of numerous books, including *Immunotics: A Revolutionary Way to Fight Infection, Beat Chronic Illness and Stay Well.*

Good choice: CleanWell, $15.99 for two one-ounce spray bottles and two 10-count packs of wipes, *cleanwelltoday.com.*

• **Take a pass on sugar.** Sugar, refined carbohydrates and high-fructose corn syrup can impair the effectiveness of our immune cells. As soon as you notice cold or flu symptoms, cut these foods out of your diet.

Beware: The caramelized sugar found on cinnamon rolls, donuts or sticky buns is particularly harmful to our immunity. Certain molecular structures in this type of sugar resemble bacteria, and our immune system receptors mistakenly bind to them, interfering with their ability to respond effectively to true infections.

If you need a sweetener: Try raw honey, which has immune-building properties.*

• **Watch out for pesticides.** Most nonorganic produce gets showered with pesticides, which damage your immune system.

What to try instead: Load up on fresh, organic fruits and vegetables to arm your immune system with disease-fighting vitamins and nutrients. Organic berries, citrus fruits, grapes and spinach are especially rich in antioxidants that support immune function. When fresh berries aren't available, try frozen organic berries. You can save money by opting for nonorganic citrus fruits and other peelable items (such as bananas) that are less likely to harbor dangerous pesticides than produce without peels.

POWER UP YOUR IMMUNITY

Many people rely on well-known immunity boosters such as vitamin C and/or echinacea, but you're likely to get better results from using the following on a daily basis as a preventive during cold and flu season (or year-round if you work directly with the public)...**

• **Probiotics.** By far, probiotics are the best way to enhance your immunity. These "good" bacteria, including Lactobacillus and Bifidobacterium, reside in your digestive tract, where they keep intestinal microbes in check and elevate your number of infection-fighting T cells.

*Infants under age one and people who are allergic to pollen or immunocompromised should not consume raw honey.

**Consult your doctor before trying dietary supplements—especially if you take prescription medication and/or have a chronic medical condition.

Fermented foods, such as kefir, yogurt, kimchi, sauerkraut and kombucha, are all naturally rich in probiotics. Aim for two (four- to six-ounce) servings a day.

In general, however, probiotic supplements are more potent and may be more reliable than probiotic-rich foods. If you opt for a supplement, use a combination of Bifidobacterium and/or Lactobacillus species.

A probiotic found in studies to boost immunity: Culturelle, $33.80 for 80 capsules, *amazon.com.*

• **N-acetylcysteine (NAC).** The body easily converts this amino acid into a usable form of glutathione, an immunity-protecting antioxidant that itself is poorly absorbed from the gastrointestinal tract.

Scientific evidence: Italian researchers found that taking 1,200 mg daily of NAC throughout flu season reduced the frequency, severity and intensity of flu-like symptoms.

Typical dose: 600 mg to 1,200 mg daily as a preventive...at the first sign of infection, increase the dose to 3,000 mg daily (taken in doses of 600 mg each throughout the day).

• **Elderberry syrup.** When used within the first 48 hours of feeling flu-ish, this syrup (made from naturally antiviral elderberries) has been shown to relieve symptoms four days faster than a placebo.

If you are not taking elderberry syrup as a daily preventive, start using it within the first two days of developing cold or flu symptoms. Follow label instructions.

Good choice: Sambucol Black Elderberry Immune System Support, $19.99 for 7.8 ounces, *drugstore.com.*

DON'T GO IT ALONE!

What do close relationships have to do with immunity? A lot, according to research.

When researchers exposed 276 adults to a rhinovirus (a cause of the common cold), subjects with only one to three relationships (such as fulfilling marriages or friendships with colleagues, neighbors and religious community members) were four times more likely to get sick than those who had more than six relationships.

Possible explanation: Social interactions help ease the negative effects of stress—a known threat to immunity.

One-Minute Immunity Boost

Take a one-minute cold shower to ward off illness. Research at the Thrombosis Research Institute in London has found that cold water stimulates immune cell production.

Theory: The body tries to warm itself during and after a cold shower, which speeds up the metabolic rate, activating the immune system.

DailyMail.com

Drug-Free Cures for Colds, Sore Throats and the Flu

Jamison Starbuck, ND, a naturopathic physician practicing in Missoula, Montana.

Viruses are the tiniest life form in existence—smaller, even, than a single cell. However their impact is huge as they are responsible for various infectious illnesses or diseases, from the common cold to chicken pox to much deadlier ones including HIV.

Natural medications are great at helping the body gear up to fight viruses, says Dr. Starbuck. They work by revving up the white blood cells of the immune system to target the bad guys causing the symptoms, boosting antibody production to encourage it to stop replicating. And, like pharmaceuticals, natural medicines can ease symptoms.

IMMUNE BOOSTING

Echinacea is high on Dr. Starbuck's list for treating viruses. This common immune booster comes in tea, capsules and tincture. Dr. Starbuck recommends the tincture because it is generally more potent and has superior bio-availability. (Test the tincture for freshness by putting a drop on your tongue—it should create a slightly numbing feel. If not, get another bottle. A good choice is Eclectic Institute's Specific Echinacea.)

Dr. Starbuck most often prescribes Echinacea tincture to be taken by her patients at the first sign of sickness as follows: Place about 30 drops into an ounce of water…take every four hours away from meals. It's a good idea to drink additional water as well.

Dr. Starbuck often uses Echinacea in combination with other herbs, too. She advises Ligusticum porteri (also named Osha root) to soothe congested tissue and stimulate circulation, again usually prescribing its tincture form. You can find "do it yourself" anti-viral herbal formulas prepared with one or several immune-strengthening herbs in natural stores such as Whole Foods Market—Dr. Starbuck likes the herbal mix Throat Mist for sore throats, by Wise Woman Herbals (*wisewoman herbals.com*). Take these herbs at the first sign of sickness. The sooner you catch the virus, the easier it is to beat back—as always, under the oversight of a physician trained in natural healing.

Vitamin C does more than any other vitamin to boost immune function. Vitamin A is helpful in moistening mucus membranes in the upper respiratory tract.

Note: Too much vitamin A can be toxic so Dr. Starbuck advises her patients to get beta carotene, the water soluble, precursor molecule of vitamin A, by eating foods that are high in it rather than taking vitamin A in supplement form. One way is to drink fresh carrot juice (two ounces, twice a day), or blended with fresh orange juice for a combined A/C hit. Oranges, tangerines and, in fact, orange-colored produce of any kind (including pumpkin and sweet potatoes) are helpful. You can continue vitamin therapy for two to three weeks.

MANAGING FEVER

Fever is the body's natural weapon for killing viruses, so it's best to let it do its work. However if a fever becomes too uncomfortable for you or your child (adults get fevers

317

far less often) or if it is sudden, higher than is typical for you when you get sick and causes bright red cheeks, it may require treatment. Be sure to alert your physician to the fever, as an intense one may require suppression and even hospitalization. Dr. Starbuck says that she often prescribes just one dose of the homeopathic substance Belladonna—typically two pellets of 30C strength—which frequently takes care of a high fever. However, for fevers that are low grade, persistent and dragging you down, she may prescribe the homeopathic substance Gelsemium sempervirens, also 30C strength, two pellets at one time.

KEEPING SYMPTOMS AT BAY

For a runny nose and cold, Dr. Starbuck prescribes ginger or usnea, herbs that dry out the mucus and provide antiseptic properties.

She also directs her patients as follows: Vaporizing or steam will help thin out mucus and keep it flowing—use a humidifier or simply a bowl or pan of just-boiled water to which you can add one or two drops of eucalyptus or lavender essential oil or several peppermint tea bags. Drape a towel over your head and stand over the water, to breathe in its steam, taking care to avoid burning, of course. For patients suffering from a sore throat that feels hot and dry, Dr. Starbuck prescribes slippery elm, licorice or marshmallow root, all moistening herbs. Also helpful for an inflamed throat is a cool mist humidifier.

Saline solutions, including nasal sprays, can help break up mucus. For a more exotic approach, Dr. Starbuck often prescribes treatment with the neti pot, used in the practice of ancient ayurvedic medicine. Neti pots have been boosted into the "trendy" category as the must-have saline irrigation system. But it's important to keep the pot clean and use filtered or distilled water if possible. The neti pot resembles a teapot to be filled with four ounces of saline solution and poured into one nostril, thereby forcing mucus out of the other. Dr. Starbuck often directs her patients to add a quarter teaspoon of combined Echinacea and eyebright tincture to the saline packet mix.

GENERAL RULES

When fighting a virus, it is good to give your digestive tract a break. Avoid proteins and fats, which are hard to digest, as well as dairy products, which create mucus. Warm up by eating hot foods—preferably soups, steamed vegetables and the like and of course, drink lots of fluids. Get plenty of sleep and don't forego exercise even now, says Dr. Starbuck. Though a hard workout will only stress your already over-stressed body, do get outside twice a day for a 15-minute relaxed walk in sunlight and fresh air.

You can protect others from your virus by washing your hands throughout the day and always after you blow your nose. Don't go to work when you are feeling sick, since you'll expose your colleagues and prolong your misery. Dr. Starbuck points out that illness will disappear faster if you take care of yourself—instead of being sick a week or longer, you can feel better in three to five days with rest and proper natural care.

Fight the Flu!

Marc Siegel, MD, an internist and clinical professor of medicine at NYU Langone Medical Center in New York City. He is a medical correspondent for *Fox News* and is the medical director of *Doctor Radio* on SiriusXM Satellite Radio. He is also the author of *The Inner Pulse: Unlocking the Secret Code of Sickness and Health*. DoctorSiegel.com

---

Getting a flu shot seems fairly straightforward. But these days, there may be more to it than simply rolling up your sleeve and getting a jab in the arm. There are multiple flu vaccines to choose from (including some that aren't injected), but your doctor may not offer enough guidance. *The facts you need to know…*

A DEADLY ILLNESS

People who have never had the flu may think that it's easy to manage, like a common cold. Those who have had it know better. The flu can leave you bedridden, achy and feverish—sometimes for weeks.

The CDC recommends that everyone six months and older get vaccinated. That's because every year, an average of more than 30,000 Americans die from flu-related complications. Older adults and those with other health problems, such as diabetes, asthma, heart disease or cancer, are at highest risk for flu and its complications.

GETTING THE RIGHT VACCINE

Flu season in the US can begin as early as October and last until May.

My advice: Get vaccinated as soon as the vaccine becomes available (ideally by October), so you don't forget. It takes about two weeks for the body to develop flu-fighting antibodies. *The main options—all are usually covered by insurance…*

• **High dose.** Because older adults are more likely to get seriously ill from the flu, and their immune response is often weaker than a younger person's after being vaccinated, they face a double risk. Fluzone High-Dose is a trivalent vaccine, meaning that it protects against three types of flu—two strains of Type A and one strain of Type B. The high-dose vaccine has four times more of the active ingredient than is used in regular flu shots. Studies have shown that people age 65 or older who get the high-dose vaccine have a stronger immune response, but experts aren't completely sure if this vaccine gives greater flu protection than the standard flu shot.

My advice: Since the high-dose vaccine appears to be just as safe as standard flu shots, it's a good choice for older patients.

An alternative: A vaccine booster. It's an effective way to increase immunity in older adults. I administer one dose of a standard vaccine early in the season, then give another dose about four months later.

• **Four-way protection.** Even though trivalent vaccines that protect against three flu strains have long been the standard, there are now quadrivalent vaccines, which add an additional B strain. However, the quadrivalent vaccine may not be available from your doctor or pharmacy.

My advice: If a quadrivalent vaccine is not available, get the trivalent vaccine. Both vaccines should protect against the most common flu strains. People over age 65 should ask their doctor whether the high-dose or quadrivalent vaccine is right for them based on their level of immunity and the circulating Type B strains.

• **Nasal spray.** FluMist is a nasal spray that is an effective alternative to shots—with no pain or crying children. A quick spritz and you are done.

However: It's not for everyone. FluMist is a quadrivalent vaccine that isn't approved for children under age two or for adults age 50 and older. Unlike the killed-virus vaccines that are used in injections, the spray contains a live, attenuated (weakened) form of the flu virus. For this reason, it shouldn't be used by those with an impaired immune system or chronic lung disease, such as asthma.

• **Ouchless.** What if you do not want a shot, but you have a health condition that prevents you from using the nasal vaccine? You can now opt for an intradermal quadrivalent shot, which is less painful because it uses a needle that is 90% smaller than those used for regular flu shots. It is injected into the skin, unlike other flu shots, which are injected deep into muscle.

Also: In 2014, the FDA approved Afluria, a trivalent vaccine that's administered via "jet injection"—a device is used to shoot a high-pressure stream of liquid through the skin. (It feels like the snap of a rubber band.)

The downside: Both intradermal and jet injections may be more likely to cause redness, swelling and itching than standard shots.

On the other hand, they are believed to provide the same level of protection as standard injections…and are less upsetting for those who don't like shots.

• **Egg-free.** Traditional vaccines are made by culturing viruses in chicken eggs—a potential problem for those with severe egg allergies. Now there are two options (Flucelvax and Flublok) that rely on cell-based technology instead of using the flu virus and eggs in the manufacturing process. The egg-free vaccines are just as effective as the standard flu vaccines and can be produced more rapidly in a sudden flu outbreak.

However: In my experience, most people with mild egg allergies can tolerate the older, egg-based vaccines—a cell-based vaccine might be helpful, though, if your allergies are unusually severe. Ask your doctor for advice.

More from Dr. Siegel...

The Truth About Two Flu "Dangers"

Anyone who has ever gotten a flu shot knows that some arm soreness, swelling and/or redness may occur for a day or so around the injection site. But what are the recent reports of SIRVA (it stands for shoulder injury related to vaccine administration) all about? This condition, marked by severe pain, limited flexibility and/or weakness in the shoulder, is actually quite rare and occurs only when an injection of any kind in the shoulder's deltoid muscle is given too deep or too high. If you're concerned about injection site side effects, including SIRVA, consider getting your flu shot from a trained professional who can provide follow-up care...or ask for a flu vaccine that doesn't require an injection.

And what about the mercury-based preservative known as thimerosal? No link has ever been found to autism. Very credible research has repeatedly shown that the low doses used in vaccines do not cause harm.

However: You can ask for a single-dose vial. Unlike the multidose vials, which contain thimerosal to avoid possible contamination, single-dose units are free of the preservative.

Better Flu Recovery

New research: Researchers divided 154 healthy adults (age 50 and older) into three groups—one that was trained to meditate daily for 45 minutes, one that exercised daily for 45 minutes and a control group that did neither.

Result: During a single flu season, the meditation and exercise groups had similarly fewer acute respiratory infections than the control group, but the meditation group's symptoms were far less severe than those of the other two groups.

Theory: Daily meditation reduces stress, which may protect against infection.

Bruce Barrett, MD, associate professor of family medicine, University of Wisconsin School of Medicine and Public Health, Madison.

How Not to Get Pneumonia

Neil Schachter, MD, professor of medicine at Mount Sinai School of Medicine and the medical director of respiratory care at Mount Sinai Hospital, both in New York City. The author of *The Good Doctor's Guide to Colds & Flu, Life and Breath: The Breakthrough Guide to the Latest Strategies for Fighting Asthma and Other Respiratory Problems—At Any Age.* Lung.org

Most people tend to worry about pneumonia during the winter months, but it can strike at any time of year.

Latest development: For reasons that are not yet understood, older men have been found to be 30% more likely than older women to die from community-acquired pneumonia—a type of pneumonia that develops in people who have had little or no contact with hospitals or other medical settings where the illness is often contracted. Even though everyone should take precautions to avoid this potentially life-threatening illness, older men should be especially vigilant.

What you need to know to protect yourself—and loved ones...

WHAT IS PNEUMONIA?

Pneumonia is inflammation of the lungs due to infection—usually bacterial or viral. Of the estimated four million Americans who contract pneumonia each year, 1.2 million are hospitalized and 55,000 die. Pneumonia is the fifth-leading cause of death among Americans over age 65.

Symptoms include cough, chills, fever, fatigue and trouble breathing.

Caution: Since an older adult's normal body temperature is often below 98.6°, he/she may not seem to have a fever.

PNEUMONIA AVOIDANCE MADE EASY

In addition to not smoking (smoking increases risk for all respiratory illnesses), getting the seasonal flu vaccine has long been a cornerstone of pneumonia prevention. Because flu weakens the immune system and damages the airways, the illness makes it easier for bacteria and viruses to multiply and turn into pneumonia. The flu vaccine is recommended for anyone over age 50 and for people of any age with pneumonia risk factors, such as asthma, heart disease or any other chronic illness. (If you didn't get a seasonal flu vaccine this winter, it's even more crucial for you to follow the advice below.)

Important steps—besides getting vaccinated for the seasonal flu—that help guard against pneumonia…

1. Get a pneumonia vaccination. A vaccine against pneumococcal pneumonia, which is caused by Streptococcus pneumoniae (the most common cause of bacterial pneumonia), is available for adults and lasts for five years. The vaccine helps prevent pneumococcal pneumonia's most serious complications, such as bacteremia (infection in the bloodstream) and septicemia (infection throughout the body).

Important new finding: A recent report shows that a significant number of adults—more than 30% of older adults in most parts of the US—have not received the pneumococcal pneumonia vaccine.

My advice: Get this vaccine if you're over age 65 or you are any age and have pneumonia risk factors, such as diabetes…chronic obstructive pulmonary disease (COPD) or other chronic lung or heart problems…or you are on immunosuppressive medical therapy, including chemotherapy or inhaled corticosteroids.

Bonus: Recent research indicates that the pneumonia vaccine also reduces heart attack risk among people with cardiovascular risk factors—possibly by preventing arterial inflammation that can accompany pneumonia.

2. Get measles and chicken pox vaccinations, if needed. Both of these diseases can lead to pneumonia. If you didn't have chicken pox or the measles and weren't vaccinated against them as a child, get vaccinated now.

3. Wash your hands frequently. Even though most bacterial pneumonia results from germs in our own bodies—for example, on our teeth or tonsils or in our sinuses—pneumonia-causing bacteria and viruses (including those that cause the flu) can be passed among people. Frequent hand-washing with soap or alcohol-based cleansers helps minimize disease transmission.

4. If you do get the flu, discuss antiviral medication with your doctor. A review of the medical records of 70,000 patients age 60 and older found that taking *oseltamivir* (Tamiflu) decreased the incidence of pneumonia in older Americans by 59%.

5. Drink alcohol only in moderation. Alcohol depresses the cough and sneeze reflexes, making it easier for microbes to enter the lower respiratory tract. It also impairs the function of white blood cells, which are responsible for destroying bacteria in the lungs. Men should not exceed one drink daily… women should limit their alcohol consumption to three drinks weekly.

6. Brush and floss—and treat gum disease and sinus infections promptly. Gum and sinus infections increase the amount of bacteria inhaled into the airways. Good oral hygiene and treatment of such infections are key preventive measures, especially for people with impaired immunity or other risk factors that increase susceptibility to pneumonia. Be sure to brush at least twice daily, floss once daily and get a dental checkup at least every six months.

7. Use caution with inhaled corticosteroids. Treatments such as chemotherapy and prednisone are known to suppress the immune system, thus increasing pneumonia risk. Now, studies show that extended use (24 weeks or more) of inhaled corticosteroids for COPD increases pneumonia risk by 50%.

Among people age 65 and older, this figure jumps to almost 75%. However, the benefits of using an inhaled corticosteroid often outweigh the pneumonia risk. Monitor yourself closely with your physician's help.

8. Treat GERD, but follow your doctor's advice about medication. Gastroesophageal reflux disease (GERD), in which stomach contents chronically wash back up the esophagus, boosts pneumonia risk by increasing the bacteria inhaled into the airways. However, treating GERD with acid-suppressing proton-pump inhibitor (PPI) drugs, such as *lansoprazole* (Prevacid) or *esomeprazole* (Nexium), also raises pneumonia risk by encouraging bacterial growth in the stomach.

New finding: While PPIs increase risk for community-acquired pneumonia only slightly, they appear to be a major factor in hospital-acquired pneumonia, which strikes up to 1% of all hospital patients in the US and kills 18% of its victims (in part because more virulent bacteria are present in hospitals).

One recent study estimates that PPIs and other acid blockers, such as H2-receptor antagonists—for example, cimetidine (Tagamet) and *ranitidine* (Zantac)—may cause some 30,000 pneumonia-related deaths each year. The study also found that many patients were routinely given PPIs and other acid blockers despite not really needing them.

If you need to take one of these GERD drugs (even in an over-the-counter product) for more than two weeks, consult your doctor.

Drug-Free Help for Chronic Heartburn

Kristina Conner, ND, an assistant professor at National University of Health Sciences in Lombard, Illinois. She specializes in natural family medicine for women and children, naturopathic endocrinology and gastroenterology.

An estimated 20% of Americans have a chronic form of heartburn—characterized by chest pain, a persistent cough

and/or burning at the back of the throat that occur more than twice weekly—known as gastroesophageal reflux disease (GERD). Besides causing significant discomfort, if left untreated, this condition increases the risk for esophageal cancer.

Drugs are not the only way to deal with GERD. Kristina Conner, ND, an assistant professor at National University of Health Sciences in Lombard, Illinois, who specializes in women's health and digestive problems, discussed various natural therapies that ease or eliminate GERD.

But first, let's quickly review a bit of biology. To break down food, the stomach produces about one quart of hydrochloric acid daily. At the base of the esophagus is the lower esophageal sphincter (LES), a band of muscle that opens to let swallowed food into the stomach, then shuts again. When the LES fails to close properly, stomach acid backs up into the esophagus and damages the esophageal lining. This is what happens with GERD. *What helps…*

ESOPHAGUS-SOOTHING SUPPLEMENTS

Taken alone or in combination for two to four months, the dietary supplements below promote esophageal healing, Dr. Conner said. For dosages and guidelines on which supplements are most appropriate for you, consult a naturopathic physician. *Options…*

• **Calcium citrate powder** mixed with water helps tighten the LES and improves the esophagus's ability to push acid back into the stomach.

• **Deglycyrrhized licorice tablets** promote production of mucus that protects esophageal cells.

• **Marshmallow root lozenges** contain mucilage, a gelatinous substance that coats the gastrointestinal tract, soothes inflammation and heals cells lining the esophagus and stomach, Dr. Conner said.

• **Slippery elm herbal tea** also provides mucilage. Drink it hot, not iced. Warm beverages are easier to absorb than cold drinks, which can tax gastrointestinal function, Dr. Conner pointed out.

• **Vitamin B complex,** including thiamine (B-1), pantothenic acid (B-5) and choline, promotes proper smooth-muscle activity of the esophagus to keep food moving in the right direction.

ANTI-GERD DIET

Foods that can exacerbate GERD by relaxing the LES muscle and/or increasing acidity generally are those that are spicy or high in fat or sugar. Some people find that symptoms are triggered by certain other foods, such as alcohol, carbonated beverages, citrus fruits and juices, chocolate, coffee, mint, onions and tomatoes. Contrary to the popular idea that dairy foods ease GERD, they actually can worsen symptoms. "You do not necessarily need to give up all these foods forever, but you will feel better if you avoid them long enough to let your body recover," Dr. Conner said.

What to do: Eliminate all potential troublemakers from your diet for two to four weeks, then reintroduce them one at a time. If eating a particular food brings on symptoms within a day, avoid it for another three to six months, then try it again. If GERD symptoms return, it is best to avoid this food henceforth. If no symptoms develop after the three- to six-month hiatus, you may be able to eat this food occasionally. But keep portions moderate. "You can't drink eight cups of coffee or soda per day and expect GERD not to return," Dr. Conner noted.

Safe to eat: Foods unlikely to exacerbate GERD include those that are high in fiber, complex carbohydrates and/or minerals, Dr. Conner said. Good choices include most fruits and vegetables (except those identified above as potential heartburn triggers)... lean meats and skinless poultry...and whole grains.

Eat slowly and chew carefully, giving your mouth—a key part of your digestive system—and stomach plenty of time to work. Don't overfill your stomach. "Avoid eating while watching TV, driving, standing up or doing anything that takes attention away from your food and encourages you to rush or overeat," Dr. Conner said.

Celebrate your food: Put out placemats, cloth napkins, even candles...as you eat, notice each food's taste, texture and aroma.

You'll enjoy your food more and eat less—a double benefit.

Heartburn Cure in Your Pantry

If you have a bout of heartburn and you've run out of antacids or prefer a safe, natural route to feeling better, here's what to do. Take a teaspoon or two of uncooked oat flakes, and chew thoroughly before swallowing. Oatmeal absorbs the stomach acid that can cause the burning pain.

Joan Wilen and Lydia Wilen, health investigators based in New York City, who have spent decades collecting "cures from the cupboard." They are authors of *Bottom Line's Treasury of Home Remedies & Natural Cures* and the free e-letter *Household Magic Daily Tips.*

Vinegar-and-Honey Headache Cure

When you get a headache and the aspirin bottle is empty—or you'd like to try a nondrug approach—here's a quick fix from your kitchen cabinet. Mix two teaspoons of apple cider vinegar and two teaspoons of honey in a glass of room-temperature water (about six ounces). Drink it slowly, and the pain should dissipate within a half-hour.

Joan Wilen and Lydia Wilen, health investigators based in New York City, who have spent decades collecting "cures from the cupboard." They are authors of *Bottom Line's Treasury of Home Remedies & Natural Cures* and the free e-letter *Household Magic Daily Tips.*

Sweet Drink Beats Lingering Cough

In a recent study, a warm honey-coffee drink relieved persistent coughing better than corticosteroids or cough syrups.

To make: Mix one-half teaspoon of instant coffee granules with two-and-a-half teaspoons of honey. Stir into seven ounces of warm water. Drink three servings a day.

Honey is a well-known remedy for cough, and caffeine dilates bronchi and stimulates breathing. If your cough hasn't eased after a few weeks of using this remedy, see your doctor.

Neda Raeessi, MD, researcher, Baqiyatallah University of Medical Sciences, Tehran, Iran.

Headache Gone in 100 Seconds

Joan Wilen and Lydia Wilen, health investigators based in New York City, who have spent decades collecting "cures from the cupboard." They are authors of *Bottom Line's Treasury of Home Remedies & Natural Cures* and the free e-letter *Household Magic Daily Tips*.

Headaches have many causes, but the main one is tension. Daily stresses and pressures can really put the ache in headache. What you need is a form of "relaxed energizing" to make the pain disappear. *Here's what to do…*

Li Shou is Chinese for "hand swinging." Hand swinging redirects blood flow away from your head, relieving the pressure on artery walls that have contracted with tension. The exercise also releases lots of endorphins—the body's own natural morphine—helping to ease pain.

According to psychologist Edward Chang, this is how to perform Li Shou…

• **Sit down and rub your palms together for a few seconds until they feel warm.** Then stroke the front of your face from forehead to chin about 30 times—always in the same direction.

• **Stand up, relax and smile.** Your feet should be shoulder-width apart, toes pointing forward. Your arms should be hanging naturally at your sides. Let your eyes almost close as you mentally focus down toward your toes.

• **Now, extend both arms out in front of you, then relax and let your arms swing naturally back behind you.** Keep swinging your arms back and forth like this in an easy pendulum-like rhythm at least 100 times. (It's called hand swinging because, of course, your hands go along with your arms.)

• **Keep your mind focused on what you're doing.** Breathe naturally, and don't let your attention wander until the exercise is completed.

Bonus: This exercise is a great stress reducer…whether you have a headache or not!

Rx for Pain in the Back… Neck…Shoulders… More—A Simple Exercise Can Do the Trick

Joel Harper, a personal trainer in New York City who designs workouts for Olympic athletes, celebrities, musicians and business executives. He created the workout chapters for the best-selling *YOU* series of books by Michael Roizen, MD, and Mehmet Oz, MD. He is creator of the PBS best-selling DVDs *Firming After 50* and *Slim & Fit*. JoelHarperFitness.com

Before you turn to surgery or drugs for back or neck pain or carpal tunnel syndrome, try a simple exercise instead. Many of the most common injuries and disorders affecting joints, muscles, tendons, ligaments and/or nerves can be prevented, and often relieved, with targeted exercises and stretches. These work as massage for your muscles. (If the exercise or stretch starts to hurt, ease up.)

CARPAL TUNNEL PAIN

Carpal tunnel syndrome is caused by pressure on the median nerve that passes through a narrow "tunnel" in the wrist. Even a small amount of swelling or inflammation in this area can cause numbness, tingling and weakness. People who perform repetitive motions of the hand and wrist—such as assembly-line workers and those who often use computers, BlackBerries and the like—have a high risk of getting it. *Exercises that help…*

• **Wrist twists.** Get down on your hands and knees. Rotate your hands so that your middle fingers on each hand are facing directly toward the same knee, thumbs on the outside. Keep your elbows soft and your head down. Maintain this position for about five deep inhales. It helps to gently relax into the position. Gradually walk your knees away from your fingers to increase your stretch.

• **Wrist circles.** This movement "opens up" the wrist and reduces tightness. With your elbows bent, hold both hands in front of your torso, with the palms facing up. Rotate your hands/wrists in a complete circle five times. Then do five more circles in the opposite direction.

Important: It's normal for one wrist to be tighter than the other. Rotating both wrists simultaneously a few times a day will help keep the muscles balanced.

NECK PAIN

This is another malady of the computer age. People who work on computers often spend hours in the same hunched-over position without taking breaks to stretch.

Fact: Neck pain usually is caused by shoulder tension. Exercises that target the neck aren't the most effective, because they don't address shoulder tightness. *Exercises that help…*

• **Shoulder rolls.** Stand straight, with your arms relaxed at your sides. Roll your shoulders in a backward circle slowly five times. Then roll them forward five times.

• **Chicken wing.** Place the back of your right hand on your right hip, with your palm facing out. Your elbow should jut out like a chicken wing. With your left hand on your right elbow, gently pull the right elbow toward your belly button. Keep your left and right shoulders at the same height. Hold the stretch for five deep inhales with your chest lifted, then repeat on the other side.

LOW BACK PAIN

The back stretches recommended by most trainers temporarily will relieve tightness and pain, but they don't affect muscles in the hips. Tightness in the hips pulls the spine out of alignment, which can cause painful contrac-

tions in muscles in the lower back. *Exercises that help…*

• **Hip rolls.** Stand up straight with your hands on your hips and your feet perfectly together. Make a complete circle with your hips, rotating to the right. Do this five times. Repeat in the other direction.

• **Wall hammock.** Sit on the floor with your back against a wall, your left foot flat on the floor and your left knee bent. Cross your right ankle over your left knee. From this position, slide your tailbone toward the base of the wall to cause a stretch. Hold the position for about 20 seconds, then relax. Switch legs, and do the stretch again.

PLANTAR FASCIITIS

This is a painful inflammation of the plantar fascia, the band of connective tissue that runs from the heel bone along the bottom of the foot toward the toes. *Exercise that helps…*

• **Toe rolls.** Stand up straight with your hands on your waist. Keeping the toes of your right foot on the floor, raise the right heel. Rotate your right knee in a circle, keeping the toes as motionless as possible on the floor. Repeat five times clockwise and five times counterclockwise. Repeat with the other foot.

SHOULDER PAIN

Shoulders often hurt because of inflammation or a small tear in the ligaments that make up the rotator cuff, the four major muscles and tendons in the shoulder.

Start by doing shoulder rolls, described on page nine. *Another exercise that helps…*

• **Shoulder squeezer.** Lie on the floor on your right side, with your knees slightly bent. Prop your right arm up on your tricep, with the back of the upper part of your arm flat on the floor and the fingers of your hand pointing up. Place your left hand on the back of your right wrist, and very gently press until your right palm is going toward the floor. Hold for three deep inhales, relax and then repeat once. Then switch sides.

SHIN SPLINTS

They're common in runners and those who engage in stop-and-start sports, such as tennis, soccer and basketball. Repetitive and excessive force on the muscle on top of the shinbone (the same muscle that lifts the toes) can cause inflammation and/or "micro-tears" in the muscle fibers. *Exercise that helps…*

•**Knee lifts.** This is among the best exercises for reducing tightness in the muscle and, in some cases, helping shin splints heal more quickly. Do this exercise very slowly and only if you don't have knee problems. (If you have knee problems, talk with your doctor or physical therapist.)

Kneel on the floor so that you're sitting on your heels, with your shins flat on the floor. Lean back slightly, and put your palms on the floor next to each heel and your thumbs on the arches of the bottoms of your feet. Using your hands for support, press down with your arms to raise your shins slightly off the floor. At this point, you will be balancing on your hands and toes. Hold the stretch for five to 10 deep inhales, then repeat five times.

Rx: Take a Walk and Call Me in the Morning

Jordan D. Metzl, MD, a sports medicine physician at the Hospital for Special Surgery in New York City. The author of *The Exercise Cure: A Doctor's All-Natural, No-Pill Prescription for Better Health & Longer Life.*

A recent study made international headlines when it found that exercise was just as effective as—or sometimes even outperformed—drugs when treating such conditions as heart disease and stroke.

The details: After examining about 300 medical trials involving more than 330,000 patients, Harvard researchers found that frequent exercise and powerful drugs, such as beta-blockers and blood thinners, provided very similar results. And in the case of stroke recovery, regular workouts were actually more effective than taking anticoagulant medications.

A troubling fact: Only one-third of clinicians "prescribe" exercise, which could not only boost the health of Americans signifi-

cantly but also save the average patient thousands of dollars a year in medical costs.

My recommendations for condition-specific routines that contribute to a healthy, disease-free future…*

HEART ATTACK AND STROKE

Drugs such as beta-blockers help treat heart disease, but side effects can include fatigue, dizziness, upset stomach and cold hands. Meanwhile, a single 40-minute session of aerobic exercise has been shown to lower blood pressure for 24 hours in hypertensive patients, and regular workouts can reduce both systolic (top number) and diastolic (bottom number) blood pressure by five to 10 points. Consistent exercise also can improve cholesterol levels.

Why exercise works: The heart is a muscle, and cardiovascular exercise forces it to pump longer and eventually makes it stronger, preventing the buildup of plaques that can rupture and lead to a heart attack or stroke. Many heart attack and stroke survivors are afraid to exercise, but it's crucial that they move past this fear. Those who exercise require less medication…need fewer major surgeries such as bypasses…and are 25% less likely to die from a second heart attack than their couch potato counterparts.

What to do: Five times a week, do 30 to 40 minutes of cardiovascular exercise at a "Zone 2" level of exertion (see p. 328). You have lots of choices for this exercise. Options include very fast walking, jogging, swimming, using an elliptical machine or recumbent bike, or taking an aerobics class. Pick an activity you enjoy to help you stay committed. After just six weeks, you'll likely have lower blood pressure, and by three months, your cholesterol levels should be improved.

Note: People with heart failure, a condition in which the heart cannot pump enough blood to the rest of the body, should avoid resistance

*Be sure to check with your doctor before starting any fitness program. If your condition is severe, he/she may initially want you to use exercise as an adjunct to medication, not as a replacement. Never stop taking a prescribed drug without talking to your doctor. *Caution*: With any of these workouts, seek immediate medical attention if you experience chest pain, shortness of breath, nausea, blurred vision or significant bone or muscle pain while exercising.

exercises, such as push-ups and heavy weight lifting, that force muscles to work against an immovable or very heavy object. Such activities can put an excessive burden on the heart and cause further injury to it.

DEPRESSION

Exercise really is nature's antidepressant. Several studies have shown that working out is just as effective, if not more so, than medication when it comes to treating mild-to-moderate depression. Exercise also can help reduce the amount of medication needed to treat severe cases of depression...and even prevent depression in some people.

A Norwegian study that tracked about 39,000 people for two years found that those who reported doing moderate-to-high physical activity, including daily brisk walks for more than 30 minutes, scored significantly lower on depression and anxiety tests compared with nonexercisers.

There are many effective antidepressant drugs, but they are frequently accompanied by bothersome side effects, including sexual dysfunction, nausea, fatigue and weight gain. And while most of these drugs can take a month to work, a single exercise session can trigger an immediate lift in mood, and consistent aerobic exercise will make an even more lasting positive impact.

What to do: The key is to boost your heart rate high enough to trigger the release of endorphins, feel-good chemicals that elicit a state of relaxed calm. Spend 30 to 45 minutes at a "Zone 3" level of exertion (see next page), three to five days a week, to benefit.

You also may want to try exercising outdoors. A study published in *Environmental Science & Technology* found that outdoor exercise produces stronger feelings of revitalization, a bigger boost of energy and a greater reduction in depression and anger than exercising indoors.

Strength training also is effective in treating depression—lifting weights releases endorphins and builds a sense of empowerment. For a strength-training program, ask your doctor to recommend a physical therapist or personal trainer.

If it's difficult to motivate yourself to exercise when you're depressed, relying on a personal trainer—or a "workout buddy"—can help.

BACK PAIN

Back pain strikes roughly half of Americans. Pain medications are available, but many are addictive and merely mask the symptoms rather than address the underlying problem. Muscle relaxants cause drowsiness...overuse of non-steroidal anti-inflammatory drugs (NSAIDs), such as *ibuprofen,* can lead to ulcers...and steroid injections, which can be given only a few times per year, can cause infection or nerve damage and long-term side effects such as osteoporosis or high blood pressure.

What to do: There's a very powerful low-tech solution—a foam roller. Widely available at sporting goods stores, these cylindrical rollers have a record of preventing and relieving back pain. With the cylinder on the floor, move various muscles (your hamstrings, quadriceps and lower back) back and forth over the foam roller slowly. Roll each area for one to two minutes. If you hit an especially tender spot, pause and roll slowly or hover in place until you feel a release. The entire routine should take about 10 minutes.

Note: Rolling muscles can feel uncomfortable and even painful at first. But the more painful it is, the more that muscle needs to be rolled. Frequency eases discomfort.

In addition to rolling your muscles, start a back- and core-strengthening program. Avoid using heavy weights, especially within an hour of waking—that's when your muscles are tighter and you're more likely to strain a muscle.

Instead, opt for higher repetitions (three sets of 15) with lighter weights (three to five pounds for women and eight to 10 pounds for men) to build endurance in your back and core, which is more protective than sheer strength.

A good core-strengthening exercise: The plank. In a push-up position, bend your elbows and rest your weight on your forearms (your body should form a straight line from shoulders to ankles). Pull your navel into your spine, and contract your abdominal muscles for 30 seconds, building up to a minute or two at a time. Perform the plank once a day.

THE 3 EXERCISE EXERTION ZONES

There are three main levels of exertion that are based on how easy it is for you to talk...

Zone 1: **Talking is easy while moving.** An example of Zone 1 exertion might be a moderate-paced walk.

Zone 2: **Talking is tough but manageable.** In Zone 2, there should be a little huffing and puffing but no gasping for air.

Zone 3: **Carrying on a conversation is quite difficult** at this level of exertion due to panting.

Surprising Cure for Back Pain

Todd Sinett, DC, chiropractor and founder/owner of Midtown Integrative Health & Wellness in New York City. He has served as a clinical expert for many television programs, including *FoxMD* and *Good Day New York*. He is author of *3 Weeks to a Better Back: Solutions for Healing the Structural, Nutritional and Emotional Causes of Back Pain.*

If you have persistent back pain, most doctors look for structural problems—a herniated disc, for example, or a misaligned spine. These can be real issues, but they point to a solution for only a small percentage of patients.

Surprisingly, back pain can be the result of poor nutrition and poor digestion, which causes chronic inflammation that irritates muscles, ligaments, tendons and/or nerves. A recent study in *Asian Spine Journal* found that nearly one-third of women and one-quarter of men with back pain also had food intolerances or other gastrointestinal complaints.

Dietary changes won't always eliminate back pain (although they might), but they often reduce pain significantly. If you rate your pain as an eight, for example, changing your diet could reduce it to a manageable two or three. *What to do...*

•**Get enough fiber.** If you're often constipated or have infrequent bowel movements, you'll have buildups of toxins that increase inflammation and back pain. A high-fiber diet can fix this and reduce your back pain.

My advice: Look at your stool. It should be more or less smooth (and should pass easily). If it is lumpy and hard, you probably need more fiber. Increase your water, fruit and vegetable intake.

•**Cut back on caffeine.** Caffeine is a stimulant that increases levels of cortisol, a hormone that triggers inflammation. People who drink a lot of coffee or other caffeinated beverages are more likely to have painful muscle cramps and spasms.

My advice: Eliminate caffeine for two to three weeks. If this makes a big improvement, give it up altogether. If it doesn't help, you can go back to it because caffeine isn't the culprit.

•**Stay well hydrated.** Many of my patients don't drink water very often. This is a problem because you need water to improve digestion and reduce inflammation—and because people who don't drink much water often consume less healthful beverages, such as sodas. Water also helps lubricate the spinal discs and can help prevent fissures, cracks in the discs that can allow the soft middle portion to bulge out and press against a nerve.

Everyone with back pain should drink between four and 10 glasses of water a day. The first thing I do every morning is drink a big glass of water. If you're not a fan of plain water, you can spruce it up with a squeeze of lemon or lime or substitute watered-down juice (half juice, half water).

•**Eliminate all added sugar.** The average American consumes about 175 pounds of sugar a year—from soft drinks, desserts and even packaged foods that you wouldn't imagine are loaded with sugar, such as white bread, salad dressing, ketchup and pasta sauce.

The rapid rise in glucose (blood sugar) that occurs when you eat sweetened foods triggers the production of cytokines, proteins secreted by immune cells that increase inflammation. A high-sugar diet also irritates the digestive tract, which can lead to back pain.

My advice: Give up all added sugar for at least three weeks. It takes about two weeks for existing inflammation to "calm." Staying off added sugar for an additional week will help reinforce the change in your usual habits. After that, you can reintroduce a small amount of sugar—by having an occasional dessert, for example, or adding a small amount of sugar to your morning coffee.

If you add back a bit of sugar and your pain doesn't increase, you'll know that you can enjoy some sugar. On the other hand, you might notice that you're having more back pain again, in which case you'll want to cut out sugar.

•**Eat more organic produce.** Most people know that antioxidants in fruits and vegetables—substances such as vitamin C, lycopene and indole-3-carbinol—can reduce levels of cell-damaging molecules (free radicals) that cause inflammation. In my experience, getting more antioxidants isn't as effective for pain as improving digestion (with fiber, cutting back on sugar, etc.), but it can help. I tell patients to buy organic produce because it won't be tainted with pesticides or other inflammatory chemicals. Also, a recent study found that organic corn contained 58% more antioxidants and that organic marionberries (a type of blackberry) had up to 50% more antioxidants than their nonorganic counterparts.

•**Look for sensitivities.** The healthiest diet in the world won't improve back pain if you're eating foods that trigger a reaction in you. Many foods (including foods considered healthy, such as broccoli) can trigger symptoms in some people. In addition to pain, these symptoms could include digestive irritation, sleepiness after a meal, fogginess, achiness and/or congestion.

To find out whether you're sensitive to one or more foods, track what you eat with a journal. When you notice an increase in pain, you can review the journal and find the food(s) that might be responsible. In addition to the foods mentioned in this article, dairy and gluten are common offenders.

My advice: When you identify a likely food suspect—maybe you drank a beer on the day your back got worse—give it up for a few weeks. If your symptoms improve, test your conclusion by having a small amount of that food or beverage. If the pain increases again, you'll know that you have to avoid that food in the future. Or you can go to a gastroenterologist, allergist, nutritionist or integrative medical doctor for food-sensitivity testing.

Best Way to Prevent Back Pain

Do *this simple exercise to strengthen your back:* Stand, sit or lie on your back, and exhale all your breath while pulling your navel in and up toward your head. Hold for 10 seconds, and release. Repeat 12 times.

Todd Sinett, DC, a chiropractor and founder/owner of Midtown Integrative Health & Wellness in New York City. He is author of *3 Weeks to a Better Back.*

Causes of Constipation

A low-fiber diet or medications that slow gastrointestinal movement, including calcium channel blockers, diuretics and Parkinson's drugs, are among possible causes of chronic constipation.

My advice: Schedule daily bathroom times, such as 30 minutes after breakfast or dinner, when gut activity increases and prompts the bowel-movement urge. Consume about 30 g of fiber daily from fiber-rich foods, such as fruits, vegetables and whole grains, including brown rice and wheat germ. To avoid bloating and gas, slowly increase your fiber intake to this level.

If you have trouble getting enough fiber in your diet, try taking one to three tablespoons daily of the natural high-fiber laxative flaxseed, crushed or mixed with juice. Drink eight ounces of water with flaxseed or any fiber supplement to help it add bulk to stool. Lastly, don't ever ignore the urge to have a bowel movement—you could eventually lose this sensation. Rarely, constipation can signal cancer. See a doctor if it's coupled with unin-

329

tentional weight loss and/or blood in the stool and symptoms last longer than three weeks.

Brian Lacy, MD, PhD, director, Gastrointestinal Motility Laboratory, Dartmouth Medical School, Hanover, New Hampshire.

Don't Let Your Bladder Run Your Life!

Holly Lucille, ND, RN, a naturopathic doctor based in West Hollywood, California. She is the author of *Creating and Maintaining Balance: A Woman's Guide to Safe, Natural Hormone Health* and serves on the Institute for Natural Medicine Board of Directors. DrHollyLucille.com

---

Women and men who scout out restrooms wherever they are may think that others don't have to worry so much about their bladders. But that's not true.

Eye-opening statistic: One in every five adults over age 40 has overactive bladder... and after the age of 65, a whopping one in every three adults is affected. If you regularly have a strong and sudden urge to urinate and/or need to hit the john eight or more times a day (or more than once at night), chances are you have the condition, too.

Men with prostate enlargement and post-menopausal women (due to their low estrogen levels) are at increased risk of having overactive bladder. Urinary tract infections, use of certain medications (such as antidepressants and drugs to treat high blood pressure and insomnia) and even constipation also can cause or worsen the condition.

But there is a bright side. Research is now uncovering several surprisingly simple natural approaches that are highly effective for many people with overactive bladder. *Among the best...**

START WITH YOUR DIET

Most people don't connect a bladder problem to their diets. But there is a strong link. *My advice...*

•**Take a hard line with irritants.** Alcohol, caffeine and artificial sweeteners can exacer-

bate the feeling of urgency caused by overactive bladder. Cutting back on these items is a good first step, but they often creep back into one's diet over time.

What helps: Keep it simple—completely avoid alcohol, caffeine (all forms, including coffee, tea and caffeine-containing foods such as chocolate) and artificial sweeteners. Stick to decaffeinated herbal teas and coffee, and use agave and stevia as sweeteners.

Many individuals also are sensitive to certain foods, such as corn, wheat, dairy, eggs and peanuts. They often trigger an immune reaction that contributes to overall inflammation in the body, including in the bladder. If your symptoms of urinary urgency and/or frequency increase after eating one of these (or any other) foods, your body may be having an inflammatory response that is also affecting your bladder. Eliminate these foods from your diet.

•**Keep your gut healthy.** The scientific evidence is still in the early stages, but research now suggests that leaky gut syndrome, in which excess bacterial or fungal growth harms the mucosal membrane in the intestines, is at the root of several health problems, including overactive bladder.

The theory is that an imbalance of microbes, a condition known as dysbiosis, can irritate the walls of the bladder just as it does in the gut.

What helps: Probiotics and oregano oil capsules. Probiotics replenish "good" bacteria, and oregano oil has antibacterial properties that help cleanse "bad" bacteria and fungi from the gut.

•**Drink up!** People with overactive bladder often cut way back on their fluid intake because they already make so many trips to the bathroom. But when you don't drink enough fluids, urine tends to have an irritating effect because it becomes more concentrated. This increases urgency.

What helps: Drink half your body weight in ounces of water or herbal tea daily. Do not

---

*Talk to your doctor before trying any of these herbal remedies, especially if you take medication or have a chronic health condition. You may want to consult a naturopathic doctor. To find one near you, check *naturopathic.org.*

drink any fluids after 5 pm to help prevent bathroom runs during the night.

THE RIGHT SUPPLEMENTS

Cranberry supplements (or unsweetened cranberry juice) can be helpful for bladder infections, but they're usually not the best choice for overactive bladder. *My advice…*

•**Try pumpkin seed extract.** These capsules help tone and strengthen the tissue of your pelvic-floor muscles, which gives you better bladder control.

Typical dosage: 500 mg daily.

•**Consider Angelica archangelica extract.** This herb has gotten positive reviews from researchers who have investigated it as a therapy for overactive bladder.

Recent finding: When 43 men with overactive bladder took 300 mg of the herb daily, they had increased bladder capacity and made fewer trips to the bathroom.

Typical dosage: 100 mg daily.

OTHER WAYS TO KEEP YOUR BLADDER HEALTHY

Kegel exercises, which help strengthen the pelvic-floor muscles, are essential for getting control of overactive bladder symptoms. Unfortunately, most people who try doing Kegels end up doing them the wrong way.

How to do Kegels: Three to five times a day, contract your pelvic-floor muscles (the ones you use to stop and start the flow of urine), hold for a count of 10, then relax completely for a count of 10. Repeat 10 times. If you're a woman and aren't sure if you're contracting the right muscles, there is a possible solution.

New option for women: A medical device called Apex acts as an automatic Kegel exerciser. It is inserted into the vagina and electrically stimulates the correct muscles ($249 at *pour moi.com*—cost may be covered by some insurance plans). Check with your doctor to see if this would be an appropriate aid for you.

Even though there's no handy device to help men do Kegels, the exercises usually reduce urgency when they're performed regularly.

Kegels can easily be part of anyone's daily routine—do them while waiting at a red light, after going to the bathroom or while watching TV.

•**Try acupuncture.** An increasing body of evidence shows that this therapy helps relieve overactive bladder symptoms. For example, in a study of 74 women with the condition, bladder capacity, urgency and frequency of urination significantly improved after four weekly bladder-specific acupuncture sessions.

•**Go for biofeedback.** Small electrodes are used to monitor the muscles involved in bladder control so that an individualized exercise program can be created. Biofeedback is noninvasive and is most effective when used along with other treatments. To find a board-certified provider, consult the Biofeedback Certification International Alliance, *bcia.org*.

Oh, My Aching Foot! Help for Common Causes of Foot and Leg Pain

Johanna S. Youner, DPM, a podiatrist and cosmetic foot surgeon in New York City. She is a spokesperson for the American Podiatric Medical Association and a delegate of the New York State Podiatric Medical Association.

The average person walks the equivalent of four times around the world in his/her lifetime. No wonder foot problems plague more than three-quarters of US adults! The good news is that we can take steps on our own to relieve the pain. *Here are the most common symptoms and problems—and what you can do…*

ACHILLES TENDONITIS

Symptoms: Pain above the heel or in the back of the leg.

Even though the tendon in the back of the heel is the strongest and largest in the body, it's still among the most vulnerable—and when it hurts, it can hurt a lot.

Inflammation of the tendon, known as Achilles tendonitis, usually is due to overuse. The tendon gets weaker and susceptible to injuries with age. If you overwork the tendon—say, by spending a few hours on the dance floor or the basketball court—the fibers can develop small tears and get inflamed. It typically takes at least three months for it to heal completely. In the meantime, don't engage in high-impact exercises such as running, and switch to low-impact activities such as biking or swimming. *Also…*

• **Start with ice.** Ice is one of the best ways to reduce inflammation and help the tendon heal. When you first feel pain at the back of the heel, apply an ice pack for up to 20 minutes. Keep applying ice throughout the day—and keep the heel elevated as much as possible for a few days. You can further reduce inflammation by taking aspirin or ibuprofen.

• **Try heel lifts.** These are thin wedges that slip into your shoes. Raising the heel as little as one-eighth of an inch reduces stress and helps the tendon heal quicker. Use lifts in both shoes so that your body is balanced. I like Spenco Rx Heel Cushions and AliMed Heel Lifts. Both are available online and in pharmacies and some stores.

Important: If you can't stand up on your toes even for a second, there's a good chance that the tendon has ruptured (completely torn). Surgery is the only treatment for a ruptured Achilles tendon.

MORTON'S NEUROMA

Symptoms: Feels as if a pebble is in your shoe…pain in the ball of the foot.

Morton's neuroma is a thickened nerve in the ball of your foot. It typically causes sharp pain or burning that gets worse when you walk. The abnormal growth of nerve tissue is the body's response to irritation—usually from shoes that are too tight or from wearing high heels. Anything that puts repetitive pressure on the toes, including activities such as jogging, can cause Morton's neuroma.

• **Wear wider shoes.** Giving the toes more room to move reduces pressure and causes the neuroma to shrink back to normal, possibly within a month or two.

• **Stretch your toes.** The nerve may be trapped under a ligament in the foot. Stretches will lengthen the ligament and open up

space over the nerve. A few times a day, use your fingers to bend your toes up and down. Stretch them as far as you comfortably can, and repeat the stretches about a dozen times.

PLANTAR FASCIITIS

Symptoms: Stabbing pain in the heel of the foot.

A thick band of tissue (the plantar fascia) runs across the bottom of the foot. It connects the heel bone to the toes and creates the arch. Small tears in the tissue can cause burning/stabbing pain, particularly in the morning.

Important: Get a second opinion if your doctor recommends surgery. About 90% of cases heal with conservative care within a year.

• **Apply ice.** Hold an ice pack over the painful area for 15 or 20 minutes, three or four times a day.

• **Replace your shoe insoles.** The Power-step brand of insoles support and cushion the plantar fascia and help it heal more quickly. You can buy insoles at pharmacies, sporting-goods stores and online for $15 to $60. In many cases, they work as well as prescription products (which can cost $550).

• **Use a tennis ball or rolling pin** to gently roll along the bottom of your foot (while sitting).

• **Take aspirin or ibuprofen** to reduce pain and inflammation.

• **Replace worn-out athletic shoes.** They stop cushioning your feet after about 500 miles of use.

• **See your doctor if the pain isn't gone within three months.** He/she might recommend a steroid injection. Used judiciously, steroid injections can help heal a chronically inflamed area quickly.

SHIN SPLINTS

Symptoms: Pain that runs along the bone on the front of your lower leg.

Shin splints are caused by inflammation that affects muscles and the underlying bone. They usually are caused by activities that involve sudden stops and starts, such as aerobics, jogging, tennis and basketball. They also occur in people who walk a lot in hard-soled shoes.

• **Use ice to reduce inflammation.** It's the most effective treatment for bone and ligament trauma. When you are in pain, ice the area of the leg—10 minutes on and 10 minutes off, as needed.

• **Try arch supports.** They slip into your shoes and support the bottom of the foot. They reduce stress on the lower leg and will help shin splints heal more quickly. I like the brands Powerstep (see above) and Superfeet.

• **Talk to your doctor about bone stimulation.** If the pain of a shin splint lasts more than a few months, you may have a stress fracture at the tibia. Your doctor might recommend a bone stimulator, a prescription device that uses ultrasound or electrical currents to stimulate new bone growth. Bone stimulators are worn daily for a minimum of three hours per day for 90 to 180 days.

BUNIONS

Symptoms: Bump and pain at the base of the big toe.

A bunion is a bony hump that forms on the outside of the foot, where the big toe emerges from the foot. Take it seriously, even if it doesn't hurt. It means that your big toe is pushing in the wrong direction. It can lead to joint damage, as well as a misalignment of the other toes. Some people are born with a tendency to develop bunions. More often, they are caused by narrow, ill-fitting shoes (particularly high heels) that press the toes into odd positions.

• **Wear sensible shoes.** "Sensible" means that the shoes are wide enough to allow your toes to move. Avoid shoes with sharply pointed toes or heels higher than two inches.

• **Do foot exercises to relieve symptoms and increase flexibility.** Point and flex your toes, or massage the bottom of your foot with a golf ball.

• **See a doctor if the bunion is painful or getting larger.** It will get worse unless you take care of it. The treatment might be as simple as a custom-made shoe insert that will reduce pressure on the affected joint. Surgery (bunionectomy) is recommended only if the bunion is persistently painful and doesn't get better with other treatments.

How Do You Get Rid of Toenail Fungus?

Jeffrey T.S. Hsu, MD, adjunct assistant professor in medicine (dermatology), Dartmouth Medical School, Hanover, New Hampshire.

Toenail fungus, also called onychomycosis, is a relatively common condition that disfigures the nail. About 2.5 million Americans see podiatrists annually for treatment of toenail fungus. People who wear tight-fitting shoes or tight hosiery are likely to develop toenail fungus, especially if they also have poor foot hygiene—not washing and thoroughly drying their feet every day...not changing socks daily...and/or not keeping their toenails trimmed. When a toenail is infected, it typically turns yellow or brown and becomes thickened, crumbles and separates from the nail bed. Toenail fungus rarely heals on its own.

What to do: Nail fungus can be difficult to treat, and recurrent infections are common. Over-the-counter antifungal nail creams are available, but they are rarely effective. If the infection is mild, your doctor may prescribe a medicated nail polish, which should be applied twice a week until the nail is cured. If the infection is more severe, your doctor will prescribe an oral antifungal medication, such as *itraconazole* (Sporanox) or *terbinafine* (Lamisil). These medications are typically taken for six to 12 weeks, but you won't see the end result of treatment until the nail grows back completely, usually in three to six months. In rare cases, both drugs may cause side effects, such as skin rashes or liver damage.

14

Brain and Memory Health

An Alzheimer's Prevention Plan Made Simple

If someone told you that there was a pill with no side effects and strong evidence showing that it helps prevent Alzheimer's disease, would you take it? Of course, you would!

The truth is, there's no such "magic bullet," but most adults do have the ability to dramatically decrease their risk for this dreaded disease.

A window of opportunity: According to the latest scientific evidence, slowing or blocking Alzheimer's plaques (buildups of dangerous protein fragments), which are now known to develop years before memory loss and other symptoms are noticeable, could be the key to stopping this disease.

To learn more, we spoke with Dr. Kenneth S. Kosik, a renowned neuroscientist who has researched Alzheimer's for 25 years. He shared with us the habits that he incorporates into his daily routine to help prevent Alzheimer's…

STEP 1. Make exercise exciting. You may know that frequent exercise—particularly aerobic exercise, which promotes blood flow to the brain—is the most effective Alzheimer's prevention strategy. Unfortunately, many people become bored and stop exercising.

Scientific evidence: Because exercise raises levels of brain-derived neurotrophic factor, it promotes the growth of new brain cells and may help prevent shrinkage of the hippocampus (a part of the brain involved in memory).

What I do: Most days, I spend 35 minutes on an elliptical trainer, followed by some weight training (increasing muscle mass helps prevent diabetes—an Alzheimer's risk factor).

Kenneth S. Kosik, MD, the Harriman Professor of Neuroscience Research and codirector of the Neuroscience Research Institute at the University of California, Santa Barbara, where he specializes in the causes and treatments of neurodegeneration, particularly Alzheimer's disease. Dr. Kosik is coauthor of *Outsmarting Alzheimer's.* KennethSKosikMD.com

To break up the monotony, I go mountain biking on sunny days. I advise patients who have trouble sticking to an exercise regimen to try out the new virtual-reality equipment available in many gyms. While riding a stationary bike, for example, you can watch a monitor that puts you in the Tour de France!

Also helpful: To keep your exercise regimen exciting, go dancing. A recent 20-year study found that dancing reduced dementia risk more than any other type of exercise—perhaps because many types of dancing (such as tango, salsa and Zumba) involve learning new steps and aerobic activity. Do the type of dancing that appeals to you most.

STEP 2. Keep your eating plan simple. A nutritious diet is important for Alzheimer's prevention, but many people assume that they'll have to make massive changes, so they get overwhelmed and don't even try. To avoid this trap, keep it simple—all healthful diets have a few common elements, including an emphasis on antioxidant-rich foods (such as fruit and vegetables)…not too much red meat…and a limited amount of processed foods that are high in sugar, fat or additives.

Scientific evidence: Research has shown that people who consume more than four daily servings of vegetables have a 40% lower rate of cognitive decline than those who get less than one daily serving.

What I do: I try to eat more vegetables, particularly broccoli, cauliflower and other crucifers—there's strong evidence of their brain-protective effects.

Helpful: I'm not a veggie lover, so I roast vegetables with olive oil in the oven to make them more appetizing. Whenever possible, I use brain-healthy spices such as rosemary and turmeric.

STEP 3. Guard your sleep. During the day, harmful waste products accumulate in the brain. These wastes, including the amyloid protein that's linked to Alzheimer's, are mainly eliminated at night during deep (stages 3 and 4) sleep.

Scientific evidence: In a long-term Swedish study, men who reported poor sleep were 1.5 times more likely to develop Alzheimer's than those with better sleep.

Regardless of your age, you need a good night's sleep. While ideal sleep times vary depending on the person, sleeping less than six hours or more than nine hours nightly is linked to increased risk for cardiovascular disease—another Alzheimer's risk factor. If you don't feel rested when you wake up, talk to your doctor about your sleep quality.

What I do: I often take a 10-minute nap during the day. Brief naps (especially between 2 pm and 4 pm, which syncs with most people's circadian rhythms) can be restorative.

STEP 4. Don't be a loner. Having regular social interaction is strongly associated with healthy aging.

Scientific evidence: Older adults who frequently spend time with others—for example, sharing meals and volunteering—have about a 70% lower rate of cognitive decline than those who don't socialize much.

What I do: To stay socially active, I regularly Skype, attend conferences and stay in touch with other scientists and postdoc students.

If you're lonely, any form of social interaction is better than none. One study found that people who used computers regularly—to write e-mails, for example—were less lonely than those who didn't. If you can't connect in person, do a video chat or Facebook update at least once a day.

Also helpful: Having a pet. Pets are sometimes better listeners than spouses!

STEP 5. Stay calm. People who are often stressed are more likely to experience brain shrinkage.

Scientific evidence: In a three-year study of people with mild cognitive impairment (a condition that often precedes Alzheimer's), those with severe anxiety had a 135% increased risk for Alzheimer's, compared with those who were calmer.

What I do: I go for long walks.

Other great stress reducers: Having a positive mental attitude, deep breathing, yoga, tai chi, meditation—and even watching funny movies. Practice what works for you.

STEP 6. Push yourself intellectually. So-called "brain workouts" help prevent Alzheimer's—perhaps by increasing cognitive reserve (the stored memories/cognitive skills that you can draw on later in life)...and possibly by accelerating the growth of new brain cells.

Scientific evidence: In an important study, older adults (including those with a genetic risk factor for Alzheimer's) who frequently read, played board games or engaged in other mental activities were able to postpone the development of the disease by almost a decade.

But don't fool yourself—if you're an accomplished pianist, then banging out a tune won't help much even though a nonmusician is likely to benefit from learning to play. Push your mental abilities—do math problems in your head, memorize a poem, become a tutor, etc.

What I do: To challenge myself intellectually, I read novels and practice my foreign language skills—I do research in Latin America, so I work on my Spanish.

5 Surprising Ways to Prevent Alzheimer's—#1: Check Your Tap Water

Marwan Sabbagh, MD, director of Banner Sun Health Research Institute, Sun City, Arizona. He is author of *The Alzheimer's Prevention Cookbook: 100 Recipes to Boost Brain Health.* MarwanSabbaghMD.com

Every 68 seconds, another American develops Alzheimer's disease, the fatal brain disease that steals memory and personality. It's the fifth-leading cause of death among people age 65 and older.

You can lower your likelihood of getting Alzheimer's disease by reducing controllable and well-known risk factors (see next page). *But new scientific research reveals that there are also little-known "secret" risk factors that you can address...*

1. COPPER IN TAP WATER

A scientific paper published in *Journal of Trace Elements in Medicine and Biology*

theorizes that inorganic copper found in nutritional supplements and in drinking water is an important factor in today's Alzheimer's epidemic.

Science has established that amyloid-beta plaques—inflammation-causing cellular debris found in the brains of people with Alzheimer's—contain high levels of copper. Animal research shows that small amounts of inorganic copper in drinking water worsen Alzheimer's. Studies on people have linked the combination of copper and a high-fat diet to memory loss and mental decline. It may be that copper sparks amyloid-beta plaques to generate more oxidation and inflammation, further injuring brain cells.

What to do: There is plenty of copper in our diets—no one needs additional copper from a multivitamin/mineral supplement. Look for a supplement with no copper or a minimal amount (500 micrograms).

I also recommend filtering water. Water-filter pitchers, such as ones by Brita, can reduce the presence of copper. I installed a reverse-osmosis water filter in my home a few years ago when the evidence for the role of copper in Alzheimer's became compelling.

2. VITAMIN D DEFICIENCY

Mounting evidence shows that a low blood level of vitamin D may increase Alzheimer's risk.

A 2013 study in *Journal of Alzheimer's Disease* analyzed 10 studies exploring the link between vitamin D and Alzheimer's. Researchers found that low blood levels of vitamin D were linked to a 40% increased risk for Alzheimer's.

The researchers from UCLA, also writing in *Journal of Alzheimer's Disease*, theorize that vitamin D may protect the brain by reducing amyloid-beta and inflammation.

What to do: The best way to make sure that your blood level of vitamin D is protective is to ask your doctor to test it—and then, if needed, to help you correct your level to greater than 60 nanograms per milliliter (ng/mL). That correction may require 1,000 IU to 2,000 IU of vitamin D daily...or another individualized supplementation strategy.

Important: When your level is tested, make sure that it is the 25-hydroxyvitamin D, or 25(OH)D, test and not the 1.25-dihydroxyvitamin D test. The latter test does not accurately measure blood levels of vitamin D but is sometimes incorrectly ordered. Also, ask for your exact numerical results. Levels above 30 ng/mL are considered "normal," but in my view, the 60 ng/mL level is the minimum that is protective.

3. HORMONE REPLACEMENT THERAPY AFTER MENOPAUSE

Research shows that starting hormone-replacement therapy (HRT) within five years of entering menopause and using hormones for 10 or more years reduces the risk for Alzheimer's by 30%. But a new 11-year study of 1,768 women, published in *Neurology*, shows that those who started a combination of estrogen-progestin therapy five years or more after the onset of menopause had a 93% higher risk for Alzheimer's.

What to do: If you are thinking about initiating hormone replacement therapy five years or more after the onset of menopause, talk to your doctor about the possible benefits and risks.

4. A CONCUSSION

A study published in *Neurology* in 2012 showed that NFL football players had nearly four times higher risk for Alzheimer's than the general population—no doubt from repeated brain injuries incurred while playing football.

What most people don't realize: Your risk of developing Alzheimer's is doubled if you've ever had a serious concussion that resulted in loss of consciousness—this newer evidence shows that it is crucially important to prevent head injuries of any kind throughout your life.

What to do: Fall-proof your home, with commonsense measures such as adequate lighting, eliminating or securing throw rugs and keeping stairways clear. Wear shoes with firm soles and low heels, which also helps prevent falls.

If you've ever had a concussion, it's important to implement the full range of Alzheimer's-prevention strategies in this article.

5. NOT HAVING A PURPOSE IN LIFE

In a seven-year study published in *Archives of General Psychiatry*, researchers at the Rush Alzheimer's Disease Center in Chicago found that people who had a "purpose in life" were 2.4 times less likely to develop Alzheimer's.

What to do: The researchers found that the people who agreed with the following statements were less likely to develop Alzheimer's and mild cognitive impairment— "I feel good when I think of what I have done in the past and what I hope to do in the future" and "I have a sense of direction and purpose in life."

If you cannot genuinely agree with the above statements, there are things you can do to change that—in fact, you even can change the way you feel about your past. It takes a bit of resolve…some action…and perhaps help from a qualified mental health counselor.

One way to start: Think about and make a list of some activities that would make your life more meaningful. Ask yourself, Am I doing these?…and then write down small, realistic goals that will involve you more in those activities, such as volunteering one hour every week at a local hospital or signing up for a class at your community college next semester.

The following steps are crucial in the fight against Alzheimer's disease…

- **Lose weight if you're overweight.**
- **Control high blood pressure.**
- **Exercise regularly.**
- **Engage in activities that challenge your mind.**
- **Eat a diet rich in colorful fruits and vegetables and low in saturated fat, such as the Mediterranean diet.**
- **Take a daily supplement containing 2,000 milligrams of omega-3 fatty acids.**

More Than Half of Alzheimer's Cases Could Be Prevented

Many of the biggest risk factors for Alzheimer's disease are modifiable—lack of physical activity, depression, smoking, midlife hypertension, midlife obesity and diabetes, according to recent findings. Changing or eliminating these risks could potentially prevent 2.9 million Alzheimer's cases in the US.

Deborah Barnes, PhD, MPH, associate professor of psychiatry, University of California, San Francisco, and leader of a comprehensive review published online in *The Lancet Neurology*.

It Might Not Be Alzheimer's

Jacob Teitelbaum, MD, board-certified internist and founder of Practitioners Alliance Network, an organization for health-care providers dedicated to improving communication among all branches of the healing arts. Based in Kona, Hawaii, he is author, with Bill Gottlieb, of *Real Cause, Real Cure*.

If a doctor says that you or a loved one has Alzheimer's disease, take a deep breath and get a second opinion. Studies have shown that between 30% and 50% of people diagnosed with Alzheimer's turn out not to have it.

Bottom line: The symptoms common to Alzheimer's can be caused by other reversible conditions. Problems with memory and other cognitive functions often are linked to what I call MIND—metabolism, infection or inflammation, nutrition or drug side effects—or a combination of these factors. Addressing these can markedly improve cognitive function. Even people who do have Alzheimer's will see improvements.

METABOLISM

Anyone who is experiencing confusion, memory loss or other cognitive problems should have tests that look at the hormones that affect metabolism. *In particular…*

•**Thyroid hormone.** A low level of thyroid hormone often causes confusion and memory loss. It also increases the risk for Alzheimer's disease. In recent studies, thyroid levels on the low side in the normal range are associated with a 240% higher risk for dementia in women. Borderline low thyroid hormone is associated with as much as an 800% higher risk in men.

My advice: For most people with unexplained chronic confusion and memory loss, I recommend a three-month trial of desiccated thyroid (30 mg to 60 mg) to see if it helps. It is a thyroid extract containing the two key thyroid hormones. (The commonly prescribed medication Synthroid has just one of the two.) If you have risk factors for heart disease—such as high LDL cholesterol and high blood pressure—your doctor should start you with a low dose and increase it gradually.

•**Testosterone.** This hormone normally declines by about 1% a year after the age of 30. But in one study, men who went on to develop Alzheimer's disease had about half as much testosterone in their bloodstreams as men who did not.

Every 50% increase in testosterone is associated with a 26% decrease in the risk for Alzheimer's.

My advice: Men should ask their doctors about using a testosterone cream if their testosterone tests low—or even if it's at the lower quarter of the normal range. Limit the dose to 25 mg to 50 mg/day. More than that has been linked to heart attack and stroke.

INFECTIONS & INFLAMMATION

You naturally will get large amounts of protective anti-inflammatory chemical compounds just by eating a healthy diet and using supplements such as fish oil and curcumin (see the next page). For extra protection, take aspirin. In addition to reducing inflammation, it's among the best ways to prevent blood clots and vascular dementia, which is as common as Alzheimer's disease. In addition, infections leave us feeling mentally foggy. Have your doctor look for and treat any bladder and sinus infections.

My advice: Talk to your doctor about taking one enteric-coated low-dose (81-mg) aspirin daily to improve circulation and reduce the risk for ministrokes in the brain. Even people with Alzheimer's may have had a series of ministrokes, adding to their cognitive decline. This is especially important when mental worsening occurs in small distinct steps instead of gradually.

NUTRITION

The typical American diet is just as bad for your brain and memory as it is for your heart. Too much fat, sugar and processed food increase cell-damaging inflammation throughout the body, including in the brain.

In one study, Columbia University researchers studied more than 2,100 people over the age of 65 who consumed healthy foods such as nuts, fruits, fish, chicken and leafy, dark green vegetables and who limited their consumption of meat and dairy. They were 48% less likely to be diagnosed with Alzheimer's over a four-year period.

Especially important…

• **B-12.** Millions of older adults don't get or absorb enough vitamin B-12, a nutrient that is critical for memory and other brain functions. You might be deficient even if you eat a healthful diet due to the age-related decline in stomach acid and intrinsic factor, a protein needed for B-12 absorption.

My advice: Take a multivitamin that contains 500 micrograms (mcg) of B-12 and at least 400 mcg of folic acid and 50 mg of the other B vitamins. If you test low-normal for B-12 (less than 400 ng/ml), also ask your doctor about getting a series of 10 B-12 shots.

Helpful: Have one teaspoon of apple cider vinegar with every meal. Use it in salad dressing, or mix it into eight ounces of vegetable juice or water. It will increase B-12 absorption.

Caution: Vinegar is highly caustic if you drink it straight.

• **Fish oil.** The American Heart Association advises everyone to eat fish at least twice a week. That's enough for the heart, but it won't provide all of the omega-3 fatty acids that you need for optimal brain health. Fish-oil supplements can ensure that you get enough.

My advice: I recommend three to four servings a week of fatty fish, such as salmon, tuna, herring or sardines. Or take 1,000 mg of fish oil daily. You will need more if you're already having memory/cognitive problems. Ask your doctor how much to take.

• **Curcumin.** Alzheimer's is 70% less common in India than in the US, possibly because of the large amounts of turmeric that are used in curries and other Indian dishes.

Curcumin, which gives turmeric its yellow color, reduces inflammation and improves blood flow to the brain. Animal studies show that it dissolves the amyloid plaques that are found in the brains of Alzheimer's patients.

My advice: Unless you live in India, you're not likely to get enough curcumin in your diet to help, because it is poorly absorbed. Use a special highly absorbed form of curcumin (such as BCM-95 found in CuraMed 750 mg), and take one to two capsules twice a day.

Caution: Taking curcumin with blood thinners can increase the risk for bleeding.

TOO MANY DRUGS

Medication side effects are a very common cause of mental decline. This can occur even when you aren't taking drugs with obvious "mind-altering" effects, such as narcotic painkillers. Many drugs—antihistamines, antidepressants, incontinence meds and even simple muscle relaxants—can impair cognitive functions. The risk is higher when you're taking multiple medications and experience drug-drug interactions.

Doctors are far more likely to add medications than to subtract them. Many older adults are taking five or more medications daily.

My advice: Ask your doctor to review all of your medications. Make sure that you're taking only drugs that you absolutely need—not "leftover" medications that might have been prescribed in the past and that you no longer need. Then ask for a three-week trial off each medication that is considered necessary to see if those drugs are contributing to the dementia (substituting other medications or closer monitoring during those three weeks usually can allow this).

Alzheimer's: Is It "Type 3" Diabetes?

Isaac Eliaz, MD, LAc, integrative physician and medical director of the Amitabha Medical Clinic & Healing Center in Santa Rosa, California, an integrative health center specializing in chronic conditions.

For years, scientists from around the world have investigated various causes of Alzheimer's disease. Cardiovascular disease factors, such as hypertension, stroke and heart failure...other neurological diseases, such as Parkinson's disease...accumulated toxins and heavy metals, such as aluminum, lead and mercury...nutrient deficiencies, including vitamins B and E...infections, such as the herpes virus and the stomach bacterium H. pylori...and head injuries each have been considered at one time or another to be a possible contributor to the development of this mind-robbing disease.

However, as researchers continue to piece together the results of literally thousands of studies, one particular theory is now emerging as perhaps the most plausible and convincing of them all in explaining why some people—and not others—develop Alzheimer's disease.

A PATTERN EMERGES

Five million Americans are now living with Alzheimer's, and the number of cases is skyrocketing. Interestingly, so are the rates of obesity, diabetes and metabolic syndrome (a constellation of risk factors including elevated blood sugar, high blood pressure, abnormal cholesterol levels and abdominal fat).

What's the potential link? Doctors have long suspected that diabetes increases risk for Alzheimer's. The exact mechanism is not known, but many experts believe that people with diabetes are more likely to develop Alzheimer's because their bodies don't properly use blood sugar (glucose) and the blood sugar–regulating hormone insulin.

Now research shows increased dementia risk in people with high blood sugar—even if they do not have diabetes. A problem with insulin appears to be the cause. How does insulin dysfunction affect the brain? Neurons are starved of energy, and there's an increase in brain cell death, DNA damage, inflammation and the formation of plaques in the brain—a main characteristic of Alzheimer's disease.

AN ALZHEIMER'S-FIGHTING REGIMEN

Even though experimental treatments with antidiabetes drugs that improve insulin function have been shown to reduce symptoms of early Alzheimer's disease, it is my belief, as an integrative physician, that targeted nondrug therapies are preferable in preventing the brain degeneration that leads to Alzheimer's and fuels its progression. These approaches won't necessarily reverse Alzheimer's, but they may help protect your brain if you are not currently fighting this disease...or help slow the progression of early-stage Alzheimer's.

My advice includes...

•**Follow a low-glycemic (low sugar) diet.** This is essential for maintaining healthy glucose and insulin function as well as supporting brain and overall health. An effective way to maintain a low-sugar diet is to use the glycemic index (GI), a scale that ranks foods according to how quickly they raise blood sugar levels.

Here's what happens: High-GI foods (such as white rice, white potatoes and refined sugars) are rapidly digested and absorbed. As a result, these foods cause dangerous spikes in blood sugar levels.

Low-GI foods (such as green vegetables...fiber-rich foods including whole grains...and plant proteins including legumes, nuts and seeds) are digested slowly, so they gradually raise blood sugar and insulin levels. This is critical for maintaining glucose and insulin function and controlling inflammation.

Helpful: glycemicindex.com gives glucose ratings of common foods and recipes.

•**Consider trying brain-supporting nutrients and herbs.*** These supplements, which help promote insulin function, can be used

*Consult your doctor before trying these supplements, especially if you take any medications or have a chronic health condition, such as liver or kidney disease. If he/she is not well-versed in the use of these therapies, consider seeing an integrative physician. To find one near you, consult The Institute for Functional Medicine, *functionalmedicine.org.*

alone or taken together for better results (dosages may be lower if supplements are combined due to the ingredients' synergistic effects)…

• **Alpha-lipoic acid (ALA)** is an antioxidant shown to support insulin sensitivity and protect neurons from inflammation-related damage.

Typical dosage: 500 mg to 1,000 mg per day.

• **Chromium improves glucose regulation.**

Typical dosage: 350 micrograms (mcg) to 700 mcg per day.

• **Alginates from seaweed help reduce glucose spikes and crashes.**

Typical dosage: 250 mg to 1,000 mg before meals.

• **L-Taurine, an amino acid, helps maintain healthy glucose and lipid (blood fat) levels.**

Typical dosage: 1,000 mg to 2,000 mg per day.

Memory Trouble? A Neurological Exam May Be Necessary

Majid Fotuhi, MD, PhD, director of the Center for Memory and Brain Health at Sinai Hospital and assistant professor of neurology at Johns Hopkins University, both in Baltimore. He is the author of *The Memory Cure.*

If you or members of your family are concerned about your memory, a thorough neurological exam can determine with 90% to 95% accuracy whether you have normal age-related memory loss or some form of dementia.

Good news: People who are alert enough to worry about their memories are less likely to have significant problems. Declines in memory or cognition that are apparent to others—but not to the patient—are usually more serious.

Key parts of a neurological exam…

YOUR MEDICAL HISTORY

Neurologists who specialize in memory loss usually can identify underlying problems from a person's medical history alone.*

Important: A friend or family member should accompany the patient to a neurological exam to help provide information regarding the patient's memory and/or lifestyle.

Questions typically asked…

• **Does the memory loss occur often?** People who repeat themselves frequently or repeatedly ask the same question during conversations are more likely to have a significant memory impairment than those who forget only occasionally.

• **Are there recent triggers?** A patient who recently had surgery might be taking a prescription painkiller or sedative that impairs memory. A head injury—even one that occurred years ago—also can result in memory loss, particularly if the patient also has high blood pressure, diabetes or other health problems. These factors—in combination with an old head injury—can have additive effects on the brain that can result in dementia.

• **Is the patient depressed?** Depression can cause trouble with attention and focus, both of which can lead to memory problems.

• **Is the problem progressing?** Memory loss that keeps getting worse or occurs with confusion—such as getting lost in a familiar area—usually indicates an underlying problem, such as dementia.

MENTAL STATUS EXAM

The Mini-Mental Status Exam (MMSE), which is commonly used to assess memory, evaluates…

• **Recent versus long-term memory.** The doctor may name three common objects, such as an apricot, a flag and a tree, and ask the patient to repeat the objects three minutes later.

What the results may mean: In the early stages of Alzheimer's, a patient might not remember the three objects that were named

---

*Ask your doctor to refer you, if possible, to a neurologist affiliated with an academic medical center. He/she will be more likely to be up-to-date on the latest research.

just minutes earlier, but is probably able to re-call details, such as a favorite childhood song or beloved pet, from the distant past.

• **Orientation.** The patient will be asked to state his/her name, the year, season, day of the week and the date. Such questions test a patient's general awareness.

What the results may mean: Orientation can be impaired by medication side effects or substance abuse as well as different types of dementia, such as Alzheimer's. A patient is more likely to have dementia if he can't re-member major details such as the name of the city where he lives.

• **Attention span.** The patient will be asked to count backward (by sevens) from, say, 100...or to spell a short word, such as "holi-day" or "pitcher," backward.

What the results may mean: These tests measure alertness and mental focus. A poor score indicates that a patient might have de-lirium (a usually temporary decline in mental function due to an acute problem, such as a urinary tract infection) rather than, or in addi-tion to, dementia.

Example: I recently saw in my practice a 102-year-old patient who didn't know where she was. I ordered a urine test, and it turned out that she had a urinary tract infection. I gave her antibiotics, and two days later she was back to normal.

PHYSICAL EXAM

The neurologist also will perform a physical examination that tests, among other things, reflexes and muscle movements to determine whether the patient has had a stroke or has thyroid problems, heart problems, Parkinson's disease or other conditions that can contribute to dementia.

DIAGNOSTIC TESTS

Depending on the results of the medical history and clinical exam, other tests, includ-ing the following, may be performed...

• **Imaging tests.** A magnetic resonance imaging (MRI) scan can show evidence of a stroke, bleeding in the brain, a brain tumor or brain shrinkage.

• **Blood tests.** Low levels of thyroid hor-mone and vitamin B-12 (both are detected by blood tests) may contribute to dementia.

Simple Way to Test Yourself for Dementia

Douglas W. Scharre, MD, associate professor of neurology and director, division of cognitive neurolo-gy, Wexner Medical Center, The Ohio State University, Columbus. His research was published in *Journal of Neuropsychiatry and Clinical Neuroscience.*

Having trouble finding the right words... showing up for visits on the wrong day...getting confused while balanc-ing a checkbook. For people who are get-ting on in years, such experiences can spark worries about whether cognitive skills are starting to slip.

Still, no one likes to think that demen-tia might be on the horizon—which is one reason why cognitive decline often goes un-diagnosed in the early stages. In fact, pa-tients typically don't mention such problems to their doctors until three or four years af-ter symptoms begin. What's more, doctors themselves often fail to pick up on the early, subtle signs of dementia during routine med-ical exams...and many doctors don't do the time-consuming tests necessary to diagnose cognitive impairment until the problem has progressed to later stages. That's too bad—because early intervention may help delay the progression of mild cognitive impair-ment and/or provide the best opportunities for patients and their loved ones to make appropriate plans for the future regarding caregiving, finances, legal matters, etc.

Game changer: Now there's a simple screening test for cognitive impairment or dementia that you or a loved one can take anywhere, using just paper and pencil. It takes only about 10 minutes to complete, and it provides your doctor with the info he/she needs to determine whether more thorough testing is needed.

DIY SCREENING ADVANTAGE

Professionally administered screening tests for mild cognitive impairment do exist, but many take lots of time and attention—which is one reason why more than 40% of people with mild cognitive impairment are not diagnosed by their primary doctors. In addition, some tests place too much emphasis on memory and too little on evaluating other cognitive skills. There also are Web-based tests that people can take on their own, but many people are not comfortable enough with computers to use these...and often such tests have not been validated.

To address these problems, researchers from The Ohio State University developed a screening tool called the Self-Administered Gerocognitive Examination (SAGE). The test was designed to identify mild cognitive impairment (which sometimes progresses to full-blown dementia) as well as dementia. In studies, SAGE has been shown to detect cognitive problems as accurately as other established but more time-consuming screening tools, correctly identifying nearly 80% of people with cognitive impairment and excluding 95% of those without impairment.

SAGE was designed to be a self-administered exam, with simple instructions written in plain language. It is a four-page, 12-question test that looks at abilities in six different areas that can be used as early predictors of mild cognitive impairment—orientation, language, reasoning/computation, spatial ability, problem solving and memory.

Some examples: Test takers are asked to name certain objects...do simple math...draw lines that follow a pattern...remember one easy task...and so forth. The test takes about 10 to 15 minutes to complete (though there is no time limit), and scoring can be done in less than one minute.

The maximum score possible is 22 points. A score of 17 to 22 is classified as normal cognitive ability...a score of 15 or 16 is classified as mild cognitive impairment...a score of 14 or less is classified as possible dementia. To compensate for age and education level, the researchers suggest adding one point to the score when the test taker is over age 80...and adding one point when the person has 12 years or less of education.

Recently the test designers recruited more than 1,000 volunteers over age 50 from venues such as health fairs, senior centers, assisted-living facilities and educational talks, and gave them the SAGE test.

Results: 72% scored in the normal range... 10% scored in the mild cognitive impairment range...and 18% scored in the dementia range. These percentages, the researchers said, are typical for the population that was tested.

HOW TO TEST YOURSELF

SAGE can be taken in the privacy of your own home or at your physician's office, without supervision or special instruction. Simply download the test from *sagetest.osu.edu* and print it out. No calendars or clocks should be available during test-taking, but you can spend however much time you need completing it.

Of course, there's nothing to stop you from scoring your own test or from asking a loved one to score it for you. But in actuality, the test is intended to be scored and interpreted by your physician—so take your test paper with you the next time you see your doctor (scoring instructions can be downloaded from the same website). If you've done fine, ask your doctor to save the test in your file for future comparison. If your score suggests that some impairment has already occurred, talk with your doctor about getting a complete cognitive evaluation.

How Not to Worry About Your Memory

Aaron P. Nelson, PhD, chief of neuropsychology in the division of cognitive and behavioral neurology at Brigham and Women's Hospital. He is coauthor, with Susan Gilbert, of *The Harvard Medical School Guide to Achieving Optimal Memory*.

With all the media coverage of Alzheimer's disease and other forms of dementia, it's easy to imagine the worst every time you can't summon the name of a good friend or struggle to remember the details of a novel that you put down just a few days ago.

Reassuring: The minor memory hiccups that bedevil adults in middle age and beyond usually are due to normal changes in the brain and nervous system that affect concentration or the processing and storing of information. In fact, common memory "problems" typically are nothing more than memory errors. Forgetting is just one kind of error.

Important: Memory problems that are frequent or severe (such as forgetting how to drive home from work or how to operate a simple appliance in your home) could be a sign of Alzheimer's disease or some other form of dementia. Such memory lapses also can be due to treatable, but potentially serious, conditions, including depression, a nutritional deficiency or even sleep apnea. See your doctor if you have memory problems that interfere with daily life—or the frequency and/or severity seems to be increasing. *Five types of harmless memory errors that tend to get more common with age...*

MEMORY ERROR #1: Absentmindedness. How many times have you had to search for the car keys because you put them in an entirely unexpected place? Or gone to the grocery store to buy three items but come home with only two? This type of forgetfulness describes what happens when a new piece of information (where you put the keys or what to buy at the store) never even enters your memory because you weren't paying attention.

My advice: Since distraction is the main cause of absentmindedness, try to do just one thing at a time.

Otherwise, here's what can happen: You start to do something, and then something else grabs your attention—and you completely forget about the first thing.

We live in a world in which information routinely comes at us from all directions, so you'll want to develop your own systems for getting things done. There's no good reason to use brain space for superfluous or transitory information. Use lists, sticky notes, e-mail reminders, etc., for tasks, names of books you want to read, grocery lists, etc. There's truth to the Chinese proverb that says, "The palest ink is better than the best memory."

Helpful: Don't write a to-do list and put it aside. While just the act of writing down tasks can help you remember them, you should consult your list several times a day for it to be effective.

MEMORY ERROR #2: Blocking. When a word or the answer to a question is "on the tip of your tongue," you're blocking the information that you need. A similar situation happens when you accidentally call one of your children by the name of another. Some patients are convinced that temporarily "forgetting" an acquaintance's name means that they're developing Alzheimer's disease, but that's usually not true.

Blocking occurs when the information that you need is properly stored in memory, but another piece of information is getting in the way. Often, this second piece of information has similar qualities (names of children, closely related words, etc.) to the first. The similarity may cause the wrong brain area to activate and make it harder to access the information that you want.

My advice: Don't get frustrated when a word or name is on the tip of your tongue. Relax and think about something else. In about 50% of cases, the right answer will come to you within one minute.

MEMORY ERROR #3: Misattribution. This is what happens when you make a mistake in the source of a memory.

More than a few writers have been embarrassed when they wrote something that they thought was original but later learned that it was identical to something they had heard or read. You might tell a story to friends that you know is true because you read about it in the newspaper—except that you may have only heard people talking about it and misattributed the source.

Misattribution happens more frequently with age because older people have older memories. These memories are more likely to contain mistakes because they happened long ago and don't get recalled often.

My advice: Concentrate on details when you want to remember the source of information.

Focus on the five Ws: Who told you...what the content was...when it happened...where you were when you learned it...and why it's important. Asking these questions will help to strengthen the context of the information.

MEMORY ERROR #4: **Suggestibility.** Most individuals think of memory as a mental videotape—a recording of what took place. But what feels like memories to you could be things that never really happened. Memories can be affected or even created by the power of suggestion.

In a landmark study, researchers privately asked the relatives of participants to describe three childhood events that actually happened. They were also asked to provide plausible details about a fourth scenario (getting lost in a shopping mall) that could have happened, but didn't.

A few weeks later, the participants were given a written description of the four stories and asked to recall them in as much detail as possible. They weren't told that one of the stories was fictional.

What happened: About 20% of the participants believed that they really had been lost in a shopping mall. They "remembered" the event and provided details about what happened. This and other studies show that memories can be influenced—and even created—from thin air.

My advice: Keep an open mind if your memory of an event isn't the same as some-

one else's. It's unlikely that either of you will have perfect recall. Memories get modified over time by new information as well as by individual perspectives, personality traits, etc.

MEMORY ERROR #5: **Transience.** You watched a great movie but can't remember the lead actor two hours later. You earned an advanced degree in engineering, but now you can hardly remember the basic equations.

These are all examples of transience, the tendency of memories to fade over time. Short-term memory is highly susceptible to transience because information that you've just acquired hasn't been embedded in long-term storage, where memories can be more stable and enduring.

This is why you're more likely to forget the name of someone you just met than the details of a meaningful book that you read in college—although even long-term memories will fade if you do not recall them now and then.

My advice: You need to rehearse and revisit information in order to retain it. Repeating a name several times after you've met someone is a form of rehearsal. So is talking about a movie you just watched or jotting notes about an event in a diary.

Revisiting information simply means recalling and using it. Suppose that you wrote down your thoughts about an important conversation in your journal. You can review the notes a few weeks later to strengthen the memory and anchor it in your mind. The same technique will help you remember names, telephone numbers, etc.

Cholesterol Affects Future Dementia Risk

Compared to people with normal cholesterol levels, those who had borderline-high cholesterol (200 mg/dL to 239 mg/dL) at age 40 to 45 were 52% more likely to develop dementia within 40 years. For those who had high cholesterol (240 mg/dL or above) at midlife, dementia risk was elevated 66%.

Lesson: What's good for the heart is good for the brain—so no matter what your age, if you have high cholesterol, talk to your doctor about cholesterol-reducing strategies, such as dietary changes, exercise and, if necessary, medication (but see below concerning statins warning).

Rachel Whitmer, PhD, a research scientist and epidemiologist in the division of research at Kaiser Permanente in Oakland, California, and senior author of a study of 9,844 people.

Statins Can Cause Memory Problems

The FDA has reported that long-term use of cholesterol-lowering statin medications can lead to cognitive issues in some people.

Self-defense: Patients and families should stay alert for any cognitive changes that seem to go beyond age-related declines.

Examples: Difficulty balancing a checkbook, trouble recognizing people, problems remembering what was just said.

Beatrice A. Golomb, MD, PhD, associate professor of medicine, University of California, San Diego, School of Medicine, La Jolla. She has collected and studied more than 3,000 reports of side effects of statin use.

Memory Robbers That Are Often Overlooked

Cynthia R. Green, PhD, assistant clinical professor of psychiatry at Mount Sinai School of Medicine in New York City and president of Total Brain Health TotalBrainHealth.com. She is the author of *Total Memory Workout*.

Alzheimer's disease is such a dreaded diagnosis that you may be filled with panic if you experience occasional memory loss. But these worries may be unnecessary.

As people age, the brain undergoes changes that may lead to some decline in short-term memory. This is normal.

Of course memory loss that truly concerns you is another matter. *Ask your primary care physician to refer you to a neurologist or geriatrician for an evaluation if…*

• **You have noticed a significant change in your everyday memory over the past six months.**

• **Friends or family members have expressed concern about your memory.**

• **You have begun forgetting recent conversations.**

In the meantime, consider whether your occasional forgetfulness may be due to one of the following causes, all of which can be easily corrected…

NOT ENOUGH SLEEP

Poor sleep is probably the most common cause of occasional memory lapses. The ability to concentrate suffers with insufficient rest. Sleep also appears to be essential for consolidating memory—whatever information you learn during the day, whether it's the name of a colleague or the street where a new restaurant opened, you need sleep to make it stick in your mind.

Self-defense: If you're not sleeping seven to eight hours nightly, make it a priority to get more sleep. If you are unable to improve your sleep on your own, talk to your doctor.

WIDELY USED DRUGS

Impaired memory is a potential side effect of many medications. Obvious suspects include prescription sleeping pills…opiate painkillers, such as *meperidine* (Demerol)…and anti-anxiety drugs, such as *diazepam* (Valium) and *alprazolam* (Xanax).

Certain blood pressure–lowering medications, such as beta-blockers, and antidepressants also cause memory problems in some people. Even over-the-counter antihistamines, such as *diphenhydramine* (Benadryl), can have this effect.

If you're taking multiple medications, more than one may cause impaired memory, making it even more difficult to identify the culprit.

Timing is often a tip-off: When impaired memory is an adverse drug effect, it's most likely to appear when you start taking a new medication or increase the dose. But not always.

As we grow older, our bodies become less efficient at clearing medications from the body, so the same dose you've been taking safely for years may cause problems you never had before.

Self-defense: If you think medication might be affecting your memory, do not stop taking the drug or reduce the dosage on your own. Talk to your doctor or pharmacist for advice.

EMOTIONAL UPSET

When you're anxious, stressed or depressed, your ability to concentrate suffers. Whatever it is that worries or preoccupies you keeps your mind from focusing on facts, names, faces and places, so they aren't absorbed into memory.

Self-defense: To keep everyday tensions from undercutting your memory, practice some form of relaxation or stress reduction. Yoga, meditation, deep breathing—or something as simple as allowing yourself a soothing time-out to walk or chat with a friend—can relieve accumulated stress and bolster your recall.

True depression is something else: Even mild-to-moderate depression can sap your energy, take pleasure out of life and affect your memory. If you suspect that you may be depressed, be alert for other symptoms—such as difficulty sleeping, sadness, apathy and a negative outlook—and see your doctor or a mental-health professional.

TOO MUCH ALCOHOL

Moderate red wine consumption has been shown to promote the health of your heart and arteries. Because of this cardiovascular health benefit, red wine also may reduce risk for dementia.

Excessive drinking, on the other hand, is harmful to the brain. Among its devastating toxic effects is a severe and often irreversible form of memory loss called Korsakoff's syndrome, a condition that occurs in alcoholics.

Alcohol's effect on memory can be subtle. Some people find that even a glass or two of wine daily is enough to interfere with learning facts and recalling information. Pay attention to how mentally sharp you feel after having a drink. If you think your alcohol intake may be causing forgetfulness, cut back. Remember, tolerance for alcohol generally declines with age, giving the same drink more impact.

Self-defense: There is more scientific evidence supporting red wine's brain-protective effect than for any other form of alcohol. If you are a man, do not exceed two glasses of red wine daily, and if you are a woman, limit yourself to one glass daily.

ILLNESS

A simple cold or headache is enough to interfere with your concentration and recall.

Illnesses that commonly go undiagnosed also may play a role. For example, when the thyroid gland (which regulates metabolism) is underactive, the mind slows down along with the body. (Other signs of an underactive thyroid include weight gain, constipation, thin or brittle hair and depression.) An overactive thyroid can affect your memory by making you anxious, "wired" and easily distracted.

Memory impairment also may be a symptom of other disorders, such as Parkinson's disease, multiple sclerosis or Lyme disease.

NUTRITIONAL DEFICIENCY

An easily overlooked memory robber is a vitamin B-12 deficiency, often marked by general fatigue and slowed thinking. Older people are especially at risk—as we age, our ability to absorb vitamin B-12 from foods diminishes.

Self-defense: If you have occasional memory lapses, ask your doctor for a blood test to check your vitamin B-12 level.

SAFEGUARDING YOUR MEMORY: CONTROL CHRONIC HEALTH ISSUES

Studies have shown repeatedly that people with high blood pressure, atherosclerosis (fatty buildup in the arteries), obesity and/or diabetes are at dramatically increased risk of developing dementia in their later years.

The effect of these chronic medical conditions on day-to-day memory is less clear. Research shows that memory declines when blood sugar rises in people with diabetes and improves when they take dietary steps to stabilize it.

Self-defense: If you have a chronic health problem, work with your doctor to keep your symptoms under control.

Watch for Anemia to Avoid Dementia

Study titled "Anemia and Risk of Dementia in Older Adults: Findings from the Health ABC Study," published in *Neurology*.

Anemia—a shortage of oxygen-carrying red blood cells—is fairly common in older adults, affecting up to 24% of people age 65 and older. Meanwhile, Alzheimer's disease, the most common form of dementia, affects 15% of people age 65 to 74 and 44% of people age 75 to 84. And now studies have shown a link between the two disorders, and that's good news. Looking out for and addressing one (anemia) may have a strong impact on avoiding the other (dementia).

In one small study, the risk of dementia doubled within three years of an anemia diagnosis and, in another, anemia was associated with a 60% increased risk of Alzheimer's disease within 3.3 years.

WHAT TO DO

How anemia is linked to dementia is not completely understood. Possible factors include simply being in poor health, not getting enough oxygen to the brain (those red blood cells!) or having an iron or vitamin B-12 deficiency. Whatever the connection, in case it is anemia that is actually causing dementia, you'll want to do whatever you can to recognize and treat the symptoms of anemia—and, of course, prevent anemia from ever happening in the first place.

Signs of anemia can be subtle at first and include fatigue, weakness, pale skin, fast or irregular heartbeat, trouble breathing, chest pain, trouble with memory and concentration, cold hands and feet and headache. So if you've been feeling fatigued and don't know why or have other symptoms just mentioned, make an appointment with your doctor, who will order a blood test to check for anemia.

If anemia is found, additional tests will be done to find the exact cause, and the results will determine treatment.

Although rare or hereditary forms of anemia require blood transfusions, others are corrected by treating the underlying cause, whether it be loss of blood from a bleeding ulcer or complications from an infection or a medication side effect. Fortunately, the most common form of anemia—that caused by an iron or B-12 deficiency—is managed with good nutrition and vitamin and mineral supplements. It might be a simple correction that lets you avoid a horrific outcome.

PREVENTING ANEMIA

Since prevention is best, keep your diet rich in iron, folate, vitamin B-12, and vitamin C (which is essential for iron absorption). Foods that will give you the iron you need include red meat, beans, dried fruit, and green leafy vegetables, such as spinach. Besides vitamin C, citrus fruits provide folate. Other good sources of folate include green leafy veggies, beans and bananas. As for vitamin B-12, rely on salmon, shellfish, beef and dairy. And if you are vegan or vegetarian (or have a large B-12 deficiency), you likely already know that you need to get B-12 from supplementation.

Common Medications Increase Dementia Risk

Shannon Risacher, PhD, assistant professor of radiology and imaging sciences at Indiana Alzheimer Disease Center, Indiana University School of Medicine, Indianapolis, and leader of a study of 451 older adults, average age 73, published in *JAMA Neurology*.

Some frequently used medications increase dementia risk in older people. These drugs, which are used to treat common disorders such as asthma, depression and incontinence, have anticholinergic (AC) activity —that is, they block an important neurotransmitter called acetylcholine. They include *brompheniramine* (Dimetapp), *chlorpheniramine* (Chlor-Trimeton), *diphenhydramine* (Benadryl), *doxylamine* (Unisom), *oxybutynin* (Ditropan) and *paroxetine* (Paxil).

Recent finding: Older people who regularly took an AC drug had brain cavities up to 32% larger than other seniors. Increased cavity size reflects brain atrophy. AC-medication users also did worse on tests of brain function including short-term memory, verbal reasoning, planning and problem solving.

Self-defense: Older people who use an AC drug for a chronic condition should ask their physicians whether non-AC alternatives are available. A list of medications that have possible or definitive AC properties can be found by putting "Anticholinergic Burden (ACB) Scale" into any search engine. Drugs with an ACB score of 3 (found in the rightmost column) are the most problematic.

Say No to Sedatives to Cut Dementia Risk

Malaz Boustani, MD, MPH, chief innovation and implementation officer at Indiana University Health and Richard M. Fairbanks Professor of Aging Research at Indiana University School of Medicine, both in Indianapolis.

S edatives increase Alzheimer's risk. Older adults who used benzodiazepine sedatives, such as *lorazepam* (Ativan), *diazepam* (Valium) and *alprazolam* (Xanax), for more than three months within a five-year period had a 51% increased risk for Alzheimer's. These drugs often are prescribed for insomnia or anxiety, but they should not be used long term.

Better approach: The underlying cause of the anxiety or insomnia should be identified and treated without using medicines—for example, with talk therapy.

Living Alone Raises Dementia Risk

I n a study of 1,449 men and women, researchers found that those who were single or divorced during middle age had twice the risk for dementia later in life as those who were married or living with partners. The risk was seven times higher for those who were widowed during middle age and still lived without a partner 21 years later.

Theory: Social engagement promotes healthy brain function.

If you live alone: Aim to stay engaged by participating in social, cultural and recreational activities.

Krister Hakansson, research fellow, Aging Research Center, Karolinska Institute, Stockholm, Sweden.

How to Have an "Einstein Brain"—Here Are His Tricks —You Can Use Them, Too!

Rudolph E. Tanzi, PhD, Joseph P. and Rose F. Kennedy Professor of Neurology at Harvard Medical School and director of the Genetics and Aging Research Unit at Massachusetts General Hospital, both in Boston. He is coauthor, with Deepak Chopra, MD, of *Super Brain*.

A lbert Einstein was a genius, but sheer intelligence was not all that he had. The man who cracked secrets of the universe also knew the secret of using his own brain for maximum effect. But unlike Einstein, most people fail to actively use the brain in order to heighten its powers.

The first step to changing this is to recognize the various parts of the brain and how each functions…

• **Brain stem.** Sometimes referred to as the "reptilian brain," the brain stem generates instinctive drives for survival and reproduction. The fight-or-flight response to threat comes from the reptilian brain, as does stress and lust.

• **Limbic system.** Situated on top of the brain stem, the limbic system filters the instinctive drives of the reptilian brain through a network of past experiences, producing emotions such as fear, desire and jealousy.

• **Frontal cortex.** Located behind the forehead, the frontal cortex is known as the "thinking brain." It allows us to plan, create and find meaning and purpose in life.

A 10-SECOND EXERCISE

Much of the time, one part of the brain dominates. Uncontrolled rage, ravenous hunger or the health-eroding grind of stress takes over when the reptilian brain is in charge. If the limbic system is leading the way, we're filled with confidence or self-doubt, longing or delight. When the frontal cortex dominates, we plan and judge, seek knowledge and weigh costs against benefits.

The brain actually is at its best when all three parts work together.

Examples: You're falling into the grip of reptilian drives when you become furious after receiving unfair criticism from your spouse. Or perhaps you've had two slices of pizza but a powerful craving for a third is about to take over. *To restore balance to your brain functions, think of the acronym STOP...*

• **Stop what you're doing.**

• **Take three deep breaths,** then force yourself to "feel" a smile all through your body.

• **Observe yourself.** How do you feel now? Paying attention to your whole body takes you out of purely reptilian mode, bringing the limbic circuit and frontal cortex into the game. Think about what you're doing—and the consequences for your health and well-being.

• **Proceed with full awareness of yourself and those around you.** This simple 10-second process allows you to take charge of your brain.

WATCH OUT FOR THE "LOOPS"

Whatever has happened in your life has left its traces in your memory, regardless of whether you have conscious access to these thoughts.

The patterns, or "feedback loops," created by intricate connections within the brain are what shape the attitudes, beliefs, fears and desires we bring to new experiences. The limbic system takes over, and that's why if you were criticized regularly by parents for coming home with poor grades, a situation where you will be judged today is likely to activate old feelings of inadequacy and arouse fear and anxiety.

Surprisingly, even positive feedback loops have a downside. When something feels good, you want to do it again and again. Unchecked, the limbic reward circuit can cause overindulgence that leads to health problems or even addiction.

What to do: Become aware of feedback loops—both positive and negative. Ask yourself where the feeling is coming from and how past associations are shaping present feelings.

Simply observing and recognizing the source of these unproductive feelings will give your brain the new input it needs to begin changing the self-defeating circuits and start "rewiring" it with healthier connections and associations.

LET YOUR THOUGHTS RUN WILD

Einstein opened up his mind to all possibilities, which allowed his brain to form new neural connections that dramatically boosted his mental capacities.

You can do the same thing. When faced with a task or situation in which previous solutions have been unsatisfactory, the logical frontal cortex is likely to take over in an attempt to "figure out" an answer.

What to do: Instead of approaching such situations with logic alone, let your brain activity run wild—allow associations that might seem far-fetched, nonsensical or even outlandish to pop up. Step back and observe what emerges without judgment or fear of being foolish.

Then put your thinking brain to work in sifting through the creative work that the other part of your brain has done. You may very well discover interesting ideas, solutions to vexing problems and refreshing approaches.

Best Workouts to Keep Your Brain "Buff"

Cynthia R. Green, PhD, a practicing clinical psychologist and the founder and president of Total Brain Health, a brain-health and memory fitness consulting service in Montclair, New Jersey. TotalBrainHealth. com

W e all want to keep our brains in top shape. But are crossword puzzles, online classes and the other such activities that we've been hearing about for years the best ways to do that? Not really.

Now: To improve memory and preserve overall cognitive function, the latest research reveals that it takes more than quiet puzzle-solving and streaming lectures.

Even more intriguing: Some activities that we once thought were time wasters may actually help build intellectual capacity and other cognitive functions.

To learn more about the most effective ways to keep your brain "buff," we talked to Dr. Cynthia R. Green, a psychologist and a leading brain trainer.

A HEALTHY BRAIN

The most important steps to keep your brain performing at optimal levels are lifestyle choices…

•**Getting aerobic exercise** (at least 150 minutes per week).

•**Maintaining a healthy body weight.**

•**Not smoking.**

•**Eating a diet that emphasizes fruits and vegetables** and is low in refined sugar and white flour—two of the biggest dietary threats to brain health that have recently been identified by researchers.

Additional benefits are possible with regular brain workouts. In the past, experts thought that nearly any game or activity that challenges you to think would improve your general brain functioning.

What research now tells us: An increasing body of evidence shows that improved memory requires something more—you need to work against a clock. Games with a time limit force you to think quickly and with agility. These are the factors that lead to improved memory and mental focus. *Among Dr. Green's favorite brain workouts—aim for at least 30 minutes daily of any combination of the activities below…*

BRAINY COMPUTER GAMES

Specialized brain-training computer programs (such as Lumosity, Fit Brains and CogniFit) are no longer the darlings of the health community. Formerly marketed as a fun way to reduce one's risk for dementia, recent evidence has not supported that claim.

These programs do provide, however, a variety of activities that may help improve intellectual performance, attention, memory and mental flexibility. Lumosity and other programs are a good option for people who enjoy a regimented brain workout, including such activities as remembering sequences and ignoring distractions. Monthly prices range from $4.99 to $19.95.

Other options to consider trying…

•**Action video games.** These games were once considered "brain-numbing" activities that kept players from developing intellectual and social skills. Recent research, however, shows that action video games can promote mental focus, flexible thinking, and decision-making and problem-solving skills. Because these games are timed, they also require quick responses from the players.

Good choices: World of Warcraft, The Elder Scrolls and *Guild Wars*, all of which involve role-playing by assuming the identity of various characters to battle foes and complete quests, often with other virtual players. These games are available in DVD format for Mac or PC and with an online subscription for virtual play.

Caveat: An hour or two can be a brain booster, but don't overdo it. Too much role-playing takes you away from real-life interactions.

•**Free brain-boosting computer game for a cause.** At *freerice.com*, you can answer fun and challenging questions in such subjects as English vocabulary, foreign languages, math and humanities. With each correct answer, the

United Nations World Food Programme donates 10 grains of rice to a Third World country. To date, players have "earned" a total of nearly 100 billion grains of rice—enough to create more than 10 million meals.

To increase the challenge: Set a timer so that you must work against the clock.

APPS FOR YOUR BRAIN

If you'd prefer to use an "app"—a software application that you can use on a smartphone or similar electronic device—there are several good options. *Among the best fun/challenging apps (free on Android and Apple)…*

• **Words with Friends.** This ever-popular game allows you to play a Scrabble-like game against your friends who have also downloaded the app on an electronic device. The game provides even more benefits if it's used with the time-clock feature.

• **Word Streak with Friends** (formerly Scramble with Friends) is a timed find-a-word game. You can play on your own or with friends.

• **Elevate** was named Apple's Best App of 2014. It provides a structured game environment that feels more like a test, focusing on reading, writing and math skills, than a game. Still, this timed app will give Apple users a good brain challenge.

TECH-FREE OPTIONS

If you'd rather not stare at the screen of a computer or some other electronic device for your brain workout, here are some good options…

• **Tech-free games.** SET is a fast-paced card game that tests your visual perception skills. Players race to find a set of three matching cards (based on color, shape, number or shading) from an array of cards placed on a table.

Bonus: This game can be played by one player or as many people as can fit around the table. The winner of dozens of "Best Game" awards, including the high-IQ group Mensa's Select award, SET is fun for kids and adults alike.

Another good choice: Boggle, which challenges you to create words from a given set of letter cubes within a three-minute period. It can be played by two or more people.

• **Drumming.** Playing any musical instrument requires attention and a keen sense of timing. Basic drumming is a great activity for beginner musicians (especially if you don't have the finger dexterity for piano or guitar).

Even better: Join a drumming circle, which provides the extra challenge of matching your timing and rhythm to the rest of the drummers, along with opportunities for socialization.

Bonus: Research has demonstrated that some forms, such as African djembe drumming, count as a low- to moderate-intensity activity that may reduce blood pressure, which helps protect the brain from blood vessel damage.

• **Meditation.** This practice improves cognitive function and sensory processing and promotes mental focus. Meditating for about 30 minutes daily has also been linked to greater blood flow to the brain and increased gray matter (associated with positive emotions, memory and decision-making). The benefits have even been seen among some people with early-stage neurodegenerative diseases, such as Alzheimer's disease.

A good way to get started: Begin with a simple "mindful eating" exercise—spend the first five minutes of each meal really focusing on what you're eating. Don't talk, read the paper or watch TV…just savor the food. Eventually, you'll want to expand this level of attention to other parts of your day. Such mindfulness habits are a good complement to a regular meditation practice.

• **Coloring.** If you have kids or grandkids, don't just send them off with their crayons. Color with them.

Even better: Get one of the new breed of coloring books with complex designs for adults. While there hasn't been specific research addressing the brain benefits of coloring, this form of play has been shown to reduce stress in children, and it is thought to boost creativity and have a meditative quality. You can find coloring books made for adults at bookstores and art-supply stores.

Get These Minerals Out of Your Brain: Here's What You Really Need...

Neal D. Barnard, MD, president of the nonprofit Physicians Committee for Responsible Medicine, a Washington, DC–based group that promotes preventive medicine. He is author of *Power Foods for the Brain: An Effective 3-Step Plan to Protect Your Mind and Strengthen Your Memory.* PCRM.org

Chances are you're doing everything that you can to eat plenty of "superfoods"—blueberries, walnuts and other nutritious and antioxidant-rich wonders—that many scientists believe help reduce risk for a variety of chronic health problems, including Alzheimer's disease.

The missing part of the story: What you may not know is that most people get too much of certain nutrients—even those found in some superfoods—that have long been considered an important part of a nutritious diet.

Iron, copper and zinc, which are widely recognized as key nutrients, actually are metallic minerals. They are common in many of the foods you may be eating, the water you drink—and even in some of the supplements you may be taking to improve your health.

What researchers are now discovering: Excessive amounts of iron, copper and zinc can produce free radicals that impair memory.

In fact, scientists have discovered that these metals are more prevalent in the brains of Alzheimer's patients than in people without the disease. Even in healthy adults, high levels appear to interfere with normal brain functions.

3 NEWLY DISCOVERED DANGERS

Your body does need iron, copper and zinc, but only in miniscule amounts. If you exceed these levels, your brain is at risk. *What to watch out for...*

•**Iron.** Unless you have been diagnosed with a condition that requires supplemental iron, such as anemia, you probably don't need more than you're already getting from your diet—and even that might be too much.

Compelling evidence: In a study of 793 adults, those who had the most iron in their blood did worse on cognitive tests than those with normal levels.

In a study of 881 adults, those with high hemoglobin levels (a measure of iron in the blood) were three times more likely to develop Alzheimer's disease than those with normal levels. Hemoglobin levels above 13.7 g/dL were associated with increased Alzheimer's risk. Those whose iron levels are too low are also at risk for Alzheimer's.

My advice: Emphasize plant-based foods in your diet. These foods contain as much or more iron than what's found in meat—but our bodies are better able to regulate our intake of the type of iron found in plant-based foods, such as spinach, dried apricots, lima beans and wheat germ. Your body absorbs more of this nonheme iron when you need it and absorbs less when you don't.

In contrast, the heme iron in meats, poultry, fish and shellfish (particularly oysters) is absorbed whether you need it or not. Because of this, a high-meat diet is a main cause of iron overload, which potentially damages not only your brain but also your heart.

Other smart steps...

•**Don't use iron cookware.** A significant amount of iron leaches from uncoated cast-iron pots, pans and skillets into foods—particularly acidic foods, such as tomatoes.

•**Choose an iron-free product if you take a daily multisupplement.**

•**Read cereal labels.** Many breakfast cereals are fortified with iron. You don't need it.

Amount of iron you need in your diet: 8 mg per day for men age 19 and older and women age 51 and older. Women age 19 to 50 need 18 mg per day. (In general, women should get the lower amount of iron when they stop menstruating.)

•**Copper.** At proper levels, copper is essential for enzyme function and helps promote heart health and bone strength. At excess levels, copper—like iron—triggers the production of free radicals that can damage brain cells.

Important finding: A study of 1,451 people in southern California found that those who had the least copper in their blood were mentally sharper and had fewer problems with long- and short-term memory than those whose levels were high.

How copper may promote almost 20 years of aging: When high copper levels are combined with excess saturated fat in the diet—another risk factor for brain problems—the effect is particularly detrimental. Data from the Chicago Health and Aging Project found that high copper/saturated fat caused a loss of mental function that was the equivalent of 19 years of aging.

My advice: Don't take any supplement that contains copper. If you have copper plumbing, it's fine to use tap water for doing dishes and washing but not for cooking or drinking. It is better to use bottled water or water filtered with an activated carbon filter (such as those found in Brita pitchers).

You are unlikely to get too much copper from plant foods that are rich in the mineral such as whole grains, nuts and beans because they also contain natural compounds called phytates that limit copper absorption.

Amount of copper you need: 0.9 mg daily.

• **Zinc.** Our bodies need adequate zinc levels for key functions such as immunity, skin health and sexual function. Excessive amounts, however, are thought to promote the clumping of beta-amyloid proteins in the brain—the hallmark of Alzheimer's disease.

Much of the excess zinc in the American diet comes from supplements. If you take a multivitamin-mineral supplement and also eat fortified cereals or other foods that include zinc, such as oysters, pumpkin seeds or cocoa, you could be getting too much.

Amount of zinc you need: 11 mg daily for men and 8 mg for women.

TAKEAWAY ON MINERALS

Testing is not needed to check levels of iron, copper and zinc in your blood. It is wise to simply avoid the mineral sources in this article. If you are getting too much of these minerals, your levels will gradually decline when you avoid excessive intakes.

Important: Avoid multivitamin-mineral supplements.

Better choices: "Vitamin only" supplements such as No Minerals Multi-Vitamin by Nature's Blend or Vitamins Only by Solgar.

More from Dr. Barnard...

What About Aluminum?

This ubiquitous metal has never been considered a nutrient—it plays no role in the body. While questions have persisted for several years about whether aluminum interferes with brain health, recent studies suggest that the risk is real.

In the UK, researchers found that Alzheimer's cases occurred 50% more often in counties with high aluminum levels in the water. Other studies have had similar results.

My advice: While researchers search for definitive findings on aluminum, err on the side of caution...

• **Don't buy foods that contain aluminum.** Check food labels. Cheese products (such as the cheese on frozen pizza) often contain aluminum. So do baking powders and the baked goods that include them. You can buy an aluminum-free baking powder, such as the Rumford brand.

• **Don't take aluminum antacids.** Use an aluminum-free product, such as Tums. Other drugs, such as buffered aspirin, may also contain aluminum. Check the label.

• **Cook with steel-clad or porcelain-coated pots**...use wax paper instead of aluminum foil...and don't consume foods or beverages that come in aluminum cans.

• **Check your tap water.** If it's high in aluminum or other metals, use bottled water or a reverse osmosis filter. You can use the EPA website, *cfpub.EPA.gov/safewater/ccr*, to get information about the water sources in your area.

• **Avoid antiperspirants with aluminum.** Labels may say aluminum or alum to indicate an aluminum-containing ingredient.

Don't Let Your Brain Shrink

Exercise prevents brain shrinkage. People who have the APOE epsilon4 allele (e4 gene) are at increased risk for Alzheimer's disease.

Recent finding: After 18 months, the brain scans of people with the e4 gene who exercised moderately a few times a week showed dramatically less shrinkage in the hippocampus—which is associated with Alzheimer's—compared with people with the gene who were not physically active.

Stephen Rao, PhD, a professor and director of Schey Center for Cognitive Neuroimaging, Cleveland Clinic, and leader of a study of 97 people, published in *Frontiers in Aging Neuroscience*.

Brain-Boosting Smoothie

Green tea offers a nice taste contrast to pomegranate juice. Matcha (finely milled green tea available at health-food stores) has a high concentration of antioxidants, and yogurt adds texture as well as protein—an important breakfast nutrient.

Combine in a blender until smooth…

1 cup plain Greek yogurt (it has less sodium and more protein than regular yogurt)

1 ripe banana, peeled and chopped

¼ cup honey

¼ cup pomegranate juice

2 teaspoons matcha

1 cup ice cubes

Marwan Sabbagh, MD, neurologist and director of Banner Sun Health Research Institute in Sun City, Arizona. He is the author, with professional chef Beau MacMillan, of *The Alzheimer's Prevention Cookbook*.

The Diet That Cuts Your Alzheimer's Risk in Half

Martha Clare Morris, ScD, professor and director of the Section of Nutrition and Nutritional Epidemiology at Rush University, Chicago, where she is assistant provost for community research. She specializes in dietary and other preventable risk factors in the development of Alzheimer's disease and other chronic diseases in older adults.

The MIND diet blends components from DASH (a blood pressure–lowering diet) and the popular Mediterranean diet, with an extra emphasis on berries, leafy greens and a few other brain-healthy foods.

How good is it? People who carefully followed the diet were about 53% less likely to develop Alzheimer's disease in subsequent years. Those who approached it more casually didn't do quite as well but still reduced their risk considerably, by about 35%.

BLENDED BENEFITS

The MIND diet was developed by researchers at Rush University who examined years of studies to identify specific foods and nutrients that seemed to be particularly good—or bad—for long-term brain health. The MIND (it stands for Mediterranean-DASH Intervention for Neurodegenerative Delay) diet is a hybrid plan that incorporates the "best of the best."

In a study in the journal *Alzheimer's & Dementia*, the researchers followed more than 900 participants. None had dementia when the study started. The participants filled out food questionnaires and had repeated neurological tests over a period averaging more than four years.

Some participants followed the MIND diet. Others followed the older DASH diet or the Mediterranean diet. All three diets reduced the risk for Alzheimer's disease. But only the MIND diet did so even when the participants followed the plan only "moderately well."

The MIND diet specifies "brain-healthy" food groups and five groups that need to be limited, either eaten in moderation or preferably not at all.

WHAT TO EAT

• **More leafy greens.** Kale really is a superfood for the brain. So are spinach, chard, beet greens and other dark, leafy greens. The Mediterranean and DASH diets advise people to eat more vegetables, but they don't specify which ones.

The MIND diet specifically recommends one serving of greens a day, in addition to one other vegetable. Previous research has shown that a vegetable-rich diet can help prevent cognitive decline, but two of the larger studies found that leafy greens were singularly protective.

• **Lots of nuts.** The diet calls for eating nuts five times a week. Nuts are high in vitamin E and monounsaturated and polyunsaturated fats—all good for brain health.

The study didn't look at which nuts were more likely to be beneficial. Eating a variety is probably a good idea because you'll get a varied mix of protective nutrients and antioxidants. Raw or roasted nuts are fine (as long as they're not roasted in fat and highly salted). If you are allergic to nuts, seeds such as sunflower and pumpkin seeds are good sources of these nutrients as well.

• **Berries.** These are the only fruits that are specifically included in the MIND diet. Other fruits are undoubtedly good for you, but none has been shown in studies to promote cognitive health. Berries, on the other hand, have been shown to slow age-related cognitive decline. In laboratory studies, a berry-rich diet improves memory and protects against abnormal changes in the brain. Blueberries seem to be particularly potent. Eat berries at least twice a week.

• **Beans and whole grains.** These fiber-rich and folate-rich foods provide high levels of protein with much less saturated fat than you would get from an equivalent helping of meat. The MIND diet calls for three daily servings of whole grains and three weekly servings of beans.

• **Include fish and poultry**—but you don't need to go overboard. Seafood is a key component of the Mediterranean diet, and some proponents recommend eating it four times a week or more. The MIND diet calls for only one weekly serving, although more is OK. A once-a-week fish meal is enough for brain health.

There is no data to specify the number of poultry servings needed for brain health, but we recommend two servings a week.

• **A glass of wine.** People who drink no wine—or those who drink too much—are more likely to suffer cognitive declines than those who drink just a little.

Recommended: One glass a day. Red wine, in particular, is high in flavonoids and polyphenols that may be protective for the brain.

FOODS TO LIMIT

• **Limit red meat, cheese, butter and margarine—along with fast food, fried food and pastries and other sweets.** The usual suspects, in other words.

All of these food groups increase the risk for Alzheimer's disease, probably because of their high levels of saturated fat (or, in the case of some margarines, trans fats). Saturated fat has been linked to higher cholesterol, more systemic inflammation and possibly a disruption of the blood-brain barrier that may allow harmful substances into the brain.

However, most nutritionists acknowlege the importance of letting people enjoy some treats and not being so restrictive that they give up eating healthfully altogether.

Try to follow these recommendations…

Red meat: No more than three servings a week.

Butter and margarine: Less than one tablespoon daily. Cook with olive oil instead.

Cheese: Less than one serving a week.

Pastries and sweets: Yes, you can enjoy some treats, but limit yourself to five servings or fewer a week.

Fried or fast food: Less than one serving a week.

Eat This Spice for Your Brain

Turmeric. The bright yellow color indicates high levels of antioxidants. People who use this spice several times a week have significant reductions in C-reactive protein, a substance that indicates inflammation in the brain and/or other tissues.

A study that looked at more than 1,000 elderly people found that those who ate curry—which includes generous amounts of turmeric—regularly did better on mental-status evaluations than those who rarely or never ate it. All spices with bright, deep colors are high in neuroprotective antioxidants.

Examples: Both ginger and cinnamon appear to have brain-protective properties similar to those of turmeric. And sage improves memory.

Recommended: Add one-quarter teaspoon to one-half teaspoon of any of these spices to your food every day.

Daniel G. Amen, MD, and Tana Amen, BSN. Dr. Amen is medical director of Amen Clinics, Inc. He is a clinical neuroscientist, psychiatrist, brain-imaging specialist and author of *Use Your Brain to Change Your Age.* His wife, Tana Amen, is a nutritional expert and neurological intensive care nurse. AmenClinics.com

A Cup of Decaf May Prevent Memory Loss

Giulio M. Pasinetti, MD, PhD, professor of neurology and psychiatry, Mount Sinai School of Medicine, New York City, and lead researcher of a study reported in *Nutritional Neuroscience.*

When you need a boost, chances are you reach for a cup of caffeinated coffee.

And if you find that it's helping you to remember things more vividly and think more clearly while you're working on an important task, you probably chalk that up to the caffeine.

Well, the caffeine might help in the short term. But recent research conducted at Mount Sinai School of Medicine in New York City shows that coffee itself also may provide a long-term memory benefit—even when it's decaf!

In fact, the study showed that drinking a certain amount of decaf over the long term might reduce the odds of developing the neurological impairment that's associated with the early stages of Alzheimer's disease.

This is certainly promising news for those who are overly sensitive to caffeine but love the taste of coffee. And it's even more promising for people with type 2 diabetes, because they're often told by doctors to avoid caffeine to keep their blood cholesterol and blood pressure in control, and they're also at higher risk for Alzheimer's disease.

COFFEE'S SECRET WEAPON

Our team of researchers became interested in how chlorogenic acids—types of antioxidants found in coffee, as well as in grapes, cocoa and other foods—affect the brain. We were interested in seeing whether the positive health effects of chlorogenic acids could come from coffee without caffeine. And we wanted to analyze how decaf could affect people with type 2 diabetes, since, as mentioned earlier, people with that condition are usually advised by doctors to avoid caffeine.

Mice were used in the study because we could completely control what they ate. Mice were given a high-fat diet that triggered the onset of type 2 diabetes. At the same time, half of the mice were fed a daily extract of decaffeinated coffee made from unroasted coffee beans.

WHAT THE DECAF DID

Results? The decaf-drinking mice's brains used 25% more oxygen—meaning that these mice were less likely to experience neurological impairment. Researchers suspect that the chlorogenic acids in decaf are the reason for this result.

WILL IT TRANSLATE TO HUMANS?

Of course, just because decaf helps mouse brains doesn't necessarily mean that it helps human brains, but we're hopeful because a great deal of previous medical research using mice has, in fact, been followed by similar results in humans. (That's a big reason mice are so often used in research.)

How much might humans consume to get a similar benefit? Ask your doctor about taking a daily supplement that contains 400-mg extract of decaf green (a.k.a. "unroasted") coffee. (An extract called Svetol was used in the study.) Or drink the equivalent (two cups of decaf per day), but note that roasting coffee beans sucks out some of the beneficial chlorogenic acids, so the benefit would not be as much as from the extract.

Another question is whether the results would be the same with regular (caffeinated) coffee. Since we suspect that the benefits come from the chlorogenic acids in the coffee itself—and not the caffeine—caffeinated coffee is likely to prevent neurological impairment, too. Other foods rich in chlorogenic acids, such as grapes and cocoa, are also likely to have similar benefits, but more research needs to examine that.

Why a Daily Drink May Help Your Memory

Light-to-moderate drinking in later life may keep memory strong, according to a recent study. Consuming up to one drink a day was associated with better episodic memory—the ability to remember specific events. Episodic memory is the type that usually diminishes in dementia.

Theory: Alcohol may help preserve the hippocampus, a brain area that shrinks in people with dementia.

Faika Zanjani, PhD, associate professor, department of behavioral and community health, University of Maryland School of Public Health, College Park, and leader of a study of 664 people, average age 75 at the end of the study, published in *American Journal of Alzheimer's Disease & Other Dementias*.

A Good Reason to Drink Juice!

Fruit juice may lower the risk for Alzheimer's disease.

Recent finding: People who report drinking at least three servings of juice a week are 76% less likely to develop Alzheimer's than those who drink juice less than once a week. The research is preliminary and not conclusive—juice drinkers may lead a more healthful life in general.

Qi Dai, MD, PhD, assistant professor of medicine, division of general internal medicine and public health, Vanderbilt School of Medicine, Nashville, and leader of a study of 1,836 people of Japanese descent, published in *The American Journal of Medicine*.

Dietary Choline and Sharper Memory

Rhoda Au, PhD, associate professor of neurology, Boston University School of Medicine.

In a recent study, researchers examined dietary and memory-test data on nearly 1,400 adults (average age 61) over a three- to 10-year period.

Result: People whose diets contained the highest levels of the nutrient choline performed better on memory tests than those who consumed the least amount.

Theory: Choline is a precursor to a brain chemical called acetylcholine, which plays a key role in cognition.

How much choline do you need each day? The recommendation from the Institute of Medicine for men is a daily intake of 550 mg and for women, 425 mg. *The richest food sources are…*

- **3.5 ounces of beef liver**—430 mg
- **One large egg**—126 mg
- **3.5 ounces of salmon**—91 mg

•**3.5 ounces (just under one-half cup) of broccoli, Brussels sprouts, cauliflower or navy beans**—approximately 40 mg.

Other sources of choline include cod, almonds, tofu, milk and peanut butter.

Stop Memory Loss

Pamela Wartian Smith, MD, MPH, codirector of the master's program in medical sciences with a concentration in metabolic and nutritional medicine at Morsani College of Medicine at University of South Florida. She is author of *What You Must Know About Memory Loss & How You Can Stop It: A Guide to Proven Techniques and Supplements to Maintain, Strengthen, or Regain Memory.* CenterforPersonalizedMedicine.com

---

Mild forgetfulness, known as age-related memory impairment, is a natural part of getting older. By age 75, a person's memory has declined, on average, by about 43%. After age 75, the hippocampus, the part of the brain most closely associated with memory, will eventually atrophy at the rate of 1% to 2% each year.

But you can improve memory with over-the-counter supplements—if you choose the right ones. Here are the supplements I find most effective with my patients. You can take several of these if you choose. You could start with phosphatidylserine and add others depending on your personal needs. For example, if you're taking a medication that depletes CoQ10, you might want to take that supplement. Or if you're under stress, add ashwagandha root. Of course, always check with your doctor before starting any new supplement. To find a practitioner trained in this field, go to *metabolic-anti-agingspecialist.com*

•**Phosphatidylserine (PS).** Most people haven't heard of it, but PS is one of my first choices for mild memory loss. It's a naturally occurring phospholipid (a molecule that contains two fatty acids) that increases the body's production of acetylcholine and other neurotransmitters. It improves cell-to-cell communication and "nourishes" the brain by improving glucose metabolism.

Studies have shown that healthy people who take PS are more likely to maintain their ability to remember things. For those who have already experienced age-related memory loss, PS can improve memory. It's also thought to improve symptoms caused by some forms of dementia.

Typical dose: 300 mg daily. You're unlikely to notice any side effects.

•**Co-enzyme Q10 (CoQ10).** This is another naturally occurring substance found in many foods (such as fatty fish, meats, nuts, fruits and vegetables) and in nearly all of your body's tissues. CoQ10 increases the production of adenosine triphosphate, a molecule that enhances energy production within cells. It's also a potent antioxidant that reduces cell-damaging inflammation in the brain and other parts of the body.

People with degenerative brain disorders, such as Alzheimer's, tend to have lower levels of CoQ10. Studies suggest that supplemental CoQ10 improves memory by protecting brain cells from oxidative damage.

Important: If you're taking a medication that depletes CoQ10—examples include statins (for lowering cholesterol)...metformin (for diabetes)...and beta-blockers (for heart disease and other conditions)—you'll definitely want to take a supplement. I often recommend it for people age 50 and older because the body's production of CoQ10 declines with age. Hard exercise also depletes it.

Typical dose: Between 30 mg and 360 mg daily. Ask your health-care professional how much you need—it will depend on medication use and other factors. Side effects are rare but may include insomnia, agitation and digestive problems such as diarrhea and heartburn.

•**Acetyl-L-carnitine.** A study that looked at people with mild cognitive impairment (an intermediate stage between age-related memory impairment and dementia) found that acetyl-L-carnitine improved memory, attention and even verbal fluency.

Acetyl-L-carnitine (it is derived from an amino acid) is a versatile molecule. It's used by the body to produce acetyl-choline, the main neurotransmitter involved in memory. It slows the rate of neurotransmitter decay, increases oxygen availability and helps convert body fat into energy.

Typical dose: 1,000 mg to 2,000 mg daily. Check with your health-care professional before starting acetyl-L-carnitine to see what dose is best for you. If your kidneys are not functioning perfectly, you may need a lower dose. Some people may notice a slight fishy body odor. In my experience, you can prevent this by taking 50 mg to 100 mg of vitamin B-2 at the same time you take acetyl-L-carnitine.

• **Ashwagandha root.** This is an herb that improves the repair and regeneration of brain cells (neurons) and inhibits the body's production of acetylcholinesterase, an enzyme that degrades acetylcholine. It also improves the ability to deal with both physical and emotional stress—both of which have been linked to impaired memory and cognitive decline.

Typical dose: 500 mg to 2,000 mg daily. Start with the lower dose. If after a month you don't notice that your memory and focus have improved, take a little more. GI disturbances are possible but not common.

Warning: Don't take this supplement if you're also taking a prescription medication that has cholinesterase-inhibiting effects, such as *donepezil* (Aricept) or *galantamine* (Razadyne). Ask your health-care professional whether any of your medications have this effect.

• **Ginkgo biloba.** Among the most studied herbal supplements, ginkgo is an antioxidant that protects the hippocampus from age-related atrophy. It's a vasodilator that helps prevent blood clots, improves brain circulation and reduces the risk for vascular dementia, a type of dementia associated with impaired blood flow to the brain. It also increases the effects of serotonin, a neurotransmitter that's involved in mood and learning.

Bonus: In animal studies, ginkgo appears to block the formation of amyloid, the protein that has been linked to Alzheimer's disease. There's strong evidence that ginkgo can stabilize and possibly improve memory.

Typical dose: 60 mg to 120 mg daily. Most people won't have side effects, but ginkgo is a blood thinner that can react with other anticoagulants. If you're taking warfarin or another blood thinner (including aspirin and fish oil), be sure to check with your health-care professional before taking ginkgo.

• **Fish oil.** Much of the brain consists of DHA (docosahexaenoic acid), one of the main omega-3 fatty acids. It is essential for brain health. People who take fish-oil supplements have improved brain circulation and a faster transmission of nerve signals.

Studies have found that people who eat a lot of fatty fish have a lower risk for mild cognitive impairment than people who tend to eat little or no fatty fish. One study found that people with age-related memory impairment achieved better scores on memory tests when they took daily DHA supplements.

Typical dose: 2,000 mg daily if you're age 50 or older. Look for a combination supplement that includes equal amounts of DHA and EPA (another omega-3). Fish-oil supplements can increase the effects of blood-thinning medications such as aspirin and warfarin if the dose is above 3,000 mg a day.

• **Huperzine A.** Extracted from a Chinese moss, this is a cholinesterase inhibitor that increases brain levels of acetylcholine. It also protects brain cells from too-high levels of glutamate, another neurotransmitter.

Huperzine A may improve memory and could even help delay symptoms of Alzheimer's disease. A study conducted by the National Institute of Aging found that patients with mild-to-moderate Alzheimer's who took huperzine A had improvements in cognitive functions.

Recommended dose: 400 mcg daily. Don't take it if you're already taking a prescription cholinesterase inhibitor (as discussed in the "Ashwagandha root" section).

Can Aspirin Stop Alzheimer's Disease?

A study of nearly 13,500 people, published in the journal *Neurology*, found that people who regularly used aspirin or some other NSAID were 23% less likely to be diagnosed with Alzheimer's than those who didn't take one of these drugs. It's possible that the drugs reduce the accumulation of plaques in the brain, which have been linked to Alzheimer's.

My advice: Don't take aspirin as an Alzheimer's preventive. The research isn't quite strong enough yet to make it worth risking aspirin's side effects. However, if you regularly take aspirin or another NSAID for some other condition, such as arthritis, you may also be reducing your Alzheimer's risk.

Stefan Gluck, MD, PhD, Sylvester Professor, department of medicine, University of Miami Miller School of Medicine in Miami, Florida.

BP Meds That Reduce Alzheimer's Risk 50%!

P atients who took medication for high blood pressure—specifically, diuretics, angiotensin receptor blockers (ARBs) or angiotensin-converting-enzyme (ACE) inhibitors—had 50% lower risk for Alzheimer's in a recent study. Patients who took other blood pressure medications did not show this benefit. Hypertension is a known risk factor for Alzheimer's, so talk to your doctor about the right medication for you.

Sevil Yasar, MD, PhD, assistant professor of medicine at The Johns Hopkins University School of Medicine, Baltimore, and leader of a study of 2,200 people, published in *Neurology*.

Hormone Replacement Therapy (HRT) May Reduce Alzheimer's Risk

I n a recent finding, women who take hormones within five years of menopause have a 30% lower risk for Alzheimer's, compared with women who never take them. The issue of HRT remains complex and controversial—discuss your personal situation with your doctor.

Study of 1,768 women by researchers at Johns Hopkins Bloomberg School of Public Health, Baltimore, published in *Neurology*.

Four Easy Tricks to Remember Names Better

Scott Hagwood, author of *Memory Power* and four-time National Memory Champion. He is based in Fayetteville, North Carolina.

H ere are my four favorite mental exercises that will train your brain to remember names more easily—and, better yet, they're all so simple!

WHEN YOU MEET SOMEONE NEW

Try at least one of the following tricks every time you meet a new person.

•**Alliterate to learn.** It's amazing how much memory power you can get by using alliteration, the stringing together of words that start with the same sound. To do this, when you first learn someone's name, think of a characteristic that describes this person and that starts with the first letter of the person's first name. For example, you might think to yourself, Hannah wears high heels…Tom is tall…or Donna loves drama.

•**Rhyme to remember.** Rhyming is also a powerful memory booster. So in your mind, rhyme a new person's first name with an associative characteristic. For instance, Anna eats a banana…Max plays the sax…Jim likes

361

to swim. (This won't work for every person, of course, but it's worth trying whenever possible.)

•**Link new acquaintances with old ones.** Say you were just introduced to someone named George who seems to be a bit of a joker. Can you think of someone else you know well who is also named George and who has a similarly playful personality? If so, make a point of linking these two people in your mind ("the two jokers") so that the next time you see this new person, an image of the old George will pop into your mind—along with the name George. (Or maybe your old George has no sense of humor at all, so you can remember this "new George" as his complete opposite.)

•**Repeat the new name.** To firmly imprint a new name on your mind, repeat it both out loud and to yourself several times. Make a point of saying something such as "Great to meet you, Jason" at the beginning of the conversation and "Hope to see you again soon, Jason" at the end of the conversation.

WHEN YOU MEET SOMEONE AGAIN

When someone you've already met reappears and his name slips your mind…what do you do? First, think of the above tricks that you used to remember this person's name in the first place. Does he have some characteristic that you notice that starts with the first letter of his name? Does he enjoy doing something that rhymes with his first name? Is he exactly like—or the complete opposite of—someone who you know who shares the same name?

If none of those methods works, don't panic. When you're in a group, be attentive, because someone else might say the name. Or just keep talking to the person without guessing at his name, because sometimes your subconscious works while you're talking, and after a few minutes, the name might come to you. If all else fails, accept defeat and politely say, "I remember talking to you before, but I've met so many people. Can you please give me your name again?" It won't be held against you!

Leave Your Memory at the Door

Gabriel Radvansky, PhD, professor, department of psychology, University of Notre Dame, Notre Dame, Indiana. He has been researching how memory works for most of his career.

How many times has something like this happened to you? While brushing your teeth, you remember an important phone call that you need to make as soon as you're done. But by the time you have finished brushing, you walk out of the bathroom, grab your coat and car keys and head out the door…totally forgetting all about that call that you really needed to make.

We all do this—quite often, in fact—and it's not because we're getting old and addle-brained. It's actually something that our brains are hard-wired to do! Research from the University of Notre Dame in Indiana, published in *Quarterly Journal of Experimental Psychology*, demonstrates the connection between forgetfulness and walking through doorways.

DOORWAYS DRAIN MEMORY

This study confirms in a "real world" environment what previous research identified in a virtual environment—a phenomenon dubbed the "location-updating effect," showing that the simple act of passing through a doorway as you move from one room to another raises the likelihood that you'll forget what you were just thinking about.

The experiment: A set of volunteers (28 women and 32 men) were split into groups. Group A walked through a series of three rooms. In the first room, they were asked to place six objects (each a different shape and color) into a box and then cover it up and bring it to the next room. In the second room, after they had gone through a doorway, they were given a computer quiz, asking which objects they had put into the box just a few minutes earlier. Group B did the same thing, except they didn't walk through a series of rooms, they walked to different spots within the same room—in other words, they didn't encounter any doorways. The results? Group

A—the one that walked through doorways—made 5% more errors on the memory test than Group B.

BOOST YOUR MEMORY

Now, what does this act of walking through doorways mean to our brains? It is an "event boundary" that signals to your brain that your situation has changed. To understand this, think of your mind as being like a filing cabinet. When something changes—whether in time or setting—your brain acknowledges the shift by creating an "event file" as a way of keeping track of your life (without which it would be a mess!). Walking through a doorway is a signal to your brain to put what you were just thinking about into its own file... which makes information from before the location change not quite as readily available to you as it was earlier. Unfortunately, another experiment that was part of the same study showed that walking back into the original room that you were in doesn't trigger recall.

We should think of this location-updating effect as being beneficial. By creating event boundaries when entering a new space, our minds are getting refreshed, so we're able to focus on the new environment. That's helpful, when your doctor walks through the door to see you, know that she is no longer thinking about the patient that she just saw!

How can we use this information to improve our memory? One idea is to plan around it by leaving sticky notepads in every room—that way, if an idea comes to you, you can write it down immediately so you don't forget it. Another idea is to always have your smartphone handy so that you can leave yourself a voicemail or send yourself an e-mail or text. And the next time you walk purposefully into a room and instantly forget what brought you there, don't fret. It's probably nothing more than your brain's overly efficient reset button trying to get you ready for what's coming next.

15

Heart Health and Stroke

4 Must-Have Heart Tests

Heart disease is tricky. Like other "silent" conditions, such as high blood pressure and kidney disease, you may not know that you have it until you're doubled over from a heart attack.

That's because traditional methods of assessing patients for heart disease, such as cholesterol tests and blood pressure measurements, along with questions about smoking and other lifestyle factors, don't always tell a patient's whole story.

Shocking finding: In a recent study, doctors followed nearly 6,000 men and women (ages 55 to 88) who had been deemed healthy by standard heart tests for three years and then gave them basic imaging tests (see next page).

Result: 60% were found to have atherosclerosis. These study participants were eight times more likely to suffer a heart attack or stroke, compared with subjects without this fatty buildup (plaque) in the arteries.

THE MUST-HAVE TESTS

Below are four simple tests that can catch arterial damage at the earliest possible stage—when it can still be reversed and before it has a chance to cause a heart attack or stroke.

My advice: Even though doctors don't routinely order these tests, everyone over age 50 should have them at least once—and sometimes more often, depending on the findings. Smokers and people with diabetes, very high cholesterol levels (more than 300 mg/dL) and/or a family history of heart disease should have these tests before age 50. *Having these tests can literally save your life…*

• **Coronary calcium computed tomography (CT) scan.** This imaging test checks for calcium deposits in the arteries—a telltale sign of atherosclerosis. People who have little or no calcium in the arteries (a score of zero)

Joel K. Kahn, MD, a clinical professor of medicine at Wayne State University School of Medicine and director of Cardiac Wellness at Michigan Healthcare Professionals, both in Detroit. He is author of *The Whole Heart Solution*.

have less than a 5% risk of having a heart attack over the next three to five years. The risk is twice as high in people with a score of one to 10...and more than nine times higher in those with scores above 400.

While the American College of Cardiology recommends this test for people who haven't been diagnosed with heart disease but have known risk factors, such as high blood pressure and/or a family history of heart disease, I advise everyone to have this test at about age 50.* The test takes only 10 to 15 minutes and doesn't require the injection of a contrast agent.

Cost: $99 and up, which may be covered by insurance.

I use the calcium score as a one-time test. Unless they abandon their healthy habits, people who have a score of zero are unlikely to develop arterial calcification later in life. Those who do have deposits will know what they have to do—exercise, eat a more healthful diet, manage cholesterol and blood pressure, etc.

One drawback, however, is radiation exposure. Even though the dose is low (much less than you'd get during cardiac catheterization, for example), you should always limit your exposure.

My advice: Choose an imaging center with the fastest CT machine. A faster machine (a 256-slice CT, for example) gives less radiation exposure than, say, a 64-slice machine.

•**Carotid intima-media thickness (CIMT).** The intima and media are the innermost linings of blood vessels. Their combined thickness in the carotid arteries in the neck is affected by how much plaque is present. Thickening of these arteries can indicate increased risk for stroke and heart attack.

The beauty of this test is that it's performed with ultrasound. There's no radiation, it's fast (10 minutes) and it's painless. I often recommend it as a follow-up to the coronary calcium test or as an alternative for people who want to avoid the radiation of the coronary calcium CT.

*People already diagnosed with heart disease and/or who have had a stent or bypass surgery do not need the coronary calcium CT.

The good news is that you can reduce CIMT—with a more healthful diet, more exercise and the use of statin medications. Pomegranate—the whole fruit, juice or a supplement—can reduce carotid plaque, too. In addition, research has found Kyolic "aged" garlic (the product brand studied) and vitamin K-2 to also be effective.

Cost: $250 to $350. It may not be covered by insurance.

•**Advanced lipid test.** Traditional cholesterol tests are less helpful than experts once thought—particularly because more than 50% of heart attacks occur in patients with normal LDL "bad" cholesterol levels.

Experts have now identified a number of cholesterol subtypes that aren't measured by standard tests. The advanced lipid test (also known as an expanded test) still measures total cholesterol and LDL but also looks at the amounts and sizes of different types of cholesterol.

Suppose that you have a normal LDL reading of 100 mg/dL. You still might have an elevated risk for a heart attack if you happen to have a high number of small, dense LDL particles (found in an advanced LDL particle test), since they can more easily enter the arterial wall.

My advice: Get the advanced lipid test at least once after age 50. It usually costs $39 and up and may be covered by insurance.

If your readings look good, you can switch to a standard cholesterol test every few years. If the numbers are less than ideal, talk to your doctor about treatment options, which might include statins or niacin, along with lifestyle changes. Helpful supplements include omega-3 fatty acids, vitamin E and plant sterols.

•**High-sensitivity C-reactive protein (hs-CRP).** This simple blood test has been available for years, but it's not used as often as it should be. Elevated C-reactive protein indicates inflammation in the body, including in the blood vessels. Data from the Physicians' Health Study found that people with elevated CRP were about three times more likely to have a heart attack than those with normal levels.

If you test low (less than 1 mg/L) or average (1 mg/L to 3 mg/L), you can repeat the test every few years. If your CRP is high (above 3 mg/L), I recommend repeating the test at least once a year. It's a good way to measure any progress you may be making from taking medications (such as statins, which reduce inflammation), improving your diet and getting more exercise.

Cost: About $50. It's usually covered by insurance.

The Hidden Heart Disease Even Doctors Miss

Holly S. Andersen, MD, attending cardiologist and director of Education and Outreach at the Ronald O. Perelman Heart Institute of New York-Presbyterian Hospital in New York City and medical adviser to the Women's Heart Alliance. She is an expert in the field of heart disease in women.

It's hard to imagine that with all the technology available today that heart disease could be completely missed. But that's exactly what's frequently occurring with a tricky heart condition known as small vessel disease or coronary microvascular disease (MVD).

Here's what happens: Patients, most often women, have chest pain, other symptoms that suggest heart disease or even heart attacks. But when doctors examine their coronary arteries, they find no evidence of blockage and often rule out heart disease.

Result: Patients go without the vital treatment they need.

Mystery solved: The problem in these cases, researchers have recently discovered, often lies in the tiny blood vessels—which can't be seen with the naked eye or conventional heart disease testing—that branch off the larger coronary arteries in the heart.

Researchers still have much to learn about MVD, but here's what's known now and what you can do to protect yourself…

A DIFFERENT KIND OF HEART DISEASE

The most common variety of coronary heart disease (CHD) is caused by atherosclerotic plaques—cholesterol-containing deposits that pile up and narrow one or more of the large arteries that carry blood to the heart, restricting flow. When the heart gets too little blood to meet its needs—during exertion, for example—people with CHD have chest pain (angina). And if blood flow is restricted even further—usually due to a clot lodged in the narrowed artery—a heart attack and death may occur.

Plaque is often involved in MVD, too. But instead of accumulating in clumps that block off segments of specific coronary arteries, cholesterol is deposited more evenly inside whole areas of microscopic circulation. Additionally, in MVD the walls of the tiny arteries are injured or diseased—instead of opening wider to allow more blood to reach the heart during exercise or at times of emotional stress, they tighten up, constricting blood flow when it's needed most.

The reason for this is unclear, but it seems that at least some of the time, it's due to malfunction of the endothelial cells that line the blood vessels. The resulting symptoms can be indistinguishable from garden-variety CHD—and the risk for heart attack may be just as real.

DO YOU HAVE MICROVASCULAR DISEASE?

Diabetes and high blood pressure raise one's risk for MVD, as does CHD. High cholesterol, obesity, smoking and a lack of physical activity are risk factors, too, and like CHD, MVD becomes more common with advancing age.

Symptoms of MVD can be identical to the classic signs of CHD—pain, a squeezing sensation or pressure in the chest, usually during activity or emotional stress. The discomfort can also occur in the shoulders, arms, neck or jaw.

MVD tip-off: Painful episodes of MVD usually last longer—more than 10 minutes, and sometimes longer than 30 minutes—than those of classic CHD.

Other symptoms of MVD: Fatigue or lack of energy, trouble sleeping and shortness of breath. Women are particularly likely to have these vague manifestations rather than the kind of distinct chest pain that we usually associate with heart disease. Forty percent of women don't have chest pain even while having a heart attack, whether it's caused by CHD or MVD.

Another clue: With MVD, patients often notice symptoms during daily activities and/or during times of mental stress rather than during times of physical exertion as is more often the case with CHD.

GETTING A DIAGNOSIS

The standard tests for heart disease may not uncover MVD. If you suspect you have the condition, be sure to see a cardiologist with significant experience in treating MVD. An academic medical center is the best place to find such a doctor. He/she may be able to diagnose it from your symptoms, medical history and earlier test results, or he may order additional tests…

•**Nuclear imaging,** which uses a radioactive compound injected into the bloodstream to reveal a detailed image of the heart and blood flow through the arteries, including microcirculation.

•**Magnetic resonance imaging (MRI)** to produce a picture of the heart and its circulation without subjecting the patient to dye or radiation.

•**Positron emission tomography (PET),** which provides information on metabolism in the heart. This can uncover certain areas that aren't getting enough fuel and oxygen, suggesting MVD.

IF YOU HAVE MVD

If MVD is diagnosed, the goal is to keep it from progressing and to prevent heart attack and stroke. *Key strategies…*

•**Tweak your diet, and punch up your exercise routine.** A healthy eating plan, such as the Mediterranean diet, emphasizes fruits, vegetables, legumes, whole grains and nuts and fish, which contain healthy fats. Weight control and exercise reduce heart disease risk overall and also reduce blood pressure and help prevent diabetes, which are additional MVD risk factors. Beyond its general cardiovascular benefits, regular exercise appears to improve the function of the endothelial cells that line blood vessels and function poorly in MVD.

•**Get help from medication.** Doctors prescribe the same medications to treat MVD as for CHD—to reduce blood pressure and cholesterol. Aspirin or other drugs to reduce clotting risk are recommended as well.

Some evidence suggests that statins may be particularly useful because they not only reduce cholesterol but also improve endothelial function and relax the muscles around tiny blood vessels.

Similarly, calcium channel blockers, such as *amlodipine* (Norvasc), and ACE inhibitors, like *enalapril* (Vasotec), may be good choices for lowering blood pressure because they too help keep arteries open.

•**Get treated for anemia if you have it.** Anemia (low red blood cell count) may slow the growth of cells that help repair artery walls. This condition is treated with iron or B-12 supplements.

Note: If you have CHD and MVD (it's possible to have both) and have had angioplasty, a stent or bypass surgery, be aware that these procedures do not help MVD.

Keep It Down!

Ongoing and lengthy exposure to everyday noises, such as cell phone rings or traffic, increases heart rate and decreases heart rate variability—two risk factors for cardiac problems and stroke.

Self-defense: Take deep breaths to ease your body's response to noise. Block out loud noises with earplugs, sound-blocking headphones and/or white noise.

Seth Goldbarg, MD, electrophysiologist, New York Hospital, New York City, writing in *Prevention.*

A Charley Horse...or a Deadly Blood Clot?

Daniella Kadian-Dodov, MD, assistant professor of medicine in the department of vascular medicine at the Zena and Michael A. Wiener Cardiovascular Institute and the Marie-Josée and Henry R. Kravis Center for Cardiovascular Health at the Icahn School of Medicine at Mount Sinai Hospital in New York City.

If you've ever been stopped cold by a charley horse, you know just how excruciating these muscle spasms can be. But are you sure it's just a muscle spasm? Or is that leg pain due to something far more serious?

What can cause leg pain...

PERIPHERAL ARTERIAL DISEASE (PAD)

This is one to worry about. Even though the pain usually isn't intense, it can triple your risk of dying from a heart attack or stroke.

What it feels like: About 10% of people with PAD suffer leg cramps, leg aching and leg fatigue that occur only during physical activity involving the legs (any type of activity can trigger it—even just walking). When you rest your legs, the discomfort goes away, usually in 10 minutes or less. As PAD becomes more severe and blood circulation worsens, pain can occur during rest and result in leg ulcers and even gangrene.

What to do: See a doctor. PAD is usually caused by atherosclerosis, the same condition that leads to most heart attacks. Your doctor will compare the blood pressure in your arms to the pressure at your ankles. If there's a significant difference, that could mean that you have PAD and you'll need an ultrasound of the legs to determine the extent and location of arterial obstructions.

Next steps: The same practices that protect your heart—such as not smoking, controlling diabetes, maintaining healthy blood pressure and getting plenty of exercise—will help stop PAD from worsening and could even reverse it.

Important: You must walk—even when it hurts. Walking ultimately reduces pain and improves circulation by stimulating the growth of blood vessels that bypass the damaged ones. With your doctor's OK, walk five times a week, for 30 to 45 minutes each time. I usually advise my patients to walk fast for two blocks or until they feel moderate pain, then rest a moment and walk fast for two blocks again, repeating until the end of their workout.

DEEP VEIN THROMBOSIS (DVT)

It doesn't always cause leg pain, but if pain occurs, this warning could save your life. DVT means that you have a blood clot—most often deep in a leg vein. It can be fatal.

What it feels like: You might notice a sudden, pulsating or aching pain deep in your calf or thigh, sometimes accompanied by redness and/or swelling. DVT usually occurs after you've been immobile for a long time—you're laid up in bed after surgery, for example, or following a long car or plane trip.

What to do: Get to an emergency department or a physician's office where you can get an immediate ultrasound. The clot could break free, travel to the lungs and cause pulmonary embolism, a clot in the lungs that's fatal in up to 30% of cases.

If you have a DVT, your doctor will probably give intravenous or injectable heparin, a blood-thinning drug that prevents the clot from growing. After a day or two, you'll be switched to oral blood-thinning medication, such as *warfarin* (Coumadin) or *dabigatran* (Pradaxa). You'll need to take the medication for about six months. If the clot is not entirely dissolved after treatment, it should be monitored with ultrasound—and if you have had one clot, you might get another one. Prevention is critical.

Everyone—whether you've had a DVT or not—should flex the ankle and calf muscles for about 30 seconds every 20 or 30 minutes when sitting for longer than four hours. Stand up and move around at least every hour or so.

If you have risk factors for blood clots—you're over age 40, obese, have a family history of blood clots or use hormone replacement therapy—ask your doctor about such precautions as taking aspirin before travel and/or wearing compression stockings while you're immobile.

SCIATICA

This back condition is typically caused by a herniated spinal disk. The legs become involved because the disk exerts painful pressure on the sciatic nerve, which runs down the backs of the legs.

What it feels like: Intense, shooting and/or knifelike pains may extend through the buttocks and into one leg. Sciatica also can cause leg and/or ankle weakness.

What to do: See your doctor. If you do have sciatica, you may get better within eight weeks by doing physical therapy and using a nonsteroidal anti-inflammatory medication such as *ibuprofen* (Motrin)—90% of sciatica patients do.

Next steps: Consider surgery for a herniated disk/sciatica only when the pain is too intense to handle...you have responsibilities that don't permit extended downtime...or you're having additional symptoms such as muscle weakness or a loss of bowel/bladder control.

More from Dr. Kadian-Dodov

When It Really Is a Charley Horse

A muscle spasm, including the infamous "charley horse" of the leg, believed to have been named after a lame horse, can occur after hard exercise or for no obvious reason. It can cause sudden, localized pain (usually with sharp contractions) that often hits the calves.

If you're getting muscle spasms with any sort of regularity, see your doctor. Muscle spasms have a variety of causes—for example, you may have overworked your legs by doing yard work...you may be dehydrated (without enough water, muscle cells can spasm)...or a medication you're taking, such as a diuretic, may be the culprit.

Helpful: Because most muscle spasms are caused, in part, by tight hamstrings (the muscles in the backs of your upper legs), I recommend doing a standing hamstring stretch on a regular basis. Start in a standing position with your knees straight...bend at the waist...and reach for your toes or the floor until you feel a stretch in your hamstrings. Hold for a few seconds, and repeat a few times a day.

Having Shingles Can Increase Risk for Heart Attack and Stroke Later in Life

People who had shingles after age 40 had a 10% higher risk for heart attack and a 15% higher risk for mini-stroke, or transient ischemic attack. People who had shingles prior to age 40 were at much greater risk—they had a 50% higher risk for heart attack...were 2.4 times more likely to have a mini-stroke...and had a 74% higher risk for stroke.

If you have had shingles: Get a cardiovascular checkup, and be screened for risk factors, such as high cholesterol and high blood pressure.

Judith Breuer, MD, professor of virology at University College London, and lead author of a study published in *Neurology*.

Meditation Cuts Heart Attack Risk in Half

Robert Schneider, MD, director, the NIH-funded Institute for Natural Medicine and Prevention, professor of physiology and health, Maharishi University of Management (MUM.edu), Fairfield, Iowa. Dr. Schneider is author of *Total Heart Health*.

Meditation can bring about a state of deep relaxation in which your heart rate, blood pressure and respiration slow down, giving your cardiovascular system a much needed rest. TM is a particular brand of meditation that is "simple and precise," said Robert Schneider, MD, professor of physiology and health at Maharishi University of Management in Iowa. It is practiced for 20 minutes twice a day while sitting comfortably with eyes closed and silently repeating a calming word to produce "a natural state of restful alertness." Dr. Schneider said that the health benefits of regular TM potentially include not

369

only lower heart rate and blood pressure, but also reduced total cholesterol and insulin resistance, less need for blood pressure medication and a slowing or reversal of the hardening of arteries that contributes to heart disease.

Building on the results of past meditation research, Dr. Schneider and his colleagues examined the specific effect of TM on heart disease patients. In a randomized controlled trial, they assigned 201 men and women (average age 59) with narrowing of cardiovascular arteries to either a TM group or a control group. For an average of five years, all participants received regular medical care, including medication as needed and lifestyle advice about risk factors such as diet and exercise. In addition, the TM group meditated for 20 minutes twice a day at home while the control group attended classes on cardiovascular health.

Dr. Schneider and his colleagues found that participants who had meditated…

•**Experienced a 47% reduction in heart attacks, strokes and death, compared with those who did not.**

•**Reduced their blood pressure by an average of five points.**

•**Had significant reductions in psychological stress as measured by standard psychological tests.**

Sponsored by the NIH, the study was done collaboratively by researchers at the Medical College of Wisconsin and the Maharishi University. Findings were presented at a recent annual meeting of the American Heart Association in Orlando.

A POWERFUL LIFESTYLE CHOICE

Dr. Schneider equates the dramatic effect of TM on heart patients to the discovery of a whole new class of drug therapy—one that taps into the body's own natural pharmacy of healing resources.

In Dr. Schneider's opinion, TM's heart benefits cannot automatically be generalized to other meditation techniques since they weren't studied. That said, you can learn more about other ways to meditate (and meditation in general) at websites such as *relaxationresponse.org* and *how-to-meditate.org*. Additional options include

guided imagery or visualization (in which you imagine specific images during meditation)…mindfulness meditation (an increased awareness of the present moment)…and techniques such as yoga, tai chi and qi gong that combine meditation, breathing exercises and movements or postures.

---

14 Little Things You Can Do for a Healthier Heart

Joel K. Kahn, MD, clinical professor of medicine at Wayne State University School of Medicine, Detroit, and founder of The Kahn Center for Cardiac Longevity. He is author of *The Whole Heart Solution: Halt Heart Disease Now with the Best Alternative and Traditional Medicine*. DrJoelKahn.com

---

Heart disease is America's number-one killer. But just because it's a major health risk does not necessarily mean that you must make major lifestyle changes to avoid it. *Here are 14 simple and inexpensive ways to have a healthier heart…*

DOABLE DIET TIPS

1. Don't eat in the evening. Research suggests that the heart (and digestive system) benefits greatly from taking an 11-to-12-hour break from food every night. One study found that men who indulge in midnight snacks are 55% more likely to suffer from heart disease than men who don't. So if you plan to eat breakfast at 7 am, consider your kitchen closed after 7 or 8 pm.

Warning: You cannot produce the same health benefits by snacking at night and then skipping breakfast. This might create an 11-to-12-hour break from eating, but skipping breakfast actually increases the risk for heart attack and/or death—by 27%, according to one study. Our bodies and minds often are under considerable stress in the morning—that's when heart attack risk is greatest. Skipping the morning meal only adds to this stress.

2. Use apple pie spice as a topping on oatmeal and fruit. Some people enjoy it in coffee, too. This spice combo, which contains cinnamon, cloves, nutmeg and allspice, has been shown to reduce blood pressure, improve cholesterol levels and lower the risk for heart disease.

3. Take your time with your tea. Tea contains compounds called flavonoids that have been shown to significantly reduce the risk for heart disease—green tea is best of all. But you get the full benefits only if you have the patience to let the tea leaves steep—that is, soak in hot water—for at least three to five minutes before drinking.

4. Fill up on salad. It's no secret that being overweight is bad for the heart. But most people don't realize that they can lose weight without going hungry. Salad can make the stomach feel full without a lot of calories. But don't add nonvegetable ingredients such as cheese, meat and egg to salads…and opt for balsamic or red wine vinegar dressing—they are rich in nutrients, including artery-healing resveratrol.

As a bonus, vegetables…and fruits…contain nutrients that are great for the heart regardless of your weight—so great that eating a plant-rich diet could improve your blood pressure just as much as taking blood pressure medication. In fact, one study found that increasing consumption of fruits and vegetables from 1.5 to eight servings per day decreases the risk for heart attack or stroke by 30%.

One strategy: Become a vegetarian for breakfast and lunch. That way you still can enjoy meat at dinner, but your overall vegetable consumption will be increased.

5. Marinate meat before grilling it. Grilling meat triggers a dramatic increase in its "advanced glycation end products" (AGEs), which stiffen blood vessels and raise blood pressure, among other health drawbacks. If you're not willing to give up your grill, marinate meat for at least 30 minutes before cooking it. Marinating helps keep meat moist, which can slash AGE levels in half. An effective marinade for this purpose is beer, though lemon juice or vinegar works well, too. You can add herbs and oil if you wish.

6. Sprinkle Italian seasoning mix onto salads, potatoes and soups. This zesty mix contains antioxidant-rich herbs such as oregano, sage, rosemary and thyme, which studies suggest reduce the risk for heart disease and cancer.

7. Avoid foods that contain dangerous additives. There are so many food additives that it's virtually impossible to keep track of them all. Focus on avoiding foods that list any of the following seven among their ingredients—each carries heart-related health risks. The seven are aspartame…BHA (butylated hydroxyanisole)…BHT (butylated hydroxytoluene)…saccharin…sodium nitrate…sodium sulfate…and monosodium glutamate (MSG).

8. Savor the first three bites of everything you eat. When people eat too fast, they also tend to eat too much. One way to slow down your eating is to force yourself to pay close attention to what you are eating. If you cannot do this for an entire meal or snack, at least do it for the first three mouthfuls of each food you consume. Chew these initial bites slowly and thoroughly. Give the food and its flavor your undivided attention, and you will end up eating less.

9. Prepare your lunch the night before if you won't be home for your midday meal. People who intend to make their lunch in the morning often are in too much of a rush to do so…then wind up resorting to fast food.

10. Buy organic when it counts. Higher pesticide levels in the blood predict higher cholesterol levels as well as cardiovascular disease. Organic food is free of pesticide—but it can be expensive. The smart compromise is to buy organic when it counts most—when traditionally grown produce is most likely to contain pesticide residue. According to the Environmental Working Group, the foods most likely to contain pesticide residue are apples, celery, cherry tomatoes, collard greens, cucumbers, grapes, hot peppers, kale, nectarines, peaches, potatoes, spinach, strawberries, summer squash and sweet bell peppers.

Important: If your options are eating conventionally farmed fruits and vegetables or not eating fruits and vegetables at all, definitely consume the conventionally grown produce. The health risks from small amounts of pesticide residue are much lower than the health risks from not eating produce.

EASY LIFESTYLE HABITS

11. Stand two to five minutes each hour. Recent research suggests that sitting for extended periods is horrible for your heart. Sitting slows your metabolism and reduces your ability to process glucose and cholesterol. But standing for as little as two to five minutes each hour seems to significantly reduce these health consequences (more standing is even better). Stand while making phone calls or during commercials. Buy a "standing desk," then stand when you use your computer.

12. Take walks after meals. Walking is good anytime, but walks after meals have special health benefits, particularly after rich desserts. A 20-minute postmeal stroll significantly improves the body's ability to manage blood sugar. Maintaining healthful blood sugar levels reduces risk for coronary artery blockage.

13. Exercise in brief but intense bursts. Research suggests that exercising as intensely as possible for 20 seconds…resting for 10 seconds…then repeating this seven more times provides nearly the same benefits for the heart as a far longer but less intense workout. Try this with an exercise bike, rowing machine, elliptical machine or any other form of exercise. Do an Internet search for "Tabata training" to learn more. There are free apps that can help you time these intervals. Download Tabata Stopwatch in the iTunes store if you use an Apple device…or Tabata Timer for HIIT from Google Play if you use an Android device.

Caution: Talk to your doctor. High-intensity training could be dangerous if you have a preexisting health condition.

14. Get sufficient sleep. One study found that the rates of heart disease for people who get seven to eight hours of sleep a night are nearly half those of people who get too little or too much sleep.

The Easiest Diet Ever— It's Also Beneficial for Your Heart

Marla Heller, RD, a Los Angeles–based registered dietitian who developed plans to bring the DASH diet from the research phase to patients. She is the author of *The DASH Diet Action Plan: Proven to Lower Blood Pressure and Cholesterol Without Medication, The DASH Diet Weight Loss Solution* and *The Everyday DASH Diet Cookbook.* DashDiet.org

Following a healthful diet is undoubtedly one of the best things we can do to protect ourselves from chronic disease. So why is it such a struggle?

Unfortunately, many diets just aren't practical over the long haul. Sure, you may be able to white-knuckle it for the first few days or weeks. But what happens when you can no longer withstand the unhealthful temptations at parties, restaurants and just about anywhere else? *The solution…*

A POWERHOUSE DIET

Many people are surprised to learn that one of the most widely studied diets is also perhaps the easiest to follow on a long-term basis because it provides enough food choices to be truly appealing—even enjoyable—to virtually anyone.

Perhaps you've heard of the DASH diet. It is commonly known as the "blood pressure diet." Short for Dietary Approaches to Stop Hypertension, the DASH plan has long been known to effectively lower blood pressure—sometimes in just 14 days, according to research.

Now: After years of scientific scrutiny, this "sleeper" of a diet, with its wide range of foods—vegetables, fruits, low-fat and nonfat dairy, whole grains, lean poultry and fish, and nuts, beans and seeds—is winning more proponents because of its other health benefits.

In addition to being linked to a lower risk for heart disease and stroke, this diet has also been shown to cut risk for kidney stones by 45% and risk for colon cancer by 20%. If that's not enough, the DASH diet also prevents (and sometimes even reverses) diabetes by controlling blood sugar spikes. And it makes you feel younger and lighter, because the low-sodium component helps you to retain less fluid.

The "Best" Diet: Because of its many health benefits, nutritional completeness and the ease with which it can be followed, the DASH diet was named "Best Overall Diet" for several years in a row by *US News & World Report*, based on analyses by experts in nutrition and various chronic diseases. The DASH eating plan beat other better-known diets, such as the Mediterranean diet and Weight Watchers.

WHY DASH WORKS

The DASH diet might seem like nothing more than a commonsense eating plan, but very few Americans actually eat according to its basic principles. Not only are most of us sorely lacking in vegetables and fruits, but we take in an average of 3,500 mg of blood pressure–raising sodium per day—far more than the amount that's recommended for healthy adults (up to 2,300 mg daily) or the amount for people with high blood pressure (up to 1,500 mg).

The magic behind DASH lies in its high amounts of potassium, calcium and magnesium. Potassium, found in fruits and vegetables, naturally lowers blood pressure by ridding the body of excess sodium. Calcium from dairy and other sources, including broccoli and fish with bones, such as sardines, works in the same way—plus it relaxes your blood vessels, making it easier for blood to pass through. Magnesium, found in whole grains, nuts and seeds, also promotes healthy blood vessels.

MAKING IT EASY

When first considering the DASH daily eating plan, you may think that you'd never be able to eat such a seemingly large amount and wide variety of food, but that's not true.

The standard 2,000-calorie plan includes…*

• **Fruits**—Four to five servings per day (one serving equals one medium-sized whole fruit or one cup diced raw fruit).

---

*2,000 calories daily is appropriate for men age 51 and older. Women age 51 and older usually need 1,600 calories daily. Younger adults can have more calories. Weight loss requires less calories and fewer servings.

• **Vegetables**—Four to five servings per day (one serving equals one-half cup cooked vegetables or one cup leafy greens).

• **Low-fat/nonfat dairy**—Three daily servings (one serving equals one-half cup fat-free or low-fat cottage cheese or eight ounces skim or low-fat milk or low-fat or fat-free yogurt). (See page 382 for updates.)

• **Whole grains**—Three daily servings (one serving equals one slice of bread, one-half cup cooked brown rice or one ounce dry cereal).

• **Refined grains**—A few servings a week (one serving equals one-half cup pasta or one cookie as a treat).

• **Healthy fats (such as olive oil and avocado)**—Two to three daily servings (one serving equals one teaspoon olive oil or one-eighth of a small avocado).

• **Lean meat, poultry or fish**—Seven ounces daily.

• **Beans and nuts**—Four to five servings per week (one serving equals one-quarter cup beans or nuts).

Why so much food and so many different choices? The diet delivers all the disease-fighting benefits that can be derived from good nutrition. Plus, the emphasis on low-calorie, high-volume produce and hunger-fighting protein means that you'll feel satisfied and less likely to give in to cravings for unhealthful foods that cause weight gain.

If five daily servings of veggies sounds daunting, think of it this way: A dinner including one cup sautéed broccoli (two servings)…a small side salad (one serving)…and one cup roasted potatoes (two servings) equals five full servings of veggies.

Other ways to meet DASH goals…

Fruits: Try one small banana at breakfast, one plum at lunch, one cup berries as a midafternoon snack, one-half cup sliced Bartlett pears for dessert.

Low-fat/nonfat dairy: Try eight ounces nonfat milk on cereal (pour it on, then drink the rest), one ounce light Swiss cheese added to a sandwich for lunch, one cup light yogurt as an afternoon snack.

Whole grains: Try three-quarters cup whole-wheat cereal or oatmeal, two slices thin-sliced whole-wheat bread at lunch, one small whole-wheat dinner roll.

Healthy fats: Try one tablespoon salad dressing and a few avocado slices.

Lean meat, poultry or fish: Try three ounces of turkey slices at lunch and four ounces of salmon at dinner.

Beans and nuts: Try a small handful of nuts for a snack.

If you are eating out, try these DASH-friendly items…

• **A Grande Starbucks Caffé Latte with nonfat milk,** or any 16-ounce coffee drink with eight ounces milk.

• **A slice of thin-crust veggie pizza plus a salad.**

• **A Subway double-meat six-inch roasted chicken sandwich** topped with all of your favorite veggies, minus the top half of the bread.

For a tasty DASH snack at home, try celery dipped in hummus.

For a free copy of the complete DASH diet, go to *www.nhlbi.nih.gov/files/docs/public/heart/new_dash.pdf.*

"Pile It On" Chili

Didn't think you could have chili when you're following a healthful eating plan? You can! *Here's an easy-to-make and tasty chili recipe…*

1 pound ground sirloin, 95% extra-lean
½ 16-oz. bag frozen onions and sliced peppers combo (or use fresh if you like, of course)
2 to 3 garlic cloves, minced
1 14.5-oz. can diced tomatoes, no added salt
1 15-oz. can tomato sauce, no added salt
1 15.5-oz. can kidney beans
1 15.5-oz. can black beans
2 Tablespoons chili powder
2 Tablespoons paprika
½ 16-oz. bag frozen mixed broccoli, cauliflower and carrots
1 cup frozen corn

Cook ground beef at medium-high heat for three minutes. Add peppers, onions and garlic. Cook on medium until onions are browned and soft. Add tomatoes, beans and seasonings. Mix well and simmer five minutes. Then add mixed vegetables and corn. Simmer 30 to 60 minutes. Add shredded light cheese and/or baked tortilla strips as a garnish (see recipe below).

Makes 12 1-cup servings. *Per serving:* 204 calories, 13 g protein, 24 g carbohydrates, 7 g fat, 7 g fiber, 379 mg sodium.

Baked Tortilla Strips

For easy tortilla strips, cut two corn tortillas into ½-inch strips. Place on a tray in the oven, and bake at 400°F for five minutes—or until lightly browned.

(See page 382 for recent updates to the DASH diet.)

TCM for Heart Health

Mao Shing Ni, LaC, DOM, PhD, a Santa Monica, California–based licensed acupuncturist and doctor of oriental medicine, TaoOfWellness.com. He is cofounder of Yo San University, an accredited graduate school of Traditional Chinese Medicine in Los Angeles, and author of *Secrets of Longevity.*

We all know that a nutritious diet is one of the keys to living a long, healthy life.

Problem: Even health-conscious individuals get stuck in a rut of consuming the same foods and drinks all the time.

Solution: Traditional Chinese Medicine (TCM) offers a wide variety of healthful, delicious foods and drinks that have been consumed for their disease-fighting properties for thousands of years.

Best TCM foods for your heart…

• **Orange peel for cholesterol.** As we age, LDL "bad" cholesterol often accumulates in the arteries, leading to heart disease and stroke. Orange peel actually may lower cholesterol better than some medications, such as statin drugs, without the side effects.

Studies show that compounds called polymethoxsylated flavones (PMFs), found in pigments of oranges and tangerines, can reduce bad cholesterol—without decreasing the level of HDL "good" cholesterol.

My advice: Grate or chop the peel of an orange or tangerine (preferably organic to avoid potentially toxic pesticides). If cooking a 12-ounce serving of meat or chicken, use the whole rind. As an alternative, use low-sugar marmalade, which contains orange rind, in your sauce.

• **Chicory for heart health.** Chicory, an herb that is popular in China and parts of Europe, contains a compound called inulin that helps strengthen the heart muscle—and may even be useful in treating congestive heart failure (a condition that causes inadequate pumping action of the heart).

One study found that chicory helps regulate an irregular heartbeat—a potentially dangerous condition that can lead to heart failure. Other research shows that chicory helps lower cholesterol levels and may slow the progression of hardening of the arteries.

My advice: In the US, chicory root is most often roasted for use as a brewed coffee substitute that can be found in most organic food markets. For heart health, drink one to two cups daily of chicory coffee substitute. Don't use chicory if you have gallstones or are allergic to plants in the ragweed family.

My favorite: Teeccino Mediterranean Java Herbal Coffee. Radicchio, a type of leafy chicory, is also widely available. Eat it two to three times weekly (in salads, for example).

Coffee and Tea Reduce Stroke Risk

In a recent finding, drinking one or more cups of coffee daily was associated with a 22% to 25% reduction in stroke risk.

Theory: Coffee beans contain antioxidants and other disease-fighting chemicals that reduce inflammation and improve insulin activity. Moderate coffee consumption also has been linked to decreased risk for diabetes, colon cancer, heart disease, liver disease and Parkinson's disease.

Susanna Larsson, PhD, division of nutritional epidemiology at Institute of Environmental Medicine, Karolinska Institute, Stockholm, Sweden. She was lead researcher of a study of 34,670 women, published in *Stroke*.

A recent analysis of nine studies involving nearly 195,000 adults found that for each additional three cups of black or green tea consumed daily, stroke risk dropped by 21%.

Theory: The antioxidant epigallocatechin gallate or the amino acid theanine, both found in tea, may have anti-inflammatory effects that protect the heart and brain. (Processing for decaffeinated tea may remove these ingredients.)

Lenore Arab, PhD, professor of medicine and biological chemistry, David Geffen School of Medicine, University of California, Los Angeles.

The Red Wine That Does the Most for Your Health

Ramon Estruch, MD, PhD, senior consultant, associate professor, department of internal medicine, University of Barcelona, Spain, and coauthor of a study published in *Circulation Research*.

Raising a glass of red wine and drinking to your health may give you a sense of satisfaction because you've heard that a bit of wine can be good for your heart.

But: There are downsides, too—alcohol increases the risk for certain cancers, and too much of it can harm the liver and increase blood pressure.

So you'll want to toast a new Spanish study that reveals how people who enjoy the taste of red wine can indulge in the beverage and get the health benefits—without the health risks.

The secret: Opt for red wine that contains no alcohol.

RAISE A GLASS!

The study participants included men ages 55 to 75 who were at high risk for heart problems because they had diabetes or various cardiovascular disease risk factors. First, after a two-week period of abstinence from alcohol, each participant's baseline blood pressure was measured and certain blood tests were done.

Then, during one four-week period, each participant drank 9.2 ounces (about two glasses) of regular red wine with dinner each day. During a second four-week period, each man drank 9.2 ounces of nonalcoholic red wine with his evening meal. And during a third four-week period, each drank 3.4 ounces (about two shots) of gin daily with dinner. (The men knew what they were drinking, but this knowledge wouldn't affect results.) Participants all followed a similar diet and drank no other alcohol during the study. At the end of each four-week period, participants' blood pressure readings were compared with their baseline readings.

Results: After drinking regular red wine, the men's blood pressure dropped insignificantly…and after they drank gin, their blood pressure didn't change at all. However, after consuming the alcohol-free red wine, the men's blood pressure dropped, on average, nearly six points for systolic pressure (the top number of a blood pressure reading) and more than two points for diastolic pressure (the bottom number). This represents a significant decrease—perhaps more than enough to reduce heart disease risk by 14% and stroke risk by 20%!

THE REAL POWER IN WINE

Polyphenols—healthful antioxidants found in fruits, vegetables and wine—in nonalcoholic wine had more potent effects than those in regular wine, probably because alcohol interferes with antioxidant activity. Gin contains no polyphenols and thus does not have antioxidant benefits. While white wine and plain old grape juice do contain polyphenols, red wine contains more, which is why the researchers focused on it.

When participants were drinking alcohol-free wine, their blood levels of nitric oxide were four times higher than when they were drinking regular red wine. This is an important change—because nitric oxide helps blood vessels relax, thus reducing blood pressure and allowing more blood to reach the heart and other organs. Again, polyphenols get the credit for the improvement in nitric oxide levels.

We suspect that experience the same effects from drinking nonalcoholic red wine, and are planning to do an all-female study to find out.

IS IT REALLY WINE?

Unlike grape juice, nonalcoholic wine is fermented just like regular wine—in fact, it is regular wine—but then the alcohol is removed. Though the process does not affect polyphenol levels, true wine aficionados may recognize that taking out the alcohol leaves the wine lighter and less robust (and also leaves you without the buzz, of course). Many people find the nuanced taste of alcohol-free wine quite appealing—and perhaps all the more in light of this new evidence for the beverage's health benefits.

Important: It is impossible to remove all alcohol from wine, though the amount left in is small at less than one-half of 1%. Still, if you are avoiding alcohol completely, nonalcoholic wine may not be appropriate for you. Also, if you have diabetes, keep in mind that alcohol-free wines do contain some sugar, so it is best to check with your doctor to see whether it is OK for you to consume nonalcoholic wine.

There are many types of nonalcoholic wine, including various reds and whites as well. Cabernet sauvignon, petit syrah and pinot noir have the highest levels of polyphenols—and a general guideline is, the drier the wine, the higher the polyphenol content. These days, alcohol-free wines are sold just about anywhere that regular wine is sold—even in many fine wine stores—and you can find them at many supermarkets and health-food stores. They're sold online too (for instance, at *www.Ariel Vineyards.com*) and typically cost less than $10 per bottle.

Heart-Rhythm Problem? These Supplements Can Help

Michael Traub, ND, director, Ho'o Lokahi, an integrative health care center in Kailua Kona, Hawaii.

The occasional flutter...a missed beat...an unusual thump. For some people, an irregularity in heartbeat, called cardiac arrhythmia, signals only a minor glitch in the heart's complex internal electrical system. But in other cases, it indicates a serious electrical malfunction that can lead to atrial fibrillation, an abnormally fast and irregular heartbeat—and that can in turn be associated with heart failure, stroke or even sudden death.

Good news: In many cases, nutritional deficiencies cause or contribute to arrhythmias—and addressing those deficiencies with the appropriate dietary supplements can help correct or minimize the heart problem!

To find out whether nutritional therapies are right for you, consult a naturopathic physician or a functional medical doctor experienced in treating arrhythmias. One of the doctor's first steps may be to order blood tests to see what's going on inside your body at the micronutrient level—because your levels of certain nutrients can have a direct impact on your heart rhythm.

For patients with cardiac arrhythmias, Michael Traub, director of an integrative health care center in Hawaii said, it's especially important to check for deficiencies of magnesium and potassium...and the ratio between the omega-6 fatty acid arachidonic acid and the omega-3 fatty acid eicosapentaenoic acid (EPA), because too high a ratio is bad for your heart. You should also be tested for the amino acid homocysteine because high levels are associated with increased risk for heart disease and arrhythmias.

The two most common deficiencies in patients with arrhythmias are magnesium and EPA. Potassium deficiency is not as common, but your potassium level should be checked because deficiency is associated with higher risk for atrial fibrillation.

RHYTHM-REGULATING SUPPLEMENTS

Based on your blood test results, your doctor will prescribe the appropriate supplements in the proper dosages to correct your nutritional deficiencies and address other factors that can contribute to arrhythmias. *The supplements Dr. Traub typically prescribes for his arrhythmia patients include one or more of the following...*

• **Magnesium.** This mineral relaxes blood vessel walls and improves blood flow. Magnesium is so effective at helping regulate heart rhythm that it is often given to patients in the hospital to reduce the risk for atrial fibrillation and cardiac arrest.

• **Potassium.** This is known to improve and stabilize the pumping action of the heart. It protects against ventricular and atrial fibrillation...it also is used as a treatment for congestive heart failure.

• **Fish oil.** Several years ago, some studies showed that omega-3 fatty acids reduced fatal ventricular arrhythmias, although more recent studies have not confirmed these findings. Still, because omega-3 fatty acids have a positive effect on heart health, Dr. Traub believes that fish oil is an important part of a natural anti-arrhythmia regimen.

Caution: Since fish oil is an anticoagulant, its use must be medically supervised in patients who take blood-thinning medication.

• **Lumbrokinase.** This enzyme is similar to the better-known nattokinase (made from fermented soybeans). Lumbrokinase is derived from the earthworm Lumbricus rubellus—but don't be put off by that, Dr. Traub said, because it works even better than nattokinase to inhibit the formation of blood clots. Like fish oil, lumbrokinase should be taken only with a doctor's OK by anyone who is on a pharmaceutical blood thinner.

• **Hawthorn.** This herb contains antioxidants that are thought to improve blood flow.

• **B vitamins.** If your homocysteine levels are high, your doctor may prescribe supplements of vitamins B-6, B-12 and/or B-9 (folate) to bring your levels into normal range.

What to avoid: Patients with arrhythmias should not take iodine supplements because they can bring about hyperthyroidism, which worsens arrhythmia. Caffeine—whether from food, beverages or supplements—also should be avoided because the stimulant can interfere with heart rhythms.

Also helpful for arrhythmia patients: It's best to limit alcohol intake…not smoke…get enough sleep…stay adequately hydrated…eat plenty of fresh fruits and vegetables…and take steps to effectively manage stress. These lifestyle choices can make a significant difference when it comes to easing arrhythmias.

The Aspirin Question

Randall S. Stafford, MD, PhD, a professor of medicine at the Stanford Prevention Research Center and the director of the Program on Prevention Outcomes and Practices, both at the Stanford School of Medicine in Palo Alto, California. AspirinProject.org

---

It seems harmless enough…popping an aspirin from that familiar little bottle tucked away in your medicine cabinet.

In fact, millions of Americans take an aspirin daily as a blood thinner to help prevent the artery-clogging blood clots that cause most heart attacks and strokes. But for many of these people, aspirin is doing more harm than good.

Recent finding: In a study of 68,800 adults taking daily aspirin therapy for heart attack and/or stroke prevention, nearly 12% were doing so unnecessarily based on their limited chances of actually suffering from one of these conditions over the next decade. In doing so, these individuals were found to be increasing their risk for potentially dangerous side effects, such as internal bleeding, for no good reason.

A tragic toll: Among the more than 16,000 deaths each year linked to bleeding associated with use of nonsteroidal anti-inflammatory drugs (NSAIDs), about one-third of these deaths occur in those who take low-dose (81-mg) aspirin.

IS ASPIRIN RIGHT FOR YOU?

You may assume from these frightening statistics that aspirin is never worth the risk, but that would be a mistake. Whether you're trying to prevent a heart attack or stroke, to make the best decision about using aspirin, you and your doctor need to weigh your potential benefits against your potential harms and then make a choice based on your preferences. *When aspirin use may help…*

If you've already had coronary bypass surgery, a heart attack or ischemic stroke (caused by a blood clot), taking aspirin and/or another blood-thinning drug, such as *clopidogrel* (Plavix) or *warfarin* (Coumadin), is wise. That's because study after study shows that aspirin significantly reduces the risk for a second heart attack or stroke. (A person whose risk for bleeding is extremely high may be an exception.)

If your goal is to prevent a first heart attack or stroke, the decision is a bit more complicated. Guidelines from the American Heart Association (AHA) and the US Preventive Services Task Force recommend aspirin for primary prevention in people at high risk for cardiovascular disease. In 2014, the FDA weighed in, releasing a statement that warned against widespread use in people of average risk.

My advice: I advise some—but not all—of my male patients who are over age 45 to take aspirin for primary prevention. For women, I advise aspirin for most who are age 65 and older. There are exceptions, especially for those who are at high risk for bleeding. Meanwhile, men and women younger than these ages sometimes have enough risk factors for heart attack and stroke that they will benefit from aspirin.

Scientific evidence: An analysis of multiple studies published in *The Journal of the American Medical Association*, involving nearly 100,000 people, showed that daily aspirin can decrease heart attacks in men age 45 and older by 32%. In women, research has found that the greatest benefit—for reduction in ischemic stroke and heart attack—occurs for those age 65 and older.

What's my criteria for recommending aspirin? If the patient's chance of having a heart attack or stroke in the next 10 years is higher than 5% to 10%.

To determine your heart attack and stroke risk: Use the cardiovascular disease (CVD) "risk calculator" created by the American College of Cardiology and the AHA. To download the calculator onto your computer or an app onto your smartphone, go to professionalheart.org (click on "Guidelines & Statements," then on "Prevention Guidelines").

If your risk is above 5% to 10%, talk to your doctor about whether you should be taking aspirin.

Important: Once you have your result from the risk calculator, you must balance your potential benefit from taking aspirin to prevent a heart attack or stroke against possible harm. Have you had gastrointestinal (GI) bleeding in the past? Are you regularly taking another anti-inflammatory medicine such as *ibuprofen* (Motrin), which also increases your risk for GI bleeding?

Are you age 80 or over? Aspirin might help you, but there's no solid evidence to guide your decision. Nonetheless, older adults have the most to gain from aspirin, but need to be particularly careful to avoid bleeding problems.

Double Whammy for Heart Attack and Stroke

A combination drug prevents heart attack and stroke better than a statin alone. Vytorin, which contains the statin *simvastatin* plus *ezetimibe*, a drug that prevents the body from absorbing cholesterol, brought down levels of LDL (bad) cholesterol more than simvastatin did on its own. Vytorin had no more side effects than taking a statin alone. Patients who took Vytorin had 6.4% reduced risk for cardiac events. Vytorin should be considered when a statin alone leaves the patient with LDL greater than 70 milligrams per deci-

liter (mg/dL) or when the patient cannot take a full dose of a statin because of a side effect.

Robert M. Califf, MD, vice-chancellor for clinical and translational research and director of the Duke Translational Medicine Institute, Durham, North Carolina. He led a study presented at a recent meeting of the American Heart Association.

Blood Pressure Alert

Rebecca Shannonhouse, editor of *Bottom Line Health*, Botom Line Inc., 3 Landmark Square, Stamford, Connecticut 06901.

For decades, we've been told to keep our blood pressure below 140/90.

Now: New expert guidelines have plenty of doctors crying foul. According to these relaxed recommendations, people over age 60 don't need treatment until systolic (top number) blood pressure rises to 150 or higher (no change was recommended for diastolic pressure). For people under age 60, 140/90 still is the cutoff.

Why the change? The committee that created the guidelines concluded that there isn't enough evidence that the additional blood pressure–lowering prevents heart attacks and strokes. In the absence of benefit, the risk for side effects from medication is not justified. Samuel Mann, MD, a hypertension specialist at New York-Presbyterian Hospital and author of *Hypertension and You*, disagrees. *He says…*

Most of the studies analyzed by the committee followed patients for only three to five years—not long enough to observe the benefits of lowering systolic pressure to 140 versus 150.

Blood pressure reduction also has other long-term benefits that would not be evident in a three-to-five-year study, such as lower risk for dementia, erectile dysfunction and other vascular-related conditions.

With the many excellent medications available today, we usually can get the systolic pressure under 140 without side effects.

Dr. Mann's takeaway: A target below 140/90 still is best for most adults.

One exception: Adults age 80 and older may do better with systolic pressure of up to 160.

Foods That Help Control Blood Pressure

Janet Bond Brill, PhD, RD, a registered dietitian and a nationally recognized expert in nutrition and cardiovascular disease prevention. She is the author of *Blood Pressure Down: The 10-Step Plan to Lower Your Blood Pressure in 4 Weeks Without Prescription Drugs.* DrJanet.com

Mark Houston, MD, MS, director of the Hypertension Institute, Vascular Biology and the Life Extension Institute at Saint Thomas Hospital in Nashville. He is author of *What Your Doctor May Not Tell You About Hypertension.*

C onsidering all the dangers of high blood pressure (including increased risk for heart attack, stroke and dementia), we definitely want to do everything we can to keep our blood pressure levels under control. But are we?

Unfortunately, one surprisingly simple step —eating the right foods—consistently gets ignored as an effective technique for controlling blood pressure.*

Of course everyone knows that a low-sodium diet helps some people maintain healthy blood pressure levels. But there's a lot more to blood pressure control than avoiding that bag of potato chips, extra dash of soy sauce or a crunchy dill pickle (just one dill pickle contains about 875 mg of sodium, or nearly 40% of recommended daily sodium intake).

What most people are missing out on: With the right combination of blood pressure–controlling nutrients, you often can avoid high blood pressure altogether...or if you already have the condition and are being treated with medication, you may be able to reduce your dosage and curb your risk for troubling side effects, such as fatigue, depression and erectile dysfunction.

The best foods for blood pressure control...

EAT MORE BANANAS

Bananas are among the best sources of potassium, a mineral that's crucial for blood pressure control. A typical banana contains

*In addition to smart eating habits, a blood pressure-controlling action plan includes regular exercise (ideally, 30 minutes of aerobic activity, such as brisk walking or swimming, at least five times a week) and a stress-reducing regimen.

about 450 mg of potassium, or about 10% of the amount of potassium most people should aim for each day.

Potassium works like a "water pill." It's a natural diuretic that enables the kidneys to excrete more sodium while also relaxing blood vessels—both functions help control blood pressure.

Scientific evidence: In a large study of nearly 250,000 adults published in the *Journal of the American College of Cardiology*, people who increased their intake of potassium by 1,600 mg daily were 21% less likely to suffer a stroke than those who ate less.

Kiwifruit also is a concentrated source of potassium with more than 200 mg in each small fruit.

Recommended daily amount of potassium: 4,700 mg. A good potassium-rich breakfast is oatmeal made with soy milk (300 mg), one cup of cantaloupe (430 mg), one cup of fresh-squeezed orange juice (496 mg) and one cup of coffee (116 mg).

Other good potassium sources: Potatoes (purple potatoes have the most), avocados, pistachios and Swiss chard.

Good rule of thumb: To control blood pressure, try to consume three times more potassium than sodium.

PILE ON THE SPINACH

Even if you eat plenty of bananas, all of that potassium won't lower your blood pressure unless you also get enough magnesium. It is estimated that about two-thirds of Americans are deficient in magnesium—and while magnesium supplements might help in some ways, they do not reduce blood pressure. Only magnesium from food—such as spinach, nuts, legumes and oatmeal—offers this benefit due to the nutrients' synergistic effect.

Recommended daily amount of magnesium: 500 mg. One cup of cooked spinach provides 157 mg of magnesium.

Also good: Two ounces of dry-roasted almonds (160 mg).

DIP INTO YOGURT

Calcium helps the body maintain mineral balance that regulates blood pressure. Calcium also contains a protein that works like a natural ACE inhibitor (one of the most common types of blood pressure medications) and prevents the constriction of blood vessels that raises blood pressure.

Important: Stick to low-fat or no-fat yogurt, milk and cheese—the saturated fat in whole-fat dairy products appears to cancel the blood pressure–lowering effects. In addition, opt for "plain" yogurt to avoid the added sugar that's found in many brands of yogurt. If you don't like the taste of plain yogurt, add a little granola, honey, nuts, seeds, fresh berries or banana.

For a tasty "pumpkin pie" snack: Add plain canned pumpkin, walnuts, pumpkin pie spice and Splenda to plain yogurt and top it with fat-free whipped cream.

Other high-calcium foods: Leafy greens and sardines (with the bones). Calcium supplements also can help keep blood pressure down, but recent research has linked them to increased cardiovascular risk. Talk to your doctor about these supplements.

Recommended daily amount of calcium: 1,000 mg for men age 51 to 70…1,200 mg for men age 71 and older, and women age 51 and older. Eating two fat-free yogurts (830 mg), one cup of cooked spinach (245 mg) and three kiwifruits (150 mg) will easily get you to your daily calcium goal.

ENJOY SOY

Soy foods, including tofu, soy nuts and soy milk, may be the most underrated blood pressure-lowering foods. Research shows that people who regularly eat soy can reduce their blood pressure as much as they would by taking some medications. Soy increases nitric oxide, a naturally occurring gas that lowers blood pressure.

Helpful: If you can't get used to the taste (or texture) of tofu, drink chocolate soy milk. An eight-ounce glass has 8 g of soy protein. Unsalted, dry-roasted soy nuts are an even richer source with about 10 g in a quarter cup.

Recommended daily amount of soy: 20 g to 25 g of soy protein. This translates to two to four servings of soy nuts or soy milk. Women at high risk or who are being treated for breast, ovarian or uterine cancer should discuss their soy intake with their doctors—it can affect hormone levels that can fuel these cancers.

SIP RED WINE

Too much alcohol increases risk for high blood pressure—as well as heart disease and stroke. In moderation, however, red wine relaxes arteries and reduces risk for diabetes, a condition that often increases blood pressure. White wine and other forms of alcohol also reduce blood pressure, but red wine is a better choice because it contains more heart-protecting antioxidants known as flavonoids.

You'll get significant flavonoids from wines with a deep red color, such as cabernets. Specifically, grapevines that face harsher sun exposure and nutrient deprivation produce more flavonoids—cabernet sauvignon tops the list.

Red wine also is high in resveratrol, another antioxidant. One glass of red wine contains enough resveratrol to stimulate the body's production of nitric oxide. Pinot noir wine has more resveratrol than other types.

Recommended daily limit for red wine: No more than two glasses for men or one glass for women.

For people who can't drink alcohol, purple grape juice has some flavonoids and resveratrol but doesn't contain the full benefit provided by red wine.

More blood pressure–friendly foods…

• **Celery.** Celery is a centuries-old traditional Chinese medicine treatment for high blood pressure, and various contemporary research studies affirm its benefit. Besides being rich in potassium, celery also contains 3-n-butyl phthalide, a compound that allows better blood flow by relaxing muscles in the walls of blood vessels.

• **Garlic.** A review article in the *Journal of Clinical Hypertension* called garlic "an agent with some evidence of benefit" in reducing high blood pressure, with some estimates saying that it can reduce blood pressure by 2%. Garlic contains the vasodilator and muscle-relaxing compound adenosine.

• **Beet juice.** Beets contain abundant nitrates, helpful in controlling blood pressure. Research from the Queen Mary University of London found that high blood pressure returned to normal levels when subjects were given two cups of beet juice per day.

• **Brown rice.** Recent research has shown that compounds in brown rice protect against hypertension by blocking an enzyme (angiotensin II) that increases blood pressure.

More from Dr. Bond Brill...

Slow Breathing Lowers Blood Pressure

You've probably heard that yoga, meditation and other forms of relaxation can reduce blood pressure.

An even simpler solution: Merely breathing more slowly, for just a few minutes a day, can do the same thing—and research shows that for some people, combining slow breathing with relaxation techniques can be as effective as drug therapy.

What to do: Once a day, take a little time to slow your breathing. Breathe in deeply for 10 seconds, then breathe out at the same rate. Repeat the cycle for 15 minutes.

Or try Resperate, an electronic breathing device that helps you synchronize your breathing ($300, *Resperate.com).*

The High-Fat Path to Low Blood Pressure...and a Healthier Heart

Study titled "Comparison of the DASH (Dietary Approaches to Stop Hypertension) Diet and a Higher-Fat DASH Diet on Blood Pressure and Lipids and Lipoproteins: A Randomized Controlled Trial" by researchers at Children's Hospital Oakland Research Institute, Oakland, California, and College of Pharmacy, Touro University California, Vallejo, published in *American Journal of Clinical Nutrition.*

The DASH diet is one of the most healthful diets ever created. And although it's pretty straightforward, it's still a restrictive.

It's low in fat, especially the saturated fat found in "real" dairy foods that we love so much. In particular, you're supposed to give up full-fat cheese and yogurt and whole milk in favor of low-fat and fat-free versions.

Not very tasty.

And, according to the latest study, not at all necessary.

MORE SATURATED FAT, LESS SUGAR

The DASH diet started out as a way to lower blood pressure—hence the name, an acronym for "Dietary Approaches to Stop Hypertension." That it does well. People who follow the diet have also been found to have less risk for heart disease, stroke, diabetes, kidney stones, colon cancer and dementia. Oh, yes, it's also great for weight loss.

The diet emphasizes plenty of fruits and vegetables, whole grains and low-fat dairy, along with lean poultry and fish, nuts, beans and seeds.

But it's also a low-fat diet, with a particular emphasis on keeping saturated fat low.

Here's the problem: Saturated fat, especially the kind found in dairy foods, doesn't appear to be bad for the heart. Meanwhile, sugar is—and the diet allowed sugar-laden fruit juices to be counted toward the fruit servings.

So the researchers wondered: What if we allowed DASH dieters to eat full-fat cheeses, high-fat yogurt and whole milk—while asking them to cut back on fruit juices and other sugar sources?

Bingo.

A TASTIER, HEALTHIER DIET

To test out the idea that full-fat dairy could make DASH both more palatable and just as healthy, researchers put 36 men and women on different diets over about two-and-a-half years—a control diet, similar to the standard American diet...a traditional low-fat DASH diet...or a high-fat DASH diet. By letting dieters have whole-fat dairy, the total fat went up from 27% in the traditional DASH to 40%...and saturated fat nearly doubled, from 8% to 14%. By cutting back on sugar, mainly from fruit juice, daily consumption went down from 158 grams a day on the traditional DASH to 93 grams.

No doubt, the high-fat DASH was tastier. But it was also just as effective at lowering blood pressure, both systolic and diastolic, as the low-fat DASH.

Plus, it had extra benefits: Compared with the low-fat, higher-sugar traditional DASH diet, it lowered triglycerides—blood fats that raise the risk for heart disease and diabetes. The high-fat DASH also was better at reducing very low density lipoprotein (VLDL), which is particularly associated with heart disease risk.

That makes this already heart-healthy diet even heart-healthier.

And more enjoyable.

The Natural Cures for High BP and Cholesterol

C. Norman Shealy, MD, PhD, founding president of the American Holistic Medical Association, a leading advocate for the use of holistic and integrative medicine by health-care providers. He is author of *The Healing Remedies Sourcebook. NormShealy.com*

Americans take an astonishing number of medications—an average of 26.5 million pills per hour. Medications do ease symptoms, but they do little to correct the root cause of most illnesses.

I have found that most patients do significantly better when they use natural therapies that restore physical as well as emotional balance. Of course, always check with your doctor before trying any new remedy.

***PROBLEM*: High blood pressure**.

***REMEDY*: L-arginine**.

L-arginine is an amino acid found in meats, grains, fish and other foods. When you take higher, supplemental doses, it increases blood levels of nitric oxide, which dilates arteries and reduces blood pressure. Studies have shown that patients who take L-arginine can reduce their blood pressure by 20 points or more. Also, L-arginine appears to reduce atherosclerosis, buildups in the arteries that lead to most heart attacks.

How to use it: Take 1,000 milligrams (mg) twice a day. Use a time-release form—it will stay active in the body throughout the day.

Caution: L'arginine can interact with some medications, including high blood pressure medications and nitroglycerin.

***PROBLEM*: High cholesterol**.

***REMEDY*: Sustained-release niacin**.

Cholesterol-lowering statin medications, such as *atorvastatin* (Lipitor) and *simvastatin* (Zocor), are very effective at reducing LDL (bad) cholesterol and reducing the risk for heart disease. But they're rife with side effects, including memory loss and muscle pain.

Better: Sustained-release niacin. Available over-the-counter, it is less likely to cause flushing than immediate-release niacin. It lowers LDL by about 20 points—the same as some statin doses. It also increases levels of HDL (the protective form of cholesterol), which is just as important for preventing a heart attack.

How to use it: Take 500 mg of sustained-release niacin with each meal—don't exceed 2,000 mg daily.

Caution: Patients should get their liver enzymes tested before taking niacin to establish a baseline liver function and again after about six months. Liver complications are rare, and if the tests are normal, you need to repeat the test only once a year. Never stop taking a statin without your doctor's OK.

Lower Blood Pressure with This Vitamin

Stephen Juraschek, an MD-PhD student in the department of epidemiology, Johns Hopkins University, Baltimore.

Andrew Rubman, ND, medical director, Southbury Clinic for Traditional Medicines, Southbury, Connecticut.

The study was published in the *American Journal of Clinical Nutrition*.

Many of us swallow a daily multivitamin and assume that we're getting all the vitamin C that we need.

After all, most multivitamins provide 100% of the USDA's recommended Dietary Reference Intake (DRI) per day for vitamin C—75 to 90 milligrams (mg).

So we're all set, right?

Well, a new analysis from Johns Hopkins University in Baltimore shows that getting even more than the DRI each day might go a long way in terms of reducing blood pressure or maintaining healthy blood pressure.

But how much is enough?

"C" IS FOR CONTROLLING PRESSURE

Scouring 45 years of medical literature, lead investigator Stephen Juraschek, a Hopkins MD-PhD student in epidemiology, and his colleagues looked at 29 clinical trials comparing blood pressure measurements among participants taking vitamin C supplements with those taking placebos. The range of supplementation taken was 60 mg per day to 4,000 mg per day—the median amount was 500 mg per day—so most subjects were taking far more than the USDA's recommended amount. Subjects took the supplements for, on average, eight weeks. Some had high blood pressure and some didn't.

Results: Participants with normal blood pressure who took vitamin C had 3.8 points lower systolic blood pressure (the top number of the reading), on average, than the placebo group and 1.5 points lower diastolic blood pressure (the bottom number of the reading), on average...and those with high blood pressure who took vitamin C had 4.9 points lower systolic, on average, and 1.7 points lower diastolic, on average.

These reductions may not be as significant as the results you might get from blood pressure medications, but if your blood pressure is only slightly high, the vitamin might help keep your pressure in a healthy range or help you take less or no medication.

Juraschek said that the dips in blood pressure are thought to result from vitamin C's action as a diuretic—it prompts the kidneys to excrete more salt and water from the body, which can relax blood vessels.

MAY HELP, WON'T HARM

Again, this research was a meta-analysis of many studies, and each study was conducted slightly differently, so Juraschek can't tell us exactly how much vitamin C is the ideal amount to take.

But since the people in the study were taking more than the USDA's recommended amount of vitamin C and their blood pressure was lowered, then should we all be taking more than 75 mg to 90 mg per day?

There's mixed advice from experts on the topic.

Juraschek takes a very cautious approach, saying that more research is needed before people increase how much vitamin C they take. He warned that doses larger than the USDA's recommendation could lead to diarrhea or kidney stones in some people, such as those prone to those problems.

But we're talking about vitamin C here! A vitamin that's good for you that is naturally in many healthy foods. Is so much caution necessary, given that vitamin C is, generally speaking, quite benign?

Excess vitamin C is excreted in urine, so how dangerous could it really be for most people?

According to Andrew Rubman, ND, medical director of the Southbury Clinic for Traditional Medicines in Southbury, Connecticut, people who are prone to diarrhea or kidney stones might have problems consuming extra vitamin C, so those people, in particular, may want to be cautious. "But that's not most of us," he said. "Chances are that most people—especially those who are prehypertensive (blood pressure between 120/80 and 139/89) or hypertensive (blood pressure of 140/90 or higher)—would benefit from taking more than 75 mg to 90 mg per day."

If you're interested in taking more vitamin C than you already do as a way of controlling blood pressure, discuss it with your doctor.

Reduce High Blood Pressure By Tapping Your Toes

Ann Marie Chiasson, MD, family practitioner and clinical assistant professor of medicine, Arizona Center for Integrative Medicine, University of Tucson. She is the author of *Energy Healing: The Essentials of Self-Care.* AnnMarieChiassonMD.com/

High blood pressure increases your risk not only for heart attack, heart failure and stroke, but also for grave maladies that you may never have considered, such as kidney failure, dementia, aneurysm, blindness and osteoporosis.

Yeah, medications help reduce blood pressure…but their nasty side effects can include joint pain, headache, weakness, dizziness, heart palpitations, coughing, asthma, constipation, diarrhea, insomnia, depression and erectile dysfunction!

There's a promising alternative therapy that's completely risk-free—and costs nothing—"tapping," which is based on the principles of Chinese medicine. *Here's how it works…*

SOMETHING OLD, SOMETHING NEW

The tapping method was described by Ann Marie Chiasson, MD, of the Arizona Center for Integrative Medicine. For her own patients with high blood pressure, Dr. Chiasson has adapted a tapping technique that is part of the ancient Chinese practice called qigong.

Qigong involves simple movements, including tapping on the body's meridians, or "highways" of energy movement. These meridians are the same as those used during acupuncture and acupressure treatments. According to a review of nine studies published in *The Journal of Alternative and Complementary Medicine*, qigong reduced systolic blood pressure (the top number) by an average of 17 points and diastolic blood pressure (the bottom number) by an average of 10 points. Those are big reductions! In fact, they are comparable to the reductions achieved with drugs—but the qigong had no unwanted side effects.

Though Dr. Chiasson has not conducted a clinical trial on her tapping protocol, she has observed reductions in blood pressure among her patients who practice tapping. The technique she recommends also could conceivably benefit people who do not have high blood pressure if it reduces stress and thus helps lower the risk of developing high blood pressure.

TAP AWAY

Some tapping routines are complicated, involving tapping the top of the head, around the eyes, side of the hand and under the nose, chin and/or arms. But Dr. Chiasson's technique is a simpler toe-and-torso method that is quite easy to learn. It is safe and can be done in the privacy of your own home—so if it might help you, why not give it a try?

First, you may want to get a blood pressure reading so you can do a comparison later on. If the tapping technique is helpful, you eventually may be able to reduce or even discontinue your high blood pressure drugs (of course, for safety's sake, you should not stop taking any drugs without first talking to your doctor about it).

Dr. Chiasson's plan: Each day, do five minutes of toe tapping (instructions below)…five minutes of belly tapping…and five minutes of chest tapping. You may experience tingling or a sensation of warmth in the part of the body being tapped and/or in your hands, which is normal. You can listen to rhythmic music during your tapping if you like. As you tap, try to think as little as possible, Dr. Chiasson said—just focus on your body, tapping and breath.

Rate: For each tapping location, aim for a rate of about one to two taps per second.

• **Toe tapping.** Lie flat on your back on the bed or floor. Keeping your whole body relaxed, quickly rotate your legs inward and outward from the hips (like windshield wipers), tapping the sides of your big toes together with each inward rotation. Tap as softly or as vigorously as you like.

• **Belly tapping.** Stand with your feet a little wider than shoulder-width apart. Staying relaxed, gently bounce up and down by slightly bending your knees. At the same time, tap softly with gently closed fists on the area below your belly button and above your pubic bone. Try to synchronize your movements to give one tap per knee bend.

• **Chest tapping.** Sit or stand comfortably. Using your fingertips, open hands or gently closed fists, tap all over your chest area, including the armpits. Tap as softly or as vigorously as you like without pushing past your comfort level.

Cautions: If you are recovering from hip or knee surgery, skip the toe tapping (which might strain your joint) and do only the belly tapping and chest tapping. If you are pregnant, stick with just the chest tapping—lying on your back during toe tapping could reduce blood flow to the fetus…and tapping on your belly may not feel comfortable and could stimulate the acupressure points used to induce labor, Dr. Chiasson said.

Follow-up: Continue your tapping routine for eight weeks, then get another blood pressure reading to see whether your numbers have improved. If they have—or if you simply enjoy the relaxing effects of the tapping—you might want to continue indefinitely.

Heart Attack Myths

Ronald M. Krauss, MD, senior scientist and director of atherosclerosis research at Children's Hospital Oakland Research Institute.

For years, we have been told that high cholesterol causes heart attacks. But that is a dangerous oversimplification.

What most people don't know: Nearly 50% of heart attack patients who are tested for cholesterol turn out to have normal levels, according to data from the large Framingham Heart study.

What's true—and what's not—about cholesterol and heart attack risk…

MYTH 1: **LDL cholesterol is always bad.** This type of cholesterol is often referred to simply as "bad" cholesterol. But we now know that LDL cholesterol isn't a single entity. Scientists have identified seven different subtypes, and there are probably more. Some

forms of LDL do contribute much more to atherosclerosis and heart attacks—others are not as harmful.

Yet the standard cholesterol tests don't make this distinction. A patient with high LDL is assumed to have an elevated risk for heart disease and probably will be treated with a cholesterol-lowering statin drug, even though his/her LDL might consist primarily of one of the less harmful forms.

Fact: Some LDL subtypes are large and buoyant—and less likely to cause heart disease than others that are small and dense. Small forms are most likely to settle into artery walls and cause inflammation and atherosclerosis, increasing risk for a heart attack.

Example: A person with high levels of Lp(a), an extremely dense form of LDL, is up to three times more likely to develop heart disease or have a heart attack than someone with lower levels, even when the total LDL is the same in both people.

Implication: Newer, expanded cholesterol tests that measure individual types of LDL particles may prove to be more useful than standard cholesterol tests. Lp(a) screening is not yet widely used—ask your doctor whether you should have it. Some insurers cover the cost of this test.

MYTH 2: **High cholesterol numbers mean high risk.** Depending on an individual's risks and other factors, optimal cholesterol is roughly defined as having a total number below 200 mg/dL…LDL below 100 mg/dL…and HDL, the so-called "good" cholesterol, greater than 40 mg/dL for men and 50 mg/dL for women.

Fact: The standard test numbers may matter less than experts once thought.

More important: The ratio of small-to-large LDL particles, known as the size pattern.

Patients with Pattern A have a higher concentration of large, buoyant particles. Those with Pattern B have a higher concentration of small, dense particles. A patient with Pattern A is at least three times less likely to develop heart disease than someone with Pattern B.

Implication: Don't assume that you need a statin drug just because your LDL is high.

Example: Suppose that your LDL is 160. If you happen to have Pattern A, taking a statin may provide only a modest benefit. If you happen to have the more dangerous Pattern B, taking a statin may not provide maximal benefit either, so other treatment may be necessary to reduce heart disease risk. Taking high doses of a statin may result in side effects such as muscle pain or weakness. Advanced lipid testing determines one's LDL size pattern.

MYTH 3: **Saturated fat is the enemy**. We've all been told that reducing dietary fat, particularly saturated fat, is among the most important ways to lower cholesterol and protect the heart.

Fact: A diet high in saturated fat clearly increases LDL. However, much of this increase is due to a corresponding increase in large, buoyant particles. In other words, saturated fat seems to trigger the less harmful Pattern A composition. Also, saturated fat increases the beneficial HDL cholesterol.

Implication: For years, Americans have been advised to keep their intake of dietary fat under 30% of total calories, with less than 7% of the fat calories coming from saturated fat. This now seems overly cautious. Americans who slightly exceed 10% saturated fat in their diets probably experience no increase in cardiovascular risks. However, people should avoid harmful trans fats in partially hydrogenated vegetable oils, found in packaged baked goods and fast foods.

MYTH 4: **It's OK to replace fat with carbohydrates**. Doctors have routinely advised patients to eat more carbs and less fat to help manage their cholesterol levels.

Fact: A high-carbohydrate diet may be more likely than a diet high in fat to increase cardiovascular risks.

Reason: Replacing fat with carbohydrates seems to shift LDL to the more dangerous Pattern B.

Important: Researchers suspect that it's mainly refined carbohydrates, such as soft drinks, white rice, white pasta, sugary desserts, etc., that cause this shift. Unprocessed carbohydrates that are high in fiber, such as whole grains, legumes, fruits and vegetables, are less likely to increase risk.

Implication: It's more important to cut back on refined carbohydrates than to cut back on fat. Danish researchers who followed 53,644 adults for an average of 12 years found that those who replaced saturated fat with refined carbohydrates were 33% more likely to have a heart attack. Those who ate healthier carbohydrates, on the other hand, had a slightly lower risk.

MYTH 5: **Statins are the best way to prevent a heart attack**. Estimates show that 20 million Americans take statin drugs, such as *atorvastatin* (Lipitor), *pravastatin* (Pravachol) and *simvastatin* (Zocor).

Fact: Even though statins do lower LDL, these drugs appear to have a limited ability to change LDL size pattern.

Implications: If you have high LDL, first control your diet and get more exercise. If your LDL level is still high, ask your doctor about advanced lipid testing to determine your LDL size pattern. Especially if you have Pattern B, discuss taking a statin with your doctor.

If necessary, also talk to your doctor about adding niacin. In high doses, niacin lowers Lp(a) by about 30% in some patients.

If you use niacin, you should be supervised by a physician and receive periodic blood tests to ensure that your liver is functioning properly. If too much niacin is taken, it can damage the liver.

New Cholesterol Drug Is Not a Statin

A new cholesterol-lowering drug is best for high-risk individuals. An FDA advisory panel has recommended approval of two PCSK9 inhibitors—*alirocumab* (Praluent) and *evolocumab* (Repatha). These drugs are for people with a genetic condition that causes LDL "bad" cholesterol to be extremely high and for others at high risk for heart disease who can't tolerate statins. Unlike statins, which reduce LDL by curtailing its production in the liver, PCSK9 inhibitors remove cholesterol from the bloodstream. Side effects are minor—mostly injection-site irritation. They can be used alone or in combination with statins—the combination can cut cholesterol 50% to 70% more than statins alone.

Michael D. Ozner, MD, medical director of wellness and prevention at Baptist Health South Florida, Miami, and author of *Heart Attack Proof* and *The Complete Mediterranean Diet.*

Eat Your Way to Low Cholesterol

Kenneth H. Cooper, MD, MPH, founder of the Cooper Clinic and The Cooper Institute for Aerobics Research, both in Dallas. A leading expert on preventive medicine and the health benefits of exercise, he is author of *Controlling Cholesterol the Natural Way.* The *"Father of Aerobics,"* CooperAerobics.com

If you have high cholesterol, your primary objective should be to find a way to lower it without drugs and their side effects. The good news is that just eating the right foods often can reduce cholesterol by 50 points or more.

Most people know to eat a low-fat diet, but there are certain foods that can help lower cholesterol that may surprise you…

MACADAMIA NUTS

Macadamia nuts are among the fattiest plant foods on the planet, about 76% total fat by weight. However, nearly all of the fat is monounsaturated. This type of fat is ideal because it lowers LDL (bad) cholesterol without depressing HDL (good) cholesterol.

A team at Hawaii University found that study participants who added macadamia nuts to their diets for just one month had total cholesterol levels of 191 milligrams/deciliter (mg/dL), compared with those eating the typical American diet (201 mg/dL). The greatest effect was on LDL cholesterol.

Macadamia nuts are higher than other nuts in monounsaturated fat, but all nuts are high in

vitamin E, omega-3 fatty acids and other antioxidants. Data from the Harvard Nurses' Health Study found that people who ate at least five ounces of any kind of nut weekly were 35% less likely to suffer heart attacks than those who ate less than one ounce per month.

Caution: Moderation is important because nuts—macadamia nuts, in particular—are high in calories. Limit servings to between one and two ounces daily—about a small handful a day.

RHUBARB

Rhubarb is ideal for both digestive health and lowering cholesterol because it contains a mix of soluble (see "Oats" later in this article) and insoluble fibers.

A study reported in *Journal of the American College of Nutrition* found that participants who ate a little less than three ounces of rhubarb daily for four weeks had an average drop in LDL cholesterol of 9%.

This tart-tasting vegetable isn't only an ingredient in pies. You can cut and simmer the stalks and serve rhubarb as a nutritious side dish (add some low-calorie strawberry jam for a touch of sweetness).

RICE BRAN

It's not as well known for lowering cholesterol as oats and oat bran, but rice bran is just about as effective and some people enjoy it more. A six-week study at University of California, Davis Medical Center found that people who ate three ounces daily of a product with rice bran had drops in total cholesterol of 8.3% and a reduction in LDL of 13.7%.

You can buy rice bran in most supermarkets—it's prepared like oatmeal. Or you can try prepared rice-bran breakfast cereals, such as Quaker Rice Bran Cereal and Kenmei Rice Bran.

RED YEAST RICE

Made from a yeast that grows on rice, red yeast rice contains monacolins, compounds that inhibit the body's production of cholesterol.

One study found that people who took red yeast rice supplements and did nothing else had drops in LDL of 23%. When the supplements were combined with healthy lifestyle changes, their LDL dropped by about 42%.

Red yeast rice may be less likely than statins to cause the side effect myopathy (a painful muscle disease).

Recommended dose: 600 milligrams (mg), twice daily. It is available online and at health-food stores.

GREEN TEA

Green tea is a concentrated source of polyphenols, which are among the most potent antioxidants. It can lower LDL cholesterol and prevent it from turning into plaque deposits in blood vessels. In one study, men who drank five cups of green tea daily had total cholesterol levels that were nine points lower than men who didn't drink green tea.

Three to five cups daily are probably optimal. Black tea also contains polyphenols but in lower concentrations than green tea.

VITAMINS C AND E

These vitamins help prevent cholesterol in the blood from oxidizing. Oxidized cholesterol is more likely to cling to artery walls and promote the development of atherosclerosis, the cause of most heart attacks.

I advise patients with high cholesterol to take at least 400 international units (IU) of d-alpha-tocopherol, the natural form of vitamin E, daily. You might need more if you engage in activities that increase oxidation, such as smoking.

For vitamin C, take 1,000 mg daily. People who get the most vitamin C are from 25% to 50% less likely to die from cardiovascular disease than those who get smaller amounts.

THE BIG THREE

In addition to the above, some foods have long been known to reduce cholesterol, but they are so helpful that they bear repeating again...

• **Cholesterol-lowering margarines.** I use Benecol every day. It's a margarine that contains stanol esters, cholesterol-lowering compounds that are extracted from plants such as soy and pine trees. About 30 grams (g) of Benecol (the equivalent of about three to four pats of butter) daily will lower LDL by about 14%.

Similar products, such as Promise Buttery Spread, contain sterol esters. Like stanols, they help block the passage of cholesterol from the digestive tract into the bloodstream. We used to think that sterols weren't as effective as stanols for lowering cholesterol, but they appear to have comparable benefits.

• **Oats.** They are among the most potent nutraceuticals, natural foods with medicine-like properties. Both oat bran and oatmeal are high in soluble fiber. This type of fiber dissolves and forms a gel-like material in the intestine. The gel binds to cholesterol molecules, which prevents them from entering the bloodstream. A Harvard study that analyzed the results of 67 scientific trials found that even a small amount of soluble fiber daily lowered total cholesterol by five points. People who eat a total of 7 g to 8 g of soluble fiber daily typically see drops of up to 10%. One and a half cups of cooked oatmeal provides 6 g of fiber. If you don't like oatmeal, try homemade oat bran muffins. Soluble fiber also is found in such foods as kidney beans, apples, pears, barley and prunes.

Also helpful: Psyllium, a grain that's used in some breakfast cereals, such as Kellogg's All-Bran Bran Buds, and in products such as Metamucil. As little as 3 g to 4 g of psyllium daily can lower LDL by up to 20%.

• **Fish.** People who eat two to three servings of fish a week will have significant drops in both LDL and triglycerides, another marker for cardiac risk. One large study found that people who ate fish as little as once a week reduced their risk for a sudden, fatal heart attack by 52%.

I eat salmon, tuna, herring and sardines. Other good sources of omega-3 fatty acids include walnuts, ground flaxseed, tofu and canola oil.

Fish-oil supplements may provide similar protection, but they are not as effective as the natural food, which contains other beneficial nutrients as well.

Tasty Nuts Reduce Cholesterol

Pistachios contain healthy fats and are rich in plant sterols, which inhibit cholesterol absorption. The nuts also are high in antioxidants—even higher than other nuts. Substituting one or two one-and-a-half-ounce servings of pistachios a day for fatty meats or other sources of saturated fat can lower LDL (bad) cholesterol by 10% to 12%.

Penny M. Kris-Etherton, PhD, Distinguished Professor of Nutrition, department of nutritional sciences, Penn State University, University Park, Pennsylvania, and leader of a study published in *The Journal of Nutrition.*

This Vitamin Supplement Fights Cholesterol

In a recent study, 120 adults (average age 47) with total cholesterol levels lower than 200 mg/dL (putting them at low-to-moderate risk for cardiovascular disease) followed a healthful diet while taking either a placebo or pantethine, a derivative of vitamin B-5.

Result: After 16 weeks, LDL "bad" cholesterol fell by 4% in the supplement group.

Implication: Because pantethine's side effects, such as gastrointestinal upset, are milder and less common than the side effects of statin drugs, which include muscle pain and increased risk for memory loss, the supplement may be useful for some patients.

John Rumberger, MD, PhD, director of cardiac imaging and lipid management program, Princeton Longevity Center, New Jersey.

Vitamin B-3 Beats Cholesterol Drug

Many cardiovascular disease patients who take cholesterol-lowering statins also take *ezetimibe* (Zetia) to further combat cholesterol.

Recent study: Ezetimibe reduced LDL "bad" cholesterol but also reduced HDL "good" cholesterol and had no effect on artery wall thickness. In comparison, among patients who took 2 grams (g) daily of niacin (vitamin B-3) instead of Zetia, LDL dropped…HDL rose… arterial wall thickness was reduced (a desirable effect)…and there were significantly fewer adverse cardiac events.

Best: Ask your internist or cardiologist about how to use niacin safely since the various B vitamins are best taken in a balanced combination.

Allen J. Taylor, MD, director of advanced cardiovascular imaging, Washington Hospital Center, Washington, DC, and leader of a study of 208 cardiovascular patients.

Berberine Can Lower Cholesterol by 30%

Berberine is a natural substance extracted from barberry, goldenseal, Oregon grape and other plants. It can be tried before going on cholesterol-lowering statin drugs, or it can be taken by statin users who need further cholesterol reductions.

Typical dosage: 500 milligrams (mg) to 1,000 mg daily. Consult your physician before starting any supplement.

Jacob Schor, ND, a naturopathic physician and primary health-care provider at Denver Naturopathic Clinic, Denver. He is author of a review of berberine published in *Natural Medicine Journal.*

Stop a Heart Attack Before It Happens: Watch Out for These Warning Signs

John A. Elefteriades, MD, the William W.L. Glenn Professor of Surgery and director of the Aortic Institute at Yale University and Yale–New Haven Hospital. He serves on the editorial boards of *The American Journal of Cardiology*, the *Journal of Cardiac Surgery, Cardiology* and *The Journal of Thoracic and Cardiovascular Surgery* and is the author of several books, including *Your Heart: An Owner's Guide.* HeartAuthorMD.com

Chest pain…shortness of breath…feeling faint…and/or discomfort in the arm—or even the neck, jaw or back. If you are overcome by such symptoms and perhaps even have an intense and sudden "sense of doom," you're likely to suspect a heart attack and rush to a hospital.

But wouldn't it be better to get a heads-up beforehand that a heart attack is on the way?

What most people don't realize: For about 60% of heart attack victims, warning symptoms do occur days or even weeks before the actual heart attack. But all too often, these signs are missed or shrugged off as something trivial.

What's behind this early-warning system? The blockage that creates a heart attack often develops over time and its symptoms, though they may be mild and elusive, should not be ignored.

Knowing the early red flags—including those you might not immediately connect to a heart problem—can allow you to see a doctor before a life-threatening heart attack occurs. Women, especially, can have symptoms that do not immediately bring heart disease to mind.

Important: If these symptoms are extreme and last for more than a few minutes—especially if they are accompanied by any of the more typical symptoms such as those described above—call 911. You could be having an actual heart attack. Even if these symptoms are mild to moderate but seem unexplained, call your doctor. If he/she cannot be reached but you're still concerned, go to the emergency room.

The following are examples of the subtle symptoms that can precede a heart attack—sometimes by days or weeks…

• **Fatigue.** If you feel more tired than usual, it's easy to tell yourself you're just growing older or getting out of shape. But pay attention! It could be the early-warning sign of heart trouble.

If your usual daily activities, whether it's walking the dog or cleaning the house, leave you feeling more tired than normal, talk to your doctor.

• **Flulike symptoms.** If you get hit with extreme fatigue, as well as weakness and/or feelings of light-headedness, you may think you're coming down with the flu. But people report having these same symptoms prior to a heart attack.

Call your doctor if you experience flulike symptoms but no fever (a telltale flu symptom).

Another clue: The flu generally comes on quickly, while flulike symptoms associated with heart disease may develop gradually.

• **Nausea and/or indigestion.** These are among the most overlooked symptoms of a heart attack—perhaps because they are typically due to gastrointestinal problems.

But if you are feeling sick to your stomach and throwing up, it could be a heart attack rather than food poisoning or some other stomach problem—especially if you're also sweating and your skin has turned an ashen color. If indigestion comes and goes, does not occur after a meal or doesn't improve within a day or so—especially if you're using antacids or antinausea medication—this could also mean heart problems. See a doctor.

• **Excessive perspiration.** If you are sweating more than usual—especially during times when you're not exerting yourself—it could mean that there are blockages. This can cause your heart to work harder, which may lead to excessive sweating. See your doctor. Clammy skin and night sweats also can be warning signs. This is likely to be a cold sweat, instead of the heat experienced in menopausal hot flashes. If sweating occurs with any of the classic heart attack symptoms described above, don't think twice—call 911.

• **Shortness of breath.** If you notice that you are beginning to feel more winded than usual, see your doctor. Shortness of breath can be a precursor to heart attack. If shortness of breath becomes stronger or lasts longer than usual, call 911. Shortness of breath may be your only symptom of a heart attack and may occur while you are resting or doing only minor physical activity.

• **Sexual dysfunction.** Men with heart problems that can lead to heart attack often have trouble achieving and/or keeping an erection. Because poor blood flow to the penis can be a sign of possible blockages elsewhere in the body, including the heart, erectile dysfunction can be an early-warning sign to get checked for cardiovascular disease. Men should absolutely discuss this symptom with their doctors.

More from Dr. Elefteriades

Women, Pay Attention!

After a woman goes through menopause—when the body's production of heart-protective estrogen declines—her risk for a heart attack dramatically increases.

Important facts for women: More women die of heart disease each year than men. Nearly two-thirds of women who died from heart attacks had no history of chest pain. The higher death rate for women is likely due to the fact that women don't seek medical attention as promptly as men because they are afraid of being embarrassed if the symptoms turn out to be nothing serious. Don't let this fear stop you from seeking immediate care. If the symptoms turn out to be nothing serious, the emergency medical team will be happy!

What to watch for: While most (but not all) men experience crushing or squeezing chest pain (usually under the breastbone), women are more likely to have no chest pain (or simply a feeling of "fullness" in the chest). Also, women are more likely than men to suffer dizziness, shortness of breath and/or nausea as the main symptoms of heart attack. Most

women (71%) experience sudden onset of extreme weakness that feels like the flu.

Flu Vaccine Reduces Heart Attack Risk

Recent Australian research found that people who had not been vaccinated against influenza and got the flu were almost twice as likely to experience a heart attack over a two-year period as people who had received the vaccine.

Likely reason: The flu can cause severe inflammation that leads to rupture of arterial plaque and the formation of potentially dangerous blood clots.

William Schaffner, MD, professor of medicine in infectious diseases, Vanderbilt University School of Medicine, Nashville.

Sunlight Helps Prevent Heart Attacks

Tobias Eckle, MD, PhD, associate professor of anesthesiology, cardiology, and cell and developmental biology, University of Colorado School of Medicine, Denver. His study was published in *Nature Medicine*.

Ah, sunlight. There's nothing like being outdoors on a summer morning.

What you may not know is that sunshine doesn't just boost your mood and your vitamin D level—it also may help you ward off a heart attack or minimize the damage that one can cause, according to a recent first-of-its-kind study.

Our circadian rhythm—the physical, mental and behavioral changes prompted by light and darkness that occur over each 24-hour period—helps determine the level of a certain protein that can minimize the cell damage and cell death caused by a heart attack. This protein might even stop a heart attack in its tracks.

In the study, researchers divided mice into two groups. One group was exposed to light boxes emitting light that was the same level of brightness as daylight ("bright light"), and others were exposed to regular room lighting ("regular light"). Both groups were exposed to the light first thing in the morning at 6:00 am.

Then the mice were given anesthesia and heart attacks were triggered in them. Researchers found that mice that had been exposed to three hours of "bright light" had three times the amount of the protective protein as the mice that had been exposed to "regular light"—and, incredibly, the "bright light" mice's hearts had experienced only one-fifth as much damage!

HOW SUNNY ARE THE FINDINGS?

There are, of course, unanswered questions—for example, how the findings might apply to humans and how lasting the benefit of the protein might be.

That said, the results are promising. What's especially interesting is that it's the light exposure on the eyes—not the skin—that affects the protein levels, said Dr. Eckle. So humans wearing sunscreen or long sleeves wouldn't blunt the effect.

SAFE WAYS TO LET IN THE LIGHT

Several forces have conspired over recent decades to keep people out of the sun during the day, such as indoor work and fear of skin cancer. But many people would be likely to benefit from getting more sunlight exposure as early in the morning as possible.

Here are some safe ways from Dr. Eckle to shed more light on your daily routine…

1. Take a daily walk outdoors, and keep wearing sunscreen. Even 10 to 20 minutes a day is better than nothing. Since, as I mentioned earlier, it's the way that light affects your eyes (not your skin) that matters, apply sunscreen—that won't dampen the benefits. The added exercise will boost your heart health, too.

2. Get sunlight while indoors. Sit near large, bright windows.

3. Use a light therapy box. If you can't follow either of the first two tips, or if you're at high risk for skin cancer and want to avoid UV rays at all costs, this may be the best option for you. Available online for about $50 and up, light therapy boxes mimic the brightness of sunlight while filtering out most damaging UV rays.

Lower Your Heart Disease Risk with Testosterone

Study titled "Cardiovascular Impact of Testosterone Therapy in Men with Low Testosterone Levels" by researchers at Intermountain Medical Center Heart Institute in Murray, Utah, presented at the 2014 annual meeting of the American Heart Association.

Low testosterone is considered a risk factor for cardiovascular disease in men, but doctors have been saying that testosterone replacement therapy isn't the answer. Instead of preventing heart attack and stroke, they say studies show that testosterone supplements can put you at risk for them. But a team from the Intermountain Medical Center Heart Institute at the University of Utah decided to take another look at the impact of testosterone supplements on cardiovascular health in men—and they came up with a different answer about testosterone therapy.

Their findings may be lifesaving.

A RAY OF HOPE

The researchers looked through 15 years of their institute's patient records to identify men given a diagnosis of low testosterone. They found 5,700 of them, of whom 28% had diabetes and 22% had coronary artery disease. The team then tracked the records of each of these men, whose average age was 62, for three years from the time of their low-testosterone diagnoses to see how many ultimately had a heart attack or stroke and how many died (either of cardiovascular disease or any cause). They also recorded and compared the men's testosterone levels and supplementation statuses over the three-year period.

The results: First, the researchers discovered that the overall rate of heart attack and stroke after three years was 9% and the overall death rate was 6%. From there, the researchers found that the men given testosterone replacement therapy whose testosterone levels increased to the normal range had a 55% reduced risk of heart attack and stroke and a 43% reduced risk of death compared with the men who had persistently low testosterone levels (either because they weren't on testosterone supplements or weren't responding to them strongly enough). The researchers cautioned that higher-than-normal testosterone levels, however, were associated with risk of heart attack or stroke.

PROCEED WITH CAUTION

This is good news for men with low testosterone. But the findings probably also mean that men should use testosterone supplements under careful supervision to make sure that they—and their doctors—know what their testosterone levels actually are and that they are taking the right amount of testosterone to get those levels to normal.

Unlike this study, studies showing a link between testosterone supplements and cardiovascular risk didn't always define why study participants were taking the supplements or whether their testosterone levels were being properly monitored. For example, a doctor might have prescribed a testosterone supplement to a man because the fellow was feeling tired and depressed and had sexual performance problems—but never have checked the man's testosterone level to make sure it was the reason for those symptoms. Or a doctor could have prescribed testosterone to a patient and never seen him again until side effects drove that patient back to his office. And testosterone supplementation does come with side effects, which can include breast enlargement and enlarged prostate and, as mentioned, high levels are associated with cardiovascular risks.

The bottom line is to not to fear testosterone replacement therapy, but to use it wisely. Rather than self-treat with testosterone

supplements, get a full health work-up from your doctor. If he or she thinks a testosterone supplement is right for you, discuss whether a bioidentical or a synthetic formulation is best—and make sure that he or she tests and keeps track of your testosterone levels while you are using the supplement.

Heart Attack: All About The Hidden Risk Factors

Robert M. Stark, MD, a preventive cardiologist in private practice in Greenwich, Connecticut. He is also a clinical assistant professor of medicine at the Yale University School of Medicine in New Haven, Connecticut, and medical director of the Cardiovascular Prevention Program at Greenwich Hospital (affiliated with the Yale New Haven Heart Institute). Dr. Stark is a Fellow of the American College of Cardiology.

We've all been told how important it is to control major risk factors for heart attack and coronary artery disease. We know, for example, not to smoke…to maintain LDL (bad) cholesterol at safe levels…raise HDL (good) cholesterol as high as possible…keep blood pressure below 120/80…and monitor our blood levels of C-reactive protein and homocysteine—a protein and amino acid that, when elevated, indicate increased heart attack risk.

What you may not know: Cardiovascular risk factors are synergistic, so any one of the risk factors mentioned above increases the effect of other risk factors.

Example: Even slightly elevated cholesterol or blood pressure becomes more dangerous in the presence of smaller, lesser-known risk factors such as…

•**Steroid medications.** Most people now know that nonsteroidal anti-inflammatory drugs, including the prescription medication *celecoxib* (Celebrex) and over-the-counter products such as *ibuprofen* (Advil) and *naproxen* (Aleve), increase heart attack and stroke risk by making blood platelets sticky. However, steroid drugs are perhaps the most dangerous of the "stealth" risk factors for heart attack.

Steroids, which include *cortisone, prednisone* and *prednisolone* (Orapred), are prescribed for inflammatory conditions such as colitis, inflammatory bowel disease, psoriasis, asthma and rheumatoid arthritis.

Besides raising cholesterol levels and blood pressure slightly, steroids also tend to promote the entry of cholesterol into the artery wall to form atherosclerotic plaque deposits.

Important: Only oral and injectable forms of steroid medications carry these risks—the inhaled form used to treat asthma does not.

Taking steroid medications also raises risk for atrial fibrillation, an irregular heartbeat associated with increased risk for stroke.

Self-defense: Avoid using oral and injectable steroids if at all possible. If you must use them, make sure your cholesterol levels and blood pressure are well-managed…take the lowest possible dose…and, whenever possible, avoid using them for more than a week or two.

Important: Abrupt discontinuation of steroids, without gradually tapering off, may cause serious side effects. Always consult your physician before stopping a steroid medication.

•**Stress.** Both chronic and acute stress can be hard on the heart—but in slightly different ways.

Chronic stress, such as from ongoing financial pressures or a strained relationship, raises blood levels of the stress hormones epinephrine (adrenaline), norepinephrine and cortisol, accelerating buildup of dangerous plaque in the coronary arteries much as steroid drugs do.

Self-defense: Address the underlying cause of the chronic stress…engage in daily aerobic exercise, which burns off excess epinephrine in the bloodstream and reduces anxiety…and practice stress-reduction techniques, such as biofeedback and meditation, which have been shown to lower epinephrine and norepinephrine levels.

Acute stress, such as from the sudden death of a spouse, not only increases stress hormones but also causes the coronary arteries to constrict. In addition, acute stress increases the heart's need for, and consumption of, oxygen. If you already have a partially blocked coronary artery due to plaque buildup, this constriction and increased oxygen consumption can contribute to a dangerous shortage of blood flow to the heart.

Self-defense: If you are confronted with acute or chronic stress, ask your doctor to consider prescribing a beta-blocker, such as *propranolol* (Inderal), *atenolol* (Tenormin) or *metoprolol* (Lopressor). These drugs are typically used to treat heart conditions and high blood pressure. However, beta-blockers also protect against the harmful arterial effect that occurs with stress and can be taken as long as stress-related symptoms occur. These drugs are not recommended for those with low blood pressure, asthma or abnormally low heart rate.

•**Sleep apnea.** People who suffer from this condition stop breathing during their sleep for a few seconds at a time many times per night. Sleep apnea not only disrupts sleep but also is associated with an increased risk for heart attack and heart disease.

Self-defense: Half of people with mild sleep apnea (those who stop breathing five to 15 times per hour) and 20% of those with moderate apnea (15 to 30 breathing stoppages per hour) have so-called positional sleep apnea—that is, the disturbed breathing occurs only when the person is sleeping on his/her back.

Good solution: A relatively new strap-on foam device called Zzoma, which forces you to lie on your side, appears to help prevent positional sleep apnea (available for $189.95 from the manufacturer at 877-799-9662 or *zzomasleep.com*).

For more serious cases, continuous positive airway pressure (CPAP), a type of therapy in which the sleeper wears a mask that blows air into his nostrils, helps reduce apnea symptoms. For those who find the CPAP mask uncomfortable, oral appliances, prescribed by dentists, also help reduce apnea symptoms.

•**Anemia.** With this condition, the blood's ability to carry oxygen is impaired. This can trigger chest pain (angina) or even a heart attack in people whose coronary arteries are partially blocked. Always seek immediate medical attention if you have chest pain.

Self-defense: Anemia often can be treated with iron, vitamin B-12 or folic acid supplements or medications. After you've sought medical attention for chest pain, be sure that your physician tests you for anemia.

•**Chlamydia infection.** Chlamydia pneumoniae is a bacterium found in the respiratory tract of more than two million Americans. Different from the germ that causes the sexually transmitted disease chlamydia, C. pneumoniae is associated with increased risk for coronary artery disease, possibly because it contributes to arterial inflammation.

Self-defense: If you have signs of a respiratory infection, your doctor may want to order a blood test for C. pneumoniae. Antibiotics can effectively treat an infection caused by this bacterium.

•**Vitamin K deficiency.** Vitamin K (found mostly in meats, cheeses and leafy green vegetables) has been shown to reduce cardiovascular risk in people by more than 50% and also has prevented hardening of the arteries in animal studies. Vitamin K is also produced by the bacteria naturally residing in the intestine. Researchers have found, however, that most people don't get enough vitamin K in their diets.

Self-defense: To ensure that you get enough of this crucial vitamin, ask your doctor about taking a high-dose vitamin K supplement (100 mcg daily for adults). Because vitamin K can reduce the effects of blood-thinning medication, it is never recommended for people taking *warfarin* (Coumadin) or other blood thinners.

•**Horizontal earlobe creases.** Though no one knows why, some research has shown that people who have a horizontal crease in one or both of their earlobes may be at increased risk for coronary artery disease.

Self-defense: While there's nothing that can be done to change this risk factor, anyone with such creases should be especially careful about monitoring other cardiovascular risk factors.

Do You Have a Heart Attack Gene?

Bradley F. Bale, MD, cofounder of the Heart Attack & Stroke Prevention Center, Nashville, and medical director of the Heart Health Program, Grace Clinic, Lubbock, Texas. He is coauthor, with Amy Doneen, ARNP, and Lisa Collier Cool, of *Beat the Heart Attack Gene: The Revolutionary Plan to Prevent Heart Disease, Stroke, and Diabetes.*

Even if you do everything right—you don't smoke, you're not overweight and you manage your cholesterol and blood pressure—your odds of having a heart attack might be higher than you think.

An eye-opening case: One of our patients, a 44-year-old executive whom we nicknamed "Superman," looked very healthy. His Framingham Risk Score—a standard measure of heart disease risk predicted that he had only a 1% risk of having a heart attack over the next 10 years. That should have been good news—except that other tests we did, which most doctors do not routinely give, showed that his real risk was about 40 times higher.

THE TESTS YOU NEED

Many of the tests that are used to detect heart disease are decades old. Some look for risk factors (such as arterial narrowing) that have less to do with the actual risk of having a heart attack than most people think. Many of the tests that can make a difference still aren't used by most doctors.

Most cardiologists routinely recommend angiography, an imaging test that looks for large blockages in the coronary arteries. If a blockage of 70% or more is found, a patient might be advised to receive a stent or undergo a bypass, surgical procedures that don't always help and can have a high rate of complications.

Severely blocked arteries can be a problem, but a more common, and typically overlooked, threat is from small deposits inside artery walls. A patient might have dozens or even hundreds of deposits that are too small to be detected with angiography.

The risk: When these "hidden" deposits are exposed to inflammation—triggered by insulin resistance, smoking, a poor diet or stress, for example—they can rupture, tear the blood vessel lining and trigger a clot, the cause of most heart attacks.

New approaches: Doctors can now predict the risk for a heart attack with far more accuracy than in the past—if you know which tests to ask for. Tests I recommend…

•**Carotid intima-media thickness (CIMT).** This is an effective way to measure atherosclerosis inside an artery wall (between the intima and media layers). The FDA-approved test uses an ultrasound wand to look for the thickening of the carotid arteries that occurs when plaque between the two layers accumulates and pushes outward.

An isolated area of thickness measuring 1.3 mm or greater indicates plaque—and an increased risk for a heart attack or stroke.

Most patients who have excessive arterial thickening will be advised by their doctors to exercise more, eat a healthier diet and take a daily baby aspirin to reduce the risk for clots. A cholesterol-lowering statin drug also may be prescribed.

•**Genetic tests.** More than half of all Americans have one or more gene variations that increase the risk for a heart attack and a stroke. According to research published in *Circulation*, up to 70% of patients who are given the genetic tests described below will be reclassified as having a higher heart attack risk than their doctors originally thought. The cost of testing has dropped to about $100 per gene. Your insurance may cover the cost. *Important gene tests…*

•**9P21.** If you inherit two copies of this "heart attack gene" (one from each parent), your risk of developing heart disease or having a heart attack at an early age (in men, under age 45…in women, under age 55) is 102% higher than that of someone without the gene.

And increased risk continues if you are already past these ages.

You'll also have a 74% increased risk for an abdominal aortic aneurysm, a dangerous weakening in the heart's largest blood vessel. If you test positive, your doctor will advise earlier and more frequent abdominal aortic ultrasounds. If you smoke, stop now. Most aortic aneurysms occur in smokers.

You should also exercise for at least 22 minutes daily (the amount found in research to be protective) and maintain healthy cholesterol and blood pressure levels.

Important: Patients with the 9P21 gene often are advised to have an ankle-brachial index test, which involves measuring blood pressure in the arms and ankles. It's used to diagnose peripheral artery disease (PAD), plaque buildups in the legs that quadruple or even quintuple the risk for a heart attack or stroke.

•**Apo E.** This gene affects how your body metabolizes nutrients. There are different types of Apo E. The 3/3 genotype—64% of Americans have it—increases cardiovascular disease, but not as much as the 3/4 or 4/4 types. Those with 3/4 or 4/4 need to eat a very low-fat diet (with no more than 20% of calories from fat). Those with the 3/3 genotype are advised to eat a Mediterranean-style diet—focusing mainly on plant foods…fish…and olive oil.

∗**KIF6.** Patients with the so-called arginine gene variant have up to a 55% increased risk for cardiovascular disease. There are no particular lifestyle changes known to be especially helpful for these patients. It's also useful to know if you're a noncarrier of KIF6—as such, you won't receive significant risk reduction if you are prescribed either *atorvastatin* (Lipitor) or *pravastatin* (Pravachol), two of the most popular statin drugs. Instead, you'll need a different statin, such as *lovastatin*.

ANOTHER CRUCIAL TEST

An oral glucose tolerance test can detect insulin resistance years or even decades before it progresses to diabetes. But many doctors still use the simpler A1C test. It's more convenient—it doesn't require fasting—but it often fails to detect insulin resistance, one of the main causes of heart attacks and strokes. Insulin resistance leads to inflammation that can trigger plaques to rupture and form clots.

With an oral glucose tolerance test, your blood sugar is measured. Then you drink a sweet solution, and your blood sugar is measured again two hours later. A level of 100 mg/dL to 139 mg/dL could indicate insulin resistance. Higher levels may indicate prediabetes—or, if they're high enough, full-blown diabetes.

Next steps: Regular exercise is critical if you have insulin resistance or diabetes.

Also helpful: Weight loss, if needed, reduced intake of sugary beverages and foods, and a diet rich in fruits, vegetables and grains.

Antacids That Can Cause a Heart Attack

Popular antacids are associated with heart attack, says Nigam H. Shah, MBBS, PhD. Analysis of the medical records of more than three million people found that taking proton pump inhibitors (PPIs), such as Prilosec, Protonix and Nexium, had a modest association (20%) with heart attack risk. The analysis showed no increased heart attack risk among patients taking acid-suppressing histamine blockers, such as Tagamet, Pepcid and Zantac.

Nigam H. Shah, MBBS, PhD, assistant professor of medicine, Biomedical Informatics Research at Stanford University School of Medicine, California, and leader of a data analysis published in *PLOS ONE.*

Calcium Supplements May Cause Heart Attacks

According to a recent study, people who took calcium supplements were more than twice as likely to have heart attacks as people who did not take the supplements. (Foods with added calcium were not studied.)

Best: Get calcium naturally from foods such as dairy products, sardines and kale.

Sabine Rohrmann, PhD, MPH, head of cancer epidemiology and prevention at Institute of Social and Preventive Medicine, University of Zurich, Switzerland, and coauthor of a study of 23,980 people, published in *Heart.*

How to Avoid a Heart Attack in Extreme Weather

Barry A. Franklin, PhD, director of preventive cardiology and rehabilitation at William Beaumont Hospital in Royal Oak, Michigan. He has served as president of the American Association of Cardiovascular and Pulmonary Rehabilitation and the American College of Sports Medicine. Dr. Franklin is coauthor of *109 Things You Can Do to Prevent, Halt & Reverse Heart Disease.*

The arctic blast that brought tundralike temperatures to much of the country last winter has left behind more than frozen pipes and frost-nipped noses. During a typical winter, there are up to 36% more circulatory-related deaths than during warmer months.

And it's not just cold weather that puts you at risk. Researchers have identified other types of weather—throughout the year—that trigger spikes in hospitalizations and death.

For details on the effects that weather can have on your heart, we spoke to Barry A. Franklin, PhD, a leading expert in cardiac rehabilitation.

We hear a lot about cold weather being hard on the heart. At what temperature does this really become an issue? When it's cold enough to wear a winter jacket, it is cold enough to think about the health of your heart. In fact, research that was recently presented at the European Society of Cardiology Congress 2013 shows that the risk of having a heart attack increases by 7% for every 18°F drop below 73°F.

Why exactly is cold weather so dangerous? Cold temperatures cause blood vessels throughout the body to temporarily constrict, raising blood pressure. Since the arteries that supply the heart are only about the thickness of cooked spaghetti, even a slight narrowing can cause reduced blood flow.

Winter temperatures aren't generally a problem if you are young and active. But risk rises as you hit middle age and beyond. The risk is highest for adults who are ages 65 and older, particularly those with underlying health problems, such as diabetes, obesity or preexisting heart disease. For people in these groups, spending even a few minutes in below-freezing temperatures can trigger a 20- to 50-point rise in blood pressure.

That's why I advise older adults, in particular, to stay indoors on the coldest days if possible. When you do go outdoors, don't depend on a light jacket—you should really bundle up by wearing a hat and gloves and dressing in multiple loose layers under your coat. Each layer traps air that's been heated by the body and serves as insulation.

And what about hot weather—does it harm the heart? Actually, heat kills more people every year than any other type of weather.

High temperatures, generally above 80°F, but especially greater than 90°F, can cause heat syncope (sudden dizziness and/or fainting)…heat edema (swelling in the feet/ankles)…and heat stroke, in which the body's core temperature can rise above 104°F. People with atrial fibrillation or dementia are at a 6% to 8% increased risk of dying on hot days. Dementia affects the brain's ability to regulate the body's heat response.

Why is strenuous exertion so dangerous for many people during weather extremes? Snow shoveling provides a good example. This activity creates a "perfect storm" of demands on the heart. With snow shoveling, the real danger—particularly for those who are older and/or sedentary—is the exertion itself.

Moving snow is hard work. Each shovelful weighs about 16 pounds (including the weight of the shovel). If you lift the shovel once every five seconds and continue for 10 minutes, you'll have moved nearly one ton

of snow. This exertion can have adverse effects on the heart.

Here's why: Snow shoveling involves isometric exercise and unaccustomed muscle tension, which increases heart rate and blood pressure. Your legs may stay "planted" when you shovel, which allows blood to pool and reduces circulation to the heart.

Also, people tend to hold their breath (this is known as a Valsalva maneuver, and it often occurs when people are straining to lift heavy loads) when they are wielding a shovel, which causes a further rise in heart rate and blood pressure. That's why every year, we read or hear about people who dropped dead while shoveling snow.

Is there any way to reduce the risk associated with snow shoveling? If you have or suspect you have heart disease, I suggest that you don't shovel your own snow. Hire someone to do it for you.

If you are in good shape and want to shovel your own snow, it may be safer in the afternoon. In general, most heart attacks occur between 6 am and 10 am, when heart rate and blood pressure tend to be higher. You're also more likely to form blood clots early in the day.

Then be sure to shovel slowly…work for only a few minutes at a time…and keep your legs moving to circulate blood. And remember, it's best to push snow rather than lift it. This helps keep your legs moving and takes less exertion than lifting. There are snow shovels designed for pushing snow.

What types of exertion are especially dangerous during hot weather? Racket sports, water skiing, marathon running and certain highly competitive sports seem to be associated with a greater incidence of cardiac events in hot, humid weather. Why? Heart rates are disproportionately increased. Electrolytes, such as sodium and potassium, also are lost, which can lead to dangerous heart rhythms.

What steps should people take to protect themselves in hot weather? Everyone knows to drink water when it's hot. But even people who are consciously trying to stay hydrated often do not drink enough. Drink plenty of cool liquids before, during and after heat exposure. If you're sweating a lot, you might want to drink an electrolyte-rich sports drink such as Gatorade or Powerade. And be sure to wear lightweight, loose-fitting clothing when you go outdoors.

In addition, think about any medications you may be taking. Many common drugs, including certain antihistamines and antidepressants, have anticholinergic effects—they inhibit your body's ability to cool off.

To help your body adapt to heat and humidity: As the weather grows hotter, gradually increase your daily exposure to the heat. The body's circulation and cooling efficiency increases, generally in eight to 14 days. Afterward, the body is better able to cope with extremes in heat and humidity.

Resting Heart Rate Linked to Heart Attack

In a recent study of 130,000 postmenopausal women, those with a resting heart rate of more than 76 beats per minute (bpm) were 26% more likely, on average, to suffer a heart attack than those with a resting heart rate of 62 bpm or less. Previous research has shown a similar finding in men.

Self-defense: If your doctor has told you that you have a high resting heart rate, discuss treatments to help keep your heart healthy.

To check your own resting heart rate: Sit quietly for five minutes. Then place your index and middle fingers on the inside of your wrist at the base of your thumb. Count how many beats occur in 15 seconds and multiply this number by four.

Judith Hsia, MD, professor of medicine and director of the Lipid Research Clinic, George Washington University, Washington, DC.

Five Foods Proven to Prevent Heart Attacks

Bonnie T. Jortberg, RD, CDE, senior instructor, department of family medicine at University of Colorado at Denver and Health Sciences Center. She was program director of Colorado Weigh, a weight-loss and healthy-living program offered throughout the Denver metropolitan area. She is coauthor of *The Step Diet Book*.

Cardiovascular disease is still the number-one killer in America. It accounts for about 37% of all deaths, according to the American Heart Association.

Most of us know that a diet rich in fruits, vegetables and whole grains and low in saturated animal fats lowers the risk of heart disease. But certain foods have been shown to be particularly beneficial. Of course, no food is a magic bullet—you still need to exercise daily and maintain a healthy weight—but eating the recommended amounts of the following can go a long way toward preventing heart disease...

SPINACH

Like most fruits and vegetables, spinach is rich in vitamins and minerals. What makes spinach stand out for keeping the heart healthy is folate, one of the B vitamins. According to several studies, including an extensive report from the Harvard School of Public Health, folate helps prevent the buildup of homocysteine, an amino acid in the blood that is a major risk factor for heart disease and stroke.

How much: Two cups of raw spinach (about two ounces) has 30% of the daily value (DV) for folate...one-half cup of cooked spinach provides 25%. Frozen and fresh spinach are both good, but beware of canned spinach—it may have excessive amounts of salt. Too much salt increases blood pressure, and high blood pressure is another major risk factor for cardiovascular disease.

Alternatives: Asparagus. Four spears have 20% of the DV of folate. Also, many breakfast cereals are fortified with folate—check the labels.

SALMON

Salmon is rich in omega-3 fatty acids. Omega-3s reduce inflammation and make your blood less "sticky," which prevents plaque—fatty deposits—from clogging your arteries. Having unclogged arteries reduces the risk of heart attack and stroke.

How much: The American Heart Association recommends two to three three-ounce servings of salmon a week. Fresh or frozen, farmed or wild, is fine, but go easy on canned salmon, which may be high in salt.

Alternatives: Other cold-water fish high in omega-3 fatty acids include mackerel, lake trout, sardines, herring and albacore tuna. If you don't like fish, have one teaspoon of ground flaxseeds daily—sprinkle on cereal, yogurt or salads, and drink plenty of water to avoid constipation.

TOMATOES

Tomatoes are loaded with lycopene, a carotenoid that gives them their color. Lycopene reduces cholesterol in the body. Too much cholesterol can lead to atherosclerosis (hardening of the arteries), which decreases blood flow to the heart—and that can lead to heart attack and stroke.

Cooked and processed tomato products, such as spaghetti sauce and tomato juice, provide the greatest benefits. Researchers at Cornell University found that cooking or processing tomatoes boosts lycopene levels and makes lycopene easier for the body to absorb. Look for low-sodium or no-salt-added products.

If you like ketchup, another source of lycopene, buy an organic brand, made with pure cane sugar, not processed high-fructose corn syrup. Organic ketchup can contain up to three times as much lycopene as nonorganic brands, according to a study published by the United States Department of Agriculture. Other organic tomato products weren't studied, so it is not yet known if they're also higher in lycopene.

How much: One cup of tomato juice (about 23 milligrams, or mg, of lycopene) or one-half cup of tomato sauce (20 mg) daily. A medium raw tomato has 4.5 mg.

Alternative: Watermelon (one and a half cups of cut-up watermelon contain 9 mg to 13 mg of lycopene).

OATMEAL

Oatmeal is one of the best and most studied sources of soluble fiber. Soluble fiber absorbs water and turns to gel during digestion. It then acts like a sponge to absorb excess cholesterol from your body. That's good for your heart. Studies show that five grams (g) to 10 g of soluble fiber a day can reduce LDL "bad" cholesterol by about 5%.

Soluble fiber also helps remove saturated fat in your digestive tract before your body can absorb it. That's also good for your heart.

How much: One and a half cups of cooked oatmeal daily. This provides 4.5 g of fiber, enough to lower cholesterol. Rolled oats and steel-cut oatmeal work equally well to help lower cholesterol, but beware of flavored instant oatmeal—it is likely to have sugar added. Too much sugar in your diet increases the chance of inflammation, a risk factor for atherosclerosis. Sugar also can lead to weight gain, which is another risk factor for cardiovascular disease.

Alternatives: Kidney beans and brussels sprouts each have three grams of soluble fiber per one-half cup cooked.

POMEGRANATES

Pomegranates are loaded with polyphenols, antioxidants that neutralize free radicals, which can damage the body's cells. Polyphenols help maintain cardiovascular health by scooping up free radicals before they damage arteries. They also are believed to reduce LDL "bad" cholesterol. Red wine and purple grape juice are great sources of polyphenols, but pomegranates have the highest amount.

How much: 1.5 ounces of concentrated pomegranate juice daily. This is the amount used in most studies. Look for products that are labeled 100% juice, or concentrated, with no added sugar.

Caution: Pomegranate juice may affect the metabolism of prescription drugs and may cause blood pressure to decrease too much when combined with certain blood pressure medications. Check with your doctor.

Alternatives: Red wine (no more than two five-ounce glasses a day for men and one for women) and purple grape juice (four to six ounces a day).

Six Ways to Liven Up Your Heart-Healthy Diet

Janet Bond Brill, PhD, RD, an expert in nutrition and cardiovascular disease prevention based in Valley Forge, Pennsylvania. She is the author of *Prevent a Second Heart Attack*. DrJanet.com

Just about everyone knows that a Mediterranean-style diet can help prevent heart disease. Even if you've already had a heart attack, this style of eating—emphasizing such foods as fish and vegetables—can reduce the risk for a second heart attack by up to 70%.

Problem: About 80% of patients with heart disease quit following dietary advice within one year after their initial diagnosis. That's often because they want more choices but aren't sure which foods have been proven to work.

Solution: Whether you already have heart disease or want to prevent it, you can liven up your diet by trying foods that usually don't get much attention for their heart-protective benefits...

SECRET 1: Popcorn. It's more than just a snack. It's a whole grain that's high in cholesterol-lowering fiber. Surprisingly, popcorn contains more fiber, per ounce, than whole-wheat bread or brown rice.

Scientific evidence: Data from the 1999–2002 National Health and Nutrition Examination Survey found that people who eat popcorn daily get 22% more fiber than those who don't eat it.

Important: Eat "natural" popcorn, preferably air-popped or microwaved in a brown paper bag, without added oil. The commercially prepared popcorn packets generally contain too much salt, butter and other additives. Three cups of popped popcorn, which contain almost 6 g of fiber and 90 calories, is considered a serving of whole grains. Studies have shown that at least three servings of whole grains a day (other choices include oatmeal and brown rice) may help reduce the risk for heart disease, high cholesterol and obesity.

SECRET 2: Chia seeds. You're probably familiar with Chia pets—those terra-cotta figures that sprout thick layers of grassy "fur." The same seeds, native to Mexico and Guatemala, are increasingly available in health-food stores. I consider them a superfood because they have a nutrient profile that rivals heart-healthy flaxseed.

In fact, chia seeds contain more omega-3 fatty acids than flaxseed. Omega-3s increase the body's production of anti-inflammatory eicosanoids, hormonelike substances that help prevent "adhesion molecules" from causing plaque buildup and increasing atherosclerosis.

Scientific evidence: A study published in the *Journal of the American College of Cardiology*, which looked at nearly 40,000 participants, found that an omega-3 rich diet can prevent and even reverse existing cardiovascular disease.

Other benefits: One ounce of chia seeds has 10 g of fiber, 5 g of alpha-linolenic acid and 18% of the Recommended Dietary Allowance for calcium for adults ages 19 to 50.

Chia seeds look and taste something like poppy seeds. You can add them to baked goods, such as muffins, or sprinkle them on salads and oatmeal or other cereals.

SECRET 3: Figs. They're extraordinarily rich in antioxidants with an oxygen radical absorbance capacity (ORAC) score of 3,383. Scientists use this ORAC scale to determine the antioxidant capacity of various foods. An orange, by comparison, scores only about 1,819. Fresh figs are among the best sources of beta-carotene and other heart-healthy carotenoids.

Scientific evidence: In a study published in the *Journal of the American College of Nutrition*, two groups of participants were "challenged" with sugary soft drinks, which are known to increase arterial oxidation. Oxidation in the arteries triggers atherosclerosis, a main risk factor for heart disease. Those who were given only soda had a drop in healthful antioxidant activity in the blood…those who were given figs as well as soda had an increase in blood antioxidant levels.

Bonus: Ten dried figs contain 140 mg of calcium. Other compounds in figs, such as quercetin, reduce inflammation and dilate the arteries. Perhaps for these reasons, people who eat figs regularly have much less heart disease than those who don't eat them, according to studies. Most dried figs contain added sulfites, so it's best to buy organic, sulfite-free dried figs.

SECRET 4: Soy protein. Tofu, soy milk and other soy foods are "complete proteins"—that is, they supply all of the essential amino acids that your body needs but without the cholesterol and large amount of saturated fat found in meat.

Scientific evidence: People who replace dairy or meat protein with soy will have an average drop in LDL "bad" cholesterol of 2% to 7%, according to research from the American Heart Association. Every 1% drop in LDL lowers heart disease risk about 2%.

A one-half cup serving of tofu provides 10 g of protein. An eight-ounce glass of soy milk gives about 7 g. Edamame (steamed or boiled green soybeans) has about 9 g per half cup. Avoid processed soy products, such as hydrogenated soybean oil (a trans fat), soy isoflavone powders and soy products with excess added sodium.

SECRET 5: Lentils. I call these "longevity legumes" because studies have shown that they can literally extend your life. Best choices: Brown or black lentils.

Lentils contain large amounts of fiber, plant protein and antioxidants along with folate, iron and magnesium—all of which are important for cardiovascular health.

Scientific evidence: A Harvard study found that people who ate one serving of cooked beans (one-third cup) a day were 38% less likely to have a heart attack than those who ate beans less than once a month.

Caution: Beans have been shown to cause gout flare-ups in some people.

Important: Lentils cook much faster than other beans. They don't need presoaking. When simmered in water, they're ready in 20 to 30 minutes. You need about one-half cup of cooked lentils, beans or peas each day for heart health.

SECRET 6: Pinot Noir and Cabernet Sauvignon. All types of alcohol seem to have some heart-protective properties, but red wine offers the most.

Scientific evidence: People who drink alcohol regularly in moderation (one five-ounce glass of wine daily for women, and no more than two for men) have a 30% to 50% lower risk of dying from a heart attack than those who don't drink, according to research published in *Archives of Internal Medicine*.

Best choices: Pinot Noir, Cabernet Sauvignon and Tannat wines (made from Tannat red grapes). These wines have the highest concentrations of flavonoids, antioxidants that reduce arterial inflammation and inhibit the oxidation of LDL cholesterol. Oxidation is the process that makes cholesterol more likely to accumulate within artery walls.

Bonus: Red wines also contain resveratrol, a type of polyphenol that is thought to increase the synthesis of proteins that slow aging. Red wine has 10 times more polyphenols than white varieties.

In a four-year study of nearly 7,700 men and women nondrinkers, those who began to drink a moderate amount of red wine cut their risk for heart attack by 38% compared with nondrinkers.

If you are a nondrinker or currently drink less than the amounts described above, talk to your doctor before changing your alcohol intake. If you cannot drink alcohol, pomegranate or purple grape juice is a good alternative.

Chocolate Helps Heart Attack Patients

Survivors of a first heart attack who ate chocolate at least twice weekly were 66% less likely to die from heart disease than those who never ate chocolate. Other sweets were not linked to reduced mortality.

Theory: Antioxidants in cocoa improve blood pressure and blood flow. If you eat dessert, consider chocolate—but keep portions small to avoid weight gain.

Imre Janszky, MD, PhD, postdoctoral research fellow, department of public health sciences, Karolinska Institute, Stockholm, Sweden, and leader of an eight-year study of 1,169 people.

Stroke: You Can Do Much More to Protect Yourself

Ralph L. Sacco, MD, chairman of neurology, the Olemberg Family Chair in Neurological Disorders and the Miller Professor of Neurology, Epidemiology and Public Health, Human Genetics and Neurosurgery at the Miller School of Medicine at the University of Miami.

No one likes to think about having a stroke. But maybe you should.

The grim reality: Stroke strikes about 800,000 Americans each year and is the leading cause of disability.

Now for the remarkable part: About 80% of strokes can be prevented. You may think that you've heard it all when it comes to preventing strokes—it's about controlling your blood pressure, eating a good diet and getting some exercise, right? *Actually, that's only part of what you can be doing to protect yourself…*

• **Even "low" high blood pressure is a red flag.** High blood pressure—a reading of 140/90 mmHg or higher—is widely known to increase one's odds of having a stroke. But even slight elevations in blood pressure may also be a problem.

An important recent study that looked at data from more than half a million patients found that those with blood pressure readings that were just slightly higher than a normal reading of 120/80 mmHg were more likely to have a stroke.

Any increase in blood pressure is worrisome. In fact, the risk for a stroke or heart attack doubles for each 20-point rise in systolic (the top number) pressure above 115/75 mmHg—and for each 10-point rise in diastolic (the bottom number) pressure.

My advice: Don't wait for your doctor to recommend treatment if your blood pressure is even a few points higher than normal. Tell him/her that you are concerned. Lifestyle changes—such as getting adequate exercise, avoiding excess alcohol and maintaining a healthful diet—often reverse slightly elevated blood pressure. Blood pressure consistently above 140/90 mmHg generally requires medication.

• **Sleep can be dangerous.** People who are sleep deprived—generally defined as getting less than six hours of sleep per night—are at increased risk for stroke.

What most people don't realize is that getting too much sleep is also a problem. When researchers at the University of Cambridge tracked the sleep habits of nearly 10,000 people over a 10-year period, they found that those who slept more than eight hours a night were 46% more likely to have a stroke than those who slept six to eight hours.

It is possible that people who spend less/more time sleeping have other, unrecognized conditions that affect both sleep and stroke risk.

Example: Sleep apnea, a breathing disorder that interferes with sleep, causes an increase in blood pressure that can lead to stroke. Meanwhile, sleeping too much can be a symptom of depression—another stroke risk factor.

My advice: See a doctor if you tend to wake up unrefreshed…are a loud snorer…or often snort or thrash while you sleep. You may have sleep apnea. (For more on this condition, see page 395.) If you sleep too much, also talk to your doctor to see if you are suffering from depression or some other condition that may increase your stroke risk.

What's the sweet spot for nightly shut-eye? When it comes to stroke risk, it's six to eight hours per night.

• **What you drink matters, too.** A Mediterranean-style diet—plenty of whole grains, legumes, nuts, fish, produce and olive oil—is perhaps the best diet going when it comes to minimizing stroke risk. A recent study concluded that about 30% of strokes could be prevented if people simply switched to this diet.

But there's more you can do. Research has found that people who drank six cups of green or black tea a day were 42% less likely to have strokes than people who did not drink tea. With three daily cups, risk dropped by 21%. The antioxidant epigallocatechin gallate or the amino acid L-theanine may be responsible.

• **Emotional stress shouldn't be poohpoohed.** If you're prone to angry outbursts, don't assume it's no big deal. Emotional stress triggers the release of cortisol, adrenaline and other so-called stress hormones that can increase blood pressure and heart rate, leading to stroke.

In one study, about 30% of stroke patients had heightened negative emotions (such as anger) in the two hours preceding the stroke.

My advice: Don't ignore your mental health—especially anger (it's often a sign of depression, a potent stroke risk factor). If you're suffering from "negative" emotions, exercise regularly, try relaxation strategies (such as meditation) and don't hesitate to get professional help.

• **Be alert for subtle signs of stroke.** The acronym "FAST" helps people identify signs of stroke. "F" stands for facial drooping—does one side of the face droop or is it numb? Is the person's smile uneven? "A" stands for arm weakness—ask the person to raise both arms. Does one arm drift downward? "S" stands for speech difficulty—is speech slurred? Is the person unable to speak or hard to understand? Can he/she repeat a simple sentence such as, "The sky is blue" correctly? "T" stands for time—if a person shows any of these symptoms (even if they go away), call 911 immediately. Note the time so that you know when symptoms first appeared.

But stroke can also cause one symptom that isn't widely known—a loss of touch sensation. This can occur if a stroke causes injury to the parts of the brain that detect touch. If you suddenly can't "feel" your fingers or toes—or have trouble with simple tasks such as buttoning a shirt—you could be having a stroke.

It's never normal to lose your sense of touch for an unknown reason—or to have unexpected difficulty seeing, hearing and/or speaking. Get to an emergency room!

Also important: If you think you're having a stroke, don't waste time calling your regular doctor. Call an ambulance, and ask to be taken to the nearest hospital with a primary stroke center. You'll get much better care than you would at a regular hospital emergency room.

A meta-analysis found that there were 21% fewer deaths among patients treated at stroke centers, and the surviving patients had faster recoveries and fewer stroke-related complications.

My advice: If you have any stroke risk factors, including high blood pressure, diabetes or elevated cholesterol, find out now which hospitals in your area have stroke centers. To find one near you, go to *hospitalmaps.heart.org.*

Be Vigilant About These Stroke Risk Factors

Louis R. Caplan, MD, senior neurologist at Beth Israel Deaconess Medical Center and a professor of neurology at Harvard Medical School, both in Boston. He has written or edited more than 40 books, including *Stroke (What Do I Do Now?)* and most recently *Navigating the Complexities of Stroke.*

W hat if there were more to preventing a stroke than keeping your blood pressure under control...getting regular exercise...watching your body weight...and

405

not smoking? Researchers are now discovering that there is.

New thinking: While most stroke sufferers say that "it just came out of the blue," an increasing body of evidence shows that these potentially devastating "brain attacks" can be caused by conditions that you might ordinarily think are completely unrelated.

Once you're aware of these "hidden" risk factors—and take the necessary steps to prevent or control them—you can improve your odds of never having a stroke. *Recently discovered stroke risk factors…*

INFLAMMATORY BOWEL DISEASE

Both Crohn's disease and ulcerative colitis can severely damage the large or small intestine. But that is not the only risk. Among patients who have either one of these conditions, known as inflammatory bowel disease (IBD), stroke is the third most common cause of death, according to some estimates.

During flare-ups, patients with IBD have elevated blood levels of substances that trigger clots—the cause of most strokes. A Harvard study, for example, found that many IBD patients have high levels of C-reactive protein (CRP), an inflammatory marker that has been linked to atherosclerotic lesions, damaged areas in blood vessels that can lead to stroke-causing clots in the brain.

If you have IBD: Ask your doctor what you can do to reduce your risk for blood clots and inflammation. Some patients with IBD can't take aspirin or other anticlotting drugs because these medications frequently cause intestinal bleeding. Instead of aspirin, you might be advised to take an autoimmune medication such as *azathioprine* (Azasan, Imuran), which suppresses the immune system and reduces inflammation. During flare-ups, some patients are given steroids to further reduce inflammation.

Side effects, including nausea and vomiting with azathioprine use and weight gain and increased blood pressure with steroid use, usually can be minimized by taking the lowest possible dose.

Some physicians recommend omega-3 fish oil supplements for IBD, which are less likely to cause side effects. Ask your doctor whether these supplements (and what dose) are right for you.

Important: Strokes tend to occur in IBD patients when inflammation is most severe. To check inflammatory markers, CRP levels and erythrocyte sedimentation rate (ESR) can be measured. Tests for clotting include fibrinogen and d-dimer. The results of these tests will help determine the course of the patient's IBD treatment.

MIGRAINES

Migraine headaches accompanied by auras (characterized by the appearance of flashing lights or other visual disturbances) are actually a greater risk factor for stroke than obesity, smoking or diabetes (see below), according to a startling study recently presented at the American Academy of Neurology's annual meeting.

When researchers use MRIs to examine blood vessels in the brain, they find more tiny areas of arterial damage in patients who have migraines with auras than in those who don't get migraines. (Research shows that there is no link between stroke and migraines that aren't accompanied by auras.)

If you have migraines with auras: Reduce your risk by controlling other stroke risk factors—don't smoke…lose weight if you're overweight…and control cholesterol levels.

Also: Women under age 50 who have migraines (with or without auras) may be advised to not use combined-hormone forms of birth control pills—they slightly increase risk for stroke. In addition, patients who have migraines with auras should not take beta-blockers, such as *propranolol* (Inderal), or the triptan drugs, such as *sumatriptan* (Imitrex), commonly used for migraine headaches. These drugs can also increase stroke risk. For frequent migraines with auras, I often prescribe the blood pressure drug *verapamil* (Calan) and a daily 325-mg aspirin. Ask your doctor for advice.

RHEUMATOID ARTHRITIS

Rheumatoid arthritis, unlike the common "wear-and-tear" variety (osteoarthritis), is an autoimmune disease that not only causes inflammation in the joints but may also trigger it in the heart, blood vessels and other parts of the body.

Arterial inflammation increases the risk for blood clots, heart attack and stroke. In fact, patients with severe rheumatoid arthritis were almost twice as likely to have a stroke as those without the disease, according to a study published in *Arthritis Care & Research*.

If you have rheumatoid arthritis: Work with your rheumatologist to manage flare-ups and reduce systemic inflammation. Your doctor will probably recommend that you take one or more anti-inflammatory painkillers, such as *ibuprofen* (Motrin). In addition, he/she might prescribe a disease-modifying antirheumatic drug (DMARD), such as *methotrexate* (Trexall), to slow the progression of the disease—and the increased risk for stroke. Fish oil also may be prescribed to reduce joint tenderness.

Strokes tend to occur in rheumatoid arthritis patients when inflammation is peaking. Ask your doctor if you should have the inflammation tests (CRP and ESR) mentioned in the IBD section.

DIABETES

If you have diabetes or diabetes risk factors—such as obesity, a sedentary lifestyle or a family history of diabetes—protect yourself. People with diabetes are up to four times more likely to have a stroke than those without it.

High blood sugar in people with diabetes damages blood vessels throughout the body, including in the brain. The damage can lead to both ischemic (clot-related) and hemorrhagic (bleeding) strokes.

If you have diabetes: Work closely with your doctor. Patients who achieve good glucose control with oral medications and/or insulin are much less likely to suffer from vascular damage.

Also important: Lose weight if you need to. Weight loss combined with exercise helps your body metabolize blood sugar more efficiently. In those with mild diabetes, weight loss combined with exercise may restore normal blood sugar levels...and can reduce complications and the need for medications in those with more serious diabetes.

CLOTTING DISORDERS

Any condition that affects the blood's normal clotting functions can increase risk for stroke.

Examples: Thrombocytosis (excessive platelets in the blood)...an elevated hematocrit (higher-than-normal percentage of red blood cells)...or Factor V Leiden (an inherited tendency to form blood clots). Clotting tests (fibrinogen and d-dimer) are recommended for these disorders.

If you have a clotting disorder: Ask your doctor what you can do to protect yourself from stroke.

Example: If you have an elevated hematocrit, your doctor might advise you to drink more fluids.

This is particularly important for older adults, who tend to drink less later in the day because they don't want to get up at night to urinate. I recommend that these patients drink approximately 80 ounces of noncaffeine-containing fluids during the day, stopping by 7 pm. People who don't take in enough fluids can develop "thick" blood that impedes circulation—and increases the risk for clots.

Check Your Stroke Risk

Can you balance on one leg unassisted for 20 seconds? In a study of nearly 1,400 men and women, one-third of those who couldn't do this had mild memory loss and brain MRIs that showed two or more microbleeds (common precursors of serious strokes). These small strokes are caused by narrowing or leakage of tiny blood vessels deep within the brain. If you fail this balancing test, see your doctor to find out why.

Yasuharu Tabara, PhD, associate professor, Center for Genomic Medicine, Kyoto University Graduate School of Medicine, Japan.

Few Women Know Their Risks for Stroke

Few women understand their unique risk factors for stroke. Only 11% of those surveyed knew that being pregnant, having lupus or migraine headaches or taking oral contraception or hormone replacement therapy are stroke risk factors specific to women. And only 10% knew that hiccups combined with atypical chest pain can be an early warning sign of stroke. Some risk factors, such as high blood pressure and smoking, are the same for both men and women.

National survey of 1,000 women by The Ohio State University Wexner Medical Center, Columbus.

Do You Get Enough of the Anti-Stroke Mineral?

Susanna Larsson, PhD, an associate professor at the Institute of Environmental Medicine at the Karolinska Institutet in Stockholm, Sweden, and lead author of a study on dietary magnesium and stroke risk published in *The American Journal of Clinical Nutrition*.

Our moms always told us to eat our greens and beans...and now a new study reveals yet another important reason why these wise women were right. People who consume plenty of foods rich in magnesium—such as leafy green veggies and legumes—appear to have fewer strokes.

Researchers analyzed data from seven studies involving a total of 241,378 people from the US, Europe and Asia who were followed for an average of nearly 12 years.

What they found: For every additional 100 mg of magnesium consumed daily, a person's risk for ischemic stroke (the most common type, which is caused by a blood clot) was reduced by 9%.

Concern: Study participants from the US fell far short of the ideal, consuming foods that pro-

vided, on average, just 242 mg of magnesium per day—though the RDA is 320 mg for most adult women and 420 for most adult men.

Because this study focused specifically on food, researchers did not make a recommendation regarding the use of magnesium supplementation. However, it is easy to boost your intake of the brain-protecting mineral with food. For instance, you can get about 100 mg of magnesium each from...

- **Beans** (black, lima, navy, white), 1 cup
- **Beet greens,** 1 cup cooked
- **Bran cereal,** ½ cup
- **Brazil nuts,** 1 ounce
- **Cashews,** 1¼ ounces
- **Halibut,** 3 ounces
- **Lentils,** 1¼ cups
- **Okra,** 1 cup cooked
- **Spinach,** ⅔ cup cooked

New Stroke Fighter: Red Peppers

Eating red peppers and other vitamin C–rich fruits and veggies may reduce your risk for intracerebral hemorrhagic stroke (a blood vessel rupture in the brain). And what's so great about red peppers? At 190 mg per cup, they contain three times more vitamin C than an orange. Other good sources of vitamin C—broccoli and strawberries. Researchers believe that this vitamin may reduce stroke risk by regulating blood pressure and strengthening collagen, which promotes healthy blood vessels.

Stéphane Vannier, MD, neurologist, Pontchaillou University Hospital, Rennes, France, from research being presented at the annual meeting of the American Academy of Neurology.

More Vitamine C...Two Citrus a Day to Lower Stroke Risk

Citrus fruits cut stroke risk. The fruits contain antioxidants called flavanones, which have anti-inflammatory and neuroprotective properties.

Recent finding: Women who ate the most citrus had 19% fewer ischemic strokes (the most common kind) than women who ate the least. The effect is likely to be similar in men.

Recommended: Two servings of citrus a day—preferably whole fruit. Juice also has flavanones but is high in calories and has little fiber.

Kathryn Rexrode, MD, MPH, associate professor of medicine at Harvard Medical School and associate physician at Brigham and Women's Hospital, both in Boston. She is senior author of a study of 69,622 women published in *Stroke*.

Dietary Fiber Cuts Stroke Risk

For every 7 grams (g) of fiber daily, the risk for a first-time stroke decreased by 7%, in a recent analysis. One serving of whole-wheat pasta or two servings of fruits and vegetables contain about 7 g of fiber. Other top fiber sources include brown rice, spelt, quinoa and other whole-grain foods...almonds and other nuts...lentils and other dried beans.

Recommended daily fiber intake: People age 50 or younger, 38 g (men) and 25 g (women)...over age 50, 30 g (men) and 21 g (women).

Victoria J. Burley, PhD, senior lecturer in nutritional epidemiology at University of Leeds, England, and coauthor of an analysis of eight studies, published in *Stroke*.

Folic Acid Cuts Stroke Risk

According to a large study, supplements of the B vitamin decrease incidence of a first stroke in people with high blood pressure by 21%. People with normal blood pressure are likely to benefit, too. A standard daily multivitamin should provide adequate folic acid.

Better: Getting the vitamin from food, especially broccoli, beans (cooked from dried) and dark, leafy greens.

Also: Enriched grain products.

Meir Stampfer, MD, DrPH, professor of medicine at Harvard Medical School, Boston, and coauthor of an editorial published in *JAMA*.

Potassium Lowers Stroke Risk

People who ate at least three pieces of potassium-rich fruit daily had a 21% lower risk for stroke than those who didn't consume that much of the mineral, say researchers from University of Naples Medical School in Italy. When people think of potassium, they usually think of bananas, but prunes and apricots (if dried, look for sulfite-free versions), honeydew melon and cantaloupe also are high in potassium. Eat up!

Mark A. Stengler, NMD, naturopathic medical doctor and founder and director of the Stengler Center for Integrative Medicine Encinitas, California...author of many books, including *The Natural Physician's Healing Therapies*.

A-fib Patients and Stroke

Atrial-fibrillation patients at the highest risk for stroke can be identified with a cardiac MRI. People suffering from the common heart-rhythm disorder atrial fibrillation (A-fib) already have five times higher risk for stroke.

Recent finding: A-fib patients with a specific alteration in the function of the heart's left atrium have slower blood flow and are at even higher risk for blood clots and future stroke.

Hiroshi Ashikaga, MD, PhD, assistant professor of medicine and biomedical engineering at Johns Hopkins University School of Medicine, Baltimore.

The Truth About Blood Thinners

Stephen Kimmel, MD, MSCE, professor of medicine and epidemiology at the University of Pennsylvania School of Medicine in Philadelphia. Dr. Kimmel is the editor of two textbooks about pharmacoepidemiology and the author of nearly 200 medical journal articles.

For people at risk of developing dangerous blood clots—a main cause of stroke and other serious conditions—*warfarin* (Coumadin) has long been the granddaddy of anticoagulant medication. This pill is taken by about 3 million Americans.

Now: The FDA has approved four newer oral anticoagulants. (Other anticoagulants such as *enoxaparin* and *heparin* are available only as injections.) While the newer oral anticoagulants may offer certain benefits over warfarin, they are not the best choice for everyone.

Why this matters: Using the wrong anticoagulant drug (or dose) can have dire consequences, such as life-threatening bleeding in the brain or gastrointestinal tract.

WHY AN ANTICOAGULANT?

Anticoagulants are used by people who are at increased risk for ischemic (caused by a blood clot) stroke and transient ischemic attacks, or "ministrokes"…or deep vein thrombosis (a blood clot in a deep vein), which can lead to a deadly pulmonary embolism (a blood clot in the lung). Anticoagulants also help prevent clots from forming in people who have

an abnormal heartbeat (atrial fibrillation)…or have received a heart-valve replacement.

THE WARFARIN STANDARD

Warfarin has been used in the US for decades and is very effective at protecting high-risk people from blood clots. It's the only anticoagulant approved for use in people with mechanical heart valves.

Here's the catch: The amount of warfarin in the body must be regularly measured via a blood test called the International Normalized Ratio (INR). This allows doctors to monitor and customize the dosage for each individual patient, but it also means that you'll need frequent blood tests—weekly or monthly—to make sure that the drug is working properly. This testing is crucial, but not all patients do it as often as they should.

In addition, when you take warfarin, you must closely monitor your diet. Foods that contain vitamin K, such as leafy greens, broccoli and spinach, help your body make normal clotting proteins, which means they will work against the drug's action. For this reason, you should be consistent in the amounts of vitamin K–rich foods that you eat. Otherwise, the drug's effectiveness will be affected.

Also, warfarin interacts with more than 700 prescription and over-the-counter drugs as well as many supplements, including ginkgo biloba, St. John's wort, coenzyme Q10 and others. You need to keep your doctor informed about everything you take. The newer drugs have far fewer interactions.

BETTER THAN WARFARIN?

Four alternatives to warfarin are now available in the US—*dabigatran* (Pradaxa), *rivaroxaban* (Xarelto), *apixaban* (Eliquis) and *edoxaban* (Savaysa). Clinical trials show a lower risk for hemorrhagic (bleeding) stroke with the newer drugs compared with warfarin. There is also a reduction in overall strokes with some of the newer drugs.

Other differences include…

• **No regular blood work.** There is no good way to monitor levels of these new drugs in the body, but they have proved effective without monitoring levels, so you won't have to endure weekly or monthly blood tests, as needed when using warfarin. However, the complete safety profile of new drugs is also unknown, and doctors cannot customize dosing for each individual.

• **There are no foods that work against the newer drugs,** as there are with warfarin. The newer drugs are as effective as warfarin no matter what you eat.

• **No antidote.** If a patient's blood becomes too thin and bleeding becomes uncontrollable, there is nothing to reverse it when using one of the newer anticoagulants. Warfarin does have an antidote.

Editor's note: More than 100 lawsuits have been filed on behalf of patients who were injured or died due to a major bleeding event after taking Xarelto. The manufacturer of Pradaxa recently agreed to pay $650 million to settle about 4,000 similar claims.

• **A link to kidney function.** The newer drugs can be affected by your kidney function, so your doctor will need to consider this when choosing a medication and its dose.

HOW TO CHOOSE?

Remember, newer drugs don't have as long a track record as older ones. That's why it's important to thoroughly discuss your medication options with your doctor.

What to consider...

• **If you have difficulty remembering to take pills throughout the day,** once-a-day Xarelto or Savaysa may be best for you.

• **If you play sports or have a hobby that may cause a bleeding accident,** warfarin might be best, since it is the only anticoagulant with an antidote that allows doctors to stop uncontrolled bleeding.

• **If you have a history of stomach problems or gastrointestinal bleeding,** you may want to avoid Pradaxa and Xarelto—both medications have the highest risk for these complications.

• **If cost is an issue,** you may want to consider warfarin. The newer anticoagulants are marketed only in brand-name versions that are much more expensive (even with insurance coverage) than warfarin, which is available in generic form. With warfarin, you also have the cost of the necessary routine blood work, but this expense may be covered by your insurance.

Caution: Do not stop using an anticoagulant without consulting your physician—this drug helps control your increased risk for stroke and other blood clot complications. Because of the bleeding risk associated with anticoagulants, people who use these drugs should wear a medical identification bracelet.

Can Antidepressants Help With Stroke Recovery?

Robert Robinson, MD, Penningroth professor and head of psychiatry, Carver College of Medicine, The University of Iowa, Iowa City. Dr. Robinson is internationally recognized as an expert in the study of poststroke depression.

Scientists keep working to try to make further improvements in stroke prevention and rehabilitation. Recently, they have come up with a novel way to speed recovery...and extend progress. Would you believe it's as simple as taking a short course of antidepressants?

ENCOURAGING NEW BRAIN CELLS TO GROW

Recent research shows that poststroke depression slowed recovery and made patients more likely to die. The much better news is that additional research has discovered antidepressants improve recovery both in stroke patients who are depressed—and also in those who are not.

The Modified Rankin Scale, a measure of physical and motor disability, is used to evaluate stroke and brain injuries. Study participants who took an antidepressant improved 1 to 1.5 categories, on average, over the placebo group when measured on the scale. For example, in some instances, people who initially could not manage daily activities such as dressing or feeding themselves were once again able to do so without help. Other patients who were unable to walk without assistance or were bedridden were able to walk independently or with assistance.

The placebo group also improved for several months, but their progress then leveled off. The antidepressant group continued to make progress for at least nine additional months after they had stopped taking the medication. It's possible that improvements lasted even longer, but the study ended at one year.

Other research demonstrates that antidepressants encourage cognitive recovery and, perhaps most impressively, nearly double your chances of survival six to nine years poststroke, according to researchers. Although scientists don't know exactly how antidepressants work this particular magic, it's likely that they block inflammation. When you have a stroke, your body releases inflammatory proteins that block cellular growth. By inhibiting the release of these proteins, antidepressants encourage the growth of new cells and allow your brain to recover more rapidly from its injury.

Study results were published online in the *American Journal of Geriatric Psychiatry*.

HEALING CONTINUES AFTER MEDICATION STOPS

The idea that antidepressants might benefit early recovery from stroke has been around for a number of years. But one major question left unanswered by previous studies was, "Does the effect last after the medication stops?" What the recent study demonstrates is that not only does the beneficial effect last, but the improvement in physical recovery continues to increase even after the patients stop taking the medication.

Researchers continue to confirm the valuable role that antidepressants can play in stroke recovery. Meanwhile, if you or a loved one suffers a stroke, it seems logical to ask your doctor whether a short course (at least) of an antidepressant makes sense.

To locate a stroke rehabilitation center near you, contact the Commission on Accreditation of Rehabilitation Facilities (888-281-6531, *carf. org/advancedprovidersearch.aspx*).

Remedy for Poststroke Disability

A promising new treatment cuts poststroke disability in women. According to a preliminary study, 42% of female patients who received IV uric acid in addition to the usual treatment, the clot-busting drug tPA, were relatively free of disability three months after a stroke compared with 29% of women given tPa and no uric acid. Little difference was found among men.

Theory: Men tend to have higher blood levels of uric acid.

Ángel Chamorro, MD, PhD, director of the Comprehensive Stroke Center, Hospital Clinic, University of Barcelona, Spain, and senior author of a study of 411 patients, published in *Stroke*.

Device Reduces Stroke Risk

The Enroute Transcarotid Neuroprotection System (TNS) provides a way for doctors to access neck arteries through an incision in the neck, rather than through the groin. The system is for patients with narrowed carotid arteries who have twisted blood vessels that don't allow access via the groin. Enroute TNS has been approved by the FDA for people undergoing procedures to restore normal blood flow in neck arteries.

William Maisel, MD, MPH, acting director, Office of Device Evaluation, Center for Device and Radiological Health, US Food and Drug Administration, Silver Spring, Maryland.

16

Live Cancer Free

4 New (and Delicious) Cancer-Fighting Foods

Researchers are continually investigating foods that may help prevent cancer. But which ones have the strongest evidence?

The American Institute for Cancer Research (AICR), a nonprofit group that keeps tabs on cancer and diet research, recently identified the following foods as being among those having the strongest scientific evidence for fighting cancer…*

PUMPKIN

Under the hard rind, orange pumpkin flesh is rich in carotenoids such as beta-carotene, alpha-carotene, lutein and zeaxanthin. A high intake of foods containing carotenoids has been linked to a lower incidence of many can-

*The studies cited in this article are only a small portion of the research supporting these cancer-fighting foods. The AICR and its international panel of experts review a much larger spectrum of research.

cers, including those of the esophagus, mouth and larynx. Scientists have recently uncovered another protective compound in pumpkins—cucurmosin, a protein that has been shown to slow the growth of pancreatic cancer cells.

Smart idea: Eat pumpkin (plain, canned pumpkin is a convenient option) and the seeds.

What to do: Eat a handful of pumpkin seeds (store-bought are fine) daily as a snack. To prepare your own, rinse fresh seeds in water, air-dry, add a touch of oil and bake at 350°F for 10 to 20 minutes.

GRAPEFRUIT

Grapefruit is a rich source of dietary fiber and vitamin C. The pink and red varieties also contain carotenoids (such as beta-carotene

Alice G. Bender, MS, RDN, associate director for nutrition programs at the American Institute for Cancer Research (AICR), a nonprofit organization that analyzes research and educates the public on the links between diet, physical exercise, weight loss and the prevention of cancer. AICR.org and lycopene) that decrease the DNA damage that can lead to cancer.

Scientific evidence: Strong research shows that foods like grapefruit help reduce risk for colorectal cancer. Other evidence suggests that it reduces risk for such malignancies as those of the esophagus, mouth, lung and stomach.

Helpful: Put red or pink grapefruit slices in a green salad with avocado. The tart grapefruit and creamy avocado are delicious together—and the fat in the avocado boosts the absorption of lycopene.

Caution: Grapefruit contains *furanocoumarins*, compounds that block a liver enzyme that breaks down some medications. (More than 85 medications interact with grapefruit, including cholesterol-lowering statins.) If you're thinking about eating more grapefruit and currently take one or more medications, talk to your doctor first.

APPLES

An apple a day is good for you—but two may be even better!

Scientific evidence: In a study published in the *European Journal of Cancer Prevention*, people who ate an apple a day had a 35% lower risk for colorectal cancer—and those who ate two or more apples had a 50% lower risk.

Apples are protective because they contain several anticancer nutrients (many of them found in the peel), including fiber, vitamin C and flavonoids such as quercetin and kaempferol—plant compounds that have stopped the growth of cancer in cellular and animal studies. Research does not specify any particular type of apple as being more protective, so enjoy your favorite variety.

A quick and easy apple dessert: Core an apple, stuff it with raisins and cinnamon, top the stuffing with one tablespoon of apple cider or water, cover the apple with waxed paper and microwave for two minutes.

MUSHROOMS
(USED IN A SURPRISING WAY)

When it comes to preventing cancer with diet, it's not only what you eat—it's also what you don't eat.

Scientific evidence: The evidence is convincing that eating too much red meat is linked to colorectal cancer. The AICR recommends eating no more than 18 ounces a week of cooked red meat (such as beef, pork and lamb).

A cancer-fighting meal extender: An easy, delicious way to lower your intake of red meat is to replace some of it in recipes with mushrooms. They're a perfect meat extender, with a savory, meaty taste and texture. What to do: In a recipe that uses ground meat, replace one-third to one-half of the meat with chopped or diced mushrooms.

In a recent study, people who substituted one cup of white button mushrooms a day for one cup of lean ground beef consumed 123 fewer daily calories and lost an average of seven pounds after one year.

If you're heavier than you should be, losing weight means decreasing cancer risk—the AICR estimates that 122,000 yearly cases of cancer could be prevented if Americans weren't overweight or obese.

Cancer in the Family? Too Few Doctors Recommend Genetic Tests

Katrina Trivers, PhD, MSPH, an epidemiologist at the Centers for Disease Control and Prevention in Atlanta and lead author of an article reporting on a survey of 1,878 US physicians.

You are probably aware that if two or more of your close family members (or just one family member for those of Ashkenazi Jewish descent) had breast or ovarian cancer, you are at increased risk for such cancers yourself. That is why various health organizations, such as the US Preventive Services Task Force, issue guidelines on who should consider genetic counseling and possibly be tested for the abnormal genes (BRCA1 and BRCA2) associated with most inherited breast and ovarian cancers. Test results can help determine your risk level and identify appropriate self-defense strategies.

Problem: According to a recent article published in *Cancer,* only 34% of family physicians, 41% of general internists and 57% of gynecologists surveyed reported adhering to guidelines in referring high-risk patients for genetic counseling and testing.

Among the reasons for the low adherence rates: The guidelines are complicated…and the various organizations define high risk differently.

Protect yourself: Visit *uspreventiveservices taskforce.org/* (search "BRCA testing") or *can cer.gov/cancertopics/factsheet/risk/BRCA* for more information on genetic risk…then talk with your doctor about your family history of breast and ovarian cancer, including who was diagnosed and at what age, if this information is available.

Reassuring: For women whose genetic test results show that they do carry an abnormal BRCA1 or BRCA2 gene, additional screening tests, medication and/or prophylactic surgery can greatly reduce the risk of succumbing to cancer.

Hot Off the Grill: Increased Cancer Risk

Karen Collins, RD, a registered dietitian, syndicated columnist and nutrition adviser to the American Institute for Cancer Research, Washington, DC. She was the expert reviewer for the Institute's international report, "Diet, Nutrition, Physical Activity and the Prevention of Cancer: A Global Perspective." KarenCollinsNutrition.com

Grilling can be among the healthiest types of cooking because it gives foods a delicious flavor while using little or no added fat. But grilling also can produce toxic compounds.

Study: Researchers at University of Minnesota analyzed data on the cooking methods, amount of meat eaten and the doneness of meat for nearly 63,000 participants. They found that those who preferred their steaks well-done and who used grilling and other high-heat cooking methods were about 60% more likely to develop pancreatic cancer than those who cooked their meat at a lower temperature and/or for less time.

Other studies have confirmed that the high heats used in grilling increase the risk for a variety of cancers, including cancers of the colon and rectum.

Example: Another study based on data from the Ontario Cancer Registry found that people who ate well-done red meat more than twice a week had a 57% higher risk of developing colon cancer than those who ate their meat medium or rare.

To reduce cancer risk, it's always wise to limit your intake of red meat to no more than 18 ounces (cooked) a week and minimize consumption of processed meats, such as hot dogs, bacon and sausage. *There also are simple steps to take to reduce grilling dangers…*

TOO HOT, TOO LONG

Grills that burn gas, briquettes or hardwood charcoal easily can achieve temperatures of 500°F or more…covered ceramic grills can exceed 1,000°F. High heats are ideal for searing meats and sealing in the juices, but prolonged cooking at high temperatures produces dangerous chemical by-products. *These include…*

•**Heterocyclic amines (HCAs),** which form when animal proteins, including the proteins in meat, chicken and fish, are cooked at high temperatures for extended periods. "The Report on Carcinogens," produced by the National Toxicology Program, lists IQ (one type of HCA) as a compound reasonably anticipated to cause cancer.

•**Polycyclic aromatic hydrocarbons (PAHs),** which are formed when the fat from cooking meat drips onto a heat source (such as hot coals or metal or ceramic "smoke bars") and produces a smoky flare-up. Like HCAs, PAHs are thought to be potent carcinogens.

Advanced glycation end products, chemical compounds that might increase the risk for cancer. They are produced at higher levels when foods are cooked at hot temperatures for prolonged periods.

SAFER GRILLING

Take the following steps to reduce risk…

•**Marinate.** Meat that is marinated for as little as 15 to 20 minutes prior to grilling produces up to 90% less HCAs than unmarinated meat. We don't know why this happens. It might be because the acidic ingredients used in marinades, such as lemon juice and vinegar, change the molecular structure of meat protein and inhibit HCA production.

•**Season with spices.** Meats that are coated with antioxidant herbs and spices, such as rosemary, turmeric, ginger and cumin, as well as garlic, produce fewer HCAs during grilling than unseasoned meats. Again, we're not sure why.

•**Cook cooler.** For cancer prevention, the temperature of the grill is more important than the time on the grill. One study found that meats cooked at a lower-than-usual temperature but for two minutes longer had only about one-third of the HCAs as meat that was cooked at a higher temperature for a shorter time and to the same doneness.

After searing the meat, move it to a cooler part of the grill…or raise the grill rack a few inches so that the meat is farther from the heat. With gas grills, you can use the high-heat setting to quickly sear the meat, then lower the flames for slower cooking.

•**Shorten the cooking time.** Meat that is cooked rare, medium-rare or medium will produce significantly lower levels of HCAs than meat that's well-done. When grilling a medium-rare steak, the internal temperature should be 145°F—that's hot enough to kill disease-causing microorganisms but cool enough to limit the production of HCAs.

A steak cooked to medium doneness will be 160°F inside.

Important: Always cook poultry to an internal temperature of 165°F to kill salmonella and other organisms.

You also can shorten cooking time by precooking in a microwave or an oven. Do this with foods such as chicken and ribs. I wouldn't recommend it for burgers or steak, though, because precooking removes some of the juices that make these foods flavorful.

•**Cut meat into small pieces before grilling.** Chunks of beef or pork (when making kebabs, for example) will cook more quickly than a whole steak or roast, which will reduce the level of HCAs.

•**Cook lean to avoid flare-ups.** Slicing off the visible fat from meats before grilling reduces fatty flare-ups and the production of PAHs. Also, avoid fatty cuts of meat (such as rib-eye steak), and choose lean beef for hamburgers.

•**Avoid smoking foods.** People often use mesquite or other types of wood chips when grilling and smoking meats. The smoke produced by these chips may increase cancer risks.

•**Use more vegetables.** HCAs are produced only when animal proteins are subjected to high-heat cooking…and PAHs are produced by fat drippings.

You can avoid both risks by grilling vegetables, such as onions, broccoli, mushrooms, zucchini, eggplant and peppers. A little olive oil brushed on veggies before grilling is fine.

By shifting the balance in a meal to a smaller portion of meat, fish or poultry and adding more vegetables, there are two benefits—less meat automatically means less of meat's cell-damaging compounds, and more plant foods means more of the protective phytochemicals that inactivate those compounds.

---

5 Cancer Risks—Even Your Doctor May Not Know About

Lynne Eldridge, MD, medical manager of the Lung Cancer site for About.com and a former clinical preceptor at the University of Minnesota Medical School in Minneapolis. She is the author of *Avoiding Cancer One Day at a Time*.

If you don't have any of the well-known risk factors for cancer, including smoking, a family history of cancer or long-term exposure to a carcinogen such as asbestos, you may think that your risk for the disease is average or even less than average.

What you may not realize: Although most of the cancer predispositions (genetic, lifestyle and environmental factors that increase risk for the disease) are commonly known, there are several medical conditions that also can increase your risk.

Unfortunately, many primary-care physicians do not link these conditions to cancer. As a result, they fail to prescribe the tests and treatments that could keep cancer at bay or reduce the condition's cancer-causing potential. *Medical conditions that increase your risk for cancer...*

1. Diabetes. The high blood sugar levels that occur with type 2 diabetes predispose you to heart attack, stroke, nerve pain, blindness, kidney failure, a need for amputation—and cancer.

New research: For every 1% increase in HbA1c—a measurement of blood sugar levels over the previous three months—there is an 18% increase in the risk for cancer, according to a recent study published in *Current Diabetes Reports.*

Other current studies have linked type 2 diabetes to a 94% increased risk for pancreatic cancer...a 38% increased risk for colon cancer...a 15% to 20% higher risk for postmenopausal breast cancer...and a 20% higher risk or blood cancers such as non-Hodgkin's lymphoma and leukemia.

What to do: If you have type 2 diabetes, make sure your primary-care physician orders regular screening tests for cancer, such as colonoscopy and mammogram.

Screening for pancreatic cancer is not widely available, but some of the larger cancer centers (such as the H. Lee Moffitt Cancer Center & Research Institute in Tampa, Florida, and the Mayo Clinic in Rochester, Minnesota) offer it to high-risk individuals. This typically includes people with long-standing diabetes (more than 20 years) and/or a family history of pancreatic cancer. The test involves an ultrasound of both the stomach and small intestine, where telltale signs of pancreatic cancer can be detected.

Also work with your doctor to minimize the cancer-promoting effects of diabetes. For example, control blood sugar levels through a diet that emphasizes slow-digesting foods that don't create spikes in blood sugar levels, such as vegetables and beans...get regular exercise—for example, 30 minutes of walking five or six days a week...and consider medical interventions, such as use of the diabetes drug *metformin* (Glucophage).

2. Helicobacter pylori infection. This bacterial infection of the lining of the stomach can cause stomach inflammation (gastritis) and ulcers in the stomach or upper small intestine. It also causes most stomach cancers.

Startling statistic: An infection with H. pylori triggers a 10-fold increase in your predisposition to stomach cancer. Getting treatment for an H. pylori infection lowers your risk for stomach cancer by 35% but does not eliminate the risk—perhaps due to lingering inflammation. What's most important is to avoid other inflammation-causing habits such as smoking.

What to do: If you are diagnosed with gastritis or a stomach or intestinal ulcer, ask your doctor to check for an H. pylori infection—and to treat it with antibiotics if it is detected. Research shows that a fecal analysis is the most accurate way to detect H. pylori.

3. "Iron overload" disease. This hereditary condition (known technically as hemochromatosis) affects one out of every 200 people, causing them to absorb and store too much dietary iron—in the liver, heart, joints and pancreas. Hemochromatosis also increases a person's risk for cancer (particularly liver cancer).

New research: In a study of more than 8,000 people reported in the *Journal of Internal Medicine,* iron overload increased the risk for any cancer nearly fourfold.

Iron overload should be suspected if you have or had a relative (including a second-degree relative such as a grandparent) with the condition...you have a family history of early heart disease (beginning at age 50 or earlier)...you have a family history of cirrhosis without obvious reasons such as alcoholism or hepatitis...or you have the symptoms of hemochromatosis (joint pain, fatigue, abdominal pain and a bronze appearance to the skin).

What to do: Ask your doctor for a serum ferritin test. If the test confirms iron overload, your doctor can simply and quickly correct the problem with regular bloodletting—a pint of blood once or twice per week until iron levels return to normal, and then three to four times per year.

4. Inflammatory bowel disease (IBD). This autoimmune disease attacks the lining of the intestine, causing symptoms such as abdominal cramping and bloating, bloody diarrhea and urgent bowel movements. The disease takes two main forms—ulcerative colitis (affecting the colon) and Crohn's disease (usually affecting the small intestine). Both forms predispose you to colon cancer.

Recent research: People age 67 and older with ulcerative colitis have a 93% higher risk for colorectal cancer...people of the same age group with Crohn's disease have a 45% higher risk, according to a 2011 study reported in *Digestive Diseases and Sciences*.

Problem: IBD can come and go in flare-ups that occur only once every five or 10 years. This can lead your primary-care physician to underestimate the severity of the problem and your risk for colon cancer.

What to do: IBD usually is diagnosed between the ages of 15 and 30. If you have ulcerative colitis that involves the entire colon, you should have your first colonoscopy eight years after diagnosis or at the standard age of 50 (whichever comes first) and then have another every one to two years thereafter.

If you have ulcerative colitis that involves only the left colon (which represents a somewhat smaller cancer risk than when the entire colon is affected) or Crohn's disease, you should receive your first colonoscopy 12 to 15 years after your diagnosis or at age 50 and then another every one to two years thereafter.

5. Polyps detected in a relative. Most people think that a hereditary predisposition to colon cancer means that you have a first-degree relative (parent, sibling or child) who was diagnosed with the disease.

Surprising fact: If you have a first-degree relative who had a colonoscopy that detected an adenomatous polyp (adenoma)—a type of growth that can turn into cancer within two to five years—you also have a predisposition to colon cancer.

New research: Having a first-degree relative with an adenoma appears to make you four times more likely to develop colorectal cancer, according to a report in *Annals of Internal Medicine*.

What to do: Have a first colonoscopy 10 years earlier than the age at which your relative's adenoma was detected and repeat it every five to 10 years (depending on results). That should give plenty of time to detect (and remove) an adenoma so it can never turn into cancer.

Interesting: Some cancer centers also advise earlier screening if a second-degree relative, such as a grandparent, had colon cancer.

How Coffee Fights Cancer

Frank B. Hu, MD, PhD, an epidemiologist, nutritional specialist and professor of medicine at Harvard Medical School and the Harvard School of Public Health, both in Boston. He is codirector of Harvard's Program in Obesity Epidemiology and Prevention.

I t's not a substitute for sunscreen, but drinking coffee could protect you from the most common type of skin cancer.

In a recent report presented at the American Association of Cancer Research meeting in Boston, researchers found that coffee drinkers were less likely to develop basal-cell carcinoma than noncoffee drinkers.

In the study, researchers followed more than 112,000 people for up to 24 years. During this time, they tracked the incidence of basal-cell carcinomas and other skin cancers. Men who drank the most coffee had a 13% lower risk for basal-cell carcinomas than those who drank the least…in women, the risk was 18% lower.

Decaffeinated coffee didn't provide the same protection, so it appears that caffeine is responsible—but the reason isn't known.

Coffee reduced the risk for only this one type of skin cancer. Other skin cancers, such as melanoma and squamous-cell carcinoma, weren't affected. Because this is the first large study to find this effect, it will have to be repeated—by different researchers and with different groups of people—to confirm that coffee does, in fact, protect the skin.

Caffeine may protect against other cancers as well.

PROMISING, BUT NOT PROVED

New finding: Women who drink four or more cups a day of caffeinated coffee reduced their risk for endometrial cancer by 30%. And drinking two or more cups of decaffeinated coffee reduced risk by about 22%.

It's important to remember that the majority of research about coffee is observational. Researchers interview large numbers of people…ask them about their coffee consumption and other habits…look at their health status…and then make conclusions about what caused what.

Unlike double-blind, randomized clinical trials, which are considered the gold standard of scientific research, observational studies cannot prove cause and effect, but they do offer evidence.

CAUTION

Some caveats about coffee…

•**Moderation matters.** Some people get the jitters or have insomnia when they drink coffee. In rare cases, the caffeine causes a dramatic rise in blood pressure. It's fine for most people to have three, four or five cups of coffee a day—or even more. But pay attention to how you feel. If you get jittery or anxious when you drink a certain amount, cut back. Or drink decaf some of the time.

•**Hold the milk and sugar.** Some of the coffee "beverages" at Starbucks and other coffee shops have more calories than a sweet dessert. Coffee may be good for you, but limit the add-ons.

•**Use a paper filter.** Boiled coffee, coffee made with a French press or coffee that drips through a metal filter has high levels of oils that can significantly raise levels of LDL, the dangerous form of cholesterol.

Better: A drip machine that uses a paper filter. It traps the oils and eliminates this risk.

Lung Cancer Breakthroughs: Prevention and Detection

Peter Bach, MD, epidemiologist and lung cancer specialist, Memorial Sloan-Kettering Cancer Center, New York City. He has done extensive research and development on lung cancer prediction models and has authored numerous articles on lung cancer for medical journals.

Men worry about prostate cancer…women worry about breast cancer…everybody worries about colon cancer, skin cancer and brain cancer. But there's another cancer that claims more Americans' lives than those five other types combined. It's lung cancer, the number-one cancer killer in the country, responsible for more than 157,000 deaths each year.

The good news: Recent advances in prevention and detection are helping in the battle against this fearsome disease. For instance, there's a new screening tool that can cut the odds of dying from lung cancer by 20%. Is it right for you or for someone you love? For answers to that question and more, we turned to Peter Bach, MD, an epidemiologist and lung cancer specialist at Memorial Sloan-Kettering Cancer Center in New York City.

OVERDUE PREVENTION TACTIC

Not all cases of lung cancer are caused by cigarette smoking, but up to 90% are. The percentage of Americans who smoke has declined significantly over the past few decades, from 42% in 1965 to 19% in 2011…but it's still way too high.

Public education campaigns and high cigarette taxes do help reduce smoking, but now the FDA is exploring a new tactic—regulating or even banning menthol cigarettes. The reason? Because menthol may make it easier to become addicted to smoking and harder to quit.

Why it has taken the FDA so long to consider regulating menthol is a mystery. Back in 2009, when the FDA banned the candy, clove and fruit flavorings that made cigarettes more palatable to young smokers, it also called for an investigation on the impact of mentholated cigarettes on public health. Two years later, the FDA's advisory committee concluded that it is "biologically plausible" that adding menthol to cigarettes makes them more addictive, and that removing menthol from cigarettes would improve public health.

Menthol's allure: The addition of menthol is a trick used by tobacco companies—in fact, the flavoring is added to all cigarettes, not just those not marketed as menthol. Menthol-flavored cigarettes have about 10 times more added menthol than regular cigarettes, but even at the lower levels, the menthol helps mask the harshness of tobacco and the irritation associated with nicotine. Without the added menthol, the harshness and irritation could be turnoffs for new smokers—making them less likely to stick with the dangerous habit.

Menthol works by stimulating the cold receptors on nerve endings in the mouth, nose and skin, creating a cooling sensation. When menthol is added at higher levels, the cooling sensation also is felt in the lungs. At the same time, menthol contains substances that enhance nicotine's "bite," a sensation that smokers seem to crave, further reinforcing smoking behavior.

The FDA is considering banning menthol because it lures smokers and keeps them, but other studies suggest that menthol also makes cigarettes more harmful. Last year, *Daily Health News* reported that smokers of menthol cigarettes had more than twice the risk for stroke as smokers of regular cigarettes. People who smoke menthol cigarettes also show decreased elasticity and increased stiffness of the carotid arteries (the main arteries feeding the brain) compared with smokers of regular cigarettes. In addition, menthol's cooling action slows respiration, increasing breath-holding time and, in turn, leading to greater exposure to the cigarette's toxins. What's more, the cilia (tiny hairlike structures in the airway that move things along) slow down when exposed to menthol, impairing clearance of toxins from the airway.

Our opinion: It's way past time for menthol to be banned from cigarettes.

LIFESAVING SCREENING: FOR WHOM?

Lung cancer has one of the lowest five-year survival rates of all cancers mainly because it usually is diagnosed too late to be cured. About 90% of people who get lung cancer die because of it.

Recently, the US Preventive Services Task Force, an independent panel of experts in prevention and evidence-based medicine, sought to update its previous determination against routine lung cancer screening for smokers. The task force reviewed relevant studies, relying most heavily on the National Lung Screening Trial (NLST).

The NLST included more than 53,000 smokers who were randomly assigned to undergo three annual exams with either chest x-rays or low-dose CT scans.

Findings: In each of the three rounds of screening, CT exams found more cancers than X-rays. In the first round alone, CT scans identified 270 people with lung cancer, compared with 136 in the X-ray group. CT screening reduced lung cancer deaths by 20%.

Based on these findings, a task force recommendation now in draft form advises annual CT screening for people at high risk—those between the ages of 55 and 79 who have a smoking history of at least 30 pack-years. (A pack-year is an average of one pack per day for one year. So, for example, if you smoked two packs each day for 15 years, you have a 30-pack-year history.) The recommendation applies even to ex-smokers who have quit smoking within the past 15 years. (The NLST did not look at ex-smokers who quit more than 15 years ago.)

If you fall in to the high-risk category, should you go get a CT scan? Probably—but there are several factors to consider first, Dr. Bach said, because the benefits to you may not be quite as great as the NLST findings suggest. The NLST was conducted at 33 academic medical centers around the country, all with expertise in diagnosing and managing lung cancer—whereas the same high-quality results may not be found outside of a top-notch academic community. Also, Dr. Bach believes that the task force's estimate of 20,000 lives saved every year from annual CT screening is overly optimistic. He explained that his institution's analysis of the data, using different statistical methods, estimates about 4,000 lives saved each year.

Why does it matter whether the true benefits are somewhat less than the NLST suggests? Because CT scans are not without risk. Although low-dose CT exposes you to much less radiation than a standard chest CT, it's still much higher than the exposure you'd get from a regular chest X-ray. CT scans also may result in false-positive findings or incidental findings (abnormalities that don't cause harm), both of which can lead to unnecessary invasive testing and anxiety.

Bottom line: If you clearly fall into the high-risk category (age 55 to 79 with a smoking history of at least 30 pack-years and less than 15 years since you quit), you should be aware of the screening option and seriously consider the trade-offs of benefits versus risks. "The most aggressive we should be is to suggest that such patients discuss screening with a doctor who is disinterested—meaning someone who is not the owner of a CT scanner or radiology center," Dr. Bach said.

Lower-risk people should not be offered screening, in his opinion. "Outside of the high-risk group, the potential danger of radiation vastly exceeds the possible benefits of screening. That's even more true for women than for men because the radiation also can contribute to breast cancer risk."

GENDER EQUALITY?

Speaking of women, let's consider the issue of gender as it relates to lung cancer risk. Lung cancer used to be considered primarily a man's disease. But several years ago, the pendulum swung in the opposite direction when some studies suggested that female smokers were more susceptible to the harms of cigarettes than male smokers…and that women who had never smoked were more likely to get lung cancer than men who had never smoked.

However, those theories did not hold up in more rigorous studies. Most experts agree, Dr. Bach said, that lung cancer is neither predominantly a man's disease nor a woman's disease. Women and men have the same risk of developing lung cancer and dying from it…and it is the leading cause of cancer death for both men and women in the US.

HELP FOR SMOKERS AND EX-SMOKERS

If you smoke or used to smoke, visit these three important websites…

•**The CDC's Tips from Former Smokers public service campaign** has been instrumental in convincing more than 100,000 smokers to drop their smoking habit, *cdc.gov/tobacco/campaign/tips/*.

•**Calculate your pack-years**—an important number when considering whether CT screening is appropriate for you, *smoking packyears.com*.

•**Memorial Sloan-Kettering Cancer Center,** one of the nation's top cancer hospitals, has developed its own online tool that can help you decide whether you should be screened. The criteria used are slightly different than those developed by the task force—so it will be helpful to discuss the guidelines with your own doctor, *mskcc.org* (search "lung screening decision tool").

New Personalized, Precision Approach to Lung Cancer Treatment

Peter Bach, MD, epidemiologist and lung cancer specialist, Memorial Sloan-Kettering Cancer Center, New York City. He has done extensive research and development on lung cancer prediction models and has authored numerous articles on lung cancer for medical journals.

Prasad Adusumilli, MD, thoracic surgeon and researcher, Memorial Sloan-Kettering Cancer Center, New York City. He has researched and published extensively on lung cancer topics, including the personalization of lung cancer surgical resection procedures.

Although the odds of surviving lung cancer admittedly still aren't great, these days a lung cancer diagnosis is not an automatic death sentence—even in the case of late-stage cancer. We have many more options for treating the disease than we did just a decade ago...and treatment today is more personalized and precise than ever.

For instance, doctors now can look at the individual characteristics of a tumor, including particular cell patterns and genetic mutations. This information helps them to set treatment plans that are more likely to work—and to avoid recommending treatments with low chances of success. In fact, Peter Bach, MD, an epidemiologist and pulmonologist at Memorial Sloan-Kettering Cancer Center in New York City, said that he is "extremely enthusiastic" about the progress that's been made over the past decade.

The problem: Despite the remarkable advances, not all hospitals have the needed tools in their arsenals...and not all doctors understand which patients will benefit from such a personalized approach. It's best to be in-the-know about the newest ways to beat lung cancer—in case you end up battling the country's number-one cancer killer.

SECRETS FOUND IN CELL PATTERNS

The term lung cancer actually is misleading because the disease is not just one entity. Rather, there are two major types of lung cancer, each with different risk factors, probable prognoses and treatments. And then even within one of those types, different tumors can have different characteristics that affect how aggressive the cancer may be and which treatment may work.

The majority of lung cancers fall in to the non–small cell category. Adenocarcinoma is the most common non–small cell cancer, accounting for about half of all lung cancers. It's the type found most often in current and former smokers—and also in people who never smoked.

When adenocarcinoma is detected before it has had a chance to spread, it's treated surgically. Most of the time, the surgeon performs a lobectomy by removing the entire lobe that has the cancer in it (a pair of lungs has five lobes, three on the right side and two on the left). In some cases, the surgeon does a limited resection, removing just part of the affected lobe.

Tricky: The decision about which procedure to do can be a tough one, according to Prasad Adusumilli, MD, a thoracic surgeon and scientist at Memorial Sloan-Kettering Cancer Center. That's because the surgeon wants to remove enough lung tissue to prevent a cancer recurrence, but at the same time leave enough tissue to preserve lung function. Until now, there hasn't been an evidence-based system to guide surgeons, so the size and location of the tumor (for example, how far the tumor is from the edge of the lung) often have been used as criteria in deciding how much to remove.

Breakthrough: Surgeons at Memorial Sloan-Kettering perform about 1,000 of these operations each year. With all the data they have accumulated over the years, Dr. Adusumilli and his research team have developed an algorithm to help surgeons decide which operation is best for patients with adenocarcinoma.

The research that led to the new algorithm was complicated, but basically the researchers performed microscopic examinations of many hundreds of samples of early-stage adenocarcinoma, classifying each according to the proportion of the five major cell patterns (acinar, papillary, lepidic, micropapillary and solid) seen in the tumor. Then they analyzed the follow-up data to determine the chances of cancer recurrence based on the cell pattern and the type of surgery that was done.

Overall, the five-year incidence of cancer recurrence was 21% for patients who had a limited resection and 15% for patients who had a lobectomy. When the specific cell patterns were analyzed, though, it became clear that tumors with a higher percentage of cells showing a micropapillary pattern had a much higher risk for recurrence within the same lobe if patients underwent limited resection.

Bottom line: Doctors can now use this knowledge about cell patterns to opt for the tissue-sparing limited resection procedure in patients whose tumors do not have the aggressive micropapillary pattern…and save the more extensive lobectomy for patients whose cell pattern indicates a high risk for recurrence.

Only a limited number of hospitals have the expertise needed to determine a lung tumor's cell pattern right on the spot, in the operating room, at the time of the actual surgery. "This requires expert pathological experience and a large volume of tumors for the pathologists to get experienced," Dr. Adusumilli explained. At hospitals that do not currently have this ability, some patients who get a limited resection may end up needing another operation later if their cancer subsequently is found to have the micropapillary pattern…or, worse, they may have a cancer recurrence.

Hopefully, that will change soon. Dr. Adusumilli and his team of researchers are now trying to develop tools that can more easily determine the cell's pattern—preferably before surgery—sparing patients the need to go under the knife a second time.

SECRETS FOUND IN GENETIC MUTATIONS

When lung cancer is diagnosed after it has spread to the lymph nodes or beyond, as it is most of the time, treatment involves more than just surgery—it also requires medication. Now, in what Dr. Bach refers to as a "very exciting" development, the particular medications that will work best often can be determined based on specific genetic mutations in the tumors.

How it started: About 10 years ago, during clinical trials for two new lung cancer drugs, doctors observed that some people receiving the drugs *gefitinib* (Iressa) and *erlotinib* (Tarceva) had a much better response than others—even though all the patients had advanced adenocarcinoma. This led to the discovery that the patients who responded well had tumors that showed a specific mutation in the epidermal growth factor receptor (EGFR) gene. People with the mutation survived nearly twice as long on the drug regimen as those without it. It turns out that the mutation is present in about 20% of people diagnosed with advanced adenocarcinoma.

A few years later, researchers discovered another mutation on the anaplastic lymphoma kinase (ALK) gene, which is present in 7% of people with adenocarcinoma. A drug that inhibits ALK activity, called *crizotinib* (Xalkori), is very effective in people who have that particular mutation.

All three of these drugs have been approved, and the required genetic testing is available. Many experts now recommend that all patients with advanced adenocarcinoma have their tumors analyzed for mutations of EGFR and ALK—including patients who have mixed cancer types, even with just a small component of adenocarcinoma. Referring to molecular testing in its entirety, not just for EGFR and ALK, Dr. Bach said, "Now, 60% to 70% of adenocarcinomas have important molecular information that affects therapeutic choices. That's huge! Lung cancer might be the poster child for this kind of precision, personalized medicine."

If you are diagnosed with lung cancer: If at all possible, see an oncologist at a hospital associated with a university, Dr. Bach advised. Academic medical centers usually have the technology and expertise to take advantage of these new tests and procedures. If you live too far away to see a doctor there regularly, consider having a consultation with an appropriate expert at such a facility—that person can advise you and your doctor on the best treatment for you.

Better Lung Cancer Follow-Up

ACT scan follow-up program after surgery for lung cancer significantly increases survival rates.

Details: About 400 patients who received CT scans of the thorax (chest) and upper abdomen every three months for two years and then every six months for three more years had a survival rate during the study of 67.8% versus a survival rate of 55.7% for those who did not receive CT scans.

If you have had surgery for lung cancer: Ask your doctor about getting regular CT scans.

Niels-Chr. G. Hansen, MD, pulmonologist, Odense University Hospital, Denmark.

Secrets to Getting the Best Colonoscopy

Douglas K. Rex, MD, a Distinguished Professor of Medicine at Indiana University School of Medicine and director of endoscopy at Indiana University Hospital, both in Indianapolis. He is coauthor of the colorectal cancer screening recommendations of the American College of Gastroenterology as well as current chair of the US Multi-Society Task Force on Colorectal Cancer and coauthor of the recommendations on quality in colonoscopy for this group.

If you're age 50 or older, chances are you've had a colonoscopy—and maybe more than one. If so, you've taken a crucial step in protecting your health.

Why this test is so important: It's estimated that if every person age 50 and older had a colonoscopy, 64% of people with colorectal cancer would have never developed the disease.

But since you are going to the trouble to get this test (and we all know the bowel-cleansing prep is no picnic), then it also makes sense to make sure you're getting

the best possible screening. How to ensure that you get the maximum cancer protection from your colonoscopy...

HOW GOOD IS YOUR DOCTOR?

One of the most important aspects of a colonoscopy is the doctor's ability to detect a type of polyp called an adenoma—the doctor's so-called "adenoma detection rate" (ADR). This varies widely depending on the doctor's skill.

If your doctor has a low ADR, you're more likely to get colon cancer before your next colonoscopy. Gastroenterologists are more likely to have good ADRs than primary care physicians and general surgeons who might perform colonoscopies, but there's a wide range of performance within each group.

Precisely defined, a doctor's ADR is the percentage of screening colonoscopies in patients age 50 or older during which he/she detects one or more adenomas. My advice: Look for a doctor with an ADR of 20% or higher in women and 30% or higher in men (who have more adenomas)...or a "mixed-gender" rate of 25% or higher—in other words, the doctor detects at least one adenoma in 25% of the screening colonoscopies he conducts.

Startling recent finding: A 10-year study published in *The New England Journal of Medicine* evaluated more than 300,000 colonoscopies conducted by 136 gastroenterologists—and found that for every 1% increase in ADR, there was a 3% reduction in the risk of developing colorectal cancer before the next colonoscopy. This means that having your colonoscopy performed by a doctor with a high ADR (as described earlier) is a must for optimal screening. But how does a patient ask about his doctor's ADR without seeming to question the physician's competence?

My advice: Ask about your doctor's ADR on the phone, during the colonoscopy scheduling process, when you are talking to an administrator or a nurse. If that person doesn't know, request that someone get back to you with the number. That will make your query less confrontational.

However: Even your doctor may not know his own ADR. Monitoring of ADRs is endorsed by several professional medical societies, such as the American Society for Gastrointestinal Endoscopy and the American College of Gastroenterology, but there is no law mandating that doctors must track it. Or your doctor may refuse to disclose his ADR—a response you should find concerning. If you don't get the information you need from your doctor, it's probably a good idea to find a new one.

Also important: Make sure your colonoscopy is being performed with a high-definition colonoscope, the current state-of-the-art in colonoscopy. Inquire about this when you ask about a doctor's ADR.

A BETTER BOWEL PREP

Another key to a truly preventive colonoscopy is the preparation. Before the procedure, a patient drinks a defecation-inducing liquid (prep) that cleanses the rectum and colon of stool so that the doctor can clearly see the lining. In some patients, a four-liter prep (about one gallon), or even more, is best for optimal cleansing. If you don't have a condition associated with slow bowel motility, such as chronic constipation, or use constipating medications such as opioids, you may be eligible for one of the regimens that requires only two or three liters of fluid. (A pill preparation is also available, but it is seldom used because it can cause kidney damage.) Ask your doctor what regimen will give you the best combination of excellent cleansing and tolerability.

A common mistake: Many people think that they can drink the prep one to two days before the procedure and then drink nothing but clear fluids (such as Gatorade, apple juice or water) until the day of the colonoscopy.

But even during the prep, the small intestine (the section of bowel after the stomach and before the colon) continues to produce chyme, a thick, mucousy secretion that sticks to the walls of the ascending colon—so that seven to eight hours after drinking the prep the colon is no longer completely clean.

Best: A split prep, with half the prep ingested the day before the procedure and half ingested four to five hours before (the middle of the night when the colonoscopy is scheduled

for the morning...or the morning when the colonoscopy is scheduled for the afternoon). Scientific evidence: Split preparation improves ADR by 26%, according to a study in *Gastrointestinal Endoscopy*.

Also helpful: Drinking the prep can be difficult, even nauseating. How to make it more palatable...

Chill the liquid thoroughly, and drink it with a straw. Follow each swallow with ginger ale or another good-tasting clear liquid. Suck on a clear menthol lozenge after you drink the prep. And if you throw up the prep, wait 30 minutes (until you feel less nauseated) and then continue drinking the prep as instructed—it can still work.

Several recent studies have found that eating a fiber-free diet all or part of the day prior to colonoscopy allows for better cleansing of the colon. Some doctors advise avoiding high-fiber foods such as corn, seeds and nuts for about a week before a colonoscopy. Ask your doctor what he advises for you.

Should You Be Screened for Melanoma? Check Your Arm

If you have more than 11 moles on your right arm, you're at increased risk for melanoma, the deadliest form of skin cancer, finds a new study. It means that you likely have more than 100 moles over your entire body, a known risk factor.

The arm check is a quick way to see if you need further screening. If your count is high, schedule regular full-body exams with a dermatologist. Early detection is a lifesaver when it comes to melanoma.

Got fewer moles? You're not off the hook! Not all melanomas emerge from existing moles. It's important to know what's normal for your skin and to let your doctor know if

425

you see any change in the size, shape, color or feel of a mole—or any other patch of skin.

Study titled "Prediction of High Naevus Count in a Healthy UK Population to Estimate Melanoma Risk" by researchers at King's College London published in *British Journal of Dermatology*.

Deadly Melanoma: Best Prevention, Detection and Treatment Breakthroughs

Albert Lefkovits, MD, an associate clinical professor of dermatology at Mount Sinai School of Medicine and codirector of the Mount Sinai Dermatological Cosmetic Surgery Program, both in New York City.

Melanoma is the most dangerous form of skin cancer. It's particularly frightening because it's more likely than other cancers to spread (metastasize) to other parts of the body. More than 76,000 Americans are diagnosed with melanoma each year, and between 8,000 and 9,000 will die from it.

Good news: New technology increases the chances that a melanoma will be detected early—and when it is, you have a 95% to 97% chance of surviving. The prognosis is worse after the disease has spread. However, therapy has been revolutionized to extend survival times, particularly in the last two years.

WHO'S AT RISK?

A study published in *Journal of Investigative Dermatology* found that melanoma rates increased by 3.1% annually between 1992 and 2004—and the incidence continues to rise.

The increase is due to several reasons. The US population is aging, and older adults are more likely to get melanoma (though it is a leading cause of cancer death in young adults). Public-awareness campaigns have increased the rate of cancer screenings (though officials would like the screening rates to be even higher), and more screenings mean an increase in melanoma diagnoses.

If you are a fair-skinned Caucasian, your lifetime risk of getting melanoma is about one in 50. The risk is lower among African Americans, Hispanics (although over the past decade incidence has increased 20% among Hispanics) and Asians, but they're more likely to die from it. Reason: They often develop cancers on "hidden" areas (such as the soles of the feet), where skin changes aren't readily apparent.

Important: Don't be complacent just because you avoid the sun or use sunscreen. Many cancers appear in areas that aren't exposed to the sun, such as between the toes or around the anus.

STATE-OF-THE-ART SCREENING

Melanomas grow slowly. Patients who get an annual skin checkup are more likely to get an early diagnosis than those who see a doctor only when a mole or skin change is clearly abnormal.

Doctors used to depend on their eyes (and sometimes a magnifying glass) to examine suspicious areas. But eyes-only examinations can identify melanomas only about 60% of the time.

Better: An exam called epiluminescence microscopy. The doctor takes photographs of large areas of skin. Then he/she uses a device that magnifies suspicious areas in the photos. The accuracy of detecting melanomas with this technique is about 90%.

The technology also allows doctors to look for particular changes, such as certain colors or a streaked or globular appearance, that indicate whether a skin change is malignant or benign. This can reduce unnecessary biopsies.

Few private-practice physicians can afford the equipment that's used for these exams. You might want to get your checkups at a medical center or dermatology practice that specializes in early melanoma detection. If this isn't possible, ask your doctor if he/she uses a handheld dermatoscope. It's a less expensive device that's still superior to the unaided eye.

NEW TREATMENTS

In the last few years, the FDA has approved several medications for patients with late-stage melanoma. These drugs don't cure the disease but can help patients live longer.

•*Ipilimumab* (Yervoy) is a biologic medication, a type of synthetic antibody that blocks a cellular "switch" that turns off the body's ability to fight cancer. A study of 676 patients with late-stage melanoma found that those who took the drug survived, on average, for 10 months after starting treatment, compared with 6.4 months for those in a control group.

• *Vemurafenib* **(Zelboraf) may double the survival time of patients with advanced melanoma.** It works by targeting a mutation in the BRAF V600E gene, which is present in about 50% of melanoma patients. Researchers who conducted a study published in *The New England Journal of Medicine* found that more than half of patients who took the medication had at least a 30% reduction in tumor size. In about one-third of patients, the medication slowed or stopped the progression of the cancer.

• **Combination treatment.** Each of these medications attacks tumors in different ways. They can be used in tandem for better results. Drugs such as Yervoy and two additional newly approved drugs, *nivolumab* (Opdivo) and *pembrolizumab* (Keytruda), have been shown to work in combination with each other, affording much more effective therapy and giving new hope to melanoma patients. Also, new developments in vaccine therapy offer promise for the future, but are not FDA-approved at this time.

Both drugs can have serious side effects. For now, they're recommended only for a select group of patients.

SELF-PROTECTION

Take steps to protect yourself...

• **Check your skin monthly.** It's been estimated that deaths from melanoma could be reduced by 60% if everyone would do a monthly skin exam to look for suspicious changes. Look for asymmetric moles in which one part is distinctly different from the other part...moles with an irregular border...color variations...a diameter greater than 6 millimeters (mm), about one-quarter inch...or changes in appearance over time.

• **Get a yearly checkup with a dermatologist.** It's nearly impossible to self-inspect all of the areas on your body where melanoma can appear. I advise patients to see a dermatologist every year for full-body mapping. The doctor will make a note (or photograph) of every suspicious area and track the areas over time.

Important: New moles rarely appear in people over the age of 40. A mole that appears in patients 40 years and older is assumed to be cancer until tests show otherwise.

• **Use a lot of sunscreen.** Even though melanoma isn't caused only by sun exposure, don't get careless. Apply a sunscreen with an SPF of at least 30 whenever you go outdoors. Use a lot of sunscreen—it takes about two ounces of sunscreen (about the amount in a shot glass) to protect against skin cancer. Reapply it about every two hours or immediately after getting out of the water.

• **Don't use tanning salons.** Researchers who published a study in *Journal of the National Cancer Institute* found that people who got their tans at tanning salons—that use tanning lamps and tanning beds that emit UV radiation—at least once a month were 55% more likely to develop a malignant melanoma than those who didn't artificially tan.

A Cancer-Fighting Vitamin

Risk for some types of skin cancer can be reduced by taking a vitamin B-3 derivative called nicotinamide, in addition to using sunscreen.

Details: Nearly 400 adults who previously had basal cell or squamous cell carcinomas took 500 milligrams (mg) of nicotinamide twice daily. After a year, their rate of new skin cancers was 23% lower than that of those who didn't take nicotinamide, which enhances the DNA in sun-damaged cells.

Note: Talk to your doctor before taking nicotinamide—it can interact with medications.

Diona Damian, PhD, professor of dermatology, The University of Sydney Medical School.

Do You Really Need a Mammogram?

Russell Harris, MD, MPH, professor of medicine and adjunct professor of epidemiology, University of North Carolina School of Medicine and Gillings School of Global Public Health, Chapel Hill, North Carolina.

While American doctors follow guidelines that screening should be offered at least every two years to women who are 50 to 74 years old, and although we definitely know that risk of breast cancer increases with age, do you really need a mammogram when you hit 70? A Dutch study says no. In fact, it found that breast cancer screening for women age 70 and older may actually cause more harm than good, leading to unnecessary treatment that puts elderly women at even higher risk than they already are for anemia, gastrointestinal problems, fatigue, infection, memory loss, effects of bone loss (osteoporosis) and heart disease. This all boils down to quality of life in your later years.

And statistics bear this out.

If 1,000 women started biennial mammography screening when they were 50 years old and continued for 10 years, one to three breast cancer deaths would be prevented over the next 15 years. If 1,000 60-year-old women had biennial screenings for 10 years, three or four deaths would be prevented over the next 20 years. For women in their mid-70s, however, their average remaining life expectancy—about 13 more years—is shorter than the 17-year lag time in which a death attributed to breast cancer could be prevented. Suddenly the number of women being helped by screening starts going down, not up.

But maybe you are 72 and expect to live until 102. Fair enough. In that case, breast cancer screening and next steps if breast cancer is detected should be a personal, individualized decision between you and your health-care provider, according to Russell Harris, MD, MPH, professor of medicine at University of North Carolina School of Medicine.

APPROACHING BREAST CANCER DETECTION FROM ANOTHER ANGLE

Dr. Harris said he is not suggesting that all breast cancer screening guidelines should completely go out the window and leave women and their doctors high and dry. His wish—and what he expects to happen, based on discussions with his colleagues in the public health field—is that for older women, at least, there will be new, more individualized guidelines that will be conveyed to gynecologists and primary-care physicians over the next few years. *The same broad leeway being proposed for elderly women should be extended to all women, of every age—and these downsides of breast cancer screening are the rationale…*

• **Cumulative radiation exposure.** Although the amount of radiation received per mammogram is minimal, every time you get a mammogram or are otherwise exposed to radiation in the medical setting, it has a cumulative effect on your body.

• **Possible unneeded treatment.** Some breast cancers are so slow-growing that they would not have caused any harm if they had gone undetected.

• **Side effects of treatment.** As we all know—cancer therapy itself is wrought with side effects. Surgery, radiation, chemotherapy and hormone therapy all come with risks that become riskier with age. Radiation to the breast can damage the heart and lead to lung cancer, and hormone therapy raises a woman's risk for serious blood clots and stroke. For some women, the treatment can be just as devastating as the disease it's meant to conquer.

WHY IT'S A PERSONAL DECISION

Each woman—young, old and in between—needs to evaluate the pros and cons of her own screening in relation to her personal health, family history and life situation. The physician's role is to help women make informed, individualized decisions about breast cancer screening—not to automatically pressure them into decisions based on screening statistics.

Part of being informed means recognizing that screening isn't the only way to protect yourself. There are other approaches to prevention that we've de-emphasized at our peril. It's time to stop putting all our eggs in the screening basket. Screening is not our only hope to reduce the scourge of breast cancer. Maintaining a healthy weight, remaining physically active, not smoking, being moderate in our drinking habits and proactively working with a gynecologist and primary-care physician to know and address personal risk factors are important ways for women to protect themselves against cancer, stay all-around healthy and have a great quality of life.

False-Positive Mammograms Mean More Breast Cancer Risk

Study titled "Increased Risk of Developing Breast Cancer after a False-Positive Screening Mammogram" by researchers at University of North Carolina-Chapel Hill School of Medicine published in *Cancer Epidemiology, Biomarkers & Prevention.*

Half of all women who get mammograms regularly will have a "false positive" within 10 years—a "suspicious" finding that turns out to not be cancer after all. When they find out that their "positives" are false, they're relieved.

But a large new study shows that women who get false positives may be at higher risk for breast cancer after all. Researchers analyzed data from 1.3 million women aged 40 to 74. Compared with women who had only negative mammograms, those who had had false positives were 39% more likely to get breast cancer in the next 10 years—and those who had gotten biopsies because of their potentially positive results were 76% more likely to get breast cancer.

Researchers aren't sure why false positives would be an indicator of greater cancer risk, but it's possible that what medical science currently labels as "false" results could actually indicate changes in breast tissue that are not cancer but that stand a reasonable chance of developing into it.

The increased risk percentages sound scary but the actual level of risk for women who had false positives is much smaller than you might think. That's because the vast majority of women, even those who have had false-positive mammogram results, don't get breast cancer. In the study, women with true negative mammograms had a 10-year risk of developing breast cancer of 0.4%, while those with a false positive had a 0.5% risk, and those who had a false positive and then a biopsy had a 0.7% risk. Even in the highest-risk biopsy group, then, 99.3% will not get breast cancer in the next decade.

It may be that as the science improves, some of today's mammogram results that are simply considered "false positives" and forgotten about will come to be considered actual positives—not for cancer, but for increased risk, albeit small.

Women with a strong family history of breast cancer, especially those with genetic markers for the disease, are already at higher-than-average risk. While this study didn't look at these groups of women in particular, they already have reason to be extra vigilant.

For women who aren't aware of any extra risk, however, this study may be an added incentive—if you've ever had a false-positive mammogram result, you now have even more reason to monitor your breast health.

What's a Good Reason to Have a Healthy Breast Removed?

Deborah Axelrod, MD, medical director, clinical breast services and breast programs, Laura and Isaac Perlmutter Cancer Center, NYU Langone Medical Center, New York City. She is on the medical advisory board of the Susan G. Komen Foundation, Dallas, on the board of directors for SHARE, and is coauthor of *Bosom Buddies,* a guide for women with breast cancer.

Call it the Angelina Effect. More women are choosing to have double mastectomies.

Some, like the actress and director Angelina Jolie, don't have cancer at all but have both breasts removed as a preventive measure. Others are diagnosed with cancer in one breast but have both breasts removed for prevention. Many celebrities have gone that route—Sharon Osbourne, Wanda Sykes, and more recently, Amy Robach and Sandra Lee.

Nor is it only celebrities. Between 1998 and 2011, the rates of women with breast cancer having a double mastectomy for single-breast disease zoomed from less than 2% to more than 11%, according to a recent study published in *JAMA Surgery*.

Here's the catch: Some women are choosing to remove healthy breasts even when doing so isn't likely to help them avoid cancer...or live longer.

What's a good reason to have a healthy breast removed? What's a bad reason? To help women faced with this difficult decision, we spoke with Deborah Axelrod, MD, surgical oncologist at NYU Langone Medical Center and coauthor of *Bosom Buddies*, a guide for women with breast cancer.

REASONS TO REMOVE A HEALTHY BREAST— OR NOT

"There are indeed many reasons why you may want to remove the 'other' breast...and they're not all purely medical," said Dr. Axelrod. "But you shouldn't be pressured. It's important to understand that most women overestimate their risk for breast cancer returning or getting a cancer in the other breast."

In her practice, when Dr. Axelrod asks patients what they are thinking about their condition and treatment options, she hears a number of reasons for choosing a double mastectomy. *Here are the four reasons she hears most often—and the science that supports or negates them...*

REASON #1: "I never want to have worry about breast cancer again."

"This is possibly the worst reason to choose a double mastectomy," said Dr. Axelrod. That's true whether you are newly diagnosed with cancer in one breast...or have already gone through treatment. Why? "Removing the second breast won't have any effect on the cancer that you have been diagnosed and treated

for," said Dr. Axelrod. "A bevy of credible research has found no meaningful survival benefit in women who have had cancer in one breast and elect to undergo a double mastectomy. Women who die of breast cancer most likely die of cancer that has spread outside the breast and the lymph nodes. If your breast cancer is going to recur, it will happen locally in the same breast—we can never remove all of the tissue—or systemically, meaning it traveled from the lymph nodes to another part of your body, most typically the bones, liver, lungs and brain. Removing the other, healthy breast is not going to prevent either type of recurrence from happening."

REASON #2: "I've got the breast cancer gene."

As a carrier of the BRCA1 gene mutation, Angelina Jolie had an 87% lifetime risk of developing breast cancer and a 50% lifetime risk of developing ovarian cancer. Her diagnosis hit close to home, too—her mother died of ovarian cancer at the age of 56. Angelina Jolie eventually had not only both her breasts but also her ovaries removed as a preventive measure. Said Dr. Axelrod, "Carriers of the well-publicized BRCA1 or BRCA2 genes, as well as a number of other genes that have been discovered more recently, including TP53 (Li-Fraumeni syndrome), pTEN (Cowden's disease), CDH1, and PALB2 have a significantly higher risk. And as in Jolie's case, removing the breasts and ovaries even when there is no cancer present will greatly reduce the odds of both forms of the disease and bring peace of mind.

"Still, you don't have to go to this extreme—with your breasts anyway. Ovarian cancer is harder to diagnose in the early stages, so there is a good argument for having your ovaries removed." With your breasts, however, it's a more complicated decision. You can chose to be closely monitored for very early signs of breast cancer, which is 98% curable if caught in Stage 0 or 1. "However, women who are BRCA1 carriers have a higher rate of small aggressive cancers," she said, "and preventive mastectomy substantially reduces that risk."

REASON #3: "I have a family history of breast cancer."

"Many women have close relatives—mothers, sisters, grandmothers—who have been diagnosed with breast cancer, yet testing has not revealed any genetic link." That's actually the case most of the time, since only 5% to 10% of women who get breast cancer have known genetic risk factors. "That doesn't rule out a genetic predisposition," she said. "It could well mean that we haven't yet discovered the particular gene mutation that you have yet. But it's not a good argument for removing a healthy breast. You can avoid unnecessary surgery with close monitoring."

***REASON #4*: "I want both my breasts to look the same."**

"While this is not a medical reason, it is a valid personal reason why one may choose to remove a healthy breast along with a diseased one," Dr. Axelrod said. "Breast reconstruction has come a long way, but there is still a big difference between a natural breast and a reconstructed one, and if you're going to have both reconstructed, better symmetry can be achieved if you choose to have them done at the same time. In addition, if you choose to have a TRAM (transverse rectus abdominis) flap (in which some of the abdominal muscle is used to create the new breast) or a DIEP flap (which uses abdominal skin and tissue but no muscle), it can be performed only once, so choosing to have both breasts done makes sense to many women. Bear in mind, however, that the length of time you will spend on the operating table for this procedure is at least double that of traditional reconstruction with implants, and your recovery time will be longer because you're also having abdominal surgery, which also increases the risk for complications. You'll likely be in the hospital for five days as opposed to two or three. And not every woman is a candidate for this procedure: If you're thin, you likely won't have enough belly tissue. Women who have had multiple cesarean deliveries or other abdominal surgeries also may not be candidates."

All of this adds up to a very personal decision in which you must consider your comfort, convenience, recovery, appearance, family history and fears. "Take your time and consider all the options," said Dr. Axelrod. No doctor should tell you that you need to be on the operating table ASAP, nor should any doctor casually say, 'how about taking off the other breast?' Both kinds of comments are warning signs that you need another opinion."

Women Testing Negative for the Breast Cancer Gene Still May Be at Risk

It was originally thought that women who come from families with BRCA mutations but who test negative for any BRCA mutations had the same risk for breast cancer as the general population.

Recent finding: Women from such families with negative BRCA2 mutation had four times the risk for breast cancer as the general population.

Gareth Evans, MD, honorary professor of medical genetics and a cancer epidemiologist at The University of Manchester in England and lead author of a study of 800 families, published in *Cancer Epidemiology, Biomarkers & Prevention*.

Take a Walk to Reduce Breast Cancer Risk

An hour walk each day lowered breast cancer risk by 14% among postmenopausal women. And women who did at least one hour of strenuous physical activity daily had 25% lower risk for breast cancer. Physical activity is thought to lower risk by reducing hormones…improving weight control, glucose metabolism and insulin sensitivity…and lowering inflammation.

Alpa Patel, PhD, strategic director of the Cancer Prevention Study-3 (CPS-3) for the American Cancer Society, Atlanta, and leader of a study of 73,615 postmenopausal women, reported in *Cancer Epidemiology, Biomarkers & Prevention*.

Skip the Midnight Snack

Longer periods of overnight fasting may reduce risk for breast cancer.

New study: For every three hours women didn't eat at night, glucose decreased by 4%, regardless of how much they ate the rest of the day.

Theory: Since diabetes is a risk factor for breast cancer, keeping normal blood sugar levels is a good way to stave off both conditions. Prolonged overnight fasting may also reduce risk for other types of cancer and heart disease.

Ruth E. Patterson, PhD, program leader, cancer prevention, Moores Cancer Center, University of California, San Diego.

Doctors Don't Follow Cervical Cancer Prevention Guidelines

American Journal of Preventive Medicine.

Here's a question for women (and for the men who love them): How often should most women get a Pap test to check for signs of cervical cancer?

If you answered "every year," you would have been correct many years ago...if you think it's "every other year," you would have been correct up to about four years ago...if you responded "every three years," you're not only correct, but you also know more than most doctors.

Another question: Can anything prevent people from getting the human papillomavirus (HPV) that causes most cervical cancers? Answer: Yes, because a vaccine has been available for seven years. Since its introduction, the HPV rate among teenage girls has been slashed in half, and rates of cervical precancers are declining in women under age 24.

Problem: Neither the Pap test nor the HPV vaccine are being used properly, a new report reveals—because only 4% of doctors are following all of the guidelines.

Now, I'm not saying that all medical guidelines are infallible and should be followed without question. You know me better than that! For instance, I was outraged several years back when guidelines were issued that suggested eliminating breast cancer screening for women in their 40s...and now new research supports my view that those guidelines were misguided.

But in the case of cervical cancer, I think the new guidelines are an improvement—so I'm disturbed that so few doctors are following them. *Here's the story...*

CHANGING RECOMMENDATIONS

The Pap test that detects cervical cancer undoubtedly saves lives. But cervical cancer generally grows very slowly...so slowly that screening every year, as was done for many decades, was actually doing harm. How so? Countless women were told that their Pap tests had detected abnormal cells, so they underwent a lot of additional testing and biopsies—and experienced a lot of anxiety—all to check out abnormal cells that never would have ended up causing cancer. Because experts in cancer prevention believed that the harms of too-frequent screening were outweighing its benefits—and because a test for HPV was developed that made screening much more effective—the recommended interval between testing was increased twice in the past four years.

In 2009, the American Congress of Obstetricians and Gynecologists (ACOG) changed its guidelines to recommend Pap tests every two years starting at age 21 (even for women who become sexually active earlier)...every three years from age 30 to 69...and stopping at age 70 or after a woman had a hysterectomy for a benign condition (because she no longer has a cervix). ACOG also recommended that the test for HPV—which causes more than 99% of cervical cancers and more than 70% of throat cancers, as well as some vaginal, vulvar and other cancers—be done every two years from age 30 to 69. (Just like the Pap, the HPV test is done with a cervical swab, and both tests are easily done at the same time, a method called co-testing.)

Then in 2012, the guidelines were changed yet again, increasing the recommended interval between Pap screenings to every three years...and offering the alternative, starting at age 30, of having Pap-plus-HPV co-testing every five years. (The guidelines do not make exceptions for women in monogamous relationships.) The new guidelines also indicated that Pap tests and HPV screening should stop at age 65 for women with no history of abnormal tests and at least two negative tests in the past 10 years...or earlier for women who had hysterectomies for benign conditions.

Reason: This screening schedule retains about 95% of the benefits of annual screening but reduces the harms associated with false alarms (the painful biopsy, the expense and inconvenience of additional testing, the anxiety) by two-thirds.

DISTURBING SURVEY

In early 2012, before the newest Pap test guidelines were endorsed by ACOG, a survey was sent to obstetrician-gynecologists across the country to see how they were doing at following the then-current recommendations. Because old habits die hard, the survey results carry some worrisome implications about the current state of cervical cancer detection. Here are the survey results as they pertain to...

Pap testing—starting and stopping: Scarcely more than half of doctors waited to the recommended age of 21 to start Pap screening...many started at age 18 or even earlier. More than one-quarter of doctors continued ordering Pap tests after age 69, with no upper age limit...and 39% continued doing Pap tests even after a woman had had a hysterectomy for a benign condition.

Pap testing—proper intervals: The majority of doctors reported that they still did annual Pap tests despite the recommendations—74% screened annually during a woman's 20s...53% screened annually from age 30 and up...and 18% offered annual screening to all women. Their reasons? Many said that they were concerned that patients would skip their annual checkups if the Pap were not offered...and 8% of doctors admitted to being worried about losing income if they didn't do annual Pap tests.

HPV testing: 23% of doctors did not offer the recommended HPV screening test at all. Just 45% offered the recommended Pap and HPV co-testing as a matter of course...21% offered co-testing (recommended for women age 30 and up) only if requested by the patient.

VACCINATION STATUS

The survey also included questions about HPV vaccination.

ACOG recommends that both female and male patients get the three-injection vaccine series starting at age 11...people who didn't get the vaccine as adolescents can receive it up through age 26. Why would boys or men get a vaccine that guards against cervical cancer? Because males can transmit the HPV virus to their female partners, increasing women's risk for cervical cancer...and because HPV also is associated with cancer of the penis in men and with cancers of the throat and anus in men and women.

Again, the survey results were disappointing. Although more than 90% of physicians surveyed offered the HPV vaccine in their practices—and very few had any concerns about the vaccine's safety or effectiveness—only 6% said that at least four out of five of their eligible patients even began the series...and of those who did begin, fewer than one-third completed the series. Oddly, 10% of doctors reported offering the vaccine to pregnant women, which is against the recommendations.

TAKEAWAY MESSAGE

Overall, just 4% of surveyed doctors adhered to all of the 2009 guidelines—a disappointing showing that does not bode well at all for compliance with the newer 2012 guidelines.

It's worth noting that male doctors generally were less likely than female doctors to comply with the guidelines. (My feeling? Perhaps women doctors, who undergo Pap and HPV testing themselves, are more attuned to the inconvenience, expense, discomfort and anxiety that can accompany unnecessary testing.)

Also of interest is that guideline compliance was lower among doctors in solo practices than among doctors in hospital-based or group practices—perhaps because solo practitioners don't have the same access to shared knowledge among colleagues. Still, as licensed physicians, all doctors should keep up with the literature and latest guidelines.

Exceptions: Of course, the same guidelines don't apply to everyone. Women who need more frequent screening include those at increased risk for cervical cancer due to a suppressed immune system (for instance, from an autoimmune disease, HIV infection or immune-suppressing drugs)…a history of moderate-to-severe cervical dysplasia (abnormal cells)…or exposure to the drug DES. But for the vast majority of women at normal risk, the screening and prevention guidelines are the best tools we have today to protect against both cervical cancer and the unnecessary testing that just causes anxiety and leads to more testing.

Women, take note: Many of the doctors surveyed said that they thought patients were uncomfortable with the idea of screening less frequently than every year—so if you are such a patient, talk to your doctor about your concerns.

If your doctor is the one pushing for annual Pap testing, remind the doctor that the guidelines suggest testing every three years, and ask for a clear explanation of why he/she believes that you need more frequent testing. I'd hate to think that a doctor would insist on yearly testing simply to hang onto the revenue that tests generate. Yet a recent commentary in *The New England Journal of Medicine* pointed out that the bill for a Pap test, which used to run about $20 to $30, now can top $1,000 if unnecessary add-ons (such as tests for multiple infections) are included when a doctor unthinkingly clicks on a single box in the electronic medical record!

I also urge you to talk to your doctor about any concerns you may have about the HPV vaccine, particularly if you have teenaged children or grandchildren. Though some people question the moral implications of vaccinating adolescents against a sexually transmitted disease, studies have shown that the vaccine is safe and effective, with over 100 million doses given around the world to date—and your doctor (not YouTube!) is your best resource for answering your questions. It's important to realize that avoiding HPV infection altogether is the best way to prevent cervical cancer in women and various other cancers in both men and women.

Prostate Cancer Action Plan—Better Than Watchful Waiting

Aaron E. Katz, MD, chairman of urology at Winthrop University Hospital in Mineola, New York. He is author of *The Definitive Guide to Prostate Cancer: Everything You Need to Know About Conventional and Integrative Therapies.*

More than 33,000 American men die from prostate cancer annually. But this type of cancer can also be relatively harmless, growing slowly, if at all, and never spreading beyond the gland itself.

This poses a dilemma: While a life-threatening condition requires aggressive action, the standard treatments for any form of prostate cancer—including the slow-growing kinds—are surgery and/or radiation, and these treatments can result in impotence and/or incontinence in a significant number of men.

For cancer confined to the prostate when diagnosed, one strategy has been watchful waiting—doing nothing unless a patient develops symptoms indicating that the cancer has spread. This was usually reserved for men with limited life expectancy (typically less than 10 years) and those who have significant other health problems or whose medical condition made surgery or radiation inadvisable. *But there are two newer, more effective, approaches…*

•**Active surveillance,** which is for men of any age whose cancer looks unlikely to progress quickly. With this strategy, the situation is closely monitored with regular tests—beyond digital rectal exams and prostate-specific antigen (PSA) tests. If the cancer seems to be growing, treatment is initiated.

• **Active holistic surveillance,** which adds diet and lifestyle changes to optimize the odds that a minor prostate cancer will stay that way.

NOT FOR EVERYONE

In 2011, a panel of experts convened by the National Institutes of Health (NIH) reviewed available research and endorsed active surveillance as "a viable option that should be offered to patients with low-risk prostate cancer."

According to the NIH committee, 100,000 of the 240,000 American men diagnosed annually with prostate cancer might be candidates for active surveillance. (Right now, only 10% of them are treated this way. The other 90% go on to some form of treatment, usually surgery or radiation.)

Active surveillance may be considered an option if the cancer is confined to the prostate, and lab tests and biopsy results indicate the tumor is unlikely to become dangerous. This calculation takes into account the concentration of PSA circulating in the blood...the Gleason score, which is based on the pathologist's reading of the cells and estimates of how aggressive the tumor will be...and the amount of cancerous tissue in the biopsy.

Ultimately, it's a decision for you and your doctor to make together. If you have other chronic diseases that make surgery or radiation especially risky, this can weigh in favor of active surveillance. But if the idea of leaving cancer in your body makes you unbearably anxious despite the low risk that it will progress, the approach is not for you.

ACTIVE-SURVEILLANCE STRATEGIES

PSA testing every few months is part of active surveillance. A marked increase in PSA indicates the need for more extensive tests.

Many doctors also repeat the prostate biopsy periodically, sometimes as often as every year, to see if the cancer has become more aggressive. But because biopsy is invasive and carries a small risk for infection and inflammation, some opt for an annual MRI or ultrasound instead, performing a biopsy only when rising PSA, MRI findings and/or symptoms, such as increased difficulty urinating, suggest the situation may have worsened. If this is the case, standard treatments for prostate cancer are usually necessary.

ACTIVE HOLISTIC STRATEGIES

In addition to keeping tabs on your cancer, you can enhance the body's natural defenses and attack the processes that support the growth of cancer by...

• **Fighting free radicals.** These highly active molecules, produced in the course of normal metabolism and increased by toxic chemicals and certain foods, damage healthy cells and allow cancer to flourish. Diet improves the body's own antioxidant system.

• **Reducing chronic inflammation.** The immune system produces chemicals and mobilizes cells to attack infection and heal injury. But when inflammation becomes chronic, it creates a steady stream of free radicals that damage cells and promote cancer growth.

PROTECTIVE DIET

The eating plan to subdue low-risk prostate cancer includes elements of the Mediterranean diet and traditional Japanese diet that are recommended for cardiovascular and brain health as well.

Key elements...

• **Consume plenty of fruits and vegetables.** Cruciferous vegetables (such as broccoli and cauliflower), highly colored fruits (especially berries), and garlic and onions are particularly rich in antioxidants and other cancer-fighting chemicals.

• **Include nuts and seeds,** which appear to reduce prostate cancer risk.

• **Avoid saturated fats,** which promote inflammation, and eliminate or limit red meat, which is associated with higher rates of advanced prostate cancer. Cured meats (such as bacon or salami), processed meat (such as cold cuts) and—especially—grilled, charred meats increase cancer risk and should be avoided.

●**Eat fatty fish** (such as wild-caught salmon or sardines) at least one or two times a week for its inflammation-fighting omega-3 fatty acids.

●**Substitute whole grains for foods with refined flour and sugar** (they promote inflammation).

●**Limit dairy products**—high dairy intake corresponds to higher risk for prostate cancer, probably due to its fat and calcium content.

●**Watch your weight**—obesity promotes oxidation and inflammation and alters hormones in a way that increases risk for aggressive prostate cancers.

SUPPLEMENT POWER

In addition to diet, nutritional and herbal supplements add protective power. *The most important…*

●**Vitamin D.** Most people don't get enough of this nutrient, which normalizes cell activity and thus may reduce the risk for cancer. Ask your doctor to test your blood level of vitamin D. If it is below 50 ng/ml, take a supplement.

●**Fish oil.** It can be hard to get enough omega-3 fatty acids in the diet. Therefore, some men may benefit from fish oil supplements (1 g to 4 g daily). Check with your doctor first if you take a blood thinner.

●**Anti-inflammatory herbs.** Certain herbs—such as turmeric, rosemary and holy basil—and green tea have strong anti-inflammatory effects. The supplement products *Zyflamend* (New Chapter) and *ProstaCaid* (EcoNugenics), which combine these herbs and others, have been shown to fight prostate cancer. Both products are available online and at health-food stores.

AN OUNCE OF PREVENTION

Men with low-risk prostate cancer who followed a program of exercise and stress reduction combined with a low-fat, plant-based diet were significantly less likely to need conventional treatment within the next two years, compared with a control group, according to recent research.

It's not surprising. Exercise reduces inflammation and enhances immune protection. Reducing stress lowers inflammation and promotes cellular repair. *What to do…*

●**Exercise at least a half hour a day**—brisk walking, biking or swimming—at a pace that seems comfortable. Add strength training three times a week to build muscle.

●**Incorporate a stress-reducing activity into your daily schedule.** Relaxation exercises, such as yoga or meditation, are ideal, but anything that releases tension (reading, listening to music) will be helpful.

IS IT SAFE TO WAIT?

Delaying treatment does not seem to risk a worse outcome. Results from a 2011 multi-center study of 731 men diagnosed with early-stage prostate cancer showed that those who had no initial treatment were no more likely to die in the next 12 years than those who had surgery.

Additionally, in a recent study at Johns Hopkins University, none of 769 participants in an active-surveillance program died of prostate cancer in the 15 years after being diagnosed, and 41% had no need for surgery or radiation.

The Right Selenium Supplement for Prostate Health

Study titled "Comparative Effects of Two Different Forms of Selenium on Oxidative Stress Biomarkers in Healthy Men: A Randomized Clinical Trial," published in *Cancer Prevention Research*.

S elenium has strong antioxidant properties, and many studies have shown that cancer is less likely to develop in people who have more selenium in their diets. But there has been a lot of controversy about how effective it is in preventing prostate cancer. One large study showed selenium supplementation cut risk of prostate cancer by up to two-thirds, while another large study showed that it was no better than a placebo.

Where does the truth lie? In the not-so-fine print, actually, because some new research has brought to light what may be obvious but easily missed. It turns out that the particular type of selenium supplement used may make it a hit or miss when it comes to protection against prostate cancer.

The study that showed a drastic reduction in prostate cancer used a supplement made of selenium yeast, which is yeast that has been enriched with selenium. The study that showed no effect used a supplement made of selenomethionine, which is the amino acid that contains selenium. To find out why one type of a selenium supplement was effective and another not in terms of prostate cancer protection, a research team recruited 69 healthy men between the ages of 23 and 78 to participate in a year-long study. The men were divided into four groups—one group received a placebo, one group received the maximum daily recommended dosage of selenium (200 micrograms per day) in the form of seleno-methionine, another group received the maximum daily dosage in the form of selenium yeast and, because higher doses of selenium yeast are currently being studied as therapy for prostate cancer, the last group received a higher dosage (285 micrograms per day) of selenium yeast.

Before starting the study and at three, nine and 12 months, all of the men had blood and urine tests to evaluate levels of selenium and prostate specific antigen (PSA, a marker for prostate cancer) as well as signs of oxidative stress related to prostate cancer development.

The results: Although blood levels of selenium increased in all of the men taking any form or dose of selenium, they substantially increased in the men taking selenomethionine (by 93%) and high-dose selenium yeast (86%). You would think that the higher the blood level, the higher the prostate cancer protection, but the study findings hinted that this may not be the case—the only form of selenium that had an impact on oxidative stress in this particular study was high-dose selenium yeast. The researchers theorized that, al-though selenomethionine may be able to get more selenium into the blood than selenium yeast, it may be missing the compounds that reduce oxidative stress in the prostate gland or allow sufficient absorption of selenium into prostate gland tissue.

Selenium is naturally found in seafood, meats, grains and eggs. Adults should get 55 micrograms per day, according to the National Institutes of Health. Most people in the United States who maintain well-balanced diets get enough selenium, although studies show that selenium levels are commonly low in men with prostate cancer. But if you are a man concerned about prostate health, get your selenium level checked first to find out whether taking a selenium yeast supplement is right for you. Getting too much selenium, such as from going overboard with supplement use, can cause gastrointestinal, cardiovascular and kidney problems.

High Cholesterol Caution

Cholesterol is linked to prostate cancer recurrence.

Recent finding: Patients with high blood levels of triglyceride fats—above 150 milligrams per deciliter (mg/dL)—had a 35% increased risk for recurrence following prostate cancer surgery. Elevated total cholesterol—above 200 mg/dL—also was associated with increased risk (9% for every 10-mg/dL rise).

But: Higher levels of HDL ("good") cholesterol were linked to reduced risk (39% decrease for each 10-mg/dL improvement) in men with low HDL. Cholesterol and triglyceride levels can be improved through lifestyle changes and/or statin drugs.

Emma Allott, PhD, a former researcher at Duke University School of Medicine, Durham, North Carolina, and lead author of a study in *Cancer Epidemiology, Biomarkers & Prevention.*

More Bad News About Inflammation

Inflammation contributes to prostate cancer, especially the aggressive form. Men with chronic inflammation in benign prostate tissue had almost twice the risk of developing prostate cancer as did men without inflammation.

To reduce inflammation: Get regular exercise...maintain a healthy weight and diet... and don't smoke.

Elizabeth A. Platz, ScD, MPH, professor and Martin D. Abeloff, MD Scholar in Cancer Prevention and deputy chair of the department of epidemiology, The Johns Hopkins Bloomberg School of Public Health, Baltimore. She is coauthor of a study published in *Cancer Epidemiology, Biomarkers & Prevention*.

Better Prostate Cancer Screening

Two new tests help men avoid unnecessary treatments for prostate cancer. The PCA3 test measures urinary levels of prostate cancer gene 3, found only in cancerous prostate cells. Men with higher-than-normal PSA levels should ask for a PCA3 test before getting a biopsy. A PCA3 score of 25 or lower means that a biopsy likely is not needed. The Prolaris test uses cancer cells taken during a biopsy to determine how aggressive a tumor is. This helps doctors pursue the best course of treatment.

Prevention. Prevention.com

Statins Stave Off Barrett's Esophagus

Statins may reduce risk for Barrett's esophagus, a precursor to esophageal cancer. Barrett's esophagus is mainly caused by long-term gastroesophageal reflux disease (GERD), obesity and/or a family history of GERD.

Recent finding: In older men, the use of statins—mainly simvastatin—was associated with a 43% lower risk for Barrett's esophagus.

But first-line prevention involves controlling GERD, maintaining a normal weight and eating a balanced diet.

Hashem B. El-Serag, MD, a professor of medicine at Baylor College of Medicine, Houston, and leader of a study of 1,212 men, published in *Gastroenterology*.

A New Blood Test Detects Pancreatic Cancer Earlier

Early detection and tumor removal can help increase life expectancy for pancreatic cancer patients. Currently the five-year survival rate is less than 5%. Further testing is needed before the test becomes available.

Study of 271 patients and volunteers by researchers at Kobe University Graduate School of Medicine, Japan, published in *Cancer Epidemiology, Biomarkers & Prevention*.

Get the Very Best Cancer Care

Barrie R. Cassileth, PhD, the former Laurance S. Rockefeller Chair and chief of the integrative medicine department at Memorial Sloan Kettering Cancer Center in New York City. She is also the author of *Survivorship: Living Well During and After Cancer*.

A cancer diagnosis is always fraught with fear and anxiety—not to mention nagging questions about the best possible treatments.

Bridging the gap: While surgery, chemotherapy and radiation have long been the mainstay treatments for cancer, major cancer centers throughout the US now offer a variety of additional "complementary" therapies that help patients cope with a wide range of cancer-related problems.

Latest development: Recent studies continue to be added to the growing body of evidence supporting the use of such nondrug and nonsurgical therapies, which are used along with conventional cancer treatment.

LOOK FOR PROVEN BENEFITS

Only a small number of complementary therapies have been thoroughly tested with randomized, placebo-controlled clinical trials—the gold standard of scientific research. Some of these approaches have now been proven to work.

Common cancer symptoms that can be relieved with complementary approaches—some services may be covered by insurance, so check with your health insurer…

•**Less nausea.** Nausea and/or vomiting are among the most common symptoms cancer patients have—and among the most feared. Antinausea medications help, but they're not a perfect solution. That's why they're sometimes used in tandem with acupuncture, a complementary therapy that has been shown to be particularly effective.

Scientific evidence: When acupuncture was tested in a group of breast cancer patients being treated with a form of chemotherapy that's notorious for causing nausea, those who were given acupuncture for five days had one-third fewer episodes of nausea than those who were treated only with medications that were used for nausea, such as lorazepam and diphenhydramine. Self-acupressure, in which patients merely press on certain points, such as the PC6 point on the wrist (without using needles), can also help.

To find the PC6 point: Turn your hand so your palm is facing up and locate the area, which is between the tendons three finger widths from the base of the wrist. Massage the area for four to five seconds…or longer, as needed.

•**Pain relief.** Both gentle massage and acupuncture can reduce the pain that's caused by cancer (such as bone cancer) and cancer treatments (such as radiation)—and sometimes allow patients to take lower doses of medication, which can help reduce troubling side effects, including constipation.

Scientific evidence: A study that looked at nearly 1,300 cancer patients found that massage improved their pain scores by 40%…and the improvements lasted for hours and sometimes days after the massage.

Imaging studies show that acupuncture also helps by deactivating brain areas that are involved in pain perception. In one study, patients with chronic cancer pain were treated with either auricular acupuncture (needles placed in the ear) or with sham treatments. After two months, patients in the acupuncture group reported reductions in pain intensity of 36% versus 2% in the placebo group.

•**Less fatigue.** Only about 10% of cancer patients are physically active during treatment. But the vast majority can safely exercise before, during and after treatments…and exercise is among the best ways to reduce treatment-related fatigue.

Scientific evidence: When researchers at the University of Connecticut analyzed 44 studies focusing on patients with cancer-related fatigue, they found that those who exercised had more energy than those who were sedentary.

Any form of exercise seems to help. Yoga that focuses on gentle postures and breathing is good because it's easy on the body and has been shown to reduce anxiety and other stress-related symptoms.

Bonus: Cancer patients who exercise tend to live longer than those who don't stay active. A study of more than 900 breast cancer patients found that those who engaged in brisk walking for two and a half hours a week—the same level of exercise that's recommended for the general population—were 67% less likely to die during the nine-year study period than those who were sedentary.

•**Fewer hot flashes.** Both men and women who have hormone-dependent cancers (such as breast and prostate cancers) often experience hot flashes when they're given hormone-based treatments. Once again, acupuncture seems to help.

Scientific evidence: One study found that nearly 90% of patients with breast or prostate cancers who were given acupuncture had a reduction in hot flashes of nearly 50% that lasted at least three months.

HOW TO STAY SAFE

Virtually all oncologists and respected cancer centers in the US now support the use of complementary therapies, such as acupuncture and massage, to help cancer patients cope with nausea, pain, anxiety and other symptoms. These and other complementary therapies are used in addition to conventional treatments. To find an evidence-based complementary oncology program: Look for a comprehensive cancer center at the National Cancer Institute's website, *cancer.gov/research/nci-role/cancer-centers/find.*

Very important: When seeking complementary care, it's vital that the practitioner (including massage therapists, acupuncturists, etc.) be properly trained to work with cancer patients. Getting therapy at a comprehensive cancer center helps ensure that.

Also crucial: Cancer patients should always talk to their doctors before taking any supplements (herbs, vitamins, etc.). They can sometimes interfere with chemotherapy and other cancer treatments. For more on specific supplements, go to Memorial Sloan Kettering's website, *mskcc.org/aboutherbs.*

After Cancer: You Really Can Get Back to Normal

Julie K. Silver, MD, who cofounded Oncology Rehab Partners, a Northborough, Massachusetts–based firm that trains and certifies hospitals and cancer centers in evidence-based cancer rehabilitation, and developed its Survivorship Training and Rehabilitation (STAR) Program. She is the author of *After Cancer Treatment: Heal Faster, Better, Stronger.* StarProgramOncologyRehab.com

Until relatively recently, there was no such thing as "cancer rehab" to help cancer patients cope with the grueling and sometimes lasting physical and psychological effects of chemotherapy, radiation, surgery or other treatment. Patients, many of whom considered themselves lucky just to be alive, dealt with the problems largely on their own.

Now: Just as patients who have suffered a heart attack or stroke are likely to receive guidance on how to cope with the aftereffects of treatment, more and more cancer patients are beginning to get the help they need to regain the quality of life they had before getting sick.

Who can benefit: Of the 12.6 million cancer survivors in the US, an estimated 3.3 million continue to suffer physical consequences of their treatment, such as fatigue and/or chronic pain…and another 1.4 million live with mental health problems, such as depression and/or a form of mild cognitive impairment known as "chemo brain."

Latest development: As cancer rehab becomes more prevalent throughout the US—hundreds of facilities nationwide offer such programs—there is mounting evidence showing how this type of care can help accelerate recovery, improve a patient's quality of life and perhaps even reduce risk for cancer recurrence.* In fact, the American College of Surgeons' Commission on Cancer now requires cancer centers in the US to offer rehab services in order to receive accreditation.

WHEN CANCER REHAB HELPS

Even though it was first conceived as a resource for patients immediately after their acute phase of treatment, cancer rehab can help long after treatment has taken place. For example, people who were treated years ago and are now cancer-free—but not free of side effects from treatment—can benefit from cancer rehab. Just because you went for, say, physical therapy two years ago after you finished cancer treatment, it doesn't mean that you can't get more help now for the same problem or a different one.

Insurance picks up the tab: Because the benefits of cancer rehab are now so widely accepted, insurance generally covers the

*To find a medical center near you that offers cancer rehab services, consult Oncology Rehab Partners, *StarProgramOncologyRehab.com.*

cost—regardless of when you were treated for cancer—including consultations with physiatrists (medical doctors who specialize in rehabilitation medicine), physical therapists, occupational therapists, speech language pathologists and others.

Even though cancer rehab therapies tend to be short term (typically requiring two to three sessions weekly in the provider's office for a period of a few weeks), insurance plans often limit the number of visits for such therapies. Be sure to check with your insurer for details on your coverage.

Each cancer patient's situation is different, but here are some common problems and how they are treated with cancer rehab…

MILD COGNITIVE IMPAIRMENT ("CHEMO BRAIN")

Cancer patients who have received chemotherapy often complain that they don't think as well and that they have less energy and decreased attention spans. If anxiety or hot flashes due to chemo interfere with sleep, that can decrease cognitive functioning, too.

How cancer rehab helps: A physical therapist might work with a cancer patient by using a specific therapeutic exercise plan. Exercise has been shown to improve cognitive functioning—perhaps by improving blood flow to the brain.

An occupational therapist or speech therapist may recommend strategies to help concentration, attention and memory. This may involve computer-based programs that improve short-term memory.

ANEMIA AND FATIGUE

Anemia is common with many hematological (blood) cancers, such as leukemia and lymphomas.

How cancer rehab helps: In a young person who has just undergone a bone marrow transplant, for example, if there is a low red blood cell count (an indicator of anemia) or a risk for infection, a tailored exercise program can build strength and endurance to help fight fatigue.

For an older adult, exercise is also a key part of a fatigue-fighting regimen that improves endurance and overall fitness. If fatigue results in problems with balance and gait, an occupational therapist can help the patient remain independent at home by suggesting a smartphone-based monitoring device such as a motion sensor that notifies a family member or friend if the patient falls.

BREATHING PROBLEMS

Difficulty breathing and feeling short of breath are common problems in lung cancer survivors. These patients also may experience pain after surgery and have trouble exercising and performing their usual daily activities due to shortness of breath.

How cancer rehab helps: In addition to improving strength and physical performance through targeted exercises, a cancer patient who is having breathing problems would need to improve his/her ability to get more air into the lungs. This may involve "belly breathing" exercises that will allow him to complete his daily activities without getting out of breath so quickly.

More from Dr. Silver…

Cancer "Prehab" Can Help, Too

Cancer "prehab" is useful during the window after a patient is diagnosed with cancer but before treatment begins to help boost his/her physical and emotional readiness for cancer treatment. For example, a specific exercise program, such as interval training, may be advised to increase strength before surgery. A nutrition program may be used to improve a patient's nutritional status before treatments that may sap appetite or lead to nutrition problems such as anemia. Working with a psychologist can help identify and deal with anxiety and stress before treatment starts. Cancer prehab usually is offered at centers that provide cancer rehab services.

PART 4

Money Matters

17

More Money in Retirement

The Biggest Mistakes Seniors Make with Their Money Can Be Avoided

E ven the smartest people can run into trouble managing their money. *Serious mistakes can be hazardous to your wealth…*

MISTAKE: **Becoming too conservative.** Seniors may feel that they must quickly shift their investment portfolio from stocks to bonds and other income-oriented instruments.

Reality: At age 60 or 65, your investment portfolio might have to last for 30 or 40 years, or even longer. Married couples, in particular, face the probability that at least one spouse will live for many years.

Over long periods, stocks have outperformed bonds, and that probably will be true in the future. Giving up on stocks can mean crimping your future lifestyle.

Strategy: Early in retirement, the best portfolio is a blended one that includes a large portion of stocks or stock funds.

With an average risk tolerance, a 60-40 split, stocks to bonds, may be appropriate. As you grow older, gradually tilt your portfolio toward bonds and other fixed-income investments to reduce the risk of incurring heavy stock market losses that you won't be able to make up. A retiree with a 60% allocation to stocks at age 65 might drop that to 55% by age 70…50% at 75, etc.

MISTAKE: **Tapping retirement accounts too soon.** Many people start to withdraw funds from their IRAs and other retirement plans as soon as they retire.

Trap: Such withdrawals reduce the tax-deferred growth enjoyed inside a retirement plan. Also, withdrawals before age 59½ may be subject to a 10% penalty tax.

William G. Brennan, CPA/PFS, CFP, principal, Capital Management Group, LLC, wealth management firm for high-net-worth individuals and families, 1730 Rhode Island Ave., Suite 800, Washington, DC 20036.

Strategy: Assuming that you have enough other assets to leave your retirement account in place, tap taxable accounts for spending money during the year. In November or December, once you can project your taxable income (and tax bracket) for the year, take low-taxed withdrawals, if possible.

Example: At year-end, your tax pro tells you that you can withdraw $10,000 from your IRA this year and remain in the 15% federal tax bracket. You should take the money out at the 15% rate, because future withdrawals may be taxed at higher rates, depending on your personal circumstances and changes in tax law.

This strategy can be repeated each year (after you turn 59½ and the 10% penalty no longer applies). After you pass age 70½, though, you'll have to take minimum withdrawals from most retirement accounts to avoid a 50% penalty.

MISTAKE: **Ignoring Roth IRA conversion opportunities.** You can convert all or part of a traditional IRA to a Roth IRA.

Advantages: After five years, all withdrawals will be tax free, assuming that you're at least 59½ years old. (Contributions can be withdrawn tax free at any time.) Also, there are no minimum required withdrawals from Roth IRAs.

Trap: Some seniors fear Roth IRA conversions because they think a total conversion is necessary, which will require a large tax payment to gain eventual tax-free distributions and/or relief from required distributions. In fact, partial conversions are allowed.

Example: Len Johnson has $200,000 in a traditional IRA.

However, converting the entire IRA would generate $200,000 in additional taxable income and cost Len around $66,000 in tax, assuming a 33% effective rate. Len does not have $66,000 in cash, so he chooses not to convert.

Strategy: Len can do partial conversions, year after year.

Example: Len converts $40,000 of his traditional IRA to a Roth IRA each year. Even if he still owes tax at 28%, that would be an annual tax obligation of only $11,200. After five years of such conversions, Len's entire IRA will be a Roth IRA.

The five-year period for tax-free Roth IRA withdrawals starts on January 1 of the year of the first partial conversion. The five-year test, which applies to each separate conversion, is met five years from January 1 of the year of the first partial conversion. Assuming that the Roth IRA owner is beyond age 59½, the account can be tapped at will, tax free.

MISTAKE: **Overspending.** You may be tempted to spend as much after retirement as you did while you were working. However, chances are that your retirement income is substantially less than when paychecks were coming in.

Best: Be realistic. You might, for example, spend what you receive from pensions, Social Security, part-time earnings, etc., after paying income tax.

It also makes sense to withdraw no more than 4% of your total investment portfolio for spending in Year One of retirement, then increase that withdrawal amount annually to keep pace with inflation. Academic studies have shown that such a drawdown rate, accompanied by a well-balanced investment plan, is likely to keep a portfolio viable for 30 years or more.

If you already have been retired for some time and your age is around 65, you can start this year to take 4% from your portfolio. Next year, adjust what you take to keep up with inflation.

If you're around 70, you can start with a 5% withdrawal, then increase for inflation. Older retirees might start with 6% or even 7%.

MISTAKE: **Halting retirement plan contributions.** Many "retirees" actually have earned income from part-time employment, self-employment, director's fees, etc.

This allows you to contribute to any of a number of retirement plans—defined-benefit, simplified employee pension, profit-sharing and 401(k) plans, for example.

Advantages: Contributions reduce the tax that you'll owe today and the retirement fund will provide an additional income stream for your later retirement years.

***MISTAKE:* Canceling life insurance prematurely.** Once your children are living independently and you have enough assets to provide for yourself and your spouse, you may wish to stop paying insurance premiums.

However, you might want cash from your life insurance at your death to pay taxes, your funeral costs, unpaid medical bills, etc. In addition, if you are going to leave one asset (such as your house) to one of your children, cash to other heirs can make for a fairer division. Life insurance can play other valuable roles, such as benefiting your favorite charities.

Best: Talk with a financial adviser and proceed cautiously before letting your coverage lapse.

Rule of thumb: If you can enjoy your desired lifestyle while still paying insurance premiums, you might as well keep paying.

***MISTAKE:* Giving away too much, too soon.** Affluent retirees may give assets to children or grandchildren to help them and to reduce their own taxable estate.

There may even be pressure from family members to start doing this. However, such gifts should not begin too early, from a personal comfort standpoint. You may be concerned that you or your spouse will need those assets someday.

Strategy: Make formal loans instead, as needed, to your children. As they prosper, they may be able to repay the loans, providing you with additional retirement assets.

A formal loan is one that's written down and signed by all the parties involved in the transaction. Terms (interest rate, repayment obligations) should be similar to loans from an unrelated lender.

Bonus: If you determine one day that you really don't need the loan money back, you can forgive the loans and elect to treat the transactions as gifts.

Good News! Retirement Costs Less Than You Think

Michael Finke, PhD, CFP, professor and director of retirement planning and living in the personal financial-planning department at Texas Tech University, Lubbock.

It's easy to wildly miscalculate how much money you'll need in retirement—even if you are already retired. And that can have major consequences. Underestimate what you will need, and you might retire too soon…and/or run out of money in your retirement years. Overestimate, and you might keep working longer than is necessary…and/or unnecessarily deprive yourself of trips, restaurant meals and other enjoyable endeavors.

Here's how we all can do a better job calculating our own personalized retirement-spending needs…

FORGET THE 80% RULE

Many financial advisers suggest that in retirement, you will need to replace 80% of the gross income you earned in your final years of work. That means, for example, that if your work earned you $100,000 a year before taxes, you would need annual income of $80,000 in retirement to avoid cutting back on your lifestyle.

But after looking at thousands of retirees' spending patterns, my research suggests that retirees are able to maintain the same lifestyle as in their working years with even less than 80%. In fact, they actually spend an average of 60% of their last working year's gross income in the first few years of retirement, although that percentage varies widely depending on income, ranging from 40% for people with very high incomes to 100% for those with very low incomes.

What's more, traditional guidelines assume that overall retirement expenses remain fixed every year or even rise due to increasing medical expenses. They don't necessarily do that. Typically the percentage of preretirement income that is spent each year in retirement starts to decline steadily by about one percentage point each year. In fact, by the time most retirees hit their mid-70s, increasing physical limitations cause average spending to start falling by two percentage points a year. My research found that by age 85, overall expenses tend to be nearly one-third less than when people first retired.

Important: Medical expenses can ruin the above scenario. For relatively healthy people, medical expenses do rise, but they are naturally offset by lower spending in the rest of the budget. For most retirees, average annual health-care expenses aren't more than their health insurance costs before retirement. A small percentage of Americans, however, will pay exorbitant costs for extended nursing-home care (see the next page).

FOCUS ON YOUR SPENDING

The best way to estimate your future retirement spending is not to look at your income, but at how much you actually spend in the year or two before you retire. This sounds straightforward, but my research has shown that many people actually have a poor idea of how much they spend and what they spend it on. *A detailed spending analysis isn't that hard to do…*

STEP 1: **Add up your essential spending.** This includes "must-haves" that you have to pay monthly or on a regular basis, such as groceries, insurance premiums, housing, transportation, property taxes and utilities. Also include essential expenses that may not occur on a regular schedule, such as clothing…medical deductibles and co-pays…and home- and car-repair bills.

STEP 2: **Total your discretionary spending.** These include nonessential expenses ranging from cable-TV bills and gym memberships to restaurant meals, gifts and vacations.

Helpful: Technology can make it easier to monitor all expenses. For example, I try to make all my purchases with a single credit card that provides a tally of annual spending by category at the end of each year. You also can use a free online service such as *mint.com* to track and aggregate your credit card and bank transactions automatically.

STEP 3: **Adjust estimates of future expenses that are likely to decrease or dis-** **appear in retirement.** These may include business clothing…mortgage payments if your house is paid off…educational costs for children…changes in lifestyle such as downsizing to just one automobile or moving to a state with no income tax. Talk to your accountant to check whether you will be in a lower tax bracket when you stop working. If you elect to start taking Social Security benefits, no more than 85% of those benefits are taxable. You also get a higher standard deduction on your tax return starting at age 65.

STEP 4: **Adjust estimates of expenses likely to rise in retirement.** These include additional travel and entertainment costs in your initial years of retirement and health-care expenses.

HEALTH-CARE COSTS

On average, a 65-year-old woman is likely to live until 87 and spend $130,000 on health care. That figure includes premiums, co-pays, deductibles and out-of-pocket expenses that Medicare doesn't cover. A 65-year-old man is likely to live to 85 and spend $115,000 on health care. But medical costs are unpredictable. The best way I have found to work around this unpredictability is to start with what you currently spend on health care annually. Or if that figure has fluctuated greatly, take the average you have spent over the past five years. If you already have complex medical problems, consider reviewing your future health-care expenses with a financial planner. *Common mistakes I see individuals make…*

MISTAKE: **Overestimating how much will be covered by Medicare.** You might assume that when you turn 65, your health-care costs are covered. But Medicare pays for only 62% of recipients' total health-care costs, on average. Out-of-pocket expenses include Medicare co-payments and deductibles, premiums on supplemental policies such as drug coverage and items not covered, such as dentures, hearing aids and eyeglasses. Also, if you plan to retire early, you will have to pay for private health-care insurance until you reach age 65 and become eligible for Medicare.

MISTAKE: **Underestimating health-care inflation.** Medical costs are rising more quickly than the cost of most other consumer goods. Plan on 4.5% annual inflation.

MISTAKE: Not factoring in the possibility of long-term care, which Medicare generally does not pay for. The average stay in a nursing home is three years at a median annual cost today of $92,378 for a private room. It's important to see how the costs might affect your retirement spending and whether you should consider long-term-care insurance. (See chapter 19 for more information on saving for and spending on health care.)

Scrutinize Your Bills for Waste

V. Raymond Ferrara, a Certified Financial Planner (CFP) and Certified Senior Advisor (CSA). He is president and CEO of ProVise Management Group, LLC, a financial planning firm in Clearwater, Florida. Provise.com

Seniors are often victims of overbilling and outright fraud. Trimming bills can improve your financial situation without costing you a dime.

You may discover a lot of ways that you were being taken advantage of through unnecessarily high charges...illegitimate charges...and double billing. Go through your checkbook register, credit card statements and bills. This frames the issue as "us against them," rather than "I know better than you how to spend your money."

Examples: Are you still renting a phone from the phone company? Are you paying massive interest rates on credit card debt? Are you being billed for services that you no longer need or even receive? Are there charges on your credit card statements that are not yours? Is there double billing on your medical bills?

If you are having trouble paying your bills, apply for programs designed to help seniors in financial need. Churches, long-term-care facility development directors and elder-law attorneys' offices in your area should be able to point you to local assistance programs for seniors in financial need. Also contact your state or local Department of Health and Human Services (sometimes called the Department of Social Services) to see if you qualify for Medicaid, tax breaks, subsidized heating bills or utility bills or other programs for low-income seniors.

Financial Help for Seniors

Jim Miller, an advocate for older Americans, writes "Savvy Senior," a weekly column syndicated in more than 400 newspapers nationwide. Based in Norman, Oklahoma, he also offers a free senior e-news service at SavvySenior.org.

Retirement is not "golden" for all seniors. More than 25 million Americans age 60 and older are living with limited assets and incomes below $30,000 per year. And even with a higher income than that, it can be difficult to make ends meet.

There are numerous financial-assistance programs, both public and private, that can help struggling seniors, as well as give relief to family members who help provide financial support for their loved ones. And because of a comprehensive resource called *benefitscheckup.org*, a free service of the National Council on Aging, locating these benefits and applying for them have never been easier.

The website is a confidential tool designed for people age 55 and older and their families. It includes information on more than 2,000 programs. Many are available to anyone in need who qualifies, while others are available only to older adults and can help them retain their independence.

To use the site, you enter basic information about the person in need—date of birth, zip code—and check boxes for what the person needs assistance with. The site generates a report instantly, listing links to the programs and services that the person may qualify for.

Some assistance programs can be applied for online...some have downloadable application forms to be printed and mailed, faxed or e-mailed in...and some require that you contact the program's administrative office directly.

It's also possible to get help in person at a Benefits Enrollment Center. There currently are 36 centers in 24 states, with 12 more centers being added in 2016. Visit *ncoa.org/cen terforbenefits/becs* to locate a nearby center.

TYPES OF BENEFITS

Here are some benefits that a senior may be eligible for…

• **Food assistance.** Programs such as the Supplemental Nutrition Assistance Program (SNAP)—previously known as "food stamps"—can help pay for groceries. The average monthly SNAP benefit currently is around $126 per person. Other programs that may be available include The Emergency Food Assistance Program (TEFAP)…Commodity Supplemental Food Program (CSFP)…and the Senior Farmers' Market Nutrition Program (SFMNP).

• **Health care.** Medicaid and Medicare can help or completely pay for out-of-pocket health-care costs. And there are special Medicaid waiver programs that provide in-home care and assistance.

• **Prescription drugs.** There are hundreds of programs offered through drug companies, government agencies and charitable organizations that help reduce or eliminate prescription drug costs, including the federal low-income subsidy known as "Extra Help" that pays premiums, deductibles and prescription copayments for Medicare Part D prescription drug plan beneficiaries.

• **Utility assistance.** There's the Low Income Home Energy Assistance Program (LIHEAP), as well as local utility companies and charitable organizations that provide assistance in lowering home heating and cooling costs.

• **Supplemental Security Income (SSI).** Administered by the Social Security Administration, SSI provides monthly payments to very-low-income seniors, age 65 and older, as well as to people of any age who are blind or who have disabilities. SSI pays up to $733 per month for a single person and up to $1,100 for couples.

In addition to these programs, there are numerous other benefits that are available such as HUD housing (affordable housing for low-income families, the elderly and people with disabilities)…tax relief…veterans' benefits…respite care (short-term care that gives regular caregivers a break)…and free legal assistance.

Financial Fraud Red Flags

Elderly adults often are financial-fraud victims because they are more likely to give out personal information over the phone, including bank-account and credit card numbers. Adult children should be alert for signs that this is happening.

Also watch for: Parents who say that they have won prizes or sweepstakes or who get lots of mailings about sweepstakes…seniors who have unneeded medical equipment at home…ones who are seriously considering unsolicited offers of reverse mortgages—these often are scams, in which seniors lose the title to their home…seniors who go to financial or investment seminars offering free meals—these often are high-pressure sales gatherings where older adults are pressured to open investment accounts and buy unsuitable products or services.

Roundup of experts on financial fraud, reported at GoBankingRates.com.

Protect Yourself and Your Loved Ones from Financial Abuse

Robert M. Freedman, Esq., a partner at Schiff Hardin, New York City. SchiffHardin.com

---

If it could happen to the heiress Brooke Astor, it could happen to anyone. Anthony Marshall, Astor's son, was accused of misusing his aged mother's nearly $200 million fortune prior to her death at age 105 in 2007—and tricking the Alzheimer's patient into altering her will in his favor. He was convicted on 14 counts, which included grand larceny.

There's no doubt that systematic theft from elderly Americans by disreputable financial advisers and family members, among others, is on the rise. Total losses are estimated to be in the billions each year.

Some victims never realize that they are being robbed, while others do not wish to press charges against family members or feel powerless to stop the thefts.

Seniors suffering from dementia or living in isolation are at the greatest risk—but anyone can be a target.

Good news: There are ways to prevent a loved one—or yourself—from becoming a victim of elder financial abuse.

TO PROTECT YOURSELF

Here are five ways to identify financial abuse in your own life and prevent further damage…

• **Review your bank account and credit card statements,** paying particular attention to any automated teller machine (ATM) withdrawals and cash advances that you do not recall taking…and checks paid to "cash" that you do not recall writing.

• **Review investment account statements for questionable withdrawals and transfers.**

• **Scan your credit report at least once each year for loans or credit cards that you did not sign up for.**

Helpful: Request one free credit report each year from each of the three credit reporting agencies at *annualcreditreport.com*.

• **Keep careful track of any valuables in your home, including cash, jewelry, stamp or coin collections, art and antiques.** If something goes missing, mention it to caregivers and family members who have access to your home. Be suspicious if one of them tries to convince you that you must have misplaced it…that you must have forgotten that you gave the item away…or that the missing item has been moved to a bank safe-deposit box or sent out for cleaning.

• **Be very suspicious of relatives, caregivers or anyone else who asks you to sign legal documents and tells you there's no need to read them first.** He/she might be trying to get you to take out a loan or tap your home equity with him as beneficiary…or to

get you to amend your will or estate plan in his favor.

TO PROTECT RELATIVES AND FRIENDS

Watch for these warning signs that someone you care about might be the victim of elder financial abuse…

• **A family member or caregiver makes it difficult for you to see this friend** or relative or insists on being present at all times during visits.

• **The friend or relative starts spending less time with friends or engaged in social activities and more time at home.** The abuser might be preventing or discouraging the elderly victim from going out.

• **He seems anxious or fearful around one particular family member or caregiver.**

• **The person's appearance is increasingly disheveled.** This can suggest that the relative or caregiver whose task it is to look after this person does not really have his best interests in mind.

• **Valuables are missing from the person's home.**

• **Unpaid bills or even collection notices pile up on the elderly person's desk.**

• **He unexpectedly changes attorneys or financial advisers.** An unscrupulous relative might be steering him away from professionals who truly have his best interests in mind.

• **The person answers all questions about money topics by saying that a particular relative or caregiver is handling them.**

CONFIRMING SUSPICIONS

If you think that you might be the victim of financial abuse, contact an attorney, or the local Adult Protective Services or the police. At least take steps to stop further abuse by cutting off the thief's access to your accounts and contacting lenders or credit bureaus to warn of fraudulent activity.

If you are concerned that an elderly relative or friend might be the victim of financial abuse, proceed with caution. Though you are trying to help, the potential victim might think you are snooping into financial matters that are none of your business…or you might make him feel too embarrassed about being victimized to discuss the problem.

Besides, there could be innocent explanations for what appear to be indications of elder financial abuse. The suspected victim might be giving away cash or valuables to avoid estate taxes...he might be experiencing financial problems or depression unrelated to theft...or the relative or caregiver who seems controlling might just be protective. *Before taking any action, take these steps to prove your suspicions...*

• **Confirm the ownership status of the person's home.** A thief might trick an elderly home owner into signing over the deed or taking out a second mortgage with the money going to the thief...or the thief might simply forge the necessary documents.

Real estate ownership is a matter of public record. Contact the elderly person's town or county and ask how you can track down title information. Some jurisdictions provide access to title information online.

• **Offer to help the relative or friend review his credit report "for errors."** Explain that you recently reviewed your own report, so you know what to look for. This approach minimizes the implication that you think the elderly person is not competent to handle his own financial affairs.

• **Similarly, ask him to let you review bank and credit card statements with his help to search for fraudulent checks and charges.** Say you found errors in your own accounts, so you know how to correct them.

• **Try to spend time with him one-on-one, and see how the suspected financial abuser reacts.** If this person tells you that your friend or relative doesn't want to see you, respond that you would need to be told this directly.

Helpful: Keep careful notes of the dates and times when you request to see the person and what you were told when you were turned away. These denials of access could help you make a legal case against the financial abuser later.

STOPPING THE ABUSE

If your investigation suggests that financial abuse is occurring, don't just tell the elderly relative. The thief could claim that you are attempting to take control of the elderly person's finances for your own gain.

Better: Present your evidence of financial abuse to the victim's other close family members and friends. Then warn the victim or confront the thief as a group.

At this point, suggest that the victim contact an attorney or the police—or at least deny the thief further access to his home and assets. *If the victim resists your suggestions...*

• **Contact the local Department of Social Services office** in the victim's town or county and ask to have an Adult Protective Services employee perform an in-home visit. These visits send the message that someone is watching, which often is enough to scare off those who financially take advantage of the elderly.

• **Arrange for a "durable power of attorney" (the legal right to handle this person's financial affairs on his behalf),** and ask the victim to authorize you to monitor his finances. Since the power of attorney is durable, it would continue in effect if the elderly person subsequently loses capacity.

Last resort: If all else fails, consult an attorney about bringing a guardianship proceeding. This means that the courts will determine whether the individual has the capacity to make his own financial decisions, and, if necessary, appoint a guardian to act on his behalf.

Financial Security for Unmarried Couples

U nlike married couples, unmarried partners aren't entitled to each other's Social Security benefits when one partner dies. Older unmarried couples should consider buying life insurance as a replacement for Social Security income, especially if one partner is financially dependent on the other, and even to cover funeral costs. Most insurance companies will accept the designation of an unmarried partner as the beneficiary, but some may take issue with it. Check in advance, and choose another insurer if there is a problem.

Sheryl Garrett, CFP, founder of Garrett Planning Network, an international network of fee-only financial advisers, Shawnee Mission, Kansas. She has been recognized five times by Investment Advisor as one of the most influential people in financial planning. She is author of *Money Without Matrimony: The Unmarried Couple's Guide to Financial Security.* Garrett PlanningNetwork.com

After a Spouse Dies... Important Financial Steps to Take Right Away

Kathleen M. Rehl, PhD, CFP, a fee-only financial planner based in Land O'Lakes, Florida, and a widow herself. Her husband and business partner died of cancer in 2007. She is author of *Moving Forward on Your Own: A Financial Guidebook for Widows.* www.KathleenRehl.com

The death of a spouse is among life's most traumatic experiences. Survivors must cope with more than grief—they also must deal with crucial financial matters. *Here is a checklist of financial actions required during the difficult days, weeks and months after a spouse's death...*

TACKLE FUNERAL EXPENSES

Funerals can cost $5,000 or more, a major expense that must be worked out within a few days of the death, assuming that arrangements haven't already been made. *Before spending this money...*

• **Determine whether the deceased had prepaid burial expenses.** If you aren't sure this is the case but recall your spouse mentioning something along these lines, search filing cabinets, safe-deposit boxes and checkbook registers. You might find a deed to a cemetery plot or a contract with a funeral home.

• **Contact the VA if the deceased served in the military** (800-827-1000, *www.cem.va.gov*).

He/she could be eligible for benefits, including free burial or a $300 burial allowance.

• **Discuss burial options with funeral directors.** Consider cremation, which can cost as little as $1,000.

• **Order 15 copies of the death certificate from the funeral home or local health department.** These will have to be sent to life insurers to claim benefits and to banks and other financial companies to transfer titles of assets.

ALERT KEY PEOPLE

• **Contact the executor of the estate.** If you are the executor, ask your estate attorney to help you manage the estate-settlement process. If you don't already have an attorney experienced with the court-supervised probate process, ask friends for referrals.

Warning: Before agreeing to work with an attorney, ask him/her how much this service will cost. A flat fee of a few thousand dollars is appropriate for a simple estate, but if you don't ask about rates first, an attorney might charge you based on a percentage of the assets that pass through probate, which could add up to a hefty bill.

An attorney might not be needed at all if you or a family member feels up to navigating the legal system on your own, particularly if most of your partner's assets were jointly owned or owned through accounts that named you as beneficiary, limiting the assets that must pass through probate. Some states require an attorney's involvement, however.

• **Contact your tax preparer and financial adviser,** if you have them, to ask whether there are any decisions that must be made or actions that must be taken quickly.

Example: If your spouse was older than 70½, you might have to take distributions from his IRAs to avoid a steep penalty.

If your spouse previously handled the investing and taxes without help from professionals but you do not feel qualified to do so, ask friends if they can recommend financial pros.

Warning: Make sure that the planner you work with is a fee-only planner. Other types of planners might boost their commissions by selling inappropriate financial products.

GATHER IMPORTANT DOCUMENTS

A lot happens after a spouse's death. You'll need a good system to make sure that nothing falls through the cracks...

• **Buy folders to organize all the paperwork that arrives in the weeks following the death,** and separate it into categories, such as "Funeral" and "Financial Statements."

• **Locate your spouse's estate documents.** These include the will and trust documents. Also, gather his key personal documents, such as a birth certificate, your marriage certificate, Social Security card (or at least the Social Security number), citizenship papers and military discharge papers.

• **Gather paperwork that details the deceased's assets,** including financial account statements, insurance policies and real estate documents.

• **Update your own estate documents and accounts** to name someone other than your spouse as your beneficiary or agent.

TAKE CHARGE OF FINANCES

Postpone, if possible, major financial decisions until things settle down emotionally, even if that means waiting a full year after your spouse dies. This most likely isn't the time to sell your house or liquidate your portfolio to buy an annuity.

• **Check bank accounts and income streams** to confirm that you have enough cash to pay household bills for the initial months following the death. If you think your cash flow might be insufficient to cover costs, determine which of your investments could be cashed in without penalty if necessary.

Example: Some certificates of deposit (CDs) have "death puts" that allow them to be cashed in early without penalty if the owner dies.

• **Pay bills when they arrive,** or immediately write their due dates on a calendar.

Exception: Medical-related bills can wait if you expect that insurance payments and/or Medicare will pay a portion or all of the bill.

Explain this to the billing source. If you incur a penalty for a late payment, explain the circumstances to a customer service phone rep and request that the penalty be waived.

• **Make a list of all of your debts, including credit card balances and mortgages.** Notify creditors of the death, and examine loan agreements for any mention of insurance that pays the debt off in the event of the borrower's death.

You might not be legally responsible for paying loans or credit card balances that are exclusively in the deceased partner's name—though debt collectors sometimes try to convince widows/widowers otherwise. It often is the responsibility of the deceased's estate to pay these. However, you are responsible for continuing to make payments if you are a co-signer on the loan or credit card...the loan is secured by property that you do not wish to see repossessed...or you live in a community property state where you legally are required to pay your deceased partner's debts. Consult your attorney.

• **File a Social Security benefits claim form online or at the nearest Social Security office** (800-772-1213, *ssa.gov*). A widow/widower typically can begin receiving survivor's benefits as early as age 60 based on the deceased partner's earnings, though those benefits will be higher if you wait until your "normal" retirement age, between 65 and 67. There also is a death benefit of $255, and minor children might be entitled to certain benefits as well.

• **Decide whether to roll over your spouse's IRAs and 401(k)s into your own IRA or continue them as beneficiary IRA/401(k)s.** (Many 401(k) plans insist that surviving spouses remove money from the deceased partner's account plan.) Rolling over this money usually makes the most sense because it often delays required distributions.

But the beneficiary IRA/401(k) option—maintaining the departed spouse's IRA, only now with you named as its beneficiary—may be worth considering if you are younger than 59½ and have little choice but to tap these savings soon because of a lack of other assets. Money typically can be withdrawn from a beneficiary IRA without incurring early withdrawal penalties regardless of the beneficiary's age.

• **Inform college financial-aid offices of the death if you have children in college.** You might qualify for increased financial aid or special hardship aid.

• **Contact your partner's employer if he still was working at the time of his death.** Ask the human resources department about unpaid salary and commissions, bonuses, stock options and compensation for unused sick and vacation days. Ask whether any life insurance was provided through the workplace and whether any other benefits are available to surviving spouses.

Also, if your spouse belonged to a union or trade association, contact it to check on any benefits available.

FOLLOW UP ON INSURANCE

• **Inform your life insurance agent of the death.** Depending on the type of policy, you may have payout options, such as a lump-sum payment or fixed monthly payments.

• **If you have been receiving health insurance through your spouse's employer or former employer,** contact the plan administrator to find out if you can retain this coverage. CO-BRA rules typically allow a widow/widower to remain on the former employer's plan for up to 36 months, twice the normal time limit.

If COBRA is not an option—and you are not yet 65 and eligible for Medicare—contact health insurance providers or insurance brokers about individual coverage.

• **Cancel policies,** services and subscriptions that are no longer needed, or have your partner's name removed from these if you both used them. You no longer need your former spouse's long-term-care insurance policy, for example, and you can remove the spouse from your auto insurance policy.

Divorce After 50— Watch Out for the Big Financial Traps

Janice L. Green, JD, an attorney specializing in divorce and family law. She is a partner with Farris & Green in Austin, Texas, and author of *Divorce After 50: Your Guide to the Unique Legal & Financial Challenges.* JaniceLGreen.com

D ivorce rates among those age 50 and older more than doubled between 1990 and 2008, according to researchers at Bowling Green State University. These older couples now account for one-quarter of all US divorces.

Splitting up after age 50 can be particularly problematic for those with limited assets and limited time to recover financially. And those who divorce after age 50 but before Medicare eligibility kicks in at age 65 may struggle to obtain affordable health insurance.

Here's what you or someone close to you might need to know to get the best possible settlement in a divorce after age 50…

RETIREMENT PLANS

An IRA or a 401(k) might be in the name of just one spouse, but the other spouse has a legal right to claim a share in a divorce. In community property states, both partners are considered joint owners of these accounts. In noncommunity property states, these assets will be divided according to the divorce agreement. A divorce decree can include language that spells out how the retirement plan's sponsors should divide the benefits. It's crucial that older divorcees obtain a fair share of this money—retirement savings often are an older couple's most valuable asset.

Four things that older people should consider before agreeing to a division of retirement plan assets…

• **Taxes.** Divorce attorneys tend to pay little attention to future taxation of retirement plan withdrawals. Remind your attorney that these taxes must be taken into account when dividing assets.

Exception: Money can be withdrawn tax-free from Roth IRA accounts in retirement.

• **Fluctuating asset values.** It typically takes months for a divorce to be finalized. If the divorce agreement is poorly written, a sharp swing in asset values during this time could result in an unintended and unfair division of assets.

Example: A divorce agreement gives the wife $100,000 from her husband's $400,000 401(k), plus the couple's house. The value of that 401(k) falls by $120,000 in a market downturn before the divorce is finalized, leaving the wife with 38% of its value rather than the intended 25%, and the husband with no house and only $180,000 in savings with retirement looming.

Ask your attorney to explain how the proposed division of assets would be affected if your portfolio were to rise or fall by 25% or 30% before the agreement is finalized. If the result seems unfair, suggest dividing retirement savings by a percentage rather than specifying that one partner receive a certain dollar amount.

• **Pension plan rules.** Many older Americans still have traditional defined-benefit pensions—pensions that pay a steady monthly income during retirement. Former spouses typically are entitled to a share of this money, but the rules are complicated. A divorce court can issue a "qualified domestic relations order" (QDRO) to the retirement plan's sponsor spelling out how benefits are to be divided. If your spouse has a defined-benefit plan, obtain a copy of the summary plan description from the employer or plan administrator.

Plan rules sometimes specify that an ex cannot claim benefits as an "alternate payee" until the plan member retires, even if the plan member works for many years beyond normal retirement age. If so, ask your attorney to attempt to negotiate for alimony or some other compensation to make up for your lost pension income should your ex work past normal retirement age.

Also, if your former spouse's pension pays joint and survivor benefits, scan the plan rules to determine whether the original spouse or a later spouse is considered the survivor if the plan member remarries. If it's the new spouse, have your attorney take this into account when dividing assets.

If you're the divorcing spouse who has the pension plan and you intend to remarry, be aware that your new spouse might not receive the survivor benefits you expect—check the plan rules for details.

• **Transfer of assets.** Make sure that any money shifted from your partner's IRA or 401(k) to your IRA when assets are divided is handled as a trustee-to-trustee transfer. You could incur penalties and taxes if these assets pass through your hands.

LIFE INSURANCE

Many older couples have been paying into life insurance policies for years, and such policies can be valuable assets. But when couples appear headed toward divorce, partners who are insured sometimes stop paying these premiums—they see little reason to pay for a policy that only benefits the soon-to-be ex.

If you are the spouse who is insured, do not stop paying these premiums. This policy can be a useful bargaining chip in your divorce. Agreeing to continue funding it might let you obtain a larger share of other assets or reduce your future alimony payments.

If you are the spouse who is not insured, explain to your spouse that he/she can use this policy as a bargaining chip, as discussed above, and seek an agreement that it will continue to be funded.

If the relationship is too strained for such an agreement, obtain a court order to this effect. You want an agreement in place before the next premium is due—even one missed payment could forfeit the coverage.

Alternative: Suggest that the policy be altered to benefit the children, not the ex.

If your divorce agreement dictates that your ex continue to fund a life insurance policy, instruct your attorney to be certain that you will have some way to confirm that these premiums continue to be paid.

HEALTH INSURANCE

Individual health insurance coverage under the Affordable Care Act is available for people in their 50s or early 60s to obtain individual health insurance. Visit Healthcare.gov to find out just how expensive it will be as soon as possible. Take these costs fully into account in the settlement.

Other potential options...

•**COBRA rules let divorcees continue to receive coverage through an ex-spouse's employer group plan for up to 36 months.** Contact the plan administrator within 60 days after the divorce is finalized. Your divorce agreement should specify whether you or your spouse is responsible for paying the COBRA premiums.

Warning: Obtain an agreement—or, if necessary, a court order—from your spouse agreeing not to drop you from the employer's group plan.

•**Delay finalizing your divorce until you turn 65 and qualify for Medicare**—or until you turn 62 if COBRA is available to bridge the remaining 36-month gap. Read your health insurance plan's rules carefully before attempting this, however. Some plans require that spouses live under the same roof to qualify for coverage.

THE HOME

Some older divorcees decide, I just want the house...he/she can have the 401(k). That may be a bad idea, given the real estate market's recent uncertainty. You could get stuck in a home that is larger than you need and that you cannot sell at a reasonable price. It's wiser to seek a diversified portfolio of assets in the divorce, even if that means selling the home and splitting the proceeds. If it cannot be sold at a reasonable price or in a timely manner in this real estate market, you and your ex could agree to...

•**Rent the house out until prices rebound.** The divorce agreement should specify how this rent will be divided, who will pay home-related expenses until it is sold and how the proceeds of the eventual sale will be split.

•**Have one spouse continue to live in the home until it is sold.** This spouse could pay rent to the other and pay home owner expenses.

BENEFICIARY DESIGNATIONS

Update the beneficiary designations in your investment accounts and estate plan as soon as divorce seems inevitable. Ex-spouses are automatically removed as beneficiaries in some states, but this won't occur until the divorce is finalized.

Exception: Some states issue automatic restraining orders preventing the alteration of beneficiary designations until the details of the divorce are agreed upon. In other states, attorneys might obtain restraining orders preventing this.

RELOCATION

Older couples often move to different states or even different countries when they retire. If you suspect that your marriage could be headed for divorce, speak with a family law attorney before relocating. Divorce laws in the new state or country might be less advantageous to you than the laws where you currently reside. If so, it might make sense to postpone or refuse relocation.

Social Security Secrets: You May Be Entitled to More Than You're Getting

Laurence J. Kotlikoff, PhD, professor of economics at Boston University, a fellow of the American Academy of Arts and Sciences and a former senior economist with the President's Council of Economic Advisers. He is co-author of *Get What's Yours: The Secrets to Maxing Out Your Social Security.* MaximizeMySocialSecurity.com

Social Security might end up being your most valuable retirement asset...and the most difficult to understand. The system has more than 2,700 core rules and thousands more codicils. A single misstep could cost you as much as one-third of the money you might have received. *Here's a closer look at four Social Security guidelines that are poorly understood, even by financial planners...*

•**You might have more than one benefit available to you, but you can't claim more than one at a time.**

Examples of benefits in addition to your standard retirement benefit…

•If your spouse (or former spouse if you are divorced and your marriage lasted at least 10 years) is alive, you might qualify for a monthly spousal benefit equal to as much as 50% of your spouse's "full retirement benefit"—the amount your spouse would receive if he starts his benefits at his "full retirement age," which is 66 for people born between 1943 and 1954…between 66 and 67 for people born between 1955 and 1959…and 67 for people born in 1960 or later.

•If your spouse or ex passes away, you might be entitled to a monthly survivor benefit of as much as 100% of the retirement benefit that he could have received if he were still alive.

Social Security rules make it difficult to understand that you can't get more than one of the benefits at the same time. The rules seem to indicate that you can receive your own retirement benefit plus the portion of another benefit that is in excess of your retirement benefit—but that's really just a confusing way of saying that the smaller of the two benefits is eliminated.

What to do: It sometimes is worth claiming first one benefit, then switching to a different one later on. Doing this delays the start of the second benefit, which could increase the size of the check that you receive each month from that benefit for the rest of your life.

There are many complex rules governing this. It's easy to make a mistake and apply for two benefits even though you intended to apply for just one. If this happens, you might eliminate any upside to switching benefits later. *Three important benefit-switching guidelines…*

•It may not be wise to claim a spousal benefit before you reach your full retirement age. Doing so would cause you to be deemed to be filing for your own retirement benefit at this early age, too, forever reducing your monthly retirement benefit.

•If you are married, you cannot file for a spousal benefit until your spouse has filed for his own retirement benefit (though if you are divorced, you can).

•Although your monthly retirement benefit continues to increase in size for each month you delay starting it until age 70, spousal and survivor benefits stop increasing once you reach your "full" retirement age, so there is no advantage to delaying the start of these benefits any further.

•**If you claim your benefit early, your spouse might pay the price.**

Many people start their retirement benefits as soon as they become eligible at age 62. That can be a very costly decision—especially if you are a man who is both older and higher-earning than your wife. If your spouse outlives you, as is usually likely, her survivor benefit will be based on the monthly retirement benefit you are receiving (or entitled to) when you pass away. And the retirement benefit you are receiving will be larger the longer you wait, up to age 70.

Example: A 67-year-old man was diagnosed with cancer and told he had two years to live. His local Social Security Administration office suggested that he file for benefits immediately—better to receive two years of benefits than nothing at all. But that advice assumed the man's goal was maximizing his own benefits rather than the combined amount he and his wife would receive. The couple would have been better off if he continued to delay the start of his benefits until he turned 70 or died. If this man's monthly benefit was $2,000 at age 67, two years of benefits would net him $48,000—but delaying benefits by two years would increase his wife's future monthly survivor benefits by 16%, putting an extra $3,840 in her pocket for every year that she survived him (actually a bit more, because Social Security benefits are inflation-adjusted). She would steadily earn back that forgone $48,000 over a period of 12.5 years, and after that all of the additional benefit amount would be a bonus.

•**Social Security's earnings penalty often is not much of a penalty at all.**

You might have heard that the "earnings penalty" makes it foolish to continue to work while receiving Social Security benefits, whether it's standard retirement benefits or spousal or survivor benefits. After all, this penalty can claim $1 of your benefits for every $2 you earn above a very low income limit (currently

$15,720). But this earnings penalty may not be as bad as it seems for two reasons. It applies only to people who have not yet reached their full retirement age...and benefits lost to the penalty are paid back later in the form of a higher monthly benefit starting at full retirement age (unless you are receiving benefits as a survivor because you are caring for a minor or disabled child).

Your monthly benefit will be adjusted by the amount that would fully compensate you for the withheld money if you live to a certain age. If you don't live to that age, you will come out behind...live longer, and you will come out ahead.

What to do: Most people should not let the earnings penalty stop them from earning more than $15,720. But if you have not yet reached your full retirement age and poor health or family history suggests a short life span, it is worth avoiding. And anyone who does incur the earnings penalty probably shouldn't switch from one type of benefit to another during retirement. Only the specific benefit that is subject to the penalty will be adjusted upward later.

Example: If you are receiving a survivor benefit when the earnings penalty is imposed, only this survivor benefit will be increased at your full retirement age to pay back the earnings penalty.

Take income taxes into account when you decide whether to continue earning income while receiving Social Security benefits, however. Your benefits could be taxable if you earn more than $25,000 a year ($32,000 for joint filers). Unlike money lost to the earnings penalty, money lost to income taxes is gone forever.

Marriage Pluses and Minuses for Older Couples

Getting married provides access to federal and state spousal and survivor benefits...and to Medicare if you do not qualify on your own. Marriage makes it simpler to make health-care decisions for each other, provides better tax benefits when inheriting an IRA or HSA and sometimes saves on taxes through a joint return. But some veterans and some widows and widowers of public employees may lose pensions by remarrying...survivor benefits on a deceased spouse's Social Security account will be lost in a remarriage before age 60...and in many states, spouses—but not unmarried partners—are responsible for each other's medical bills, including long-term care. Ask your tax adviser and an elder-care attorney for details.

AARP.org.

Best Ways Now to Boost Social Security: Smart Strategies for Married Couples

Michael Kitces, CFP, director of planning research for Pinnacle Advisory Group, Inc., a wealth-management firm based in Columbia, Maryland. He is publisher of the financial-planning blog *Nerd's Eye View.* Kitces.com

---

Since Congress voted in October 2015 to end two Social Security loopholes, many married couples have been searching for other strategies to maximize their benefits.

Couples who already started taking advantage of the file-and-suspend loopholes can continue to do so. *For people who can't use the file-and-suspend loopholes, here are the best alternative strategies...*

Best option for most couples: The spouse with the higher earnings history postpones claiming benefits, while the spouse with the lower earnings history starts collecting benefits as early as age 62. Your level of Social Security benefits depends, in part, on your earnings history and the age at which you start collecting benefits. Postponing the start of the higher earner's benefits increases the size of that spouse's future monthly benefits by 6% to 8% for each year of postponement, up to age 70. (There is no advantage to postponing the start of benefits past 70.)

Whether it pays to do this depends in part on how long the higher earner expects to live, making the choice difficult. But keep in mind that by postponing the start of the higher earner's benefits, you also can increase the amount that the spouse with the lower earnings history ends up receiving—that's because of "survivor benefits." When one spouse dies, the surviving spouse can, in effect, opt to claim the deceased partner's benefits. Because of that option, delaying the start of the higher earner's benefits until age 70 typically will produce the highest total benefits for a married couple if either spouse lives to at least 83. Based on actuarial tables, it's likely that for the typical married couple, if both reach age 65, at least one will live past 90. (Be aware that benefits claimed before full retirement age are subject to a Social Security earnings test, which could reduce or even eliminate benefits if the lower earner still is working and earning $15,720 or more.)

Example: Say a husband is entitled to monthly benefits of $2,000 if he starts collecting at age 62...or around $3,500 if he waits until age 70.* And say he decides to start collecting at age 70 and dies at 80, so he receives just $420,000 in total benefits, less than the $432,000 he would have received if he had started his benefits at age 62. But his wife lives to 90, so the combined benefits they receive from his account, including her survivor benefits, total $840,000—much more (a difference of $168,000) than the $672,000 they would have received if he had started at age 62.

Meanwhile, the wife started collecting Social Security benefits at age 62 based on her own earnings history and kept collecting those benefits until she switched to survivor benefits. That way, the couple receives at least some benefits while waiting for the higher earner to start collecting at age 70. (Of course, if the wife had not earned much at all, these benefits might be very small. If her benefits are much

less than half the husband's benefits, it might make sense for the husband to start collecting before age 70—more on that below.)

Possible alternative when the lower earner has an extremely low earnings history or no earnings history: Rather than waiting until age 70, the higher earner starts collecting benefits when the lower earner reaches "full" retirement age. One downside to waiting until age 70 to claim benefits, as the husband in the previous example did, is that under the new rules, the wife in the example could not claim spousal benefits based on the husband's earnings unless the husband is collecting his benefits. (Under the old rules, the husband could file for benefits to allow his wife to claim spousal benefits, and then he could immediately suspend his own benefits, allowing his eventual monthly benefits to continue to increase in size.)

The new barrier to claiming spousal benefits is not a major problem if the wife has a significant earnings history of her own, but for couples where one spouse earned virtually all the income, it could mean that the low-earning spouse loses out on substantial benefits for many years. And be aware that although most Social Security benefits increase in size for each month you wait to claim them up to age 70, spousal benefits stop increasing once the spouse reaches what the government refers to as "full" retirement age, which is 66 for people born between 1943 and 1954.

That means it might make sense for the higher earner to start collecting his benefits when the low earner reaches full retirement age so that the low earner can start collecting spousal benefits at that point.

Example: Say the husband is the higher earner and is eligible to start collecting monthly benefits of $2,500 when he reaches full retirement age of 66...or $3,300 if he waits until age 70. Say his wife, who is the same age, did not have significant earned income during her working years. The husband chooses to start collecting his benefits at age 66...the wife starts collecting spousal benefits at age 66...and both live to 80. The couple receives a combined $630,000 versus just $594,000 if they had waited until age 70 to start collecting benefits.

---

*Social Security amounts cited in this article are based on current levels. Actual benefits may increase each year based on a measure of inflation.

However, in some cases, it might make more sense for the high earner to wait, possibly until age 70, even though that means the low earner sacrifices some spousal benefits. The correct choice depends on such factors as whether the couple has enough assets to tide them over and their expectations about their life spans. (If the high earner is at least four years older than the low earner, this is a nonissue—by the time the low earner reaches full retirement age, the high earner will have started his benefits anyway.)

Example: Say the wife in the example above lives to 90 rather than 80. As a result, the couple would have been better off waiting until age 70 to start collecting benefits, which would have meant the couple earned a total of $990,000 versus a total of $930,000 if the husband started at age 66.

Possible alternative when both partners are in poor health: Claim benefits as soon as possible. If health and/or family history strongly suggest that neither spouse is likely to live past his/her early 80s, the best way to maximize total benefits is for both partners to start their benefits as soon as possible, meaning at age 62 or immediately if they already are past age 62.

IF YOU HAVE DEPENDENT CHILDREN...

When a Social Security recipient has children who are unmarried and not yet 18, each of those children might be eligible to receive dependent benefits equal to as much as 50% of a parent's full retirement age benefit. But under new rules that were part of legislation passed by Congress last year, the child can receive these "auxiliary" benefits only if a parent is receiving his/her own benefits. So the question is, should the parent claim at age 62 or as soon as possible after that to take advantage of these auxiliary benefits...or postpone benefits to age 70 based on considerations discussed above?

The answer depends in part on how many auxiliary benefit payments the family is likely to receive. If there is one child in the household who is just months away from 18 when the older parent turns 62, it almost certainly isn't worth claiming early. But if there are multiple children in the household who will be el-

igible for benefits for many years, it very often makes sense. (A parent or other designated adult receives and controls the payments.)

Key details: The 18-year-old age limit is extended to 19 and two months if the child still is in high school. There is no age limit if the child is disabled, but the disability must have begun before age 22. If the child is younger than 16 and the spouse who is not starting his/her own benefits is providing child care, that spouse might be eligible to receive a spousal benefit. This is possible even if the spouse is not yet old enough to receive spousal benefits under normal circumstances. (Dependent grandchildren also may be eligible to qualify for dependent benefits, but there are extensive rules that restrict this eligibility.)

Social Security Traps: Singles, Widows and Widowers

William Meyer, founder and managing principal of Social Security Solutions, Inc., which offers personalized Social Security benefits optimization strategies, Leawood, Kansas. SocialSecuritySolutions.com

S ome of the traps that ensnare current and future Social Security recipients apply especially to people who are single or widowed...

FOR SINGLES...

TRAP: **Bad timing.** If you're single, there are certain ages when it is most advantageous to wait a little longer to start receiving benefits. That's because your monthly benefit amount increases in size for every month that you delay starting Social Security from age 62 to 70—but it doesn't increase at a consistent pace throughout those years.*

*To calculate the amounts that you could get at each age, go to *ssa.gov/oact/quickcalc/index.html*. Decisions about when to start Social Security also depend on your life expectancy (go to *ssa.gov/oact/population/longevity.html* for a guide to life-expectancy calculations) and on whether you still are earning substantial employment income, which could mean much of your Social Security benefits would be lost to taxes.

For instance, if you start your benefits at age 66, or whatever your so-called "standard" or "full" retirement age is, you probably are doing so exactly at the moment when continuing to postpone the start offers the greatest rewards—even though it's the age that the Social Security Administration (SSA) considers the "normal" time to retire.

When you crunch the numbers, it turns out that there actually are two windows during which it is especially inopportune for most single people to claim benefits if they wish to maximize the total amount they receive. One window runs from age 62 and one month through age 63 and 11 months...while the other is centered around your standard retirement age—age 65 and five months through age 66 and seven months if your standard retirement age is 66.

If your standard retirement age is higher than 66, the windows during which it's best not to start benefits are within eight months before or after your standard retirement age and within approximately 12 months before or after the date that is three years prior to your standard retirement age.

Example: If your standard retirement age is 67, the windows to avoid are between 66 and four months and 67 and eight months...and between approximately age 63 and age 65.

All this is true for married people, too, but married people have additional benefits options, such as spousal benefits and switching strategies that mean starting benefits at standard retirement age sometimes makes sense.

WIDOWS AND WIDOWERS...

TRAP: **Permanently choosing between survivor benefits and your own retirement benefits.** The best option usually isn't one or the other—it's one and then the other. Many widows and widowers depend on their Social Security checks to pay the bills. Yet most receive less from the Social Security system than they should because of this simple trap.

When widows and widowers explore their benefit options, they typically are told that they must choose between claiming a ben-

efit based on their own earnings and claiming survivor benefits based on their departed spouse's earnings—not both. The vast majority select whichever of these is larger and then receive that amount each month for the rest of their lives. These checks often are relatively small because survivors tend to start their benefits as soon as they're eligible—some don't have any other way to pay the bills.

Widows and widowers are allowed to start their survivor benefits as early as age 60, but the sooner they claim them, the lower their monthly checks will be. Start benefits at age 60, and you will receive just 71.5% of the amount you would receive if you start benefits at your standard retirement age (assuming that is age 66).

What most widows and widowers don't realize is that while they can't receive both their retirement benefit and their survivor benefit at the same time, they can—and, in most cases, should—eventually switch from one to the other. This switching strategy can produce tens of thousands of dollars in additional benefits, particularly when both spouses had significant earnings during their working lives.

Example: A woman is widowed at age 62. She has a standard retirement benefit of $1,657** and a standard survivor benefit of $2,245. In this situation, most widows simply would take the survivor benefit and receive $1,862 per month for life (that's the $2,245 survivor benefit minus a reduction for starting benefits at 62, four years prior to standard retirement age). If this woman lives to age 85, she will receive a total of $506,464 from the Social Security system.

Much better: If this woman instead claimed her own retirement benefit at age 62, she would receive $1,277 per month ($1,657 minus the reduction for starting four years before standard retirement age) until age 66...at which point she could switch to her standard $2,245 survivor benefit. This strategy would

---

**Estimates of future Social Security income provided in this article do not include future inflation adjustments.

produce additional benefits of more than $62,000 if she lives past age 85.

TRAP: Your standard retirement age for survivor benefits might be different from your standard retirement age for retiree benefits. The SSA is slowly phasing in a higher standard retirement age. If you were born in 1937 or earlier, you can retire at age 65 and receive your standard retirement benefit. But if you were born after 1937, your standard retirement age falls somewhere between age 65 and two months and age 67, depending on the year of your birth.

What most people don't realize: The SSA is using a slightly different schedule to increase the standard retirement age for survivor benefits. This could cause widows and widowers to accidentally delay the start of survivor benefits beyond their survivor benefits standard retirement age, costing them some monthly checks without increasing the size of future checks. (Those born between 1945 and 1956 are not affected—for them, both standard retirement ages are 66.) To find your survivor standard retirement age: Go to *www.SSA.gov/survivorplan/survivorchartred.htm.*

Example: If you were born in 1956, your standard retirement age for retiree benefits is 66 and four months—but your standard retirement age for survivor benefits is exactly 66.

Social Security Online Scam Alert!

Steven J. Weisman, JD, senior lecturer in the department of law, tax and financial planning at Bentley University in Waltham, Massachusetts. He is founder of the scam-information website Scamicide.com.

Your Social Security account is a tempting target for scammers whether you are already collecting benefits or will be in the future. *Watch out for these scams…*

•**Online account hijacking.** The Social Security Administration is encouraging beneficiaries and future beneficiaries to set up "My Social Security" accounts on its website, *SSA.gov.* If you set up an account, you can check on the size of future Social Security benefits or make changes to your account, such as altering your mailing address or bank information, without visiting an office or waiting on hold for a phone rep. Unfortunately, this system is proving convenient for scammers, too. They have been setting up accounts in the names of benefit recipients (and people who are eligible to receive benefits but have not yet done so)…and then routing benefits to the scammers' bank accounts or debit cards.

Scammers can do this only if they know a victim's Social Security number, date of birth and other personal information, but thanks to recent data breaches, that information often is easily accessible. If a scammer hijacks your benefits, Social Security will reimburse you, but it could take months to sort this out, during which time you could have financial trouble if you depend on your benefits.

What to do: Set up an account at *ssa.gov/myaccount* before a scammer sets up a bogus account in your name—the sooner, the better. You can set up an account even if you have not yet reached retirement age and/or do not yet wish to start receiving your benefits (accounts may be set up only for people who are at least 18 years old). When you set up your account, click "Yes" under the "Add Extra Security" heading on the online form. That way, a new security code will be texted to your cell phone each time you try to log onto your account. Access to the account will be allowed only if you enter this code, making it extremely unlikely that a hacker would be able to hijack your account.

•**Fake data-breach scam.** The scammer contacts a victim, claims to work for the Social Security Administration and says that its computers have been breached. The scammer says that in order to find out which accounts have been hacked and altered, he/she must check whether he has the correct bank and account number for the beneficiary. Victims are asked to provide the correct bank information and perhaps other information as well. In reality, victims who provide the requested information might have their benefits and/or identity stolen as well.

What to do: Always ignore calls and e-mail messages about Social Security data breaches—the Social Security Administration never initiates contact with recipients via phone or e-mail. If you receive a letter claiming you must take action because of a data breach, this, too, could be a scam—call the Social Security Administration at 800-772-1213 (not at a number provided in the letter) to ask whether the letter is legitimate. The real Social Security Administration would never ask for personal information.

Is This Customized Portfolio Right for You?

Charles Rotblut, CFA, vice president, American Association of Individual Investors, Chicago. AAII.com

When you invest in most mutual funds in a taxable account, you depend on an expert to manage the fund portfolio—leaving you with no control and with tax consequences that you share with thousands of investors. When, instead, you create your own portfolio at a brokerage, you get control and greater ability to save on taxes, but success depends on your own expertise. Neither way is ideal. Now brokerages are offering an increasingly popular alternative that features advantages of both approaches, and they are making it available to investors with as little as $25,000, compared with previous minimums as high as $1 million.

The alternative? A "separately managed account" (SMA). With SMAs, you choose the kind of portfolio you want, including what kinds of sectors, stocks and bonds you favor. Based on those preferences, an SMA specialist chooses investments—typically a few dozen. The SMA team then manages the portfolio, deciding when to buy and sell investments and trying to minimize your tax bite by balancing gains and losses.

Keep in mind that fees tend to be higher than for mutual funds, and because they are customized, SMAs don't have track records.

Examples of SMAs: Fidelity has six basic SMAs with a range of options. The lowest minimum is $50,000, and annual fees range from 0.2% to 1.7% depending on the strategy and the size of your investment. TD Ameritrade and E*Trade require a minimum of $25,000.

Collect Social Security If You Retire Abroad

You can collect your Social Security no matter where you live. You even can have it directly deposited in your foreign bank account if the bank allows it. And more people are doing it. The Social Security Administration sent benefit checks to more than 346,000 retirees living outside the US in 2011, the latest year for which figures are available. That's up from about 307,000 in 2008.

Dan Prescher, senior editor, InternationalLiving.com, and coauthor of *The International Living Guide to Retiring Overseas on a Budget.*

Divorced? You Could Be Entitled to Much More Social Security

Barbara Shapiro, CFP, a certified divorce financial analyst (CDFA) and vice president of HMS Financial Group, a financial-planning, wealth-management and investment firm based in Dedham, Massachusetts. BShapiro-cdfa.com

Breaking up is hard to do—but on the bright side, it may provide some extra retirement benefits.

The Social Security system has special rules and options for people who have divorced—

rules that allow some to claim significantly larger benefits than they otherwise would receive.

But don't expect the Social Security Administration (SSA) to inform you that you're eligible for those higher benefits. It's up to a divorced person to inform the SSA of a past marriage and to request benefits based on his/her former spouse's earnings history (800-772-1213, *ssa.gov*). Otherwise, you may be leaving thousands of dollars on the table, particularly if your former spouse earned significantly more than you did.

Here's what you need to know about Social Security benefits if you have divorced…currently are going through a divorce…or are considering divorce now…

IF YOU WERE THE LOWER EARNER

If your marriage lasted at least 10 years and you have not remarried, you likely will be eligible to claim Social Security benefits based on your former spouse's earnings history—assuming that those benefits exceed the benefits that you would receive based on your own earnings. Unlike a current spouse, who must wait for the wage earner to file for benefits before claiming spousal benefits, an ex need not wait unless the marriage ended within the past two years. Inform the SSA that you wish to file as an "independently entitled divorced spouse." There is no downside to doing this—it will have no effect on your ex's benefits, and if it turns out that your own benefits exceed those available to you through your ex's earnings, you simply will receive your own benefits instead.

Your benefits as a divorced spouse likely will be very similar to those that would have been available to you had you remained married, and like a married person, you must opt for either benefits based on your own earnings or benefits based on the earnings of the current or former spouse. You can't claim both at the same time.

What you will be eligible for…

While your ex is alive, you will be eligible for a monthly "spousal benefit" equal to 50% of this former spouse's full retirement benefit, starting at your full retirement age. You could begin these benefits as early as age 62, but doing so would permanently reduce your monthly checks by as much as one-third. For larger monthly checks, wait until full retirement age.

The cochairs of a bipartisan deficit commission proposed capping spousal benefits at 50% of the average wage earner's benefit, which would reduce the monthly benefits of some spouses and ex-spouses of high earners. Even if such a rule is ever adopted, however, it likely would exempt those already in or near retirement.

After your ex passes away, you will be eligible for monthly "survivor benefits" equal to 100% of the monthly amount that your former partner was entitled to receive, instead of the 50% spousal benefit. Survivor benefits can be started as early as age 60—age 50 if you are disabled—but your checks will be permanently reduced if you start receiving them before your full retirement age. Divorced former spouses are not eligible for the special lump-sum death benefit paid to surviving spouses.

Even though you cannot simultaneously receive Social Security benefits based on your own earnings history and benefits based on your ex's earnings, you can switch between these if future Social Security reforms or life events affect the amount that you would receive.

Example: A divorced woman claims benefits based on her own earnings, which are greater than the 50% spousal benefits she would receive based on her ex-husband's earnings. When her ex passes away, she switches because the 100% survivor benefits she would receive based on his earnings exceed her own benefits.

IF YOU REMARRY

You likely will lose your right to benefits based on your ex's earnings history if you remarry. *Two exceptions…*

If this new marriage also ends—whether due to divorce, annulment or your new spouse's death—you once again will become eligible for benefits under your first ex's earnings history, regardless of how long the second marriage lasted. If you also are eligible for benefits based on the second partner's earnings—you are likely to be eligible if this marriage lasted at least 10 years, or if it ended because of the death of this second partner—you will be allowed to choose whichever partner's earnings history is more beneficial to you.

Remarriage will not prevent you from claiming survivor benefits based on your ex's earnings if the new marriage occurs after your 60th birthday—after your 50th birthday if you are legally disabled. This is true whether your ex dies before or after you turn 60 and remarry. If you are nearing 60 and considering remarriage, it could be worth delaying the wedding.

IF THERE ARE MINOR CHILDREN

If you are caring for your ex's natural or legally adopted child…this child is younger than 16 and/or legally disabled …and your ex passes away, you might be eligible for benefits of up to 75% of the ex's full retirement benefit as a surviving divorced parent. These parental benefits are different from the 100% survivor benefits mentioned above that could be available to you when you reach retirement age and are available even if you have not yet reached retirement age and even if your marriage did not last 10 years. They end when the child turns 16 unless the child is disabled. The child also is entitled to benefits based on the deceased parent's earnings, typically up to age 18, or 19 if he/she is attending high school full-time.

Note: All of the minor children and caregiving parents combined cannot receive more than 150% to 180% of the deceased wage earner's benefit. If there are numerous claimants and this cap is reached, each claimant will receive a reduced benefit.

Example: When a husband passes away, his ex-wife is caring for his 14-year-old son while his new wife is caring for his four-year-old daughter. Because there are four total claimants—two wives and two children—each is likely to receive between 37.5% and 45% of the husband's full benefit amount, rather than the 75% each would have received had the ex-wife and oldest child not filed for these benefits.

IF YOU ARE THE HIGHER EARNER

If you earned more than your former spouse during your career, filing as an "independently entitled divorced spouse" will not increase your benefits. On the bright side, as discussed above, your ex's right to claim spousal and survivor benefits based on your earnings will not reduce your Social Security benefits or the benefits available to your current spouse except, perhaps, if you pass away while your ex is caring for your minor or disabled children, as described earlier.

Your ex's Social Security benefits could become an issue for you if your ex requests a modification to your alimony agreement after age 62, however. You and your attorney or a financial professional should take a close look at the ex's use of the Social Security system. An alimony increase is less likely to be granted if you can establish that your ex could boost his/her income by maximizing Social Security benefits instead.

Example: A 66-year-old woman took her ex to court to request an increase in alimony until age 70, stating that she wished to delay the start of her Social Security spousal benefits until then. Her ex-husband's advisers successfully countered that there was no good reason for this woman not to start her Social Security spousal benefits immediately. Unlike the benefits available to wage earners, spousal benefits do not increase by waiting beyond full retirement age.

IF YOU ARE CURRENTLY DIVORCING

The right of one former spouse to claim Social Security benefits based on the other's earnings does not need to be negotiated during divorce proceedings. These benefits are legal entitlements, not a negotiable component of the marital assets. Do consider the precise length of the marriage before the divorce is finalized, however. If it ends even one day short of 10 years, you will not be entitled to potentially valuable Social Security benefits based on your former partner's earnings. Reaching the 10-year mark is particularly important for spouses who have limited earnings histories of their own. If the marriage appears on course to end just shy of the 10-year mark, ask your divorce lawyer if the process could be dragged out slightly, or ask your spouse to agree to a brief postponement. The date the divorce is finalized is what matters, not the date of legal separation.

Appeal Social Security Decisions Within 60 Days

Nancy Shor, executive director, National Organization of Social Security Claimants' Representatives, an association of more than 4,000 attorneys and other advocates who represent Social Security and Supplemental Security Income claimants, based in Englewood Cliffs, New Jersey. NOSSCR.org

You can file an appeal if you receive a decision from Social Security denying your claim (for example, your claim for disability benefits or other benefits is denied)… you believe that an agency employee made an error…or you did not get credit for certain working years. The general rule is that you have 60 days from the date you receive a decision, but in some cases, you may need to act sooner. On Social Security's website, review Your Right to Question the Decision Made On Your Claim (*ssa.gov/pubs/EN-05-10058. pdf*). The pamphlet explains the different appeals levels, how to file an appeal and what to expect if you appeal.

If you appeal: Be sure to assemble all the documents and facts that support your claim. If your first appeal is denied, you can appeal to the next level and will be able to file additional paperwork. The process can take considerable time, but initial negative decisions can be reversed if you have the facts on your side.

You Could Lose Retirement $$$ If You Don't Know About These Age-Based Rules

Austin A. Frye, JD, CFP, a financial planner with more than 30 years of experience. He is president and founder of Frye Financial Center in Aventura, Florida, which tracks important age-based milestones for clients. FryeFinancial.com

What do you want for your next birthday? If you're going to be 50 or older, various government benefits become available as you reach certain milestones—but new requirements also pop up.

Among the most important financial-planning milestones, and what you can and should do when you reach them…

AGE 50

• **"Catch-up" contributions.** The calendar year in which you turn 50 is the first in which you can make extra annual contributions to your qualified retirement plans. In 2016, that means you can contribute an extra $6,000 to a 401(k)…an extra $3,000 to a SIMPLE 401(k)… and/or an extra $1,000 to an IRA, above the usual limits, tax-deferred.

• **Disabled survivor benefits.** Permanently disabled widows and widowers are eligible to begin receiving Social Security survivor benefits based on their former spouses' earnings. Survivor benefits are instead of, not in addition to, benefits based on your own earnings, but they could be larger than your own benefits if your late spouse earned more than you.

These monthly survivor benefit checks will be permanently reduced if you begin them before reaching normal retirement age, however, which is between 65 and 67, depending on your year of birth.

AGE 59½ (55 FOR SOME)

• **Retirement plan withdrawals.** Age 59½ generally is the earliest that savers can withdraw money as needed from qualified retirement plans without incurring a 10% "early withdrawal" penalty. Before that, to avoid any penalty, you typically must commit to a schedule of "substantially equal periodic payments" based on your life expectancy (or your joint life expectancy together with your beneficiary) for at least five years or until you reach 59½.

Penalty-free IRA withdrawals also might be possible before age 59½ if the money is used to pay for medical expenses, college bills, the purchase of a primary residence or for certain other costs. See IRS Publication 590, Individual Retirement Arrangements, for details (*irs.gov*).

The IRS does allow penalty-free withdrawals from 401(k)s as early as age 55 if the employee separated from the employer sponsoring the 401(k) in or after the calendar year in which he/she turned 55.

AGE 60

•**Nondisabled survivor benefits.** Widows and widowers who are not disabled can begin receiving Social Security survivor benefits based on a deceased spouse's earnings when they reach age 60. Survivor benefits will be permanently reduced, however, if they are begun before the survivor's normal retirement age, which is between ages 65 and 67.

AGE 62

•**Social Security benefits.** If you're not widowed or disabled, the month of your 62nd birthday or the month that follows is likely the earliest you can start receiving your Social Security benefits. But these benefits will increase for each month you wait until you turn 70, at a rate of 7% to 8% per year. If you don't need the money when you turn 62 and you expect to live many more years, delaying the start of benefits is a good way to protect against the risk of outliving retirement savings, although many people choose to collect right away and possibly invest the early payments. Starting benefits at age 62 is a bad idea if you're still working. If you earn more than $15,720 while receiving Social Security benefits, as much as half of your monthly benefits will be withheld.

AGE 65

•**Medicare.** You have a seven-month window surrounding this birthday to enroll in the program—the three months before the month of your birthday through the three months after. Your Medicare coverage, which includes Part A (hospital insurance), Part B (physician and outpatient services) and Part D (prescription drug coverage), can begin as soon as the first day of the month of your 65th birthday. If you prefer, you also can select a Medicare Advantage Plan, known as Part C, instead of Part A and B. These are offered by private companies but approved by Medicare and have somewhat different costs and coverage levels. If you miss this seven-month window, you not only will have to wait until an open-enrollment period (from November 15 to December 31 each year) to sign up, but you also may have to pay higher rates for Medicare Part

B, the part of the system that pays for doctor bills, for the rest of your life.

Exception: Late-enrollment penalties don't apply in most cases if you still have health insurance through your employer or your spouse's employer, assuming that your coverage is deemed to be at least equal to Medicare coverage. This exception applies only with group plans obtained through an employer. If this applies to you, you must sign up for Part B within eight months of the end of that coverage to avoid penalties.

•**Higher income tax deduction.** You can claim a higher standard federal income tax deduction than younger taxpayers can. That deduction boost is $1,550 if you are single or the head of household…$1,250 per person if married, filing jointly. This will not affect you if you itemize your deductions.

The IRS considers you to be 65 the day before your 65th birthday, so those born on January 1 can claim this one year early. Many states also offer tax breaks for property owners who have reached age 65. To find out whether you qualify, read the directions for your state's income tax forms, speak with an in-state accountant or contact your state's department of revenue.

AGE 66

•**"Normal" retirement age for Social Security.** If you were born between 1943 and 1954, your 66th birthday is your "normal," or "full," retirement age. That is the earliest you can start receiving your Social Security benefits without an "early retirement" reduction in the rate. That doesn't mean that age 66 is the best time to begin your benefits—your monthly checks will increase each month that you wait until age 70. *But your full retirement age still is an important date…*

Once you reach full retirement age, you can earn in excess of $15,720 per year and claim Social Security benefits without having any of those benefits withheld because of earned income limits. This is true whether you claimed your benefits early or waited.

If you are married, the spousal benefits you can claim based on your partner's earnings—and the spousal benefits your partner can claim based on your earnings—max out as soon as both of you reach your respective full retirement ages. Some couples mistakenly believe that spousal benefits, like wage-earner benefits, will continue to increase if they wait until age 70.

AGE 70

If you have not already started your Social Security benefits, do so no later than the month of your 70th birthday. Your benefit checks have reached their maximum potential size, and delaying any longer will cost you money.

AGE 70½

• **RMDs—Required minimum distributions.** Starting in the year in which you reach age 70½, you likely will be required to take annual withdrawals from tax-advantaged retirement accounts, such as your traditional and Roth 401(k)s and traditional IRA. The size of these required withdrawals will be based on your life expectancy or the joint life expectancy of you and your spouse using figures found on the tables in Appendix C of IRS Publication 590. If you fail to make these withdrawals, the IRS can impose a massive 50% penalty based on the amount you failed to withdraw.

If you neglect to take RMDs in the year in which you turn 70½, you can take them by April 1 of the following year without incurring penalties. In ensuing years, however, RMDs must be taken by December 31 of each year.

Exceptions: You do not have to take RMDs from employer-sponsored retirement plans if you are still working unless you own 5% or more of the business. And there never are any RMDs from Roth IRAs during the account owner's lifetime, so you might want to roll over any Roth 401(k)s you have to a Roth IRA before age 70½. (Your heirs other than your spouse will have to take RMDs from your Roth IRA spread over their lifetimes. A surviving spouse generally can roll inherited Roth accounts into his/her own IRAs and delay distributions.)

Daring Strategy to Protect Your Nest Egg

Michael Kitces, CFP, partner, director of planning research, Pinnacle Advisory Group, a private wealth-management firm in Columbia, Maryland, that oversees more than $1 billion in client assets. PinnacleAdvisory.com

Most retirees may have it backward when it comes to making a nest egg last through their retirement.

Here's why: Common wisdom says that to protect your retirement assets you should slowly scale back your exposure to stocks throughout your retirement years.

But the truth is, it may be safer and smarter to slash your stock holdings as you near retirement or in early retirement, then slowly increase the allocation to stocks over time during retirement.

Here's why this approach may be more effective and how to use it in your own retirement planning...

CUSHIONING THE CRASH

Before the 2008 stock market crash, many investors were heavily overweighted in stocks on the eve of their retirement or relatively early in retirement. When the market crash came, many suffered devastating losses.

Fearful of further losses, they became more conservative, selling their stocks at terribly low prices and missing out on much of the stock market's enormous five-year rebound. They also tended to cut way back on their spending—scrimping at a time when they probably wished they could have been enjoying their first few years of retirement.

This was more than just bad luck and unfortunate timing. Many prospective retirees were overlooking something fundamental—how you fare in trying to preserve and extend your money over a typical 30-year or longer retirement is heavily driven by the "sequence" of investment returns you get, especially in the years right before and after you stop working. As a result, strategies with a heavy stock allocation early in retirement may leave you too vulnerable to a stock market crash. Even if there's no dramatic crash, if you retire at the start of a prolonged period of mediocre returns, you may face severe constraints on your spending in your later years.

RETHINKING THE MIX

A recent research study that Wade D. Pfau and I published provides an alternative. We used computer simulations to see how various mixes of stocks and bonds that change throughout retirement could help determine how long a retiree's money would last.

What we found is that if you maintain a 60% stock/40% bond allocation throughout retirement—the sort of strategy recommended by many advisers—you have a 93% chance of never running out of money. That doesn't sound too bad. If you trim your stocks during retirement as you get older—for instance, cutting 1% per year and finishing at 30%—the situation is the same, also with a 93% chance of success.

However, reversing the pattern—starting with a 30% stock/70% bond split and finishing with a 60% stock/40% bond split—produced a better outcome, a 95% probability of never running out of money. Although this may not seem like a huge difference, it is a very significant one when it comes to helping most people prolong their assets, especially since it involves allocating less to stocks for most of your retirement, including when your portfolio may be largest and most prone to disaster (at the start of your retirement).

WORST-CASE SCENARIOS

In addition, when we looked at some of the worst-case scenarios from the simulations, this "increasing-stock-allocation" portfolio still would produce enough money to last an average of more than two years longer than the traditional "decreasing-stock-allocation" portfolio.

This also may not sound like a monumental difference when you are middle-aged and in good health. But imagine that you are in your late 80s, and you realize that you're almost out of money. It's especially frightening at an advanced age when you have far fewer options for generating income. To put it mildly, in retirement planning, it pays to skew the odds in your favor as much as possible.

Our strategy can be useful even if you are already retired, as long as you might live for another 20 years or more. It also was a superior strategy using a higher initial spending rate (5% instead of 4%) and when the assumed average returns were much lower (3.4% for stocks and 1.5% for bonds).

However, if your spending rises too high relative to your returns, your only choice becomes owning a lot of stocks throughout retirement and praying things go well. (At that point, the only way to reduce risk and prolong retirement is to spend less!)

Why it works: If there is a big stock market crash and/or bear market around the year in which you retire, owning much less in stocks means that you take much less of an immediate hit. In the ensuing years, as you gradually raise your stock allocation, you essentially are loading up on stocks when they are cheap. If, on the other hand, the stock market soars around your retirement year, owning much less in stocks may mean that you don't leave quite as large of an inheritance, but you still will be on track to make your money last until age 95.

TO MAKE IT WORK

To make this strategy work, you need to carry it out in the following way…

•**Decrease your stock allocation when you retire (or in the years leading up to retirement).** Our research suggests that you need only about 30% of your portfolio in stocks the day you retire (as long as you're ready to gradually increase later).

Note: Many investors are nervous about increasing their bond exposure right now, given the potential for bond values to decline as interest rates rise, as they are likely to do in the next several years. But the key here is that the bonds we used—US Treasuries with maturities from three to 10 years—still aren't nearly as risky as the stock component of the portfolio. Owning less in bonds and more in stocks still is the greater retirement risk. Bond risks can be further managed by using individual bonds in a bond ladder, rather than bond funds, or buying shorter-term bonds (which lose less when rates rise) and waiting to reinvest at higher rates in the future.

•**Upon retirement, start increasing your stock allocation by one percentage point a year.** If you enter retirement with a 30% stock/70% bond portfolio, after the first year, rebalance to 31% stocks/69% bonds…the second year, 32% stocks/68% bonds…and so on.

You also can help manage year-to-year volatility by keeping one year's worth of living expenses in cash, perhaps in a high-yield online savings account, and using money from whichever investment has fared best to replenish it.

You may want to reassess your need for an increasing-stock-allocation strategy once you reach what you estimate to be the latter half of your retirement. If your portfolio is much larger than you expected at this point, you can do one of the following—decide to become more conservative and dial back on stocks…continue increasing your stock allocation annually but start withdrawing more each year…or plan on leaving a bigger inheritance for your heirs.

Important: No retirement strategy is foolproof. Retirement strategies of all sorts still are subject to the risk that investment returns in the future are even worse than any disasters we have ever seen in history, so there always is a possibility that a few further adjustments will be necessary. If one of those true economic disaster scenarios unfolds, you can either tighten your belt and draw down less annually for a period of time, especially in down years for the stock market…or try to further diversify your portfolio, for instance, with foreign and small-cap stocks.

HOW THE RETIREMENT STUDY WAS CONDUCTED

To do our analysis, we started by using two simple asset classes—large-capitalization stocks (the kind of big companies found in the Standard & Poor's 500 stock index) and intermediate-term US Treasuries that mature in three to 10 years. We tested a number of situations, including average returns consistent with history and lower-return environments where stocks alone or both stocks and bonds are less rewarding.

We ran these criteria through computer simulations to consider thousands of possible market-performance scenarios for a 30-year-period, allowing us to evaluate the risk to a retirement plan and the implications of good and bad markets and various sequences of returns. We assumed that retirees would start out spending either 4% or 5% of their initial-portfolio and would adjust that dollar amount each subsequent year for inflation (so "real" spending remained consistent for life).

How to Spend More in Retirement Without Running Out of Money

Scott Burns, chief investment strategist at AssetBuilder, Inc., an investment-management firm in Plano, Texas, with more than $455 million under management. He is coauthor with economist Laurence J. Kotlikoff of *Spend 'til the End: The Revolutionary Guide to Raising Your Living Standard (Today and When You Retire).* assetbuilder.com

It's one of the most important questions you face in retirement—how much of my nest egg can I spend each year? If you choose too high an amount, you eventually could run out of money. Choose too small an amount, and you may feel that you are depriving yourself. At a time when a volatile stock market and paltry bond returns have made it difficult to gauge whether your nest egg is sufficient, relying on standard methods to pick a withdrawal rate may not work.

HOW THE 4% RULE WORKS

Using the standard approach, in the first year of retirement you withdraw 4% of your savings and investments to help cover living expenses. Every year after that, you increase the dollar amount by the previous year's rate of inflation. The strategy is meant to sustain a retirement of about 30 years whether you start with $100,000 or a few million dollars, but there are no guarantees.

Example: If you start with a nest egg of $1 million, you withdraw $40,000 in year one.

Then if annual inflation is running at 2.5%, you withdraw $41,000 in the second year…$42,025 in the third year…and so on. With this strategy, if you have invested your money in a standard mix of 60% large-cap US stocks and 40% US intermediate-term bonds (and rebalance each year to maintain that mix), there is only a 10% chance that if you retire at age 65 you will run out of money by age 95, according to a study by T. Rowe Price.

But the best withdrawal strategy for you depends on factors such as how well you are able to stomach volatility…how long you expect that you and your spouse will live…how much you will receive from other sources of income, such as Social Security, pension benefits and part-time work…and whether you want to leave a sizable inheritance to your heirs.

Here, assorted alternatives to the 4% rule, as designed by several experts…

CONSERVATIVE
THE 4%-PLUS ANNUITY STRATEGY

Asset-allocation authority Ibbotson Associates uses annuities to increase the odds that you won't run out of money. This strategy guarantees that you will have enough money for basic expenses for as long as you live, even if the market plunges, while allowing your nest egg to grow over the long term.

How it works: Use a portion of your assets to buy an immediate annuity, and use a percentage formula, such as the 4% rule, for the rest of your assets so that they will continue to grow over the long term. The annuity's payouts should be just big enough to cover the estimated costs of your essential monthly living expenses, such as mortgage payments, utility bills, basic food costs and health insurance premiums. In exchange for handing over a lump sum for the annuity, you get steady monthly income that can be adjusted for inflation.

Caution: The lump sum that you initially hand over will not be available for your heirs, and the payouts typically stop when you die.

Example: A 65-year-old man living in Connecticut who has $1 million available for investments and savings needs to generate $1,300 a month for basic living expenses. He can purchase an immediate annuity with a cost-of-living rider (assuming an average of 3% inflation each year) for about $350,000. With the remaining $650,000, he can use the 4% rule, allowing withdrawals of an additional $26,000 per year, with adjustments for inflation.

Withdrawals can be used for optional expenses, such as a big trip overseas or a new car, and for emergency expenses, such as unexpected health-care costs. Even in the unlikely event that he exhausts his remaining portfolio in less than 30 years, he still can count on his annuity checks in later years.

For more information on annuities and price quotes, go to *immediateannuities.com* or *personal.vanguard.com/us/funds/annuities*.

AGGRESSIVE
THE 5% MULTI-ASSET STRATEGY

Brigham Young professor Craig L. Israelsen, PhD, found that increasing diversification raises returns and allows a higher withdrawal rate. This strategy allows you to withdraw 5% per year, instead of 4%, without running out of money and without greater risk, but it's much more complicated than other strategies and requires a greater variety of investments.

How it works: Withdraw 5% of your initial nest egg in the first year of retirement instead of 4%…increase the amount for inflation each year…and rebalance your investment portfolio annually. Instead of a 60% stocks/40% bonds split, divide your portfolio evenly among 12 asset classes (about 8.33% of your portfolio in each).

You can do this by investing in exchange-traded funds (ETFs), which track specific sectors and typically have lower expenses than mutual funds, to focus on the following segments—large-, mid- and small-cap US stocks…foreign stocks in developed markets…emerging-market stocks…global real estate…natural resources (energy, precious metals)…commodities (agriculture)…US bonds…US Treasury Inflation-Protected Securities (TIPS)…foreign bonds…and cash. Although there are no guarantees, extensive research and computer simulations indicate that you are likely to be safe withdrawing more each year than with the 60/40 portfolio because over the past 40 years, this kind of multi-asset portfolio has generated an additional percentage point in annual returns.

VERY AGGRESSIVE
THE 6.2% FLEXIBLE STRATEGY

Financial adviser Jonathan Guyton, CFP, has focused on "sustainable" withdrawals and how they are affected by volatility. This strategy allows you to withdraw even higher amounts if you are willing to face sharp ups and downs in the value of your portfolio.

How it works: You withdraw 6.2% of your portfolio's initial value in the first year…you increase the dollar amount of the withdrawals each year based on the inflation rate but within strict limits…and you rebalance each year.

To make this higher withdrawal rate work and keep up with inflation, you will need higher returns.

That means taking more risk by raising the stock portion of your overall portfolio to 80% rather than 60%. It also means a mix of stock ETFs that includes 30% US large-caps…20% US small-caps…20% foreign stocks…and 10% REITs…as well as putting 10% of your overall investment portfolio in US intermediate-term bonds and 10% in cash.

The biggest danger with an aggressive portfolio and high withdrawal rates is that you might face sharp market drops in some years and periods of very high inflation. So you need to follow some strict rules if you want your money to last for at least 30 years.

Rule 1: **Regardless of the inflation rate or how much your portfolio grows, you cannot increase the dollar amount of your withdrawals by more than 6% in any year.** So if you withdraw $62,000 from a $1 million portfolio in your first year, the most that you can increase the withdrawal in the next year is $3,720 (6% of $62,000), even if inflation soars beyond 6%.

Rule 2: **If the value of your portfolio shrinks in any year, you cannot increase your annual withdrawal at all the next year to compensate for inflation, and there is no** "catch-up" for that missed increase in subsequent years.

Rule 3: **At the end of each year, raise the money you need to fund next year's withdrawal by selling shares of your ETFs in a very disciplined way.** First, trim back your stock ETFs that have appreciated the most so that they are in line with your original target percentage allocations.

Next, if necessary to finish making the year's withdrawals, trim back your bond ETFs that have experienced the greatest appreciation to their target allocations. If those profits aren't enough, dip into your cash. The idea is to avoid being forced to sell shares in any asset class that has temporarily lost money. That way, the shares have an opportunity to recover.

Retirement Income for Life

Michael Finke, PhD, CFP, professor and director of retirement planning and living in the personal financial-planning department at Texas Tech University, Lubbock.

Do you think you'll live past 85? If so, there's a surprisingly attractive type of investment you can make now that starts paying off big once you reach that age—and never stops as long as you live. And thanks to a new twist, you can easily dip into your retirement accounts to fund it.

Don't be scared off by its name. It's called a Qualified Longevity Annuity Contract, or QLAC for short. And don't be frightened by the fact that it's an annuity—even though there are many types of annuities that have bad reputations and should be shunned.

Unlike many of those annuities, which can be extraordinarily complex and charge exorbitant annual fees, QLACs are easy to understand and have no annual fees. And your payout amount is fixed and guaranteed, unlike with some annuities that are linked to the performance of stocks.

For many people, a QLAC is the best way to guarantee that they won't run out of money if they live past age 85. And it has big tax advantages (see below).

How a QLAC typically works: You hand over a lump sum of money, which can come from a taxable account or a retirement account such as a traditional IRA or 401(k), to an insurance company that provides the annuity. You don't get anything back at first. But once you turn 85, the insurer starts paying you a guaranteed fixed monthly amount. This amount will depend on your age when you purchased the annuity, how much money you paid, your gender (women will receive a lower monthly amount than men because they tend to live longer) and how high interest rates were when you bought the QLAC.

The payments typically are a lot bigger than what you could earn from a long-term bond portfolio that you might invest in on your own.

THE NEW DIFFERENCE

Why are QLACs such a big opportunity now? In the past, there was a serious drawback to longevity annuities for people who had most of their money tucked away in retirement accounts. That was because upon turning age 70½, all investors in traditional IRAs, 401(k)s and some other accounts are required to begin taking required minimum distributions (RMDs) from those accounts—but if a big chunk of the money in those accounts was tied up in a longevity annuity, these people might not be able to withdraw enough to meet the RMD requirement. The result would be substantial penalties.

New solution: Two years ago, the IRS approved a twist on the longevity annuity and called it a QLAC, which too many investors still are not taking advantage of. With this type of longevity annuity, you don't have to start meeting RMD requirements from the portion of the account devoted to the QLAC until age 85, when you will start receiving payouts from the annuity. Even better, the payouts themselves are deemed to fulfill the RMD requirements for the invested amount. (Some investors buy QLACs that start paying out at a younger age, but that is uncommon because it diminishes the size of the payouts

and the advantage of delaying RMDs.) Only a limited amount of money can be used to buy QLACs—a total up to 25% of the value of all your retirement accounts or up to $125,000, whichever is less.

KEY ADVANTAGES

Because you are not taking RMDs for all those years between age 70½ and 85, you are not paying taxes on those RMDs. You also benefit from what insurance companies call "mortality pooling," which means that the monthly payout amount that the QLAC offers reflects, in part, the money that the insurer won't have to pay out to QLAC holders who die before age 85.

Example of how much a QLAC might pay out: A 65-year-old man who buys a $125,000 QLAC today can expect to receive about $60,000 in income each year starting at age 85 and then as long as he lives. In comparison, if he invested in a portfolio of 20-year AAA-rated corporate bonds at age 65 and wanted to re-create the same payouts from age 85 to 100, he would have to start out with a $304,000 investment, not $125,000 (thus costing $179,000 more), assuming a 4% interest rate. Since women live longer, a 65-year-old woman who pays $125,000 for a QLAC today would get $50,000 of annual income.

WHO SHOULD NOT BUY A QLAC

The many advantages don't mean that QLACs are perfect for everyone. *They probably won't work for you if one or more of the following applies…*

●**Because of your health and/or family history, you don't expect to live much past age 85.** (Go to the life-expectancy calculator at *ssa.gov* to determine how long you are likely to live.) If you die before age 85, your heirs get nothing from a QLAC unless you bought a "return-of-premium" death benefit guarantee (see below under strategies).

●**Your assets total enough that you are sure you will have sufficient money to live on no matter how long you live.** In that case, buying a QLAC would not make sense because you don't need the guaranteed income.

●**Your assets total so little that you are likely to exhaust them before the age of 85.** In that case, buying a QLAC would not make sense because you need the money to live on.

Important: Even if you will have plenty of income from such sources as pensions and Social Security, be sure not to invest so much in a QLAC that you are not able to also maintain a sufficient emergency cash fund.

STRATEGIES FOR BUYING A QLAC

Ways to get the most out of a QLAC…

●**Buy only from a major, highly rated insurance company.** Check quotes for QLACs from various insurers at *immediateannuities. com*. Check that insurers' credit ratings are A+ or better at ambest.com or *standardandpoors. com*. However, if an insurer runs into financial problems and is unable to meet its QLAC payouts, each state has an insurance guarantee fund that takes over the obligation but is subject to coverage limitations.

Example: Florida pays out a maximum of $300,000.

●**Calculate how much a QLAC will cost and end up paying out based on a purchase at different ages.** You can do this at *immediateannuities.com* for various annuity providers. The younger you are, the cheaper it is to get a QLAC that offers a certain level of income starting at age 85.

Example: If a 65-year-old man wants guaranteed income of about $35,000 a year, he must pay about $70,000 for a QLAC now. A 70-year-old man would have to pay $82,750 to obtain the same income.

Because it is likely that long-term rates will rise, it may make sense to spread QLAC purchases over several years, perhaps buying one per year over four years. That's because higher rates when you buy a QLAC mean higher payouts.

●**Consider adding riders to your QLAC,** but keep in mind that riders will reduce your eventual payouts. *Common riders…*

●Cost-of-living-adjustment (COLA) rider. This adjusts payouts starting in the second year. The rider generally pays for itself within five to eight years after payouts begin, depending on how high inflation is.

●Return-of-premium rider. With this, your spouse and other heirs receive the initial amount you invested in the QLAC if you die before you get any payouts. For couples, I often suggest that both spouses get a QLAC, if they can afford to, likely making this rider unnecessary. Costs vary widely.

Dividends Every Month

Richard J. Moroney, CFA, chief investment officer at Horizon Investment Services, Hammond, Indiana. He is editor of the *Dow Theory Forecasts* newsletter. DowTheory.com

You can design a stock portfolio that provides income every month of the year. It provides a steady cash stream with a decent yield and potential gains in share price and dividend growth.

How to do it: Companies pay stock dividends on a quarterly basis—but not necessarily at the end of the usual calendar quarters. So you can pick a few attractive companies that pay in January and every three months after that…a few that pay in February and every three months after that…and a few that pay in March and every three months after that.

The 27 stocks below have paid dividends reliably, are attractively priced and have the potential for share price gains. Purchased in equal dollar amounts, the stocks offer an annual yield that recently totaled nearly 3%.

Dividends in January, April, July, October: AmTrust Financial (AFSI)…Comcast (CMCSA)…Dow Chemical (DOW)…Fifth Third Bancorp (FITB)…JPMorgan Chase (JPM)…Macy's (M)…Schlumberger (SLB)…UGI (UGI)… Union Pacific (UNP).

February, May, August, November: Alliant Energy (LNT)…AmeriGas Partners (APU)…Apple (AAPL)…Capital One Financial (COF)…CMS Energy (CMS)…CVS Caremark (CVS)…electricity provider Idacorp (IDA)… PNM Resources (PNM).

March, June, September, December:
Energy provider Avista (AVA)...BlackRock (BLK)...railcar leaser GATX (GMT)...Kroger Co. (KR)...automotive supplier Magna International (MGA)...Norfolk Southern (NSC)... Penske Automotive Group (PAG)...Qualcomm (QCOM)...Wells Fargo & Co. (WFC).

How to Find Your Lost Pension Money

Jim Miller, an advocate for older Americans, writes "SavvySenior," a weekly information column syndicated in more than 400 newspapers nationwide. Based in Norman, Oklahoma, Miller also offers a free senior news service at SavvySenior.org.

It's not unusual for a worker to lose track of a pension benefit. Perhaps you left an employer long ago and forgot that you left behind a pension. Or maybe you worked for a company that changed owners or went bellyup many years ago, and you figured the pension went with it...but you might have been wrong.

Today, millions of dollars in benefits are sitting in pension plans across the US or with the Pension Benefit Guaranty Corporation (PBGC), a federal government agency, waiting to be claimed by their rightful owners. The average unclaimed benefit with PBGC is $6,550.

To help you look for a pension, here are the steps to take and some free resources that can help you search if your previous employer has gone out of business, relocated, changed owners or merged with another firm...

CONTACT THE EMPLOYER

If you think you have a pension and the company you worked for still is in business, your first step is to call the human resources department and ask how to contact the pension plan administrator. Ask the administrator whether you have a pension, how much it is worth and how to claim it. Depending on how complete the administrator's records are, you may need to show proof that you once worked for the company and that you are pension eligible.

If you haven't saved your old tax returns from these years, you can get a copy of your earnings record from the Social Security Administration, which will show how much you were paid each calendar year by each employer. Call 800-772-1213, and ask for Form SSA-7050, Request for Social Security Earnings Information, or you can download it at *ssa. gov/online/ssa-7050.pdf*. You will pay a small fee for the report, depending on the number of years of data you request.

Some other old forms that can help you prove pension eligibility are summary plan descriptions that you should have received from your employer when you worked there...and any individual benefit statements that you received during your employment.

SEARCH PBGC

If your former employer went out of business or if the company still is in business but terminated its pension plan, check with the PBGC, which guarantees pension payouts to private-sector workers if their pension plans fail, up to annual limits. Most people receive the full benefit they earned before the plan was terminated. The PBGC offers an online pension-search directory tool at *search.pbgc. gov/mp/mp.aspx*, or call 800-400-7242.

GET HELP

If you need help tracking down your former company because it may have moved, changed owners or merged with another firm, contact the Pension Rights Center, a nonprofit consumer organization that offers seven free Pension Counseling and Information Projects around the US that serve 30 states. For more information, visit *pensionrights.org* or call 888-420-6550. If you, your company or your pension plan happens to be outside the 30-state area served by the projects, or if you're trying to locate a federal or military pension, use Pension Help America at *pensionhelp.org*. This resource can connect you with government agencies and private organizations that provide free information and assistance to help your search.

Also, the PBGC has a free publication called *Finding a Lost Pension*. Go to *pbgc.gov/documents/finding-a-lost-pension.pdf* to see it online, or call 800-400-7242 and ask for a copy to be mailed to you.

Find Unclaimed Funds

Do a search for unclaimed money to which you might be entitled. Funds in financial institutions or companies that have had no activity and no contact with the owner for a long time—usually three years or more—may go to state unclaimed-property offices. To find out if any funds are being held for you, search the websites *missingmoney.com* and *unclaimed.org*...check the Treasury site for the state where you live and any in which you lived in the past...search under any names you have ever used, and try a first initial plus your last name as well as first and last names. Search *irs.gov* for any possible unclaimed tax-refund money. The Pension Benefit Guaranty Corporation (*pbgc.gov*) has a searchable database for unclaimed pensions...*treasuryhunt. gov* helps in searches for unclaimed savings bonds...websites of individual life insurers let you search for claims or payments.

Jean Chatzky, financial editor, NBC's *Today* show. Today.com

Need Cash? How to Borrow from Your Life Insurance Policy

Lee Slavutin, MD, CLU, principal, Stern Slavutin-2 Inc., an insurance and estate-planning firm in New York City, SternsLavutin.com.

Many types of loans are difficult to obtain in these credit-crunch times. However, you might get needed cash by borrowing against your life insurance policy.

Advantages: Such loans require no complicated paperwork, no credit check and no proof of income. Interest rates are reasonable—and you don't have to pay the interest if you choose not to.

Downside: The loan balance, including any accrued interest, will be subtracted from the insurance benefit that you presumably bought to protect your loved ones. And if you borrow more than the policy's cash value, you can wind up with a big tax bill (explained below).

Moreover, any loan interest you pay to preserve your policy's benefits is not tax deductible. *To know whether a life insurance loan makes sense for you, consider...*

FOREVER FUNDS

Life insurance policy loans are available if you have a so-called "permanent" cash value policy—one designed to stay in effect as you grow older. You can't borrow from a term life policy, which remains in effect only for a specific period and has no cash value.

There are various kinds of permanent life insurance, including whole life, universal life and variable life policies. Policyholders pay much higher initial premiums for such policies than they do for term life. In return, the policies accumulate "cash value" over time. Ultimately, that cash value can pay the increasing cost of life insurance premiums as you grow older. In addition, the cash value can serve as collateral for loans.

THE COST OF CASH

An example can illustrate the pros and cons of policy loans.

Example: Jane Jones bought a permanent life policy at age 50. Ten years later, she had paid in $100,000 and had accrued $120,000 in cash value ($100,000 of premiums plus $20,000 of investment income). At that point, she borrowed $100,000.

Note: Jane did not actually borrow from her policy. She borrowed from her insurer, using the insurance policy's cash value as collateral.

With $120,000 in cash value, Jane was able to obtain a $100,000 loan, less than the $108,000 (90% of cash value, which is the maximum you are allowed to borrow) limit on loans in her case. She can use that money in any way she wants, and she owes no income tax on it.

Downside: Policy loans usually charge interest rates comparable to the yields on highly rated corporate bonds.

Assume that Jane is charged compound interest of 6% a year but chooses not to pay any of this interest for 12 years. At that point, her loan balance would be around $200,000.

Trap: Although Jane continues to earn money on her $120,000 in cash value, which earns money because it is treated as an investment account, she won't earn as much as she would have earned if she hadn't borrowed any money.

Typically, the amount borrowed ($100,000 in this example) will earn interest at a rate that's one to two percentage points lower than the rate earned on the rest of the cash value ($20,000).

Result: The loan balance will grow faster than the cash value. Jane's cash value might be only $190,000 when the loan balance reaches $200,000.

NEGATIVE THOUGHTS

As mentioned, a policy loan uses the borrower's cash value as collateral. Jane's $190,000 in cash value is no longer enough to back a $200,000 policy loan balance.

What will happen: The insurance company will ask Jane to pay the $10,000 difference.

Each year, the loan balance may grow faster than the cash value. The amount that Jane will have to pay probably will increase each year.

Trap: If Jane does not make any of the required catch-up payments, her insurance company will report Jane's income to the IRS. That income will be the amount by which her loan exceeds the total of premiums she has paid for the policy.

Suppose that this occurs when Jane's loan is $200,000. She has paid $100,000 in premiums, so she will owe tax on $100,000 in income. That's phantom income—income she'll never pocket—because the entire cash value will be used to pay off the policy loan.

Not only will Jane owe a substantial amount of income tax, she'll also no longer have the life insurance coverage she wanted.

CUTTING COVERAGE

If Jane dies while her policy is still in force but with an outstanding policy loan, the loan will be repaid to the insurer and the death benefit will be reduced by that amount.

Suppose that Jane dies when her policy's cash value is $190,000 and her loan balance is $188,000. Further suppose that the policy's death benefit is $300,000.

Result: Of the $300,000 death benefit, $188,000 will go to the insurance company, settling the loan. Only $112,000 will go to Jane's beneficiary.

DON'T BORROW TROUBLE

Considering how policy loans are treated, pursue the following strategies...

•**Treat life insurance policy loans as a last resort.** Borrow only if you have a vital need for cash, not for nonessentials, such as a luxury vacation, a second home or your daughter's wedding.

If you do have a critical need for cash and it's not possible or practical to get another type of loan, borrowing against your policy can generate cash at a reasonable interest rate.

•**Don't borrow the maximum amount.** Rather than borrow 90% of the amount of your cash value, borrow a smaller portion. That will reduce the risk that your loan balance will grow to exceed your cash balance.

•**Pay the loan interest each year.** That will prevent the loan balance from growing and enable you to maintain a death benefit for your beneficiaries.

•**Monitor statements from your life insurer carefully.** If the loan balance exceeds the cash value, promptly pay enough to make up the shortfall. This will keep you from incurring a huge tax bill.

House-Rich but Cash-Poor: Unlock the Value of Your Home to Help Pay for Retirement

Steven A. Sass, PhD, program director of the Financial Security Project with the Center for Retirement Research at Boston College. He previously was an economist with the Federal Reserve Bank of Boston. CRR.BC.edu

Many retirees and soon-to-be retirees are house-rich but cash-poor. Their mortgages are mostly or fully paid off, and their houses have climbed in value since they bought them, creating thousands and thousands of dollars in equity—yet their other savings are too limited for them to enjoy the retirement they want…if they can retire at all.

There are three common approaches to unlocking the value of your home—downsizing …obtaining a reverse mortgage…or using a home-equity line of credit. *There are advantages and disadvantages to each…*

DOWNSIZING

You could sell your home and then either rent or buy less expensive housing. This may not be an attractive option for people who hoped to continue living in the homes they are used to. But financially it often is the best choice.

That's because downsizing not only frees up assets—it can dramatically reduce ongoing expenses. Nationally, property taxes, utilities, maintenance, insurance and the like tend to total approximately 3.25% of a home's value each year—so downsizing can produce big savings.

Example: Downsize from a $400,000 home to a $200,000 home, and you not only free up $200,000 for your retirement, you also are likely to save around $6,500 a year in ongoing housing costs, which would add up to $130,000 over a 20-year retirement. You might save even more by choosing a new home that is especially energy-efficient and/or in a town with low property taxes.

People in or near retirement often can downsize without any significant decrease in quality of life because their existing homes are not well suited to their current needs. Their kids generally have moved out, so they no longer need a large home or one in an area with great (and high-tax) public schools. And once home owners retire, they no longer need to live close to employers. Moving might mean being farther away from friends—but keep in mind that as your friends age, they, too, may choose to move.

Downside: Selling a home is expensive. Broker fees, moving costs and the cost of fixing up your current property before putting it on the market could add up to 10% of the property's value.

Selling your home could trigger capital gains tax, though this is not common. Married people who file jointly (and people widowed within two years of the home sale) generally will not have to pay taxes on the sale of a primary residence as long as their profit on the sale does not exceed $500,000 (the limit is $250,000 for single filers). A couple who bought a home for $250,000 and spent $50,000 improving it over the years could sell it for as much as $800,000 without triggering taxes, for example. See IRS Publication 523, Selling Your Home, for details.

Downsizing could come back to bite you if you or your spouse later require an extended nursing home stay. This care can cost upward of $80,000 a year, and Medicaid will not start paying these bills until you have exhausted virtually all of your assets. In most states, the primary residence can be excluded from Medicaid's eligibility calculations, potentially allowing a spouse or heirs to hang onto this asset—but if you downsize and pocket the profit, that profit would be at risk.

There are limits and restrictions that can complicate Medicaid's primary residence exclusion. For more details, visit *longtermcare. gov* and select the "Medicare, Medicaid & More" link on the left…or enter your state's name and "Medicaid" into a search engine to find contact information for the agency that manages your state's Medicaid program.

Bottom line: Because of its potential to greatly reduce ongoing expenses, downsizing is the first option to consider if you want to free up equity from your home. If you think you are likely to downsize at any point during your retirement, do so as soon as possible to maximize these savings. Yes, there are steep costs involved in selling a home, but those costs will have to be paid at some point, either by you or your heirs. There are emotional reasons to not downsize, but financially, downsizing tends to be a bad choice only in very exceptional circumstances—for example, if you or your spouse has a degenerative health condition that makes a Medicaid-financed extended stay in a nursing home likely.

What about renting rather than buying? If you are 70 or younger and downsizing, buying has an advantage—it protects you against the possibility that rents could rise sharply in the future. If you are 80 or older, renting is preferable because there's a good chance that you won't be able to live independently long enough to justify the transaction costs generated by buying and later selling a new home. If you are in your 70s, a case could be made for either renting or buying, depending on your preference and what's available in your new location.

A REVERSE MORTGAGE

If you are 62 or older and own your home outright (or have a relatively low mortgage balance), you likely can qualify for a reverse mortgage. This is a type of loan that lets you borrow against the equity in the home with no loan payments required during your lifetime as long as you continue to live in the home. The amount that you can borrow depends on the value of your home and your age, among other factors—the older you are, the more money you can get, all else being equal. This money can be received as a lump sum, a line of credit or monthly payments.

Example: A 65-year-old with $250,000 in equity in his/her home could obtain a $127,000 lump sum…while a 75-year-old with a similar property could get a $139,000 lump sum.

Reverse mortgages have earned a bad reputation because of high costs, misleading advertisements and confusing contracts. One major complaint was recently eliminated. In the past, if only one spouse in a couple took out a reverse mortgage because the other was not yet 62 and thus not eligible, that younger spouse could later be forced out of the home when the borrower died or moved into a nursing home. Recent reforms allow the younger spouse to remain in the home.

The proceeds from a reverse mortgage are not subject to income tax or capital gains tax, and they typically will not affect your Social Security or Medicare benefits.

Downsides: Reverse mortgages are expensive. Example: For a $100,000 loan, upfront costs may be $8,000. To find a calculator that shows maximum allowed charges, go to *re versemortgage.org/about/reverse-mortgage-cal culator.*

Because reverse mortgages typically are repaid through the sale of the property after the borrower's death, heirs usually will not be able to inherit the home, and there could be little or no equity left as a bequest.

Bottom line: A reverse mortgage lets you access your equity and remain in your home for the rest of your life. But you'll pay steep up-front costs, which can be paid out of the proceeds of the loan, and funds withdrawn are charged a relatively high interest rate. So if you do not remain in your home for the rest of your life, these costs will significantly reduce the equity you'll get when you move.

Be realistic—are you sure you will want to continue to live here even as your friends retire to other areas and your health and mobility decline?

Consider speaking with a fee-only financial planner before signing reverse mortgage documents.

WHEN TO USE A HELOC

Home-equity lines of credit (HELOCs) are an easy and inexpensive way to tap home equity—they have low up front costs and reasonable interest rates. But they are not a good option for retirees who wish to use their homes to supplement their retirement income. Borrowers typically make only interest payments at first but must start repaying the principal as soon as the "draw period" ends. (The "draw period" is a predetermined time, often 10 years, during which the line of credit can be tapped.)

Other HELOC drawbacks include the fact that these loans almost always have a variable interest rate, so your cost of borrowing could increase even after you obtain the line of credit…and lenders sometimes have the option of canceling HELOCs at any time. They don't commonly do so, but it means there is a chance that the cash you were counting on might not be there when you need it.

Still, a HELOC's low costs and flexibility make it a great option if you are seeking financial flexibility to pay for occasional expenses such as when your home suddenly needs a new furnace.

When Reverse Mortgages Are a Bad Idea

Jane Bryant Quinn, who has been a columnist for *The Washington Post*, *Newsweek* and Bloomberg.com. She is author of *Making the Most of Your Money Now*, which was named the best personal finance book by Consumers Union and has been updated for the new decade. JaneBryantQuinn.com

Reverse mortgages are tempting to people whose retirement savings and home values have had recent losses—but don't take out a reverse mortgage if you're in your 60s.

A reverse mortgage loan is a way to borrow against the value of one's home without selling the home in this slow market. These loans now are being aggressively marketed to home owners as young as 62—but they are a very bad idea for anyone younger than 70, and even then, they should be used only as a last resort.

Lenders offer extremely unappealing reverse mortgage loan terms to those still in their 60s. These loans are not to be repaid until the home owner dies or moves out. That might take decades if the borrower is in his 60s, so lenders adjust their offers to make up for the delayed payback. Reverse mortgage contracts are so complex that it often is difficult to spot the steep fees and interest rates.

Rent Out Your Home

Scott Shatford, founder of RentingYourPlace.com, which helps property owners maximize their rental income on Airbnb. He is author of *The Airbnb Expert's Playbook*.

Thanks to the website Airbnb, more home owners are earning extra cash by taking in guests. But many home owners worry that inviting strangers into their homes could be an invitation to disaster. A guest could steal or damage their property or even do them physical harm. *Here's what you need to know to successfully rent out your home or a room on Airbnb…*

ATTRACTING GUESTS

Airbnb (*Airbnb.com*) is not the only short-term property rental website—competitors include *homeaway.com* and *vrbo.com*—but it is the best choice. It can market rental properties to literally millions of potential guests…it's the easiest home-rental site to use…it does not impose any upfront or annual fees (hosts pay 3% of their rental income)…and it offers the strongest safety features, including free insurance (see next page) and "Verified ID"—most guests must provide Airbnb a copy of a passport or driver's license or verify personal information in other ways.

To rent out your place…

•**Advertise yourself, not just your property.** Include a smiling, friendly picture of yourself in your listing and personal details, such as your hobbies and how long you have lived in the area. Potential guests are much more likely to rent from you if they form a positive first impression of you.

•**Set a low initial rate.** When you're starting out, price your property around 25% below the rates charged by the most comparable Airbnb properties in your area. A low price also increases the odds that guests will feel they got their money's worth and post positive reviews of your property. Those positive reviews will attract future guests…even after you have raised your price.

•**Target peak-demand weeks.** If your plan is to rent out your primary residence when you're away on vacation, take your vacations when lodging in your area is in greatest demand. *To identify these weeks, consider…*

•Do other Airbnb properties and hotels in your area charge higher rates during particular weeks?

•Is there a festival, marathon, bowl game, golf tournament or other event that annually draws large numbers of visitors to your area?

•When do area colleges have their homecoming, graduation and parents' weekends?

•**Don't oversell your home.** Giving an overly rosy picture of your property will lead to disappointed guests. Disappointed guests are likely to post negative reviews.

Examples: Don't say your home is on the beach if it is really two blocks away…don't call the property tranquil if it is on a busy road.

Use the listings of highly rated Airbnb properties in your area as a template for what to mention in your listing.

The photos you include should tell an honest story as well. Don't take a picture of the beautiful view from your rooftop if the view from the inside of your home is far less impressive.

• **Clean, then clean again.** Some guests have very high standards for cleanliness. Better to spend extra time cleaning than receive a negative review—particularly when you're new to Airbnb and have not yet received the numerous positive reviews needed to balance a bad one.

• **Form a personal connection.** Greet your guests in person when they arrive, if possible. Check in with them during their visit to see if there's anything they need. Send a note thanking them for their visit shortly after they depart. These connections will help guests see you as a person, not just a property owner, which increases the odds that they will take good care of your property and give you a good review.

SAFETY AND SECURITY

Airbnb does not disclose statistics about how often rentals go wrong, but theft and serious property damage appear to be rare. There were more than 10 million Airbnb rentals last year, yet mentions of major problems are uncommon on social media and in the press. I've never had a single problem in more than 50 rentals at my private home and 500 rentals at my full-time rental properties—not so much as a broken dish.

Still, it is prudent to be cautious…

• **Install digital door locks.** With these you can give guests a code that they can use to enter, then you can change the code after their visit. That's safer than handing over a key, which a guest could have copied in order to sneak in later. Digital locks cost $100 to $300 in home centers and from online retailers.

• **Rent only to guests who have excellent reviews and "verified IDs."** A guest who has received uniformly glowing feedback after five or more rentals is unlikely to cause problems.

Guests with "Verified ID" badges on their profiles almost certainly are who they claim.

Also: Read what the guest has written about himself/herself in his profile…what he has written about Airbnb properties he previously has visited…and what the owners of those prior Airbnb properties have written about this guest. Does this seem like someone you want in your home?

• **Exchange e-mails with a potential guest.** Try to get a feel for this person and anyone he will be traveling with. Families and retirees tend to be especially low-risk guests.

• **Lock up portable valuables, or store them off-site.** Buy a safe…rent a bank security-deposit box…or store items of particular value with a friend or relative.

LEGALITY

Many cities and some towns have laws that restrict property owners' right to rent out their homes on a short-term basis or require them to pay hotel taxes if they do so. Call your town's or city's zoning or development office to ask about applicable laws in your area. Or enter the terms "Airbnb," "legal" and the name of your town into a search engine to see if a local newspaper or other reliable source has written anything on the subject.

In practice, however, these laws are almost never enforced even when they exist…unless neighbors complain.

Also worth noting…

• **Even if local laws restrict your right to rent out your property on a short-term basis,** you probably still have the right to rent out a room in your property while you are on hand.

• **Homeowner's associations (and condo or co-op boards)** often have rules blocking short-term rentals. These groups may enforce rules strictly.

• **Tenants often are prohibited by the terms of their rental contracts** from subletting their dwellings without the property owner's permission.

NEW AIRBNB INSURANCE—IS IT ENOUGH?

Homeowner's insurance often does not cover claims related to paying guests. Airbnb recently addressed this concern—starting

January 2015, the company began providing $1 million in liability insurance at no extra charge to protect property owners should a guest be injured or killed. That's in addition to the $1 million in coverage it already supplies for property theft and/or damage stemming from rentals.

Airbnb's million-dollar liability and theft/damage coverage greatly reduces insurance concerns, but...

•**The liability component of Airbnb's coverage is new and untested.** If you want to be certain that you are well covered—or if you rent out your home through a service other than Airbnb—consider purchasing coverage designed specifically for properties that are rented out on a short-term basis. Providers include CBIZ Insurance Services (*cbiz.com*) and Peers Marketplace (*peers.org*).

•**Cash and securities are not covered by Airbnb's million-dollar theft insurance.** Coverage for jewelry, collectibles, artwork and certain other high-end items is limited. Airbnb's coverage also does not protect property owners from losses due to identity theft if a guest gets hold of, say, credit card account information, Social Security numbers or other sensitive information.

There have been reports of homeowner's insurance companies threatening to cancel the coverage of homes that are rented out. Ask your insurer if renting out your property through Airbnb will affect your coverage—and get the answer in writing.

7 Fun Jobs for Retirees

Nancy Collamer, a career coach in Old Greenwich, Connecticut. She is author of *Second-Act Careers: 50+ Ways to Profit from Your Passions During Semi-Retirement* and founder of MyLifeStyleCareer.com.

You may have retired, but you still can get a job—and have fun doing that job! *Here are seven options...*

•**National Park Service employees get paid to work in spectacular natural or his-**torical settings. They work at the gift shops and entrance gates, give talks to guests, maintain trails and perform all the other tasks that keep the National Park system running. These jobs tend to be seasonal—don't expect many openings until spring. Age is not an issue. More than one-third of National Park employees are over age 50. Salaries typically are between $12 and $15 an hour, sometimes higher. Lodging might be provided as well.

To learn more: Visit the National Parks website (*nps.gov*) or *usajobs.gov* to find openings. Private website *coolworks.com* lists National Park job openings, too (select "National Park Jobs" from the "Find a Job" menu).

•**English language teachers are in heavy demand in Asia and elsewhere.** It is a great opportunity to get paid to live abroad. Some of these positions pay only travel expenses, lodging and a small stipend, but others pay $50,000 a year or more. A one-year commitment often is required. Passing a certificate program on teaching English as a second language can improve your odds of landing good jobs in this field, but it's not required.

To learn more: Visit the sites of Teach English as a Foreign Language (*tefl.com*) or Transitions Abroad (*transitionsabroad.com*).

•**Adjunct professors share their expertise while working in an intellectually stimulating environment.** Impressive academic credentials usually are required to land an adjunct professor position at a prestigious college—but at junior colleges, community colleges and technical colleges, these jobs are within reach of many retirees. If you had a successful career in marketing, for example, a local community college might hire you to teach a marketing course. Adjunct professors typically earn a few thousand dollars per course taught at four-year colleges but often just $1,000 to $2,000 per course at two-year colleges.

To learn more: Visit the websites of two-year and technical colleges in your region to see if they are looking for an instructor in your area of expertise.

•**Caretakers look after homes or other properties while their owners are away.**

483

Retirees are in particular demand as caretakers because property owners consider them mature and responsible. Often all a caretaker has to do is live in the property and care for it as any resident would—having someone there reduces the odds of break-ins or that a major maintenance issue will go unnoticed.

Caretaking doesn't tend to pay very much—sometimes nothing at all—but it can be a great way to reduce retirement travel costs by staying in interesting properties in interesting locations with no out-of-pocket housing costs. (Income should be provided if the caretaker is asked to do significant maintenance or groundskeeping.)

To learn more: Subscribe to *The Caretaking Gazette*, which lists caretaking opportunities worldwide ($29.95/yr, *caretaker.org*).

• **Inn sitters take care of inns and bed-and-breakfasts while their owners are away.** Duties might include handling guest check-ins and checkouts, cooking breakfast and cleaning rooms. Compensation varies greatly depending on the inn sitter's level of experience and other factors, but experienced inn sitters or inn-sitting couples often earn $100 to $200 a day plus lodging and perhaps travel expenses.

To learn more: Ask innkeepers and B&B owners whether they ever hire inn sitters. The website of the Interim Innkeepers Network offers some additional details (*interimInnkeepers.net*).

• **Stadium ushers help fans find their seats on game days.** The job doesn't pay much—often little more than minimum wage—but it's a way to get paid to attend sporting events. Usher jobs can be difficult to land with top teams, but the odds can be better at minor league stadiums or at baseball spring-training facilities in Florida and Arizona.

To learn more: Visit the websites of local teams and stadiums to find openings, or call the team offices.

• **Museum docents serve as guides, helping visitors to understand the museum exhibits.** Docent jobs typically are unpaid, but they can be an enjoyable opportunity to share your passion for a topic and further your knowledge of it by attending museum lectures, events, exhibitions and training programs for free. (Some museums offer extensive training programs for their docents.)

To learn more: Call local museums, and ask about their docent or volunteer programs. Or visit a museum's website, and look for a section labeled "Volunteer" or "Docent Program."

How a Job Impacts Your Retirement Benefits

Kiplinger's Retirement Report. Kiplingers.com

If you want to return to work after retirement, find out how the job will affect your retirement benefits. Social Security is not reduced if you are past "full" retirement age. But if you are within the year in which you reach that age, you forfeit $1 of benefits for every $3 you earn above the $41,880 earnings limit up to the month of your birthday…and if you are taking benefits earlier than your full-retirement year, you forfeit $1 for every $2 of earned income over the $15,720 earnings limit. However, at full retirement age, your Social Security benefit will be adjusted upward to take into account the amounts that were withheld.

If you receive annuity or pension payments: They will continue if you go back to work—but you may be able to stop periodic withdrawals from a variable annuity's investment portfolio if you wish. In retirement accounts, you can again contribute to an IRA or a 401(k) if you meet eligibility and age requirements…and you won't have to take required minimum distributions (RMDs) from your employer's 401(k) as long as you work there. Consult a financial adviser. Social Security, annuity and retirement account rules are complex and vary widely.

Finding a Work-at-Home Job—Most Are Scams, but These 7 Are for Real

Michael Haaren, CEO of Staffcentrix, a training and development company. He is coauthor of *Work at Home Now: The No-Nonsense Guide to Finding Your Perfect Home-Based Job, Avoiding Scams, and Making a Great Living.* RatRaceRebellion.com

A growing number of employers are willing to use home-based employees, assuming those employees have access to a phone, computer and high-speed Internet connection. That's good news for people with disabilities or who are caring for children or an elderly relative or who live in an area where jobs are scarce. It's also good news for people who could find work outside the home but prefer to spend more time with their families and less time sitting in traffic.

The bad news is that there are roughly 60 "work from home" job scams on the Internet for each legitimate opportunity, according to our research.

Here's how to avoid the scams and land a good work-at-home position…

LANDING WORK-AT-HOME JOBS

• **Tweak your résumé before you start applying for work-at-home jobs.** Stress any work experience that shows that you can work productively without direct supervision or handle projects outside the workplace. Be sure to mention any experience you have with communications technology, such as video-conferencing tools and tablet computers.

If your work history is light on projects outside the workplace, consider taking a virtual volunteer position and listing this on your résumé.

Example: The United Nations Volunteers program offers plenty of volunteer-from-home opportunities and looks impressive on a résumé (*onlinevolunteering.org*).

• **Interviews for online positions often are conducted via phone or Skype video call.** If you are not naturally comfortable speaking on the phone or you lack experience with Skype video calls, practice with friends before the interview.

Helpful: If the interview is a Skype video call, make sure that the backdrop behind you is uncluttered and looks professional.

HOME-BASED CAREERS HIRING NOW

Among the career opportunities open to the home-based…

1. Customer service agents field calls from their employers' customers and prospective customers—they do not place telemarketing calls. Major employers of home-based workers in this field include Live-Ops (*join.liveops.com*)…Alpine Access (*jobs.alpineaccess.com*)…and Arise (*partner.arise.com*).

Other well-known companies that frequently hire home-based customer service agents include American Express (on *careers.americanexpress.com*, enter "Work at Home" in the keyword search box)…Amazon.com (on *amazon.com*, select "Careers" from the "Get to Know Us" menu near the bottom of the page, then enter "Work at Home" in the keyword box)…and the Home Shopping Network (on *hsn.com*, select "Careers" from the "Get to Know Us" menu near the bottom of the page, then select "Work at Home" from the "Category" menu). To find other companies hiring in this field, select the "Call Center & Cust. Service" listing on the left of the home page of my company's website, *ratracerebellion.com*.

Pay typically is $9 to $12 an hour, though it can reach $20 an hour or more.

2. Internet ad assessors conduct Internet searches and make sure that search results are appropriate for the search terms used. Extensive tech skills are not needed—just basic Internet skills. Companies hiring home-based workers in this area include Google (on *google.com/about/careers/jobs*, search for the job "Ad Rater")…Lionbridge (on *www.lionbridge.com*, select "Careers," then "Work-at-Home Opportunities") and Leapforce (*leapforceathome.com*). Pay is about $10 to $15 per hour.

3. Website testers visit websites and record their impressions of those sites. It's like being part of a focus group except that you can do it from home. Employers offering home-based employment in the field include Userlytics (on *userlytics.com*, select "Join Our Tester Panel" near the bottom of the page) and UserTesting.com (on *usertesting.com*, click on "Sign up today to become a tester").

Reviews typically take around 10 to 20 minutes apiece and pay perhaps $10 per review. But don't expect to make a lot of money or make this a full-time career—testers typically get occasional assignments, not regular work.

4. Online moderators oversee website communities, Facebook groups and interactive online games, stepping in to remove offensive comments or ban troublemakers. Employers that hire home-based moderators include LiveWorld.com (*liveworld.com*) and Zynga.com (on *zynga.com*, click on "Jobs, then "Open Positions"). The job requires tact, interpersonal skills and experience with social media. The pay for this work tends to be toward the lower end of the scale—often $10 an hour.

5. Virtual task freelancers perform chores posted on websites such as TaskRabbit.com. Some of the chores require travel and thus are not appropriate for the exclusively home-based—picking up a client's dry cleaning or assembling new IKEA furniture, for example. But others can be performed from home, such as conducting online research or doing data entry.

Job seekers typically bid on tasks. If their bid is accepted, they are paid directly by the individual or company that needs the work done.

Comparable websites include Amazon's Mechanical Turk (*mturk.com*) and Clickworker (*clickworker.com*). Also, the site Fiverr (*fiverr.com*) lets people post tasks that they're willing to perform for $5.

6. Transcriptionists type verbatim accounts of board meetings, presentations, conference calls, etc., from audio recordings. Some of the companies that hire home-based transcriptionists include Tigerfish (*tigerfish.com/employment.html*)…Ubiqus (on *ubiqus.com*, select "Employment" under "Contact Us")…and Cambridge Transcriptions (*ctran.com/employment*).

The pay for transcriptionists can vary with typing speed but generally is around $10 per hour.

7. Freelance posters are paid to post content to blogs. Topics vary widely, depending on the theme of the blog. Pay can range from a few dollars per post to $50 and beyond, and usually is made directly to the poster by the owner of the blog. Short posts on generic themes such as lifestyle and fashion generally pay less, while specialized posts requiring more research (on economic issues, for example) pay more. These are listed on such websites as *problogger.net* (click on "Jobs") and *bloggingpro.com* (click on "Jobs")…and Postloop (on *postloop.com*, click "Join").

WORK-AT-HOME SCAM ALERT

Some work-from-home scams are easy to spot—they require applicants to pay upfront "membership" fees or similar fees—but other work-at-home scams are very subtle.

The best way to avoid these scams is to search for work-at-home jobs only on websites that make some effort to weed out scammers. These include *indeed.com* (click "Advanced Job Search," type "Work From Home" without quotes into the "exact phrase" field, and leave the location field blank) and the Work From Home section of About.com (*thebalance.com/jobsearch-4074003*, search "Work from Home Jobs"). Screened job leads are posted on *ratra cerebellion.com*.

Warning: Con artists are constantly fine-tuning their scams, and occasionally a bogus offer will slip through at Indeed.com and similar "job aggregator" websites. Job seekers should always proceed with caution. Use a search engine to research the potential employer to make sure it appears legitimate before applying. Also visit work-at-home forums such as *wahm.com* to learn what other home-based employees and job seekers have to say about the employer. If your search turns up little or no mention of an employer, be wary—it could mean that it isn't really an employer at all.

Retire Happily on $25,000 a Year

Dan Prescher, senior editor of InternationalLiving.com, and Suzan Haskins, Latin America editor of InternationalLiving.com. The couple currently resides in Ecuador. They are coauthors of *The International Living Guide to Retiring Overseas on a Budget*. InternationalLiving.com

Retirees can live very comfortably in Latin America for $25,000 a year or less—that's about half of what it would cost in some parts of the US. We pay property taxes of less than $55 a year for our 1,100-square-foot condo in Ecuador. Health care is inexpensive. Great meals cost just a few dollars. Homes can be very affordable. Some Latin American nations even offer special discounts to retirees.

Example: Panama's "pensionado" program offers retirees 50% off many entertainment-related costs and the closing costs of a home loan, among many other savings.

And despite what many Americans fear, you can live in Latin America without sacrificing safety or high-quality health care...and without feeling isolated or out of place. Residency permits tend to be easy to obtain, and US pensions and other US retirement income often are not taxed. (But US citizens are required to report income annually to the US government and pay US income taxes no matter where they live.)

Here's what you need to know...

HEALTH CARE

Many parts of Latin America now have excellent—and affordable—health care. Urban and suburban areas popular with foreign retirees often have modern hospitals and doctors who speak English well and who were educated in well-regarded US or European universities. (The quality of health care may not be up to par in rural parts of Latin America, however.)

Paying for medical care in Latin America usually isn't a problem, either. Most countries in the region have a socialized health-care system that is open to foreign residents. If this public system does not meet your medical needs, there's often a high-quality private health-care system as well.

Prices in this private health-care system are likely to be much lower than in the US. Doctor and dentist appointments typically cost $20 to $40...hospital procedures tend to cost one-quarter of what similar procedures cost in the US...health insurance for people of retirement age can cost as little as $50 a month—sometimes with no deductible. (Alternatively, many top hospitals in Costa Rica, Nicaragua, Panama and Uruguay have plans that provide steep discounts on hospital services for perhaps $25 to $75 per month.)

In some ways, medical care in Latin America is even better than in the US. Doctors tend to spend more time with their patients than they now do in the US...and some doctors make house calls and/or give patients their personal cell-phone numbers.

Examples: Costa Rica has a very good national health-care system and an excellent private system. Areas of Mexico popular with expatriots, such as Lake Chapala and Puerto Vallarta, have very strong private medical providers who are used to treating American retirees. Panama City has a Johns Hopkins–affiliated hospital that is as technologically advanced as an elite US hospital.

If a major medical issue arises and you are enrolled in Medicare, you also could return to the US and use Medicare to pay for treatment. However, Medicare does not cover medical treatment in foreign countries.

SAFETY

When Latin America is mentioned in American news reports, the story is often about political instability or violent crime. That is not typically the reality faced by American retirees. There are very legitimate safety and stability issues in Venezuela, El Salvador, Argentina and near the US/Mexican border, but most of Latin America is quite safe. Even countries such as Nicaragua and Colombia that are associated with war and drugs in Americans' minds now are safer and more stable than before.

Staying safe in Latin America is like staying safe in the US—stay out of the bad areas. The local expat community can warn you about places to avoid. In our 13 years living in seven different parts of Latin America, we've never felt unsafe, much less witnessed or experienced violent crime. The most serious crime we've encountered is pickpocketing on trolley cars.

ISOLATION

One of the major complaints of Americans who retire abroad used to be that they felt cut off from their families, friends and culture. The Internet has significantly reduced this problem. Today's expats can use the Internet-calling service Skype to make video calls back to the US for free. They can watch US television shows, movies and certain US sporting events over the Internet, too. And certain Latin American expat communities have become so large and well established that they feel almost like US communities.

Examples: Large, well-established expat communities include Lake Chapala, Puerto Vallarta and San Miguel de Allende in Mexico... Boquete, Coronado and Panama City in Panama...and the Central Valley of Costa Rica.

In some parts of Latin America, many locals speak English, too, further easing any feelings of isolation. Still, you will enjoy living in Latin America more if you learn to speak Spanish.

If you live in or near a Latin American city that has a major airport in a country not too far from the US, flying back home for visits won't be much different from flying back to a northern state from, say, Florida or Arizona.

CLIMATE AND CULTURE

Americans tend to associate Latin America with warm winter weather and relaxing beachfront living. If that's what you're looking for, there are plenty of options.

Examples: Puerto Vallarta, Mexico... Coronado, Panama...Dominical, Costa Rica... Ambergris Caye and Placenia, Belize.

But if you consider steamy summer temperatures a turnoff, head to higher elevations. We live in the mountains of Ecuador and never need air-conditioning or heating.

Examples: For nice temperatures year-round, consider Costa Rica's Central Valley...the Sierra (mountain) region of Ecuador, including Quito and Cuenca...the Mexican highlands including San Miguel de Allende and Lake Chapala...Medellín, Colombia...and Boquete, Panama.

And if cosmopolitan city life is more your speed, there are plenty of culturally vibrant cities in Latin America.

Examples: Panama City, Panama...Mérida, Mexico...Quito, Ecuador...and San José, Costa Rica.

TO FIND YOUR RETIREMENT SPOT...

Visit Internet bulletin boards aimed at expats to learn more about potential Latin American retirement destinations. Just type the name of a Latin American city, region or country and the word "expat" into a search engine to find these.

Examples: Gringo Tree offers bulletin boards for Cuenca and Quito, two popular spots for expats in Ecuador (gringotree.com). Facebook is another resource where you will find plenty of expat-related pages.

On these bulletin boards, you'll find expats chatting about what life really is like for Americans in these places. Post any questions that you have about retiring to the area.

Spend at least one month, preferably longer, visiting an area before deciding to retire there. Rent a home rather than stay in a hotel or tourist condo during this trial phase—the touristy parts of Latin America tend to be very different from the areas where people actually live. Latin America does not have many property-rental agencies, but some real estate agents rent out homes on behalf of clients. Request real estate agent recommendations on the area's expat bulletin boards. In addition to some sightseeing during this visit, try to do the everyday, ordinary things you actually would do if you lived there. For more information, go to our website, *internationalliving.com*.

18

Tax Savvy

How to Save Big on Taxes in Retirement

Once retired, you decide when you get paid—and from which accounts to draw that money... which means you have the ability to save big on your tax bill. *Here are three strategies...*

LOW-INCOME YEARS

Conventional wisdom says retirees should tap their taxable accounts first, traditional retirement accounts next and Roth retirement accounts last. That way, you squeeze more tax-deferred growth out of your traditional retirement accounts, such as your 401(k) and IRA, and more tax-free growth out of your Roth 401(k) and Roth IRA.

But if you follow the conventional wisdom and pay for your initial retirement years by dipping into, say, savings accounts and certificates of deposit held in taxable accounts, you may find yourself paying little or no taxes—which in the long run is a terrible waste.

Better strategy: Take advantage of these low-income, low-tax-rate years to withdraw some money from a traditional IRA or 401(k). You even could convert part of your traditional IRA to a Roth IRA. The conversion would trigger a tax bill on the sum converted, but thereafter the money in the Roth would grow tax-free.

By shrinking the size of these traditional retirement accounts in your 60s, you may avoid big tax bills once you're in your 70s and you have to take required minimum distributions (RMDs) from your retirement accounts. Those RMDs will boost your taxable income and could, in turn, trigger taxes on up to 85% of your Social Security benefit!

Suppose you expect to be in the 25% federal income tax bracket once you start RMDs in your 70s. To reduce those big tax bills, you

---

Jonathan Clements, a personal finance journalist and columnist for *The Wall Street Journal*. He is author of *The Little Book of Main Street Money* and *Jonathan Clements Money Guide 2015*. JonathanClements.com

489

might want to generate enough taxable income in your 60s to get to the top of the 15% bracket. In 2016, that would mean generating at least $75,300 in total income if you're married filing jointly or $37,650 if you're single. Because income that high could lead to taxes on your Social Security benefit, consider delaying your Social Security benefits until as late as age 70. That can be a smart move anyway because your monthly check will be significantly larger as a result of the delay.

HIGH-DEDUCTION YEARS

Got a year with large itemized deductions, perhaps because of hefty medical expenses or large charitable contributions? Those deductions will reduce your taxable income, and you could find yourself in a lower tax bracket than normal. To get more value out of your deductions, consider making larger-than-usual withdrawals from your traditional IRA.

HIGH-COST YEARS

Suppose you need to buy a new car or replace your home's roof. To generate the necessary spending money, you might be tempted to take an extra-large withdrawal from your traditional IRA. But not only could that withdrawal get taxed at a high rate, the extra taxable income also might trigger taxes on your Social Security benefit.

What to do instead? Consider tapping your savings account or money-market fund held in a regular taxable account or, alternatively, making a tax-free withdrawal from your Roth IRA.

Smart Ways to Withdraw Money from Retirement Accounts

Robert Keebler, CPA, partner, Keebler & Associates, LLP, a tax advisory firm in Green Bay, Wisconsin. He is a contributing author to the *American Bar Association's The ABA Practical Guide to Estate Planning.* KeeblerAndAssociates.com

We spend decades putting money into our retirement accounts, then the moment finally arrives to start pulling it

out. Only it isn't entirely up to us to choose when that moment is upon us—or how much to withdraw each year. IRS rules require that we begin making withdrawals from tax-deferred retirement accounts such as 401(k)s and traditional IRAs by the year in which we turn 70½. Failure to make these required withdrawals triggers extremely steep penalties—50% of the amount that we were supposed to withdraw.

These mandated withdrawals, officially called required minimum distributions (RMDs), sometimes cause complications, forcing us to liquidate investments that we would rather leave undisturbed...putting an end to tax-deferred appreciation for whatever amounts we withdraw...and potentially triggering hefty tax bills.

Here are seven ways to minimize the impact that RMDs have on your retirement savings...

•**Take RMDs late in the year.** IRS rules don't specify when during the year you must take RMDs. If you don't need the money right away, it usually is best to wait until late in the year to get every possible month of tax-deferred growth.

There is one potential downside to such a delay, however—if you pass away or develop a serious health issue that prevents you from handling your financial affairs before making the withdrawal, your spouse or heirs will have to do it for you. The IRS doesn't accept death or disability as an excuse. Give your spouse and/or heirs specific instructions about how to make RMDs on your behalf if necessary, and include a durable power of attorney in your estate plan to ensure that they can.

Warning: The IRS offers a special grace period in the first year that you are required to make withdrawals—for this first year only, you can make RMDs as late as April 1 of the following year without penalty. But it usually does not pay to take advantage of this grace period.

If you postpone making your initial RMD until the following year, you also will have to make your second annual RMD during the same calendar year.

Because the amounts withdrawn count as income, that double withdrawal could push you into a higher income tax bracket and/or make a higher percentage of your Social Security benefits taxable.

What to do: Postpone your initial withdrawal past December 31 only if your income—and resulting tax bracket—happen to be exceptionally high in that first year. Discuss this possibility with your tax preparer and/or financial planner before year-end if you believe it might apply to you.

• **Do a Roth rollover to reduce or eliminate future withdrawal requirements.** The IRS doesn't require people to make withdrawals from their Roth IRAs and Roth 401(k)s (the only exception is that heirs are required to make withdrawals from an inherited Roth).

If you have money in a tax-deferred account, rolling it over to a Roth could be a smart strategy—if you can afford to pay the income taxes triggered by such a rollover without dipping into your tax-deferred savings.

In addition to the RMD advantage, Roth accounts allow your money to grow without facing additional taxes. The math behind Roth rollovers can get complex, however, so discuss this with a financial planner first.

• **Consider withdrawing more than the required amount in years when you fall into an unusually low tax bracket.** Estimate your taxes before each year ends. For these purposes, don't sweat the details—just try to get a general idea of what your adjusted gross income will be.

If you discover that your income will be short of the point where Social Security benefits start to become taxable—currently $25,000 for single filers, $32,000 if married filing jointly—it's probably worth withdrawing as much additional money from your tax-deferred accounts as possible without going over these income levels.

It even might be worth increasing your withdrawals—or doing a Roth conversion—until your income approaches the top of the 15% tax bracket, if you usually fall into a higher bracket. For 2016, the top of the 15% tax bracket is $37,650 for single filers…$75,300 for married people filing jointly.

Here's the reasoning: You or your heirs eventually are going to have to pay income taxes when you take money out of your tax-deferred accounts, so you might as well do so in years when your tax rates are as low as possible. (Excess withdrawals made in one year cannot be applied to the following year's withdrawal requirement, however.) If you don't need the additional money that you withdraw, consider reinvesting it in a taxable investment account.

• **Withdraw money from the tax-deferred investments that seem least promising.** You get to choose which investments to liquidate within a tax-deferred account each year—you don't have to pull money out of every investment. In fact, if your tax-deferred accounts are traditional IRAs, you don't even have to withdraw money from each of your IRAs each year, as long as the overall amount that you withdraw from all of your traditional IRAs meets or exceeds withdrawal requirements. Instead, sell off the investments that seem likely to earn the lowest returns in the coming year or two. For example, you might want to scale back on long-term bond investments, especially since rising interest rates are expected to hurt the performance of such bonds in coming years.

Warning: If you have tax-deferred savings in "qualified-plan accounts," such as 401(k)s, inherited IRAs or Keogh accounts, you must withdraw at least the minimum required percentage from each separate account each year.

• **Speak with your tax adviser before withdrawing highly appreciated company stock from a 401(k).** Special tax rules might allow you to pay income tax only on the cost basis of these shares—the amount that you originally paid for them—rather than their current value.

You also would pay long-term capital gains tax on the "net unrealized appreciation" of the shares—but that rate could be much lower than your income tax rate. The tax savings from this can be substantial, but the rules are complex. Speak with a tax professional if the rules might apply to you.

• **Consider rolling your IRAs and/or your 401(k)s from prior employers into your current employer's 401(k) if you work past**

age 70½. You are not required to take distributions from your current employer's 401(k) while you still are working (unless you own 5% or more of the company).

You are required to take them from your non-Roth IRAs and previous 401(k) accounts, however. That can lead to hefty tax bills on your withdrawals if the income from your job pushes you into a high tax bracket.

Ask your current employer's benefits department if it allows rollovers into its 401(k). If so, rolling other tax-deferred retirement savings into this account will shield them from RMDs as long as you continue to work.

Warning: Use this strategy only if your current employer offers attractive investment options and charges reasonable fees within its 401(k).

HOW MUCH MUST YOU WITHDRAW?

Your age and the amount you had saved in tax-deferred retirement plans at the end of the prior year typically determine how much you must withdraw from your tax-deferred accounts each year, starting in the year that you turn 70½.

There is an exception: If the primary beneficiary of your tax-deferred retirement account(s) is your spouse and he/she is more than 10 years younger than you are, that will lower your withdrawal requirements.

The Financial Industry Regulatory Authority (FINRA) offers a calculator that can help you determine the amount you must withdraw each year (*apps.finra.org/calcs/1/rmd*).

Tax Traps to Avoid In Retirement Plan Distributions

Ed Slott, CPA, editor, *Ed Slott's IRA Advisor*, 100 Merrick Rd., Rockville Centre, New York 11570, IRA help.com. He is a nationally recognized IRA distributions expert.

Tax-deferred retirement plans, such as IRAs and 401(k)s, enable you to build up a sizable nest egg. However, you need to be careful when taking distributions and naming beneficiaries. *Tax traps to avoid…*

WITHDRAWALS

Trap: Withdrawals before age 59½ usually trigger a 10% penalty.

Loophole: There are several exceptions to this penalty, permitting you or your heirs to take some cash from your plan before age 59½.

Examples: Disability, death.

Also, if you retire or change jobs, you can withdraw money from an employer-sponsored plan, penalty free, if the separation occurs during or after the year you turn age 55.

In addition, you can take substantially equal periodic payments (SEPPs), penalty free, for at least five years or until the age of 59½, whichever comes later.

Caution: The rules for SEPPs are complex, so you need to work with a savvy tax pro.

Trap: If you don't start to take required minimum distributions (RMDs) by April 1 of the year after you reach age 70½, you could face a 50% penalty.

Once you reach that age, you must withdraw the minimum amount each year and pay tax on it. As long as you're alive and there is money left in your account, you will be required to continue to take these minimum distributions.

You can choose to take larger distributions from your retirement account, if you wish. However, you must withdraw at least the minimum amount each year.

Example: Suppose you are 76 years old and have $220,000 in your IRA. According to the IRS's Uniform Lifetime Table—found in Publication 590, Individual Retirement Arrangements (IRAs), 800-829-3676 or *irs.gov*—you have a distribution period of 22 more years. Thus, you must withdraw at least ½₂ of your IRA this year, or $10,000.

If, instead, you withdraw only $2,000, you have an $8,000 shortfall. As a result, you'll owe a $4,000 penalty, which is 50% of the $8,000 shortfall.

Again, calculating the minimum withdrawal can be complicated. Consult your tax adviser (don't rely on bank information).

Loophole: There are no lifetime RMDs for Roth IRAs. And you don't need to take required distributions at age 70½ if you're still working. That's true as long as you don't own more than 5% of your company. If you begin working after having started RMDs, you can discontinue RMDs from that company's plan, assuming the plan allows it. You still have to take RMDs from other plans and IRAs.

The exception applies only to withdrawals from employer-sponsored plans. If you roll your account balance to an IRA, the minimum distribution rules apply, even if you're still working.

Loophole: You can roll IRA money into an employer-sponsored plan if the plan will accept it.

Strategy: If you're working after age 70½ and you don't need to take distributions, roll your IRA into your employer's plan, if possible. You will forgo having to take distributions and avoid the 50% penalty.

SAFE BUT SORRY

In order to avoid the 50% penalty, you might take out more money than you really need.

Example: Before you reach age 79, your required distribution will be less than 5% per year. Thus, if you withdraw 5% of your balance each year, you'll avoid a penalty.

Trap: Taking 5% per year from your retirement plan is fine if you need the money. However, if you currently don't need income and you withdraw more than the minimum, you'll pay more income tax than you need to pay and sooner than you need to pay it. More important, excess withdrawals reduce the amount of tax-deferred wealth-building that you (and possibly your beneficiaries) can enjoy.

If you do not need the money for living expenses, withdraw only the bare minimum.

NAMING BENEFICIARIES

Trap: If you don't name a beneficiary, whoever inherits your account will have to withdraw more money sooner and pay more income tax. The same is true if you name your estate as the beneficiary.

Strategy: Name one or more individuals as beneficiaries on the form provided by the custodian or on a custom form you provide.

If you have doubts about your beneficiary's ability to handle a large inheritance, name a trust as the beneficiary, then name your heirs as trust beneficiaries.

Loophole: If handled properly, setting up such a trust can permit your heirs to stretch out required withdrawals. Work with an experienced trust attorney.

COMPANY STOCK

If you work for a publicly traded company, chances are that your retirement plan account contains some company stock.

Trap: Mishandling the withdrawal of that stock could cost you a prime tax break.

Example: Your 401(k) is $200,000, including $50,000 of company stock. When you retire, you roll over the entire $200,000 to an IRA. All subsequent IRA withdrawals will be subject to ordinary income tax, at rates up to 39.6%.

Strategy: Before you execute the rollover, ask about your basis in the company stock. That's the amount it was worth when the shares were contributed to your retirement account.

Loophole: You can pull out those shares and pay tax only on your basis, and not on their current value.

Example: Say your company shares are now worth $50,000 but your basis in those shares is only $10,000. You could withdraw the $50,000 worth of shares but owe tax on only $10,000 worth of income.

The other $40,000 won't be taxed until you sell the shares, which might be right away or many years in the future. In the meantime, you can receive dividends from all the shares and you can borrow against them, if you wish.

Result: Whenever you decide to sell the shares, the $40,000 will be taxed as a long-term capital gain, at a top tax rate as high as 23.8%, depending on your income level instead of at ordinary income tax rates of up to 39.6% on regular IRA withdrawals. After more than one year, any additional gains will also qualify for the bargain tax rate.

The remaining assets in your 401(k) can be rolled into an IRA, tax free. You won't pay income tax until you begin making withdrawals.

Surprising Medical Deductions

Lawrence K.Y. Pon, CPA/PFS, CFP of Pon & Associates, Redwood City, California. He is a US Tax Court practitioner, authorized to represent clients in Tax Court. LarryPonCPA.com

---

Family medical costs continue to rise, with more than half the respondents in a recent national survey reporting that medical costs "seriously" or "very much" impact their household budgets—and two-thirds saying they had been surprised by medical bills in the past 12 months.

But surprising tax deductions for medical expenses exist, too—ranging from big-dollar home improvements that help people deal with medical conditions to many small items that you might not expect to be deductible, such as clarinet lessons to help remedy a child's overbite. (For the essential rules on medical deductions and strategies to use them, see "How to Maximize Medical Deductions" on page 495.)

Here's a guide to dozens of possible medical deductions—many of them surprising...

• **Home improvements and modifications.** A client of mine was able to deduct the cost of an elevator that he installed in his multistory house for $17,000 to help him go from floor to floor after a leg injury.

Deductions also have been allowed for...

• Swimming pools, when swimming is prescribed as medical treatment and no suitable public facility is available.

• New siding on a home when old siding had become infested with mold, contributing to a medical problem.

• Central air-conditioning to alleviate a respiratory condition.

Operating and maintenance costs for such improvements are deductible, too, such as the service cost for maintaining a pool or elevator.

When an improvement increases the value of your home, the deductible amount is the improvement's cost minus the increase in value. So if a $20,000 expense increases your home's value by $5,000, the deductible amount is $15,000. Document any increase in value by obtaining an appraisal. The cost of the appraisal is deductible, too, not as a medical expense but among your miscellaneous itemized deductions.

Many home modifications are assumed by the IRS not to increase the value of a home and so are fully deductible when made to meet the needs of a family member with a limiting physical condition. *These may include...*

• Relocating or modifying kitchen cabinets.

• Grading the ground around a house to provide easier access.

• Widening doorways and hallways.

• Installing railings and support bars anywhere in the house.

• Shifting the location of or otherwise altering electrical outlets and fixtures.

• **Vehicle modifications.** Another client of mine was able to deduct $20,000 of changes made to a minivan to meet the needs of a family member with disabilities. Smaller modifications such as special hand controls or pedals to help deal with a physical disability also are deductible. If you buy a new vehicle customized to meet the physical needs of a family member, the extra cost over a standard model is deductible.

• **Travel and transportation.** Local transportation to medical appointments and treatments is deductible, including the cost of transport by taxi, bus, train and car. And despite general IRS limits on long-distance travel deductions, you can deduct the cost of long-distance travel undertaken for medical reasons, such as travel to...

• A doctor in a distant city who has special knowledge of your medical condition or your medical history (such as your former doctor in a location from which you've moved).

• A conference where you can learn about a condition that afflicts you or a family member.

• **Ask for and keep receipts.** If you drive your own car, you can deduct either your expenses for gas, oil changes and the like or, to keep things simple, 19 cents per mile (for 2016), plus parking and tolls. Lodging and meals generally are not deductible on such trips.

• **Costs paid for nondependents.** You can, of course, deduct medical expenses for your dependents—and sometimes you can deduct costs paid for nondependents, too. *These include…*

• People who do not qualify as your dependents only because their income is too high (more than $4,050 in 2016). *Example*: A retired parent who doesn't live with you but gets more than half of his/her support from you—such as when the parent is in a nursing home. Medical costs may be very high in such cases.

• A child who is claimed as a dependent by your ex-spouse. *Rule*: When either divorced spouse claims a dependency exemption for a child, each spouse can deduct medical expenses that the spouse actually pays for the child.

• **Insurance.** As health insurance costs continue to rise, make the most of deducting premiums. *Examples…*

• Health insurance premiums for self-employed people are deductible to the extent that you have earned income.

• Long-term-care insurance is a defense against the risk of potentially huge costs for nursing home care. Premiums are deductible in an amount that rises with age—ranging in 2016 from $390 annually for people age 40 or younger to $4,870 for people over 70.

• Medicare Part B and Part D premiums are deductible, as are Medigap policy premiums.

Your share of premiums for an employer's group plan generally is not deductible because premiums usually are deducted from wages before taxes.

Various additional surprising deductions include…

• Medical services that are included in a tuition bill—you may have to ask the school to itemize the bill.

• Legal expenses necessary to obtain authorization for medical treatment.

• Equipment used to alleviate a medical condition, such as portable air conditioners, humidifiers and dehumidifiers—and their operat-

ing cost. (It helps if the doctor is specific about brands and specifications.)

• Service animals with special training used to alleviate disabilities. *Examples*: Cats trained to react to sound for the deaf…Seeing Eye dogs for the blind.

• Weight-loss programs to remedy a specific medically diagnosed condition, such as hypertension or diabetes (but not for simply being overweight).

• A diet prescribed by a doctor to the extent that its cost exceeds that of standard meals.

• Fees paid to a note taker for a deaf person. Telephone equipment for the deaf. Closed-caption television decoder.

• The cost of a wig prescribed for mental health reasons following hair loss due to disease.

• A musical-instrument remedy, such as clarinet lessons prescribed to help treat a child's dental bite problem.

• Batteries for hearing aids.

You may discover new surprising deductions of your own for many activities incurred primarily for the "diagnosis, cure, mitigation, treatment or prevention" of disease or a medical or physical condition.

However, having a prescription or a doctor recommendation is not necessarily going to make any expense a medical expense. Vacations and pianos, for instance, sound dubious even if prescribed. The IRS may hire medical experts to review diagnoses and treatments. Don't get carried away or too creative.

For more on deductible and non-deductible expenses, see IRS Publication 502, *Medical and Dental Expenses*, at *ira.gov/pub/irs-pdf/p502.pdf.*

How to Maximize Medical Deductions

Medical expenses are deductible on an itemized federal tax return to the extent that the total of these expenses exceeds 10%

of adjusted gross income (AGI), or 7.5% of AGI for taxpayers age 65 or older and joint returns where the older spouse is 65 or older. So if a return reports $50,000 of AGI, expenses exceeding $5,000, or $3,750 for a taxpayer age 65 or older, are deductible.

By claiming all the deductions that you are entitled to—and timing them wisely—you can minimize your medical costs in after-tax dollars. Time a deduction by choosing to pay an expense before or after year-end. *Examples*...

• **If you expect your medical expenses to be over the 10% (or 7.5%) of AGI limit** for the current year or next year but not both, you will want to take as many deductions as you can in that one year.

• **If you will be over the limit in consecutive years,** take as many deductions as you can in the year in which you expect to be in the highest tax bracket if that will vary between the two years.

Now is an excellent time to figure out timing strategies, because enough of the year has passed to judge your tax position while enough remains to plan year-end medical appointments and expenditures.

Tax Breaks for Older People

The standard deduction for 2016 is $7,850 for a single taxpayer age 65 or older—compared with $6,300 for younger taxpayers. Taxpayers age 65 and older who itemize can deduct medical expenses that exceed 7.5% of adjusted gross income—the threshold for younger taxpayers is 10%. Those who become self-employed after leaving a job can deduct the premiums paid for Medicare Part B and Part D, the cost of Medigap policies or the cost of a Medicare Advantage plan. The working spouse of a retiree can contribute up to $6,500 a year to the retiree's IRA. There are limits and special circumstances affecting some of these tax breaks—consult your financial adviser.

Fidelity.com

When a Dog Can Be a Tax Deduction

Service-dog costs are tax deductible as a medical expense. And guard dogs—for example, for junkyards—can be business deductions. Under some circumstances, if an animal earns money for you—perhaps your dog was in a pet-food commercial—costs associated with the animal's training or care may be deductible.

Roundup of experts in tax deductions, reported in *The Wall Street Journal*.

Refinancing Your Mortgage? Maximize the Tax Breaks

Diane Kennedy, CPA, founder, TaxLoopholes, LLC, 1503 E. San Juan Ave., Phoenix 85014, TaxLoopHoles. com. She is author of *The Insider's Guide to Tax-Free Real Estate Investments*.

Interest rates may not be low for long, so now might be a good time to refinance. As of this writing, the average rate on a 30-year fixed-rate mortgage is below 4%, according to Freddie Mac.

As recently as July 2015, the average rate was 6.7%.

Payoff for good behavior: Today, lenders are penalizing borrowers with subpar credit scores by making them pay higher interest rates. Conversely, borrowers with good scores pay lower rates.

Example: According to Fair Isaac, developer of the FICO credit score used by most lenders, someone with a 680 credit score might pay 3.47% for a 30-year loan. With a 720 score (around the national median), you would likely pay 3.29%, and 3.07% with a superior 760 score.

You can purchase your credit score at my FICO.com (*myfico.com*).

Bottom line: If your credit score has improved since you took out your mortgage, perhaps because late mortgage or late credit card payments from prior years no longer count in your score, you might be able to trim your costs by refinancing now.

TAX TACTICS

If you're refinancing your mortgage, knowing the tax rules can help you make the most of available tax deductions.

Strategy: To be sure that all of your interest will be deductible, refinance with a dollar-for-dollar replacement loan.

Example: Your current loan balance is $200,000 on a 6.7% loan. If you refinance with a $200,000, 3.7% loan, all of the interest will be tax deductible as long as the total of your home loans is $1 million or less.

Cashing out: Even after the recent slump in home prices, many houses are still worth far more than the outstanding balances on their mortgages. In such cases, home owners often refinance for larger amounts, pulling out cash.

Example: Your home is appraised at $300,000, and your current loan balance is $200,000. You find a lender willing to provide you with an 80% loan-to-value mortgage, so you borrow $240,000.

Thus, you pay off the old $200,000 loan and pocket $40,000.

Strategy: The best time to get a cash-out mortgage is when you're planning an addition to your home, or if you plan a substantial renovation. If you spend the cash from the home loan in this manner, all the interest on the refinanced loan will be deductible.

If you don't use any or all of the cash for home improvement, the excess will be considered home-equity debt.

Example: You refinance a $200,000 loan with a $240,000 loan, as above, and spend $20,000 putting in a new bathroom. You use the other $20,000 to buy a car.

Result: Of your new loan, $220,000 is considered "home-acquisition debt," so interest on this amount is deductible. The other $20,000 is considered "home-equity debt," which falls under different rules.

How it works: The interest on home-equity debt of $100,000 or less is deductible no matter how it's spent. If you use the $20,000 from your cash-out mortgage to buy a car, the interest on that $20,000 probably will be fully deductible (as long you don't owe more than $80,000 on a home-equity loan or line of credit, which would push you over the $100,000 deductibility threshold).

Trap: For home-equity debt to be fully deductible, the total mortgage debt on the house cannot exceed its value.

In the above example, where the home is appraised at $300,000 and home-acquisition debt after refinancing is $220,000, interest on only $80,000 of home-equity debt will be deductible.

Caution: Be especially careful about using cash-out mortgage money for expenses other than home improvements if you must pay the alternative minimum tax (AMT).

Why: If you are subject to the AMT, home-equity debt is subject to the same $100,000 limit for deducting the interest. However, the deduction is available only if the money is used for home improvement.

If you are subject to the AMT and use home-equity debt to pay off consumer debt, buy a boat, etc., you can't take a deduction for the interest.

AHEAD ON POINTS

When you refinance a mortgage, you may pay "points" up front.

Example: You refinance a $200,000 loan and pay two points (2%), or $4,000. Paying points will reduce the interest on a loan, so it may be worthwhile if you'll be in the house for at least several years.

Tax treatment: When a mortgage is refinanced, points you pay can be deducted over the life of the loan.

Example: You pay $4,000 in points for a 30-year (360-month) loan. Every month that this loan is outstanding, you can deduct $11.

Payoff: If the loan is paid off early, all of the not-yet-deducted points can be deducted at once. This might be the case when the house is sold or when the refinanced loan is refinanced once more.

In the case of a re-refinance, the old points can be deducted immediately and you can begin a monthly schedule for deducting points on the new loan.

Exception: If you refinance with the same lender, you can't deduct the old points. Instead, those points are folded into the new point-deduction schedule.

Example: You have $3,000 worth of non-deducted points when you refinance with the same lender and pay $4,000 in points on the new loan. Now you have $7,000 in points to deduct. On a 30-year loan, you would deduct $19 ($7,000 divided by 360) each month.

Loophole: If you use a cash-out mortgage and use some of the proceeds to improve your principal residence, a corresponding portion of the points can be deducted up front.

Example: You refinance a loan secured by your principal residence, borrowing $240,000 and paying $4,800 in points. Of the $240,000 that you borrow, $40,000 (one-sixth) is used for home improvements.

Result: You can deduct $800 (one-sixth of $4,800) immediately. The other $4,000 paid for points can be written off over 360 months (30 years). However, if the refinancing and home improvements were done on a second home, the entire $4,800 would have to be written off over the life of the loan.

In all cases, you take deductions for points paid on Schedule A of your tax return—as an interest expense—so the tax break is available only if you itemize deductions.

Financial Risks of Renting Out Your Home

Stephen Fishman, JD, who writes about legal and tax issues at Nolo.com, publisher of do-it-yourself legal guides. Based in Alameda, California, he is author of *Every Landlord's Tax Deduction Guide*. Fishman LawAndTaxFiles.com

If you'd like to bring in some extra money by renting out your home—as a growing number of people are doing, thanks to websites such as Airbnb—you may take comfort in the protections that home-rental websites offer.

Example: Airbnb offers $1 million in insurance coverage against liability claims in case a guest sues you over an injury and up to $1 million for property damage caused by guests.

But beware: There still are potential financial consequences if you take in paying guests…

• **Taxes.** The IRS lets you rent out your home only up to 14 days a year without having to pay tax on the income.

Self-defense: Ask your accountant whether you owe any state and city taxes on the income in addition to federal tax. If you rent your home for more than 14 days per year, you can deduct certain related expenses from your rental income, such as fees you pay to Airbnb, as well as mortgage interest and real estate taxes for the rental portion of your home. But your expense deduction cannot exceed your rental income for the year.

• **Penalties for illegal subletting or renting.** Many municipalities have restrictions on short-term rentals.

Self-defense: Check with the local housing authority. Also, make sure you are not violating the terms of your lease if you yourself are a renter…or the rules of your condo association, homeowners association or other relevant body.

• **Items not covered by the Airbnb property damage "guarantee."** It's called a guarantee because Airbnb itself, not an insurance company, provides coverage and establishes its own rules. For instance, damage to any fine art or antiques you own isn't covered by Airbnb. Neither are losses due to guests stealing items.

Self-defense: Add a "security deposit" to your listing. Guests are charged if Airbnb later determines that a guest is responsible for damages not covered by the Airbnb guarantee. Airbnb allows the host to set the security deposit from $95 to $5,100. Browse other local listings to help choose an amount that's right for your home.

The IRS Will Rob Your Heirs

Martin M. Shenkman, CPA, JD, founder of Shenkman Law, a law firm specializing in wealth planning and protection, Fort Lee, New Jersey. He is coauthor of *The Tools & Techniques of Estate Planning and Powers of Attorney*. ShenkmanLaw.com

Don't make the common mistake of neglecting tax planning for your estate just because it's unlikely that the estate will owe estate tax. It's true that few taxpayers will ever face any federal estate tax—that's because the amount exempt from tax has increased to $5.45 million for 2016 ($10.9 million for a married couple after the second spouse dies) or higher when adjusted for inflation in future years. However, the estate and heirs still might owe income tax, reducing the amount that the heirs will inherit, and that's where estate planning can make a big difference.

A combination of wise estate planning now and prudent steps taken by your executor and/or trustee later can save on taxes. Here's what you need to know about cutting taxes for estates of all sizes*…

INCOME TAX CAN HIT ESTATES HARD

An income tax return must be filed for an estate for every year that it has income of as little as $600 until the estate is dissolved. The estate's income tax, which applies to income received beginning on the date the person dies, is different from the deceased individual's personal income tax, which applies to income received before the date of death and requires that an individual 1040 return be filed. (The heirs do not owe income tax when they inherit assets, but they may owe capital gains tax when they sell inherited assets such as stocks or property.)

And unfortunately, income tax brackets for an estate return are triggered at much lower levels than for personal tax returns. For example, for the 2016 tax year, the top 39.6% bracket doesn't apply on an individual tax return until taxable income hits $415,050. But it applies to an estate (and a trust) when its taxable income hits $12,400. An estate's income

*Some states have inheritance and estate tax rules that differ from federal rules, so consult a state tax expert.

may include interest and dividends from investments, items owed to the deceased (such as rent), income from a private business, compensation paid by an employer after death and any other income received by the estate.

Generally, you want to reduce the amount of income tax that the estate will owe by reducing the amount of income it will receive and directing that money elsewhere. This may be more complex than it sounds and may include what you can do now and what you should make sure the executor of your estate or trustee of a trust knows to do.

WHAT TO DO NOW

•**Consider donating income-producing assets to charity now while you're still alive rather than making bequests to charity in your will.** That's because the rules have changed. It used to be advantageous for an estate to reduce estate tax by making charitable donations. But if an estate doesn't owe estate tax, then no tax deduction will be available for charitable donations made by the estate. By donating now, while you're alive, you can take a tax deduction that your estate wouldn't get—and by reducing the amount of income-producing assets that will be left in your estate, it also will reduce the estate's taxable income. These assets might include stocks, bonds, mutual fund shares and real estate.

If you have already included in your will a bequest to charity and you don't want to redo your will, you may be able to simply tell the charity that you will make a gift to it now in exchange for the charity sending you a letter that waives its right to receive the bequest that is already in your will, acknowledging that the current donation is an advancement of that bequest.

•**Designate individuals as beneficiaries in retirement plans.** Retirement accounts often are the most valuable financial assets owned by an individual, so they should be a key consideration in any estate plan.

If you don't designate individual beneficiaries for your IRA, the IRA may be included in the assets to be distributed according to the provisions in your will…and income tax on it will be due within five years under IRA rules.

In contrast, if you do designate your spouse, children and/or other individuals as beneficiaries of your IRA, they may be able to stretch distributions from it over an entire lifetime, providing them with decades of tax-favored investment returns—a big difference. Keep in mind that unlike with a 401(k), your spouse is not automatically the beneficiary of your IRA.

• **Consider creating a trust.** If you create a trust and designate assets to put into the trust rather than into your estate, the trustee can manage the assets after your death to minimize taxes. You can give the trustee as much or as little discretion as you wish over how to distribute the assets and who receives them. The trustee could, for instance, stretch out distributions from the trust over a number of years and decide which are the most tax-efficient ways to make those distributions. A trustee could be anyone ranging from a spouse or an adult child to a financial institution.

Distributions include the income generated by assets in the trust. Be sure that the trust document permits inclusion of capital gains as a form of income that can be distributed in this way.

Example: The trustee, in conjunction with your heirs, might decide that in certain years it is best to give bigger distributions to young beneficiaries who have minimal income and so are in low tax brackets, such as those beneficiaries who are in college or starting out in their careers, rather than those who are in high tax brackets.

REDUCE FUTURE CAPITAL GAINS TAX

When an heir inherits certain of your assets, such as shares of stock or a piece of art, the asset's tax basis is reset at the market value at the date of your death, instead of your original cost to acquire the asset. Future taxable capital gains or losses when an asset is sold by an heir are determined based on this tax basis, which is called the stepped-up basis if it is higher than your initial cost or the stepped-down basis if it is lower. The tax basis is subtracted from the eventual sale price to determine the capital gain or loss. A stepped-up basis lowers the capital gains taxes that heirs eventually must pay.

Example: A parent buys stock at a price of $20 per share...the share value is $50 when a child inherits the stock...and the child later sells the shares for $55 each. The child's taxable capital gain is just $5 per share, even though the stock price rose by $35 since the parent bought it, because the stepped-up tax basis is $50.

How to make sure capital gains taxes will be minimized...

• **Maximize the advantages of a stepped-up tax basis.** Make sure that your executor or your trustee knows that he/she will need to carefully record the adjusted basis for each asset on your date of death so that your beneficiaries can use that basis whenever they sell assets in the future. This is especially important for valuable items that don't trade regularly, such as real estate, shares in a private business, artwork, antiques and other collectibles that might require an appraisal. An appraisal obtained for a modest price may avoid a costly conflict with the IRS in the future. The executor or trustee also should make sure that your heirs who inherit shares in a mutual fund know to tell the firm that operates the fund to start using the stepped-up basis in its calculations of capital gains for the 1099 form it provides to the IRS each year.

• **Beware the trap of a stepped-down basis.** If the asset that you bequeath to an heir diminished in value from the time you acquired it, it could mean a greater eventual capital gains tax—or a smaller capital loss that is less effective in offsetting capital gains. To avoid this trap, review the assets now that will likely be in the estate and consider selling those that have diminished in value since you acquired them.

Caution: Keep in mind that the strategies described in this article have technicalities that may require advice from a financial professional.

19

Better Ways to Save and Pay for Health Care

Better Way to Plan for Retirement Health Expenses

Health-care costs can wallop consumers as they get older, even though some expenses remain stable. A recent study by the nonprofit Employee Benefit Research Institute (EBRI) suggests that the best way to plan for retirement health-care expenses is to divide them into two separate categories...

• **Recurring expenses include doctor and dentist visits and prescription medications.** These generally are consistent throughout retirement.

Exception: Prescription drug costs can spike with certain medical problems, adding $1,000 to $2,000 to annual costs for possibly 10% of retirees.

Strategy: If you already are covered by Medicare, add up your yearly out-of-pocket expenditures for these recurring medical costs over the past year, then build this amount into your annual budget allowing for a 2% rate of inflation and a 3% return on savings. If you are not yet Medicare eligible, budget around $1,885 a year.

• **Nonrecurring expenses include nursing home stays,** outpatient surgery, hospital stays and treatments, and special facilities such as rehabilitation programs.

Strategy: Create an investment account specifically to pay for these expenses. Earmarking a separate account this way, rather than keeping health-care money in a general account, is the best way to ensure that it is not misspent. Another EBRI study found that to have a 90% chance of covering retirement health costs, a man should plan for $116,000 in costs...a woman $131,000. The good news is that be-

Sudipto Banerjee, PhD, research associate at EBRI, Washington, DC. He is author of the study "Utilization Patterns and Out-of-Pocket Expenses for Different Health Care Services Among American Retirees." EBRI.org

cause nonrecurring health costs tend to occur mainly late in retirement, people still in their 60s can invest this money in a relatively aggressive portfolio of investments.

Use Your Health Savings Account to Boost Your Nest Egg

Roy Ramthun, founder and adviser, HSA Consulting Services, LLC, a health-care consulting practice specializing in HSAs and consumer-driven health-care issues, Silver Spring, Maryland. *HSAConsultingServices.com*

More than 13.5 million people now use Health Savings Accounts (HSAs) to set aside pretax dollars for their medical expenses. But because you don't have to use the money in an HSA by any particular deadline, HSAs also can serve as powerful savings tools to supplement your retirement accounts or to provide some emergency cash.

As a former senior adviser to the Secretary of the US Treasury for health initiatives, I helped implement HSAs nationwide a decade ago. Their features make them far more useful, flexible and valuable than most people realize.

One of the greatest advantages is that, unlike the more popular Flexible Spending Account (FSA) that requires employees to predict their medical spending for the year in advance and contribute a defined amount, the IRS allows you to fund your HSA with pretax dollars after a medical expense* has occurred, then immediately reimburse yourself.

Smart strategies for using HSAs…

*HSA money can be used tax-free for only "qualified" medical expenses, which include most ordinary procedures, treatments and prescribed medications but not over-the-counter medications, vitamins or cosmetic surgery. HSA contributions are deductible for federal income tax and for state income tax in all states except Alabama, California and New Jersey. If you withdraw HSA funds for unqualified medical expenses before age 65, you are subject to a 20% penalty plus income tax on the amount withdrawn.

•**Pay insurance premiums.** You might know that if you change jobs or lose your job, you still keep your HSA and have access to all the money you have contributed. That means that even if you aren't eligible to make contributions because you are no longer enrolled in a high-deductible health insurance plan, the money still can be withdrawn tax-free and penalty-free to cover medical expenses.

But you might not know that if you get fired, laid off or quit your job, the IRS allows you to use HSA money to pay premiums for temporary COBRA health insurance coverage. Moreover, if you are receiving federal or state unemployment benefits, you can tap your HSA to pay the premiums for any health-insurance coverage.

Once you turn 65, HSA flexibility increases even further. At that point, the IRS allows you to withdraw your HSA money tax-free and penalty-free to cover your premiums for Medicare and long-term-care insurance.

•**Supplement your nest egg.** You might know that the money in your HSA account can be invested and can grow tax-deferred just like your IRA assets in investments such as certificates of deposit, stocks, bonds and mutual funds, depending on which kinds of investments your HSA provider offers.

But you may not know that once you turn 65, HSA money can be used—without paying a penalty—for any reason, medical or otherwise, although if you use it for purposes other than qualified medical costs or insurance premiums, you have to pay income tax on the withdrawn amount.

That makes the HSA so attractive that I often recommend that while someone is employed, he/she should fund it to the maximum allowable amount year after year—even before fully funding IRAs and even if he doesn't expect to spend nearly that amount in the same year he makes the contribution.

I also recommend that if someone can afford to, he should consider paying for all or a portion of medical expenses with non-HSA money in years when he is contributing to his HSA. That way, HSA investments can grow tax-free, as they would in an IRA, for many years.

• **Leave your HSA to your spouse.** When you die, your HSA can be transferred to your spouse tax-free, and it becomes his/her HSA. The surviving spouse can continue to make contributions if otherwise eligible to do so and can use the HSA money to pay for qualified medical expenses or for other purposes outlined above. But, if your HSA is left to another beneficiary, it converts to a regular bank account and loses any tax advantages.

HSA RULES

To qualify for an HSA, you need to be enrolled in a high-deductible health insurance plan, which means that insurance does not pick up your health-care costs until you meet your annual deductible, which must be at least $1,300 for singles and $2,600 for families in 2016. After that, your insurance will cover additional expenses. Your maximum annual out-of-pocket expenses under the plan (including all of the deductibles, co-pays and coinsurance) cannot exceed $6,550 in 2016 for an individual with self-only coverage or $13,100 in 2016 for an individual with family coverage.

To contribute: You can put up to $3,350 for individuals and $6,750 for families in your HSA in 2016. Figures include money your employer may contribute to your HSA. If you are over age 55, the IRS allows you to add an additional $1,000 annually over your HSA contribution limits.

Transferring an HSA

Todd Berkley, president, HSA Consulting Services, LLC, a health-care consulting practice specializing in HSAs and consumer-driven health-care issues, Minnetonka, Minnesota. HSAConsultingServices.com

If you're getting a new job, you are allowed to keep your old HSA and add money to it—and contribute to a new one—as long as total contributions to the two accounts do not exceed $3,350 for individual coverage or $6,750 for family coverage (plus an additional $1,000 if you are age 55 or older). Or you can shift the money in the old HSA to the new one. The best way to do this is to "transfer" the funds—have the old HSA administrator send a check to the new one, and it will be deposited into your new account. (Keep in mind that to contribute to any HSA, you must be enrolled in a high-deductible health insurance plan.)

Alternatively, you can do a "rollover" by having a check for the old HSA money sent to you in your name, and then you can send a check to the new HSA, which you must do within 60 days to avoid paying taxes and a penalty. You can do just one HSA rollover every 12 months. If you do keep your old HSA, your former employer may no longer cover the annual fees paid to the administrator of your old HSA, which is why most people elect to shift the assets of an old HSA into a new one. However, you may want to keep the old HSA if you have substantial savings built up there and prefer the choice of investments that it offers.

Another Way to Finance Your HSA

A tax-free rollover from an IRA to an HSA is allowed once in your lifetime. The allowable amount is limited to the maximum health savings account (HSA) contribution permitted for the year (which is $3,350 for a single person and $6,750 for a family in 2016) minus any HSA contributions that you, or your employer on your behalf, have already made in that year. To qualify to make HSA contributions this year, you must have a health insurance policy with a deductible of at least $1,300 for individual coverage or $2,600 for family coverage—these numbers may change in future years. The transfer can be made from a traditional or Roth IRA, but it is better from a traditional one. If you were to withdraw money from a traditional IRA, rather than making a tax-free transfer to an HSA, you would pay tax on the withdrawal. But by rolling over the assets into an HSA, you can use the money tax-free for medical costs. Ask your financial adviser for details.

Kiplinger.com

Health Insurance Alert...If You're Over 65 and Still Working

Aaron Tidball, manager of Medicare operations at Allsup Inc., a nationwide service based in Belleville, Illinois, that helps guide people with Social Security disability and Medicare. AllsupInc.com

Two-thirds of baby boomers plan to work past age 65—the age at which they become eligible for Medicare—according to a study by the Transamerica Center for Retirement Studies. One of the challenges they might face is determining whether they can and should remain on an employer's health insurance plan or make the switch to Medicare. And it often is a very tricky choice that even human resources departments may not fully understand. *What you need to know if you plan to work (or already are working) past age 65...*

•**The number of workers that your employer employs dramatically affects your health-care options.** If there are 20 or more employees, the employer is required to offer you the same coverage after you turn 65 that it offers its younger employees. This means you generally can remain on this group plan—and it is considered "primary coverage"—unless the employer's prescription drug coverage is not considered "creditable." For more information, put "CMS: creditable coverage" into a search engine and go to the CMS.gov site listed.

If your employer has fewer than 20 employees, you almost certainly should sign up for Medicare. That's because Medicare generally is considered to be your primary health coverage...and your employer-based insurance, should you choose to continue to be covered, becomes "secondary" coverage (unless your employer opts to provide primary coverage to employees age 65 and over, though this is rare). That means the employer-based coverage will pay only the portion of your eligible health-care bills that Medicare does not cover. In this case, if you failed to sign up for Medi-

care, you would have to pay the lion's share of your medical bills out of pocket.

For details and exceptions to these rules, including how they apply to disabled employees, go to *medicare.gov/pubs/pdf/02179.pdf.*

Caution: It sometimes is difficult to know whether a company has 20 or more employees under Medicare rules. A seemingly small company might legally be part of a larger organization...while a seemingly large company might actually have many part-time or contract workers who do not count toward the 20-employee threshold. Ask your company's human resources department.

•**Medicare could be the better option even if you can choose your employer's plan as primary coverage.** In decades past, employer health insurance plans almost always were more attractive than Medicare. But many employer plans have become less appealing in recent years—deductibles, co-pays and premiums have grown larger, while in-network medical-provider options have shrunk. So an increasing percentage of employees age 65 or older now would be better off switching to Medicare.

To figure out whether Medicare is the better choice for you, start by going to *medicare.gov* and putting "Which insurance pays first?" in the search box.

If your employer's coverage has a four-figure deductible and a 20%-or-higher copay after that, for example, there's a good chance that Medicare would be better.

Helpful: Although ordinarily you must enroll with Medicare within a few months before or after you turn 65 to avoid late-enrollment penalties, if you stick with your large employer's plan as primary coverage, you don't have to sign up for Medicare at that point. The penalties do not apply as long as you sign up within eight months after the date your employer coverage ends or your employment ends, whichever comes earlier.

If you are at a small company and do sign up for Medicare, it sometimes makes sense to also keep your employer plan despite the extra cost. This isn't common because the combined premiums of Medicare Part B (which covers medical services and supplies), Medicare Part D (which covers prescription drugs) and employer health coverage get pricey. But dual coverage could be best if you have a serious medical condition whose costs would be well covered by the employer plan but not by Medicare. Ask your health-care providers if they can help determine whether you would face significantly different out-of-pocket costs or coverage gaps for your current needs if you don't keep your employer coverage in addition to Medicare.

• **Your spouse and dependents cannot stay on your employer's health plan if you leave it for Medicare.** It might be worth continuing your employer coverage even if Medicare makes more sense for you as an individual, especially if your employer's plan is the best way for your family members to obtain affordable high-quality health insurance.

However, there might be a way you could keep family members on your large-company employer plan even when you switch to Medicare for your own coverage. This involves COBRA coverage, which might be available to extend your family coverage, typically for up to 18 months, after you switch to Medicare. Ask your employer's human resources department for details.

THE HSA MEDICARE MISTAKE

Medicare often is discussed as if it is a single service, but it actually includes several components that eligible Americans could opt to sign up for at different times. Among these components is Medicare Part A, which covers hospital costs. There generally are no premiums for Medicare Part A, so people often are advised that they might as well go ahead and sign up for this "free" part of Medicare as soon as they become eligible even if they intend to remain on an employer's coverage.

For many employees, that can be a costly mistake. That's because more and more employer plans now include high deductibles and a Health Savings Account (HSA), a type of tax-advantaged savings account that can be used to pay medical bills. If you sign up for Part A and continue to make HSA contributions, you will face tax penalties. So if you opt

to remain in an employer plan that includes an HSA, do not sign up for Part A until you leave this plan. (Rules differ for a spouse covered under your plan. For details, type into a search engine, "AARP: Can I have a health savings account as well as Medicare?" and go to the AARP website.)

Caution: Do not file for Social Security retirement benefits if you wish to continue contributing to an HSA. Starting Social Security anytime after age 65 automatically begins your Part A coverage up to six months retroactive to your Social Security signup date. If you made HSA contributions during that six-month period, you likely will face tax penalties.

Understanding Medicare Options

Frederic Riccardi, MSW, director of programs and outreach with the Medicare Rights Center, a nonprofit consumer rights organization with offices in New York City and Washington, DC. MedicareRights.org

Medicare's many options can be quite confusing. *What each is…*

• **Medicare Part A helps cover the cost of inpatient care in hospitals,** skilled nursing facilities and hospices, plus certain home health-care costs. For most people, there is no premium because they paid Medicare taxes while working.

• **Medicare Part B helps cover the cost of doctors' services,** outpatient care and certain other medical services. There usually is a premium for Part B that is deducted from your monthly Social Security check.

• **Traditional Medicare,** sometimes called original Medicare, consists of Medicare Part A and Part B.

• **Medicare Part D helps cover the cost of prescription medications. It is offered by private Medicare-approved companies. Part D plans vary somewhat in premiums,** co-pays, co-insurance and deductibles.

●**Medicare Advantage plans,** also called Medicare Part C, are an alternative to traditional Medicare. Unlike traditional Medicare, which lets participants choose virtually any health-care provider, many Advantage plans operate like HMOs or PPOs, using financial incentives to steer members toward in-network providers. Advantage plans often charge premiums (beyond those for Medicare Part B).

●**Medigap policies,** also called Medicare Supplement Insurance, help pay health-care costs not covered by traditional Medicare, including co-payments, co-insurance and deductibles. While Advantage plans replace traditional Medicare, Medigap policies just supplement it. Costs and coverage details depend on the Medigap plan selected.

Veterans Medical Benefits and More...

Christopher Michel, a former naval flight officer and founder of Military.com, America's largest military membership organization, located in San Francisco. He is author of *The Military Advantage: A Comprehensive Guide to Your Military & Veterans Benefits.*

No country in the world offers more benefits to those who have served in its armed forces than the United States. Some of the benefits are available only to active service members or military retirees (those who have retired after at least 20 years of service), but many are offered to all of America's 24 million veterans and their families.

MEDICAL BENEFITS

The Department of Veteran's Affairs is required by law to provide eligible veterans with "needed" hospital care and outpatient care. VA defines "needed" as care or service that will promote, preserve and restore health. This includes treatment, supplies and services, such as physical exams and immunizations. The decision of "need" will be based on the judgment of the vet's health-care provider at the VA and in accordance with generally accepted standards of clinical practice. There are also VA clinical health programs that vets may be eligible for, including treatment for blindness rehabilitation, Agent Orange exposure and HIV/AIDS.

Veterans' dependents are also eligible for these VA health-care programs in many cases. Final eligibility depends on several factors for each program. These factors include the nature of a veteran's discharge from military service (e.g., honorable, other than honorable, dishonorable), length of service, service-connected disabilities, income level and available VA resources, among others. Generally, the vet must be enrolled in the VA health-care system—there are 1,326 VA facilities throughout the country—to receive benefits.

More information: Visit the United States Department of Veterans Affairs site (*va.gov/healtheligibility*).

BURIAL BENEFITS, TOO

Veterans are eligible for free burial in any of 125 VA national cemeteries, space permitting. Veterans' spouses are also eligible. The cemetery plot, headstone, transportation of the remains, burial with military honors, if requested, and grave upkeep are provided by the government at no charge. The casket and other funeral home expenses remain the responsibility of the family.

More information: Call the VA at 800-827-1000 for more information. You will need a copy of the vet's discharge papers. Burial at Arlington National Cemetery is subject to greater restrictions. For more information call 703-607-8585. If a vet prefers to be buried in a private cemetery, the VA still can provide a free headstone. Call the VA for more details, or visit *military.com* and submit VA Form 40-1330.

HOME LOANS

Under the GI Bill, vets can buy homes worth up to $417,000 with no money down and without a monthly mortgage insurance premium. The Veterans Administration (VA) doesn't actually lend money—it simply guarantees a portion of the loan with your lender. (Of course, you have to meet your lender's credit standards.)

More information: Call 800-827-1000 or go to the Loan Guaranty website (*homeloans. va.gov*), where you can download VA Form 26-1880.

CAREERS

Thousands of jobs are listed on Military. com (*military.com/careers*) by companies that are eager to hire vets. Or head to the Veteran Career Network (*benefits.military.com/vcn/ search.do*) to find a helpful vet in the company, industry or city where you would like to work. There are more than 600,000 veterans willing to provide fellow vets with career assistance.

TRAVEL

•**Air travel.** Veterans who are retired from the military and family members who fly with them can fly for free or close to free on certain military flights, space permitting. This is standby travel, so it's only appropriate when your schedule is flexible. Military flights aren't always comfortable and might not be well heated or include meal service, so bring a jacket and snacks.

More information: Visit Military Living's SpaceA.info (*spacea.info*) or Military.com (*military.com/spacea*).

•**Lodging.** Military retirees and their families have access to inexpensive lodging—either on-base lodging or at Armed Forces Recreation Centers—on a space-available basis.

Examples: Shades of Green resort within Walt Disney World and Hale Koa Hotel on the beach at Waikiki.

More information: Air Force retirees, visit Air Force Services Agency (*www.afsv.af.mil*)... Army retirees, US Army MWR (*armymwr. com*)...Coast Guard retirees, the US Coast Guard site (*uscg.mil/mwr*)...Marine Corp retirees, the MCCS site (*usmc-mccs.org*)...and Navy retirees, visit Navy Lodge (*navy-lodge. com*).

CORPORATE DISCOUNTS

Many companies offer discounts to active military personnel, and some extend these discounts to vets. Military.com lists more than 700 discount programs, including some for airfare, computers and electronics, dining and entertainment.

Examples: Veterans can get 20% off all floral and gift items at *fromyouflowers.com*.

Can You Afford Long-Term Care? Big Insurers Are Bailing Out...What to Do Now

Robert Carlson, JD, CPA, managing member of Carlson Wealth Advisors, LLC. Based in Fairfax, Virginia, he is editor of the monthly newsletter *Retirement Watch*. RetirementWatch.com

---

B uying long-term-care (LTC) coverage is supposed to ease your financial anxieties about retirement by guaranteeing that you can afford extended nursing care if needed. But lately the LTC insurance sector has been in such a state of upheaval that buying and owning a policy have been anything but reassuring.

Half of the 20 largest providers have stopped issuing policies, including giants such as Unum and MetLife. Many of the insurers that remain have been dramatically increasing premiums for new and existing policyholders. The average annual premium now is around $3,500 per year.

Helpful: Existing policyholders can remain with insurers that stop issuing new policies. Even if the issuer increases premiums, switching likely would be even more expensive because you would be signing up at a higher age.

Providers have been tightening underwriting rules, too, making it difficult for someone who has a significant health issue to obtain coverage except perhaps through very expensive "high-risk" pools. But despite the drawbacks, for many people the right kind of LTC insurance could make sense if they shop carefully. *Here's what you need to know...*

WHO SHOULD BUY IT

If you have less than $300,000 in assets when you reach your 50s or 60s, you're probably better off skipping the coverage and spending down your assets to qualify for Medicaid if you later require long-term care. If you have more than $2 million in assets, you probably can skip the coverage and just pay for any care that's needed out of pocket unless you have a family history that suggests that a long nursing home stay is likely. But if your savings fall between $300,000 and $2 million, an LTC policy likely makes sense. If so, it's best to obtain coverage while still in your mid-to-late 50s because insurers are dramatically tightening their underwriting standards. The older you are when you attempt to obtain coverage, the greater the odds that you will have a health problem that disqualifies you from the best rates—or from obtaining coverage at all. Buying at a younger age also means that you'll pay a lower annual premium.

WHAT TO BUY

Today's high premiums make it even more important to buy only coverage that you really need. *Among the options…*

•**The daily benefit.** The average daily rate for a private room in a nursing home reached $253 in 2016. But that's a national average that hides the extreme regional differences in nursing home costs. Daily rates are several times higher in some places than others.

Strategy: Use the survey of regional LTC costs available at Genworth Financial's website (*Genworth.com*) to determine nursing home daily rates in the region where you would most likely receive care. Your insurance need not cover 100% of this daily amount if you would have enough assets to pay the difference out of pocket, but it should cover more than 50%—and significantly more, if possible. If you can't afford insurance that pays at least that portion, it probably isn't worth buying coverage at all. An extended nursing home stay would likely eat up all of your savings anyway, at which point you would qualify for Medicaid.

•**Maximum length of coverage.** Lifetime coverage has become rare and prohibitively expensive when it is offered.

Strategy: Two to five years of coverage usually is sufficient. Two-thirds of those who enter a nursing home stay less than one year. Only 10% stay five years or longer. If you do outlive your coverage, you will have to spend down your assets and rely on Medicaid—but if you purchase a "partnership policy" (see below), you might not have to spend down your assets.

•**Inflation protection.** Inflation has been minimal in recent years, and even nursing home bills and other LTC costs have been increasing at "only" a 4% annual rate, down from 7% previously. But don't be fooled. If your policy does not include strong inflation protection, even 4% annual price increases could render it almost worthless decades from now when you need it.

Strategy: Opt for the best inflation protection you can afford. An inflation rider offering a compound—not simple—5% rate of inflation protection is ideal. Compound 3% inflation protection is the least you should accept.

•**Elimination period** is the number of days of care that the policyholder must pay out of pocket before benefits begin.

Strategy: Opt for a 90-day elimination period. Insurers now charge prohibitively steep prices for policies with shorter elimination periods, and longer periods mean huge amounts must be paid out of pocket before benefits kick in.

•**Joint coverage.** This allows married couples to purchase one policy for both partners to share—typically for much less than the cost of separate policies.

Strategy: Joint coverage usually is the best option for married people. There is some danger that couples might exhaust the policy's coverage if both spouses require lengthy nursing home stays, but this is very unlikely.

•**Partnership policies.** Those who exceed their policy time limits typically must pay for care out of pocket until their assets are almost completely depleted and they qualify for Medicaid LTC benefits. But if your policy is written under the public/private "partnership" program, which now is available in about 40 states, you can keep much more of your savings and still qualify for Medicaid. Your assets will be protected up to the total amount of coverage you received from your policy before you exceeded the coverage limits, which is likely to be hundreds of thousands of dollars.

Strategy: Check whether your state participates in this program. If so, strongly lean toward choosing a policy that qualifies. It's an extra measure of asset protection at no added cost.

•**Hybrid option.** Some insurers now offer "hybrid" policies that combine elements of LTC insurance and either life insurance or an annuity. Trouble is, the LTC insurance element of these hybrids tends to be fairly limited, and the life insurance or annuity portion can be expensive.

Strategy: Hybrid policies typically make sense only if you intended to purchase life insurance or an annuity similar to what's included anyway…and/or you cannot pass the medical underwriting standards of a typical LTC insurance policy—hybrid policies often feature more lax underwriting.

COMPARING OFFERS

Obtain quotes from at least three LTC insurance agents or brokers. Rather than just one quote from each insurer, request a matrix of quotes at different daily benefit levels, lengths of coverage and inflation protection percentages.

Don't just purchase the policy that offers the lowest premiums for a given level of coverage. Historically, the LTC insurers that offer the lowest premiums tend to later impose the steepest rate increases and/or decline the highest percentage of claims. Instead, ask agents for the premium increase history and claim-approval history of every LTC insurer from which you receive quotes. Your state insurance department also should be able to provide these figures.

The 7 Worst Long-Term-Care Insurance Mistakes

Bunni Dybnis, director of professional services at LivHome, an at-home senior-care company with 16 locations across the US. She is a certified care manager, a member of the Older Adults Task Force for the city of Santa Monica, California, and a Fellow in The Leadership Academy of the National Association of Professional Geriatric Care Managers. LivHome.com

People who consider buying long-term-care insurance to cover future nursing home or in-home care costs often focus on a single key issue—is it worth the high price? But even if long-term-care coverage is worth the cost for you, there are many additional crucial questions that you must ask about this costly and complex product before buying—otherwise you might wind up paying for a policy that does not cover your long-term-care needs as well as you expect.

The challenge has become even more difficult in recent years. Leading long-term-care insurers, including MetLife and Unum, have stopped selling this kind of coverage…premiums have been rising, sometimes dramatically, for both new and existing policies…and new products that combine long-term-care insurance with life insurance offer a potentially appealing option—and a new source of confusion.

Seven potentially costly consumer mistakes and how to avoid them…

Mistake: **Buying a policy that you won't be able to afford in retirement.** A typical long-term-care insurance policy might cost a 55-year-old man around $2,000 a year. But the greatest challenge isn't fitting those premiums into your budget when you obtain the policy, typically in your 50s or early 60s (or even later than this, with higher premiums)—the problem is fitting them into your retirement budget down the road. Compounding the problem, insurers often increase the premiums of existing policies, sometimes by as much as 40% to 60%. Many people end up dropping no-longer-affordable policies just as they approach an age when they are increasingly likely to require care.

What to do: Speak with a fee-only financial planner about fitting the premiums into your projected retirement budget—not just your current budget—before buying coverage.

And consider buying a hybrid life insurance/long-term-care insurance policy. With these, you pay up front for a life insurance policy rather than pay annual premiums that likely would stretch into your retirement. If you require long-term care, the policy provides benefits like a long-term-care policy does—and if you die without ever requiring long-term care, your heirs receive a death benefit, as they would with a conventional life insurance policy. These do require a hefty upfront investment, however—the average buyer plunks down around $130,000.

Helpful: If you already have a policy that has become prohibitively expensive during retirement, do not drop the coverage without first investigating options for limiting the policy's premiums by reducing benefits.

Important: People who have less than $100,000 saved for retirement typically are better off skipping long-term-care insurance and relying on Medicaid to pay for any future nursing home stays. Those with more than $500,000 saved that could be spent on long-term care may be better off paying out of pocket.

Mistake: Buying a policy that overly restricts your care options. Some policies cover only certain types of care—in-home care but not nursing home care, for example. Other policies cover all types of care but not equally—the maximum daily benefits for in-home care might be 50% of the per-day maximum for nursing home care, for example.

What to do: As far as you can afford, choose a policy that provides strong benefits for all types of care, including nursing home care, assisted-living care and home care.

Mistake: Misunderstanding waiting periods. Modern policies have various types of "elimination periods"—a specified number of days (often 90) that the policyholder must pay for long-term care out of pocket before benefits kick in. "Calendar day" elimination periods simply count 90 days from when care begins…

while "service day" elimination periods count only days when care actually is provided.

Example: If you receive in-home care every other day, a 90-day service-day elimination period actually will last 180 days.

What to do: If you compare two similarly priced policies, the one with the calendar-day elimination period is a better buy than the one with the service-day elimination period, all else being equal.

Mistake: Ignoring limits on the type of care provider you can hire. Some policies will pay for in-home care only if you hire a state-certified care provider and/or work through an agency licensed by the state. That could prevent you from hiring someone you know and trust, such as a family member or a caregiver recommended by a trusted friend. And it could cause major headaches if your state does not license home-care agencies at all.

What to do: Favor policies that are not restrictive about who can supply in-home care.

Mistake: Ignoring important inflation-protection details. To be effective for you, a policy must protect against climbing long-term-care costs. Without an annual cost-of-living adjustment (COLA) of at least 3%—preferably 5%—the policy is unlikely to cover anything close to the full cost of your care 20 or 30 years down the road. Unfortunately, even consumers who understand the importance of inflation protection often fail to notice crucial nuances in how this inflation protection is worded in their contracts.

Some contracts use compound COLAs…others use simple COLAs (explained below).

Some policies offer COLAs but do not include them for the basic price. Policyholders must pay an additional fee—potentially a very substantial one—to get the inflation protection that they thought was included in their policy when they signed the contract.

What to do: Although for some people low cost is most important, generally favor policies that don't charge extra for inflation protection…and that use compound COLAs, which add up much faster than simple COLAs. For example, a policy with a $200 daily benefit and a 5% simple COLA will pay a maximum of $450 per day 25 years later…while a similar policy with a 5% compound COLA will pay a maximum of $677.27 a day—a difference of nearly $83,000 per year in potential benefits.

***Mistake:* Overlooking subtle differences in benefit caps.** A policy that caps benefits at $200 per day is not similar to one that caps them at $6,000 per month, even though $6,000 divided by 30 days equals $200. A monthly cap of a given amount provides far more flexibility, and potentially far more reimbursement, than a daily cap. If, for example, you require in-home care costing $400 every other day, a policy with a $6,000 monthly benefit cap would pay more or less the whole thing—15 of those $400 visits per month would equal $6,000. But a policy with a $200 daily cap would pay only half of each $400 visit for a total of just $3,000 in monthly coverage.

What to do: Favor policies that have monthly benefit caps over policies that have daily ones, all else being equal. Carefully read the section of the policy describing benefit limits—in addition to the overall benefit cap, some policies have caps covering specific types of services.

***Mistake:* Not understanding how disabled you must be to receive benefits.** Policies generally provide benefits only when the policyholder requires assistance with a specified number of "activities of daily living." These include bathing, dressing, eating, toileting and transferring (such as from a bed to a wheelchair).

What to do: Lean toward a policy that provides benefits when you require assistance with two activities. It can be significantly more difficult to receive benefits when this figure is higher—many people require assistance with dressing and bathing long before they require assistance with a third activity.

Also: Favor policies that specifically include dementia coverage even when the policyholder does not yet meet the policy's activity triggers.

Long-Term-Care Warning If You Live Overseas

Phyllis Shelton, president of LTC Consultants, Nashville, which trains long-term-care insurance agents. She is author of *Protecting Your Family with Long-Term Care Insurance*. GotLTCI.com

Many LTC policies do not cover foreign care at all, and those that do tend to significantly restrict benefits, sometimes slashing them to half what the policy would pay in the US…or to just one year of coverage. Even those restricted benefits might be difficult to use abroad if the policy pays for only licensed caregivers and there is no licensing procedure in the country. For details, look for a heading labeled "International Benefits" (or something similar) in your policy or check the sections of the policy that list exclusions.

If your policy does not offer extensive foreign benefits, you still could retire overseas and then return to the US if you require extensive long-term care.

Currently the insurer MedAmerica offers policies that provide full international coverage with an option to receive the benefits in cash, which allows more flexibility in selecting caregivers. MedAmerica policies can be pricey, but women and couples might find that they're no more expensive than other companies' coverage at the moment—MedAmerica is one of the few issuers that has not yet imposed higher premiums on women.

The Federal Long Term Care Insurance Program, which is available to current and retired federal and postal employees as well as members of the military, also offers relatively strong international coverage. It provides up to 80% of the policy's normal benefit amounts when policyholders seek care outside the US.

John Hancock policies provide 100% of the normal benefit amount abroad, but for only one year. Genworth policies tend to cover up to four years of nursing home coverage abroad with benefits capped at 50% of the normal benefit amount…and one year of home health care capped at 25%.

Index

A

ACE (angiotensin-converting enzyme) inhibitors, 198, 215, 361, 367. *See also specific*

Acetyl-L-carnitine, 251, 359–60

Achilles tendonitis, 331–32

Achromycin V (*tetracycline*), 194, 195, 211, 216, 223, 251

Actifed, 209

Activity monitors, 81–82

Actonel (*risedronate*), 112, 114

Actos (*pioglitazone*), 248

Acupressure, 266, 313

Acupuncture, 260, 266, 331, 439–40

Adipex, 209

Advanced lipid test, 365

Adverse events, in hospitals, 182

Advil (*ibuprofen*), 194, 206, 218, 222, 253–54, 259, 394

Afrin, 193

Aging. *See also* Longevity
  anti-aging secrets, 5–7

color vision and, 248–49

daily living issues, 275–76

drug addiction risk and, 190–92

fraud risk and, 151

hearing loss related to, 254 (*see also* Hearing loss)

herbs in slowing, 9–11

looking younger (*see* Appearance)

memory loss and, 359

normal signs of, 7–9

posture and, 7–8, 60–62

sarcopenia affecting, 14–16

sense of smell and, 261–62

slowing process of, 3–5, 11–13

Aging in place
  home safety tips (*see* Home; Safety)
  information sources for, 80–81
  in-home caregivers, 92–93, 509, 510

technology for, 81–82, 85–91

tools for, 82–85

virtual village concept, 79–81

AIS (Active Isolated Stretching), 300–301

ALA (alpha-lipoic acid)
  for brain health, 341
  in diabetes control, 284
  for eye health, 238–39
  hearing link to, 251, 260
  longevity link to, 4
  in Parkinson's treatment, 298

Alcohol consumption
  affecting mood, 71
  bone density and, 112
  in brain-healthy diet, 356
  driving and drinking, 140
  fish consumed with, 36–37
  heartburn link to, 36
  heart health and, 375–76, 381, 403

513

night time strategies, 133–34, 135–36

safety tips, 128–30, 133–35

for small-car owners, 132–33

texting and, 135

Drugs. *See also specific conditions; specific drugs*

abuse of prescription, 190–92

for bone strength, 112, 114–16

causing disease, 199–201

cognitive function and, 346–47, 348–49

diabetic supply scam, 161

dizziness caused by, 180

dosage warnings, 196–98

driving affected by, 128–29, 134, 139–40

dry mouth from, 270

eye health risks, 208–10

fall risk and, 100–101

financial aid programs, 450

food and drink interacting with, 221–25

gait problem link to, 304

interactions between, 210–13

mistakes to avoid, 187–90

multiple, and Alzheimer's risk, 339–40

online pharmacies, 160–61

osteoporosis link to, 112

overprescribing, 167

overuse of OTC, 192–94

questioning pharmacists about, 188–89, 190

remembering to take, 85–86

side effects, 196–98, 203–5

supplement interactions, 194–96, 214–16

Duopa (*carbidopa-levodopa enteral suspension*), 296–97. *See also Carbidopa*; Sinemet

DVT (deep vein thrombosis), 368

DynaCirc (*isradipine*), 223

Dyrenium, 118

E

Ears. *See also* Hearing loss

heart attack risk and, 396

infections, 213–14

inner-ear dizziness, 111

wax in, 259, 260–61

Echinacea, 317

Education

college financial aid, 455

driving refresher courses, 134–35

Effexor (*venlafaxine*), 139, 200, 210

Eggs, 27, 37, 177

Eldepryl (*selegiline*), 222, 297

Elderberry syrup, 316

Eliquis (*apixaban*), 410–11

Elixophyllin (*theophylline*), 220, 222, 312

E-mail safety warnings, 152–53

Emotional connections, and immunity, 7. *See also* Relationships; Social connections

Emphysema, breathing technique, 305

Employment

after retirement, 483–87, 493, 504–5

veteran benefits, 507

Enbrel (*etanercept*), 173, 200

Endurance, exercises for, 106

Enoki mushrooms, 21

Enoxaparin, 410

Environment, and immunity, 7

Erectile dysfunction, 212, 220, 392

Erythromycin, 194, 211, 251

Esophageal cancer, 438

Estate planning. *See* Money; Retirement

Estrogen, low, 302

ETFs (exchange-traded funds), 472–73

Evening primrose, 194, 220–21

Exercise. *See also specific*

in Alzheimer's prevention, 334–35

with arthritis, 278

for belly fat reduction, 14

for better posture, 60–62

for bone health, 115, 121–22

in cancer treatment, 439, 441

choosing best, 39–41, 310–11

dancing as, 294

in diabetes treatment, 282, 286–87

do-it-anywhere workout, 44–46

eye strength, 232–33

for fall prevention, 104–6, 107, 108–10

finding time for, 47–49

flu recovery and, 320

for foot strength, 52–53

functional training, 38–39, 109–10

for hands, 50–52

hearing link to, 251

home gym safety, 123

for immune system health, 6–7

intensity of, 328, 372

longevity link to, 5

in muscle loss prevention, 15–16

for pain relief, 42–44, 300–301, 324–28, 329 (*see also specific conditions*)

for Parkinson's patients, 298

for prostate health, 436

skin health and, 66

strength training for seniors, 49–50

tips for enjoying, 46–47

Eyebrows, and aging, 56

Eyeglasses, 56, 73, 102–3, 234–35

Eye health. *See also* Vision

cataracts affecting, 177, 227, 230, 238–40

color vision changes, 248–49

diabetes link to, 230, 247, 248, 290–91

diet link to, 36, 245

exercises improving, 232–33

fall risk and, 102

foods for, 231–32

glaucoma, 228, 236–37, 240–43

medications affecting, 208–10

occlusion treatment, 247

Eyes, dry, 209, 226

Eylea (*aflibercept*), 245, 247

519